THE OPERAS OF VERDI

The Operas of Verdi, Volume 2

Il Trovatore   *La Traviata*
Les Vêpres Siciliennes   *Simon Boccanegra*
Aroldo   *Un Ballo in maschera*
La Forza del destino

The Operas of Verdi, Volume 3

Don Carlos   *Aida*
Otello   *Falstaff*

JULIAN BUDDEN

The Operas of Verdi

I

From *Oberto* to *Rigoletto*

Revised edition

CLARENDON PRESS · OXFORD

Oxford University Press, Walton Street, Oxford OX2 6DP
Oxford New York
Athens Auckland Bangkok Bombay
Calcutta Cape Town Dar es Salaam Delhi
Florence Hong Kong Istanbul Karachi
Kuala Lumpur Madras Madrid Melbourne
Mexico City Nairobi Paris Singapore
Taipei Tokyo Toronto
and associated companies in
Berlin Ibadan

Oxford is a trade mark of Oxford University Press

Published in the United States by
Oxford University Press Inc., New York

First published in 1973 in Great Britain by
Cassell & Company Ltd., London, and in the
United States by Praeger Publishers, Inc., New York

Published in 1978 in the United States by
Oxford University Press, Inc.

First issued in paperback in 1984

This revised edition published in 1992 by
Oxford University Press, Oxford,
and by Oxford University Press, New York

ISBN 0-19-816261-8

3 5 7 9 10 8 6 4 2

Printed in Great Britain
on acid-free paper by
St Edmundsbury Press Ltd., Bury St Edmunds, Suffolk

CONTENTS

ACKNOWLEDGEMENTS

My grateful thanks are due to G. Ricordi & Co. for permission to examine and quote from the autographs in their possession, and especially to Luciana Pestalozza and Fausto Broussard for their personal kindness and co-operation; to the late Sandro Della Libera, Archivist of the Teatro la Fenice, Venice, for allowing me to research into the Theatre's archives; to the late Mario Medici and the staff of the Istituto di Studi Verdiani for putting at my disposal their collection of documents, scores and reference books; to François Lesure of the Bibliothèque Nationale, Paris, Giampiero Tintori of the Museo del Teatro alla Scala, Milan, and Anna Mandolfi of the Biblioteca del Conservatorio San Pietro a Majella, Naples, for providing me with valuable photocopies and microfilms; David Lawton, of the State University of New York at Stony Brook, and David Rosen, of Cornell University, Ithaca, NY, for information regarding the insert arias; and to my friends and colleagues in England and Italy—Giorgio Pestelli of Turin University, Pierluigi Petrobelli, Rome University, Luigi Innocenti, Patric Schmid, Don White and the late John Davies, B.B.C. Music Librarian—for practical help and moral encouragement in my researches; and finally to Barbara Barker for endless work done on the typescript.

PREFACE TO THE FIRST EDITION

'Do we really need another book on Verdi?' The question, twice put by a well-known critic during the last few years, will no doubt be asked yet again. The present author must be ready with his answer.

Verdi's life spanned a relatively backward period in Italian music. Having for more than two centuries led the world in the invention of new forms and techniques, Italy found the reins firmly taken out of her hands by the first Viennese school and its successors. Instrumental music languished; the quartet, the symphony, the tone-poem gained only the slenderest foothold south of the Alps; even song was mostly reduced to the short, strophic romanza with a perfunctory piano accompaniment. There remained only opera organized on an old-fashioned system and with an eye to commercial values. Here too the conventions of musical expression failed to keep pace with those of the rest of Europe. Italian opera was the chief bogy from which Wagner claimed to be rescuing his contemporaries.

It was at the end of this period that the English musical renaissance began. Inevitably its gods were almost exclusively German. Largely anti-operatic by conviction (Stanford being an honourable exception) it was tolerant of Wagner, Gluck and Mozart. But in general it set its face against Covent Garden and the public who thronged there night after night—to be described by Sir Hubert Parry as 'having the lowest mentality of any who presume to call themselves musical'. The fact that Verdi's works formed the largest single contribution to the repertoire was unlikely to commend their author to the new Establishment.

As a result the voices raised on his behalf have tended to be defiant rather than persuasive. The English books which deal with his works, beginning with Bonavia's still eminently readable monograph of 1930, are full of arbitrary judgements which give the reader no idea as to the standard by which they are being made. There is general recognition of a steady progress from *Oberto* to *Otello* and *Falstaff*—two works which have usually inspired the respect if not the affection of the die-hards— but even here opinion has changed over the years, as successive writers find more and more to admire in what had previously been dismissed or apologized for. But if you proclaim *I Masnadieri* a neglected masterpiece, how do you avoid throwing it into the same scale as *Aida*? Only by going into the hows and the wherefores to a greater extent than has been attempted hitherto. The present vogue for Verdi among the literary intelligentsia is of course welcome, but not wholly musical in origin. The belief that Verdi's worst naïveties are somehow morally and spiritually healthier than the ruminations of Wagner is seldom due only to liberal sentiments (for was not Verdi a man of the left, while Wagner...?) but also to a certain lack of musical appetite, and the inability to digest the kind of sustained musical argument which Wagner never fails to provide. How many of these enthusiasts would ever sit through a symphony concert? Not enough, it seems to me, has been written to demonstrate (as in Wagner's case) what Verdi has to offer the informed musician.

Curiously enough the situation in other countries is not so very different. When Verdi died in 1901 opera had already entered an idealist phase, much under Wagnerian influence, in which literary and dramatic values were held to be as important to the finished result as those of music, and libretti were expected to stand up as plays in their own right. Debussy's *Pelléas*, Pfitzner's *Palestrina* and all the works of Strauss and Hoffmansthal conform to this canon; of Verdi's only the last two. Hence the tendency among writers brought up in such a climate to lay far too much stress on the merits or demerits of the libretti when assessing his work. The views set forth by Helmut Ludwig in the Atti of the Second International Congress of Verdi studies deserve to be printed in letters of gold above every opera-critic's desk. The plot, he maintains, is a vital matter to the composer but not to us. A libretto is an important donnée; it conditions the outward form of the opera; it affects the composer's invention in so far as it affords more or less scope for emotional expression; it can affect an opera's popularity in so far as it offers situations or characters which engage the ordinary opera-goer's sympathy (witness the failure of Mozart's *Titus* to gain a hold in the repertory). But its own merits as a drama are quite irrelevant. Therefore the statement that 'X is a bad opera because the libretto is badly constructed/ill-motivated/unbelievable, etcetera' is nonsense. Yet one comes across it over and over again in Verdi's biographies, from Monaldi to Abbiati.

At the opposite pole there have always been those who consider that 'ideal' opera in any form is not Verdi's métier; that *Otello* and *Falstaff* represent a diminution of the composer's real voice. Such was the view of Soffredini, one of the earliest writers to attempt a comprehensive critical survey of the operas. Ridiculous, you may think; but it was endorsed by Igor Stravinsky, by Shaw and in a sense by Vaughan Williams, who infinitely preferred *Rigoletto* to *Falstaff*. In the German-orientated world this often goes hand in hand with the 'irrational' approval of Verdi. We are all familiar with the person who announces with a laugh both patronizing and defensive that he *adores Il Trovatore*—as one who confesses a weakness for Danny La Rue. For such people this book is emphatically not intended.

Many leaders of the English musical establishment have had good and penetrating things to say about Verdi—Dent, Tovey and Blom, to name but a few; but for anyone brought up on the German classics, and taught to regard the '48', in Parry's words, as his daily bread, Verdi's development as a composer presents a good many puzzles and problems. Even the sympathetic Wagnerian Edward Dannreuther could be dismayed by the apparent backsliding from the music-drama of *Rigoletto* to the old-fashioned melodrama of *Il Trovatore*. The clue to all such mysteries lies in a deeper study of form and convention in the works of Verdi and his contemporaries, and their relation to those of the rest of Europe. In this area there will, I imagine, be plenty of room for further writing since there has been so little in the past. What I have endeavoured to do is to fill in some of the gaps left by my predecessors (though inevitably being obliged to go over the same ground as they); to describe in greater detail the musical procedures of Verdi's day, the extent to which he used, modified or departed from them and why; to chart the evolution of one of the most personal of nineteenth-century styles, showing how, as the long, somewhat inflexible melodic limbs of the early operas give way to smaller, more plastic units, susceptible of variation and development, so the music gains in range and depth of expression. I have dwelt sparingly on the subject of influences since not only are these often a matter of speculation, but the similarities which are supposed to prove them too often exist in the ear of the individual, as do personal likenesses in the eye. If by contrast I have dealt at length with anticipations it is to show the fundamental consistency of Verdi's style throughout his composing life. To find pre-echoes of pieces by other composers is a temptation no writer can resist. However, when faced with a theme such as heralds the arrival of Malcolm and his forces in Act IV of *Macbeth*, rather than regard it like Spike Hughes in his stimulating *Famous Verdi Operas* as a precursor of the army song 'One-eyed Reilly', I would prefer to hear it as a martial variation on the stretta finale-theme of Bellini's *Beatrice*—as Verdi's contemporaries would have done. In discussing individual operas I have followed the method of Spike Hughes and Ernest Newman (*Wagner Nights*), combining exposition of the plot with commentary on the music, so as to be able to relate the two without repeating myself more than is strictly necessary.

Yes, there will always be a need for more books about Verdi, if only because more relevant material is continually coming to light: the so called insert-arias (not so far discussed in any of the standard works), revisions, 'puntature' and sketches, some of which are here discussed for the first time; and of course—though of more marginal interest—letters. The *Copialettere*—some of which Charles Osborne has performed the invaluable service of translating into English—is, if not the tip of the proverbial iceberg, a small fragment of a very much larger whole. Letters totalling several thousand are scattered in publications now mostly out of print, ranging from books devoted to a single correspondent to the odd letter printed in a periodical now defunct. There is hardly a museum in Italy which does not have at least one letter from the maestro bussetano tucked away in its archives. But there is still a vast range of correspondence—some of it in the hands of private collectors—between Verdi and his librettists which the Verdi scholar is waiting to see and which may enable him to discover why such-and-such a passage was changed, why this or that singer was dropped from the cast and so forth. The Verdi Institute at Parma has made a valuable start in assembling a complete catalogue, and we may all look forward to the forthcoming publication under their auspices of the composer's complete business correspondence with his publishing house.

J.B.

October 1972

PREFACE TO THE
REVISED EDITION

Research is unending, and since this study was written a number of discoveries and exhumations have occurred of which even the present reprint has not always been able to take account. A performance of the composite *Messa per Rossini* for which Verdi supplied the 'Libera me', mentioned as a possibility in Vol. III, p. 161n., has in the mean time become a reality, having been given at the European Music Festival of Stuttgart, 1988, in an edition prepared by the Istituto di Studi Verdiani. A commercial recording on Hannsler Classic 981 949 (CD) followed soon after. Among documents a copy of Piave's original libretto for *Macbeth* with corrections by Andrea Maffei has recently come to light at the Museo Teatrale alla Scala, Milan, and will in due course be published with a critical commentary by Francesco Degrada. Its chief interest lies in the evidence it provides of Verdi's readiness to throw out Maffei's ideas as well as Piave's if they did not meet his musical needs. Although the bulk of Verdi's musical sketches remain shrouded from public view, occasional items surface in Sotheby's catalogues, usually to disappear again into the hands of private collectors, though sometimes, more fortunately, into the Pierpont Morgan Library, New York. A recent instance is a sketch for the soprano–baritone duet, 'Amai, ma un solo istante' (*Giovanna d'Arco*), a comparison of which with the definitive version shows how Verdi adapted the soprano part to the particular means of Erminia Frezzolini with her penchant for the stepwise-moving legato line. Still more tantalising is the first, fully scored page of a discarded aria (later replaced by 'Se al nuovo dì pugnando') from (*La battaglia di Legnano*, reproduced in facsimile in George Martin's *Aspects of Verdi* (London, 1989) p. 156. The same study contains two previously unpublished letters from the composer to Ferdinand Gravure and Léon (or Marie) Escudier respectively (pp. 245–6), from which it would appear that Verdi supplied some ballet music for the Brussels première of *Nabucco* given on 29 November 1848. Has the score perhaps passed into the archives of Choudens et Cie, along with that of *La Force du destin*?

During the 1970s a valuable collection of letters forming part of Verdi's correspondence with the house of Ricordi during the years 1880–90 appeared on the international antiquarian market. Negotiations for its purchase by the Italian government came to nothing at the time; but fortunately the bulk of the collection was offered again in 1980 and was (like the Sibylline books) duly bought by the state, which granted exclusive publication rights to the Institute of Verdi Studies. A selection of these letters edited by Franca Cella and Pierluigi Petrobelli was published in the *Catalogo Giuseppe Verdi: corrispondenza e immagini 1881–90* (Milan, 1981), printed in association with an exhibition of the material mounted at La Scala in that year. One letter, written to Giulio Ricordi on 14 November 1881, gives the lie to Maurel's statement (see vol. III, p. 324) that Verdi disapproved the notion of a beardless Iago. 'I'm much in favour of Iago without a beard,' Verdi observed. And indeed until comparatively recently every famous exponent of the role, from Titta Ruffo to Tito Gobbi, played it thus, as contemporary photographs show.

Further light is shed on Verdi's last two masterpieces by James A. Hepokoski's *Falstaff* (Cambridge, 1983), with its detailed account of the variants to be found in successive vocal scores, and the same author's *Otello* (Cambridge, 1987), where Verdi's and Boito's delineation of the leading characters is viewed in the context of nineteenth-century Italian traditions of Shakespearean performance. Meanwhile a contemporary document which seems to have eluded all Verdian scholars, with the exception of Marcello Conati (to whom I am indebted for a copy), is a series of three lectures on *Falstaff* delivered in 1894 to the Royal Institution of Great Britain by Alexander Campbell Mackenzie, then Principal of the Royal Academy of Music, London. These were printed in a pamphlet (now, alas, vanished without trace), and in this form evidently came to the attention of Ricordi who had them translated and published under the title *Tre letture di Falstaff*, Verdi himself was so touched by them that he sent Mackenzie a photograph of himself inscribed 'with great admiration and deep gratitude' (see A. C. Mackenzie, *A Musician's Narrative* (London, 1927) p. 251). True, the lectures tell us nothing new about the opera itself, but they are full of a lively appreciation which must have gone straight to the composer's heart. The conclusion is particularly charming. After a reference to Verdi's charitable works — the hospital at Villanova, the projected Rest Home for Musicians in Milan — Mackenzie continues:

> You will surely know that centuries ago German theologians used to enjoy putting to each other the most bizarre and abstruse questions; and when the argument grew too heated they would break off and listen to a piece of music. One subject that used to concern them mightily on such occasions was: 'How many angels could in the same moment dance upon the point of a needle?' Well now, faced with this wonderful creation of the human spirit coupled with so beneficent a heart, like the unimaginative Scot that I am, I can only invite you to solve a similar problem: 'How many angels do you think could at this moment unite in joyous celebration on Verdi's last laugh?'

On a still lighter note, the so-called 'Maddalena aria' (*Rigoletto*) deserves a mention as the kind of false trail on which even the most careful of scholars may sometimes be led. In 1977 a Belgian bibliophile announced that he had in his possession in a reduction for piano and voice an aria for Maddalena written for a French version of *Rigoletto*. There was great excitement all round. Photocopies were obtained and distributed amongst the faithful. The directors of Opera Rara were determined to have the aria sung in a performance planned for Belfast later in the year. The music was clearly Verdi's; the words, 'Prends pitié de sa jeunesse', etc., were eminently suited to a girl who was pleading with her brother to spare the life of a young man; and the fact that the piece was published by Escudier ruled out the possibility of piracy. Accordingly, one scholar scored it in true Verdian style; two others set to work on an Italian translation; another, who possessed a French libretto containing the text, was able to indicate the exact point where the music could be slotted into the existing score. The moment of truth arrived when, in my capacity as External Services Music Organizer of the B.B.C., I commissioned an interview on the subject with Patric Schmid of Opera Rara for the World Service.

The broadcast was heard by a Mr Gerry Zwirm, resident in Italy, who wrote back to say that the music of the aria was identical with that of one of Verdi's salon pieces, 'Il poveretto', of which he enclosed a photocopy. A glance at the entry on 'Il poveretto' in the first volume of Hopkinson's bibliography confirmed that it had indeed been adapted as an area for Maddalena; but that there was no evidence that the composer was even aware of this, let alone responsible for it. There were a few red faces in Verdian circles that day.

Yet our gaffe was perhaps less shaming than it might seem. Verdi, so insistent on maintaining the integrity of a work in the initial stages of its career, would sometimes, once its popularity had been assured, adopt an attitude of 'If they want such-and-such let them have it'. To this we owe the high C's in 'Di quella pira' and probably the reinstatement of the Fontainebleau act in *Don Carlos*. Moreover, until their quarrels of 1876 Verdi himself was on terms of the closest intimacy with Escudier, who knew only too well the danger of flouting the Master's wishes. The chances that 'Il poveretto', adapted to form Maddalena's aria for provincial performances in the French-speaking countries, may have had his permission, if not his approval, are considerable.

Indeed, in these days in which every cut, however small, is frowned upon by the cognoscenti and the 'edizione integrale' enjoined by leading critics the world over, it is instructive to come across more and more evidence of the ruthless attitude of star singers of the past with regard to a composer's intentions. The list of transpositions and 'puntature' in the part of Lady Macbeth as sung by the mezzo-soprano Pauline Viardot-Garcia can be found in *My Reminiscences* by the conductor Luigi Ardiri (London, 1896), pp. 58ff. Adelina Patti's score of *La Traviata*, in the possession of Jonathan Ruffer, proves no less revealing. Not only does it contain all the traditional cuts; the whole of her first 'scena ed aria' from 'È strano' down to the end of the cabaletta 'Sempre libera' is marked *Un tono sotto* after the first three bars. The 6/8 section of the duet with Germont beginning 'Non sapete' is removed, leaving only Germont's pendant 'È grave il sagrifizio'. So is the entire final cabaletta ('Morrò, la mia memoria'). The rhythmic augmentation in the final phrase of 'Amami, Alfredo' is rewritten and shorn of two bars so as to make it conform to the melody as it appears in the prelude. (As Spike Hughes has pointed out, many singers do this automatically; but it takes a star of Patti's egotism to alter Verdi's notation.) In the final act the cabaletta 'Gran Dio, morir si giovine is reduced to thirty bars shared out between soprano and tenor. If nowadays we err in the direction of inflexibility in our fidelity to the composer's intentions it is a fault on the right side.

It remains to signalise the steady progress of the Critical Edition of Verdi's works published by the House of Ricordi in conjunction with the University of Chicago Press. Inaugurated in December 1976, its first fruits have been *Rigoletto*, *Ernani* and *Nabucodonosor* (*Nabucco*). Of these the first and third have each received a prestigious baptism under Riccardo Muti at the Vienna State Opera (March 1983) and La Scala, Milan (December 1986) respectively. *Ernani* was mounted by the Associazione Teatrale de Emilia-Romagna in December 1984 under Roberto Abbado with a predominantly young cast, most of whom had been prepared for the occasion by a two-month seminar. The production by Gianfranco De Bosio aimed at recreating the style of the opera's period, using contemporary scenic designs, a proscenium and simulated candle-light which extended to the auditorium and was never extinguished during the performance. The orchestra included contemporary brass instruments and played on stage level. The result proved profoundly illuminating as to the composer's dramatic intentions and constituted a landmark in practical Verdian scholarship — happily a still thriving industry.

J.B.

July 1990

I VERDI AND THE WORLD OF THE PRIMO OTTOCENTO

The primo ottocento (a term loosely used to cover the first half of the nineteenth century in Italian music) has up to now received scant attention from scholars; nor does it form any part of the ordinary music student's education. Most professors, with the authority of Berlioz, Schumann, Mendelssohn and Wagner to support them, have been content to dismiss it as a provincial backwater, an era of decadence in taste and craftsmanship. (They might do well to remember, however, that 'Wop-bashing' was always a favourite occupation of Germans—the result of two centuries of artistic subjection.) Even so staunch a champion of Italian music as E. J. Dent describes the period as, comparatively speaking, a desert, 'golden only in so far as it is glittering'.* It is not the purpose of this chapter to challenge such a view: rather to try to explain the aims and values of an age which formed the background of one of music's supreme geniuses.

The early masterpieces of German opera—*Die Zauberflöte, Fidelio, Der Freischütz* —all represent a personal, an ideal synthesis of several traditions, of which the most important are eighteenth-century opera buffa and opéra comique. Both genres represent opera's left wing. They are concerned with the development of character, the conflict of personalities; and they ally themselves far more closely with the symphonic tradition than does opera seria, whose function was to express different, contrasted states of mind in a succession of exit-arias. Works such as Rossini's *Tancredi*, on the other hand, descend in a direct line from the so-called 'Neapolitan' operas of Metastasio's time, using many of the same verse-forms, expressing the same ideals, making the same concessions to performers and audiences as though Gluck's famous manifesto of 1767 had never been written. The reason is partly institutional. The French Revolution and the Napoleonic Wars had caused profound upheavals in European society and created new conditions in the world of art and entertainment. In Italy empires might rise and empires might fall, but La Scala, Milan, and the Teatro la Fenice, Venice, still needed their two opere d'obbligo (new operas) for the winter season. Even in the darkest days of warfare and military occupation Italian opera remained a thriving industry with a wide market at home and abroad, largely due to the prowess of Italian singers.

This is not least among the factors that kept Italian opera with one foot in the eighteenth century, when the singer, not the composer, was the starting-point. When Mozart was a youth no one would dream of composing an aria until he had first heard the artist who was to perform it; and this might be no more than a fortnight before the premiere. Thus, for instance, Leopold Mozart to his wife during the composition of *Mitridate Re di Ponto* in Milan in 1770—'Wolfgang has composed only one aria for the primo uomo, since he has not yet arrived and Wolfgang doesn't want to do the same work twice over'.† More than sixty years

* E. J. Dent, 'Donizetti, an Italian Romantic', in *A Fanfare for Ernest Newman* (London, 1955), p. 86.
† Emily Anderson, *The Letters of Mozart and his Family* (London, 1938), I, p. 252.

later, when Bellini was writing *I Puritani* for the Théâtre des Italiens in Paris, the situation was no different. 'The whole of the first act is now finished, except for the trio, because I want first to try it out (*provarlo*) on Rubini.'* *Provare* is the word used for trying on a suit. Bellini's contemporary, Giovanni Pacini, one of the most prolific operatic practitioners of his day, wrote in his memoirs that he always tried to serve his singers as a good tailor serves his clients, 'concealing the natural defects of the figure and emphasizing its good points'.† The dangers of not making to measure are illustrated by an incident in Bellini's career. For the revised version of his opera *Bianca e Fernando* (Genoa, 1828) he wrote a new entrance-aria, or cavatina, for the prima donna Adelaide Tosi. 'She tried it out with orchestra, and as she sang it like a pig and it went for nothing she wanted another one, and she wouldn't sing the stretta because there was no agility in it and it was music for boys; and if I didn't change it she would sing one of her pezzi di baule instead.'‡ In fact Tosi did not carry out her threat; she merely called in another master-tailor to make adjustments.

> David [*the tenor*] told me that the changes had come from D. [*Donizetti*] and I'd already suspected that because Tosi herself told me that when D. went over the part with her he said that the stretta was no good. I believe he said this as his own honest opinion and without spite and because he was concerned about her; but his having gone over it with so many changes of tempo and all quite different from my own makes me certain that it is *absolutely impossible* to have friends in the same profession; and the fact that his opera comes on immediately after mine doesn't suggest that he's going to take kindly to my success.§

Donizetti too had his problems—a soprano who insisted on a cabaletta finale in *Lucrezia Borgia*, two prima donnas who fought each other during rehearsals for *Maria Stuarda*, a 'friend' of the management who had to be accommodated in a breeches-role in *Pia de' Tolomei*. None of these ladies could be treated lightly. It was only in England that Handel was able to hold a prima donna out of the window until she complied with his wishes. Verdi himself took a bold step in 1844 when he refused to provide Sofia Loewe with a rondò-finale for *Ernani*; and even he thought it wise to write to the baritone Felice Varesi offering him three differently scored versions of the final scene of *Macbeth* ('Mal per me che m'affidai') and asking him which he preferred.

Once the composer had fulfilled the terms of his contract by composing and rehearsing the music, and attending the first three nights in the orchestral

---

* Letter to Count Pepoli, 19.9.1834. L. Cambi, *Bellini: Epistolario* (Verona, 1943), p. 433. See also letter to Florimo, 21.9.1834. Cambi, p. 439.

† G. Pacini, *Le mie memorie artistiche* (2nd ed., Florence, 1875), p. 72.

‡ Letter to Florimo, 5.4.1828. Cambi, p. 74. *Pezzi di baule* or 'suitcase-pieces' were the arias which were designed to fit stock operatic situations and which all singers liked to carry about with them to be used at discretion, particularly in revivals of operas at which the composer himself was not present.

§ Cambi, p. 75. The cabaletta which Adelaide Tosi wanted changed ('Contenta appien quest'alma') eventually found its way into *Norma* as 'Ah bello, a me ritorna', the movement which follows 'Casta diva'. See F. Pastura, *Bellini secondo la storia* (Parma, 1959), p. 133.

pit,* his control over the work for all practical purposes ceased. He might in certain cases be commissioned to mount (*mettere in scena*) a revival of one of his operas, adapting it (*puntare*) to the new cast and even composing fresh numbers; but this version too would pass right out of his hands once he had launched it. Any piece which was given as an opera di ripiego (that is, a fill-up when the expected novelty of the season was delayed) would be treated quite ruthlessly. Maria Malibran regularly performed Bellini's *I Capuleti e i Montecchi* with a penultimate scene lifted from Vaccai's *Giulietta e Romeo*. Most performances of Verdi's *Nabucco* after the first run at La Scala suppressed the death of Abigaille.† When *Oberto Conte di San Bonifacio* was put on at Turin during rehearsals of Nicolai's *Il Templario* the first-act duet between tenor and mezzo-soprano was omitted and an aria from Mercadante's *Elena da Feltre* put in its place. Neither composer nor publisher could have any say in the matter. It was a state of affairs which composers of this time accepted as had their eighteenth-century forebears, and from which they were always ready to profit. Rossini, Bellini and Donizetti transferred individual numbers from one opera to another, and so, for all his idealism, did Gluck. Mozart wrote several arias for individual singers to interpolate into the operas of Anfossi and others; Bellini was invited to compose an aria for insertion into Rossini's *Otello* and would have complied if they had paid him enough.‡ All of them from Gluck to Verdi wrote extra pieces for revivals of their own works, whether or not they themselves were present at the occasion. Verdi wrote a new tenor cabaletta for *I Due Foscari* and a new cavatina for *Giovanna d'Arco* to oblige the singers Mario and Sofia Loewe respectively. As late as 1863 he supplied a new romanza for *Les Vêpres siciliennes* of 1855. By that time, however, the situation had changed considerably. Ricordi's practice of bringing out complete authentic vocal scores soon after the first performance made it very difficult for composers to borrow from their own works without detection (Bellini, it may be noticed, never borrows from a score which has already been printed outside Naples); while, with the signing of the convention of 1840 between Austria and Sardinia for mutual protection in matters of copyright, a limit was put to the liberties that could be taken with a composer's work. True, it was some time before its conditions took full effect. But as early as 1847 Verdi was writing to Ricordi suggesting that in his contracts with the various theatres he should include a clause forbidding a single note of the score to be altered, on pain of a heavy fine. Naturally that was too much to expect at the time, but it shows the direction in which composers' thoughts were tending. Such an attitude would have been unthinkable at the time when Verdi began his career.

---

* According to Pacini (p. 35) it was the custom at the San Carlo theatre, Naples, for the composer to turn the pages for the leading cello and double bass players on opening nights— 'a rule which remained in force up till 1839 and which I abolished when I mounted a production of *Saffo* on that very stage'. Clearly this practice was a relic from the early years of the century when the composer used to act as maestro al cembalo for his own works. By the 1820s and '30s the keyboard had vanished but the player was still at his post. Even in Verdi's time the leading bass player was often referred to as the 'contrabasso al cembalo'—i.e., the player who would have accompanied the recitativo secco, had there been any.

† See M. Lessona, *Volere è potere* (Florence, 1869), pp. 297–8; A. Basevi, *Studio sulle opere di Giuseppe Verdi* (Florence, 1859), p. 17; also P. Petrobelli, 'Nabucco', in *Conferenze 1966–7* (Associazione Amici della Scala, Milan), p. 24.

‡ Letter to Florimo, 21.4.1828. Cambi, p. 88.

Generally speaking, then, Italian romantic opera was written under the same conditions as eighteenth-century opera seria—rapidly and to a great extent piece-meal according to the availability of the singers; what is more, the parts themselves had to be replaceable. Naturally this presupposes a heavy reliance on convention as well as an inherent conservatism of taste such as had ceased to operate north of the Alps. In Paris audiences wanted novelty; in Italy they wanted the mixture as before. Italians who aimed at the kind of ideal composition represented by Weber's *Euryanthe* or Schubert's *Alfonso und Estrella* were forced to go abroad. Cherubini and Spontini became expatriates; Rossini and Bellini ended their careers in Paris; Donizetti spent his last few years between Paris and Vienna. It could be said that Italian composers had always tended to produce their best work for France, if only because the *tragédie-lyrique*, being free from the tyranny of good voices, offered the composer more scope for his invention, while the inherently more intellectual nature of the French libretto required him to take more thought.

The Italian scene in the early nineteenth century was further darkened by the steep decline in its instrumental tradition. Previously opera had represented only part of a professional composer's activity; now it was the whole of it, since nothing else could earn him a living. Paisiello and Cimarosa wrote chamber music and concertos throughout their careers. Their successors put all such things behind them once they had left their conservatoires. Nowhere was the gap between the schoolroom and the stage so wide as in Italy. Composers fought like rats to secure *scritture* (contracts) and discharged them as quickly as possible so as to be able to take on others. Writing somewhat apologetically in 1865, when the situation had improved, Pacini admits that: 'I was never sufficiently careful [*accurato*] in my scoring, and I particularly neglected the strings [*quartetto*].'* One never fails to be struck by the improvement in Italian instrumentation after contact with the Parisian stage. Rossini's French scores are far richer in texture and variety of colour than those he composed for Italy. Bellini wrote to Florimo with some justification that in *I Puritani* he had scored 'more carefully' than ever before. For his Viennese operas *Linda di Chamounix* and *Maria di Rohan* Donizetti added full-length over-tures in symphonic first-movement form. In Italy they would have been drowned in audience chatter. Verdi's orchestration also benefited from ultramontane influences, as we shall see.

Another retarding feature of ottocento opera is the persistence, particularly in its early years, of 'genres'. In the eighteenth century opera seria and opera buffa constituted two separate worlds, each with its own tradition of musical organization and even of voice-casting. In the first the hero was an alto-castrato, the heroine a soprano, the father and/or villain a tenor. In the second the hero was a tenor or basso cantante, the heroine a light soprano and the father a basso buffo—generally meaning a good actor and a poor singer, as Mozart's Buff indicates in *Der Schauspieldirektor*; hence his habit of declaiming against an orchestral melody, rather than vocalizing in the usual way. By the second half of the century the two genres were already beginning to mingle in Italian operas composed outside Italy. The reason was largely economic. For the average German ruler Italian opera was an expensive commodity; and he could not afford two separate casts for the comic and the high style respectively. Thus in Mozart's *La Finta Giardiniera* the

* Pacini, p. 71.

hero and the father are both tenors, and there is a castrato all of whose arias are in the grand manner. Likewise in Haydn's *L'Infedeltà Delusa* while the heroine is a direct descendant of Pergolesi's archetypal Serpina the father is once more a tenor. In Italy on the other hand opera, as they say, grew on trees. Most of the major cities had more than one theatre, each specializing in a particular genre. As late as Berlioz's time Naples could offer the San Carlo for serious opera, the Fondo for comic. In Venice, where Rossini began his career, there were three theatres—the Teatro la Fenice for opera seria, the San Benedetto for opera buffa, the San Moisè for one-act *farse*. One curious result of this segregation was that when the castrato began to disappear his place in serious opera, together with his title of *musico*, was taken not by the tenor but by the female contralto. Incredible as it may seem, right up to 1830, with Weber, Schubert and Beethoven already in their graves, the usual distribution of voices in an opera seria was soprano-heroine, contralto–hero, tenor–father or villain. Even such virile types as Byron's Conrad and Hugo's Hernani were conceived as prancing 'principal boys', the first by Pacini (*Il Corsaro*), the second by Bellini in sketches for an opera that he never wrote. Nothing in the ottocento indicates the survival of eighteenth-century values so clearly as this. In Metastasian opera seria, with all its moral uplift, its concern for the triumph of right over wrong, of order over chaos, we are not expected mentally to cheer the hero, boo the villain (when there is one) and weep with the temporarily wronged heroine, if only because all three are equally unreal, not to say unsympathetic. What we enjoy is the musical expression of martial ardour in one piece, anger in the next, sorrow in the next and so on. Dramatic truth was the province of opera buffa, not of its sister-species. Yet when faced with an increasing number of romantic plots which require direct sympathy with their characters, Italian composers at first preferred to treat them on Metastasian lines, adding a happy ending, even in cases where the tragic outcome is the whole point of the story. Rossini was indeed stepping out of line when in 1816 he allowed Otello to smother Desdemona and then kill himself;* and for a later performance in Rome he sanctioned (or at least was paid for) the substitution of a duet of reconciliation set to music from his opera *Armida*. In due course the flood-tide of romanticism, lower in Italy than elsewhere, swept away the contralto–hero, and the 'noble unreason' of the tenor voice assumed its sway. But throughout the 1830s and even later the contralto retained a place as sub-hero. Maffio Orsini (*Lucrezia Borgia*), Gondì (*Maria di Rohan*), Pierotto (*Linda di Chamounix*) are among the Donizettian examples. Apart from Oscar in *Un Ballo in Maschera*, who belongs to a different tradition anyway, there are no trouser-roles in Verdi. But in the *King Lear* he was never to write the Fool was projected as a contralto musico. Connected with this survival of the breeches-role is the fact that even at a time when romanticism had come to dominate the Italian libretto, and when most plots were, as Massimo Mila has neatly put it, a mere retelling of the Romeo-and-Juliet story, classical subjects taken from Voltaire, Marmontel or even Metastasio continued to be set with great success—Donizetti's *Belisario*, Mercadante's *Orazi e Curiazi* and *La Vestale*. A less successful instance is Verdi's *Alzira*.

---

* Only classical legends were exempt from the rule (see Mayr's *Medea in Corinto*). Shakespeare, Tasso and Voltaire were not. Yet for a revival of *Tancredi* at Ferrara in 1813 Rossini had ventured to restore Voltaire's dénouement.

Of course, the values of opera seria would never have survived if the genre itself had been quite so static as historians sometimes imply. Even in Gluck's day it was being modified by influences from two directions: from French tragédie-lyrique with its vast choral tableaux (Traetta regularly set adaptations of French libretti, as did Paisiello in his *Fedra* of 1787) and from opera buffa with its concerted finales, its ensembles, its smaller, more flexible forms. The two influences are well illustrated in Mozart's *Idomeneo* and *La Clemenza di Tito* respectively. But if the outward form changed the spirit essentially did not. The exit-aria remained the staple unit, even when it was expanded into two movements, preceded by a chorus and a page of declamatory recitative, and interspersed with comments from by-standers and snatches of dialogue. If it marked the first entrance of the character concerned it was called a cavatina; if it brought down the final curtain it was called a rondò-finale. Long before Verdi's time both terms had lost any formal connotation they may once have had; they refer to position and nothing else.* Whatever its context it was always advisable for a singer to leave the stage after a two-movement aria (unless of course it ended the opera), as Verdi indicated in a letter to his librettist Piave during their collaboration on *I Due Foscari*.†

None the less, in obedience to the spirit of the times Italian opera was slowly moving in the direction of greater continuity. The process can be seen in the last act of Rossini's *Otello*, in the last four operas of Bellini with their wealth of melodic recitative, in the more dramatic works of Donizetti such as *Lucrezia Borgia*. Yet the cleavage of genres remained below the surface like class distinctions in a modern democracy; and composers continued to employ certain procedures in one convention which they would never consider using in another. Leaving out of account such obvious examples of opera buffa as *L'Elisir d'Amore* or *Don Pasquale* with their patter songs and duets, the difference can be sensed in such works as *Norma* and *La Sonnambula*; the first a solemn, high tragedy whose heroine for all her beautiful music commands more veneration than sympathy, the second an unashamed 'weepie'. *Norma* makes use of the 'serious' opera forms at their most expansive; *La Sonnambula* employs shorter, freer designs.

When Verdi began his career, then, the operatic tradition in which he was launched was a deeply conservative one, linked far more strongly with the previous century than were contemporary traditions in France, Germany or even Russia. From this fact springs the special nature of its forms and language. But a study of both cannot proceed without reference to that key figure, the reluctant architect of Italian romantic opera, Gioachino Rossini—a composer who sums up all the paradoxes and ambiguities of the ottocento.

He arrived on the scene in 1810, at a time when Italian opera had almost lost

---

* In the case of *cavatina* a certain confusion has been caused by its association with the German usage of *Cavatine* to denote an aria in one, slow movement—e.g., Agathe's 'Und ob die Wolke' from *Der Freischütz*. Hence the practice amongst modern writers and critics (Italians included) of designating the slow movement of a double aria as a cavatina. In the primo ottocento there was no universally recognized term to cover such a movement. Composers referred to it variously as the 'andante', the 'largo', the 'adagio' or just the 'first movement'. If it stood by itself with no cabaletta to follow it was generally called a 'romanza' even when the words were as unromantic, say, as those of Giacomo's 'Speme al vecchio' from *Giovanna d'Arco*. Verdi himself often used the word *cantabile* in this connection.

† Letter to Piave, 22.5.1844. G. Cesari and A. Luzio, *I Copialettere di Giuseppe Verdi* (Milan. 1913), p. 426.

its way. Of the two acknowledged masters of the late eighteenth century Cimarosa was dead, Paisiello had retired from composition. Valentino Fioravanti was keeping alight the torch of Neapolitan comedy. But among the younger composers Italy had no one of greater consequence to offer than Ferdinando Paër and Simone Mayr, a Bavarian émigré more famous as the teacher of Donizetti than as a composer in his own right. In ten years, from his double triumph with *Tancredi* and *L'Italiana in Algeri* in 1813 till his departure for Paris in 1823 after *Semiramide*, Rossini had revitalized the world of Italian opera, refashioning it in his own image. How far the formal patterns which his successors accepted without question can be directly ascribed to Rossini himself has been disputed on the perfectly reasonable ground that we do not know sufficient of the work of his contemporaries to be certain about the matter. But the few extracts of Generali, Guglielmi and Mosca that have been recently brought to light either in concert performance or in the form of quotations by scholars such as Friedrich Lippmann* suggest that his influence has been under- rather than over-estimated. Pacini was in no doubt about it at all. '. . . Everyone followed the same school, the same fashions, and as a result they were all imitators of the great luminary. But, good heavens, what else was one to do if there was no other way of making a living? If I was a follower of the great man of Pesaro, so was everyone else.'†

Yet this was the romantic age; and Rossini was certainly no romantic. His own talent was for comedy, as he was always ready to admit. The world of serious lyric drama he had inherited by default. His phenomenal success in this field was due to the sheer strength of his musical personality and also to the robustly Italianate quality of his style—for this was an Italophile age in which even Cherubini must have wondered whether he had been wise to renounce his birthright. Relevant here too is the time-lag which operates between literature and music. The romantic poets and writers projected their own outlook into the music they knew and loved, rather than the compositions which most nearly expressed their ideals. For E. T. A. Hoffmann Mozart and Beethoven were romantics avant la lettre. Byron and his contemporaries recognized their own image in *Semiramide* rather than *Der Freischütz*. Nor is this surprising. Musical expression is at once vivid and vague, almost chameleon-like. Much depends on the listener's own perspective. To those who have experienced Wagner *Tancredi* will seem relatively cold. Yet Stendhal could contrast favourably the introduction to 'Di tanti palpiti' with the orchestral writings of Germans such as Weber, Marschner and Conradin Kreutzer. '*They* use their instruments to furnish us as crudely as possible with certain necessary information which the singer on the stage should properly speaking convey to us in words.'‡ And he goes on to compare the voice in German opera to the sovereign who refers the most important decision to his state ministers. This is typical of an attitude which was to obstruct the appreciation of Wagner in France.

Yet there was a certain falsity in Rossini's position as musical king of romantic Europe; and he himself knew it. He knew, further, just how long he could profit

---

* F. Lippmann, *Analecta Musicologica*, VI: *Vincenzo Bellini und die italienische Opera seria seiner Zeit* (Cologne, 1969).

† Pacini, p. 54.

‡ Stendhal, *Vie de Rossini* (trs. R. Coe) (London, 1956), p. 57.

from his supremacy and how far his own temperament and integrity would allow him to come to terms with a movement with whose ideals he was fundamentally out of sympathy. In 1829 he retired from the operatic scene at the age of thirty-seven, having defined the form and language of early Italian romantic opera once and for all. He had created the masterplan, leaving Bellini, Donizetti and Verdi to fill it out each in his own way. If their operas could never have come into existence without Rossini's example, the magnitude of their achievement depends in each case mostly on the extent to which they were able to overcome the limitations of formal procedures designed to meet the needs of a temperament quite different from theirs.

So many of the distinctive features of Italian romantic opera derive from the flamboyant musical personality of its founder. The orchestral technique is one of the most obvious. The scoring of Cimarosa or Paisiello was plain, neat, unobtrusive; but with the first known Rossini overture—*La Cambiale di Matrimonio*—a subtly but unmistakably new manner is evident. The coat is styled to fit its wearer. To convey the mischief and ribaldry of his comedies Rossini devised a slightly fantastic manner of scoring with a hint of parody in it. The tone colours are separated rather than blended—as for instance in his favourite combination of chattering strings and sustaining horns—and the woodwind are treated as solo voices. Because of the ingenuity and elaboration of Rossini's instrumental patterns his compatriots often accused him of 'germanizing'—quite wrongly, for this is entirely distinct from the organic scoring of a Beethoven or a Weber. The Germans themselves called it meretricious, with more reason; for without the taste and stylishness of Rossini to guide it meretricious is just what it became. The ranz des vaches from the *Guillaume Tell* overture has much to answer for.

Likewise in his writing for the voice Rossini gives full play to his own personal exuberance. How far a Rossini aria would have sounded more elaborate than one by Anfossi or Zingarelli can never be determined, because in those days the singer was expected to add his own embellishments. Performer's licence amounted to a disease, and Rossini treated it homeopathically. By devising for the singers ornaments more ingenious than any that they could invent themselves, he was able to assert his composer's authority in a subtler way, at the same time integrating into his structure what could easily have become an unwanted excrescence. In comedy his roulades and flourishes are wholly delightful, a vital element in the belly-laugh that he brought to music. In opera seria the effect is not so much inappropriate as rather frigid and 'baroque' in the architectural sense. In his later French operas Rossini simplified his vocal writing and enriched his orchestral textures; but the structures of his arias remained more or less constant with symmetrical phrases, closely patterned accompaniments and simple harmonies.

'Baroque' describes the spirit of a good many of Rossini's opere serie, and this in itself indicates an essentially eighteenth-century quality in his genius. In making his terms with the new age he was faced with a problem of vocabulary which he never fully solved until his last works for the stage. The wide range of expressive harmony that made possible such a romantic tour de force as the 'Wolf's Glen' scene in *Der Freischütz* was not for Rossini, and in his search for dramatic truth he often found himself driven in the opposite direction towards Italian popular melody. One hesitates to call it 'folk' melody because the word carries heavy romantic overtones. It suggests too a primitive idiom divorced from the musical language of the time. Italian folk music had long since come to terms with tonality. It had fertilized Neapolitan opera since the time of Alessandro Scarlatti; and opera had enriched it in return. It was the music of a people who had never wholly lost touch with sophistication; and for Rossini it was the language of dignity and sincerity. The folk or popular idiom underlies all that is most deeply felt in Rossini's music. The famous 'Di tanti palpiti' from *Tancredi* is really a folk-tune beneath its finery. The Gondolier's Canzone, on the face of it a mere interpolation, is the emotional centre of Act III of *Otello*. The pastoral sung by Helen in *La Donna del Lago* counts for more than all the baroque duets and ensembles which make that opera difficult to perform today. Moses's prayer and the trio from *Le Siège de Corinthe*, Act III, are both examples of the popular idiom raised to the status of a high style. What more natural than for Rossini to use the Fisherman's Song to paint the backcloth against which the drama of *Guillaume Tell* unfolds? However, such a style as this—'folk' without being what the Americans call 'folkloric'— has certain limitations. Folk-songs are formal, symmetrical even; their expression is general and diffused if only because being strophic they repeat a single tune over and over again to words with a different sense. Their harmonies are straightforward; the melodic shape is all-important. The voice alone is the vehicle of expression; hence the emotional climax will be determined less by the harmonic progressions than by the tension of the vocal cords, i.e. the contours of the singer's line. There is no room here for subtleties of personal expression, and it is no coincidence that in Rossini's last three serious operas the choral element should have become more and more prominent. Moses and Tell are the embodiments of a whole people— that is their strength, musical as well as dramatic. Arnold, Mathilde, Aménophis and Anaïde are secondary figures, however beautiful the music they sing. For the extremes of personal feeling Rossini never devised an adequate musical vocabulary; yet this was precisely what contemporary taste, and contemporary libretti were beginning to demand.

Once the folk or popular element came to predominate in Italian opera the split with Germany opened wide. Weber also drew on native folk song, though in a more consciously romantic spirit than Rossini; but it is folk music with an entirely different physiognomy. A feature of Italian folk song is its tendency to change from minor to major mode with little shift of emotional significance beyond a certain feeling of release at the point of transition (the implications of this in relation to Verdi's use of tonality will be touched upon later). Another is the fondness of melodies in thirds, persisting to the point where the thirds clash with the accompanying chords. As the popular element becomes more pronounced in Rossini's successors, so we meet more and more often pentatonic phrase-ends such as these:

1

What is truly remarkable about Rossini's last work for the stage, which he wrote not for Italy but for France, is the extent to which it *anticipates* the course of Italian opera over the next twenty years, at a time when younger composers such as Mercadante, Pacini and Donizetti were still conscientiously exploiting the florid vein of *Semiramide*.

When Tell and Walter inform Arnold of his father's murder by the Austrians, Arnold reacts in the language which will serve Violetta at the height of her sorrow.

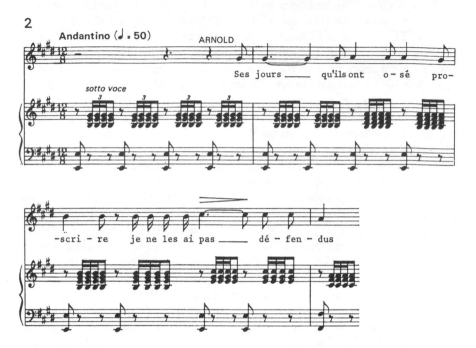

Another example is the famous 'Sois immobile', where Tell addresses his son as he prepares to take aim (see Ex. 3, facing page).

The feelings of Tell are not conveyed by means of poignant harmony. Rather they are externalized in the melodic figure given to the cello, which is extended formally like a frieze. Note the descending semitonal figure (*x*) like a lament. It is not so much an expression of sorrow as a symbol of it, like the symbols which occur in the accompaniments of a Bach cantata. Verdi uses it again and again in his early operas, and nearly always in recurrent, self-perpetuating patterns, as here. The vocal line is rigidly controlled in its expression, but the feeling rises to the surface as the melody winds its way into the major key, and is then repressed as it returns to the minor. The same procedure, even down to the use of the solo cello, will depict another suffering father: Rigoletto.

To set forth in detail all the forms of what might be called the Code Rossini would take too long. Like the da capo aria of the previous century and the various binary and ternary structures associated with the sonata and the symphony, they were partly designed to meet the needs of rapid production, as well as the tastes of an essentially conservative audience. There is a certain problem of terminology here. Nineteenth-century scholars and academics have devised neat labels for the different features of sonata form ('first subject', 'second subject', 'exposition', etcetera), which would doubtless have puzzled Haydn and Mozart. Nobody has

defined the forms of Italian opera in that way, though they are no less complex. Hence the present-day student of the period will often find himself obliged to invent his own technical terms for purposes of classification.

Any survey of operatic design in the primo ottocento must begin with the double aria, since this is in a sense the opera's point of departure—and for many people its raison d'être. The practice of dividing an aria into two sections contrasted in tempo was not new in Rossini's time. One has only to think of Donna Anna's 'Non mi dir' and the Queen of the Night's 'O zitt're nicht'. But it was Rossini who set the seal on the convention whereby every principal should have at least one aria in two self-contained sections—the first slow and expressive, the second fast and brilliant and known as the cabaletta. It was he, too, who carried furthest the expansion of this two-part structure into the 'scena' with its long preceding recitative, and its short interlude (with or without chorus) between the contrasted sections of the aria.*

---

* Lippmann (*op. cit.*) has charted meticulously the evolution of the Metastasian exit aria into the scena and aria of Rossini's time.

Nothing illustrates the essentially conservative nature of Italian opera so clearly as the persistence of certain verse-forms in the elements of which it is composed. The double quatrain (three lines of seven syllables followed by one of six) was the basis of the Metastasian *da capo* aria, the second verse forming the middle contrasted section. It continues into the age of Mozart and Haydn; and in Verdi's time it is still one of the commonest verse-forms in opera, though not the only one. Variants of it exist in five-, eight- and ten-syllable metre.* The librettist Cammarano had a predilection for the double sestet. Yet in all except narrative arias two verses were the rule, and in conformity with the trend towards popular melody they were set far more simply and schematically than in Hasse's or Mozart's day. The musical result is invariably bipartite, both in andante and cabaletta, with coda and—in the andante—a cadenza to follow. Bipartite; but not necessarily binary, since the structure usually contains a strong element of reprise and therefore of ternary form. Of the two movements the andante lent itself more readily to romantic expression, and is therefore one of the areas in which Rossini's successors headed by Bellini moved furthest away from their master. What Friedrich Lippmann describes as the 'open' melody,† that is, one which begins with recitative-like declamatory flourishes and then assumes a more periodic character as it proceeds—and he instances 'Pensi alla patria' from *L'Italiana in Algeri*—is a speciality of Rossini's. It cannot be found in any of Bellini's operas later than his first, though Donizetti gives a fine example of it in 'O tu che desti il fulmine' (*Pia de' Tolomei*). Verdi invariably follows Bellini's more periodic style of melody in all his first movements, not surprisingly; for Bellini was the greatest master of the vocal andante. No one devised such a wide variety of slow melodies as he. Some, like 'Ah non credea mirarti' (*La Sonnambula*), proceed from first note to last without ever repeating themselves. Others, like 'Qual cor tradisti' (*Norma*), are spun from repetitions of a short rhythmic pattern (this is a favourite method with Donizetti too). But whatever their character the bipartite feeling is always present. Not only that: the traditional move towards the dominant in the first part of a binary structure plays little or no part in Bellinian melody. Whereas Rossini and Donizetti generally have a central cadence on the dominant side of the key, Bellini tends to conclude his first section in the tonic, even in cases where the melody is of the non-repeating kind. 'Casta diva' never touches on the dominant at all. 'Qui la voce sua soave' from *I Puritani* makes a gesture in its direction at the words 'quì giurava essere fedele' only to contradict it in the next phrase with a descent to supertonic harmony (II) on the word 'crudele'; an unequivocal tonic cadence follows on 'sparì'. The commonest pattern in Bellini is the one identified by Lippmann‡ as $a^1 a^2 b a^2$, each letter representing a half-stanza. A typical instance is Riccardo's 'Ah per sempre' from *I Puritani*, where the section *b* is introduced by a fidgety figure in the woodwind which for the moment takes the weight from the voice (see Ex. 4, facing page).

This device is several times copied by Verdi in the course of a larger but still bipartite structure which may be described as $a^1 a^2 b a^3 c a^3$—cf. 'Dio di Giuda' (*Nabucco*), 'Ernani, Ernani involami' (*Ernani*), 'Sempre all' alba' (*Giovanna d'Arco*).

---

*For a technical description of Italian metres see Vol. II, p. 17.

†Lippmann, *op.cit.*, p. 170.

‡Lippmann, 'Verdi e Bellini', *Atti del I° Congresso Internazionale di Studi Verdiani 1966* (Parma, 1969), p. 189.

4

But the significant feature of all these andante designs is that they are tonally static. Even in Donizetti arias with their central cadences on V or III the gravitational pull of the tonic is still felt. The home key never disappears below the horizon as in the middle section of Fiordiligi's adagio 'Per pietà, ben mio, perdona' from *Così fan tutte*; hence a very clear distinction from the binary and ternary forms on which the German symphony and sonata are based. The binary movement of an eighteenth-century suite has the character of a question put then answered. The design of a Bellini andante is like a statement commented on and confirmed. Now, as any Bach fugue will show, the simplest, most fundamental form of antithesis is the juxtaposition of tonic and dominant. State the subject in C major, answer it in G major, and at once you have the basis of a musical argument. On this elementary sense of polarity the whole structure of German symphonic thought and logic rests, and with it the architectonic use of key-relationships, evident at its most spectacular in the first movement of Beethoven's 'Eroica'. The move towards the dominant is the first step in any symphonic exposition. The high point of drama occurs at the point where the opening subject is restated in the tonic key, usually after prolonged dominant preparation. Significantly enough, even in the eighteenth century the Italians were much slower than their German colleagues to exploit this tonic–dominant polarity. There is plenty of drama in Haydn's recapitulations, very little in Boccherini's. Conversely Germans who wrote Italian romantic opera found it very difficult to shake off their symphonic habit of thought. Ivanhoe's cavatina from Nicolai's *Il Templario* shows a typically German *Drang nach der Dominant* in its first quatrain.

A corollary of all this is that it is useless to look in the operas of Verdi and his contemporaries for any large-scale key-scheme such as can be found in Wagner's scenes or Mozart's finales. In Italian opera even andante and cabaletta may be in totally unrelated keys. 'Casta diva' (*Norma*) was written originally in G major;[*] its cabaletta is in F major. Verdi's 'Parmi veder le lagrime' (*Rigoletto*) is in G flat major, the cabaletta in D major; and examples could be multiplied indefinitely. There is no way of explaining the connections or lack of them. There is no structural reason why the Act II duet in *Rigoletto* should begin in E minor and end with a cabaletta in A flat major; it was merely that what Schoenberg called the 'tonal regions' were no part of Verdi's way of thinking.

* Though often printed in F.

For andantes in a minor key the most usual procedure was for the first quatrain to form a complete statement in the minor mode. The first two lines of the second quatrain would be set as an episodic comment ending on the dominant; the last two would be extended so as to form a complementary section in the tonic major. Examples of this are numerous and not confined to Italian opera. Another method was for the second quatrain to be sited entirely in the relative major, so that the movement ends in a different key to the one in which it began—a procedure which no German would countenance for a moment. Rossini adopts it in the Willow Song from *Otello*. Bellini found it especially congenial. Examples include 'Nel furor della tempesta' (*Il Pirata*) and—most moving of all—'Ah non credea mirarti' (*La Sonnambula*). A notable instance in Verdi is 'D'amor sull'ali rosee' (*Il Trovatore*). A subtle blending of both procedures—tonic minor to relative major, tonic minor to tonic major—is to be found in Donizetti's famous 'Una furtiva lagrima' (*L'Elisir d'Amore*).

The cabaletta also has a two-quatrain structure; normally a simple sixteen- or thirty-two-bar unit, which loosens up towards the final cadence so as to provide the singer with opportunities for display. It is a form handled more expertly by Donizetti and Pacini (known in his day as the 'master of the cabaletta') than by Bellini; but altogether it must be accounted among the less fortunate parts of the Rossinian legacy. In a scene such as Arsace's 'Eccomi infine in Babilonia' (*Semiramide*), where both movements are an expression of sexless musico–heroics, it is wholly appropriate. In cases where the preceding andante is filled with romantic feeling it can all too easily strike a jarring note. As late as 1880 Verdi was ready to defend the cabaletta in theory;* but once he had made enough money to be able to write the kind of opera he wanted the cabaletta was one of the earliest features to disappear. Its function would be summed up in a few long sweeping phrases, as in 'O voluttà del soglio' from the revised *Macbeth*. For it must be pointed out that the cabaletta had another purpose besides that of display. It provided a 'vent' for the emotion which was strictly controlled in the andante. For an Italian of the period emotion was like a charge of electricity to be earthed, not a warm bath in which to soak. It was not until Puccini and the 'Veristi' that composers enjoyed pricking the heart to make it bleed. Significantly, where an andante occurs on its own as a 'romanza' it is usually in the minor–major form, which carries its own 'vent' in the concluding section in the major. Minor-key cabalettas are not uncommon, though usually in the context of a so-called 'rondò-finale'. Mostly they conclude in the tonic major, e.g. 'Era desso il mio figlio' (*Lucrezia Borgia*) or 'A brani a brani o perfido' (*Luisa Miller*), but for conclusions in the relative major see 'Or sei pago o ciel tremenda' from Bellini's *La Straniera* or 'Ah se un giorno' from Donizetti's *Maria Stuarda*. A common feature of the Donizettian cabaletta is the move to the flat side of the key that occurs in 'Quando rapita in estasi' (III) and 'Spargi d'amaro pianto' (VI), both from *Lucia di Lammermoor*. This is one of the stock methods of giving an element of surprise to a type of melody that can become all too predictable; also it is a peculiarly Italian type of modulation, its harmonic logic depending on the equation of tonic minor and tonic major which is inherent in the Italian folk song. In the second case G flat is the relative major of E flat minor; and a native tradition extends the relationship to E flat major as

* Letter to Giulio Ricordi, 20.11.1880. *Copialettere*, p. 559.

well. The point is worth stressing since Verdi carries the principle still further, linking the tonic major with all other keys related to the tonic minor and drawing some of his most beautiful effects from the resulting modulations.

Ever since Rossini's time it had been customary to repeat the cabaletta with a ritornello intervening. One cannot talk of two verses here, since the words are always repeated together with the tune. The object was usually to give the singer an opportunity of embellishing the melody the second time round without new words to distract the listeners' attention. At what time the practice of decoration ceased it is impossible to say, since the evidence is conflicting. We cannot even be certain up to what point if at all Verdi expected his own cabalettas to be embellished in this way.* But he continued to construct them on the basis of an obligatory repeat, introducing into the ritornello material which is later taken up in the coda. In certain of his earlier cabalettas the ritornello will be cast in the form of a Rossinian crescendo. If there is a chorus present, as in most rondò-finali, it will give tongue in the ritornello and coda. Many cabaletta texts are marked in parentheses. This means quite simply that the singer must advance to the footlights and sing directly at the audience. The chorus will be confined to comments like 'How dark his brow!' or 'How joyful he appears!'; in other words they are supposed, somewhat improbably, to be out of earshot.

Next in importance to the aria came the duet. Here the same andante–allegro design is normally expanded by a preceding allegro. In the so-called 'gran duetto' the favourite pattern is that of the Semiramide–Assur duet in Act II of *Semiramide*. It can be found in the duets between Alaide and Arturo in Bellini's *La Straniera*, Gulnara and Seid in Pacini's *Il Corsaro*, Lucia and Enrico in Donizetti's *Lucia di Lammermoor*, Oberto and Leonora in Verdi's *Oberto Conte di San Bonifacio*—to name only a few. It consists of three movements: A. An allegro in which the same finite melody is given out successively, though to different verses, and in certain vocal combinations at different pitches, by each singer, ending in a substantial cadence. This is followed by a passage of dialogue during which the music modulates towards a new key and so leads into B, an andante which yokes the two voices in a chain of thirds (if they are soprano and contralto, or two sopranos), sixths (soprano and tenor), tenths (soprano and baritone or bass). Sometimes they sing together from the start, as in the Leonora–Cuniza duet in the appendix of Verdi's *Oberto*. More often they begin separately and with different material, since the text of B tends in most cases to imply a double soliloquy, with the characters turned away from each other. Sometimes only one voice will have a solo verse (Lucia–Enrico) and will be joined by the other immediately afterwards; and sometimes they will state the same melody one after the other as in the first movement, and then combine in a new idea (Alaide–Arturo). But the sixths, thirds or tenths will arrive sooner or later, and the movement will end with a swooning cadence. A brief transition, usually in brisk rhythm and prompted by some kind of intrusion (as for instance the sound of distant hunting-horns in *La Straniera*), will usher in C: a moderato or allegro in which once more the two voices will sing the same melodic period successively; then there will be a ritornello and the melody will occur yet

---

* In the original version of the tenor cabaletta ('Come poteva un angelo') from *I Lombardi alla Prima Crociata* Verdi provided a few simple embellishments of his own for the repeat. See p. 134.

again sung by both voices in unison, in dialogue, or linked together in whatever way the combination will allow. Sometimes it will be a straight cabaletta for voices in thirds, as in Bellini's 'Sì, fino all'ore'. This too has a precedent in the final movement of the duet between Semiramide and Arsace.

A number of variations on this basic pattern are possible. Donizetti is particularly skilful at ringing the changes. One finds two-movement duets (usually A and C, or B and C); even duets of which the first movement is in dialogue virtually throughout and held together by an orchestral rather than a vocal design, as in 'Soli noi siamo' (*Lucrezia Borgia*). This is a characteristic device of Donizetti's and used to good effect in 'Donna chi sei' (*Nabucco*). In Verdi's treatment of the duet in general one salient feature emerges. Whereas his predecessors preferred on the whole to entrust the same material to both voices, Verdi likes to keep his singers as far apart from one another musically as possible; in other words to give them different entries. Examples of both A and C where each voice enters with a different idea can be found in Rossini and Donizetti, but they are rare; and in Bellini rarer still. In Verdi they are an essential element of his musico-dramatic art with its roots in the clash of personalities and voice-types. Lacking a technical term for both species of movement we may refer to that in which the two voices sing the same melody successively as 'similar' and that in which the entries are different as 'dissimilar'. The 'similar' pattern in Verdi occurs mostly in love duets or duets of reconciliation.

At the other end of the scale there is the 'central finale'. A curious feature of early Italian romantic opera is that it throws the main weight of its musical elaboration in the middle rather than at the end—in the finale of Act I if there are two acts, of Act I or II if there are three. This is a legacy of eighteenth-century opera buffa, where the chief interest lies more in the comic complexity of the plot than in its often purely formal dénouement. Its origin is the 'ensemble of perplexity' which occurred regularly at the mid-point of the comedy and which offered to a composer like Mozart the opportunity for construction on a symphonic scale. Rossini was certainly not the first to introduce this feature into opera seria; but what is unmistakably Rossini's is the form and character which it took and which, like so many features of Italian romantic opera, is essentially the work of Rossini the comedian. As a humorist he particularly delighted in the spectacle of human beings transformed by emotion into puppets. The more alive they think they are the more mechanically they behave. The big ensemble or finale provides unlimited opportunity for exploiting this joke. When the captain of the city guard in Seville asks for a simple explanation of the uproar in Dr Bartolo's house he is confronted by one gibbering, gesticulating automaton after another, each convinced that his or her own account alone is true; yet viewed with the ribald objectivity of Rossini all their protestations fall into a grotesquely mechanical pattern. From this it follows Rossini will treat the ensemble–finale much more schematically than Mozart. However elaborate it may be its kernel is usually a pattern of three movements. The first is fast, and based on one or more orchestral themes which are repeated, extended sequentially into different keys, or even developed. The second movement is slow. Here everyone is 'struck all of a heap', as the result of some unexpected revelation. The dramatic development comes abruptly to a halt, as all express their utter astonishment, sometimes in a false canon, as in the *Barber*, sometimes in an elaborate unaccompanied ensemble, as in *Le Comte Ory*. Then suddenly the music breaks into furious activity. No longer numbed by shock the singers become only too articulate. But the beauty of the joke is that they are far too excited to do anything but shout and gesticulate. Each may complain, as in *L'Italiana in Algeri*, about the noise everyone else is making, while doing his or her best to aggravate it.

The scheme is a musical elaboration of that most universal and elementary of all jokes—the pratfall. The victim strides purposefully along, then steps on a banana-skin. His legs fly up and he lands on his coccyx. There follows a split second of innocent wonder as he surveys the universe from a new and unexpected angle; then, as his ganglia awake to life and transmit painful messages to his brain, he lets out a howl of agony. In these three stages we have the three movements of the Rossinian finale.* The disadvantage of this formula when applied to genuinely dramatic music is not only that it may introduce a note of caricature but that it interferes even more drastically than the aria with the dramatic evolution, freezing the action for long stretches at the very points where it ought to move forward. As in the aria Rossini's successors achieved more with the largo concertato or slow section than with the stretta. To the false canon Bellini and Donizetti preferred a sequence of two ideas, corresponding to the two stanzas of an aria first movement. The first will be given out by one singer, then perhaps by two others; the second, in which the full ensemble joins, will give the composer an opportunity to exploit his skill in voice-leading and the achievement of rich sonorities. The 'groundswell' in such concertati as 'D'un pensiero' from *La Sonnambula* and the famous sextet from *Lucia* (which is really the largo concertato from the Act II finale) is a Bellinian contribution. The effect is often to transfigure the most tense and tragic situations in accordance with a purely Italian lyric tradition, which finds no echo in German opera. But the final section or 'stretta del finale' is more often than not an anti-climax. Usually it is started by one singer; but before long everyone else is weighing in, each contributing his own unintelligible stanza to the general mêlée. One can almost speak of a standard stretta rhythm which occurs over and over again in Rossini and his successors (♩ ♫ | ♩. ♫ , etcetera), with an accompaniment of plucked chords and continual use of cymbals and bass drum. Rossinian crescendos are not uncommon in this context.

Here too Verdi had no alternative but to follow his predecessors, and once again it was a long time before he found a more convincing solution than they. There are few riper examples of unconscious comedy in music than some of the central finales of his early operas. The score flames and crackles with energy, the stage is filled with people standing poised to fly at each other's throats, and there they remain until rescued by the fall of the curtain. But at least in the stretta no soloist's honour was involved, so that Verdi could afford to dispense with it earlier than with the cabaletta. By the time of *Luisa Miller* it is no longer de rigueur; and once

---

* For a more detailed and slightly different analysis of the Rossinian finale see P. Gossett, 'The Candeur Virginale of Tancredi', in the *Musical Times*, Vol. CXI, No. 1538 (April 1971), pp. 326–9. Gossett sees the formula as one of four movements, two 'kinetic' and two 'static'. The second 'kinetic' movement he identifies in the transitional music that usually bridges the andante or largo concertato and the stretta. In fact this section of the scheme varies so widely in length and scope from opera to opera that it is difficult to speak here of a formula. Sometimes (e.g. in *Il Barbiere di Siviglia*) it is too short to qualify as a movement in its own right. Elsewhere (e.g. *Tancredi*) it is no more than a varied reprise of the first movement.

it has fallen away, the preceding slow movement, deprived of the contrast, loses its original identity to become merely one of those moments of lyrical expansion such as one expects at the high point of any opera. In *Il Trovatore* Verdi winds up the finale to Act II in much the same way as his mature arias, with a single phrase of cantilena from a soloist.

Rossini had given the coup de grâce to the old recitativo secco in *Elisabetta Regina d'Inghilterra* and *Otello* (though he returned to it temporarily in one or two of his later works).* But at no time did he attempt a symphonically constructed opera even in the limited sense of Weber's *Euryanthe*. Obviously once the so-called closed forms have been stamped with a finite mould, recitative will remain recitative however cleverly it may be interwoven with them. In the same way thematic reminiscence, of which all composers of the period with the strange exception of Mercadante made liberal and successful use, was bound to remain that and nothing more. It will be discussed further in connection with Verdi's *I Due Foscari*.

Other less important devices of Rossini's remained in vogue long after his own retirement from the musical stage. Clearly a dark day dawned for Italian opera when in *Ricciardo e Zoraide* (1818) he introduced a stage band.† From then on the banda became de rigueur for any context in which its presence was faintly plausible. Rossini's own use of it was always naturalistic and perfunctory; and as usual what is perfunctory in Rossini is apt to become banal in Donizetti and Bellini. It was left to Verdi to plumb the depths of vulgarity with his banda marches, even at a time when his style as a whole had reformed. It was not entirely his fault. The banda, a miscellaneous collection of wind instruments with clarinets predominating, always operated as a separate unit. It had its own conductor whose business it was to score in detail what the composer wrote out on two staves as for piano; and it was used to playing only one kind of music. The so-called Kinsky band at Venice had a very high reputation, and Verdi, who had refused to write for it in *Attila*, took good care to include it in all his subsequent Venetian operas.

Perhaps the most remarkable instance of Rossini's authority is the way in which all his successors take over as a matter of course the one musical device which has always been associated with his name, namely the crescendo—that excited reiteration of a phrase usually with tremolo violins and more instruments added with each repetition. A purely mechanical formula on the face of it; and no one can be certain who used it first. It has been credited to Guglielmi, to Mosca, to Mayr and various others, but only Rossini made it into a personal fingerprint, for he alone had the secret of making it sound new-minted with every recurrence. When it passed into the common language of opera it took on a secondhand quality, like the imitation of a great actor's mannerisms. To Bellini with his hatred of excessive noise the crescendo is as ill-suited as can be; yet he sometimes uses it to bridge two statements of a cabaletta, and so does Donizetti. Verdi dispenses with it in the body of his operas quite early on. As late as the *Vêpres Siciliennes* he was still drawing on it for the overtures. But, as we shall see, it is a slightly different style of crescendo.

The language of Italian romantic opera, then, is a creation of Rossini, whose personality it reflects. The difficulty arose when this same idiom was forced on

---

* It was not an innovation. String-accompanied recitative was already the rule in Naples by 1815.

† A precedent exists in Paisiello's *Pirro* (1787). See G. Roncaglia, *Rossini l'Olimpico* (Milan, 1946), p. 174.

those with a different temperament and outlook. This is especially true in the matter of dramatic expression. Rossini, like the classicist he was, remained outside the action he was depicting; his successors tried to enter in. His own attitude to the Swiss uprising in *Guillaume Tell* is purely aesthetic. He was no dyed-in-the-wool patriot— indeed he professed a horror for the 'spirit of the barricades'. Verdi on the other hand was emotionally involved with the Risorgimento, and his music shows it.

The circumstances which combined to keep operatic form in a relatively fixed mould also influenced the libretto. If opera plots in Italy seem less interesting than in France and Germany; if their dramatic content is both lower and less varied; if they make heavier demands on the listener's 'willing suspension of disbelief', it must be remembered that there was no flourishing native tradition of spoken tragedy to act as a yardstick. French opera was a product of the Grand Siècle; Lully himself modelled his operatic declamation on that of the Comédie Française. German opera was born at the time of the literary renaissance, and performed side by side with the plays of Goethe and Schiller. Not that the plots of *Die Zauberflöte* and *Der Freischütz* are anything but naïve fairy-tales. But in general German composers were more conscious of literary values than their Italian colleagues. The position of an Italian librettist was that of a master-craftsman. He was called a poet; and he wrote not 'libretti' but 'melodrammi'. His name was given pride of place on the playbill and still is (*La Traviata* is described in Italy as an opera by Francesco Maria Piave, with music by Giuseppe Verdi). But he was not expected to show any originality. In a well-known letter to the Countess Maffei,* who was trying to raise funds to help the by now indigent Solera, Verdi blamed the librettists themselves for their subservience to literary models; yet in this they were merely catering for public taste. The opera of the 1830s was the cinema of a hundred years later. Audiences wanted the film of the book, or the play as the case might be. Librettists therefore never strayed far from the beaten track of well-known plays and novels, classical or popular, and nearly always foreign. Besides the dramas of Schiller, Shakespeare, Byron and Hugo, the novels of Scott and Bulwer Lytton, a favourite hunting-ground was the Parisian theatre world, which produced on an average fifty new plays in a year. Many of these found their way into Italy either in translation or in the form of ballets. Anicet-Bourgeois, Pineu-Duval, d'Ancelot, Soumet, Souvestre, Méry, are the sources of many a Verdi or Donizetti opera. Given the somewhat rigid code of the musical theatre it was inevitable that they should all tend to assume a family likeness (*Anna Bolena* and *Beatrice di Tenda* are sisters under their music). Successful librettists were busy men and tended even more than composers to revert to their own fixed procedures and turns of phrase. The language of Cammarano and his kind was both stilted and monotonous. Bells are never bells but 'sacred bronzes'; midnight is always 'the hour of the dead'. In a brilliant essay Luigi Dallapiccola has compared these circumlocutions to Homeric epithets, evidence of the essentially 'epic' quality of the Italian nineteenth-century opera.† What is certain is that the verse structures which had remained in current use since the previous century were a determining factor in keeping Italian opera in its highly formal mould. 'New subjects, new verse-forms,' is Verdi's cry

---

* 3.9.1861. Copialettere, p. 521.

† 'Parole e musica nel melodramma', in *Quaderni della Rassegna Musicale*: 2 (Turin, 1965); A Grazebrook, in W. Weaver and M. Chusid (eds.), *The Verdi Companion* (London and New York, 1979), pp. 193–215.

during the preparations for *Il Trovatore*.* Indeed for anyone who wanted to change the pattern of opera, the verse must be the starting-point, as Wagner had begun to realize at the same time. The variety of metres provided by the libretto of *Les Vêpres Siciliennes* was as vital to Verdi's efforts to enlarge his scope as was the Stabreim to Wagner's. Pacini comments in his memoirs that the originality of *Norma* was partly made possible by the novelty of one of Romani's verse-forms.† Felice Romani certainly stands above the average librettist. But he too was over-worked and, like Cammarano and Solera, notoriously dilatory in supplying his verses—another factor in making the composition of an opera such a hurried affair.

But all criticism of Italian opera libretti must take into account the all-important fact that printed copies were not only cheaply available at every theatre but could be consulted during the performance, since the house-lights were never lowered. This is why even so experienced a composer as Donizetti never hesitated to make two characters sing different verses at the same time, each killing the other's words, as in the largo of the Bertucci–Faliero duet in *Marino Faliero* or in the sextet from *Lucia*; or why Verdi will drown an all-important exclamation like 'mio PADRE!!' in a burst of orchestral sound. Wagner the poet was prepared to write three preliminary operas to explain the action of one (*Siegfrieds Tod*); Piave and Romani preferred where necessary to print an antefatto on the fly-leaf of the libretto, summarizing the events which precede the rise of the curtain. In *Robert le Diable* Meyerbeer and Scribe used the narrative ballad, written in the iambic metre of ordinary speech and composed in a conversational 6/8 rhythm in such a way that every word was clearly audible. Narrative arias occur plentifully in Italian opera—they account for a large proportion of *Il Trovatore*—but happy the man, English or Italian, who could follow their sense by ear alone. It was not until well into his mid-career that Verdi became concerned to set his words intelligibly.

Another factor which no composer of the time could disregard was the 'convenienze', a system which divided singers into definite categories. Most operas contained only three principals, of which the commonest distribution was soprano, tenor and baritone (usually referred to as 'basso cantante'). If there was a fourth principal it was usually a full bass as in the famous '*Puritani*' quartet at the Théâtre des Italiens; or it might be a second soprano or mezzo-soprano (the two voice-types had not yet been officially distinguished).‡ Then there were the secondary parts—the heroine's confidante and 'feed', the messenger or henchman who brings that vital piece of news which provides the bridge between andante and cabaletta. He or she might also have to sustain a separate line in an ensemble—as does Arminio in *I Masnadieri* or Viclinda in *I Lombardi*, but nothing more. There was also an intermediate category known as '*comprimarii*', who qualified for a part in an ensemble of soloists, a duet, or even a cantabile or romanza; not, however, for a whole scena or double aria. Such roles if too elaborate could be very difficult to fill, since the singer had all the work of a principal without any of the réclame. Smeton (*Anna Bolena*), Rodrigo (*Pia de' Tolomei*), Wurm and Federica (*Luisa Miller*) are all instances of the use of *comprimario* singers to increase the range of characters.

---

*Letter to Cesare De Sanctis, 1.1.1853. *Copialettere*, p. 531. †Pacini, p. 54.

‡ The recognition of the dramatic mezzo-soprano as a separate voice-type had to wait for the advent of Pauline Viardot-Garcia. The singer Rita Gabussi of whom Verdi first thought in connection with Azucena in *Il Trovatore* is described in a notice of 1841 as a 'soprano sfogato for whom everything has to be adapted, transposed and manipulated'.

Finally there was the censorship. Libretti had always been subject to control from a higher authority. But the eighteenth century had been one of stability and tolerance; and it was not until the first grumblings of the French Revolution that censorship became a serious consideration. With the fall of Napoleon it was established throughout Italy as a political necessity, and woe betide the composer who dared to ignore it. In the preface to *Hernani* Victor Hugo equated modernism in literature with liberalism in politics. The government of Metternich favoured neither the one nor the other. Up till the abortive risings of 1848 strictness of censorship tended to vary according to latitude. In Lombardy–Venetia the Austrians rode the population with a light rein. So long as the Milanese flocked to La Scala and the Venetians to the Fenice and all enjoyed themselves, there was little to be feared. None the less a composer had to be prepared for last-minute intervention from the police, as happened to *I Lombardi alla Prima Crociata*; and threats of censorial interference induced Bellini and Romani to give up their *Ernani* and write *La Sonnambula* instead. But in the Papal States every line was scrutinized for subversive meanings, religious or political. In Rome Bellini's *Norma* had to revert to the play's original title, *La Foresta di Irminsul*, since 'norma' was a technical term in the liturgy. Likewise, in the days before Joan of Arc's canonization she could not be the subject of any opera given on the Roman stage. Verdi's *Giovanna d'Arco* became *Orietta di Lesbo*. The implication is clear. Better a lesbian than a heretic.

In the Kingdom of the Two Sicilies censorship reached preposterous lengths. It was partly a quarrel with the censors that caused Donizetti to break his connection with Naples in 1837. More than twenty years later Verdi withdrew his *Un Ballo in Maschera* from the San Carlo theatre for the same reason. *Maria Stuarda*, though based on a German classic, could only be presented under the title of *Buondelmonte*, since the conflict of Catholic faith and Protestant conscience was judged to be offensive. Very few of Verdi's 'Risorgimento' operas retained their original titles on the stages of Naples or Palermo; and where the subject was changed the situations tended to lose their force. In the case of an opera di ripiego the censors were both ruthless and infinitely painstaking. No line was too innocent to harbour a suspicious meaning. Any word which could evoke religion even in the most everyday metaphor must be changed. Thus in a libretto of *Oberto*, given at the San Carlo theatre in Verdi's absence in 1840, we find the following couplet altered out of recognition:

> Io sognava ai Cherubi
> Su dorate e bianche nubi

to become:

> Io contenta allor sognava.
> Sventurata! Io m'ingannava

and why? Because the word *Cherubi* (cherubim) was unacceptable. But in the meantime the second line has been given a completely different emotional slant, and one which the music was never intended to convey. As Verdi was never tired of pointing out, 'I don't write my music at random, however good or bad it may be; I always take care to give it a definite character.'*

* Letter to Marzari, 14.12.1850. *Copialettere*, pp. 109–11.

But what applied to Naples and Rome before 1848 extended to the whole of the peninsula after, until the proclamation of the Kingdom of Italy in 1861 brought a happy release. During those years of national frustration and disappointment even Verdi became reconciled to the necessity of altering the titles, characters and venues of certain well-known subjects. *Les Vêpres Siciliennes* in its Italian version was first published as *Giovanna de Guzman*. On the autograph score of *La battaglia di Legnano*, produced during the false dawn of the Roman republic in 1849, the alterations of names and places to fit *L'Assedio di Arlem* are in Verdi's own handwriting. In the case of this as of *Stiffelio* Verdi toyed with the idea of refurbishing the opera to fit a new plot altogether. *Rigoletto* emerged after a long battle with the Austrian police with its situations blessedly intact and only a change of place, name and epoch. But even these modifications were considered inadequate elsewhere. The most frequent casualty, however, was *La Traviata*; and Verdi had some bitter words to say about those 'holy priests who cannot bear to see represented on stage what they do every night behind closed doors'.* Ricordi's have in their possession a copy of Piave's libretto suitably 'emended' by one canon of the cathedral for a performance at Bologna. The alterations pass belief. Alfredo's drinking song ('Libiamo nei lieti calici') was considered far too licentious and therefore rewritten. Naturally 'croce e delizia' is disallowed and altered to 'pena e delizia'. Certain changes involve an extra syllable and therefore an extra note. Well might Verdi complain to his publisher that when certain theatres perform his works they ought to print under the title, *Words and music by Don . . .* , and then fill in the name of the censor. 'What would you say,' he wrote to his friend the sculptor Luccardi, 'if someone tied a black ribbon round the nose of one of your figures?'†

To all these circumstances which tended to limit the range of an Italian opera might also be added the public taste. It was impossible for a composer to think of educating his audience. They had come to be entertained. They knew what they wanted and if they failed to get it they made their feelings very plain. Sometimes an opera would be withdrawn after a single night because of audience hostility. A succès d'estime was of no value whatever. The opinion of critics counted for nothing, nor was it much heeded. (Indeed the critic's worst crime in a composer's eyes was to report that an opera had failed when it had in fact triumphed.) Verdi and his contemporaries had to carry their public with them; they could not afford, as Wagner could, to write for the future. Verdi's most remarkable achievement as an Italian opera composer was to reach to a point at which he could say of his last opera, 'I have written it to please myself.'‡

*Letter to C. De Sanctis, 16.2.1854. A. Luzio, *Carteggi Verdiani* (Rome, 1935–47), Vol. I, p. 24.
† Letter to Luccardi, 1.12.1851. *Copialettere*, p. 496.
‡ Letter to Giulio Ricordi, 9.6.1891. *Copialettere*, p. 712.

2 CHARACTERISTICS OF THE EARLY OPERAS

Verdi was twenty-six when his first opera was produced at La Scala, Milan, in the autumn of 1839. By the standards of the time it was a late start. The previous three years he had spent as a music-teacher and conductor of the local orchestra in Busseto. The training he had received from Vincenzo Lavigna after the Milan Conservatoire had shut its door in his face was strictly academic and old-fashioned. Original compositions were corrected in the style of Paisiello. 'In the three years I spent with him I did nothing but study canons and fugues. . . . Nobody taught me orchestration or dramatic technique. . . .'* On the subject of musical education Verdi became perverse in his later years and as usual inclined to exaggerate. Great composers often like to represent themselves as entirely self-taught—as indeed they are in everything that matters; and Verdi was more prone than most to look back in anger.

In his exercise books the names of Mendelssohn and Beethoven occur beside those of Corelli and Palestrina. The trouble was not that his training had been neglected or that it was out of date; merely that it had not been absorbed at a sufficiently early age to equip him with that natural fluency and resource which is its basic purpose. Accustomed from adolescence to write marches for the amateur orchestra of Busseto he found difficulty in bringing the rules of more advanced composition to bear on his 'native woodnotes wild'. It is not an uncommon phenomenon.

Indeed Verdi had a long and laborious road to travel before becoming, in the words of Ildebrando Pizzetti, 'a master of harmony'.† It began with the discovery in *Nabucco* of that broad vein of popular melody which did so much to bring about the opera's success, uniting with the traditions of Donizetti and Bellini to produce a style that is simple, direct and grandiose. The public liked it and asked for more, and Verdi gave it to them. Patriotic choruses, rousing or nostalgic, figure in most Verdi operas from *Nabucco* to *La Battaglia di Legnano*. Bellini provides the nearest precedent in the duet 'Suoni la tromba' (*I Puritani*), a square, simple tune a hair's breadth away from banality. Naïve though they are, Verdi was never ashamed of these patriotic choruses, any more than Elgar was ashamed of his 'Pomp and Circumstance' marches. They were written with the greatest sincerity of purpose. He was very much a man of his age, a passionate believer in the cause of Italian freedom. For him the nationalism of the Risorgimento was the gateway to a wider and grander conception of humanity. The path that begins with 'Va pensiero' and 'O Signore dal tetto natio' leads to the council chamber scene in *Simon Boccanegra*.

But there was a negative side to the picture. So long as Verdi continued in this path just so long he was confined to what Abramo Basevi as early as 1859‡ has called his 'grandiose' manner. In *Nabucco* style and subject are perfectly matched.

* Letter to Florimo 9.1.1871 quoted by C. Gatti, *Verdi* (1st ed., Milan, 1931), Vol. I, p. 68. English edition, trs. E. Abbott (London, 1955), p. 24.
† See I. Pizzetti, 'Contrappunto ed armonia nell'opera di Verdi', in *La Rassegna Musicale*, No. 3, Anno XXI, July 1951, pp. 189–200.
‡ Basevi, pp. 156–9.

As in Rossini's revised *Mosè* its hero is not a person so much as a people. Nabucco himself is like a force of nature; Abigaille is a monster; Zaccaria is the mouthpiece partly of a nation, partly of Jehovah; and Verdi always referred to him as 'the prophet'. Only the comprimarii Ismaele and Fenena are human-sized. When the drama is strictly individual, as in *Alzira*, the effect is often one of exaggeration. A notable feature of the early arias and duets is the elaboration of their accompanimental patterns, far surpassing anything to be found in Rossini or Donizetti. These enable Verdi to carry over the 'grand manner' of the choruses into the solo numbers, at the same time providing the singer with a far more magnificent platform than the simple see-sawing violins of Bellini. But, as Massimo Mila has pointed out, they rarely bear an organic relation to the melodies they support.[*] They give them emphasis but not always meaning; and what the melodies gain in force they sometimes lose in distinctiveness, and indeed distinction, so that the whole score takes on the quality of a poster rather than a painting. Only when these fidgety accompaniments begin to fall away do the characters acquire depth and humanity.

The 'grandiose' manner of the early operas is matched by a style of scoring which has often been harshly criticized, and sometimes irrationally praised. It is best described as utilitarian. It serves its purpose and little more. In this area Verdi had started with every possible disadvantage of time and place. What may be called Rossini's 'false democratization' of the orchestra had debased the tradition of instrumental writing throughout Italy. What was stylish with him became cheap with his successors. In the 1830s and '40s voice was all that mattered, and the orchestra had two main functions: to support the singer in such a way as to bring out the variety of the vocal line; and to stimulate applause by making as much noise as possible. Solo instruments were featured a good deal—wind, rather than strings, because of their more voice-like quality. Often there would be a virtuoso clarinettist or trumpet-player whose talents it was desirable to parade in some prelude or obbligato; for this was the age when every virtuoso whether on double bass or cornet aspired to play Paganini's variations on *Le Carnaval de Venise*. Hence the miniature concertos like circus acts, such as the clarinet prelude to Act III of Pacini's *Saffo*; and even the violin solo in the third act of *I Lombardi*, though cleverly written for the instrument, is little better as music. Generally speaking all instrumental obbligati tended to follow the same bel canto style, even in the case of a trumpet, which is hardly a bel canto instrument.

The composition of the orchestra was always the same; and a glance at the way it was set out in manuscript is revealing. There was no attempt as now to group the instruments in 'families'—strings, woodwind, brass. At the top were the violins and the violas. Next came first flute and piccolo, in that order, and on separate staves; then the two oboes, two clarinets, four horns (each pair crooked in a different key, since long after the invention of valve horns the delusion persisted that four instruments were needed to do the work of two),[†] two trumpets, two bassoons, three trombones and a brass bass known as the cimbasso, which seems

[*] M. Mila, *L'arte di Verdi* (Turin, 1980), p. 61.

[†] The first composer to employ valve-horns in an opera was Halévy in *La Juive* (1835). Italian composers however continued for many years to insist on the natural horn with all its disadvantages. As late as 1883 Verdi opened the four-act *Don Carlos* with a passage for four horns in unison, each crooked in a different key!

to have been a variety of bombardon.* Timpani and bass drum follow as the usual percussion instruments, with side-drum, cymbals, triangle and tam-tam added as required; likewise the harp. At this point in the score we find the voice parts, solo and then chorus; the last two staves were allotted to cello and double bass respectively. The division is roughly into melody, harmony and bass instruments. The first group includes first violins, first flute, oboe, clarinet, trumpet and piccolo.† The harmony instruments are second violins, violas, horns and trombones, and the woodwind when used in pairs. The bass are bassoons, cimbasso, cellos and basses. It is a very approximate division, and a Rossini or a Mercadante would not abide by it; but Verdi in his early days almost invariably did. His accompanying patterns are normally beaten out by strings; where he wants them underlined, as in the introduction to a martial cabaletta, he adds horns and sometimes bassoons. His trombones operate as a self-contained unit together with the cimbasso.

As a melody works to its climax he will reinforce it with more and more 'melodic' instruments, possibly rounding off the highest three or four notes with trumpet and piccolo.‡ The result of all this is that in the cabalettas particularly the orchestral score is full of short fragments of phrases whose only purpose has been to set in relief a certain contour in the singer's line. This habit persisted with Verdi well into his middle years, and is one reason why so many orchestral players, particularly violinists, dislike performing his operas. In his use of sustaining instruments he follows a native tradition, pointing the modulations that colour the melody; and this practice also remained constant with him for most of his career. The voice will begin over an accompaniment of strings alone. At the first accidental, woodwind (usually clarinets and bassoons) will add sustaining chords, other wind instruments will join in as he approaches the end of the first section, and the scoring will thicken even more towards the final cadence. Verdi also shares Donizetti's and Bellini's fondness for wind instruments in thirds, particularly in introductions to arias,§ and in the kind of orchestral melody that so often forms the basis of a rapid dialogue (see overleaf, Ex. 5).

So much, then, Verdi took over from his predecessors. Certain procedures, however, bear his own personal stamp right from the beginning, as for instance the use of the rapid pizzicato arpeggios on cello to create a sudden access of energy within a slow melody (see overleaf, Ex. 6).

More arresting still are the pieces—at least one in each opera—in which the instrumentation is on the scale of chamber music and the sonority carefully if empirically calculated. Here more than anywhere the future composer of *Falstaff*

---

*See R. Meucci: 'Il cimbasso e gli strumenti affini nell'Ottocento italiano', *Studi Verdiani* V (Parma, 1989), pp. 109–47.

| The practice of setting out the piccolo on a separate stave below that of the first flute was apparently of fairly recent origin. Rossini normally placed his two flutes on the same stave making either double piccolo as required. His successors tended to dispense with second flute in favour of piccolo. The orchestra of the San Carlo Theatre at Naples, exceptionally, contained two flutes *and* a piccolo—an amenity of which Donizetti in *Lucia di Lammermoor* and Verdi in *Alzira* and *Luisa Miller* took full advantage.

‡ To achieve the various gradations of emphasis the instruments are usually added in the following order: flute and clarinet, oboe, first violins, trumpet, piccolo. In the case of the lower male voices bassoon and cellos might be added at some stage.

§ The woodwind introduction can be traced back in opera seria to the turn of the century in the works of Mayr and his contemporaries. See Lippmann, VI, p. 68.

and Act III of *Aida* is revealed. Early instances of this include Zaccaria's prayer (*Nabucco*) with its six solo cellos; Giselda's prayer (*I Lombardi*) with its eight violins, one cello, one bass, flute and clarinet; the romanze of Carlo (*Giovanna d'Arco*) and Odabella (*Attila*) and on a larger scale the duet from Act I and the sleepwalking scene from *Macbeth*. In every case the colour and texture remain constant throughout the number, which is thus carefully marked off from the rest of the score. Rarely before the first and third acts of *La Traviata* does Verdi mix chamber and orchestral instrumentation.

In general the sensitiveness of Verdi's scoring matches the refinement or otherwise of his musical thought, which is why even at its most coarse it is never ineffective. True, an opera as well integrated as *Nabucco* still has one or two jarring moments, as when bassoon arpeggios are added to the bass line of the andante of Zaccaria's cavatina, giving it a most unprophet-like roguishness. The progress of Verdi's orchestral technique can best be seen in those operas which he revised or refashioned after several years. In Oronte's cavatina 'La mia letizia infondere' (*I Lombardi*) he underlines the return to the main key with a drum roll and full sustaining wind including trombones and cimbasso. In the revised version from *Jérusalem* the same effect is obtained by means of woodwind alone. Gradually he begins to break down the old divisions, to imagine a wider variety of possibilities. The exquisite wood-wind passage which introduces 'Caro nome' (*Rigoletto*) he could never have written in his early operas because it would not have occurred to him to treat the full double woodwind as a separate self-sufficient organism.

For Verdi, as for Donizetti and Bellini, the starting-point of opera was the voice; and his early scoring shows that he was often unable to think of the orchestra except in relation to it. As early as *Ernani* he refused to supply the full score a month before the first night of the opera 'since I am accustomed to begin the orchestra-tion during the piano rehearsals'.* In other words how he scored an aria depended often on how the singer sang it. As time went on the orchestra took an ever stronger hold on his imagination. The sketches for *Rigoletto* show that the all-important motif which begins the storm scene occurred to Verdi straight away in its orchestral guise; and it is significant that in this opera he was accused of sub-ordinating the singers to the orchestra far too often.† But many of his most original and striking instrumental effects, as for example the soft accompaniment for full orchestra that begins the 'Miserere' scene from *Il Trovatore*, are like the best piano effects of Schubert; they would never have occurred to a born virtuoso of the medium.

The initial roughness of Verdi's orchestral technique partly accounts for the flatness of the descriptive passages in the early operas—the clearing of the sky in *Attila*, the sunrise in *Jérusalem*, the storm in *Giovanna d'Arco*; but there is another factor. Italy, then so conservative, still preserved some traces of the baroque tradition whereby an object or concept referred to in the text was *externalized* in some imitative figure in the music that accompanied it.‡ During the eighteenth century this practice was still universal. But with the dawn of romanticism musical description took a new turning; it became in Beethoven's words 'mehr Ausdruck der Empfindung als Malerei'. The musical images of Liszt and Wagner have an extra dimension. They may imitate the sound and shape of the objects to which they refer; but they endow them with a wealth of poetic and psychological over-tones. The storms in *Die Walküre* and *Les Préludes* are not just imitations of nature. In one can be heard the shuddering anxiety of the hounded Siegmund; in the other the agony of the pseudo-Lamartine hero buffeted by life's tribulations. This kind of description made its way very slowly into Italian music. There is a hint of it in Act IV of *Guillaume Tell* where the sun, gradually emerging from the clouds, is associated with the dawn of liberty. But the preceding storm is onomatopoeia and little else. Bellini's tempest in *I Puritani* comes nearer to the German ideal with an essentially melodic storm intended to 'portray the sadness of nature beneath the lightnings of heaven';§ but Verdi's musical descriptions remain for a long time on

---

* Letter to Mocenigo, 9.4.1843. M. Conati: *La bottega della musica: Verdi e La Fenice* (Milan, 1983), p.39.

† See A. Della Conte, 'Saggio di bibliografia delle critiche al "Rigoletto"', *Bollettino dell'Istituto di Studi Verdians*, no. 9 (Parma, 1982), pp. 1634–95.

‡ This is in itself a legacy from the sixteenth-century madrigal where similar 'imitations' often occur in the vocal lines. 'Madrigalisms' are not infrequent in Verdi's voice parts.

§ Letter to Florimo, 21.9.1834. *Epistolario*, p. 437.

the imitative level. The wind that blows fitfully in Riccardo's romanza (*Oberto*) and Pagano's cavatina (*I Lombardi*) is an external effect grafted on to the accompaniment. In the same way the descriptive interludes in *Attila* and *Jérusalem* are mere exercises in sonority with no more musical depth than a Czerny study. In *Jérusalem* the sunrise immediately follows Giselda's (now Hélène's) prayer with its chamber-scoring and so Verdi is able to add to the suggestion of growing brightness by gradually augmenting the strength of the orchestra. It is a rather naïve tour de force but little more. *Macbeth* is the first opera in which Verdi's tone-painting begins to take on an extra dimension; where the wind-swept bleakness of Shakespeare's 'blasted heath' is absorbed into the heart of the drama. From then on we may indicate the storm in Act III of *Il Corsaro*, the opening of *Luisa Miller* with its matutinal freshness, the prelude to Act II of *Stiffelio*, as instances of description in depth, where the music goes beyond an external imitation of nature's sounds and shapes. Finally there is the motif which introduces the storm scene in *Rigoletto* and which imitates nothing; yet it sets the emotional atmosphere with all the precision of a Wagnerian leitmotiv.

For Verdi opera was music-drama right from the start. No composer took so much thought over the choice of his plots except perhaps Bellini; and certainly no other composer was so insistent on keeping close to the original literary source as he. Indeed it was often through the determination to follow a twist of the plot that he was led to new formal solutions. But his concern with dramatic pace coupled with an initially blunt technique resulted in a different attitude to the conventions from that of his predecessors. Both Rossini and Bellini tended increasingly to expand the formal units; both to some extent liked to submerge the boundaries that marked them off from recitative, one by incorporating declamatory flourishes in his arias, the other by treating the recitatives themselves as extensions of arias in low relief. Verdi tends not to expand but to contract. At first his arias are more schematic than those of his predecessors, and the movements shorter and plainer. Not for him the 'heavenly length' of Bellini—or not yet. Long-windedness of any kind he detested: 'As for the duration of the pieces, brevity is never a fault . . . I do recommend brevity since that is what the public likes.'* This injunction, from one of Verdi's earliest letters to Piave, runs like a burden through their correspondence during the first years of the partnership. In general recitative is kept to a minimum: 'You won't find more than a hundred lines of recitative in all four acts of *Nabucco* or *I Lombardi* put together.'† In Verdi's view, recitative of the free, conversational type, successor to the old recitativo secco, slackened the interest. Hence his preference, wherever possible, for other means of connecting set numbers or effecting his dramatic transitions: conversation against a background of dance music, isolated formal strophes, and that species of quasi-formal declamatory dialogue between voice and orchestra which makes Don Carlo's confrontation of Ernani so impressive. At the same time no one can make more powerful use of *declamatory* recitative or what in the previous century would have been called 'accompagnato' than the young Verdi.

---

* Letter to Piave, 8.8.1843. F. Abbiati, *Giuseppe Verdi* (4 vols) (Milan, 1959), I, pp. 471–2.
† Letter to Brenna, 15.11.1843. Conati, p. 102. A comparison of Acts I of *Lucia di Lammermoor* and *Ernani* will show 78 bars of recitative in the latter as against the former's 109. Both acts last for approximately the same length of time.

In a word, Verdi never dawdles. His movements make their effect less by their individual beauty than by swift succession and mutual contrast. It is possible to speak here of a 'dialectic of drama' in which the logic evolves through a system of statement and counter-statement. That this was fundamental to Verdi's whole conception of large-scale composition transpires clearly enough from one of Muzio's letters. Verdi had received the flattering commission from the Società dei Nobili in Milan to compose a cantata to celebrate a congress of learned men to be held in Milan in 1844. The text was by Andrea Maffei, a knight of the Roman Empire and a poet and translator of no mean standing. He was also a friend of Verdi's with whom he was to collaborate in *I Masnadieri*. But in this case no collaboration was possible.

> [Maffei] had written the most beautiful, sublime piece of poetry ever; it was the breath of the Eternity creating the spirit of wisdom; but it was decidedly impossible to set to music; here there were lines in free metre, there three-line stanzas, elsewhere quatrains; and in general there was no dialogue; and the Signor Maestro couldn't divide the poem into separate pieces so as to alternate the chorus with the principals; he wanted something dramatic.*

This sense of dialogue or dramatic dialectic expressed in a succession of short, contrasted movements each carrying the musical argument a stage further forward provides the basis of an entirely new synthesis, which is fully achieved for the first time in *Rigoletto*. Of previous composers only Donizetti may be said to have pointed the way in such works as *Lucrezia Borgia*, an opera which Verdi knew well and from which he learned much. In the duet between Lucrezia and Alfonso in Act I there is also a sense of dialectic, but far less pith and urgency than in Verdi. The older composer remains tied to a more leisurely conception of music-drama.

Hand in hand with the evolution of Verdi's dialectic goes his sharp characterization of voice-types, and also what is perhaps his most striking single innovation— the 'discovery' of the high baritone. The term baritone is traditionally vague in its application. Before the nineteenth century it referred not to a voice but a string instrument, and most of those who style themselves baritone today would have been called bassi cantanti. The Germans have never until recently recognized it as an independent voice category; their lower male voices are either 'bass' or 'high bass'. The French 'baryton martin' is essentially a low tenor. The Verdian high baritone, whose range is similar, needs a much fuller consistency of tone. Shaw accused Verdi of crimes against the human voice; of confining the baritone to the top fifth of his range in contrast to Wagner who distributed his vocal writing much more evenly. But Wagner wrote for basses and bass baritones or 'high basses'. Verdi demanded a true baritone with an area of comfort roughly a tone higher than that of the old-fashioned basso cantante; a voice that can move smoothly and easily above the bass stave and open out round about F and G. Such singers are rarer than is generally supposed. Many of them want to turn heroic tenor. The Count of Luna and Rigoletto are too often assigned to the commoner species of

---

*Letter to Barezzi, 30.6.1844. Garibaldi; *Giuseppe Verdi nelle lettere di Emanuele Muzio ad Antonio Barezzi* (Milan, 1931), pp. 169–70.

high bass, with results which the forty-five-year-old Bernard Shaw described with deadly accuracy.*

But for Verdi the true baritone was to become the nub of his essentially masculine dramatic art, a central point from which he reached out to encompass every variety of emotion and character. For him the baritone above all is an embodiment of *force*. Having once defined its scope Verdi was able to bring the other voice-categories into an equally sharp focus. The key work here is *Ernani*, where once and for all the three types—tenor, baritone and bass—are clearly marked off from one another, each with his own emotional properties and characteristic line: the tenor ardent, lyrical and despairing; the bass dark, granite-like, inflexible in his purpose for good or ill; the baritone iridescent with all the colours of the emotional spectrum, a dynamo of energy. He is Jupiter to the bass's Saturn. Their encounter is the irresistible force meeting the immovable object. *Ernani* is the first opera of what might be called vocal 'scontro'; an opera whose dramatic force and musical interest derive from the clashing of characters embodied in vocal archetypes. There is no precedent for this in Rossini or Donizetti; the confrontation of Balthasar and Alfonso in *La Favorita* is static by comparison. Each party remains encapsulated within his own world. In *Ernani* and many subsequent works the principals are like dodgem-cars in a fairground. They collide, strike sparks off one another, and so drive the opera forward.

It took longer for Verdi to define his female types quite so clearly. Giovanna in *Giovanna d'Arco* is one of the few instances in early Verdi of a heroine fully individualized; Abigaille (*Nabucco*) and Lady Macbeth are also sharply if extravagantly drawn. But most of the pre-*Rigoletto* heroines have a certain undifferentiated quality (though no more so than their predecessors in Donizetti and Bellini). One or two even lack consistency, as, for instance, Odabella in *Attila* and Luisa in *Luisa Miller*. One reason for this is that among the female categories there was less occasion for definition by contrast. Verdi's discovery of the mezzo-soprano begins with Azucena in *Il Trovatore*, four years after Meyerbeer had presented in Fidès the first of the great 'mother figures' of opera. From then on the mezzo-soprano assumed in Verdi's works the function and characteristic that he had previously associated with dramatic sopranos such as Abigaille and Lady Macbeth. She became a female equivalent of the baritone with less poetry than the soprano but more power. Azucena can always steal the show from an indifferent Leonora.

The conflict of personalities embodied in voice-types—this is perhaps the young

---

* G. B. Shaw, 'A Word More about Verdi', first published in the *Anglo-Saxon Review* (March, 1901), reprinted in *London Music in 1888-9 as heard by 'Corno di Bassetto'* (London, 1937), pp. 395-6. 'The whole secret of healthy vocal writing lies in keeping the normal plane of the music, and therefore the bulk of the singer's work, in the middle of the voice. Unfortunately the middle of the voice is not the prettiest part of it; and in immature or insufficiently trained voices it is often the weakest part. There is, therefore, a constant temptation to use the upper fifth of the voice almost exclusively; and this is what Verdi did without remorse. . . . He practically treated the upper fifth as the whole voice and pitched his melodies in the middle of it instead of in the middle of the entire compass. . . . The upshot of that, except in the case of abnormally pitched voices, was displacement, fatigue, intolerable strain, shattering tremolo, and finally, not, as could have been wished, total annihilation, but the development of an unnatural trick of making an atrociously disagreeable noise and inflicting it on the public as Italian singing.' Bülow echoed this stricture when he dubbed Verdi 'der Attila der Kehlen' ('the Attila of the throat'). *See* G. B. Shaw, *Shaw's Music*, ed. Dan H. Lawrence (London, 1981), III, p. 580.

Verdi's most striking contribution to the resources of Italian opera. It explains his preference for the 'dissimilar' rather than the 'similar' pattern of duet, since in this way he can achieve the greatest degree of tension between the characters. It provides another reason why, in the early works, the duets and ensembles are generally more striking than the solos. *Ernani* really springs to life with the entry of Don Carlo into Elvira's apartment. Francesco's vision of the Last Judgement (*I Masnadieri*) is musically an ambitious failure; but his duet with Moser immediately afterwards transports us to a different world. That same duet affords a good instance of another Verdian characteristic: his ability to make a tremendous effect through a bass voice conjured up seemingly from nowhere. Tenor, soprano and baritone, to establish themselves as characters of any significance, have to be principals or at least sub-principals (e.g. Medora in *Il Corsaro*, Macduff in *Macbeth*), but a Verdian bass can crown a scene with just a few phrases, even if he has never appeared before and will never appear again. Barbarossa (*La Battaglia di Legnano*), Leo (*Attila*) are further instances of this.

Inevitably then the early operas are greater than the sum of their parts. Verdi's melodic style in those years is not one that draws attention to itself as does Bellini's. Basevi acutely observes the lack in Verdi of those appoggiaturas (i.e. resolving discords on strong beats) which are a notable characteristic of Bellini's melodic style.* More than once Verdi was accused of lacking originality; and it is true that he was mostly content to use the stock procedures of the time in somewhat blunter, more 'popular' form. But even at their least distinctive his melodies have one salient feature: they tend to increase in interest towards the final cadence. 'Tacea la notte' from *Il Trovatore* is a marvellous example of an aria illumined from its final phrase. In all this Verdi stands at the furthest remove from Berlioz, whose melodies usually trail away into an unemphatic ending. Bellini, Donizetti and Rossini all distribute their melodic interest more evenly. But Verdi's tendency in this matter is all part of the essentially forward thrust of his music. Akin to this is his invariable practice of elaborating however slightly the accompaniment of a melody when it is repeated. This too contributes to the sense of gathering momentum. Sometimes in the earlier works the momentum gets the better of him; and then we have the riot of noise, that over-use of displaced accent for which he was often criticized (see overleaf, Ex. 7).

The duets are remarkable for their wide range of expression and contrast, even when their material is not intrinsically striking. Best, generally speaking, are those between soprano and baritone where the tension is most marked. The standard love duet evoked less of a response from Verdi than from his contemporaries. An early exception is the duet between Carlo and Giovanna in *Giovanna d'Arco* in which, significantly, the situation is complicated by the heroine's sense of guilt and betrayal. It is not until the masterpieces of the middle years that Verdi realizes all the simple poetry of romantic love.

But it is in the large ensembles, the concertati, that Verdi shows his originality most clearly. Right from the beginning he showed an ability to float a succession of contrasting ideas on a single rhythmic impulse without ever allowing the structure to fall apart—a feat possible only to one who is a master of rhythm. That Verdi was such a master is evident even from the most primitive of his early pieces,

* Basevi, pp. 16–17.

where there is usually some quirk to relieve the squareness. If at first his harmonic touch falters his feeling for rhythm never does. In the overture to *Un Giorno di Regno* he already shows his ability to build a powerful unit from a succession of irregular phrases. How many people realize that the main section of the brindisi in *La Traviata* consists of a ten-bar phrase? So skilfully are the melodic stresses calculated that the asymmetry passes unnoticed.

Of the two standard methods of introducing an opera Verdi succeeds better with the short prelude than with the formal overture, largely because it enables him to sum up more pithily the dramatic essence of the entire score, and even to begin the drama before the rise of the curtain. The eight overtures written between 1839 and 1850 are generally insubstantial for their length. Ever since the Italians had begun to neglect the symphonic principles of construction and the architectonic use of tonality the classical overture was an anachronism; yet for years they continued to pay it lip-service. Rossini, in whom the symphonic sense was still present, flattened its perspective when he omitted the development and second transitional passage, making the second subject follow the first without a break during the recapitulation. But this was a personal formula. Verdi on three occasions (*Un Giorno di Regno, Luisa Miller, Stiffelio*) uses a variant of sonata form current in Mayr's day, in which a short development leads from the end of the exposition straight into the second subject reprise. *Oberto, Giovanna d'Arco, Nabucco, Alzira* are more primitive in their design, each having the character of a pot-pourri. *La Battaglia di Legnano* offers a more unusual solution which will be discussed in its place. Most striking of all is the overture to *Luisa Miller*, if only because it contradicts almost every tendency in Verdi's art noticed so far. It is strictly monothematic; its one subject is treated with a logic worthy of Schubert, and the whole movement is scored with a delicacy and brilliance recalling Weber. This feat of 'musical science' recalls the anecdote told about him during his days of study with Lavigna. A colleague of Verdi's teacher who taught at the Milan Conservatoire was complaining that none of the students in his class had been able to write a correct fugue on the subject he had set them. Lavigna promptly handed the theme to Verdi who returned after a while with a correctly worked out fugue in which the subject was embellished with 'double canon', 'as,' said Verdi, 'it seemed to me rather uninteresting and I wanted to enrich it'.* But the overture to *Luisa Miller* is not just a feat of academic technique; it is a beautiful piece of music. It illustrates very clearly the dangers of generalizing about Verdi's procedures. Even in his youth he was far too wide-ranging an artist ever to confine himself within narrow formulae. If at first he generally avoided the 'melodie lunghe lunghe lunghe'† of Bellini he could none the less write in the Sleepwalking scene from *Macbeth* a melody far longer than any written by his predecessor. If he tended to load his 'larghi concertati' with a greater variety of ideas than anyone before him, he could also, in the Act I finale of *Il Corsaro*, evolve an entire largo movement most effectively from a single thematic cell.

In tracing the course of Verdi's development Abramo Basevi noted that with *Luisa Miller* came the beginning of a new style or manner.

> The first manner [*says Basevi*] is marked by a predominance of the grandiose, which betokens the influence of the last operas of Rossini. In the second the grandiosity becomes less, vanishes even: every character stands only for himself; and because the emotions are those of individuals they have less need of exaggeration; hence the vocal lines, however impassioned, proceed more calmly. The melodies are lighter and less broad, the rhythms more fluent and less involved, the themes are more homely and grateful to the ear. . . . In his second manner he moves closer to Donizetti.‡

Like Wilhelm von Lenz's celebrated division of Beethoven's work into three periods, Basevi's distinction has been taken up by later biographers as a vague but useful point of reference. But it should be remembered that Basevi was writing in 1859, with five of Verdi's greatest operas yet to come; and shrewd though his comments undoubtedly are it would be foolish to pretend that the perspective on Verdi's output has not changed since then or that there are not more important turning-points in his career—*Les Vêpres Siciliennes*, for instance, where he entered on a new scale of operatic thought from which he never subsequently departed. The tendency towards individualism that Basevi first notices in *Luisa Miller* is present from the beginning. Some of the most grandiose of the earlier operas resolve themselves in their final pages into dramas of individuals—in the case of *Attila* with results that are faintly ludicrous. What is new in *Luisa Miller* is the delicacy and subtlety with which personal feelings are explored. Verdi's musical resources had by then advanced to the point where he could penetrate below the turbulence of surface emotion to a clear well of lyrical poetry. Here the influence of two years spent in Paris was decisive. Indeed one can never over-estimate the role

---

*G. Monaldi, *Verdi 1839–1898*, 3rd edition (Turin, 1951), p. 17. H. Gerigk, *Giuseppe Verdi* (Potsdam, 1932), p. 12, cast well-merited doubts on the truth of this anecdote whose only source is Monaldi's frequently inaccurate biography. True or false, it has a characteristic flavour.

† Verdi's own description. See letter to C. Bellaigue, 2.5.1898. *Copialettere*, p. 416.

‡ Basevi, pp. 156–9. In fact, up to the time of *Aroldo* (1857) Basevi discovered no less than four successive 'manners' in Verdi. The third, introduced by *La Traviata*, was marked by the influence of French opera, the fourth (*Simon Boccanegra*) by that of German!

played by French music in the enlargement of Verdi's vocabulary and the refinement of his instrumental style. The three operas written in Paris during the
years 1847–9—*Jérusalem, Il Corsaro, La Battaglia di Legnano*—all contain numbers
or scenes which reek of the Opéra. In *Luisa Miller* these French traits are
gathered up in a synthesis that is wholly Italian, and that points the way to the
great triad of Verdi's mid-career. But the process of growth and assimilation is,
we repeat, gradual and continuous. Even *Luisa Miller* reverts here and there to the
'grandiosity' of the earlier operas: while the simplicity noted by Basevi can be
found as early as *I Due Foscari*.

Well before *Luisa Miller*, too, an individual harmonic style is beginning to
emerge. There is nothing revolutionary about it; no definite break with the current
language of its time. It reveals itself, like Beethoven's, in elliptical progressions, in
the by-passing of standard procedures. There are harmonic side-slips, non-functional
chromatic inner-parts, bass notes displaced, unexpectedly anticipated or protracted.
Such traits are purely personal, owing nothing to academic training and, unlike
the unorthodoxies of *Oberto* and *Un Giorno di Regno*, they are unfailingly and
unselfconsciously *strong*.

Two instances may suffice.

In Ex. 8 the harmonic jump (*x*) is acceptable as a variation of the orthodox
progression (I–V) which had occurred beneath the same melody in the first four
bars of the period. But there is no defending these ugly sevenths produced by
conflicting patterns in Ex. 9. It is just bad craftsmanship.

In the operas from *Macbeth* onwards we shall have occasion to notice a very
personal use of second-inversion chords 6-4 and 6-4-3, particularly the former.
Indeed a whole book could be written on this subject alone. Perhaps the reason

is that, as Massimo Bruni suggests,★ the 6–4 is the propulsive chord par excellence and therefore especially suited to Verdi's continually forward-moving operas. Also it is traditionally the chord of expectancy, and as such regularly introduces the main cadenza in a concerto. At all events second inversions, often unprepared and often sited in a remote key, come to play an increasing part in the transformation of Verdi's style and language.

Certain features of this style are not so much 'modernisms' as is sometimes claimed as survivals from an earlier mode of expression, such as one would expect to find in a conservative people. Roman Vlad, in an interesting and perceptive essay,† finds genuine bitonality in the following passage taken from Act IV of *Ernani* (piano score):

A glance at the orchestral score would have shown that any hint of bitonality was effectively stifled by a sustained chord of A major on woodwind and brass, firmly anchoring both scales to the key of D minor. The discords and false relations in the second half of the bar are merely the survival of a linear way of thinking that goes back to the sixteenth and seventeenth centuries: an extension of the principle whereby both ascending and descending forms of the melodic minor scale could be used simultaneously despite the fierce discord that results for those with vertically trained ears. Such 'bitonality' is much more common in Verdi than modern editions would allow us to suppose. In *I Due Foscari* the following figure is given out three times by the orchestra, ascending a degree with each repetition.

★ M. Bruni, 'Funzionalità drammatica dell'accordo di quarta e sesta nello stile di Verdi', in *Atti del 1° congresso verdiano*, pp. 36–9.

† R. Vlad, 'Anticipazioni nel linguaggio armonistico verdiano', in *La Rassegna Musicale*, Vol XXI, 1951, pp. 238–9.

All printed scores give a C sharp in the descending scale; but the autograph leaves no doubt that C natural was meant; likewise D natural not D sharp in the second statement, E natural not E sharp in the third. It is amusing to note that at the very time that he was writing such passages, well-meaning English editors were busy 'correcting' similar 'audacities' in Purcell. In later Verdi the persisting habit of linear thought reveals itself in a very personal use of harmony to colour and inflect a melody.

In accounting for the unity of a Verdi opera we cannot speak of tonal schemes since these operate when at all only within the compass of a separate number. One of the consequences of the Italian equation of major and minor mode is the fondness for modulations by keys a third apart (a propensity shared by Chopin and due in part to their common heritage from Bellini). Thus the final trio from *Ernani* moves on an axis F major–D minor–D major: the Act I quartet of *I Masnadieri* D flat–F minor–F major–D minor; and in both cases the progressions are summed up epigrammatically in the concluding bars. But the scheme never extends to entire scenes, still less acts. Nor is Verdi in any real sense a motivic composer.

The early works (to a great extent the late ones too) remain 'number' operas, so that we cannot speak of their having the same kind of unity as Wagner's. There are no leitmotivs to be combined and developed like subjects in a symphonic design. Yet Basevi is not far wrong when he talks about a distinctive colouring or 'colorito' to be found in the more successful operas and revealed in certain details of melodic, harmonic or rhythmic procedure: the upward thrust of so many melodies in *Ernani* and the abundance of andantino in broken 6/8 to be found in *I due Foscari*. These procedures, to which we may add the bow-shaped melodic designs of *Attila* and the minor-third figurations of *Macbeth*, are undoubtedly a unifying element in Verdian opera. But in an age which loves to analyse music in terms of tiny melodic cells bent and stretched according to the analyser's convenience one should distinguish between those cases where too great a similarity of melodic pattern leads to monotony of effect and others in which the unifying process operates much more subtly, as for instance in the predominance of triple rhythms and melodies characterized by stepwise motion and a somewhat narrow compass to be found in *La Traviata*. In other words the merit of a Verdi opera in no way depends on the ease with which it lends itself to this style of anatomy.

To sum up: throughout these early years Verdi both explored and consolidated. He improved year by year his mastery of the traditional components of Italian opera—the aria, the cabaletta, the stretta and so forth; yet he also seized at plots which gave him the opportunity of bypassing them and creating new forms. To the first tendency we owe *Il Trovatore* and *Il Corsaro*, to the second *Rigoletto* and the original *Macbeth*. *Il Trovatore* is a remarkable case of new wine in old bottles; for in form it is a very old-fashioned piece, more opera than music drama. When, eight years before, Cammarano had provided him with just such another libretto in *Alzira* the result, though lively and vigorous, was rather below the best of Donizetti, simply because it was the kind of opera which was based on extended solo melody—one cavatina after another—and Verdi's melodic style had not yet attained true individuality. It was still too much like a homespun version of that of his predecessors. Generally speaking it is the unusual plots that bring out the best in him during that time, and he knew it. Yet there is no opera which does not show an interesting musical advance in some quarter, even if the work is unsatisfactory as a whole. Certain features of traditional opera remained as impediments to dramatic expression. It is fascinating to follow the various ways in which Verdi circumnavigates them, neutralizes their effect, or at times turns them to good advantage. An instance of 'neutralization' occurs at the outset of *Rigoletto*. Here as in *I Lombardi* the curtain rises to banda music. But in the earlier opera the effect is one of comical bathos. In *Rigoletto* the same means are used to point up the drama. First we hear the prelude, heavy with menace; then the banda strikes in with a note of deliberately jarring cheerfulness. The music is no less vulgar in the second case but its vulgarity is harnessed to a dramatic purpose. Then there is the unwritten but very strict law of early Italian romantic opera that *any extended piece in the minor key must end in the major*. To violate this rule as Pacini did in *I Cavalieri di Valenza* is to incur the sinister-sounding charge 'abuso dei minori'.* In a work such as *I Lombardi* Verdi observes it only too well; and the stretta of the finale to Act I begins impressively in C minor, only to dissolve into lilting banality as it moves into C major. Seven years later in the stretta of Act I of *Stiffelio* he confines the major section to a brief, unthematic coda, so avoiding all sense of anticlimax. As always Verdi prefers to transform the conventions of his time rather than to overturn them.

---

*See the polemic in *I Teatri* (Milan, 28.6.1828), quoted in *Cambi*, pp. 125–33.

3 OBERTO CONTE DI SAN BONIFACIO

OBERTO CONTE DI SAN BONIFACIO

Opera in two acts
by
TEMISTOCLE SOLERA*

*First performed at the
Teatro alla Scala, Milan,
17 November 1839*

CUNIZA, sister of Ezzelino da Romano	PRIMA DONNA MEZZO-SOPRANO	Mary Shaw
RICCARDO, Count of Salinguerra	PRIMO TENORE	Lorenzo Salvi
OBERTO, Count of San Bonifacio	PRIMO BASSO	Ignazio Marini
LEONORA, his daughter	PRIMA DONNA SOPRANO	Antonietta Rainieri-Marini
IMELDA, confidante to Cuniza	SECONDA DONNA MEZZO-SOPRANO	Marietta Sacchi

Knights—ladies—vassals

The action takes place in Bassano in and near the castle of Ezzelino

Epoch: 1228

* So described on all printed libretti, although most of the text was probably by Antonio Piazza.

A certain air of mystery surrounds Verdi's first published opera. It is the only one whose literary source cannot be traced; and recent scholars have been in some doubt as to whether or not it is remodelled from an earlier one.

In the biographical summary that he gave to Giulio Ricordi in 1879 Verdi is quite explicit. During his student days at Milan he had been introduced by his teacher Lavigna to the Philharmonic Society, one of those associations of aristocratic dilettanti that formed the chief basis of concert life throughout Austria during the years that spanned the decline of the private musical establishment and the rise of the professional orchestra. At the time they were rehearsing Haydn's *Creation*. One day, in the absence of one of their regular maestri, the director, Pietro Massini, asked Verdi to accompany from the piano, feeling unequal to the task himself.

> I was then fresh from my studies [*Verdi continues*] and a full orchestral score held no terrors for me; I agreed, and sat down at the piano to begin the rehearsal. I well remember the sarcastic smiles of some of these dilettanti, and it seems that my youthful figure, thin and not too fastidiously dressed, was not calculated to inspire much confidence. Well, the rehearsal began and as I got more and more worked up and excited I didn't confine myself only to accompanying. I began to conduct with my right hand playing only with my left. . . . Once the rehearsal was over, compliments, congratulations on every hand! . . .

In the end he was asked to take charge of the concert, which he did with great success. Some time later: 'Massini, who it seems had confidence in the young maestro, suggested that I should write an opera for the Filodrammatici Theatre of which he was the director and gave me a libretto which, in part modified by Solera, became *Oberto Conte di San Bonifacio*. . . .'* If this is true it is very elliptical and we have to return to contemporary letters and events to fill out the picture.

During his third year of study with Lavigna in 1834 Verdi was suddenly called back to Busseto. The old organist Provesi had died. The clergy appointed a temporary successor until a competition for the post could be held; then arbitrarily confirmed the appointment in perpetuity. At once the town was thrown into a state of faction. The clergy's case was that Ferrari, their nominee, had a wife and six children to support, while Verdi was an able-bodied youth with no dependants. The other side maintained that the appointment was illegal, that Ferrari would be useless as a conductor of the local Philharmonic Society, and that priests were not to be trusted anyway. Verdi was placed in a difficult moral position. He was no longer interested in being the cathedral organist or Director of the Music School.

* A. Pougin, *Giuseppe Verdi: vita aneddotica* (Milan, 1881), Appendix to Chapter VI, p. 41.

Yet his chief sponsor for the post, Antonio Barezzi, was the man who had provided most of the money for his training and Verdi was in love with his daughter. Eventually he returned for the second time to Busseto, entered for the competition —held in the teeth of the clergy as the result of intervention from the government at Parma—and won it. Ferrari was allowed to remain as organist, however, while Verdi became Director of the Music School with a salary which enabled him to marry Margherita Barezzi. The appointment was for a minimum period of three years; but in the event the municipal authorities allowed Verdi to leave for Milan after two and a half, in February of 1839.

Writing to Lavigna from Busseto back in August of 1834, Verdi had asked him to remind Massini about the opera libretto he had promised him; it was to have been written by one Tasca.* Nothing further is heard about the matter until 1836 when Verdi returned to Busseto to take up his appointment as Director of the Music School; and this time he had a libretto. Several letters to Massini follow in which he talks about the opera which was to be given in Milan at a time when he himself could come and direct it. By September he actually describes it as complete 'except for those little passages that will have to be retouched by the poet'.† The difficulty was that the council only allowed him two months' vacation in September and October, and an amateur performance at the Filodrammatici Theatre needed more time to set up. So next year he tried to get the opera performed at Parma, this time by professionals. His letter to Massini tells us for the first time the title and the name of the librettist: *Rocester*, by Antonio Piazza. Verdi was anxious that Piazza should expand 'the duet for the two women so as to give it more grandeur . . .'.‡ Again he was to be disappointed. The impresario at Parma was not interested in putting on new works; so Verdi had still not had his opera performed when he finally left Busseto in 1839. The biographical summary goes on:

I set out again for Milan taking with me the complete score in perfect order, having taken the trouble to extract and copy out all the solo voice parts. But here the difficulties begin: Massini was no longer director of the Filodrammatici; therefore it wasn't possible to give my opera there. However whether Massini really had confidence in me or whether he wanted in some way to show his gratitude to me for having helped him a number of times after the *Creation* (and conducting various shows for him including a *Cenerentola*) without ever claiming any financial return, he didn't lose heart . . . but said that he would try every means to get my opera performed at La Scala on the occasion of the Benefit concert for the Pio Istituto. . . . In this he was strongly supported by the cello player Merighi, who knew me from the days when he played in the orchestra of the Filodrammatici. Eventually all was arranged for the spring of 1839; in which case I would have had four really outstanding singers: Strepponi, the tenor Moriani, the baritone Giorgio Ronconi and the bass Marini. No sooner were the parts allotted and the piano rehearsals begun than Moriani fell seriously ill . . . so that everything was

* See Abbiati, I, p. 147.

† Letter to Massini, 16.9.1836. C. Sartori, 'Rocester, la prima opera di Verdi', in *Rivista Musicale Italiana*, Jan.–Feb. 1939, p. 100.

‡ *Ibid.* This disposes of the statement by Giuseppe Demaldè in his unpublished *Cenni Biografici* of 1856 that *Rocester* was completed in 1838.

broken off and the idea of giving my opera was now out of the question. I was completely at a loss and I thought of returning to Busseto, when lo and behold one fine morning an employee of La Scala came to see me and said very abruptly, 'Are you the maestro from Busseto who was to have given an opera for the Pio Istituto? . . . Come to the theatre, the impresario wants to see you. . . .' 'Is that possible?' said I, and the other replied, 'Yes, sir, I've been ordered to send for the maestro from Parma who was to have given an opera. . . . If you're the man come along.' And I came.

The impresario was at that time Bartolomeo Merelli; one evening on the stage he'd heard a conversation between Signora Strepponi and Giorgio Ronconi in which she spoke well of the music of *Oberto* and that impression was shared by Ronconi.

So I presented myself to Merelli, who came straight to the point and said that as he had received favourable information about my music he wanted to perform it the next season; if I agreed to this I would have to make some adjustments to the range of the voice parts as I wouldn't have the same four artists as before. It was a good offer: young and unknown as I was I had fallen in with an impresario who took the risk of putting on a new work without asking me for any indemnity against a failure—which I wouldn't have been able to give anyway. Merelli, then, shouldering all the production costs at great risk to himself, merely suggested sharing with me the sale of the opera if it should turn out to be successful. Let it not be thought that this was a hard condition for me; it was a beginner's opera . . . and after the favourable outcome the editor Giovanni Ricordi acquired the rights of the score for only 2,000 Austrian lire.

Oberto Conte di San Bonifacio had, I won't say a rapturous reception, but quite a good one; it was given a fair number of times, and Merelli had actually prolonged its run beyond the fixed schedule. The opera was performed by Rainieri-Marini, mezzo-soprano, by Salvi, tenor, and by Marini, bass, and as I said I had to modify parts of the music for reasons of tessitura and to write a new piece, the quartet, whose placing in the drama was suggested by Merelli himself and for which I got Solera to write the verses. It turned out to be one of the best pieces in the opera.*

There are two mistakes here, the first perhaps more apparent than real. Antonietta Rainieri-Marini called herself a soprano; but a glance at the part of Leonora will show that she must have possessed a remarkably low range. Nowadays she would qualify as a light mezzo-soprano, as distinct from the contralto Mary Shaw who created the lower part of Cuniza. Quite wrong, however, is Verdi's description of the cast of the projected spring performance. One woman and three men! Something more than adjustments of tessitura would be needed to adapt the opera to its present form. A letter written to Demaldè, one of his friends at Busseto, in April 1839 puts the record straight. It seems that Verdi had originally been content with the idea of mounting his opera at some lesser theatre in Milan—the Carcano, the Canobbiana or even the Filodrammatici—and had withdrawn it because the singers were unsatisfactory; 'but,' Verdi adds, 'though my score is still wrapped up

* Pougin, p. 41.

it is not sleeping. I will tell you a secret: perhaps it will be performed at La Scala with Moriani, Ronconi, La Strepponi and La Kemble. . . .'* *Not* Marini, therefore, but Adelaide Kemble. It is a little unflattering to our national pride that Verdi should have completely forgotten the two English singers concerned in his first opera, while remembering everybody else.

According to the biographical sketch the opera to be performed at the Pio Istituto was by this time *Oberto*. At what point then did Solera take over? And what became of *Rocester*? A letter of Verdi's written in 1871 to Emilio Seletti in Milan confuses the issue still further. Seletti was collecting facts for a book about Busseto and had asked Verdi whether the Bussetan poet Luigi Balestra had had a hand in the libretto of *Oberto*. Verdi replied: '*Oberto Conte di San Bonifacio* was altered and added to by Solera on the basis of a libretto entitled *Lord Hamilton* by Antonio Piazza, a government employee, then writer of feuilletons for the *Gazzetta di Milano*. Neither in *Lord Hamilton* nor in *Oberto* is there a line by Luigi Balestra.'† No, but there might have been; since Balestra had written the words for a duet that Verdi intended to add to the score for a revival of *Oberto* in Genoa in 1841. Unfortunately it was never performed, although the music had already been composed—so he told Balestra. It would be interesting to know what became of it.

Clearly then Verdi's memory was not to be trusted. The early biographers followed the account of 1879 implicitly and assumed that *Oberto* was the finished result of an opera which had been begun as early as 1836. Then in his book *The Man Verdi* Frank Walker subjected the facts to his usual careful scrutiny, and concluded that there was no reason for believing that *Oberto* was a revised version of *Rocester* or of any other opera. He points out that there is no duet for two women in *Oberto* such as we know to have existed in *Rocester*; and though in the manuscript score of *Oberto* there are signs of revision and alteration, the names of the characters, he says, are unchanged. Likewise the autograph of the libretto, preserved in the museum of La Scala, is in Solera's hand throughout. Moreover, the letter to Seletti suggests that if *Oberto* was a reworking of anything it was of *Lord Hamilton*, not *Rocester*.

Abbiati, on the other hand, postulates a double change: from *Rocester* to *Lord Hamilton*, then to *Oberto*. Others have been content to leave the matter open. We may take the argument a stage further, however, with the aid of a few facts which Verdi's biographers appear to have overlooked.

(1) At the end of the autograph of *Oberto* there are three fully scored numbers which are not included in the printed score, though they appear as separate items in Ricordi's catalogue as late as 1875.‡ Their provenance will be discussed later; in the meantime we may just note that one of them is a large three-movement duet for the two women. Whether it was the piece which Piazza was required to expand for Parma; whether it was the duet with words by Balestra composed for Genoa but never performed there: whether in fact it was written before or after

---

* Letter to G. Demaldè, 22.4.1839. *Carteggi Verdiani*, IV, p. 77.

† Letter to E. Seletti, 14.5.1871. Original in the Museo alla Scala, Milan. Quoted Abbiati, I, p. 326.

‡ The first study to deal with these three extra pieces in *Oberto* was David R. B. Kimbell in 'Poi . . . diventò *l'Oberto*' in *Music and Letters*, Vol. LII, No. 1, Jan. 1971, pp. 1–7. He assumes, somewhat arbitrarily, that they were written *before* the first performance and relegated to an appendix (see also note on p. 64).

the first performance we cannot be sure. But it proves beyond any doubt that in the scheme of *Oberto* there was a place for a duet such as we know to have existed in *Rocester*.

(2) At the start of the quartet in Act II the name RICCARDO is superimposed on another which is crossed out. But the original word can be read clearly enough—ROCESTER. It is still very puzzling. If the quartet was one of the last numbers to be written, long after it had been decided to give the opera its present title, why in that of all pieces should Verdi revert to the original nomenclature—if such it was? Obviously it was a *lapsus calami* such as must occur often enough, but especially when working on an opera in which the names of the characters have been altered. It can be paralleled in the autograph of *Rigoletto* where Monterone is referred to as Castiglione, the name originally decided upon for Hugo's St Vallier then discarded for fear of offending a local family.

(3) Both Oberto and Leonora use the words 'questi lidi' ('these shores'), implying that each has crossed the sea, from Mantua and Verona respectively. Since the action of the opera takes place at Bassano neither would have had to cross anything more substantial than the Piave and the Adige. There is no shore within plausible distance of any of the three cities. So this would appear to be further evidence of a change of plot or at least locale. Such changes were common enough if only for reasons of censorship. In any case Verdi states unequivocally that the story of *Oberto* was remodelled from a different plot. However untrustworthy his memory for detail, is this a point over which he or any other composer would be likely to be mistaken; or on which he would want to mislead his public?

(4) As the reader will have gathered, no opera in those days could be said to exist until it had been performed. If it never reached the stage or proved a failure when it did, the composer invariably used the best of it in a new work. Throughout all his correspondence in the 1830s Verdi talks always of 'my opera'; never once does he suggest that there was more than one. Probably what he took with him to Milan in 1839 was a rough and ready operatic structure in the conventional mould, to be expanded, or shortened or generally modified in accordance with the singers available for the first performance, and based on a story which could adapt itself, chameleon-like, to medieval Italy no less than to Restoration England.

For, although again there is no proof, we may be reasonably certain that the Rocester of the title was John Wilmot, 2nd Earl of Rochester (1647–80), joint archetype with George Villiers, Duke of Buckingham, of the witty Restoration rake, and familiar on the Continent partly through the memoirs of Count de Grammont which Walter Scott edited, and partly through Victor Hugo's drama *Cromwell* of which he is in a sense the sub-hero. Riccardo, the tenor lead of *Oberto*, is also a deceiver of women; but as there is nothing in Hugo or de Grammont that resembles his situation we must look elsewhere for the origin of the plot: possibly to the play *Rochester* by Antier Benjamin and Theodor N....(*sic*) given at the Théâtre Porte St-Martin on 17 January 1829. The distribution of characters would fit—Rochester, Wilkins, Mrs Wilkins and Clarisse. With the jealous husband turned into an outraged father, the two women (both wooed by Rochester) changed from sisters into more ordinary rivals and a moral ending to replace the bloodbath that finishes the play, we should have the basic situations of Verdi's first published opera. Rochester presents himself to Mrs Wilkins under a false name; Riccardo, according to the antefatto, has conquered Leonora by a similar ruse. But any connection between the two plots must remain a matter of speculation until Piazza's libretto comes to light. *Lord Hamilton* remains even more of a mystery. He may have been the baritone to Rochester's tenor: Count Anthony Hamilton, perhaps, who was the author of the de Grammont memoirs or else the young Hamilton who was Rochester's boon companion and a partner in many of his escapades. Equally 'Hamilton' could be the librettist's alteration of 'Campbell', Rochester's assumed name in the play; doubtless to an Italian one Scots name is as good as another, and Hamilton would at least be easier to sing (it would be scanned '[H]am*i*lton'). It is even possible that the plot had been invented by Piazza from the start. True, Italian librettists did not usually make up their own stories; but Piazza was never a professional in this field. Years later he was to publish a romance about Pergolesi and the daughter of the British ambassador to Naples. A fictitious episode in the life of Rochester would not be beyond his powers.

Another argument in favour of the identity of the two operas is that no separate provenance has ever been established for *Oberto*. Rolandi speaks of an 'origine walterscottiana' but offers no proof of this.* Even the scenario of the ballet *Ezzelin da Romano sotto le mure di Bassano* (Milan, 1838) which is concerned with a similar time and place turns out to be something quite different. Certainly a great many problems are avoided if we assume that Verdi's account of how he came to write his first opera is substantially true.

The first performance took place on 13 November 1839. The greatest star was Ignazio Marini. A low basso cantante of great power and authority he was to prove a staunch friend to the young composer. Seven years later he created the name part of *Attila* and carried it triumphantly up and down the peninsula. About the same time he suggested that Verdi revise his first opera giving more prominence to the title role; 'but,' wrote Muzio, 'the Signor Maestro wouldn't agree because it would mean the whole of the first act and only a month and a half to do it in and he just hasn't the time'.† Marini was also a great exponent of Moses in the revised version of Rossini's opera.

His wife was by all accounts an excellent artist despite a somewhat limited range (Verdi never takes her above an A in this opera); and it is worth noting that in all the Italian performances without exception she was the prima donna. The implication is that she was partly responsible for their taking place at all. Lorenzo Salvi seems to have been a good but unremarkable lyric tenor. Mary Shaw's brief contact with Italy does not seem to have been especially glorious. 'She has a good voice and clear diction,' wrote the critic of *La Fama*, 'but being a novice in both singing and acting she is not for a leading theatre such as ours.'‡ But it was from her letters home that people in England first came to hear of a brilliant young composer who was beginning to make a name for himself.

Critical reaction to the opera itself was encouraging on the whole if contradictory in detail. The correspondent of the *Figaro* found evidence of taste if not of originality or imagination and advised Verdi to study the great classics so as to 'open his mind to those brilliant conceits in which his present score is far from rich'. The *Moda*, unreservedly favourable, insisted that Verdi's inspiration owed

* U. Rolandi, *Libretti e librettisti verdiani dal punto di vista storico bibliografico* (Rome, 1941), p. 4.
† Letter to Barezzi, 3.9.1846. Garibaldi, p. 268.   ‡ Monaldi, p. 15. This was less than fair. As

nothing to Donizetti; Bellini, Mercadante nor even Rossini. *La Fama* chose to beat the reformist drum. It attacked the libretto as typical of everything that was most absurd in contemporary musical theatre; while the score, with its Bellinian overtones, contained, it said, too much melody in the wrong places and of the wrong kind, 'languid and monotonous where it ought to be energetic and passionate'. The *Gazzetta Privilegiata* supported all the criticisms of the *Figaro* and sternly bade the young composer not to pay too much attention to the ephemeral applause of the public.★ A bad notice, certainly, but not one that a composer of the time would have minded. The fact emerged that, rightly or wrongly, the public had enjoyed it sufficiently to warrant another thirteen performances that season, and Ricordi had thought the opera worth buying straightaway. An oblique tribute to it was paid barely a year later by the Mantuan composer Achille Graffigna, who specialized in resetting the libretti of operatic perennials. To the list comprising *Il Barbiere di Siviglia*, *La Buona Figliuola*, *Il Matrimonio Segreto* was now added a certain *I Bonifazi e i Salinguerra* on Solera's libretto.

Critical reaction was to some extent conditioned by the fact that Italian opera was going through a slightly self-conscious phase at the time. Donizetti's style was beginning to take on a Parisian sophistication. The outstanding successes of 1838–40 —Mercadante's *Il Giuramento*, Nicolai's *Il Templario* and Pacini's *Saffo*—are all intensely studied, almost reformist works. Verdi in his first opera set his sights much lower. The correspondent of *La Moda* was wrong in saying that his inspiration owes nothing to Donizetti, Mercadante, Bellini or Rossini. In detail it owes a little to all of them. But what finally emerges is often subtly different, with a flavour of its own. Above all it has that ultra-Verdian quality of gathering momentum as it proceeds. The *Figaro* noted that at the second performance applause was meagre in the first act but tremendous in the second. The same was true when *Oberto* was revived in the Camden Town Hall a few years ago. The superior smile, the cosy giggle gradually died away; the crudities seemed to take on a craggy grandeur; and one left the hall purged by the pity and terror of a genuine melodrama.

The published libretto carries the following antefatto.

> Oberto, Count of San Bonifacio, being defeated in battle by Ezzelino da Romano who came to the help of the Salinguerra party in Verona, escaped to Mantua. Leonora, his daughter, being without a mother, was left at Verona in the care of an elderly aunt. A young count of Salinguerra under a false name seduced Oberto's beautiful daughter with a promise of marriage. Later he fell passionately in love with Cuniza who had been left in the castle of Bassano by her brother Ezzelino, while he, already the lord of Verona, attended to the conquest of Monselice, Padua and Montaghana; and the count offered to marry her. Since Ezzelino owed his position in Verona to the count of Salinguerra he was not averse to the marriage. Too late Leonora learned the truth and came in despair to Bassano on the day of the wedding to denounce her betrayer. It is at this point that the action of the drama begins.

Mrs Alfred Shaw she enjoyed a huge reputation in England, being much admired by Mendelsohn, in whose *St Paul* she had performed at the Birmingham Festival of 1837.

★ Abbiati, I, pp. 327–8. For other, more favourable notices from foreign correspondents see M. Conati, 'L'Oberto Conte di S. Bonifacio in due recensioni straniere poco note e in una lettera inedita di Verdi', in *Atti del 1⁰ congresso verdiano*, pp. 67–92.

Ezzelino da Romano, who never appears in the opera, would be well known to Italian audiences as an early prototype of the vicious medieval despot. The family, which ruled Bassano, was originally German; hence the somewhat Teutonic name of Cuniza.* Ezzelino da Romano acquired substantial territory in Northern Italy, including the city of Verona, which he held from 1227 until 1259.

The overture, one of Verdi's shortest, is typical in its mixture of the original and the derivative. It is in two movements, both based on themes taken from the opera. The opening andante features a slow melody, folk-like in character but Austrian rather than Italian (Beethoven or Brahms might have worked it into a symphony). Italian audiences however would have traced it to the invocation to Mahomet from Rossini's *Le Siège de Corinthe*. To make the derivation even clearer both melodies have a similar context in the opera itself: each is a nuptial chorus before a wedding which never happens. But Verdi makes no attempt to imitate Rossini's subtlety in conveying through harmony any feeling of impending disaster. He is content to remain Rossini in homespun, writing for two trumpets as though they were horns.†

12

This same tune, restated with an altered but still naïvely colourful scoring, leads directly into a stormy allegro transition with music later to be associated with the duel. The second theme (see Ex. 13, facing page), given out by the clarinet, has a typically Verdian climb. Characteristic too is the enrichment of the harmonies at the sixth bar. Here, having established the dominant key, Verdi seems to have felt that he has done his duty by traditional overture form; and he allows the music to slide back into D major before unfolding a succession of amiable march tunes. The first (Ex. 14) is worth quoting, not because it is particularly distinguished, but because it is the earliest form we have of an idea which recurs in various guises in later operas (*Alzira, La Battaglia di Legnano, La Traviata*). Quite effective in drawing the loose-knit structure together is the new theme that Verdi presents, *à la* Schumann, in the coda.

ACT I

Scene 1: a delightful countryside with the castle of Bassano in the distance
In the overture we have had another illustration of how little the tonic–dominant polarity, so dear to the German composer, meant to the Italians of that time—

* Both she and her notorious brother are mentioned in Dante's *Divine Comedy* where their two destinies are very different. Ezzelino is in the lower reaches of Hell (*Inferno*, XII, 109); Cuniza rates a place beside Beatrice in Paradise (*Paradiso*, IX, 13–66).

† He had a precedent here in the orchestral prelude to Elvino's aria 'Pasci il guardo' in *La Sonnambula*, printed at length in Boosey's vocal score, drastically cut in Ricordi's.

and still less the complex system of relationships erected on it. So there is nothing unusual in the procedure, unthinkable in Beethoven, Mozart or Weber, whereby Verdi ends his overture in D major and begins his introductory chorus a tone higher. A host of knights, ladies-in-waiting, courtiers and vassals have come out to meet Riccardo, Count of Salinguerra, their master's ally and future brother-in-law, on his return from the wars; and they do so in a chorus (*Di vermiglia amabil luce*) decorated by those fluttering woodwind figures which the notion of dawn always seemed to call forth from Italian composers.* As they see him approaching, the rhythm changes to the familiar bolero pattern and a fresh melody is introduced— in effect a choral cabaletta to balance the choral adagio. Riccardo replies with two lines of recitative which lead straight into the andante of his cavatina (*Son fra voi! Già sorto è il giorno*). He returns the chorus's greeting and courteously disclaims their praises, which, he says, are due not to him but to his bride. It presents the charac-teristic Bellinian design mentioned earlier (a^1 a^2 b a^2) with b entrusted to the chorus. But as a melody it is plain and schematic to a fault and the main theme is too short and commonplace to bear the weight of repetition that Verdi puts upon it. The coda is more effective, though, and takes the lower theme excitingly up to a high B. A cabaletta follows in G major (*Già parmi udire il fremito*) in which Riccardo in-veighs against his enemies while the chorus bid him come 'where love awaits him'. It is a clumsy affair with an inadequately prepared climax occurring twice.

* Compare the introduction to 'Ecco ridente in cielo' (*Il Barbiere di Siviglia*); the opening bars of *Luisa Miller*, I, i; *Simon Boccanegra*, I, i.

Moreover the jump to the flat side of the andante in B major gives an inappropriately relaxing effect; but it was a happy idea to quote (not quite literally) the march (Ex. 14) in the ritornello and in the final coda as the assembled company all leave in the direction of Bassano.

Next the heroine, Leonora, makes her entrance with one of those meandering, chordal introductions which suggest an impromptu organ voluntary. No wonder Verdi remembered Antonietta Rainieri-Marini as a mezzo-soprano; for the part includes at one point an A to be sung forte below the stave. Leonora describes her plight during the familiar progress through declamatory recitative to arioso, then more emphatic recitative culminating in a two-octave descent in preparation for the aria. It is all a little abrupt and rough-hewn; but the heroine's conflict of moods is vividly expressed. Characteristically the most pathetic accents are reserved for the passage where Leonora talks about her father's grief, for the paternal relationship always struck a responsive chord in Verdi's imagination. The mood of the andante (*Sotto il paterno tetto*) is one of gentle sorrow as Leonora recalls the 'angel of beauty' whom she sheltered beneath her father's roof and who betrayed her love. Here we have the first instance of a typical Verdian phenomenon: an ordinary tune in the standard form ($a^1 a^2 b a^2$), but transfigured by its final bars—in this case, a spacious arching phrase in the coda.

15

It is in such moments that Leonora shows her kinship with her great namesake from *Il Trovatore*. No such distinction marks the cabaletta (*Oh potessi nel mio core*) with its crude foretaste of 'Caro nome', its Rossinian crescendo between statements of the melody, and its awkward dissolution into semi-bravura for the last two lines of the second quatrain. Nor is it effectively situated. Four years later Verdi was to impress upon Piave the need for contrast ('distacco di pensiero') between andante and cabaletta.* Here the cabaletta merely continues the thought of the andante, so that the change of movement remains unmotivated. It is an exit-aria and nothing more.

* Letter to Piave, 25.3.1844. *Copialettere*, p. 426.

But now the opera takes a leap forward. Another orchestral introduction, full of drooping chromatic lines and displaced accents, announces the arrival of Oberto, Leonora's father. The scoring shows signs of unusual care. Oboe, clarinets and bassoons begin; strings enter at bar 7 followed by the full orchestra at bar 9, where the tortuous melodic idea resolves itself into a phrase supremely Verdian in its boldness and simplicity.

16

The soliloquy which follows contains some of the finest arioso–recitative in early Verdi. It is flexible and expressive; and above all it creates a specific character —sorrowful, weary, yet full of a dark determination. Already there are pre-echoes of another outraged father, Rigoletto; and indeed, like Rigoletto, Oberto is especially impressive in recitative. Elements of the introduction interwoven into the scene all contribute to the sense of inner conflict: pleasure at seeing again his native land; sorrow that he must leave once more, this time for ever; love for his ungrateful daughter; and a thirst for vengeance.

Leonora returns declaring that she will go to the castle that night during the wedding festivities. Oberto recognizes her voice. Confrontation . . . and a Grand Duet. Here for the first time Verdi has the two contrasted vocal elements (low male and high female) from which he was to distil much of the finest music of his early works; and it prompts him to a formal solution of surprising boldness. The duet is the usual three-part scheme. In the first movement the librettist supplied each character with a double Metastasian quatrain, implying an identical setting for both pairs. Verdi not only sets the first quatrain of each pair quite differently, but he avoids any suggestion of a regular melodic period in either. Oberto's verse (*Guardami! Sul mio ciglio*) with its extended note-values and irregular phrase-lengths suggests a continuation of his previous arioso–recitative. Leonora's reply (*Padre, mi strazii l'anima*) though couched in the same tempo seems to move more swiftly, being set as a series of exclamations punctuated by rapping, busy orchestral figures. Only in the second quatrains (*Non ti bastò il periglio*—Oberto; *A una tradita e misera*—Leonora) do we find anything like a formal melody. This is the lyrical core of the movement and also its unifying element. True, it is the same for both singers, but since both the pitch and the context are different each time, the sense of musical conflict remains.

The rest of the duet is more conventional. Eight bars of expressive woodwind writing lead to the central andante (*Del tuo favor soccorrimi*) where father and daughter each pray to heaven for aid. Here again Verdi employs the 'dissimilar' pattern, but the two ideas are too close to each other for the device to be effective. The coda, however, works up to a strong climax. Distant trumpets are heard from the castle. Oberto commands his daughter to go there and denounce her seducer; only then will he forgive her. Musically, Leonora repeats the lesson like an obedient schoolgirl; and so to the last part of the duet (*Un amplesso ricevi, o pentita*), a standard final movement after the manner of Donizetti's 'Verranno a te sull'aure', with an accompaniment of string pizzicato chords where the voices sing separately, and the same, fortified by arpeggios (clarinet instead of harp), where they join. As father and daughter are now reconciled it is appropriate that they should sing the same music in the same key, but being bass and soprano respectively they cannot do this with equal comfort. Verdi opts for an uneasy compromise whereby they both start their verses in the same way, but from the third bar onwards the soprano sings two degrees higher than the bass. This enables them to combine in tenths at the final statement of the theme without disturbing the harmony, but the usual 'clinching' effect is lost because the theme itself has never been properly defined.

Scene 2: a magnificent hall in the castle of Bassano

Riccardo's bride Cuniza is being dressed for the wedding while Imelda and her ladies sing an elaborated version of the melody that began the overture (Ex. 12), the rest of the chorus joining in at the first episode. The chorus at Milan was clearly a strong one; so Verdi was able to avoid that automatic doubling of sopranos and tenors which safety required elsewhere. Next one would expect a cavatina for Cuniza; but doubtless the inexperience of Mary Shaw made this inadvisable. Instead she thanks and dismisses her attendants in a few lines of recitative and is at once joined by Riccardo, to whom she confides the secret forebodings that cloud her dream of love. The first movement of their duet (*Il pensier d'un amore felice*) suggests Bellini at his most languid and Victorian ballad-like, though Verdi attached sufficient importance to the melody to quote it later in the opera.

17

Riccardo replies reassuringly with the same theme, slightly cramped by the change of pitch from G to C major. Then follows a most original stroke. From the dialogue of what would normally be set as the first of a two-movement duet, Verdi extracts in effect a new movement. If no change of tempo is marked for the E major section (*Fra il timor e la speme divisa*) with its long overlapping phrases, it is certainly implied; for this is an excited 'lovers' meeting' passage such as introduces the last-act duet in *La Traviata*. True, Verdi has not yet discovered the advantage of a long dominant pedal at such moments; nor has he paid much attention to the sense of the words, according to which Cuniza is still in doubt. But the duet as a whole gains immensely from this episode, which prepares far more effectively than any conventional setting would have done for the final movement of reconciliation (*Questa mano omai ritorni*). Here again Verdi employs the similar pattern at contrasted pitches (Cuniza in D, Riccardo in G); and a ritornello based on a Rossinian crescendo ensures that in G the music remains till the end. The result is curiously lop-sided. Also it is a poor way of suggesting characters in conjunction. In Verdi's own most successful use of this device, in Act II of *Rigoletto*, not only are Gilda and her father still in opposition, but Verdi dispenses with a ritornello after the second verse, so as to allow a natural return to the original tonality.

After Riccardo and Cuniza have left by opposite doors a 'heartbeat' figure heralds Leonora, who enters in conversation with Cuniza's waiting-woman, Imelda. She waits apprehensively as Imelda goes to fetch her mistress. The sharp rapping figure which accompanies Leonora's prayer for strength is entirely conventional, but it is characteristic of the young Verdi to give it trumpets and trombones. Cuniza receives her guest graciously. At the mention of Oberto she shows alarm. 'Behold him,' says Leonora as her father steps melodramatically out of the shadows.

In the first movement of the terzetto (*Son io stesso! A te davanti*) we again have the shape of things to come: definition of characters by contrast, yielding an exciting new musical structure. Verdi has set the text as a continuous succession of variegated ideas, each reflecting the mood of the singer. Oberto's music combines sorrow with a hint of menace; and his opening phrase despite its major mode carries unmistakable overtones of Mozart's Commendatore—'Don Giovanni, a cenar teco'. Cuniza (D minor) is all agitation and foreboding; Leonora (A major) is resolute. Her opening phrase (*Tutto puoi, lo puoi tu sola!*) is the only theme to be repeated, as she pours out the story of her betrayal. It is left to Oberto himself to give the traitor's name in a thunderous outburst: 'The Count of Salinguerra.' The revelation gives rise to a new, slow movement (*Su quella fronte impressa*) in which Oberto threatens, Cuniza soothes and promises to help, while Leonora expresses deep gratitude to her rival. With the slackening of dramatic tension comes a similar drop in the musical interest. Verdi has cast the movement as a 'false canon', a form requiring far more delicacy of craftsmanship than he possessed at this time; and the blunt, three-bar phrase which ends each quatrain seems especially clumsy. The stretta (*Ma fia l'estremo, o misera*) in which each singer resolves to bring Riccardo to justice is a cheerful march, based on a very Donizettian main theme, complete with Donizetti's favourite mannerism of a feminine ending falling from the fifth to the third degree of the scale.

After leading Oberto into an adjoining room Cuniza summons her guests, among them Riccardo at whom she points an accusing finger. Riccardo recognizes Leonora and goes pale. But first he tries to brazen it out. 'Yes, I loved her once: but she was false to me.' In a passionate outburst, like a more formidable Donna Elvira, Leonora denounces him before the assembled company, all of whom take her side. But once again it is Oberto who, with his penchant for the melodramatic appearance, creates the real sensation as he steps out of hiding. So far all is convention; but for the 'moment of calm' (*A quell'aspetto un fremito*) Verdi gives a new display of his powers as a musician, and a dramatist as well. Bold and simple in its conception it is worked out with a skill that would satisfy any professor of counterpoint. The slow G minor tramp of the opening with its rolls on the kettledrum; the plunge into a diminished seventh fortissimo on the word 'fremito'; the *genuine* canon at the second occurrence of the opening phrase—these are features which point to the future composer of the *Requiem*.

18

By the nature of things one cannot expect the stretta following Oberto's challenge to be anything but an anticlimax. True, Oberto's verse (*Non basta una vittima*), half recitative, half arioso, with its impressively prolonged final phrase acts as an effective launching-pad to the main theme of the movement. But for the most part it is all Rossini without Rossini's knack of avoiding the perfunctory with some happily placed modulation. By comparison Verdi's switch into A flat is mere routine. The movement has a certain impetus, a purely physical vigour rare in Verdi's predecessors. But of musical distinction there is not a trace.

ACT II

Scene 1: the private apartments of Princess Cuniza

With an introductory chorus of attendants, recitative and double aria Cuniza proclaims her status as a full principal. The attendants are concerned at her air of sadness; Imelda enters to tell her mistress that Riccardo wishes to speak with her. After a sigh of regret for her lost dreams of happiness Cuniza decides not to admit him; he must return to his first love; and the chorus intimate their approval. The most interesting feature of this scene is the quotation of Ex. 17 as an orchestral theme round which the attendants weave their chorus of compassion (*Infelice! Nel cor tradito*). This time, however, it is anchored to a tonic pedal, as in a very similar chorus 'Piangon le ciglia' in Act II of *I Puritani*. Snatches of the same melody, delicately scored for woodwind, punctuate Cuniza's recitative. Both movements of her aria are alas purely conventional, and prove no more than that Verdi could write an effective showpiece for a low mezzo-soprano. The andante (*Oh, chi torna l'ardente pensiero*) follows the late-Bellini model even down to the woodwind figures at the end of the first quatrain; the cabaletta (*Più che i vezzi e lo splendore*) is highly Rossinian in scoring as well as in gait. In each movement the lyrical impulse, genuine enough, is weakened by some curiously inert harmonies.

Scene 2: a deserted place near the castle gardens

Such is the description on the printed score; yet one may guess that the chorus of knights (*Dov'è l'astro che nel cielo*) was meant to be played in front of a drop-curtain while the previous scene was being changed. Certainly it has no other obvious function, since the knights themselves do no more than express their pity for Cuniza. Not only that; the 26-bar orchestral introduction is so portentous as to make one surmise that originally the piece might have had a different context altogether—in *Rocester*.

The chorus opens in the manner of late Rossini with short phrases majestic in their abruptness. Less Rossinian however is the continuation (*Si consoli la tradita*), which breathes the more romantic air of the 1830s; so too the instrumental theme that decorates the chorus unisons. But with a sure instinct for stylistic unity Verdi hammers home the final phrases with a sharp rhythmic pattern recalling the opening.

The knights disperse; the drop-curtain is raised and we are now in the 'deserted place' mentioned above, where Oberto is waiting impatiently for Riccardo. Has the messenger not delivered his challenge? Is Riccardo afraid to fight him? Oberto broods for a while on his enemy's treachery. Then a chorus of knights come to announce that Cuniza has saved him from the wrath of Ezzelino and now summons him to her presence. Before leaving Oberto indulges in a fearful outburst against the viper's brood of Salinguerra.

All this is set as a scena and double aria of which protocol demanded that a principal should have at least one. A pity, since, as we have seen, Oberto expresses himself more effectively in recitative and in ensembles. The scene begins with the characteristic thrusting tune from the overture (Ex. 13), a superb preparation for Oberto's first words 'È tardi ancor'. Apart from the striking introduction with its melody for two horns, the andante (*L'orror del tradimento*) is rather poor, its first cadence being excruciatingly crude; but the final allegro marziale (*Ma tu superbo giovane*) sets the pattern for many a future baritone cabaletta. It is very much in the Donizettian mould; but it packs an infinitely greater punch (see Ex. 19, overleaf).

Oberto is not disappointed. Riccardo arrives, but like Don Giovanni he has no wish to fight an old man. However Oberto's taunts of cowardice, underlined by

19

Allegro marziale

OBERTO

Ma tu, super-bo gio-va-ne, ____ me non ve-drai fiac-ca - to!

str.

a blazing brass chord, goad him into drawing his sword. At this point Leonora and Cuniza arrive, determined to prevent bloodshed. Cuniza insists that Riccardo marry Leonora; Riccardo, full of remorse, consents. But Oberto's honour has still to be avenged, and he privately arranges to meet Riccardo later and fight it out. The situation is conveyed in the great scena and quartet which on Merelli's advice Verdi decided to add to the score during the summer of 1839.

The scena is particularly interesting for the way in which Verdi has once more carved out an extra movement in embryo from a fragment of dialogue. Oberto's taunt (*Vili all'armi, a donne eroi*) is an early version of Germont's heavy rebuke to his son in Act II of *La Traviata* ('Di sprezzo degno'). It has the same contours, is in the same key and requires the same measured delivery: a striking instance, this, of the way in which Verdi will return to identical procedures for similar dramatic situations throughout his life. At Oberto's words Riccardo's anger explodes in a resumption of the prestissimo marked a few bars earlier; and from this the new movement is generated. It is brought to a halt by the sudden appearance of Cuniza with Leonora, at which point the quartet proper begins. This was the piece which generally speaking made the greatest effect, so we are told; and indeed the correspondent of the *Allgemeine musikalische Zeitung*, Germany's leading music-periodical, quoted substantially from the score in his review of the autumn season at La Scala.* From today's standpoint it seems an odd mixture of the boldly simple and the bizarre. Its rhythmic design is very powerful and entirely Verdian, and the opening sestina (*La vergogna ed il dispetto*) presents a characteristic design which we shall meet again somewhat better executed in the next few operas: a declamatory opening made up of short vocal phrases in dialogue with the orchestra; a climax, usually a point of harmonic high tension about the fourth or fifth line, from which the music falls away in a smoother, more even motion and in longer, more 'periodic' phrases. It is a simpler, more powerful descendant of the Rossinian 'open' melody.

The G major–minor ambiguity which seems so promising at the start leads Verdi into tortuous paths. Note the ugly wrench from B flat to the dominant of D at the words *Lacerando il cor mi va*, and also the fact that D major no longer carries that sense of the dominant that makes a return to G inevitable. But somehow enough rhythmic momentum has been generated to carry a large-scale movement; and once the rolling 4/4–12/8 gait is established, we can recognize that favourite

* See Conati, *loc. cit.*

20

backcloth against which the young Verdi loved to parade the slow pageant of his ideas. Cuniza's phrase (*Sciagurato! e tanto ardiva*) will reappear note for note nine years later in *Il Corsaro*. The repeated appoggiatura on the B, the resolution by means of a two-quaver figure broadly bestriding the triplet accompaniment—all this is specifically Verdian tissue (see Ex. 21, overleaf).

Characterization is admittedly scanty. There is little to indicate that Riccardo

21

CUNIZA

Scia-gu‒ra‒to! e tan ‒ to ar‒ di‒va   mentre a me chie-de‒a‒pa-ro‒la,

is both angry and remorseful; that Cuniza is accusing; that Leonora like Gilda still loves the man who has betrayed her; only Oberto smouldering with thoughts of vengeance leaps into prominence here and there with a phrase of repressed savagery. The final stretta (*Ah, Riccardo, se a misera amante*) is again a movement of mixed feelings. Leonora is tremulously happy, Oberto exultant at the prospect of vengeance, Riccardo guilty at the thought of the duel which his honour requires, Cuniza full of sorrow at having given up Riccardo. As music it is all energetic but trite. At the end Leonora and Cuniza leave for the castle, while Oberto and Riccardo make for a near-by wood.

No drop-curtain is needed for the next chorus of knights (*Li vedeste?*) as they comment on the false reconciliation of the two counts and moralize like a Greek chorus about the horrors of fraternal strife. The music is unremarkable except for a bold leap from G major to E flat seventh at the words 'Ahi, sventura'. But there is a good touch of dramatic irony which Verdi was to re-echo years later in *La Forza del Destino*. As the knights reach the final cadence of their melody with a prayer for peace, sounds of fighting are heard off (the stormy transitional passage from the overture), and the men hurry away to see what is afoot. Then after more agitated music Riccardo appears 'with sword in hand as though pursued by some-one'. Yet he finds time to sing a Romanza (*Ciel, che feci!*)‒a lyrical andante in what may be called minor-major form (see Chapter 1) but with a curious tonal scheme: E flat minor‒B flat major. It is not an entirely happy invention. In the first two stanzas one has the impression that Verdi was concerned with providing a singable and expressive line without bothering too much about its harmonic implications. In the middle stanza the music reflects all too faithfully the naïveté of the text. Riccardo hears a groan (there is a falling minor second on clarinet and bassoon), then decides that it was only the wind (first violins oblige with a flurry of demisemiquavers). But no, it was a groan (falling minor second again) and so on. Surprisingly, the final B flat major section with its arpeggiated cello accompaniment (*Ciel pietoso*) is one of the finest things in the score. In its simple poetry and truth-fulness of expression it points forward to that other memorable tenor aria, 'Quando le sere al placido' (*Luisa Miller*).

Riccardo leaves; and then Cuniza hurries on to the scene oppressed by those vague forebodings to which she has been given throughout the opera. Verdi skilfully sustains the feeling of growing excitement, pounding out the rhythms with trumpets and trombones, up to the point where a chorus of returning knights announces that they have found the body of Oberto in the wood and beside it Leonora who had witnessed the duel. As Leonora is led on now in a state of collapse, Cuniza sings a brief adagio with chorus (*Vieni, o misera*) which prepares the way for the heroine's rondò-finale. The largo (*Sciagurata, a questo lido*), a movement in simple minor to major strophic form amplified by chorus recalls Bellini at his most lachrymose. Bellinian too is the melodic episode for Cuniza as she reads a

letter which a messenger has brought from Riccardo with the news that he has
gone into voluntary exile having left all his property to Leonora, 'his first love'.
Inevitably the heroine's final outburst (*Cela il foglio insanguinato*) takes the form of a
cabaletta with chorus, with all the tawdriness and noise that that dreariest of
conventions implies. But two points are worth noting: first, Verdi has kept the
heroine's line simple and free from fioritura; more striking still, he has dovetailed the cabaletta into the preceding music where most of his contemporaries
would have prepared the way with a full ritornello. This is an early and successful
instance of Verdi's technique of short-circuiting the traditional procedures, while
at the same time preserving the musical balance. Considered on its own, Leonora's
final cabaletta is somewhat scrappy; but it gains hugely through having been
subordinated to a much larger musical scheme. Indeed this is true of everything in
Oberto from Riccardo's romance onwards. There is little here that is distinguished,
and much that is merely rough. But the momentum is sustained right up to the
final chord.

However the history of Verdi's first opera does not end there. The following
revivals entailed significant changes, and even the composition of new music.

TURIN, *carnival season 1840*. During the preparation of what was to be the outstanding operatic success of the year, Nicolai's *Il Templario*, *Oberto* was taken up as an
opera di ripiego, presumably at the insistence of Mme Rainieri-Marini who again
sang Leonora. The Cuniza was Luigia Abbadia, a much higher mezzo-soprano
than Mary Shaw; and she was not prepared to do without a cavatina. Accordingly
the Turin libretto prints the text of an andante (*Parmi che al fin quest' anima*), some
linking recitative and a cabaletta (*Da tanta gioia assorta*)—all adopted from a

cavatina written by Mercadante for Luigia Boccabadati to sing in *Elena da Feltre* in place of the heroine's original romanza in Act I. Despite the verbal alterations the text, which is all about the unclouded happiness of a bride on her wedding day, is not particularly suited to its new context. Cuniza's happiness is very far from being unclouded then or at any other point of the opera. The duet with Riccardo is omitted altogether, doubtless for reasons of pitch.

In his memoirs Nicolai maintained that the opera was badly received; but he was hardly an unprejudiced observer. The reviewer of the *Gazzetta Piemontese*, who signed himself *R.* and may well have been Felice Romani, then its editor-in-chief, poured scorn on the opera's naïveté, contrasting it with the 'over-sophistication' of Rossini's *Guillaume Tell* which had preceded it on the cartello. He concluded with the remark that it was no use expecting the citizens of Turin to fall for everything that had been the rage in Milan. Point to be noted: *Oberto* *had* been a success at Milan.

MILAN, *autumn season 1840*. After the disastrous failure of *Un Giorno di Regno* Merelli replaced all further scheduled performances with *Oberto*. The name part was taken by the baritone Ferlotti, while Abbadia again sang Cuniza. According to the biographical sketch of 1879 Verdi did no more than 'adapt' (*puntare*) the part of Oberto to Ferlotti's somewhat higher voice. In fact he seems to have composed two entirely new pieces: a cavatina in two movements for Cuniza and a three-movement duet for Cuniza and Riccardo to replace the original one.* The cavatina is poor as music and clumsily scored. The first phrase of the andante (*D'innocenza i cari inganni*) has a resemblance to the start of the preceding chorus, which may or may not have been intentional; the cabaletta (*Ma ne' primi anni un angelo*) has a purely routine brilliance. Whether or not the author was Solera the underlying idea and even some of the phraseology can be traced easily enough to Victor Hugo's *Angélo, tyran de Padoue*. Thisbe, the actress, is recalling her mother who protected the innocence of her youth like a guardian angel. No mother appears in *Oberto*: but there is a link between the two plots. Thisbe's lover is Ezzelino da Romano!

The duet is better altogether. In point of craftsmanship it surpasses the original, though far more conventional in form. Here Verdi follows the standard Rossinian pattern without the slightest deviation. The opening allegro in F minor (*Ah Riccardo a mia ragion'*) is a 'similar' movement with the voices an octave apart—something which the low voice of Mary Shaw had made impossible. The music reflects Cuniza's agitation as she tells Riccardo of her forebodings; Riccardo, as in the earlier duet, tries to dispel her fears. Then follows a central andantino (3/4–9/8) in E flat major (*Ah de' rimorsi miei*) where both singers soliloquize, Riccardo remembering with shame his betrayal of Leonora, Cuniza rebuking herself for her unworthy suspicions. If not particularly original it is none the less a beautiful piece of vocal writing, and it has a harmonic strength and variety all too rare in this very unequal

---

* One should not, of course, exclude the view of David Kimbell (*loc. cit.*) that both pieces had been composed for the performance that was to have been given at the Pio Istituto earlier in 1839. The higher range of Cuniza's part would be appropriate, since Adelaide Kemble was a soprano, and a noted exponent of Norma. But in that case should Luigia Abbadia have sung her inserted aria at Turin if the cavatina which she was to perform in Milan had already been composed?

score. As before quality falls off in the final movement (*Tu del mio cor sei l'arbitra*), a moderato in G major with a thrumming accompaniment of pizzicato strings. But here at least Verdi can once more keep both entries in the same key, so giving the required effect of reconciliation and avoiding the tonal imbalance of the original last movement. The real drawback in using this duet in place of the other is that the quotation of Ex. 17 at the beginning of Act II will no longer have the character of a reminiscence.

NAPLES, *carnival season 1841.* As in Turin *Oberto* was revived as an opera di ripiego in Verdi's absence. Again the heroine was played by Rainieri-Marini (doubtless it was one of the few parts which really suited her voice). Cuniza was sung by Bucini, a full contralto, so the original score was used. The only changes made were the infuriating little bowdlerizations of the text referred to above (see Chapter 1). The opera was not an unqualified success, and prompted the unkind quip from a reviewer that people were 'doubly right in thinking that the San Carlo Theatre was in the red'.* The Italian expression uses a different colour—green (*verde*).

GENOA, *carnival season 1841.* This was a revival which Verdi had been commissioned to mount himself. The differences between this version and the original appear from the published libretto to be very extensive. They include:

(a) The new Cuniza–Riccardo duet but not Cuniza's cavatina.

(b) A new duet for Leonora and Oberto, in two movements,† the first beginning *Dove corri o sciagurata*, the second *Vieni, pietoso è il ciel*. This replaces the three-movement duet in Act I of the original. Its salient features are: the opening orchestral flourish suggesting someone in flight and so giving point to Oberto's first words; the gentle Bellinian lilt of the cabaletta; and the alternative transitions according to whether this last was to be sung in F or E major.

(c) A new chorus for Cuniza's attendants (*Sorge un canto; si diffonde*) in place of *Fidanzata avventurosa*. This survives only in an arrangement for piano solo from which it is impossible to deduce the vocal parts.¶

These changes are all confirmed in a recently discovered letter to Massini.‡ From the same source—as well as the letter to Balestra quoted above—we know that Verdi added the stage band to Riccardo's cavatina and it made 'a devil of a row'.

A further puzzle remains; the origin of the grand duet for Leonora and Cuniza at the end of the autograph. Verdi's exact words to Luigi Balestra are: 'I am sorry that we couldn't perform your duet which I had already set to music, but it would have been too tiring for Mme Marini and so I put in another very small one.'§ He does not say it was a duet for two women; though obviously Leonora must have been involved. But the only new duet which could possibly qualify as 'piccolissimo' is the one for Leonora and Oberto (*Dove corri o sciagurata*). The natural assumption is that the Balestra duet was for the same characters.

---

* Abbiati, I, p. 366.
† The music of this, together with the puntature for a baritone Oberto, exists in two MS. full scores in the Biblioteca S. Pietro a Majella, Naples (Fondo verdiano 32.4.5 and O.A.39).
‡ See Conati (*loc. cit.*).
§ Abbiati, I, p. 359.
¶ See also p. 169

The Leonora–Cuniza duet was obviously intended to follow Cuniza's aria in Act II. Leonora, determined to save her father from the vengeance of Riccardo, is detained by Cuniza. She tells the frightened heroine that she will protect Oberto, and that she herself is fully resolved to punish Riccardo. But first she must be quite certain that Leonora herself is without blame. Leonora swears her innocence; and the two women in effect fall into each other's arms. The form is unusually flexible. Cuniza is reassured in the course of the first movement (*Pria che scende sull' indegno*), whereupon the music following Leonora's strophe changes from A minor to A major with excited pizzicato motion in the cellos. The central section (*Nel cangiar di sorte infida*) finds the two women singing in thirds from the beginning. The melody has a haunting, romantic beauty recalling Bellini's 'Mira, o Norma'.

23

A transitional passage in B minor leads to the final movement (*Generosa, un tanto affetto*) again in D major and based on Ex. 13. It is precisely this feature that makes one wonder whether the duet dates from an altogether earlier stage of the opera; whether it could be the duet from *Rocester* referred to above. True, it is a remarkably good piece to have been written so early; but it does contain some ridiculously naïve touches, e.g. the introduction of trombones in the first movement at the words 'Giura a me'. Also, in the successive versions he made of his operas Verdi tends to entrust more and more of his melodic thought to the orchestra. This duet is the only point in the entire score where Ex. 13 is *sung*.

For a first opera *Oberto* is an interesting achievement. But let us not exaggerate. Verdi was then twenty-six, the age at which Mozart had written *Die Entführüng*, with *Idomeneo* already behind him—the first a repertory work from the day it was produced, the second beginning nowadays to qualify as such. In no circumstances could *Oberto* enter the general repertoire. At most it can be revived for occasional performances in the anniversary years; and even then its audiences will be restricted mainly to verdiani. Had Verdi died after writing it he would not be remembered today, for there is nothing here of that finite achievement to be found in the work of certain younger geniuses: in Mendelssohn's Octet or *Midsummer Night's Dream* overture, or Schubert's early songs and symphonies. We might not even recognize the great moments so easily if we were not viewing them through the telescope of Verdi's later operas. They are there none the less, and always at points where the dramatic situation spurs his invention. The weakest parts of the opera are where Verdi sets himself to write orthodox cavatinas and arias of no great dramatic application, and succeeds only in being crudely imitative. An apt comparison could be made with, say, Beethoven's Cantata on the death of Joseph II, which he wrote in his twentieth year. Here too the composer's voice can be heard in fits and starts, often muffled by an imperfect technique. Likewise *Oberto* with all its many faults and ineptitudes is unmistakably the beginning of the road.

4 UN GIORNO DI REGNO

UN GIORNO DI REGNO

(later IL FINTO STANISLAO)
Melodramma giocoso in two acts
by
FELICE ROMANI
(after *Le Faux Stanislas*, a comedy by Alexandre Vincent Pineu-Duval)

First performed at the
Teatro alla Scala, Milan,
5 September 1840

THE CAVALIERE DI BELFI-ORE, posing as Stanislaus king of Poland	PRIMO BARITONO	Raffaele Ferlotti
THE BARON KELBAR	BASSO BUFFO	Raffaele Scalese
THE MARCHESA DEL POGGIO, a young widow, the Baron's niece, in love with Belfiore	PRIMA DONNA SOPRANO	Antonietta Rainieri-Marini
GIULIETTA DI KEL-BAR, the Baron's daughter in love with Edoardo	PRIMA DONNA MEZZO-SOPRANO	Luigia Abbadia
EDOARDO DI SANVAL, a young officer	PRIMO TENORE	Lorenzo Salvi
SGR. LA ROCCA, Edoardo's uncle, treasurer of the States of Brittany	BASSO BUFFO	Agostino Rovere
THE COUNT IVREA	SECONDO TENORE	Giuseppe Vaschetti
DELMONTE, squire to the supposed Stanislaus	SECONDO TENORE	Napoleone Marconi

Servants—chambermaids—vassals of the Baron

The action takes place near Brest in the castle of Kelbar

Epoch: 1733

Having recounted the success of *Oberto* Verdi continues in his summary:

> Merelli then made me what was a very generous proposal for those days: he offered me a contract for three operas at intervals of eight months to be given at La Scala or at the theatre in Vienna of which he was also the impresario. In return he was to pay me 4,000 Austrian lire for each opera, sharing with me the proceeds from the sale of the scores. I accepted the contract straight away; and a little while later Merelli set off for Vienna, having charged the poet Rossi to provide me with the libretto; and this was to be *Il Proscritto*; however I was not entirely happy about it and I hadn't even begun to set it to music when Merelli came back to Milan in the early months of 1840 and said that he absolutely must have a comedy for the autumn season for special reasons of repertory; he would like to find me a libretto straight away and after that I could set *Il Proscritto*. I didn't refuse this request, and Merelli gave me various libretti by Romani to read, all of which had lain forgotten on the shelf, either because they hadn't been successful or for some other reason. I read them over and over and didn't like any of them, but because the matter was of some urgency I chose the one which seemed to me the least bad; and that was *Il Finto Stanislao*, which was then christened *Un Giorno di Regno*.*

Then follows the curious mis-statement that his wife Margherita and two children died within three months of each other during the summer of 1840. In fact the first child died in 1838 when Verdi was still at Busseto; the second during the rehearsals of *Oberto* the following year. However, an entry in the diary of Antonio Barezzi for June 1840 attests: 'In Milan at midday on the feast of Corpus Christi my beloved daughter Margherita died in my arms of some terrible disease perhaps unknown to medical science; she was in the flower of her years and at the height of her good fortune, for she had become the lifelong companion of that excellent young man Giuseppe Verdi, maestro di musica.'† Verdi returned to Busseto with his father-in-law. He wrote to Merelli asking to be released from his contract; but Merelli refused. So after two months Verdi returned to Milan where 'so as not to fall short of my obligations I was forced in the midst of terrible sorrow to compose and see through to its production a comic opera!'‡

Un Giorno di Regno was produced on 5 September 1840 and was an unqualified disaster. The public whistled and jeered; the critics wrote in varying degrees of pity and contempt. Least unkind was the *Figaro*:

> The near impossibility of finding nowadays a verse comedy which is not utterly insipid, the size of the theatre which ruins the effect of half-tones and light melodies and the lack of aptitude shown by present-day singers for the

* Pougin, pp. 43 ff.   † F. Walker, *The Man Verdi* (London, 1962), p. 33.   ‡ Pougin, *ibid.*

comic genre; all this makes it twice as difficult for a new score of this kind to succeed. Add to all this the special circumstances that Verdi was forced to clothe his latest work with gay music just at the time when a cruel and unexpected catastrophe had struck him in the innermost part of his being, and it will be easily understood how in this his second venture he fell short of the expectations aroused by his first.*

Other papers dwelt on the monotony and derivativeness of the music and the inadequacy of the performance. 'A day's reign' did not survive its first night.

At a distance of nearly forty years Verdi took a detached view. 'Certainly the music was to some extent to blame, but then so too was the performance.'† But the wound had taken a long time to heal. In a letter to Tito Ricordi in 1859 he recalled how the Milanese public:

> slaughtered the work of a poor ailing young man working under pressure and heartbroken by a terrible catastrophe. All this was known but it in no way restrained their discourtesy. I haven't seen *Un Giorno di Regno* from that day to this and I've no doubt it was a bad opera but who can say that it was any worse than many which have been tolerated and even applauded? . . . I don't intend to condemn the public; I allow its severity, I accept its whistles on condition that I'm not asked to be grateful for its applause.‡

In fact Milan's verdict of 1840 was not final. Five years later Verdi was writing to the sculptor Luccardi: 'Do you want a good laugh? That opera of mine that was hissed off the stage at La Scala is now a sensation at the Teatro San Benedetto.'§ This was the second theatre in Venice, a younger sister to the Fenice with a strong tradition of comedy. In 1854 it was to perform an even more spectacular work of reclamation with *La Traviata*. *Il Finto Stanislao*, as it was now called, enjoyed a further run at the San Carlo, Naples, in 1859. It was also deemed strong enough to be chosen by the Italian firm of Cetra as one of the three little-known Verdi operas to make commercially available at the time of the fiftieth anniversary celebrations of 1951, together with *I Lombardi* and *La Battaglia di Legnano*.

The excuses given by the *Figaro* critic were perfectly valid. Opera buffa was in decline. The days were long since past when it could offer a far wider scope for musical development than its strait-laced elder sister. Opera seria had absorbed its most fruitful forms and techniques; while the persistence of recitativo secco in comedy long after it had been abolished in tragedy meant that the serious genre allowed for a greater continuity of musical design. If opera seria remained in certain respects spiritually linked to the eighteenth century, this was even more the case with opera buffa. In Donizetti's *L'Elisir d'Amore* we regularly hear the recitativo secco accompanied by harpsichord, because it seems the most suitable instrument for what is essentially an eighteenth-century operatic element. Yet how many theatres of the 1830s would even have possessed a harpsichord? The use of piano here would strike our ears as a modernism—quite wrongly. It is the medium itself, not the instrument, that is anachronistic.

---

* Abbiati, I, pp. 352–3.   † Pougin, *ibid.*
‡ Letter to T. Ricordi, 4.2.1859. *Copialettere*, pp. 556–7.
§ Letter to Luccardi (undated), Abbiati, I, p. 596.

Yet *L'Elisir d' Amore* (1832) does come to terms with its age. It is picturesque and delicately sentimental. *Il Finto Stanislao*, written by the same author, Felice Romani, for the Austrian composer Adalbert Gyrowetz in 1818, is a very different matter. It was conceived at a time when the vogue for Rossinian comedy was at its height. It calls for two bassi buffi, two sparkling unsentimental heroines, one sophisticated, the other ingenuous; and at the centre of the action a baritone or basso cantante requiring that mixture of flamboyance and irony which Rossini realizes to perfection. In the event even Gyrowetz failed to meet the challenge, which is why the libretto had been 'remaindered'. Twenty-one years later Verdi with even less experience than Gyrowetz was unlikely to succeed any better. To begin with the cast was unpropitious. It had been assembled chiefly with a view to the performance of Nicolai's *Il Templario*, to which most of the rehearsal time had been devoted. Merelli had engaged three of the original singers (Antonietta Rainieri-Marini as Rebecca, Lorenzo Salvi as Ivanhoe and Luigia Abbadia as Rowena), while for Brian de Bois-Guilbert he secured Raffaele Ferlotti, one of opera's leading baritone villains. The outcome was all that might have been expected: *Il Templario*, given on 13 August, was as successful in Milan as it had been in Turin. Immediately afterwards this same cast, hand-picked for the high heroic style, had to accommodate themselves to an old-fashioned comedy. Only the two bassi buffi Raffaele Scalese and Agostino Rovere acquitted themselves with credit. The rest hardly appeared to be trying. For the present Nicolai was up and Verdi was down. In less than two years the scales were to tilt most dramatically.

Un Giorno di Regno is based on a play, *Le Faux Stanislas* (Paris, 1808), by the French dramatist, theatre-manager, sailor, architect and jack-of-all-trades Alexandre Vincent Pineu-Duval, who was still alive and in his seventies when Verdi's opera was produced. The Stanislas of the original title is Stanislas Lescinski who was King of Poland off and on during the first half of the eighteenth century. His last successful election to the throne occurred in 1733 when he travelled to Warsaw disguised as a coachman; and at the same time a French chevalier, Beaufleur, was chosen to impersonate him, so as to give his enemies the impression that he was still in France. The play concerns an episode in which Stanislas's double, staying as an honoured guest at the house of Baron Kelbar in Brittany, brings about the wedding of two young lovers in the teeth of parental opposition, and effects a reconciliation with his own mistress, who is just on the point of marrying somebody else.

Romani fashioned this into a libretto with his usual consummate skill, omitting only the complication whereby the treasurer has by fraudulent means dispossessed the hero of his family estates, and reducing an informative servant (Delmonte in the opera) to the briefest of secondary parts. Belfiore retains all the central importance of Morange, his counterpart in the play, whose character Duval thought it necessary to define very precisely in a stage direction: 'He has two different physiognomies, both well-pronounced. He must move between the gravity of a wise prince and the thoughtlessness of a young soldier. The whole effect of the role depends on this.' He shows one face to his fellow-actors, another to the audience. He must not only be a likeable humorist in himself; he must appear to be the stage manager of the entire opera. *Un Giorno di Regno* is the Belfiore Show. Rossini could have set it convincingly enough. To Verdi the protagonist presented a problem he was unable to solve at this stage of his career. His Belfiore is the mere shell of a buffo baritone; which would matter less if he were not the raison d'être of the opera.

But that is not the only reason why *Un Giorno di Regno* failed at the time. The main strength of *Oberto* was its sustained momentum. In its successor Verdi was writing in a genre in which this momentum was far more difficult to achieve because the various numbers were marked off from each other by recitativo secco. Again, how much thought, discussion and revision were needed to produce the *Oberto* that has come down to us we shall never know. At no point did Verdi even discuss *Un Giorno di Regno* with its author. The cuts and variants of the original text are probably the work of Solera, then the effective 'dramaturge' of La Scala.★ *Oberto* is a shortish opera; paradoxically *Un Giorno di Regno*, written under far greater pressure, is too long. The fault is partly Romani's who had six principals to accommodate and therefore spun out the end of the plot so that none of them should feel overlooked. Finally, comic opera in the 1840s was expected to show delicacy and grace, two qualities in which Verdi was as yet totally lacking. In tragic opera he was better able to conceal his defects. In the more discontinuous genre of comedy his immature technique is cruelly exposed. There is no rising tide of dramatic emotion to carry him over the harmonic miscalculations. Naturally the audience began to fidget, being reminded not so much of what other composers had done as of how much better they did it.

Yet in certain respects *Un Giorno di Regno* is an improvement on its predecessor. It contains fewer mistakes of musical grammar, fewer harmonic ineptitudes. It has moments of unforced lyrical sweetness and even of infectious gaiety. But by the side of *L'Elisir d' Amore* or *Don Pasquale* it cuts a clumsy figure.

The overture is once again very short; but it contains some of the most characteristic music in the opera. It is in one movement only which skips along in the rhythm of a military two-step, such as underlies the last movement of the overture to *Guillaume Tell*. Despite its primitive structure (sonata form abridged to the point where it loses its identity) the music has a sureness of touch, which is doubtless the fruit of several years' practice in writing marches for the Filarmonici of Busseto. In the second subject (G major) Verdi shows for the first time the ability which he shares with Haydn and Beethoven, to tease an irregular theme into a convicing rhythmic shape. Everything is preposterous about the theme itself: it is repetitive, banal and coarsely scored. By the time it returns embellished with a counter-subject on cello, bassoon, trombone and cimbasso it has acquired the kind of disconcerting logic to be found later in certain of Verdi's more boisterous choruses (e.g. 'Niun periglio in questo seno' from *I Lombardi*).

ACT I

Scene 1: a gallery in the house of Baron Kelbar near Brest

The opening scene has been laid out by Romani as an 'introduzione', according to one of Rossini's most cherished formulae: chorus—episode for subsidiary character or characters (in this case the two bassi buffi)—chorus—scena and cavatina of principal character (Belfiore) with chorus joining in the final movement. The

★ See R. Parker, 'Un Giorno di Regno: from Romani's libretto to Verdi's Opera', in *Studi Verdiani*, II (Parma, 1983), pp. 38–58.

Baron's household is in a pleasurable ferment. Never did a more glorious day dawn upon the House of Kelbar (*Mai non rise un più bel giorno*) soon to be graced by the presence of a Noble Sovereign. The same day should see a double wedding: of the Baron's daughter to Signor La Rocca, Grand Treasurer of Brittany, and his niece, the widowed Marchesa del Poggio, to Count Ivrea, Commandante of Brest. There will be splendid banquets, balls, festivities of all kinds and plenty of tips. The Baron himself and his prospective son-in-law compliment and congratulate one another in typical basso buffo style, after which the chorus is resumed.

The Baron's servant (Delmonte) announces His Royal Majesty. There is a brisk flourish of trumpets and with it a chorus of welcome; and in steps the Cavaliere Belfiore. 'No ceremony please, gentlemen,' he says, 'your hospitality is enough,' and he hints delicately that on his return to Poland the Baron's services will not go unrewarded. While the Baron retreats in ecstatic confusion, Belfiore advances to the footlights and confides to the audience: 'If only my old comrades in Paris could see me now: the most dissolute officer in the regiment turned philosopher king!' He then resumes his regal manner, as he tells his hosts once more to greet him as a friend. 'The day will come, alas, when cares of state and the sceptre of my forefathers will weigh heavily upon me.' Baron, Treasurer and household all chatter away in admiration of his modesty.

What is chiefly remarkable about Verdi's setting is his attempt to integrate all the components of this introduction into a single structure together with the overture, by a thematic working which is too clear to have been unintentional. (Note how Ex. 24 (c) provides yet another instance of his consistency of procedure throughout his life; for this is exactly the language in which he will characterize Fra Melitone in Act IV of *La Forza del Destino*.)

The components themselves are variable in quality. The opening chorus shows Verdi's style at its most homespun: sopranos and tenors cheerfully double each other in thirds; and both are doubled by the full wind, including trombones, and supported by pizzicato strings—all giving a 'clanking' sound from which Donizetti would have recoiled. Yet this was the direction which all opera buffa was taking in the hands of Donizetti's successors. Verdi's choral writing is no more primitive than Luigi Ricci's in *Piedigrotta* and is a good deal more vigorous. The first real miscalculation occurs at Belfiore's entrance. This opening moderato (*Compagnoni di Parigi*) recalls the situation of Dandini in *La Cenerentola* who also makes his entrance with a behind-the-hand aria ('Come l'ape d'aprile'). But what a build-up Rossini contrives before Dandini utters a word; and with what a widely arched phrase he eventually does so, as though making an ironical bow! There is a similar suggestion of impudence in Belcore's cavatina ('Come Paride vezzoso') from *L'Elisir d'Amore*. For Belfiore Verdi merely provides a lyrical tune in his most spacious baritone manner in 9/8 with an elaborately patterned accompaniment.

The melody is striking enough in itself, but its effect is one of boot-faced solemnity. Verdi had missed the chance of getting the audience on Belfiore's side from the start. The final movement (*Verrà purtroppo il giorno*) is more effective, even if its heady vigour contrasts strangely with the sense of the words. If in Verdi's early tragedies the final allegro movements are usually the least convincing, in his one traditional opera buffa they are often the strongest, if only because it is in them that he allows his own voice to be most clearly heard.

The first bout of recitativo secco puts an end to all further development. The Baron tells Belfiore of the 'double wedding' and the names of the parties concerned. At the mention of the Marchesa del Poggio Belfiore starts. He askes his host to leave him, and then proceeds to write a letter to his employers, begging to be released from his imposture. The real Stanislas must surely have arrived in Warsaw by this time, and if Belfiore were to 'reign' a day longer he would lose the woman he loved. In accordance with the operatic tradition the words of the letter are spoken, not sung. Strings take over from the keyboard, so anticipating the recitative idiom of *Don Pasquale*, as Edoardo di Sanval enters. Heartbroken at the prospect of losing Giulietta to his uncle he has come to ask the supposed Stanislas to take him into his service so that he may seek an honourable death on the field of battle. In short, Edoardo is one of those romantic, lachrymose young lovers that people the comic operas of Donizetti and his contemporaries. The scene is set for a duet of contrasts laid out by Romani in the standard tripartite scheme. In the first movement (*Proverò che degno io sono*) Edoardo protests eternal loyalty and gratitude to Belfiore, while Belfiore replies that the young man may indeed fight at his side, always supposing that he has to fight at all. In the transitional passage Belfiore goes further and appoints Edoardo his personal squire. This leads to the usual joint soliloquy, Edoardo overwhelmed by his sovereign's magnanimity, Belfiore chuckling over the havoc he intends to cause in the Baron's household. The stretta (*Infiammato da spirto guerriero*) is a 'shoulder-to-shoulder' movement in military style.

Verdi's setting of all this begins promisingly enough with a close imitation of Rossini's manner, each singer delivering an expansive melodic period which breaks down into shorter units before winding up with an emphatic cadence. The transition is enlivened by a characteristic tripping figure and culminates in a suitably strong, if orthodox, modulation to the key of the central movement (*Ricompensa amica sorte*). For this there is an obvious model in the Nemorino–Belcore duet from Act II of *L'Elisir d'Amore* ('Venti scudi') where the tenor soars lyrically in sustained notes above continuous buffo chatter. (The situation is very similar, since Nemorino too wants to enlist.) Verdi manages it more awkwardly than Donizetti. He sets out two contrasting ideas at full length before attempting to combine them. Not only is neither melody particularly good in itself (Edoardo's is spoiled by a clumsy progression in the seventh bar), but the second sounds too fast in relation to the first. In the event Verdi finds he cannot combine them at all, and has to be content with throwing Belfiore a few reiterated semiquavers beneath an abridged version of the tenor melody. Curiously enough no change of tempo is marked for the start of the movement; and indeed the opening melody can be sung quite comfortably and without losing its character at the pace of the preceding section. But Belfiore's comment (*Quando in fumo andrà la corte*) most certainly cannot. It almost seems as if we are dealing with the kind of miscalculation to be found later in the overture to *Nabucco*. Doubtless the cause was extreme haste in both cases. The last movement, if undistinguished—not to say maddeningly repetitive—is at least characteristic in its bluff vigour. Both voices combine in thirds from the start, and continue singing during the ritornello.

No sooner have Edoardo and Belfiore left than the Marchesa enters, having watched them from a distance unobserved. One of the two she is quite certain is her lover, Belfiore. So much the better; she will pretend to marry the old Count Ivrea in the certainty that Belfiore will declare himself. And so after a few bars of Rossini-like accompanied recitative she launches into her cavatina. The Marchesa del Poggio is the real heroine of the opera. A young widow and a merry one, she is as humorous and as determined as Rossini's Rosina; but she is an older woman with fewer illusions. Her problem is not to outwit a stupid guardian but to bring a rakish lover to heel. The words of both andante and cabaletta indicate tenderness, humour and a touch of sadness. She can never love anyone except Belfiore; if as she suspects he is deceiving her she will renounce love for ever. Neither movement is remarkable. The first (*Grave a core innamorato*) for all its steep contours keeps strictly within Antonietta Rainieri-Marini's mezzo-soprano range, never rising above A flat except in the cadenza. Its most interesting feature is a syncopated passage for flute, oboe, clarinet and horn in the coda, underlying a succession of trilling figures in the voice to the word 'sospirai', in which there is a distant glimpse of the postlude to 'Caro nome'. The cabaletta which follows at once (*Se dee cader la vedova*), is graceful and sprightly with a touch here and there of military abruptness (note the quick, almost bitten-off cadence in the fourth bar). The scoring is in Verdi's flashiest vein with statement and restatement bridged by the inevitable Rossini crescendo.

Scene 2: the gardens of Baron Kelbar's castle

Giulietta, the Baron's niece, is receiving the homage of her attendants, who have brought flowers and fruit to one that is fairer than any flower. Verdi sets the scene with a return to the essentially 'villareccio' style of the introduzione: sopranos in thirds doubled by all the upper wind including piccolo, and with triangle added. The chorus (*Sì festevole mattina*) (Ex. 25) is of a kind that recurs at Federica's entrance in *Luisa Miller* and Lida's opening scene in *La Battaglia di Legnano*.

In both the later operas it is one element in a highly variegated design. Here there is no such variety. The allegro 3/4 rhythm passes into the andantino 6/8 of Giulietta's cavatina (*Non san quant'io nel petto*) without losing its identity: and it reappears still more unequivocally in the cabaletta (*Non vo' quel vecchio*) together with the same orchestral triplets which were a feature of the opening movement. The reason for this is doubtless Verdi's wish to depict Giulietta as an *ingénue*, in contrast to her more sophisticated cousin; and popular music was his most effective resource, though at the cost of a certain monotony. However the andantino, in which she confides her sorrow to the audience, has a simple dignity about it; and the passage where the attendants comment on her 'clouded brow' beneath a sustained high note from the soprano recalls in more rustic fashion a similar moment in Bellini's 'Casta diva' (Ex. 26)'.

The effect will be recaptured even more movingly in Lucrezia's cavatina from *I Due Foscari*.

25

26

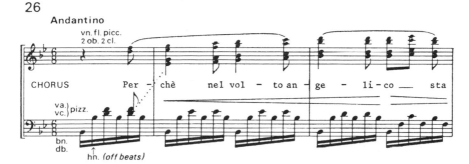

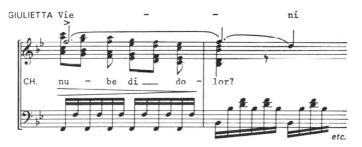

The cabaletta features what is to become one of Verdi's most well-worn rhythmic patterns ♩ ♩ ♩ | ♪. ♫ ♩ ♪, clearly of popular provenance, and indeed there are distinct echoes of the Neapolitan song 'Santa Lucia', in the melody to which Giulietta declares that she has no wish to marry an old man.* We may note in passing that,

* In the orchestral introduction the melody is broken off in mid-phrase in a manner familiar from a very similar piece: 'La donna è mobile'. It is a device used not infrequently by Donizetti; and it can be found in the Marchesa's cavatina earlier in this opera. But it is only in the context of this bouncing 3/4 rhythm that it achieves that slightly comic arbitrariness that borders on vulgarity.

though Luigia Abbadia is described as a mezzo-soprano and Antonietta Rainieri-Marini as a soprano, and though Giulietta's line is placed below that of the Marchesa in the ensembles, her solos are mostly higher, regularly rising to a B flat. Evidently the distinction between the two categories was at that time one of precedence rather than range.

Now the intrigue starts to build up as it moves first of all through the shallows of recitativo secco. The Baron enters, surprised to find his daughter looking so glum on the day of her marriage. The Treasurer who is with him prefers to ascribe her low spirits to the natural apprehensions of an innocent girl before her wedding night. Tomorrow, he assures her, she will see it all very differently. Before she can reply, Belfiore joins them with Edoardo, whom he presents as his personal squire. As he has important military matters to discuss with the Baron and the Treasurer, he proposes that Edoardo entertain his prospective aunt in the meantime—an idea which is not at all to the Treasurer's taste. But who is he to oppose the wishes of a crowned head? The stage is set for one of the most elaborate ensembles in the opera: it is also one of the most successful, despite its haphazard key-scheme, according to which it would appear that having begun the opening moderato in E flat major Verdi decided after four bars to site it in A flat major but forgot to change the key signature. Here the five characters assume their various attitudes—Edoardo and Giulietta amorous and tender, Belfiore and the Baron fussily poring over a map, the Treasurer trying to pay attention yet covertly eyeing the two lovers with increasing suspicion. The lines converge into a long lyrical tune sung by the lovers over a typically buffo accompaniment of remarks thrown out by the other three. Belfiore and Kelbar sing in staccato quavers or dotted quavers and semiquavers, while the Treasurer grumbles in semiquavers. In this way all the three elements are clearly distinguished. Soon however the laugh is to be on Belfiore. The Marchesa is announced; and no possible ruse on his part can prevent her being presented to him. His only hope is to play the monarch sufficiently well to make her uncertain. Verdi treats the Marchesa's entrance by the time-honoured comic-opera device of declamation against a rapid orchestral melody. There is an appropriate explosion at the point where she recognizes her lover; and her astonishment is expressed in a solitary stanza (*Pur dell'amante quell'è l'aspetto*) which begins in declamatory fashion in dialogue with the orchestra, then flowers most beautifully into lyrical melody with one of those phrases which in the later operas will do duty for whole movements (. . . *dell'incostante in tutto pingere gode l'amor*). The sextet ends with what is in effect a rapid 6/8 ensemble of perplexity (*Madamine, il mio scudiere*). For though Belfiore proposes to entrust the ladies to the care of his squire he makes no attempt to leave the room, but like everyone else present stands there giving vent to his private feelings. It is all Donizetti with extra horse-power and less grace. Twice there is a crescendo from *pp* to *ff* without any alteration in orchestral texture. Verdi was clearly in a hurry.

Belfiore now eventually retires with the Baron and the Treasurer on pretended military business, leaving the Marchesa alone with the two lovers. Part of her intention in coming there was to help them. But now they find to their dismay that she appears to have other things on her mind, and can only answer them distractedly and irritably. The situation and its resolution are limned in a trio whose first movement with its rippling accompaniment (*Bella speranza invero*) recall the minuet in *Don Giovanni*, a piece which will recur to Verdi's mind on more than one occasion.

Its somewhat un-Verdian softness is emphasized by the dragging, chromatic introduction on the strings. But there is a characteristic touch in the climbing figure that rounds off the main melody at the words 'So che tutt'ora, tutt'ora io l'amo'. For the Marchesa's apology and her reconciliation with Edoardo and Giulietta Verdi again has recourse to a buffo-style orchestral melody, whose model is clearly 'V'han certuni che dormendo' from *La Sonnambula*.* But the young Verdi's heavier hand is all too evident. The chattering tune is too obtrusive, too continuous for its purpose, while the use of piccolo throughout in unison with violins is enough to blot out most of the words. The voices unite in a brief final section (*Amanti siamo e giovani*) which in the autograph exists in two fully scored versions. One of them is unexpectedly dainty and gavotte-like with the three voices singing consecutively. The other, much stronger if also more vulgar, keeps the singers in unison throughout; and this is the one which was printed.

Scene 3: the gallery in Baron Kelbar's castle

Belfiore has hit upon a sure way to prevent the approaching wedding with the Treasurer. Taking the bridegroom on one side, 'What a pity,' he tells him, 'that you are pledged to the Baron's daughter! Otherwise I could have offered you an important ministry, as well as the hand of the Princess Isanska with her immense dowry . . .' The Treasurer can hardly wait to break off his engagement. The result is one of the few numbers that succeeded on the ill-fated first night: a short but effective duet between the two basses—outraged Baron, embarrassed Treasurer. There is a foretaste of the *Aida* trumpet march in the first movement (*Diletto genero, a voi ne vengo*) (Ex. 28) where the as yet unsuspicious Baron hands his prospective son-in-law the marriage contract for signing.

At its repeat Verdi characteristically elaborates the accompaniment with triplets on cello and bassoon. The final, patter-section (*Che sento? Oh nobili atavi miei*) leads straight into the first act finale, a characteristic three-part structure (allegro–adagio–presto). In the allegro the busyness of the orchestral part is not out of place, for the Baron, apoplectic with fury, is setting about the Treasurer and threatening

---

* The use in an aria of an orchestral cantilena as formed and periodic as this remains essentially an opera buffa device; and in this context it illustrates the essentially 'mixed-genre' or 'semiseria' nature of Bellini's sixth opera. The technical term for it is 'parlante'.

28

to kill him. The Marchesa arrives on the scene together with Edoardo and Giulietta and the servants. When the matter has been explained to her she has a very simple solution to offer. The Baron's most suitable revenge would be to marry his daughter straight away to the Treasurer's nephew Edoardo—a suggestion which the young couple do nothing to oppose. But for a Baron of the House of Kelbar the only fitting revenge is blood. The Treasurer must fight a duel. All further argument is then halted by the voice of Belfiore calling them to order, and so bringing about the moment of stasis, the inevitable adagio. Verdi treats it rather like the first movement of the quartet in *Oberto*, even turning the initial quatrain into a sestina by repeating the last two lines (Ex. 29).

As in the earlier adagio the melody is arresting, with bold harmonies and a climax at the end of the fourth line; but whereas Riccardo's verse has an ugly modulation at this point, Baron Kelbar rises to a high E flat over a 6/4 chord in the home key, from which point the melody gradually smoothes itself out.* Here, as previously in *Oberto*, the declamatory opening gradually relaxes into a chain of lyrical ideas. The Baron's bewilderment, his shame at the idea of brawling in the royal presence, is followed by four bars from the Treasurer, hoping now to be able to save his skin; then the long cantilena unfolds, shared mainly between Edoardo, the Marchesa and Giulietta, accompanied by the other men with Belfiore emerging now and then, Figaro-like, from the ensemble with some amused observation. At last Belfiore asserts his authority. He demands to know the cause of the quarrel; and in a rapid transitional section in 6/8 all present try to explain with the chattering incoherence of Bartolo's household when questioned by the officer of the guard. Belfiore halts the flow and announces that if either party tries to renew the dispute before he himself has been given a full explanation of its cause, then the aggressor

* The scale which leads to the climax will recur in *Ernani* at the corresponding structural point in the finale of Act I. The key is the same, and there is a reference to the restraining effect of a royal presence. Hence, no doubt, the unconscious reminiscence. See G. Roncaglia, *L'Ascensione creatrice di Giuseppe Verdi* (Florence, 1940), p. 30.

29

will incur all his regal fury. There follows the stretta (*Affidate alla mente reale*) into which Verdi has neatly woven the principal melody of the overture, scored for violins, piccolo, oboe, clarinet and trumpet just in case anyone might miss it! The assembled company is in a very chastened frame of mind and resolves outwardly at least to behave with decorum in the future.

One unexpected feature of this finale is the almost classical strictness of its key scheme (B flat–E flat–B flat). This is not usually Verdi's way, but here he makes it yield good results. The G flat major modulation in the adagio, the change to D flat in the stretta are all the stronger for being set in a wider perspective than that of the movement in which they occur.

ACT II

Scene 1: the same

It is in the nature of central finales to be inconclusive; so that when the curtain rises on the second act the action has not advanced beyond the point at which Belfiore halted the dispute between Baron and Treasurer. The various problems are still unsolved, and the principals plunged in gloom as the servants observe with some mystification. Still, that is always the way with the gentry: they change their mood with their clothes. Life is more carefree in the servants' hall—so they sing, in one of those amiable ditties of Neapolitan or Venetian provenance which were by now a staple feature of opera buffa (*Noi felici, noi contenti*). We have already heard its like in Giulietta's cavatina. The chorus serves as introduction to an aria in which the love-lorn Edoardo opens his heart to the servants. The gist of both movements is that he now has hopes of marrying his beloved after all; yet their musical character is curiously plangent. Both illustrate the young Verdi's uncertainty of touch when required to compose an orthodox undramatic aria. The largo (*Pietoso al lungo pianto*) is a simple, long-limbed but four-square melody in one structural unit with coda. Resumed at the fourth line the opening phrase is beautifully extended into a 'dying fall', after which flutes and oboes take over the accompanimental pattern with charming effect.

30

But there is real tautology in the middle of the melody, since the second and third lines end with precisely the same cadential figure, though at different pitches. (The high C in the cadenza would of course have been sung falsetto.) A choral transition leads to the cabaletta (*Deh lasciate a un alma amante*), a languid piece of music despite its martial gait and brighter instrumentation. Verdi himself must have had his doubts here, for the autograph contains part of the rough draft of another setting.

The chorus now retire as Belfiore enters with the Treasurer and Giulietta. Belfiore wants to know why the Baron objects so strongly to Giulietta's marriage with Edoardo. 'Ah,' she replies, 'the young man has no fortune, while the Treasurer is swimming in money.' 'In that case,' says Belfiore, 'he must give up to Edoardo one of his castles together with the sum of five thousand scudi,' and with this pronouncement he makes his royal exit with Edoardo and Giulietta. The Treasurer winces, but feels bound to obey his new sovereign. As if that were not enough, he sees his host approaching, obviously still in the same mind about the proposed duel. No matter; he had better bluff it out. If the Baron wants war he shall have it; and so straight into a second comic duet between the two basses, longer and more elaborate than the first one. The situation is a stock one in opera buffa (see Rossini's *Le Cambiale di Matrimonio*) but Romani gives it an extra comic twist. As the challenged party the Treasurer has the choice of weapons; and he suggests a grand tournament on horseback with kegs of gunpowder. The Baron sees through this cowardly ruse and decides to have his opponent soundly thrashed instead. Verdi sets this in three movements, all in fast tempo. The first, *Tutti l'armi si può prendere* (E major), unfolds like a typical Rossini buffo duet, each verse beginning pompously, then gradually tumbling over itself into comic patter and concluding in strong reiterated cadences. At the Treasurer's gambit (*Si figuri un barilone*) the rhythm changes to 6/8 (A major); and so it remains for the final movement (*Ardo, avvampo*, E major), stepped up in pace, as both sides threaten to burst with fury. It is all quite skilfully done strictly by means of opera buffa commonplaces, including a coincidental likeness* to the 'Rataplan' chorus from *La Fille du Régiment*, but the earlier duet is more original.

Scene 2: a veranda giving on to the castle gardens

The Marchesa has at last cornered Belfiore and is determined to make him confess who he is. They fence with each other in a sly duet whose first movement, again,

*As the Italian version of Donizetti's opera hadn't yet been prepared, V. couldn't possibly have known it!

is not unworthy of Rossini (*Ch'io non possa il ver comprendere*). It is a 'similar' duet, each verse based on a long melodic limb made up of different rhythmic elements. Note the witty foreshortening of the final phrase. What sets out as a four-bar idea is deftly turned into one of three bars.

For the second movement, where the voices join although each is singing aside (*Io so l'astuzia*), Verdi has recourse to a popular, almost 'montanaro' style of melody whose simple harmonies are later embellished with a descending counterpoint in the bass. Embellished? In intention perhaps; but the effect is horribly crude (see Ex. 9).

The Baron now joins them to say that the Count Ivrea will be arriving any moment; to which the Marchesa replies that she intends to marry him forthwith. 'And the Cavaliere?' puts in Belfiore. But the Marchesa says that she has no intention of waiting for him any longer; he has made game of her long enough. Belfiore can do no more than hint that the lover will somehow contrive to prevent her marriage with Count Ivrea. Well then, why, the Marchesa would like to know, is he so long in making his appearance? In a tender aria (*Si mostri a chi l'adora*) she declares herself ready to forgive him if he is sufficiently contrite, adding in an aside to the effect that if *that* doesn't bring him out into the open nothing will. Everything about this andante is delightful, from the organ-like wind introduction (a huge advance on a similar passage in *Oberto*) to the chuckling figure that accompanies the aside (*Se non si scopre adesso*). In short it deserves a better reception than it gets from the Cavaliere, who still honourably persists in his regal pretence. At this point the Count Ivrea is announced to the sound of a military trumpet theme; whereupon the Marchesa plunges into a defiant cabaletta (*Si, scordar saprò l'infido*). It is coarse and brassy and must have taxed the original exponent sorely, if she sang the exposed high B in the coda. Yet it is genuinely strong; and the return from the rueful aside (*Scaltro ingegno del bel sesso m'hai servito come va*) to the original thought is managed with a punch which you would not expect from Verdi's predecessors.

Dramatically it is now high time for the dénouement; but operatic protocol requires one more duet for the other pair of lovers, and the fact that their problem has really been solved must not be allowed to stand in the way. Textually what follows is a substantial piece, and Verdi, as if aware that the audience's patience might be giving out, sets all three movements allegro and with a minimum of thematic repetition. So Edoardo must be troubled with scruples; he has promised to follow 'Stanislas' to Poland, and cannot break his word (*Giurai seguirlo in campo*). Giulietta tells him not to talk nonsense. She herself will go to the King and persuade him to release her lover (*Corro al re: saprò difendere*). Hope revives in Edoardo and the two voices proceed to weave chain upon chain of rapturous sixths in the Italian operatic tradition (*Ah non sia, mio ben, fallace*). To us Edoardo hardly seems the stuff of which even sub-heroes are made. But then the spineless tenor is opera buffa's tribute to the romantic age. The Almavivas and Ramiros have languished into Ernestos, Tonios and Nemorinos. Such characters are not for Verdi and he seems to have lost interest in Edoardo altogether, since the only spark of vitality is contributed by Giulietta, with her chattering, Cimarosa-like mockery of Edoardo's sighs ('O possibile, possibile, possibile . . .').★

★ In the autograph Giulietta's semiquavers are set out in a dotted rhythm.

Next the Count Ivrea, whose arrival was so pompously announced, makes his entrance quietly in a passage of recitativo secco. The Marchesa, her eyes fixed on Belfiore, says once more that she will marry Ivrea; and Belfiore must play his one remaining trump. He forbids the marriage for 'reasons of state' and requires Ivrea to accompany him to Poland. The general consternation is expressed in the settimino—a very ample piece whose model seems to be the sextet from *La Cenerentola*. But it has twice Rossini's length and none of his decorative panache. It is virtually a piece of choral writing with only the Cavaliere and the Marchesa emerging now and again from the plodding homophony.

The finale follows directly on the heels of the settimino as a messenger enters with a letter for Belfiore. The King Stanislas has arrived safely in Warsaw, so that Belfiore is now released from his imposture. As compensation for his loss of a kingdom he is to receive the title of Marshal of France. Events now move rapidly. First Belfiore commands the marriage of Edoardo and Giulietta; then, as soon as the Baron has consented, he reads aloud the contents of the letter, declares his true identity and embraces the Marchesa. The two basses put a good face on their chagrin (buffo basses generally do) and the opera ends with a spirited chorus and ensemble based on the music of the overture. Romani's verses are subjected to the most brutal treatment imaginable. But the music is vital enough, and makes an appropriate ending.

Un Giorno di Regno cannot any more than *Oberto* be considered a repertory work. If it is more even from the point of view of technique it is far less of a musical and dramatic whole, while the level of invention fluctuates disconcertingly from one number to the next. How far Verdi's bereavement contributed to the failure it is difficult to say, since the creative mind works in unexpected ways, but pressure of time undoubtedly was a factor. *Un Giorno di Regno* was finished in a hurry; and that is possibly why there is not one piece of really imaginative scoring from beginning to end. Yet the occasional revival discreetly cut will always be of interest, for there is enough vitality there to keep the work afloat for two or three performances. It is still very much a 'prentice' work; yet it marks a further stage in Verdi's progress as a composer and above all a craftsman.*

---

* Several of its best ideas have found a suitable home in Charles Mackerras's brilliant ballet-score *The Lady and the Fool* (Sadler's Wells Theatre Ballet, 1954) compiled from the lesser-known works of Verdi.

There is some evidence that the overture is based on a 'Sinfonie' written earlier for the Busseto orchestra.

5 NABUCCO

NABUCODONOSOR

Opera in four parts
by
TEMISTOCLE SOLERA
(after the play, *Nabucodonosor*, by Anicet-Bourgeois and Francis Corñue)

First performed at the
Teatro alla Scala, Milan,
9 March 1842

NABUCODONOSOR (Nabucco), king of Babylon	PRIMO BARITONO	Giorgio Ronconi
ISMAELE, nephew of Sedecia, king of Jerusalem	TENORE COMPRIMARIO	Corrado Miraglia
ZACCARIA, High Priest of the Hebrews	PRIMO BASSO	Prosper Derivis
ABIGAILLE, slave, believed to be the eldest daughter of Nabucodonosor	PRIMA DONNA SOPRANO	Giuseppina Strepponi
FENENA, daughter of Nabucodonosor	SOPRANO COMPRIMARIO*	Giovannina Bellinzaghi
THE HIGH PRIEST OF BAAL	SECONDO BASSO	Gaetano Rossi
ABDALLO, an elderly officer in the service of the King of Babylon	SECONDO TENORE	Napoleone Marconi
ANNA, Zaccaria's sister	SECONDA DONNA	Teresa Ruggeri

Babylonian and Hebrew soldiers—Levites
Hebrew virgins—Babylonian women—magi
lords of the Kingdom of Babylon—populace

The action takes place in Jerusalem and Babylon

Epoch: 587 B.C.

* The range is mezzo-soprano.

The failure of *Un Giorno di Regno* was the bitterest moment of Verdi's career: a career which, up till then, had been far from easy. The Milan Conservatoire had rejected him. His time as Director of the Music School at Busseto was poisoned by faction. He had had to wait at least three years for the production of his first opera. Now it seemed that the progress so hardly achieved had been wiped out, and this just after he had lost the wife for whose sake he had remained at Busseto when he might have been furthering his career as an opera composer. Meanwhile time was passing. At twenty-seven Bellini, Rossini and Donizetti had all established themselves as masters or at least beyond the power of an occasional fiasco to do them harm. Verdi had been king for a day. Now it seemed that day was over. His feelings could indeed be similar to Beethoven's at the time of the Heiligenstadt testament.

The story of his bitterness, his determination never to write another note, and of the chance meeting months later with Merelli who tempted him back to opera with the libretto of *Nabucco* is too familiar to need quoting. The standard version comes from the account given to Giulio Ricordi in 1879; another less well known is to be found in *Volere è potere* ('Where there's a will . . .') by Michele Lessona, a fervent Darwinian rationalist and admirer of Samuel Smiles. Lessona had made Verdi's acquaintance at Tabbiano, a spa near Parma, and so had the story from the composer's own lips. Up to the meeting with Merelli the two accounts tally exactly, Lessona adding the detail that in those barren months Verdi's only solace lay in reading bad novels. But after that there is a notable discrepancy. According to Verdi himself:

> I . . . threw the manuscript on to the table almost violently. . . . The roll of paper opened out; and without my knowing quite how I found myself staring at the page in front of me and my eyes fell on this line:
>
> Va pensiero sull'ali dorati
>
> I ran over the lines that followed and I was profoundly struck by them especially as they were almost a paraphrase from the Bible which I have always enjoyed reading.
>
> I read one passage then two more; then still firm in my resolve never to compose again I forced myself to tie up the fascicle and went off to bed! . . . But . . . *Nabucco* kept running through my head . . . I couldn't get to sleep; I got up and read the libretto not once but two or three times so that by morning you could say that I knew the whole of Solera's libretto off by heart.[*]

Next day he returned the manuscript to Merelli with thanks. The impresario told him to set it to music, Verdi refused; and for answer Merelli thrust the libretto into the young man's pocket and pushed him unceremoniously out of the office.

[*] Pougin, pp. 43–6.

'I went back home with *Nabucco* in my pocket; one day one line, another the next, a note here, a phrase there . . . and bit by bit the opera was written. . . .' According to Lessona however:

> The young maestro . . . threw the libretto into a corner without looking at it any more, and for the next five months he carried on with his reading of bad novels; then one fine day towards the end of May he found himself with that blessed play in his hands: he read the last scene over again, the one with the death of Abigaille (which was later cut), seated himself almost mechanically at the piano—that piano which had been silent for so long—and set the scene to music. The ice was now broken . . . within three months of that time *Nabucco* was composed, finished, and in every respect the opera that it is today.*

Lessona's version has the advantage of having been written ten years nearer the event; what is more it received substantial confirmation from Verdi himself, who, when Lessona's book first appeared, wrote to his friend Opprandino Arrivabene: 'That is my story for you, as true as true can be' ('Eccoti la storia mia vera vera vera!').†

He protests too much. The more one investigates Verdi's early life, the more it becomes apparent that in later years he was concerned to weave a protective legend about himself to keep the inquisitive biographer at a distance: the legend of the peasant who made good, who owed nothing to anybody, and achieved fame and glory while remaining totally indifferent to the opinion of those about him. It was all part of his fierce independence of spirit, and it causes him not so much to falsify directly as to mislead. How serious was his intention to give up composition after the failure of *Un Giorno di Regno*? How did he propose to keep himself in Milan, since the proceeds of his first two operas would not last for ever? In fact he appears to have composed two substantial new numbers for the revival of *Oberto* at La Scala that same winter; and he supervised and rehearsed a new production at Genoa in January 1841, again adding fresh music. So much for the 'piano which had been silent for so long'.

It would seem then that youthful resilience triumphed earlier than he remembered or wanted us to believe. The removal of a new opera after its opening night was not such an unusual occurrence. It was about to happen to Nicolai, who took it far harder than Verdi. A serious young Prussian from Königsberg, he had set out in 1833 from his country's embassy in Rome to conquer Italy as his fellow-Germans Hasse and Handel had done over a hundred years earlier. Within seven years he had his wish. After *Il Templario* he was to be mentioned in the same breath as Pacini, Mercadante and Donizetti. It was to him that Merelli first offered the libretto of *Nabucco*; but Nicolai contemptuously turned it down in favour of *Il Proscritto*, which had been originally intended for Verdi. Produced in March 1841 *Il Proscritto* suffered the identical fate of *Un Giorno di Regno*. To make matters worse, the prima donna was Nicolai's fiancée, the young Italian soprano Erminia

---

* Lessona, pp. 297–8.
  † Letter to Opprandino Arrivabene, 7.3.1874. A. Alberti, *Verdi intimo (1869–81)* (Verona, 1931), p. 176.

Frezzolini. She was hissed off the stage; and Nicolai by one of those delusions common to composers was convinced that she sang badly merely to spite him. It was the end of his Italian career and of his engagement. Like Verdi he persuaded Merelli to release him from his contract and escaped over the Alps to Vienna from where he witnessed the triumph not only of the *Nabucco* that he had refused, but of *I Lombardi* and *Giovanna d'Arco* with Erminia Frezzolini as prima donna. True, he was able to salvage the wreck of *Il Proscritto* in the highly successful *Die Heimkehr des Verbannten*, but his love for Italy had turned to hatred. For Nicolai it was now 'treue deutsche Kunst' all the way. 'Look how low Italy has sunk in the last five years,' he wrote in 1844. 'The man who writes her operas today is Verdi. They are really horrible. . . . He scores like a fool—technically he is not even professional—and he must have the heart of a donkey and in my view he is a pitiful, despicable composer. . . .'* Verdi had many detractors in his life but none so virulent as Nicolai.

Although *Nabucco* was finished by early autumn of 1841 at the latest it was not produced until March of the following year, and then only after a furious remonstrance with Merelli.† Fortunately a ballet on the same subject had been given at La Scala four years previously;‡ so Merelli was spared the expense of new scenery and costumes.

'With this opera,' Verdi added, 'my artistic career may be said to have begun.'§ . . . And in the letter to Arrivabene—'after *Nabucco* I always had as many commissions as I wanted'.¶

Its triumph was total, despite formidable competition in a cartello whose novelties included Donizetti's *Maria Padilla* and Pacini's *Saffo* (already heard in Naples but new to Milan). The public went mad, insisting on an encore of the chorus *Va pensiero*. The critics followed suit, more cautiously, and with various reservations, but generally agreeing on the assurance and vitality of the new work. Once again the name of Bellini was mentioned. There was much praise too for that libretto which Nicolai had dismissed as nothing but 'Rage, invective, bloodshed and murder'. ‖

Its author, Temistocle Solera, had already collaborated with Verdi in *Oberto*. Born at Ferrara in 1817, he grew up to be an adventurer in the Casanova tradition. While still a child he ran away from his boarding school in Vienna and joined a travelling circus; he was eventually arrested by the Austrian police in Hungary, but not, it is said, before he had enjoyed the 'ripe favours' of the manager's wife (he was about thirteen at the time).** By 1842 he had made a name for himself as poet, and even composer, with two operas to his credit; and he stood in high regard with Merelli for whom he had written more than one successful libretto.

He remained Verdi's favourite librettist for the next three years; and their connection was only broken when with his work on *Attila* as yet uncompleted he followed in the wake of his singer-wife, Teresa Rosmina, to Spain. His subsequent fortunes as manager in Madrid, 'intimate adviser' to Queen Isabella of Spain,

---

* Otto Nicolai, *Tagebücher, nebst biographischen Ergänzungen von D. Schröder* (Leipzig, 1892), p. 130. The last sentence, though often quoted, does not appear in the original edition.
† For a discussion of the part supposedly played by Giuseppina Strepponi and Giorgio Ronconi in inducing Merelli to change his mind see Walker, pp. 165–8.
‡ See p. 95.   § Pougin, p. 46.   ¶ Alberti, p. 176.
‖ Nicolai, p. 121.   ** Abbiati, I, p. 311.

editor of a religious magazine in Milan, confidential courier between Napoleon III and the Khedive of Egypt, water-carrier in Leghorn and antique-dealer in Florence do not concern this book. But he was the right collaborator for Verdi at this stage of his career. He had a flair for bold, swaggering verse and the coup de théâtre—doubtless his circus training had come in useful for opera of this period. More than once he was accused of plagiarism. When *Nabucco* was first performed in Paris, Ricordi found to his annoyance that he was liable for a fee of 1,000 francs, due, it has been assumed, to the authors of the play on which the libretto was based. But if so this is extremely puzzling. For in making use of a contemporary French play Solera was merely following a long-established Italian tradition. Nor was there any secret about this particular case. The play in question, *Nabucodonosor*, by MM. Anicet-Bourgeois and Francis Cornue (Théâtre Ambigu-Comique, Paris, 1836) was perfectly well known in Italy in translation and also as a ballet. Possibly the answer is to be found in one of Muzio's letters to Barezzi. 'Vatel, the impresario of the Italian theatre in Paris, has had to pay out 1,000 francs to somebody who has done a libretto on *Nabucco* and says that Solera has taken his one from it.'[*]

The 'Biblical grandeur' that so attracted Verdi is certainly not a feature of the original play—which is remarkable none the less as a piece of ingenious plot-spinning in the manner of Scribe. If the characters do not develop psychologically they change their positions in a way that makes for theatrical excitement. Abigail, Nebuchadnezzar's adopted daughter, begins as a dare-devil heroine who rescues her sister Fenena from Israelite captivity by disguising herself as Josabeth of Marpha, a vengeful Hebrew war-widow. Ishmael, nephew of the King of Jerusalem, allows the two princesses to escape because of his love for Fenena; for this act he is solemnly anathematized by his uncle, the High Priest Zacharias, in words that will appear translated in the opera-chorus *Il maledetto*. When a little later Nebuchadnezzar invades Jerusalem at the head of his army, Abigail, still the heroine, saves Ishmael's life as he is about to be struck down by an Assyrian soldier. It is only when Nebuchadnezzar appoints Fenena as regent during his absence in the field that the elder princess turns sour.

During the Jewish captivity in Babylon Fenena is converted to the worship of Jehovah. Then an edict comes from Nebuchadnezzar in the field that the Jews are to be put to death. No sooner have Ishmael and Fenena planned to escape together than Abigail herself arrives with the news that Nebuchadnezzar has been killed in battle. Ishmael offers to arm the Jews for Fenena; the Priests of Baal rally to Abigail's side. Bloodshed is prevented by the sudden appearance of the king himself.

At this point the struggle becomes three-cornered. Nebuchadnezzar still intends to put the Jews to death; but he is also resolved to crush the conspiracy against Fenena of Abigail and the Priests of Baal. He orders a graven image of himself to be set up in the Hanging Gardens, then sends for Abigail, and shows her a document which proves her to be the daughter of a slave *by one of his own wives*. He had executed both the guilty parties, and brought up their child as a sop to his conscience. He now insists that Abigail publicly renounce all claim to the throne. The climax is reached in a scene in the Hanging Gardens. Before the assembled people the High Priest of Baal tells the king that he refuses to serve under Fenena.

[*] Letter to Barezzi, 13.10.1845. Garibaldi, p. 222.

By way of reply the king unveils the image of himself. Both the High Priest and Zacharias protest at this blasphemy; but Nebuchadnezzar gives orders for Zacharias to be dragged before the image and killed. At this Fenena cries, 'Je suis juive.' To which Nebuchadnezzar replies, 'Et je suis dieu.' Zacharias stretches out his hand. Crash of thunder; Nebuchadnezzar's crown falls from his head and he sinks to the ground in a faint. Abigail reaches into his garment and pulls out the parchment disproving her royal birth.

There follows Nebuchadnezzar's madness, his signing of an order that condemns Fenena to death with the other Hebrews, the prayer to Jehovah which restores his sanity. Fenena, already executed, is brought back to life by a divine miracle. Abigail is stabbed to death by her adoptive father.

Cortesi's ballet* inevitably simplifies, partly because the language of choreography is strictly limited, partly because in this medium, even more than in opera, it was the virtuoso star who counted. Therefore subsidiary characters are eliminated, including one Manasseh, the fanatical Jewish patriot who ends by aligning himself with Abigail. Zacharias then becomes the symbol both of the Jewish conscience and of their national pride. The incident of Josabeth is cut, Fenena remaining in Jewish hands until the arrival of Nebuchadnezzar. She is released by Ishmael only after Zacharias has offered to stab her. Abigail therefore remains a villainess from the start. From Act II on the ballet follows the play, except for the addition of a grand divertissement in the Hanging Gardens.†

From all this it should be clear that Solera's starting-point was the ballet rather than the play. But he made some notable departures from both. Abigail's unrequited love for Ishmael is entirely his invention. His too is the twist whereby Abigail remains in Babylon instead of accompanying Nebuchadnezzar on the field, and makes her own discovery of the 'fatal scritto' proving her to be illegitimate. (The adultery is passed over: she is tactfully referred to as 'the daughter of slaves'.) In this way he could condense what had been the second and third acts of the ballet into one of the opera. The ending too he made decorous, with Nebuchadnezzar arriving in time to save Fenena, and Abigail being pardoned and converted to the worship of Jehovah, after having taken poison. But Solera's greatest innovation lay in the emphasis he gave to the chorus. His *Nabucco* is a drama not of people but of *a* people. The great chorus *Va pensiero* has no equivalent either in ballet or play. Elsewhere too, what were mere cries in the play are expanded into whole verses in the opera. Clothed in Verdi's music they take on a significance far beyond anything in the original drama. Verdi himself carried the process still further. He insisted that a duet between Fenena and Ishmael be replaced by a 'prophecy' for Zacharias. In few operas of the time is the love interest quite so perfunctory.

But though *Nabucco* was an unusual type of opera for Italy, neither Verdi nor Solera would have been so foolhardy as to set his hand to a scheme for which there had been no precedent. In this case it is to be found in the French operas of Rossini, which had already made their way into Italy in translation—*Le Siège de Corinthe*, *Guillaume Tell*, and above all *Moïse*. Indeed close structural parallels between

* *Nabucodonosor*, a historical ballet in five parts composed and conducted by Antonio Cortesi, was given at La Scala, Milan, in the autumn of 1838. A copy of the printed scenario published by Truffi can be found in the Biblioteca Braidense in Milan.

† Or what *should* have been the Hanging Gardens; but a curious avvertimento in the printed scenario tells us that the action has been transferred from Babylon to Jerusalem.

Moïse and *Nabucco* can be traced, particularly in the first acts,* while the distribution of voices and characters match each other exactly, allowing for the difference of emphasis due to the diverging plots and to the particular quality of the singers for whom both operas were written. Nabucco has a larger role than Pharaoh, his counterpart in *Moïse*, not only because he is the subject of the opera but because the part was written for Giorgio Ronconi, the leading Italian baritone of the time (it was on his account that Donizetti made the hero of his *Maria Padilla* a baritone rather than a tenor). Verdi's insistence on enlarging the role of Zaccaria at the expense of the young lovers may have been partly dictated by the knowledge that its creator would be Prosper Derivis, who was that rara avis in Italy, a basso profondo of star quality. But in his astonishing realization of Abigaille the composer seems to have had no individual singer's qualities in mind—certainly not those of Giuseppina Strepponi.

Indeed, though it may have a structural model in *Moïse*, *Nabucco* is none the less overwhelmingly new in its force of language, its intense melodic vitality, and, above all, its sense of commitment. Rossini and his generation stand back from the action which they portray; Verdi is a participant. With *Nabucco* an oppressed nation had found its voice.

The opera is officially divided not into acts but into parts, each with its own title. This was a common practice of the time (Cammarano nearly always insisted on it); yet here it seems to have more point than usual. Each of the scenes is for the most part static, such action as occurs being telescoped into a moment's scuffle. *Nabucco*, more than any other of Verdi's operas, resembles a series of vast tableaux, rather than a drama relentlessly moving towards its dénouement. To the title of each part Solera has added a quotation from the Book of Jeremiah.†

The overture was written at the last moment on the suggestion, it is said, of Giovanni Barezzi, Verdi's brother-in-law.‡ Mostly it is a free pot-pourri of themes taken from the opera. The opening idea however is quite new and portrays more vividly and economically than any quotation could have done the central thesis of the opera, the steadfastness of the Hebrews in the face of persecution. Trumpets, trombones and cimbasso give out a chorale-like melody; there are two sudden outbursts from full orchestra, the second in a remote key, after which the chorale theme is resumed as though nothing had happened. The rest of the overture is rather perfunctory. First there is a section built on *Il maledetto* (Ex. 32), the chorus where the Hebrews curse Ismaele; then after a brief return to the chorale theme an

32

*See P. Petrobelli, 'Nabucco', in *Conferenze 1966–1967* (Associazione Amici della Scala, Milan, 1967). pp. 17–47.   †See p. 112 n. *.   ‡Abbiati, I, p. 407.

andantino movement consisting of a primitive variation in 9/8 rhythm on *Va pensiero*, the famous chorus from Act III, scored in what seems like a crude parody of Rossini's 'ranz des vaches' manner. There is something almost comic about the reprise, where trumpet joins oboe on the melody, while flute, piccolo and clarinet chatter like starlings in semiquaver triplets. Then *Il maledetto* returns leading this time to a triumphant movement in the major with three new melodies, whose respective sources are the chorus of Assyrian priests in Act II, the stretta of the finale of Act I, and the duet in Act III between Nabucco and Abigaille. The second of these is worked into a crescendo both in the overture and later in the opera. But it is not a Rossinian crescendo since it lacks that essential element—continuity of texture to accentuate the mounting excitement. It proceeds in a series of abrupt gestures.

33
Allegro

Finally there is a coda with *Il maledetto* in the major mode and in a still faster tempo.

There appears to be one miscalculation. When *Il maledetto* first occurs it seems to demand the same pace as in the body of the opera. When it recurs after the andantino *Va pensiero*, it must be taken more slowly if it is to lead convincingly into the following section in D major. Possibly Verdi intended to indicate this by marking the first statement *Allegro 4/4*, the second *Allegro* ₵ in doubled note values and therefore with more frequent accents. But the effect is curiously awkward. The theme hangs fire if you have heard it taken faster shortly before. Conductors sometimes try to find a way round this either by taking Ex. 32 more slowly on its first appearance, or else by playing it up to speed at its second and then slowing down for the D major section. In both cases the remedy is worse than the disease.

PART I

Jerusalem

Inside the temple of Solomon

The Assyrians under Nebuchadnezzar have defeated the Israelite army and are advancing on the city. The Israelites are cowering in terror. The Levites call upon the temple virgins to pray for deliverance, and their prayer is soon taken up fervently by the entire chorus, men and women. Zaccaria then comes forward and bids them take heart; they have a hostage in Fenena, the Assyrian king's daughter.

Let them remember how the Lord delivered them from Egypt. Ismaele hurries in to say that Nabucco's army is almost at the gates. Zaccaria hands over Fenena to Ismaele's care and predicts that God will scatter his enemies as the rising sun disperses the shades of night. In all this the parallel with *Moïse* is very close. But it is typical that in the opening chorus where Rossini gives us two contrasting ideas Verdi should give us three. Rossini's 'Dieu puissant du joug de l'impie' retains for all its poignancy a certain classical sedateness; Verdi's *Gli arredi festivi già cadono infranti* has the character of a storm chorus with rushing scales, shrieking wind and brass, and an abundance of diminished sevenths. (Its other parent would seem to be the opening scene of Bellini's *Il Pirata* [1827]—where, incidentally, there is also a hermit to soothe the people!) The Levites' melody (*I candidi veli, fanciulle, squarciate*) is for basses in unison accompanied by a chorale of brass instruments and bassoons; and the virgins' reply (*Gran Nume, che voli sull'ali dei venti*) is scored for harps and woodwind, with a touch of onomatopoeia at the word 'thunderclouds'. Altogether it is one of the longest choruses in Italian opera, and it is simply and massively constructed. There is no counterpoint, no masking of the symmetrical basis, apart from the occasional augmentation of the last line of a stanza. The result is at times reminiscent of choruses in the yet unwritten *Lohengrin* and *Tannhäuser*; and it brings home the fact that Italian music is no less prone than German to rhythmic squareness, especially in choruses where there is little opportunity for decoration or rubato. Yet Verdi has avoided monotony by various means: by contrasts of key (E minor–G major–E major), by contrasts of instrumentation, and by characteristic gestures such as the upward-sweeping figure on the flute which occurs during the prayer and the suave melody for tenors and violins which covers the interstices of the full choral phrases in the final section.

Zaccaria's recitative is much in the same vein as Moïse's; and it parades the basso profondo voice in all its glory. But the andante (*D'Egitto là sui lidi*) *is again* something new. It is in the rolling, majestic style first heard in the quartet from *Oberto*; and there is about it a quality of massive assertion that is almost Beethovenian. As in the earlier piece much of the power derives from the tension between the simple 4/4 of the melody and the implied 12/8 of the accompaniment. An earlier century would have approximated the one to the other. (See Ex. 34, facing page.)

This is the vein from which the famous *Va pensiero* is quarried. Characteristic too is the cabaletta (*Come notte a sol fulgente*) with sweeping string gestures reinforcing the conventional quasi-bolero accompaniment. Both aria and cabaletta contain a moment of surprise when the chorus in unison strikes in.* In the andante it covers the soloist's final note, almost giving the effect of an interruption. In the cabaletta it enters even earlier at the beginning of the fourth phrase. The people's confidence has revived; they have followed Zaccaria and are now ahead of him; but above all they have come right to the front of the drama with a directness that not even Rossini ever matched. After this the chorus disperse leaving Fenena alone with Ismaele. From their recitative we learn that a little while back

---

* Basevi (p. 7) claims to find a precedent in the aria 'Bel ardir' from Donizetti's *Marino Faliero*. But the parallel hardly holds, since Donizetti's use of choral repetition is so obviously less dramatic. Indeed since the conspirators are expressing different sentiments to those of the Doge they would really have been better suited with a different melody. The cabaletta which follows ('Fosca notte') is merely a variant of the 'giuramento' formula in which the followers repeat phrase by phrase the words and music of their leader.

34

Ismaele was sent as ambassador to Babylon for Judah. On arrival he was arrested and cast into prison, but he is evidently a young man of unusual attractions since *both* of the King's daughters fell in love with him. Fenena even effected his escape and so returned with him to Israel. But as they are pledging their love, Abigaille enters at the head of a column of Assyrians disguised as Israelites and announces the temple's capture. Then she catches sight of Fenena and Ismaele in each other's arms. She taunts them bitterly and curses them in one of those magnificent passages, part recitative part arioso, with which Verdi knew so well how to plant a serious character. She begins with a verse (*Prode guerrier*) which has the forced calm of sarcasm. 'Valiant warrior—with the weapons of love!' Only the hollow low B with which it begins and the shrill woodwind figure indicate the true state of her feelings. Then suddenly she loses control; the music plunges into a new key and

35

the formal phrases dissolve into irregular declamation, with wide melodic leaps.

36

Having finally vented her rage in a huge cadenza-like flourish she softens; and after a brief woodwind transition she begins the terzettino (*Io t'amava*) by reminding Ismaele of her love for him. He rejects her to the same melody; and it is left to Fenena now feeling the power of the true God to introduce new material in what is perhaps the most memorable phrase she has to sing throughout the evening (*Ah t'invoco, già ti sento, Dio verace d'Israello*). Verdi has thrown it into relief by choosing that moment to add harp to the orchestral texture.

37

As the trio winds sweetly towards its close, Abigaille's attempt to lead the music into E minor is frustrated by Ismaele's firm but gentle reassertion of the home key. In place of a stretta there is another chorus (*Lo vedeste?*) as the populace with Zaccaria come flying helter-skelter back into the temple with the Assyrians at their heels, little knowing that the temple has already been captured. This is a rudimentary essay in opera-house counterpoint which bears the same relation to the academic or church variety as do the two-dimensional façades of eighteenth-century landscape gardening to the structure they are intended to represent. It is the merest embryo of a double fugue, illustrating the physical 'flight' of the people.

But it becomes quite powerful towards the end, where the chromatic phrases start to overlap like people falling over one another in a panic rush. Verdi's Israelites are the descendants of Handel's even though in reduced circumstances.

Abigaille's voice rings out, 'Long live Nabucco'. From deep inside the temple Assyrian voices answer her; and there is a brief interchange between the three soloists almost comic in its extreme economy. ZACCARIA: 'How did the wicked ones enter?' ISMAELE: 'In lying clothes.' ABIGAILLE: 'Your pride is in vain; the king approaches.' Indeed his approach has already begun to the distant strains of the band.

38

It is not the last time that Verdi announces royalty in such a homely style. 'Like a Rossini overture,' says more than one writer; but notice a typically Verdian rhythmic quirk. The march begins, like so many of Verdi's, in the middle of the bar. But the last phrase is held back so as to begin on the first of the following bar, with the result that the main melody is resumed two beats before we are prepared for it. At La Scala the banda would have marched in accompanying Nabucco as he makes his entry on horseback, but this last formality (or, considering the nature of the place, *in*formality) is usually dispensed with. Zaccaria now seizes Fenena and, holding a dagger to her throat, forbids Nabucco to profane the house of God. Nabucco has no alternative but to dismount, which he does to a smouldering figure on the strings. It is a typically Verdian confrontation; baritone against bass.

We have now arrived at the moment of stasis, obligatory for all central finales since Rossini's day. Usually it was comprehended in the compass of one or at the most two melodic ideas. Verdi solves the problem in a personal way, one which he had adumbrated both in the quartet from *Oberto* and the finale to Act II of *Un Giorno di Regno*. He launches the movement with a solo stanza which begins in short, abrupt phrases, rises to a climax at the end of the fourth line, then takes on a rolling periodic motion, which in turn generates a succession of related ideas, each setting in relief the attitudes of the various parties—Nabucco menacing, Abigaille vengeful, Zaccaria steadfast, Fenena and Ismaele pleading, the Israelites on their knees. Here are some of the ideas as they pass on the conveyor-belt of a slow 3/4–9/8 rhythm:

39

(b) is underlined by Verdi's favourite clarinet arpeggios. As usual Abigaille's wrath is expressed not in the harmonies but by means of jagged rhythms and vertiginous leaps (c).

The calm is broken; Nabucco bursts out in open blasphemy. Where is this God in whom the Israelites believe? There was no sign of him on the field of battle; obviously He was afraid of *him*, Nabucco. Zaccaria again makes as if to stab Fenena, but before he can do so, Ismaele has grabbed the dagger from him, and Fenena rushes to her father. Now the tables are turned; and in the stretta which follows Nabucco (*con gioia feroce*) gives orders for the sacking of the temple, while the Israelites mutter curses on Ismaele (see Ex. 33).

PART II

The Ungodly One

Scene 1: the royal apartments in Babylon

The act begins with a powerful scene for the villainess herself. First an orchestral prelude, somewhat loosely prolonged perhaps but effective in its suggestion of someone frantically searching; then enter Abigaille triumphant, holding up a parchment scroll—the *fatal scritto* she has been looking for. Her recitative, stiffened by motifs from the prelude, is among the most vivid to be found in Italian opera since Monteverdi, as she vents all her bitterness and desire for revenge. Then the flute ushers in a change of mood with a phrase which Verdi will recall in a similar context in the middle of Rigoletto's soliloquy 'Pari siamo'; and Abigaille begins to reminisce about her love for Ismaele. For the andante (*Anch'io dischiuso un giorno*) Verdi employs a larger design than he has used hitherto, and one which will serve him frequently for the next few operas. In *Oberto* and *Un Giorno di Regno* the standard double quatrain is set without repetition either as $a^1 \, a^2 \, b \, a^2$—in Bellini's favourite manner—with no central cadence in the dominant, or else as $a^1 \, a^2 \, b \, a^3$ with a central cadence in the dominant or the mediant minor and the last phrase sometimes beautifully and imaginatively extended. In both cases there is a coda to follow. Here Verdi combines the two patterns. Having reached a^3 he introduces a restless woodwind figure à la Bellini and proceeds to add an extra wing to the structure using the words of the second quatrain and ending with a repetition of a^3. Then follows a coda with cadenza which is rounded off by the woodwind figure. Here the melody itself is very Donizettian, with its little clusters of fioritura at the end of each phrase; but from the reprise to the end is Verdian gold. Notice the typical soar and dip on the words 'incanto mi torna'; this is flowering in a different sense to fioritura.

40

The High Priest of Baal enters in great agitation with the news that Fenena has decided to set the Israelites free. Abigaille must assume the regency at once. To a melody already heard in the overture (*Noi già sparso abbiamo fama*) the priests or 'magi' tell Abigaille that they have spread a false rumour of Nabucco's death. Abigaille's reply (*Salgo già del trono aurato*) is Verdi's best cabaletta to date—forceful, wide-ranging in its vocal contours and a perfect expression of the singer's determination to 'mount the golden throne'. As in many of Donizetti's best cabalettas (cf. 'Scritto è in ciel il mio dolore' from *La Favorita*) the final cadence is led up to by foreshortened fragments of the opening idea.

Scene 2: a hall in the grand palace with other rooms adjoining

At this point Cortesi's ballet had a grand pas de deux for Fenena and Ismaele; and one wonders whether Verdi had in retrospect confused this scene with the prophecy of Act III, since Zaccaria's recitative and Preghiera (*Tu che sul labbro*) with its rich tapestry of six solo cellos has the quality of an inspiration that a composer will force into an opera whether the context has been prepared for it or not. It is Zaccaria's invocation to Jehovah to give strength to lighten the way of an unbeliever; to speak to the Assyrians through the mouth of His prophet; and 'Thy temples shall resound with Thy praise'. Not a note is wasted in this superb cantabile, too flexible to be called an aria. The texture varies from the sparse two-part counterpoint of the opening phrase to an almost Lisztian sonority at the words 'E di canti a te sacrati' (Ex. 41 overleaf).

It is the first instance in Verdi of that 'selective' scoring of which there will usually be at least one example in each of his early operas. The model here is presumably the first movement of Rossini's *Guillaume Tell* overture with its four cellos; but the result is wholly original.

Zaccaria now enters the royal apartment together with a Levite bearing the tablets of the law. As soon as he has left, Ismaele and the Levites enter from different doors (this complicated arrangement of exits and entrances is another feature

41

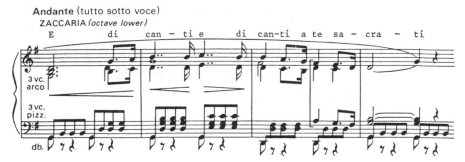

Andante (tutto sotto voce)
ZACCARIA (octave lower)

E di can - ti e di can-ti a te sa - cra - ti

which makes one suspect that the libretto may have been changed). On seeing Ismaele the Levites recoil from him in horror with that soft chorus of imprecation, reinforced by pattering side drum (*Il maledetto non ha fratelli*) (Ex. 32)—to which he replies, a more urgent Leicester pleading with Elisabetta (*Maria Stuarda*). The Levites are inexorable until Zaccaria's sister Anna enters to announce that Ismaele has saved a Jewess, meaning that he has been responsible for converting Fenena. This is confirmed by Zaccaria, now emerging with the princess-regent. But the general rejoicing is cut short by the sound of tumult. The orchestra sets up a movement of galloping triplets as the Assyrian Abdalla rushes in to warn Fenena that her father is dead and that the people have acclaimed Abigaille as their queen; and he urges the princess to fly at once. But Fenena declares that she will go out and quell the revolt. Before Ismaele and the Levites can dissuade her, the High Priest enters with a cry of 'Glory to Abigaille, Death to the Hebrews!'; and after him Abigaille who straight away orders Fenena to give up the crown.

Just as she is about to seize it by force, Nabucco enters, snatches it and puts it on his own head. (Once again Solera's compression of events has its ludicrous side, to which happily the music makes us oblivious.) Then the action freezes in a concertato ensemble, beginning as in the Act I finale with a verse from Nabucco, in which we can recognize again the design that had so fascinated Verdi in the *Oberto* quartet—six phrases with a harmonic 'strong point' at the end of the fourth, then a relaxation into more cursive rhythm (Ex. 42, facing page).

This is the pithiest realization of the design achieved yet. By compressing Solera's last two lines into four bars Verdi has been able to enhance his effect through rhythmic diminution.* The theme now evolves as a false canon, turning like a great wheel. It may not be very dignified, nor despite the sudden, instantly repressed tutti outburst (γ) does it express that sense of 'the wrath to come' which is the subject of the verse; but in strength and momentum it is unsurpassed. The unison choral entry towards the end is something that could only happen in this opera.

To a succession of trombone chords Nabucco tells the Assyrians that he renounces the god Baal who has turned them all into traitors. The god of the Israelites he has already defeated in battle. '*I* am your god,' he cries. 'Kneel before me.' Zaccaria refuses; whereupon Nabucco gives orders that he is to be put to death together with his people. Fenena protests that she too is now a Jewess and will share their

* Compare the sextet from *Maria Stuarda*, possibly the model for this movement; where Verdi shortens, Donizetti makes his effect with an extra bar.

42

martyrdom. Again Nabucco proclaims his own divinity. There is a peal of thunder, the crown is struck from his head and he falls to the ground.

From here on the finale takes a very different course from the usual one. There is no stretta but instead a formal yet half-coherent aria in F minor for the demented king, its first sentence culminating in a hysterical flurry of syncopated accents. The music turns into A flat major as he appeals to Fenena to help him. He has another outburst of terror, then a fit of weeping and again he falls down in a faint. The act ends with Abigaille magnificently asserting the glory of Baal in a single phrase. All this is real music drama, showing not only Verdi's readiness to break with tradition when in the grip of a strong dramatic idea, but also his ability to encompass a vast range of emotion within a small space. Few composers since Gluck have been willing to change from allegro to adagio in the course of a formal period as Verdi has done in Nabucco's solo.★ The depressive and manic phases of insanity are usually confined to andante and cabaletta respectively, where they are not distributed in recitative. How infinitely more impressive is Verdi's way in *Nabucco*!

PART III

The Prophecy

Scene 1: the Hanging Gardens

Abigaille is seated on a throne surrounded by courtiers who are singing her praises. Behind her is a statue of Baal. The chorus (*È l'Assiria una regina*) is introduced by the banda march from Act I (Ex. 38) and later interwoven with it. The High Priest of Baal hands Abigaille a warrant for the execution of the Hebrews and of

★ For a precedent see the curiously Gluckian finale to Act I of Bellini's *La Straniera*.

one whom 'he dare not call her sister'. Abigaille is just feigning a decent recluctance to sign, when Nabucco wanders in pathetically trying to gather his wits. She dismisses the courtiers and prepares to exact the full toll of humiliation from her adoptive father. Here occurs the first of Verdi's great duets, so often the redeeming feature of an otherwise undistinguished act. It is laid out in the traditional three sections. The first allegro (*Donna, chi sei?*) is a dialogue, Donizetti-style, to which the orchestra supplies continuity, with a sharply rhythmic melody. This resolves itself into one of the overture themes, a perfect expression of Abigaille's callous mockery!

43

Nabucco, she says, must sign the Israelites' death-warrant; or does he want them to believe that their God has triumphed after all? Nabucco obediently signs, then suddenly remembers Fenena, his own flesh and blood. 'She shall perish with the rest,' cries Abigaille. When Nabucco reminds her of her origins she produces what may be called her birth certificate and tears it up before his eyes. The second movement (*O di qual'onta aggravasi*) is one of powerful contrasts in dissimilar style. It takes the form of a double soliloquy. Nabucco pours out his grief in an F minor melody which owes something to Guillaume Tell's 'Sois immobile' not only in its dignified restraint but in its moving key change to D flat and back again. Abigaille, nourishing her dreams of glory, seems to inhabit a different world. Where he is submissive she is imperious; while his line is smooth-moving within a restricted compass hers is jagged and moves by leaps. His tonality is F minor, hers is D flat. Inevitably when the two voices sing together they do so in her key, not his, yet they retain their individual character till the end. Previous Italian composers just did not write this kind of duet movement.

There is a flourish of trumpets behind the scenes: 'the death signal of the Jews whom *you* condemned,' cries Abigaille. Nabucco calls for his guards; but the soldiers who now enter have come to take him into custody. In the last movement of the duet (*Deh perdona*) he makes a final appeal to Abigaille to pity his infirmity; but she replies mockingly to Ex. 43 as she watches him being led away. The repetition of this theme is the one doubtful feature of the duet, and a reviewer criticized Verdi for it at the time. Certainly it is something which he never did in his later duets where each movement marks a fresh stage in the relationship and there is no going back over previous material.

Scene 2: the banks of the Euphrates

'By the waters of Babylon . . . we sat down and wept.' It was Solera's idea to include this psalm, suitably paraphrased, thereby altering the emphasis of the entire drama as conceived by the original authors. Verdi's chorus, aptly described by Rossini as a grand *aria* sung by sopranos, contraltos, tenors and basses,* is the centre of the opera. No one should miss the primitive imagery in the orchestral introduction. 'Fly, thought, on golden wings,' runs the verse, 'and light upon the hills and banks where the sweet breezes of our native land blow soft and fragrant.' So after three bursts of brutal sound in bars 6 to 8, flute and clarinet detach themselves from the orchestral texture and flutter bird-like into a distant pianissimo. There is the usual pause before the cadence, then the melody begins softly in the somewhat uncommon key of F sharp major—doubtless a deliberate stroke on Verdi's part in order to heighten its colour.

44

When in 1847 the poet Giusti reproached Verdi for not having sounded in *Macbeth* that 'note of sorrow which finds an echo in our breasts'† he could well have been thinking of this chorus. It has all the elegiac quality of a Bellini; but the underlying sadness is that of a whole people, not of a single hero or heroine. The great swing, the sense of a thousand voices is something inherent in the melody even if it is sung as a solo or played on an instrument. It is blunter than anything that Bellini wrote just as a crowd is blunter, less subtle in its reactions than an individual. The burst into harmony at the words 'arpe d'or' is a stroke of genius, and a fine instance of Verdi's elementary use of dominant harmony to make a climax seem even more towering than its actual pitch. As always the reprise in verse four is copiously decorated by woodwind figures whose only purpose is to intensify the rhythm. In itself it is repetitious and naïve, but of course it is only designed to register on the fringe of one's consciousness. The melody is the thing.

For Zaccaria's prophecy of the fall of Babylon (*Del futuro nel buio*) Verdi had a model in Rossini's *Le Siège de Corinthe* had he cared to refer to it. But the chorus (*Va pensiero*) imposes its own conditions, which have nothing to do with Rossini. If Zaccaria's melody is somewhat four-square in its rhythm it contains two points of interest both prophetic of the later Verdi: the sequence of modulations by keys a major or minor apart in the second quatrain (B minor–D–B flat and F–A flat–B

---

* Gatti, 1st ed., p. 207. † Letter to Verdi, 14.3.1847. *Copialettere*, p. 449.

minor), and the harmonic bareness beneath the familiar lamenting figure on the oboe suggesting the desolation of the ruined city, where only the cry of the owl shall be heard.

45

Towards the end Verdi breaks with the sense of the words ('No stone shall be left to tell the stranger where Babylon once stood') to express the real feelings of Zaccaria and the Hebrews—their renewed hope and trust in the future—in a heartening phrase which the chorus take up in the manner of Act I; and the scene ends on a note almost of triumph.

PART IV

The Broken Idol

Scene 1: an apartment in the royal palace

The practice of beginning the last or next-to-last act with an extended prelude was not uncommon in Verdi's day, but it was a happy inspiration to have made it a montage of reminiscences passing through the disordered brain of Nabucco as he reclines in a chair sleeping fitfully. First there is a snatch from the Act II finale recalling his terror at being struck down; then a vision of the Hebrews pleading for mercy in Act I (Ex. 39b); the strains of the Assyrian march (Ex. 38); and finally with a sense of nightmare panic the king shakes himself into full consciousness. At the sound of cheering and a few chords from the off-stage banda he drags himself to the window to see a procession of soldiers conducting Fenena to execution to the sound of a funeral march.* He vainly tries to open the door. Then as the full horror of his predicament bursts on him he vents his feelings through a procedure which will become increasingly common in Verdi: a 6/4 chord outside the main key.

46

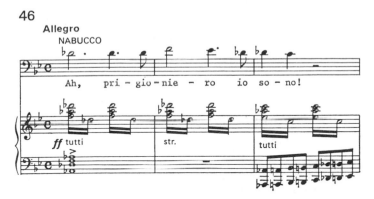

Only one hope is left. Falling on his knees Nabucco prays to the God of the Israelites. An introductory dialogue for cello and flute suggest both his supplication and the divine grace. Apart from its lack of any dominant half-close the aria itself (*Dio di Giuda*) follows the structural pattern of Abigaille's *Anch'io dischiuso un giorno* even down to the fidgeting woodwind figure after the first complete statement of the theme. It is not a great or particularly original melody, but there is a simple unaffected sincerity about it which somehow makes it seem the perfect expression of a broken and contrite heart—which, sure enough, God does not despise. When Abdalla and his still loyal guards enter they are delighted to find their master restored to sanity and strength. Fenena must be saved, he tells them; and there is no time to be lost beyond what will allow him and them a brief cabaletta (*Cadran, cadranno i perfidi*). But this is no ordinary example of the genre. The orchestral ritornello turns out to be the first statement of the melody; its second limb sung by the chorus alone is couched in the subdominant key; then Nabucco taking up the principal strain asserts the tonic. This key scheme is familiar to Donizetti (see 'Trema Bisanzio' in *Belisario*), but here Nabucco's defiance of what may be called the pull of subdominant gravity is a wonderful expression of his newfound strength. The scene ends with a reference to the by now almost too familiar banda march from Act I (Ex. 38).

Scene 2: the Hanging Gardens

As Fenena and the Israelites are led before the image of Baal the banda (brass instruments only) play an extended version of the funeral march heard in the previous scene. Once again it is too long for the average stage performance and is therefore usually shorn of its middle episode and reprise. This is not a matter for much regret; it is a lame piece of music and all too credibly ascribed to Verdi's Busseto years. Zaccaria tells Fenena to take heart, a martyr's crown awaits her; and for the third time the unhappy princess has a knife held at her throat. But she

---

* An unconfirmed tradition has it that this march dates from Verdi's years at Busseto. See S. Hughes, *Famous Verdi Operas* (London, 1968), p. 33.

is allowed one small 'preghiera' (*O dischius'è il firmamento*) where she describes a vision of the heavens parted and Jehovah seated on his throne. It is a simple touching piece with an unusually sensitive texture of pizzicato violins and cellos, viola arpeggios, and sustaining horns and bassoons. But it also lies rather low in the voice, which may explain the supplement at the end of the autograph where it is rewritten 'puntata per la Zecchini'.* As an instance of how far a composer was prepared to go in order to accommodate the singer, it is worth quoting the first quatrain side by side with the original.

With the timing of the rescue party in an old-fashioned Western, Nabucco and his men arrive on the scene. The king raises his sword and the image of Baal crumbles into fragments. To heavy chords on the brass he proclaims freedom for the Jews who may now return to their country. Abigaille, he says, has taken poison; and now a new temple is to be raised to Jehovah. Israelites and Assyrians join in one of those full unaccompanied choruses (*Immenso Jehova*) so dear to composers of that time, so often ruined today by poor blending from the soloists. It was at this point that many nineteenth-century performances ended. The fact seems incredible, since the death of Abigaille (*Su me morente esanime*) is one of the finest numbers of the opera, and it forms yet another of those selectively orchestrated passages which lighten a distinctly heavy score. The basic elements are cor anglais, solo cello and harp (another reminiscence of 'Sois immobile'), and single contrabass; but there are touches of clarinet and bassoon as well. As she drags herself dying on to the stage, Abigaille implores forgiveness. She gives her blessing to Ismaele and

* Giuseppina Zecchini was engaged as Fenena in the revival of *Nabucco* at La Scala, Milan, in August 1843.

Fenena. Her sin, she knows, is great but Jehovah is merciful. Now the melody turns into the major, decorated by those flute arpeggios which in Verdi will often signify death in a state of grace. There is a surge of choral and orchestral sound as the voice reaches its climax then dies away in broken phrases. The final word is spoken by Zaccaria as he gives thanks to Jehovah.

VENICE, *Teatro la Fenice, Carnival Season 1842–3*. It was in April 1843 during the Viennese revival of *Nabucco* at the Kärntnertor Theatre (also managed by Merelli) that Verdi first made the acquaintance of Count Nani Mocenigo, President of the Teatro la Fenice, who invited him to compose an opera for Venice the following year. At the time Verdi declined, having already promised his next-born to La Scala. For the year afterwards (1844), he might be free to accept, but as yet he would not commit himself. Such was the first step on the long and eventful road which was to lead to *Ernani*. In the meantime, however, he was willing to supply a new preghiera for the distinguished singer Almerinda Granchi, who was about to star as Fenena in the first Venice production of *Nabucco* on 26 December 1842. Early in that month the romanza was written and scored, and Verdi sent it to Mocenigo with a covering letter: 'Here is the romanza for Signora Granchi. If it is too high they can transpose it down a tone.' He adds: ' . . . Also I would beg you to point out to the conductor . . . that the tempi should not be too broad. They should all move, especially the canon in the finale of the second act'*—a piece of advice which deserves a wider circulation than it has so far received.

The romanza itself, preserved in the archives of the Fenice, is written to the same text as the original, but it is longer and more grandiose. As will happen in the case of many a future 'substitute' aria Verdi attempts here to compensate for the loss in dramatic continuity by a deliberate approximation to the basic 'colorito' of the opera as a whole. *Nabucco* takes its character from *Va pensiero* whose measured, swinging gait is reflected in many a solo and ensemble elsewhere in the work. It is particularly evident in this preghiera—far more so than in the piece that it replaces. Indeed the first melodic period (x) suggests a soprano variant of the as yet unwritten patriotic chorus 'O Signore dal tetto natio' (see Ex. 65, Chapter 6), first cousin to *Va pensiero*. The general design is one to which Verdi will return in another romanza written for Attila (see Chapter 11): an expansion of the Bellinian $a^1 a^2 b a^2$ whereby a new idea (y) is introduced at the return to the main key and a^2, varied into a^3, is held back so as to form a final culminating phrase before the codetta. The scoring is marked by plentiful use of harp, combined with flute, indicating that Fenena's thoughts are turned heavenward, but some crude melodic doubling at the climax reminds us how far the young Verdi's feet were earthbound in the matter of solo arias.

Nabucco is the supreme instance of the triumph of the whole over the parts. Many of the individual numbers are fine in themselves; many are undistinguished and one or two are trivial. Yet throughout the freshness of vision is unimpaired. Despite Verdi's debts here and there to his predecessors there is nothing here of the déjà vu. *Nabucco* is the expression of a new personality in Italian music, as opera-goers all

*Letter to Mocenigo, 19.12.1842; see D. Lawton and D. Rosen, 'Verdi's non-definitive revisions; the early operas' in *Atti del III° congresso verdiano* (Parma, 1974), pp. 189–237.

over Italy were quick to recognize. Before the end of the year it had seventy-five performances at La Scala alone. From there it spread throughout Italy. Donizetti conducted it in Vienna in 1843 and there were performances in Lisbon and Cagliari the same year. A performance in Corfu in 1844 is worth mentioning as being the first occasion when in the cartello the title was officially shortened from *Nabucodonosor* to *Nabucco*. However in most countries *Nabucco* followed in the wake of *Ernani*, the opera which gave Verdi the reputation of a European master. In London it was not given until 1846 at Her Majesty's, the title being changed to *Nino* since it was not considered proper to represent Biblical characters on stage. Nowadays *Nabucco* is more certain of a place in the repertoire than *Ernani*, if only because it is less dependent on the calibre of its performers. Opera choruses are better now than they were a hundred years ago; and the title role, though it marks the beginning of Verdi's love affair with the high baritone voice, is not beyond the reach of most members of the species. It is far less exacting than Macbeth or Rigoletto. The only problem is to find a soprano who can do justice to the part of Abigaille.

One anomaly remains. We have noticed that Michele Lessona referred to the death of Abigaille as having been cut. Verdi was familiar with Lessona's book since he recommended to Arrivabene the chapter dealing with himself as being 'really really true'. The implication is that he knew about this traditional cut and even sanctioned it. Many years later writing to Antonio Somma Verdi declared that he would never consider setting subjects such as *I Due Foscari* and *Nabucco* now—they were far too monotonous.* It would seem then that he personally had little retrospective affection for his first masterpiece.

*Letter to Somma, 22.4.1853. A. Pascolato, *Lettere di G. Verdi sul Re Lear e un Ballo in Maschera* (Città di Castello, 1902), pp. 45–8.

'Thus saith the Lord . . . Behold, I will give this city into the hand of the king of Babylon, and he shall burn it with fire.' *Jeremiah*, chap. 34[1]

'Behold the whirlwind of the Lord goeth forth with fury . . . it shall fall with pain on the head of the wicked.' *Jeremiah*, chap. 30[2]

'Therefore the wild beasts of the desert . . . shall dwell there, and the owls shall dwell therein.' *Jeremiah*, chap. 50[3]

'Baal is confounded; his images are broken in pieces.' *Jeremiah*, chap. 50[4]

[1] Page 97   [2] Page 102   [3] Page 105   [4] Page 108

6 I LOMBARDI ALLA PRIMA CROCIATA

I LOMBARDI ALLA PRIMA CROCIATA

Opera in four acts
by
TEMISTOCLE SOLERA
(after Tommaso Grossi's poem, *I Lombardi alla prima crociata*)

First performed at the
Teatro alla Scala, Milan,
11 February 1843

ARVINO ⎫ sons of Folco,	TENORE COMPRIMARIO		Giovanni Severi
PAGANO ⎭ lord of Rò	PRIMO BASSO		Prosper Derivis
VICLINDA, wife of Arvino	SECONDA DONNA SOPRANO		Teresa Ruggeri
GISELDA, their daughter	PRIMA DONNA SOPRANO		Erminia Frezzolini-Poggi
PIRRO, Pagano's squire	SECONDO BASSO (PROFONDO)		Gaetano Rossi
PRIOR OF THE CITY OF MILAN	SECONDO TENORE		Napoleone Marconi
ACCIANO, tyrant of Antioch	SECONDO BASSO		Luigi Vairo
ORONTE, his son	PRIMO TENORE		Carlo Guasco
SOFIA, wife of Acciano, and a secret convert to Christianity	SECONDO DONNA SOPRANO		Amalia Gandaglia

Nuns—city fathers—hired ruffians—armed retainers
in Folco's palace—Ambassadors from Persia, Media,
Damascus and Chaldea—knights and soldiers of the
crusade—pilgrims—Lombard women—women of the
harem—celestial virgins

The action takes place in Milan, in and around Antioch, and near Jerusalem

Epoch: 1096–7

Nabucco was, essentially, the beginning of Verdi's star career. It was also the end of Giuseppina Strepponi's. Although she was not yet thirty, ten years of unremitting stardom (interrupted by no less than three childbirths) had reduced that golden voice to a thread and now threatened the singer with consumption. She was in no position to do justice to the part of Abigaille. 'Even that Verdi of hers didn't want her in his opera . . .' wrote Donizetti after she had given a very feeble performance in his *Belisario*.[*] 'That Verdi of hers'—prophetic words! But in 1842 they probably mean no more than 'that Verdi she's always talking about'. In other words she was one of Verdi's earliest supporters, and after her partial recovery the few appearances that she made were nearly all in operas by him. As a star, even though on the wane, she was able to give him practical help. It was to her that he turned for advice as to how much he should charge for the new opera, *I Lombardi alla Prima Crociata*. She suggested the same amount that Bellini had asked for *Norma*; and Merelli, who had given Verdi a blank cheque, accepted without demur.

The subject was taken from an epic poem written in 1826 by Tommaso Grossi, a friend of Manzoni[†] and one of the most admired writers of his day. However when *I Lombardi* was first printed many critics accused him of presuming to rival Tasso. But apart from the subject matter, the length, and the use throughout of octave rhyme *I Lombardi* is no more an imitation of Tasso than the verse plays of Tennyson and Browning are imitations of Shakespeare. In fact it is very much a child of its age: a grand historical novel with a patriotic slant. Its central figure is a villain turned saint, like Jean Valjean, the hero of Hugo's *Les Misérables*. Its theme is the reconciliation of family strife through devotion to a common ideal. Throughout there is the same blend of fantasy and realism as in the work of Scott and Manzoni. The crusaders are the crusaders of history not of legend. There is no attempt to soften the atrocities committed by the Christian soldiery at Antioch, or to conceal the selfish quarrels of their leaders. The saintly Godfrey of Bouillon, whom Tasso set at the head of the First Crusade, is rightly placed below Raymond, Tancred and the crafty Boemund. Even Peter the Hermit is shown in a moment of cowardice. As these historical characters serve merely as a backcloth to the family whose fortunes are the subject of the epic, they are excluded from Solera's libretto. One of them however, by a device well known to romantic novelists, has been provided with an imaginary career linking him with the central figure of the plot. Firuz, the Syrian captain who betrayed Antioch to the crusaders, is made out to be a renegade Italian, Pirro, once the henchman of the hero-villain. Pirro therefore comes into the opera.

In 1843 any subject where Italians were shown united against a common enemy

[*] Letter to Vaselli, 4.3.1842. G. Zavadini, *Donizetti—Vita, Musica, Epistolario* (Bergamo, 1948), p. 379.
[†] Manzoni slyly quotes from *I Lombardi* in Chapter 9 of *I Promessi Sposi* by way of a 'puff preliminary' for Grossi's as yet unpublished poem.

was dangerous, especially in Austrian Milan. Yet strangely enough it was not the police but the church that took exception to *I Lombardi*. Rumours had reached the Archbishop of Milan of an ecclesiastical procession with incense and banners, a baptism performed on stage, and parts of the liturgy butchered to make an operatic aria. The police were asked to investigate. As Verdi let it be known that he would not change a note of his score, Merelli and Solera had to make their excuses and disclaimers as best they could. Fortunately the police chief, Torresani, was himself a music lover and merely insisted on one or two trifling alterations for form's sake. The heroine was required to begin her prayer in Act I with the words 'Salve Maria' instead of 'Ave Maria' (and the added *s* and the inserted *l* can be seen in the manuscript in Verdi's own handwriting).

The first night was a wild success. The newspapers spoke of long queues to the box-office, of stampedes in the theatre, of frenzied applause at the end of each number. The critics however kept their heads. The correspondent of *France Musicale* declared that the opera was not worth a sou. The *Figaro* merely pointed out that the vocal writing was too syllabic and that the accompaniment was often too heavy for the tunes. The *Gazzetta Musicale di Milano* had a few observations to the effect that Verdi was already on the right path, that he knew how to combine 'pristine simplicity of manners with modern refinements of taste[!]'.* The writer refused to compare it with *Nabucco*, both operas being equally good in their different ways— 'We would just say that if *Nabucodonosor* created this young man's reputation *I Lombardi* has served to confirm it.' This is over-generous. *I Lombardi* has its moments of grandeur, some superb flights of lyrical fantasy and a number of effective theatrical ideas. It is more adventurous than *Nabucco*, and more wide-ranging in its choice of material. Yet it lacks the central vision which gives purpose and unity of structure to the earlier work. The kernel of *Nabucco* is, in a sense, the chorus 'Va pensiero'. There is a similar chorus in *I Lombardi*, *O Signore dal tetto natio*; but it is no more than a detail in a vast, sprawling canvas. *Nabucco* is all of a piece, a unity, however crude; *I Lombardi* is an agglomeration of heterogeneous ideas, some remarkable, some unbelievably banal.

In carving out a libretto from Grossi's novel-epic Solera faced an impossible task, and nowhere more than in his first act. Grossi avails himself of the novelist's privilege of *not* beginning at the beginning. The events which occur first in time are narrated to us by a character who could not have witnessed them. The heroine Giselda, a captive in Antioch, is visited by the Sultan's son Saladin, who is in love with her and wants to know how she came to be there. She replies with the story of her family. Her mother, Viclinda, was wooed by two brothers, Arvino and Pagano. She herself chose Arvino; whereupon Pagano determined to carry her off by force. One day he ambushed two of his brother's men, killing one of them on the spot and the other at an altar where he had taken refuge. For this deed of sacrilege he was sent into exile. Meanwhile Viclinda married Arvino, and had two children by him. A third, Giselda herself, was already on the way when Pagano sent a message to his father, Folco, begging to be allowed to return home, having expiated his sin wandering amongst the holy places. Folco consented; but the sight of Viclinda proved too much for Pagano. His murderous hatred of his brother revived, and with the help of his henchman, Pirro, he set fire to the family

*Abbiati, I, pp. 447–8.

home, intending to kill Arvino during the panic and carry off Viclinda. At first he seemed to be successful, and Viclinda was carried off on horseback to Pagano's castle. It was then she vowed that if she escaped unharmed she would send her as yet unborn child on a pilgrimage to Jerusalem as soon as he or she should come of age. Meanwhile Pagano discovered that the man whom he had killed as he came out of the house was not Arvino but his father Folco. Aghast, he fled from Lombardy and was never heard of again.

All this is told in the fourth canto of the poem. But we have already been introduced to a saintly old hermit, living in a cave near Antioch and famed throughout the countryside for his powers of healing. Could it possibly be? . . . But we can only guess; and indeed are kept guessing for most of the poem. Opera in Italy does not allow any such ambiguity. There is no limit to the extent to which operatic characters can impose on one another (see *Così fan tutte*) but they cannot hope to cheat an audience in the same way. Wicked Uncle Pagano and Pagano the Hermit must be sung by the same singer, whose face and figure may be disguised but whose voice cannot. So Solera must needs straighten out the time sequence, expanding into a whole act an event which Grossi dispatches in a dozen stanzas and filling them out with every stock operatic device he can think of, however irrelevant. Nor do his difficulties end there. The obvious heroine for Act I of the opera would be Viclinda, the object of the brothers' quarrel. But this would be an untidy arrangement since she would have to give place to Giselda for the rest of the opera. Therefore Giselda must take the lead in a scene which does not really concern her. For the same reason the accidental parricide must be postponed eighteen years so that she can be there at all. Eighteen years therefore is the period of Pagano's false penitence; his conversion cannot last more than two. That he should still think of carrying off Viclinda after she has become the mother of a grown-up daughter is slightly absurd. However the audience who had read Grossi's poem would doubtless accept the shift in time as a legitimate operatic device. It had at least this advantage: it enabled Solera to show at the same time the crowds assembling for the first crusade, with a copious display of patriotic sentiment; and no one, Verdi least of all, would be worried by the fact that the event plunges Pagano into still further inconsistencies of behaviour. A more serious disadvantage for Verdi was the fact that as Pagano he was to have Prosper Derivis, the creator of Zaccaria; so that he had to cast as a basso profondo a part whose ambivalence would be far more effectively conveyed by the baritone voice.

The opera makes an uncertain start. For the first time Verdi dispenses with the overture in favour of a short prelude. Normally this is an effective procedure. But here his difficulty is that the essence of the work is far too diffused to be summed up in so short a space. Later on, faced with a similarly ramshackle dramatic framework in *La Forza del Destino*, he hit on the solution of a pot-pourri overture which is a kaleidoscope of moods, rhythms and themes and yet has the quality of a musical epigram. But in the short adagio that begins *I Lombardi* there is room only for solemnity, fervour, the dark menace of Pagano (trombone and woodwind), his repentance and hope of salvation (strings and flute). All these are conveyed in a succession of brief, mostly asymmetrical phrases thrown out with the apparent inconsequence that marks the start of a Liszt rhapsody.

PART I

The Vendetta

Scene 1: the Piazza di Sant' Ambrogio

The year is 1095 and the inhabitants of Milan are still the descendants of the Long-beards who swept into Italy from the north in the twilight of the Roman Empire. Even now they are more Teuton than Latin as their names show. The church doors are open and a crowd of men are coming out, to the cheerful plebeian strains of the banda sounding from inside the Basilica. The device of raising the curtain to banda music was not new (cf. Mercadante's *Il Giuramento*): here it is in a sense appropriate considering the huge role of the banda in this opera. The men have been mightily impressed with the scene they have just witnessed. There has been a public reconciliation between Arvino and Pagano, lately returned from exile. But for all his tears and protestations there was a look in Pagano's eye which boded ill. Can the wolf change so quickly into a lamb?* The banda gives way to orchestral strings as the female half of the chorus enter wondering why, at the midnight hour, such happy sounds should be heard from inside the Basilica. They go on to ask what had been the crime for which Pagano had been exiled. The men reply with a musical narrative, in which Solera here parts company with Grossi by making Pagano attack Arvino on the day of his wedding to Viclinda in this very same Basilica. The verses are 'syllabated' over a brisk march-like tune, picked out with first violins, oboe, clarinet, bassoon, trumpet and trombone. It is all very ugly, as well as being incomprehensible without the aid of a printed libretto.

The banda music is resumed as the Folco family issue from the cathedral in strength, giving the men of the chorus another opportunity to observe the ferocious gleam in Pagano's eye. Then Pagano's voice is heard for the first time begging his brother once more to forgive him. The accompaniment of three trombones and cimbasso is one which will frequently characterize Pagano throughout this act. Here it reveals him straight away as a creature of darkness, for all his words of penitence. Arvino raises him up, bestows on him a kiss of reconciliation. A chorus of City Fathers (Priori della Città) praise his magnanimity; and the stage is set for the first big ensemble which is also the opera's first real gem, if a rough-hewn one (*T'assale un tremito, padre che fia*). Giselda observes that her father is looking pale just at a time when he ought to be happy. Arvino replies that he is troubled by a nameless fear. Pagano metaphorically grinds his teeth and whispers villainies to Pirro; the crowd comment piously on the fraternal kiss, hoping that it is not the kiss of Judas. From all this tumult of separate thoughts, each portrayed in some characteristic phrase, Verdi distils a piece as dramatically vivid as it is original. (We shall find a similar movement in the Act I finale of *Luisa Miller*.) Giselda's worried concern for her father is conveyed not only in the string tremolo and woodwind stabs but in the three-bar pattern of her opening statement. The irregularity straightens itself out as she hails the reconciliation in a phrase which

---

* I.e., in the twinkling of eighteen years. . . .

becomes the main theme of the piece. It will appear ten years later, subtly elaborated, in the *finale ultimo* of *Il Trovatore*.

49

Arvino tries to stifle his own suspicions with a soaring melody which reverts to the three-bar design:

50

A phrase of Pagano's cuts across him—jagged, bumping, and scored for bassoons, trombones, cimbasso:

51

The chorus melody is of a different type again. The prevailing tone here is string, cellos singing together with first violins, horns filling in the harmonies with second violins and violas, and the clarinet supplying an accompaniment of placidly gurgling sextuplets.

52

Just how subtle a craftsman the young Verdi could be is amply evident in this piece, whose only weakness is a too facile return to the home key for the reprise of its main idea.

The leading City Father announces that the citizens of Milan, fired by the preaching of Peter the Hermit, have voted to send a contingent to the crusade with Arvino as its leader. Arvino accepts the charge laid upon him and all present join in a massive homophonic chorus (*All'empio che infrange*) full of sudden pauses, abrupt key-changes, steep contrasts of dynamic—in a word a piece of frank effect-mongering without any pretension to musical depth. This in turn resolves itself into one of the many march movements scattered throughout the score. It is led by Arvino and Pagano, determined to sink their differences in a common cause. The music, with its tramping anapaests, perpetual side-drum, banda weighing in behind the choruses, is vulgar but attractive. It is one of the few marches that finds its way into the revised version of 1847.

53

As night falls on the empty square a chorus of nuns are heard singing in the depth of the Basilica. The chorus (*A te nell'ora infausta*) has a sugariness more suited to the sirens of the Venusberg than to an enclosed order of nuns. Two details arrest the attention fleetingly. The chorus, mainly a cappella, is accompanied here and there not, as one would have expected, by an organ or harmonium behind the scenes but by a group of clarinets, bassoons and horns which 'must imitate the sound of an organ'. Then too the penultimate bar of this otherwise quite regular melody in 4/4 rhythm is expanded into one of 3/2. Italian composers of the time did not usually measure out their pauses so exactly.*

As the last note fades away Pagano steals in with Pirro. He comments sardonically on the nuns, whose prayers heaven will for once not hear. Yet, he tells Pirro, he was not naturally disposed to crime—it was thwarted love which led him astray; and once more the voices of the nuns float in praying for peace on earth. Then Pagano apostrophizes Viclinda in the andante of his first aria (*Sciagurata, hai tu creduto*). Here, as in most of the arias in *I Lombardi*, Verdi reverts to the simpler design (a^1 a^2 b a^2 *coda*) to be found throughout his first two operas. But the movement itself is far from simple. The vocal line leaps and plunges; the accompaniment, closely patterned, bristles with acciaccature and restless figuration, including a suggestion by scurrying cellos of the 'Italian volcano nourished by the rains' ('Qual dall'acque l'alimento tragge l'italo vulcano'), and a semitonal clash between horn and strings as he repeats the words 'gli impeti d'amor'. Pirro now summons from hiding the men who are to set fire to Arvino's house. When Pagano warns of the dangers that await them they reply defiantly with a unison melody (*Niun periglio il nostro seno*) of almost comic explosiveness. Unexpected bursts of sound against a sotto voce background are a favourite device of Verdi's for conveying mass villainy. Here the effect is crude but invigorating; like the overture to *Un Giorno di Regno* it shows the composer's early skill in shuffling with irregular accents.

Once more the nuns' dying fall is repeated, and Pagano breaks out into a cabaletta of savage glee (*O speranza di vendetta*) in the traditional quasi-polonaise rhythm, with Pirro and the chorus joining in not only at the ritornelli but also at the penultimate line of the melody, so giving weight to the reaffirmation of the home key as in Zaccaria's Act I cabaletta in *Nabucco*. Like the andante it is somewhat overstrenuous. Pagano's villainy is now fully established but it has all been hard work.

---

* This is one of the areas in which the difference between Italian and German composers is most evident, the first taking performers' rubato for granted, the second integrating their variations of pace much more precisely into the rhythmic structure. Rather than mark a passage *ritardando* Wagner prefers to lengthen his note values. Brahms's cross-rhythms and hemiolas are often no more than ritardandi written out.

Scene 2: a gallery in the Palazzo Folco, leading from Arvino's rooms
on the left to other apartments on the right. The scene is lit by a torch.

Viclinda enters with Giselda, still oppressed by an anxiety she cannot explain. She proposes a solemn vow to God that if they live through this night they will make the pilgrimage bare-footed to Jerusalem. Arvino enters briefly to tell his wife to go to their room where Folco will stay with her. He himself has heard strange stirrings in the palace and is going to investigate. The women then kneel and Giselda begins her famous prayer, *Salve Maria*. With the approach of the crisis Verdi's genius awakes once more to life. Viclinda's recitative is preceded and accompanied by music of quiet intensity; her unease is reflected in a tremolo which darts from one department of the strings to another like a morbid shiver and by a succession of obsessively repeated violin quavers.

For Giselda's prayer Verdi specifies eight violins, two violas, one bass, solo flute and clarinet—chamber-music texture. It is 'empirical' scoring with no hint of the textbook about it. But the touch never falters. Even less orthodox is the melody itself—simple, basically regular yet containing only four bars of repetition and cast in a tonality which does not declare itself unambiguously until nearly half-way through, at the words 'Vergine santa'. The final cadence is an early instance of what was to become a favourite device of Verdi's—a bold side-slipping of unrelated chords (see Ex. 54, overleaf).

In contemplating this astonishing piece of music, one of the strangest entrance arias to be given to any leading soprano, we should remember the special qualities of Giselda's creator, Erminia Frezzolini. A young singer gifted with a pure fresh voice and perfect legato,* she belonged to the generation of sopranos which in time was to lead Verdi and his contemporaries away from the more florid style of vocal writing. It was for her that Verdi composed what is perhaps the finest of his early soprano roles—Giovanna d'Arco.

The two women go off each to her own room. An ominous orchestral motif of horns over busy strings ushers in Pagano and Pirro. Pagano, told that Arvino has been seen retiring for the night, creeps into his brother's room from which he emerges a moment later dragging Viclinda. Meanwhile flames and smoke are seen reflected in the gallery windows. All the familiar elements of Verdian excitement are here – pounding strings, crescendo trumpets cutting through the texture with a sharp, rapping figure, melodies in double dotted rhythm. Pagano, every inch the villain of melodrama, cries to the protesting Viclinda, 'Call your loudest— there is no one to heed you . . .' but he is wrong, for Arvino steps forward. Then whose is the blood on Pagano's dagger? His father's! Horror! ! ! And so in the shortest possible time Pagano and the audience are made aware of the new atrocity. The action freezes for the adagio concertato of the finale. Both the adagio and the stretta have a rugged grandeur typical of the best in *I Lombardi*; yet both are vitiated by the rule which forbade Italian composers *abuso dei minori*—an abuse of the minor key. Nothing could be more striking than Pagano's hushed exclamation—*Farò col nome solo il ciel inorridir*—an abyss between two peaks of sound (Ex. 55).

* Muzio contrasts her style of execution with the more old-fashioned manner of Jenny Lind. Letter to Barezzi, 16.6.1847. Garibaldi, p. 329.

54

Less than twenty bars later the same idea returns chanted in the major key by violins and upper wind in sixths and thirds over a bass of rolling bassoon sextuplets (Ex. 56). The movement swings comfortably on to its final cadence with the dramatic tension gone out of it, so that one is quite unprepared for Arvino's outburst, demanding that Pagano should pay for their father's death with his own. But before he can run him through, Giselda steps between them and begs her father not to aggravate one crime with another. Pagano tries to kill himself but his followers hold him back. The rest turn on him and pronounce his banishment in a thrilling start to the stretta, in which there are echoes of Nicolai's overture *Il Templario* (Verdi, like Mozart, liked to profit from his contemporaries). All goes well until the inevitable switch into the major key, with its consequent lowering of emotional temperature. Only the fierce driving rhythm remains to bring down the curtain in a storm of applause.

PART II

The Man of the Cave

Scene 1: a hall in the palace of Acciano in Antioch. Acciano seated on a throne; before him ambassadors, soldiers and people.

Several months have passed since the previous act. The Crusaders have reached Asia Minor and are now laying siege to Antioch. The other Arab kingdoms have rallied to the side of Antioch's Sultan Acciano, and in the opening scene of Act II their ambassadors join with the army and people of the beleaguered city in a hymn of defiance (*È dunque vero*) led by Acciano himself. He paints a lurid picture of the invaders' brutality—rape, pillage, everywhere a pile of corpses left in their wake. The people and ambassadors swear to forget their national differences and unite against the Europeans (may Allah smite them!).

The year before *I Lombardi*, Glinka had shown his fellow-Russians how to portray the mysterious East. Slowly his example was to filter through into the rest of Europe; and by the time of *Aida* the East was comfortably within Verdi's reach—but not yet. There is little to distinguish the idiom of Asians from that of the Crusaders apart from choppy rhythms, tonic pedals and an emphasis on the Neapolitan sixth—devices which, typically, also recur in *Aida* as 'orientalisms', though of course enhanced by a far more subtle and sophisticated technique. But in general the Orientals of *I Lombardi* are merely the conventional operatic gypsies, while the incursion of the banda at the word 'Giuriam' with a motif recalling the men's narrative in Act I brings them firmly back to the piazza of Busseto.

Acciano and the assembled company file out leaving the hall empty except for the Sultan's wife and son. Sofia, the Sultana, is a secret Christian who in her heart favours the Crusaders' cause. Like Viclinda's hers is a bit-part without even Viclinda's privilege of sustaining a solo line in the ensemble. The scene belongs to her son, Saladino in Grossi's poem, but here called Oronte, doubtless to avoid confusion with his more famous namesake, Richard Cœur-de-Lion's enemy; though it is odd of Solera to have called him by the name of the river on which Antioch stands. Oronte is the opera's tenor lead, Arvino being a comprimario of the order of Ismaele in *Nabucco*, though curiously enough his is the more forceful role and requires a heavier voice. Oronte, although written for Guasco, the future creator of Ernani, is all tenderness and poetry. Verdi establishes his character at once with a graceful, rather languishing idea given out by flute and clarinet in unison as a prelude to his recitative. 'Mother, what is she doing?' 'She sighs and weeps and calls upon the names of her dear ones . . . and yet the poor girl loves you.' 'There is no happier mortal on the earth than I.' The girl is of course Giselda, who has fallen into Syrian hands at the first engagement. Oronte pours out his feelings for her in an andante (*La mia letizia infondere*), with a distinctive second-beat cadence.

57

This is the first of Verdi's aria-movements to be evolved from repetitions of a single rhythmic pattern—a procedure common enough in Donizetti. Here the pattern is subtly varied so as to avoid monotony; yet its persistence enables Verdi to bypass the usual point of reprise at the penultimate verse line by giving us not the opening idea but a rhythmic derivative of it over dominant seventh harmony. Despite the steepness of the progression, the suggestion of consecutive octaves,★ the false relation—perhaps because of all these things—the effect is wonderfully spontaneous (Ex. 58).

There is the usual pleasant surprise in the coda: a downward-spiralling figure, chromatically harmonized. Sofia then warns him that he can only hope to win Giselda if he embraces her religion. Oronte declares himself a convert there and then, adding rather naïvely that the God in whom such an angel of goodness

★ The freedom to use consecutive octaves between voice and bass combined with a sudden modulation had already been won for Italian composers by Rossini.

58

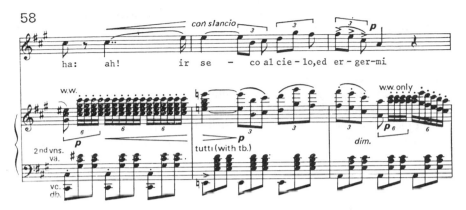

believes must be the true one. The cabaletta (*Come poteva un angelo*) is in simplest Bellinian vein, not unlike the cabaletta to be found in *La Straniera*, with a gentle pace, see-sawing strings and no decoration more elaborate than a gruppetto. If it lacks the individuality of the andante, it is a sensitive piece of writing none the less, using for once the plangent oboe by way of introduction, and in general showing a subtler use of woodwind colour than usual. The only real defect is a trite, Rossinian central crescendo through which Sofia has to make herself heard as she tells Oronte that Giselda will be his angel of redemption.*

Scene 2: the mouth of a cave in the mountains

The scene opens very impressively with what is the first instance of Verdi's 'cavern music': sombre, heavily chromatic and scored with rare economy for strings alone. Here is the desolate landscape which Grossi describes at length at the start of his novel—for that is where the opera has now arrived. Verdi acknowledges the fact with his one and only quotation from the prelude: the 'redemption' figure of flute arabesques above tremolo strings, as Pagano talks about heavenly grace. The score describes him throughout this scene as 'L'eremita' (the Hermit); but Verdi was perhaps deliberately stressing his identity with a short sequence of solemn chords for trombones and cimbasso accompanying the words 'È giusto Iddio soltanto' (God alone is just). These lead into what is in form, if not in content, a romanza (*Ma quando un suon terribile*) in the standard minor-major form. The accompaniment here is no less busy than in Pagano's aria from Act I; but what before had seemed exaggerated and mildly comic here takes on a certain rugged grandeur. The opening phrase culminates in a burst of sound to the words 'Dio lo vuole' (God wills it). These words occur like a refrain in Grossi's poem and would be recognized at once by a contemporary audience, even if by unleashing the full orchestra Verdi has made it quite impossible to hear the all-important verb. The major key brings no sense of anticlimax; and not all the woodwind chattering can spoil the simple dignity of the melodic line. The prospect of divine grace and redemption is beautifully summed up in the modulating coda.

No sooner has Pagano finished his aria than he receives a visit from a very peni-tent Pirro, who quite fails to recognize his former master. He explains that he was a Lombardian who assisted in a crime of patricide, then like a coward fled his

* For a discussion of the second setting of this cabaletta, see below, p. 134.

native land and changed his faith. Now that the crusading army has arrived in Syria he wishes to atone for his sins by betraying to them the defence of Antioch which has been entrusted to him. The compression of Grossi's time-span renders this whole episode rather ridiculous; and Verdi dispatches it in a brief march-like stanza (*Io son Pirro, e fui Lombardo*) heavily coloured by lower brass. Barely has Pagano had time to give him heaven's blessing than the sound of a banda is heard in the distance with a melody which is to become important later on. At first it is spelt out piecemeal, the final notes of each half-phrase echoed by the wind instruments in the orchestra pianissimo—a device familiar from the start of Bellini's *La Sonnambula*. Here the effect is curiously flippant:

59

While Pagano falls on his knees in an ecstasy of pious gratitude, the stage begins to fill with crusaders, military bandsmen and pilgrims of both sexes. Pagano hurries Pirro into the cave, and a little later emerges from it himself holding a sword and clad in a visor. Arvino then steps forward and engages Pagano in a duet which, musically, strikes a more genuinely heroic note than we have yet heard from the Crusaders. The style is Rossini at his most classical, but a typical Verdian detail is the sharply rhythmic figure in the violins which embellishes the accompaniment at the repetition of the main tune.

60

During all this Arvino has told Pagano about the capture of his daughter; and Pagano replies that before sunrise next day he and his men will pitch their camp in the citadel of Antioch, and that his daughter will be restored to him.

The music from here to the end of the scene belongs, alas, to the category of 'il Verdi brutto'. First there is a savage outburst in F minor against 'Allah the fool' (*Stolto Allah*); then follows the march previously heard in the orchestra, now sung by Pagano and Arvino in unison and echoed by the full chorus reinforced by banda, bass drum, side drum, cymbals. It is the same formula as in the first scene of Act I applied to an even less distinguished melody.

Scene 3: within the harem in Antioch

We return to Giselda in captivity, surrounded by a chorus of taunting fellow slaves (*La bella straniera*). It is couched in an idiom of jarring triviality that will later depict the Witches in *Macbeth*—fast 6/8 in E minor, short phrases spiked with grace notes and orchestrated as shrilly as possible. The main difference between Turkey and Scotland is a battery of percussion including that *sine qua non* of the so-called *alla turca* style, the triangle. The mockery is emphasized by copious woodwind trills (in Verdi there is nothing so savagely derisive as a trilling clarinet). For the rest the chorus is clearly a dance number, and also rather long for its musical substance, though the continual repetitions of 'La bella straniera' are doubtless intended to exacerbate. Verdi will give us a similar though much more polished chorus at the start of Act II of *Il Corsaro*.

What follows is an interesting example of how the standard conventions could be bent to serve the purpose of a particular plot. The act is closed not by an ensemble nor a duet with chorus but by a rondò-finale for the heroine, which was the kind of piece normally reserved for the last act. Giselda, left alone, prays to the spirit of her mother for comfort; for she is consumed by a love unworthy of a Christian. Shrieks of alarm are heard; the women of the harem rush in with the Crusaders in pursuit. With them is Sofia crying out that Antioch has been betrayed, and that she has seen her husband and son slain at her feet 'by *him*'—and she points to Arvino who has just entered with Pagano. Giselda is so appalled that when Arvino comes forward to embrace her she repulses him with horror. She prophesies that the crusade will fall on evil times and her tirade culminates in the final blasphemy 'God wills it *not*!' (Dio non lo vuole). Arvino, enraged, offers to stab her but Pagano restrains him.

For this scene Verdi has reverted to a more conventional style of soprano writing far removed from that of the *Salve Maria*. Giselda's soliloquy (*Se vano è il pregare*) is a suave melody with little to distinguish it apart from the disconcerting violence of its middle section (the *b* of the $a^1\ a^2\ b\ a^3$ design) which strikes in exactly half a bar before you expect it, bringing tighter, incisive rhythms, ominously punctuated by the lower brass (*Un cumulo veggo d'orribili giorni*). The reprise brings as usual an extension of the opening phrase rising successively to B flat and D flat and descending in coils of Bellinian fioritura. The cabaletta (*No, giusta causa non è d'Iddio*) recalls the rondò-finale of *Oberto* in its rhythmic cut, though it is more elaborate and brilliant. There is a portentous episode, full of chromatic sequences, where Giselda foretells desolation and ruin. Otherwise it is a piece of fairly routine vehemence. Mild insanity is usually a feature of these rondò-finali; so it is not surprising to find Giselda's line marked *quasi colpita di demenza*; though her constant refrain that the Christian God is a god of peace, not war, is quite rational if in the circumstances tactless.

PART III

The Conversion

Scene 1: the valley of Jehoshaphat. Flanked by hills of easy access,* foremost among them the Mount of Olives. Jerusalem is visible in the distance.

Across this pleasant landscape a crowd of knights, Crusaders, and pilgrims of both sexes are passing in slow procession with uncovered heads. It is a solemn moment described by Grossi in a wealth of detail. The pilgrims marching across the Syrian desert arrive on a little eminence from which they catch their first glimpse of the Holy City; and it affects them as the sight of the sea affected the weary Greek troops led back from Persia by Xenophon.

Verdi could not reproduce operatically the passing back from van to rear of the word 'Jerusalem'; nor would he wish to dwell on Grossi's vignette of the devout as they kissed the sheep and goats who had been privileged to approach the walls of Jerusalem. None the less, the general picture inspired him to write one of the loveliest pieces in the whole score. The main theme has a noble breadth and simplicity which recalls, particularly in its closing instrumental passage, the first scene of *Norma*; a favourite with the composer, as is clear from a letter to Camille Bellaigue.†

Oboes and clarinets double the voices in thirds giving an effect of soft trumpets. The men reply in a short episode pointing out the various places sanctified by the

61.

* *Praticabile*—the Italian term for scenery that can be walked on.
† Letter to Bellaigue, 2.5.1898. *Copialettere*, pp. 415–16.

Gospels—the Garden of Gethsemane, Golgotha and others. Then the melody is resumed with full choir and orchestra and with a moving bass line hammered out with the extra weight of trombones and cimbasso. There is a final episode with some effective bass writing ('Now the living God of War is here') and the piece dies away with an echo of the unaccompanied chorus with which it began and an instrumental epilogue of hushed beauty, as the pilgrims march away into the distance.

Now Giselda appears, having escaped from her father's tent. Her thoughts are with Oronte whom she believes to have been killed; but as she soliloquizes he steps out from the shadows and takes her in his arms. He tells her how he had been thrown from his horse and left for dead; how, on recovering, the desire to see her again had made him a coward. He has wandered far and wide in search of her; he has left his country, his family and his throne, and if he loses her he will lose his life too. Impulsively she insists on joining him, even though they will be forced to live wandering from place to place without a home, 'with only the cry of the hyena as their song of love'.*

The first movement of their duet has a freedom of design that is rare in early Verdi. So well is it merged into the preceding recitative that it is not easy to tell exactly at what point the formal number begins. Most of Oronte's recitative is in strict time, marked *presto*, while the allegro agitato passage (*Presi la fuga*) is strongly thematic. The tempo becomes constant at Giselda's decision to escape with Oronte (*Seguirti io voglio*) where there is a brief dialogue over an F minor orchestral melody to be recalled later at Gilda's first entrance in *Rigoletto*. Most of the movement belongs to Oronte as he describes his wanderings in a solo (*Per dirupi e per foreste*) reminiscent of Bellini's 'Nel furor della tempesta' (*Il Pirata*), the oboe, Verdi's favourite instrument of poignancy, adding a characteristic comment to the opening phrase. Then the orchestral melody is resumed, this time in the major, and with it the dialogue leading to an excited climax which prepares the way for the second movement (*Oh belle, a questa misera*). Here to a long-breathed melody accompanied only by harp with pizzicato cellos and basses the lovers bid a sad farewell to their people, each in successive stanzas. The rest of the orchestra joins in the coda where the voices instead of joining in routine sixths and thirds intertwine with a freedom which looks forward to the masterpieces of the 1850s. In how many final ensembles shall we meet again these thrusts from the soprano?

62

Distant shouts from the Lombardian camp alarm the two lovers. They decide to flee at once. Their cabaletta (*Ah vieni, sol morte*) is suitably short and free from display. Between their phrases the Lombardian 'To arms' can be heard coming steadily nearer, with thrilling effect, marred only by some needlessly crude scoring.

* The ageing Solera, now shabby and down-at-heel, told Eugenio Checchi that this comically dreadful line ('sarà l'urlo della jena la canzone dell'amor') was actually Verdi's. E. Checchi, *Verdi* (new ed. Florence, 1926), p. 52.

Scene 2: Arvino's tent

A few hours have passed since the previous scene. Arvino hints rather than tells us how he discovered Giselda and Oronte; and how Oronte carried his daughter away on horseback, with the 'man of the cavern' in pursuit. He curses Giselda in much the same words as those used by the Arvino of Grossi's poem: 'Vile, impious woman. Born to bring shame upon my house. Would that you had died in your cradle, sacrilegious maid. . . . Would that I had never begotten you!' A group of Lombardian soldiers enter to say that Pagano has been seen about the camp. Arvino, not connecting him with the 'man of the cavern', swears to hunt down his brother and kill him. All this is conveyed in a scene for men's chorus, mainly in unison (*Più d'uno Pagano*) with leading role for solo tenor in the manner of 'Il maledetto' from *Nabucco*. But whereas Ismaele had only the Levite basses to contend with Arvino must ride effectively over the entire male chorus—a further indication that although technically a comprimario he must be of real heroic calibre, especially as throughout the movement the orchestra colour is laid on with the thickest of brushes.

Scene 3: inside a cave, from the mouth of which the river Jordan can be seen

The scene begins, surprisingly, with a miniature violin concerto. Instrumental solos of this kind are commoner in Italian opera than we might suppose and understandably so at a time when there was a dearth of orchestral concerts. This one is more substantial than most. It consists of three movements: a declamatory prelude with cadenzas, a lyrical andante and a brilliant coda with echoes of Paganini. It is all effectively written for the instrument, but it hardly rises above the level of salon music, and it falls a long way short of the fine solo for cello with which Verdi was soon to introduce *I Masnadieri*. However the solo violin is with us for a long time yet. It is ready with a comment as Giselda lays Oronte by a rock on the floor of the cave. He has been mortally wounded in the clash with Arvino's men. Realizing that he is beyond help she breaks out in what sounds like a cabaletta, but is in fact the beginning of a freely constructed trio. 'God of my Fathers; Thou hast taken my mother from me; Thou hast preserved me for a life of misery; and now Thou hast taken from me my love, my sorrow's only solace; Thou art cruel . . .' But at this the voice of Pagano thunders out, 'Who dares accuse the Lord?' And to the familiar accompaniment of trombones and cimbasso he adds, 'Yours was a sinful love.' More gently he tells Oronte that he has come to bring him salvation and rebirth. Once more the solo violin is heard foretelling redemption. There is nothing in the stage directions to indicate that Pagano goes to the Jordan and brings holy water (doubtless the Archbishop's sensibilities were respected here), yet this is obviously what happens during the next few bars which Verdi has scored with particular care for cellos divided into four and double basses. Against this shimmering ethereal background Pagano pronounces his blessing, while the violin sweeps up and down in arpeggios. The music is suitably hymn-like; and at the end Giselda exclaims in a joyous allegro phrase that their love is no longer a sin. Another arpeggiated passage for the violin, marked *angelico*, prepares for the andante of the trio (*Qual voluttà trascorrere*). Here Oronte sobs out his life in a Bellini-like cantilena with a semiquaver gasp. At the end of every phrase there is the violin to remind him of salvation.

63

The best things about this trio are its huge rhythmic span, its wealth of heartfelt melody and the richness and subtlety of its scoring with harp as well as solo violin added to the texture. The one weakness lies in the tonal scheme. The music proceeds from A major through E major to B major, where it remains orientated for some time. The gravitational pull of the tonic has been so weakened that the final return sounds curiously unmotivated. This is the last time in Verdi in which such a deficiency will be felt, and it must be said that for years this trio remained the most applauded piece in the opera.

PART IV

The Holy Sepulchre

Scene 1: a cave near Jerusalem

The original libretto contains a short scene in inverted commas (indicating that it was never set to music) whose purpose is to bridge a gap in the action. How did Giselda manage to return to the Lombardian camp? Why at their next meeting do she and her father appear to be completely reconciled? If the audience would never hear the answers they could at least read them. So we are asked to imagine Giselda lying unconscious in the cave, while Pagano is explaining to her father how he has carried her back from the scene of Oronte's death; and he asks Arvino to forgive his now penitent daughter. Arvino consents; and the two men leave in search of water with which to revive her. Now hear on . . .

Giselda is dreaming of heaven—a heaven which Verdi has conjured up in a manner likely to reconcile most of us to the prospect of eternal perdition. The two harps are predictable and so is the invisible chorus; but to complete the celestial picture he can think of nothing better than to press the poor, hard-working banda into service. It is as little suited to his purpose as could be imagined. The chorus (*Componi o cara vergine*) is comically trivial, though Giselda's interjections have a certain nobility. The scene relapses still further when Oronte appears on a cloud, equipped with harp, to sing his least interesting aria (*In cielo benedetto*), whose opening phrase is no doubt consciously derived from Ex. 63. It contributes one vital piece of information. As proof of his bona fides, Oronte tells Giselda that if the Lombardians will go to Siloim they will find fresh water to relieve their distress. Readers of Tasso would not need reminding of the fearful drought which tormented the Crusaders outside Jerusalem. Grossi enlarges on this with a far greater wealth of realistic detail than Tasso. It is thirst—or rather the inability to swallow water when it is brought to her—that eventually kills Giselda in the poem. But it was Solera's idea to make her the purveyor of the good news, having received it from the most reliable source of all. First, however, she breaks out into an aria of joy (*Non fu sogno*)—a healthy, exhilarating piece, with plenty of fioritura and syncopation in the voice line, and scored in Verdi's most brilliant manner, the melody doubled now by flute, oboe and violins, now by clarinets in thirds, now by flute, oboe, clarinet, violin and trumpet. This 'cabaletta della visione' never failed to bring the house down. One small quotation will give an idea of its elemental vigour. If the basic material is commonplace, only Verdi would have punched home the return to F major with so bold a progression.

64

Scene 2: the Lombardians' camp near the tomb of Rachel

The scene opens with the most famous single number in *I Lombardi*, the large chorus, mainly unison, *O Signore dal tetto natio*. It is modelled fairly closely on the design of 'Va pensiero' and was clearly intended to repeat its success. It has one or two striking details, notably the scoring of the main section for brass with bassoons only. Characteristic too are the huge irresistible roll of the rhythm, and the effortless length of the melody.

The Lombardians are nearly dying of thirst. As they raise this desperate prayer to the Almighty, their thoughts are being drawn back to the murmuring streams of their native Lombardy. Hence the woodwind chatterings and gurglings which encrust the latter part of the chorus and which, it must be confessed, detract a little from its dignity. As the last chord dies away the voices of Giselda, Arvino and Pagano are heard crying, 'To Siloim!' Amid intense excitement Giselda delivers her message. Arvino then announces that as soon as they have quenched their thirst the attack on Jerusalem shall begin.

65

Adagio

CHORUS *cantabile con espressione*
(unison) O Si — gno — re, dal tet — to na — ti — o ci chia-

—ma — sti con san — ta pro — mes — sa;

At once the trumpet is heard calling them to battle. The Lombardians—without having had time to touch a drop of water—burst into the violent F minor chorus last heard in the second scene of Act II to different words. Here too it is followed by a Crusaders' march sung by Arvino and Pagano in unison and scored even more blatantly, in keeping with their new warlike mood. The chorus and banda join in as before, and eventually all leave the stage. The music however continues with an interlude whose model would seem to be Beethoven's Battle Symphony, with the two opposing forces represented not by anthems but by two melodies which we have already heard them sing—the Musulmans by the chorus at the start of Act II and the Crusaders by their familiar march (Ex. 59). To make the distinction even clearer the Christians have the orchestra while the enemy have to make do with the banda. By comparison with this the Battle Symphony seems a model of construction and logic. Here the respective themes are alternated without the slightest attempt at coherence, right up to the point where a fortissimo chord in F minor tells us that battle has been joined. From then on the interlude sounds like nothing so much as the first tutti of an overture, until in the general subsidence a tiny wailing figure from the banda, marked *lamentevole* and containing the Verdian minor second of grief, announces the defeat of Mahomet, while a little later the flute cocks a cheerful snook with a fragment of the Crusaders' theme flung out over a long drum roll; and the sounds of battle die away.

Scene 3: *Arvino's tent*

Pagano is being borne in by Giselda and Arvino. He is gravely wounded and delirious. 'Away from me,' he says. 'Who are you?' Hearing the reply he looks at his hands and cries that they are stained with Arvino's blood. Giselda in a phrase of exquisite tenderness tries to recall him to his senses, reminding him that he has saved her life and her reason. At the sound of her voice his mind clears; he calls her his 'angel of forgiveness' and his melody comes to rest in a cadence of which Verdi was to become particularly fond in later years.

66

Andante

PAGANO

tu se - i ___ l'an - ge-lo del per - do - no!

str.

The whole passage including the modulation from G major to E flat where Pagano replies combines delicacy with dramatic truth in a way that is all too rare in early Verdi. The time has come for Pagano to reveal his identity, so producing the inevitable fortissimo exclamation from voices and orchestra. Then in a final arioso over descending cellos with bassoons and lower brass intermittently sounding a low F of doom Pagano announces that he will now expiate his crime with death. Giselda, who has now recovered the almost mystic tone of her *Salve Maria*, declares to Arvino that her uncle has died 'in God'.

With his last breath Pagano begs to be allowed a last view of Jerusalem. The door of the tent is flung open to reveal the walls and towers of the Holy City hung with the banners of the cross and lit by the rising sun. Chorus and soloists join in a hymn of praise which, scored at first for harp and one cello and one bass, mounts in a steady crescendo to the final note of the opera. Just before the end there is a striking key-change to E flat, giving an effect not unlike that of the famous E major chord in the final bars of Ravel's Bolero. Only one palpable indication exists of the haste in which Verdi wrote this final scene. Beneath a few chords for the banda at the end of the autograph there is a note in Verdi's hand: DEAR MAESTRO: would you please score these few bars before 12.00 noon today. Sorry to be a nuisance. Friend VERDI.'

SENIGALLIA, *Summer 1843.* For a revival at this little Adriatic summer resort, with Frezzolini's husband Antonio Poggi in the part of Oronte, Verdi provided an alternative setting of the cabaletta-text *Come poteva un angelo.* Doubtless Poggi also sang it at the performance which Verdi himself directed at La Scala the following winter. It is more brilliant and graceful than the original and it takes the tenor up to a high C in the penultimate phrase. Like the andante it is built from repetitions of a single rhythmic pattern, which is virtually the same one that had served Donizetti in the cavatina 'O luce di quest'anima' (*Linda di Chamounix*). On the debit side it is very heavily not to say coarsely scored and far less suited to the sensitive, poetic character of the opera's hero. Unusually for a 'substitute' aria, this one is included in the published score.

For many years *I Lombardi alla Prima Crociata* enjoyed the same kind of popularity as *Nabucco*; indeed the chorus *O Signore dal tetto natio* almost outstripped 'Va

* See Girard's catalogue for the first quarter of 1844. Girard had replaced Cottrau as Ricordi's agents in the Kingdom of the Two Sicilies.

pensiero', and was actually commemorated in a poem by Giusti. The opera failed badly however at Venice the year after its first production, and in general was not as safe a proposition as *Nabucco*. Nor did it travel abroad to the same extent, though curiously enough it was the first Verdi opera to be heard in America. Then during the 1850s and '60s it entered a new phase of popularity. Much of this was doubtless due to sentimental rather than musical considerations. *I Lombardi* was the only one of Verdi's operas to take its theme from a purely Italian source. Even when the unity of Italy had passed from a dream to a fact people remembered with affection this early essay in Italian patriotism. After seeing a performance in 1865 Boito wrote that whereas *Rigoletto* remained eternally youthful *I Lombardi* was beginning to show its age. He was not exaggerating. Yet Verdi himself had undertaken its rehabilitation in 1847 when he converted it into *Jérusalem* for the Paris Opéra, removing the worst numbers, adding fresh ones and fitting it out with a more rational plot. But the fatal mistake here was to transform the Lombards into Franks, thereby removing all connotations of the Risorgimento. As a result *Jérusalem* never supplanted the original version. Not only that; all Italian writers beginning with the usually perceptive Basevi united in condemning it out of hand; and the foreign authors have mostly followed. Yet for *I Lombardi* they retained a disproportionate affection. Basevi, for instance, finds in it that consistency of colorito which for him is the most powerful unifying element in a Verdian opera;* whereas unity is the last quality to be found in *I Lombardi*. For revival today it presents several difficulties: eleven scenes, most of which require a certain grandeur of spectacle, two tenors of quite different calibre, the stronger having the smaller part, and worst of all an omnipresent banda. If *I Lombardi* is a very imperfect work of art, it is nevertheless a rich compost-heap which fertilized the soil of many a later opera. The quintet in Act I, unique in its wealth of ideas, is the model for some of Verdi's most powerful concerted finales. Here and there too the unusual dramatic situation spurred Verdi to find newer, less schematic ways of treating a formal number, as in the duet and trio from Act III. In years to come he throve on diffuse plots with a wealth of incident. But as yet he was not ready for them. In both the next two operas his path lay through a far greater concentration of ideas.

---

* Basevi, pp. 21–2.

7 ERNANI

ERNANI

Opera in four acts
by
FRANCESCO MARIA PIAVE
(after Victor Hugo's play, *Hernani*)

*First performed at the
Teatro la Fenice, Venice,
9 March 1844*

ERNANI, the bandit	PRIMO TENORE	Carlo Guasco
DON CARLO, King of Spain	PRIMO BARITONO	Antonio Superchi
DON RUY GOMEZ DE SILVA, a Spanish grandee	BASSO COMPRIMARIO*	Antonio Selva
ELVIRA, his niece and betrothed	PRIMA DONNA SOPRANO	Sofia Loewe
GIOVANNA, her nurse	SECONDA DONNA	Laura Saini
DON RICCARDO, the King's equerry	SECONDO TENORE	Giovanni Lanner
JAGO, equerry to Don Ruy	SECONDO BASSO	Andrea Bellini

Rebel mountaineers and bandits—Knights and members of
Silva's household—maids in attendance on Elvira—
Knights of Don Carlo's suite—members of the 'Holy
Alliance'—Spanish and German nobles and their ladies

Walk-on parts: Mountaineers and bandits—Electors and
nobles of the court of the Holy Roman Empire—pages
of the imperial court—German soldiers—ladies—followers,
male and female

The action takes place in the Pyrenees, at Aachen, and at Saragossa

Epoch: 1519

---

* Nowadays *primo basso* by virtue of the added cabaletta in Act I.

With the double success of *Nabucco* and *I Lombardi*, Verdi had won his spurs, and offers of contracts came pouring in. Unwilling to tempt providence with another premiere in Italy's leading opera house* he decided in the teeth of all Merelli's blandishments to accept a commission from the Marquis Nani Mocenigo, President of the Gran Teatro la Fenice in Venice, La Scala's biggest rival in Northern Italy. In the seventeenth century Venice had been the cradle of public opera; two hundred years later there was no city in all Italy more clamorous in its operatic enthusiasm. It was here that Rossini had first won international fame with *Tancredi* and *L'Italiana in Algeri*. Here too he closed his Italian career in a blaze of glory with *Semiramide*—wreaths flung into the water, a flotilla of gondolas escorting the maestro to his lodgings, and a water-borne band regaling him with a selection from his score. A Venetian triumph had a rare flavour of its own.

The contract was to produce two operas for the carnival-quaresima season 1843–4, the first to be a new work, the second a novelty for the Fenice (*I Lombardi*), but it was some time before Verdi could bring himself to sign it. Even at this early stage in his career he intended to dictate his own terms. He would certainly not supply the full score of the new opera on the date suggested since he was not accustomed to begin the instrumentation until the piano rehearsals were under way or to finish it until the pre-dress-rehearsal (l'antiprova generale). He would not accept less than 12,000 Austrian lire; nor would he agree to be paid in full only after the third performance, since there might not be a third performance (memories of *Un Giorno di Regno*!). A month at least must elapse between the opening nights of *I Lombardi* and the new work.† The singers for the latter were to be chosen by Verdi himself from the season's roster. The libretto was to be Verdi's responsibility entirely; he was to choose and pay the librettist, after having decided on the subject.

This was the most difficult part. Verdi toyed with a variety of ideas, mostly taken from English history or works by English authors. It was then that he first thought of *King Lear*, only to dismiss it, along with Byron's *The Corsair*, because they needed a baritone of Ronconi's calibre, such as would not be available in Venice that season. For a long time he clung to the notion of a 'prima donna' opera. He tried unsuccessfully to interest Solera and Cammarano in Byron's *The Bride of Abydos*.‡ He went so far as to make a synopsis of a *Caterina Howard*, though without much enthusiasm because the characters were so unpleasant.§ As alternatives he proposed a *Cola di Rienzi*—only the censors would never allow it; a *Caduta dei Longobardi*—only it was too diffuse and needed too big a cast of principals, including a baritone and a 'true bass'. By July he had changed course again, having as he thought found the ideal plot for Venice in Byron's *The Two*

*See letter to I. Marini, 11.6.1843. *Copialettere*, p. 423.
†Letter to Mocenigo, 9.4.1843. Conati, *La Bottega della musica*, p. 39.
‡Letter to Mocenigo, 6.6.1843. *Ibid.*, pp. 42–3.
§Letter to Mocenigo, 9.7.1843. *Ibid.*, p. 59.

Foscari: 'a Venetian story,' he told the board, 'full of passion, very easy to set to music. . . . The poet who will write me the libretto is a big name, but he does not wish to be known.'* (It was probably Romani.) But at the end of July Mocenigo wrote to say that both *Caterina Howard* and *I Due Foscari* had been forbidden by the censorship, the former because it contained too much cruelty, the latter for fear of giving offence to the descendants of such as Loredano and Barbarigo. Meanwhile Verdi had already received a letter from a certain Francesco Maria Piave, a friend of Brenna, the theatre secretary, saying that he had begun a libretto on the subject of *Cromwell*, and that if the composer were interested he would be glad to finish it. Verdi replied encouragingly but without committing himself. It was only after receiving solemn assurances from Mocenigo that Piave had a good sense of theatre and a knowledge of musical forms that he agreed to collaborate with him. So began a partnership which was to continue intermittently for more than twenty years.

The subject decided upon, and officially approved by the directorate at a meeting on 10 August, was not Victor Hugo's *Cromwell* but a certain *Allan Cameron*, which deals with the escape of the future Charles II after the Battle of Worcester with the help of a loyal Highland chieftain and his daughter Edith. An examination of the libretto, eventually set by Pacini in 1848, shows it to be based on Walter Scott's novel *Woodstock* with a change of names and locale and the elimination of various characters including Everard, the Puritan hero.† About this project, and its author, Verdi remained cautious, and with good reason.

In the theatrical world Piave was a novice. The eldest son of an unsuccessful businessman, he had been intended for the Church; but family affairs forced him to leave the seminary and he was eventually reduced to finding work as a publisher's proof-reader. In his spare time he poured out translations and light verse in which he showed great facility combined with a tendency to archaic euphuism, which caused Giuseppina Strepponi in later years to address him jokingly as 'Il grazioso'.‡ As a collaborator he was resourceful and accommodating—two qualities which Verdi was quick to appreciate. But he never forgot his initial mistrust of Piave's ability. Throughout their relationship he treated the poet sometimes with affection, sometimes with impatience—and with no respect for his judgement whatsoever.

This is precisely what makes their correspondence so interesting, since it reveals very clearly Verdi's ideas on music-drama at the time and his determination to enforce them. In his letters about *Allan Cameron* his chief concern is to prevent the public from getting bored.

---

*Letter to Brenna, 4.7.1843. *Ibid.*, pp. 58–9.

†In operatic adaptations of Waverley novels the omission of the central figure is not uncommon. In Federico Ricci's *La Prigione di Edimburgo*, based on *The Heart of Midlothian*, Jeanie Deans is reduced to a bit-part in the opening ensemble! Oddly, in A. Benedetti, *Le traduzioni italiane di Walter Scott e loro anglicismi* (Florence, 1974), *Allan Cameron* is listed as a spurious Waverley novel. (See also D. Kimbell, *Verdi in the Age of Italian Romanticism* (Cambridge, 1981), p. 118.) However, the correspondence of the situations with those of *Woodstock* is too close to be fortuitous.

‡For a detailed account of Piave's literary background and early association with the Arcadian Society of Rome see B. Cagli: '". . . Questo povero poeta esordiente": Piave a Roma', *Ernani ieri e oggi: Bollettino dell'Istituto di Studi Verdiani no. 10* (Parma, 1987), pp. 1–18.

You know better than I that in this type of composition there is no effect unless there is action, so therefore let's have as few words as possible. . . . In the finale of Act III do just as you please, whatever comes most naturally out of the plot, just so long as you keep the interest going. . . . Remember that brevity is never a fault. The metres as you like . . . I never try to shackle the genius of my poets [!]. . . . But I do insist on brevity because that's what the public wants. . . .*

There was to be no question of setting the opera piecemeal as Rossini used to do.

I'm putting this first act away in a drawer because I don't want to start work on it until I have the complete libretto. . . . I find that . . . once I've got a general picture of the poem as a whole the music comes of its own accord. . . . I hear that you've cut the drama down to two acts; so much the better. I would just point out that if the second act turns out to be longer than the first it might be better to keep to the original division.†

As a general rule Verdi liked to make each successive act shorter than the previous one.

Then towards the end of August a fateful meeting took place in Milan between Verdi and Mocenigo to discuss the completed libretto. Both decided that the plot needed drastically overhauling—if indeed anything could be done with it at all. Mocenigo was almost inclined to suggest another subject altogether: say, *Hernani* or *The Tower of* ——.‡ But *Allan Cameron* had been approved by the censorship, and Piave would certainly have to be paid for the work he had already done. Accordingly composer and president drafted a revised synopsis of *Allan Cameron* reworking the last act so as to introduce Cromwell for an important soliloquy. As for some reason the hero's name seemed vaguely ridiculous they decided to rename him Evan (Euan) Cameron, and the opera itself *Cromwell*.§

But in dropping the magic name *Hernani* Mocenigo had lit a candle which was not to be put out. Within a few days Verdi wrote to him:

This *Cromwell* is really not very compelling when you consider the requirements of the theatre. It is clear, fluent and well-made but miserably uneventful . . . the fault of the subject rather than the poet. . . . My own view—supposing we keep to this libretto—would be to retain the original division into three acts; then work out a fine ensemble-finale for King Charles's farewell,¶ and change the last act finale because it isn't gripping enough as it stands; the poet should bear in mind the finale of *Norma* or of *Beatrice*.

But oh, if only we could do *Hernani* instead that would be tremendous. I know it would mean a great deal of trouble for the poet but my first task

---

* Letter to Piave, 8.8.1843. Abbiati, I, pp. 471–2.
† Letter to Piave, 19.8.1843. *Ibid.*, p. 472.
‡ See letter from Mocenigo to Verdi, 2.9.1843. Conati, pp. 72–3. There is a lacuna in the title.
§ The title *Cromwell* was Verdi's idea. See letter from Mocenigo to Brenna, 25.8.1843. *Ibid.*, p. 71.
¶ Prince Charles had been crowned King in Scotland.

would be to try and compensate him. . . . Signor Piave has great facility in versifying and in *Hernani* all he would have to do would be to condense and tighten up; the action is there ready made, and it's all immensely good theatre. Tomorrow I'll write at length to Piave setting out all the scenes from *Hernani* which seem to me suitable. . . . I've already seen how the whole of the first act could be compressed into a magnificent introduction, and Act I could finish at the point where Don Carlos requires Silva to give up Hernani who is hidden behind the picture. Act II could be made from Act IV of the French play. And the third act would end with a magnificent trio in which Hernani dies.*

Verdi's enthusiasm is understandable. After *I Lombardi* what he needed was the discipline of a plot whose action is focused on a central issue, and whose events fall within the same range of experience. This is what led him in the first instance to *I Due Foscari*, and when that was refused to a drama by Victor Hugo. For all their defiance of convention, their mixing of comic and tragic elements, their disregard of the sacred rules of Alexandrine metre, the wide-ranging fantasy and romantic rodomontade, Hugo's plays always have an inner reinforcement of logic. Behind them there is a thesis however general, which is one reason why, like Shaw, he delights in polemical prefaces. *Hernani*, produced with tumultuous success in Paris in 1830, proclaimed the gospel of Romanticism, or 'Liberalism in literature' as Hugo called it. But the freedom with which the characters of *Hernani* are treated, the extravagance with which they behave are governed by an intellectual idea; the struggle between love and honour. True, plays with love as the spur and honour the bridle are common enough. But in *Hernani* it is not honour as understood by, say, Richard Lovelace. It is more an obsessive pride which turns all the characters into giant egoists, swearing mutual vengeance for the most trivial causes, doing each other monstrous kindnesses, destroying themselves and each other to satisfy some whim of punctilio. Arrogant even in humility, they are never so vain as when protesting their own utter unworthiness. Of the three rivals for the love of Doña Sol, only one, Don Carlo, later the Emperor Charles V, wins through to glory. His love is the least worthy; yet he alone has a sense of humour, and it is he who performs the one 'free' action in the play, when he pardons the conspirators. Doña Sol, her white-haired guardian Don Ruy Gomez de Silva and her noble outlaw of a lover Don Juan of Aragon, alias Hernani the bandit, all die victims of the code they profess. Within Hugo's scheme each illogical action follows logically from the one that precedes it, giving Verdi the pace, the eventfulness and above all the dramatic unity that he had been looking for.

The poet was deeply dismayed by this change of plan. He was convinced that *Hernani* was dangerous, and that in any case it would lose all its dramatic character if made into an opera libretto. He had a supporter in his friend Brenna, who pointed out to Verdi that Piave's own *Cromwell* based on Victor Hugo had been forbidden by the police; and that merely concerned a republican ruler who foiled a plot against his life. How much less would they be likely to tolerate the behaviour of Hernani towards his liege lord?† But at a meeting of the directorate *Hernani*

---

*Letter to Mocenigo, 5.9.1843. *Ibid.*, pp. 74–5.
†Letter from Brenna, 17.9.1843. *Ibid.*, pp. 76–7.

was approved; and Piave had to be content with financial compensation and a minute to the effect that his own *Allan Cameron* should never be performed under the title of *Cromwell*. Meanwhile in case of police obstruction to *Hernani* he would hold *Allan Cameron* in reserve. As noted, it would eventually serve another composer.

Verdi himself might have envisaged taking over Hugo's action as it stood; but Mocenigo and Piave knew that modifications were essential if the opera was ever to see the stage. No king, for instance, would ever be allowed to hide in a cupboard, as Don Carlo does in Hugo's Act I. To Piave, then, with Mocenigo at his elbow, must be ascribed the present scheme with a preliminary scene for Hernani and his men followed by a conflate of Hugo's Acts I and II. The synopsis was entitled not *Ernani* but *Don Ruy Gomez de Silva*.* This much Verdi approved but added, 'In the last two acts the closer we keep to Hugo the more effective it will be. I find those last two acts quite heavenly.'† And in the same letter, 'I would urge you . . . not to overlook some of the very beautiful sentences in the original. Also please allow for a nice cantabile at the moment of Ruy's entrance, particularly as Superchi is a very fine singer, and anyway the situation calls for it and Victor Hugo himself has these words: "Take and tread beneath your feet this token of my honour. Tear out my white hairs . . .", etc.' This insistence on a close adherence where possible to the original play marks a new outlook in Italian opera, and one which would never have occurred to Rossini or Donizetti, for whom plots were to some extent interchangeable like their music. For Verdi an opera based on *Hernani* had in some way to reflect the unique character of the parent drama.

His most serious objection to the synopsis concerned the change of scene in Act III. 'I would say that from the moment when Carlo appears and surprises the conspirators the action should move swiftly right up to the end of the act. A scene-change would worry the audience and interrupt the dramatic flow. For God's sake don't end Act IV with a rondò, but do a trio; what's more this trio should be the best piece in the opera.'

From the mention of the baritone Superchi as Ruy Gomez de Silva it is clear that Verdi had not yet arrived at the present distribution of voices. How he eventually did so provides an excellent illustration of the laws which operated in the Italian theatre of the time. Even during the preparation of *Allan Cameron* Verdi had been under pressure from the management to include a part for the musico contralto Carolina Vietti. Evidently he was unenthusiastic: for in August Brenna thought it necessary to enlist the advocacy of the tenor Antonio De Val, then about to visit the composer in Milan. Later De Val reported back that Verdi had agreed to accommodate the lady if he could find a suitable part for her but '*he is a sworn foe to the idea of making a woman sing dressed up as a man*'.‡ Surprisingly, in his eagerness to set *Hernani* at all costs Verdi promised to write for Vietti unconditionally;§ so that up till the end of October the agreed voice distribution was: Donna Sol or Elvira (soprano), Ernani (contralto), Don Carlo (tenor), Don Ruy Gomez de Silva (baritone). By this time the police had at last given their approval, stipulating merely that in the conjuration scene no swords should be

---

* *Ibid.*, p. 80. † Letter to Piave, 2.10.1843. Abbiati, I, pp. 474–5.
‡ Italics mine. Letter from De Val to Brenna, 24.8.1843. Conati, p. 70. In the management's defence it must be said that in Hugo's play Hernani is described by Don Carlos as 'a beardless youth'.
§ Letter to Brenna, 22.9.1843. *Ibid.*, pp. 84–5.

unsheathed and that in his defiance of Don Carlo Ernani's language should be that of a subject to his lawful sovereign.* Verdi could now afford, therefore, to stand his ground over the casting. Piave had already hinted to the management that Ernani would be more effective as a tenor; and Brenna had felt bound to remind the composer that Vietti had to be accommodated somehow and that if she was unsuitable for Ernani she would be even less so as Don Carlo, who was a considerably older man.† A subsequent letter from Mocenigo pointed the way to a solution. Throughout the carnival-quaresima season the Fenice could be sure of two leading tenors. If Verdi was against using Vietti for dramatic reasons, why not cast both Ernani *and* Don Carlo as tenors? Alternatively he could give the part of Carlo to the baritone Superchi, making Silva a basso profondo. Unfortunately Rosi, the only full bass on the theatre roster, was not sufficiently experienced to sustain a leading role. If Verdi knew of a suitable artist who could make himself available, they would try to engage him, though this might be expensive.‡ Verdi replied:

> I don't know what artist to suggest for the basso profondo, but I think we could manage with the company as it is now. We could even make use of two tenors; but the best solution would be to give Conti the part of Ernani, Superchi that of Carlo, and Rosi that of Gomez, since in this part there is only the finale of Act I, a few pertichini, a duet in the second act (a very powerful one with chorus); and in Act III he only has ensembles. In Act IV there's the terzetto finale, but if the poet will bear with me, we can centre all the interest on the two lovers. . . . I think this will work out well, especially as everyone assures me that Superchi is a very fine singer; and in the part of Gomez we should be forced either to falsify the part or to ill-treat the singer.§

In terms of the convenienze, therefore, Silva was to be a comprimario role—an important point to remember when we come to consider the first of the opera's later accretions (see below, p. 167).

As a result some of the instructions to Piave had to be countermanded. Previously Verdi had written:

> I find it dangerous to have Carlo, Ernani and Ruy appearing one after the other without working out a single musical number of importance. These are things that the theatre public often find rather ridiculous. At the moment of Carlo's entrance I would make a very tender little duet and so develop rather more the theme of Carlo's love. Then at Ernani's entrance shortly afterwards I would make the stretta of the Carlo–Elvira piece with him joining in. . . . Later on I would have Ruy's arrival announced by a servant or by Giuseppa in a kind of recit., as in Hugo. Then after a few words of surprise I would make him [i.e., Silva] start the adagio of the finale concertato at this point and I would like him to be the dominant figure in the vast canvas. . . .¶

---

* *Ibid.*, p. 99.
† Letter from Brenna, 26.10.1843. *Ibid.*, p. 98. He would doubtless have been surprised to know that less than four years later the part of Don Carlo would be sung at Covent Garden by the contralto Marietta Alboni.
‡ Letter from Mocenigo, 7.11.1843. *Ibid.*, p. 100.
§ Letter to Mocenigo, 10.11.1843. *Ibid.*, pp. 100–1.
¶ Letter to Piave, 10.10.1843. Abbiati, I, pp. 475–6.

But that was before the decision to allot Silva to a comprimario bass. If Rosi could not dominate the finale as originally intended too much weight would fall on the soprano. Piave complained about these constant changes of plan to his friend Brenna; to whom Verdi wrote in a tone of injured innocence:

I am the last person to worry a poet by wanting a single line changed [!] and I've set to music three libretti by Solera and comparing the originals with the printed texts which I've kept you will only find a very few lines changed and always because Solera himself wanted it. But Solera has written five or six libretti and knows all about the theatre and dramatic effect and musical form. Signor Piave hasn't yet written for the theatre and therefore it's natural that he should be wanting in these matters. But in fact where will you find a woman who is going to sing one after the other a long cavatina, a duet which ends as a trio, and then an entire finale like the one in the first act of *Ernani*? Who is the composer that can set a hundred lines of recitative such as there are in the third act without boring everybody? In the entire four acts of *Nabucco* or *I Lombardi* you will not find more than a hundred lines of recitative.

It's the same with so many other little details. You've been so kind to me— I do beg you to try and make Piave realize all this. However little experience I may have had, I do go to the theatre all the year round and I pay the most careful attention to what I see and hear. I've been able to put my finger on so many works which wouldn't have failed if the pieces had been better laid out, the effects better calculated, the musical forms clearer, etc. . . . in a word if either the composer or the poet had been more experienced. So often an overlong recitative, a phrase, a sentence that would be really fine in a book or even in a spoken drama just make people laugh in an opera.*

To solve the problem of Act I Verdi retained the idea of a short cantabile for Silva of the type that can always be given to a comprimario.

But his difficulties with the singers were not over yet. The season opened as usual on 26 December with a disastrous performance of *I Lombardi* in which the tenor Domenico Conti sang so badly that Verdi refused point blank to consider him for the title role of his new opera. Unless the production could be deferred until the arrival of Carlo Guasco he would prefer to be released from his contract. Once again Mocenigo proposed a compromise. At the time a certain Vitali was rehearsing in *Nabucco* at Verona. At his own request Verdi was allowed to go to the first performance; if Vitali appeared satisfactory he would be engaged in Conti's place. But here too the result was negative. 'I have heard Vitali,' Verdi wrote, 'and I don't like him. With time perhaps he'll develop into a fairly good tenor, but at present he's nothing and his voice gets tired and half-way through the opera he tends to go flat.'† So Verdi had his way and the premiere of the opera, now called *Ernani* or *L'Onore Castigliano*, was fixed for March.

In the meantime Verdi was becoming increasingly on edge. The Venetians it seems were in a more than usually fractious mood. The failure of *I Lombardi* was

*Letter to Brenna, 15.11.1843. Conati, pp. 102–3.
†Letter to Mocenigo, 8.1.1844. *Ibid.*, p. 116.

followed by the even greater fiasco of Pacini's *Fidanzata Corsa*, after which Mocenigo offered his resignation, but was persuaded to retract it. Levi's *Giuditta*, the
other novelty of the season, fared no better. 'If I have a fiasco I shall blow my
brains out,'* Verdi wrote to a friend: 'I couldn't bear the thought, especially as
these Venetians seem to be expecting goodness knows what.'† Next Guasco wrote
from Madrid declining the part of Ernani as being too fatiguing; but he changed
his mind when the presidency of the Fenice threatened to sue the impresario
who was acting as his agent. Sofia Loewe objected to the final trio, having presumably hoped for a rondò-finale for herself in its place.‡ Finally Meini, the bass who
was to have sung Silva (what had become of Rosi is not recorded) found the part
too low for him. At Verdi's own request he was replaced by a young bass from the
chorus called Antonio Selva, who thus owed the composer the start of a distinguished career. Five years later he was to create the part of Count Walter in
Luisa Miller.

But amid all difficulties and mishaps to which almost any operatic enterprise is
subject there were unmistakable signs that the new work would create a sensation.
'The copyists all say that this is a masterpiece,' Brenna wrote to Mocenigo;§
and in the event, neither Guasco's hoarseness, Loewe's poor intonation,¶ thought
to have been caused by her annoyance over the final trio, nor the blowing of a
horn on stage, to which Mocenigo had vainly objected, prevented *Ernani* from
being a tremendous success. With it Verdi's fame took a new leap, which carried
it at once across the boundaries of Italy. For better or worse he was now a world
composer.

From Paris, Victor Hugo protested vehemently against the 'clumsy travesty'
of his play; and when it arrived at the Théâtre des Italiens two years later he insisted
that both the title and the names of the characters be altered. The opera was given
as *Il Proscritto*: Ernani became Oldrado of Venice; Carlo a certain Andrea Gritti,
later Doge of Venice; Silva an unsuccessful rival, Zeno. This practice was followed
in other cities where the names Victor Hugo and Hernani smacked of revolution.
In Palermo (1845) it was *Elvira d'Aragona*, in Naples (1847) *Il Corsaro di Venezia*.
But wherever there was an Italian opera house, *Ernani* arrived sooner or later.

Why Hugo should have taken such exception to Verdi's work is difficult to
understand. It was not the first operatic *Ernani*. As early as 1834 Vincenzo Gabussi
had written one for the Théâtre des Italiens, which Hugo must have known about.
Bellini had contemplated an opera on the same subject; and it was fear of the
censors not of the playwright which made him break off and compose *La Sonnambula* instead. Francis Toye describes Piave as 'having taken from Hugo's drama the
situations and discarded the details that made them comparatively credible'.‖
He also accuses him of undue compression. Neither of these charges is fair. It is
true that Piave cut down the arguments and the long speeches, but nowhere so as
to affect the credibility of the drama. The speeches are for the most part either a

---

* Literally 'crack my brains'.
† Letter to Luigi Toccagni (undated). Abbiati, I, pp. 481–2.
‡ See letter to Brenna, 5.10.1850. Conati, p. 219.
§ Letter from Brenna to Mocenigo, 31.1.1844. *Ibid.*, pp. 118–9.
¶ See letter to Countess Appiani, 10.3.1844. *Copialettere*, p. 425.
‖ F. Toye, *Giuseppe Verdi: His Life and Works* (London, 1931), p. 243.

parade of historical references, such as audiences liked as a stiffening to period drama, or else they are poetic evocations of feelings which music could conjure up in sixteen bars. As for compression, not even Piave achieved a more telegraphic exchange than this:

DONA SOL Des soldats! L'empereur! O ciel! Coup imprévu! Hernani!

HERNANI   Doña Sol!

SILVA   Elle ne m'a point vu!

(She rushes into Hernani's arms but he repulses her with disdain)

HERNANI Madame!

DONA SOL   J'ai toujours son poignard!

HERNANI *(taking her in his arms)*   Mon amie!*

If the opera seems extravagant to a modern age, it is no more so than the play. Nor is there anything in Piave quite so ridiculous as Silva's history of the portraits of his ancestors. If Piave's libretto does not reflect that vein of sardonic humour in Don Carlo which gives him a wider horizon than his obsessed rivals, the essential greatness of the man is suggested by Verdi himself, and by the simplest of means: the baritone voice. This is the opera in which Verdi defines most clearly his male vocal archetypes: the granite-like, monochrome bass (Silva) older than the roots of his family pride; the heroic tenor, lyrical, ardent, despairing (Ernani); and partaking of both natures, now zephyr, now hurricane, the Verdi baritone (Carlo), the greatest vehicle of power in Italian opera. *Ernani* is built out of the clash of these three voice-types, each setting the other more and more strongly in relief. This is essentially what is new about it. In harmony and orchestration it is far less consciously adventurous than *I Lombardi*. Its range of ideas is rather narrower. Yet the work gains immensely from its greater unity of purpose, which in turn proceeds from the logic with which Hugo has followed up his dramatic premises. In two respects only is the balance of the original drama affected for the worse. As a tenor, no matter how heroic, Ernani inevitably cuts a lesser figure in the vocal tournaments beside the Verdian baritone and bass. Then too by amalgamating the first two acts of the drama in the way that he had, Piave deprived the hero of his moment of greatest glory, when he has the king at his mercy but refuses to take advantage of him. True he is compensated with an opening scene to himself: but this is not Hugo. It is Italian opera commonplace, and does nothing for the hero's stature.

Yet from the first the spirit of Hugo is there. Ten years younger than the playwright, Verdi was part of that youthful audience to which the play *Hernani* is addressed. The bounding energy of Hugo's alexandrines is reflected in the spirit of Verdi's music, which is far more forceful than anything he had written so far. Victor Hugo, one might say, was good for Verdi, and it is significant that both the operas that he based on Hugo's plays (the other was of course *Rigoletto*) were landmarks in his career.

Like *I Lombardi*, *Ernani* begins with a prelude, as superior to its predecessor as the opera to which it belongs. It consists of two elements, both central to the drama. The first, announced by trumpets and trombones in unison and preceded by a

* *Hernani*, IV, iv.

tympanum roll, is a quotation of Ernani's oath to give up his life to Silva whenever the old man should require it.

67

But for the moment the last phrase is withheld; and the transition back from the Neapolitan sixth is provided by a cello solo, quoting from a passage in Act III (see Ex. 86). The other melody proclaims itself as a love-theme; but it would be wrong to call it a quotation, for this is the fullest version in which we shall hear it.

68

Here is the essence of Verdi's early style—plain, strophic, with steep progressions towards the cadence points, and the instrumental colour laid on in thick daubs. Note the upward leap of a sixth from dominant to mediant—a fingerprint of the opera as a whole and, also, as we shall see, a touchstone whereby the main characters will be defined. Characteristic too is the way in which at the ninth bar the cello semiquavers change from arco to pizzicato (see Chapter 2), the violins divide in octaves and all the high wind instruments, trumpets included, join the melody in a great surge. The effect is of some huge bird taking wing. At the end part of the oath-theme (Ex. 67) is recalled with frightening force on the full orchestra. This time it is supplied with its proper ending, and dies away on trombones and trumpets. Ex. 68 also returns, this time played by oboe and bassoon in octaves and decorated in a manner familiar from the prelude to La Traviata, with tripping semiquavers ascending and descending. The scoring is predictably less subtle than in the later work, flutes, clarinets, violins and violas doing what in 1853 would be done by violins alone. The opening phrase is repeated twice and the prelude is wound up with the briefest of pianissimo codas.

ACT I

The Bandit

Scene 1: a lonely place in the mountains of Saragossa

Piave follows the current practice of giving each act a separate title, as does Hugo himself; but for reasons which will be obvious he uses here the title of Hugo's second act (Act I of the drama is headed 'The King'). The scene is laid in the mountains near the village from which Ernani takes his name. It is not his real name, of course; for Ernani is Don Juan of Aragon, Grand Master of Avis, Duke of Segorbe and Cardona, Marquis of Monroy, Count of Albatera, Viscount of Gor, and, as he tells Carlo in the play, Lord of more places than he can remember. But due to a family quarrel with the present king's father his estates have been confiscated and he himself has become an outlaw with a price on his head. Two thoughts sustain him: the determination to be revenged on his father's foe, and the love of the young Doña Sol, called in the opera by the more singable name of Elvira, who is soon to be married to her uncle and guardian Don Ruy Gomez de Silva. Meanwhile Ernani is living the life of a bandit chief:

> . . . among companions rude,
> Men all proscribed, of whom the headsman knows
> The names already. Men whom neither steel
> Nor touch of pity softens, each one urged
> By some blood feud that's personal.★

These then are the men discovered at the start of Act I, carousing, gaming and polishing their arms. After a drinking chorus they perceive their leader approaching, wrapped in gloomy thought. Ernani tells them of his love for Elvira, 'fresh as the dew upon the thorn', and declares that if she is taken from him he will die of grief. The men eagerly offer to help him carry her off. Whereupon Ernani advances to the footlights and apostrophizes Elvira in a typical 'cabaletta-in-parenthesis', while his men respectfully bid him take heart.

It is the most conventional scene in the opera, presenting the hero as merely a tenor in love; and much of it is conventionally treated. Nothing is less obviously original than the brisk 6/8 rhythm, the mechanically rising music which seems to push the curtain up with it, the continual side-drum tattoo, and the Neapolitan street-song cadences. But compare it with what other Italian composers wrote in similar circumstances—as for instance the chorus of drunken pirates from Bellini's *Il Pirata*, which it resembles in all externals. What a poor spavined affair Bellini's piece appears, despite the echo effects of which the composer was so fatuously proud! Verdi's superiority lies as usual in greater melodic vitality and a longer rhythmic sweep. There are four melodic ideas in this drinking chorus, each distinctively if coarsely scored and each growing naturally out of the one before. The natural symmetry is varied by that expert juggling with irregular phrase lengths that we often find in Verdi's male choruses (cf. Chapter 6). Above all,

★ *Hernani*, I, ii (trs. Mrs Newton Crosland).

the music *moves*. Even the overworked side-drum makes a special contribution to the impetus with a cluster of grace-notes at the words 'Allegri, beviam'.

The andante (*Come rugiada al cespite*) is also less conventional than it appears. Based on a double sestina instead of a double quatrain it is designed on a bigger scale than usual with elements of the narrative-aria in it. The C minor–E flat major episode where Silva is mentioned owes something to Pollione's 'Meco all' altar di Venere' (*Norma*); but, characteristically, the excited effect of Bellini's string tremolando Verdi achieves by rapid cello pizzicati and the addition of four horns to the accompaniment. Unlike Bellini, Verdi does not repeat his opening idea when he returns to the home key; and for the coda he brings in a new idea in shorter, more rapid phrases culminating in an upward scale followed by a cadence.

The intermediate chorus (*Quando notte il cielo copre*) recalls the style of Pagano's followers in *I Lombardi*; but it is more pithy and less absurdly explosive, with each phrase launched from a tiny figure on unison brass and timpani. It was a happy

69

thought to work in this same chorus as the ritornello and coda of the succeeding cabaletta (*O tu che l'alma adora*). Here too Verdi has enlarged the traditional scale slightly by setting the entire second quatrain in the dominant key as the central section of what is almost a ternary plan, and repeating the last two lines for his reprise. The scene ends in a long orchestral diminuendo as the stage empties and Ex. 69 seems to blow away like thistledown.

If despite these touches of invention the music falls short of memorability, the fault lies in the narrowness of Verdi's present idiom, here defined more sharply than ever before. The scene is essentially static, the nineteenth-century expansion of a Metastasian exit-aria. Such scenes called for a subtlety of craftsmanship Verdi had not acquired. The beginning of the andante with its rising sixth is so close to Ex. 68 that a listener might well imagine he is hearing the aria from which the prelude-theme is a quotation. Both themes are expressions of the *Ernani* colorito, the plain sinewy melodic style which characterizes the whole opera. Otherwise their similarity is not quite close enough to seem intentional, and just too close for us not to feel that it might have been better avoided. Likewise the scale in the codetta to the words 'd'affanno, d'affanno morirò' is identical in context and effect with one which occurs in a later duet between soprano and baritone. In neither case is there any cogency in the connection.

The cabaletta too is of a type that will reappear throughout early Verdi sung almost interchangeably by the various Jacopos, Carlos, Zamoros of the tenor-lead. It is full of energetic rising phrases, displaced accents, syncopations and always scored in the 'brilliant' manner, the contours picked out here and there with wood-wind and trumpet. With rare exceptions these movements are among the least valuable part of Verdi's operatic legacy.

Scene 2: the apartments of Donna Elvira in the palace of Don Ruy Gomez de Silva

There is a tiny prelude for strings, and the curtain rises on Donna Elvira sitting sadly alone. She tells us that it is midnight; that her guardian Silva has not returned; that she wishes she were rid of him for ever, that 'hideous spectre' who pursues her with words of love; that her thoughts are with her lover the young Ernani. Then she breaks into a cavatina, which is Verdi's first aria to achieve what might be called 'concert-hall' status. The andantino *Ernani, Ernani involami* is built on the same ground plan as Abigaille's 'Anch'io dischiusi un giorno'—$a^1 a^2 b a^3 c a^3$— and with the similar woodwind chatterings to introduce '*c*'; but the realization is much tauter and owes less to Verdi's predecessors. The slow 3/4–9/8 swing is typically Verdian:

70

There is a sureness of touch even about the mannerisms: the pin-pointing of the final two notes in the phrase of bar 5 with flute, oboe, clarinet and first violins, and still more the throwing-in of full orchestra during the words 'per antri e lande inospiti'. The movement contains not a note too many; and the climax on the high C where Elvira declares in effect that with Ernani 'Ah, wilderness were paradise enow' is achieved so naturally and easily.

Between andantino and cabaletta there is a chorus sung by Elvira's attendants as they come in with expensive presents from her guardian. Cast in bolero rhythm (a rare concession to local colour) it is essentially a ballet movement with female voices added. The scoring too is very much in the blatant ballet style of Pugni and his like. Elvira turns and thanks the ladies. Then she sings her cabaletta (*Tutto sprezzo che d'Ernani*). Like Ernani's in the previous scene this is a footlight piece in which she tells us that she despises all jewels and trinkets that do not speak to her of Ernani. This too is built on a more ample scale than usual but once again the attraction lies in the pith and spontaneity of the melody. It is a taxing movement, but it contains no more fioritura than seems to be implied in the opening phrase. Even the rush of semiquavers over one and a half octaves seems a natural ornamentation of what has gone before. Between statement and restatement the women beg her to show a little more pleasure at the prospect of being Silva's bride; and at the end they follow her out of the room in the approved exit-aria manner.

After a few bars of agitato music Don Carlo, melodramatically incognito, enters the empty stage followed by an agitated duenna. In the opera she needs very much less persuasion to fetch her mistress than in the play. A touch on Don Carlo's dagger and she hurries to do his bidding. In his few moments alone Carlo reflects on the ignominy of his position, rejected for a bandit by the woman he loves. His final cadence is interrupted by the sudden appearance of Elvira, alarmed and indignant. 'You, sire? and at this hour . . .' and so into a duet similar to that of Abigaille and Nabucco. Trumpet and piccolo join in the woodwind melody which forms the basis of the first movement-dialogue (see Ex. 5). But it is not repeated or developed at length—the action is moving too swiftly for that. Carlo hurls his taunt—'Is a bandit the proud master of your heart?' She answers softly and evasively, and he changes his method of attack. In the second movement he tells her of the love she has inspired in him since the day he had first seen her (*Da quel dì che t'ho veduta*). Here, keeping the melody centred in the upper third of the baritone's voice makes him sound like a richer-hued tenor, with velvet depths. The poetic feeling of the melody is enhanced by simple, delicate scoring. Here too we meet the 'rising sixth' motif, but in a more sedate form. Carlo does not take it in one bound, but through an intermediate tonic note. Elvira retorts in the musical language of Abigaille, over a busy accompaniment which is used more than once in this opera to express indignation. Not even in *Nabucco* did Verdi achieve greater contrast between two 'dissimilar' stanzas than here:

71

In due course the voices overlap with the same phrases, eventually joining in the traditional sixths and tenths. But the polarity established at the outset generates a motive power that keeps the tension sustained up to the final cadence.

The andantino concluded, Carlo loses patience and tries to seize her. She grabs the dagger from his belt and threatens to dispatch first him and then herself. Carlo calls for his followers, a secret panel opens; and there before him stands Ernani. Duets which end as trios are not so uncommon in Italian opera, but Verdi's treatment of this one is quite out of the ordinary. First there is a verse for Don Carlo in measured, declamatory style, each phrase in dialogue with the orchestra. This type of verse half-way between recitative and formal aria-movement is to serve Verdi very often in the future in some of his strongest situations. (Precedents abound in Donizetti, but rarely with the orchestra playing so bluntly assertive a role as here (see Ex. 72, facing page)).

But in the final phrase Carlo's patience gives way and the tempo accelerates into that of the stretta which begins as though launched from a catapult, with Ernani and Elvira defying Carlo in unison. Verdi is to make powerful use of this effect in *Il Trovatore*. The typical stretta rhythm is filled with an energy which here and there topples over into brashness, and what Verdi's contemporaries called 'abuse of syncopation' (see Ex. 7).

Here Piave has switched from Hugo's Act I to Act II with unfortunate results for Ernani, since it allows Carlo to take command of a situation in which both men are on equal terms. In Act I of the play the king is ready enough to fight. The lofty scorn which he exhibits here belongs to the later context where the bandit's men have surrounded his own. Ernani, stung by his contemptuous refusal to engage, tells Carlo the reasons for his mortal hatred in lines almost as concise in their

72

violence as Hugo's. But in the opera they go for nothing, because Elvira is simultaneously threatening to kill herself with Carlo's dagger unless the two men behave themselves. Once again the opportunity of establishing Ernani as more than a thwarted lover has been lost.

No sooner has the stretta reached a noisy conclusion with Elvira on a high C above the stave than Ruy Gomez de Silva enters and the action returns to Hugo's Act I. Hugo describes Silva as an elderly grandee with white hair and beard and dressed in black. In his short solo (*Infelice, e tuo credevi*) there is no attempt to retain those lines of Hugo's Silva which had so impressed Verdi as being suitable for Superchi. Instead the old man enters unannounced, sings a few lines of recitative expressing horror at finding two young men in his bride's apartment, summons his household to witness the disgrace; then he delivers a cantabile of self-pity from the footlights. Here Verdi reverts to the simple design (a^1 a^2 b a^3) but adds an ample coda in which cellos, woodwind and trumpets join the voice-part as if in compassion. In the opening phrase the shape of the rising sixth is present again; but in contrast to Ernani's confident leap, Silva's line drags itself almost painfully to its high note.

73

The action is now swiftly resumed. Silva turns to Carlo and Ernani and asks them to follow him. Old as he is he will avenge the honour of his house. Carlo and Ernani are protesting when Don Riccardo, the King's Esquire, is announced by Don Iago, chamberlain of Silva's household. 'So much the better,' cries Silva, 'he shall be witness of my revenge.' But Don Riccardo on entering uncovers and bows respectfully to Carlo with the words, 'All homage and fealty to the King of Spain!' so providing the cue for the adagio of the finale.

The concerted finale is laid out on an ample scale, well suited to a scene which has already had a miniature finale in the stretta of the trio. The adagio contains three distinct ideas, the first two being strongly contrasted. Structurally it is as though the sextet from *Lucia* had been amplified by adding to it the concertato adagio from Act I of *Le Comte Ory*—a measure of the new sense of scale Verdi was bringing into Italian operatic finales.* The surprise of Carlo's identity, elaborated into a massive E flat cadence, is followed by an unaccompanied settimino with chorus, hushed but with sudden outbursts. Here it is Don Carlo who dominates, detached from the main ensemble. It is very much a Rossinian 'moment of calm' with Don Carlo pointing Figaro-like at Silva's Dottor Bartolo: 'See how this good old man sheds all trace of his anger.' It is the only point where he shows any hint of the original Carlo's humour. With the entry of the orchestra, the movement takes on a more romantic tone. The principal melody is now with Ernani, Elvira providing a rudimentary descant; both parts are doubled by clarinets which give a creamy flavour to the ensemble. Towards the end Silva and Carlo in unison introduce a new melodic figure:

74

La pre-sen - za

which is tossed from one pair of singers to the next until brought to a glorious climax by Elvira and Ernani on a high B flat. Throughout the part-writing is remarkably skilful and clear; but as usual the sentiments are rendered obscure by the ensemble. Briefly, Ernani and Elvira are comforting one another, he with promises of rescue, she with assurances of eternal constancy; Carlo is still commenting on Silva's changed mood; and Silva is all mortification at having suspected his liege lord of dishonourable conduct.

His first action after the adagio is to kneel before Carlo asking his forgiveness. This Carlo readily grants. He explains the reason for his visit in a verse which neatly anticipates the rhythm of the stretta. His grandfather the Emperor Maximilian has died; and as candidate for the succession he has come to beg the support of one whose family had been known for their loyalty to the crown. Silva is overwhelmed. 'With your permission,' Carlo continues, 'we will spend this night in your palace.' Ernani and Elvira are appalled; but Carlo whispers to Ernani, 'I will save you,' and in the same breath he says to Silva, 'This follower of mine

* The later works of Mercadante (i.e. those written from 1838 onwards) were an important influence here. Both *Il Giuramento* and *Il Bravo* were favourites with Verdi.

will leave immediately.' 'A follower indeed,' murmurs Ernani grimly, 'one who will follow you to your death.' Here is the corresponding passage in Hugo (I, iv):

SILVA   Qu'est-ce seigneur?

CARLOS   Il part. C'est quelqu'un de ma suite.

                                   (*exeunt*)

ERNANI (*seul*) Oui, de ta suite, o roi! de ta suite—J'en suis!
           Nuit et jour, en effet, pas à pas, je te suis.
           Un poignard à la main, l'oeil fixé sur ta trace
           Je vais. Ma race en moi poursuit en toi ta race.

It is a long speech and brings down the curtain of Hugo's act with Hernani firmly in the foreground, a romantic, almost Hagen-like figure. But its effect depends upon his being alone, which is out of the question here since the adagio of the finale concertato needs a stretta to balance it. Also because of the presence of the others Ernani cannot go on at such length. Then too the pun on *suite* is poorly rendered in Italian (Piave uses the word *fido*). Yet despite all this, Hugo's speech has inspired one of the best strettas in early Verdi. Ernani's twelve-bar verse in march rhythm (*Io tuo fido? Il sarò a tutte l'ore*) is full of menace and latent power, in no way diminished when Elvira takes it up immediately afterwards. It is followed by the main stretta section which takes the form of a crescendo unambiguously major where the verse had alternated between the two modes. The crescendo is strictly in Verdi's, not Rossini's, style without tremolando violins. What makes it particularly exciting are the triplets alternating on horns and trumpets between the main beats. Here verbal confusion is at its height since every character is singing something different—even poor Giovanna, who has not caught up with events at all, and is wondering why Elvira is not happier about her wedding arrangements. Silva is protesting his devotion to the king; Carlo is talking of the delights of empire. Everyone but Elvira has forgotten all about Ernani.

ACT II

The Guest

A great hall in the castle of Don Ruy Gomez de Silva. The walls are hung with portraits of Silva's ancestors.

Hugo's title for this act had been 'Le Vieillard'. Piave's is more comprehensive, taking into account that 'L'Ospite' in Italian can mean both guest and host, and so is even more appropriate to the story of Hugo's Act III which it follows in all essentials. In the original this act contains more waste matter than any of the other four—endless self-recrimination from Hernani, Silva's preposterous display of his picture gallery, Doña Sol's unfortunate line 'Vous êtes mon lion superbe et généreux' which the original actress nearly refused to speak. All these Piave rightly throws out, while preserving most of the key lines of the play. He begins in operatic style with a chorus (*Esultiamo*) celebrating in polka rhythm the approaching nuptials between Silva and Elvira. The trite melody that Verdi shares out between orchestra and banda were better passed over if it were not for one curious feature.

The opening phrase seems to contain one half-bar too many, *but only at its first appearance.*

75

True, Verdi was not usually careless; but in a number as banal as this one it is not difficult to believe that Homer was nodding. As the guests disperse to another room, Don Iago announces a pilgrim who has come to the castle begging for shelter. Silva, to whom the laws of hospitality are sacred, gives orders for his admittance. The pilgrim enters, and in a familiar tenor voice wishes him all peace and happiness. Silva invites him to his forthcoming marriage. At that moment one of the side doors is opened, letting in an unpleasant draught of banda music (though played by the orchestra), and Elvira comes in dressed in all her finery. The effect on the 'pilgrim' is extraordinary. Flinging off his cloak he cries out that he has brought her a wedding gift—the price on his own head.

What follows is a piece of long-welded construction such as Verdi aimed at whenever the dramatic situation allowed: a two-movement trio with a two-movement duet between andante and stretta. Again one is struck by the extraordinary homogeneity of the score. The andante of the terzetto (*Oro, quant'oro ogn' avido*) is cast in 3/4–9/8 rhythm which harks back to the soprano cavatina and forward to the final trio of the opera. Even Ernani's opening phrase presents a tortured version of the rising-sixth motif.

76

There is also a parallel with the tenor cavatina in the central modulation to C minor and E flat major. Elvira introduces a contrasting idea as she despairs of her lover's life, while Silva remarks that his guest seems to have lost his wits. The situation is pointed up by the fact that while Elvira is doubled by high woodwind violins, Silva by trumpet and bassoon, Ernani's voice alone remains unfortified. The andante concluded, Silva goes out followed by his retainers to see that the defences of the castle are manned. He has not recognized Ernani from the previous act, and even if he had done so his bizarre code of honour would require him to act no differently. The ladies precede Elvira to her apartments, but she remains behind with Ernani. The tension between them is conveyed by a dark orchestral crescendo beneath which the timpani roll unceasingly. Then Ernani bursts out, 'Tu perfida,' and they launch into a dialogue duet-movement, their voices doubling the orchestral melody wherever possible. The movement reaches a climax as Elvira produces Carlo's dagger with which she means to kill herself on her bridal night, whereupon the tempo slackens abruptly. Ernani's anger vanishes; but instead of indulging like Hugo's hero in pages of remorse he merely protests his undying love. She falls into his arms with a sublime phrase which loses none of its distinction for being thundered out on the full orchestra. Could Verdi have known then that it was with single phrases such as these that he was eventually to replace both the stretta and the cabaletta?

77

There follows an andantino for the reconciled lovers scored in chamber-music style for flute, clarinet and oboe only, later joined by harp and pizzicato basses. Extremely simple throughout, the movement has a poetry and freshness recalling Weber. It contains two ideas: the first in G major with the voices singing in sixths and thirds throughout; the second, more cursive, in G minor made up of long, intertwining phrases which culminate in a repetition of *Caro accento* (Ex. 77) remoulded into the prevailing 9/8 rhythm. Finally the voices die away in a coda of harp and woodwind filigree.

At this point Silva returns to find his guest and his bride locked in an embrace. He has barely time to exclaim in fury before Don Iago announces that the King is at the gates. 'Let him be the instrument of your revenge,' cries Ernani; but Silva has other plans. In a trio/stretta similar in all but its opening to that in Act I, he tells Ernani that he will take his revenge in person. Silva's anger, be it noted, is expressed very differently from Carlo's in a line which remains relatively fixed.

78

With his sure feeling for logic Verdi reflects the repeated notes in Ernani's and Elvira's unison reply, couched as one would expect in the major. The lovers are prepared to welcome death together; but this is no part of Silva's intentions. He opens a secret panel behind the portrait of himself, and hustles Ernani inside.

Like the previous trio/stretta this forms a kind of intermediate finale to the act; so much so that Verdi does not think it necessary to make a key transition to the next movement, which begins a tone higher. A brief march-like melody heralds the entry of Carlo with his followers. He is in no friendly mood. Why, he wants to know, has Silva fortified his palace in this manner? Why did he find the draw-bridge raised? Is this a feudal rebellion? If so he will know how to suppress it. In vain Silva protests his loyalty. Carlo has it on sure authority that the bandit chief Ernani was seen to have taken refuge in the castle. Silva admits that he is sheltering a pilgrim whom the laws of hospitality forbid him to betray. 'Would you betray your king, then?' asks Carlo passionately. 'Silva does not betray,' is the answer. Carlo then requires him to give up his sword to the chamberlain Riccardo, while he himself has the house searched. 'The castle will prove as loyal as its master,' murmurs the old man. All this has taken place to one of the longest stretches of recitative in the opera. In compensation the music moves to the end of the act in an almost unbroken succession of musical numbers, short and interlocked as is often Verdi's way. The duet between Carlo and Silva (*Lo vedremo, veglio audace!*) is a wonderful illustration of Verdian 'confrontation', the clash of vocal archetypes. It is a 'dissimilar' duet, like the one between Carlo and Elvira in the previous act; only this time it is Carlo who is accompanied by the indignation pattern (see Ex. 71 (b)).★ His vocal line leaps and bounces, edged from time to time with trumpet. Silva's by contrast moves slowly and reluctantly, by never more than a degree at a time. It is the classic instance of baritone versus bass.

79

The moral victory remains with Silva as he answers Carlo's threats with the utmost dignity. Don Carlo's men return. In a unison chorus (*Fu esplorata del castello*) whose 'bassy' character has been emphasized by doubling the tune with bassoon and cimbasso, they tell him that they have made the most thorough search of the palace and have found nothing. Carlo threatens torture; but at this Elvira enters in lyrical agitation begging the king to have mercy. At the sight of her he softens. He will spare Silva if he can take Elvira with him as a hostage. Silva's mortal anguish is expressed in an outburst from full orchestra with an effective bunching of lower brass. Falling on his knees he implores Carlo not to take from him the sole delight of his declining years in a characteristic melody which makes a feature of repeated notes (*Io l'amo, al vecchio misero*, Ex. 80).† 'Well, then, give me Ernani,' says the king; and after a dramatically inadequate pause of two beats, Silva replies in effect, 'Take her away then; I will never betray my faith.' The scene ends with what is in

★ The term 'duet' is here, strictly speaking, a misnomer. The movement is in reality an 'aria con pertichini' (i.e. small interventions from another singer) for Carlo, and is so entitled in the vocal score.

† The strong resemblance of his melody (apart from its mode) to 'Fur le nozze a lei funeste' (*Lucia di Lammermoor*, Act III) has been noted more than once. E.g., Roncaglia, *L'Ascensione creatrice di Giuseppe Verdi*, p. 64; Gerigk, p. 39.

design a cabaletta with chorus for Carlo (*Vieni meco, sol di rose*, Ex. 81), as he takes Elvira's hand and addresses her passionately. In relation to Hugo's drama this is of course nonsense. Carlo has no intention at this point of revealing his love for Doña Sol to all and sundry. The movement is a concession partly to musical form, partly to a beautiful baritone voice. The structure required a piece of importance here to which the preceding formally incomplete movements could lead up. The solution, however unlikely its text, does at least convey the ambivalence of Carlo's character. For while the melody itself is full of charm, there is menace in the minor key ritornello with its Rossinian crescendo. Note too how the repeated Ds, sung in a light semi-staccato, balance the weary stresses of Silva's previous repeated A flats.

80

81

The stage gradually empties, and Silva is left alone with his ancestors and in a mood of black fury. His line of recitative over tremolo strings and trombones conveys the essence of Hugo's impressively restrained couplet:

> Roi, pendant que tu sors joyeux de ma demeure
> Ma vieille loyauté sort de mon cœur qui pleure.

But before he can proceed against Carlo, Silva still has an account to settle with Ernani. Their conversation proceeds in a duet-movement of short exchanges, a musical stychomythia in which the orchestra takes an increasing part. Silva has produced two swords and insists on a duel. Ernani has no intention of fighting an old man, though he admits Silva's right to kill him if he chooses—just so long as he can see Elvira once before he dies. When Silva tells him what has happened he bursts out with the truth that his host might reasonably have begun to suspect for himself: the king is their rival in love. There now leaps into prominence one of those orchestral figures common in early Verdi which are flashy and trivial in themselves but which increase the dramatic tension with their busyness (Ex. 82).

As Silva summons his vassals, Ernani offers to assist him in wreaking vengeance on the king. After that, he says, Silva may kill him if he wishes; and it is then that he makes the fatal promise, set unforgettably in the music and quoted in the prelude with slightly altered scoring due to the difference of pitch (Ex. 67). Ernani offers Silva his hunting-horn in pledge of his good faith. Silva has only to sound it

82

in Ernani's hearing, and Ernani will give up his life. The two men then swear an oath (*Iddio n'ascolti, e vindice*) to a formal verse of no great musical importance. Then to a development of Ex. 82 the household gathers, and all join in a massive ensemble of vengeance (*In arcion! in arcion! cavalieri*), similar to Arvino's scene in the third act of *I Lombardi*, with an additional element of feline stealth and suppleness, traceable to the contours of the opening melody.

83

This is evolved into a Verdian crescendo of abrupt gestures with side-drum beating out the melodic rhythm.

Through all this act Ernani may well seem to have played an inexplicably passive role. The reason is to be found in the act which Piave has largely omitted, and which contains one of the turning-points of the drama. Carlo has come prepared to abduct Doña Sol, with a small bodyguard. But while he is trying to force her to fly with him his men are captured by the bandits and he himself is confronted and challenged to a duel by Hernani. It is beneath Carlo's dignity to fight a bandit (in the previous act he had been unaware of his rival's identity), and he in turn challenges Hernani to murder his king in cold blood. Hernani counters by allowing Carlo to escape, lending him his cloak for the purpose. All this he does in a spirit not of Christian charity but of Castilian pride. The Greeks had a word for it; and the word is *hybris*—the excess that the gods punish in their own good time. From now on Hernani is a prisoner of his own code of honour. He accepts the hospitality of his rival Silva in order to continue his vendetta against the king. His feelings for the moment get the better of him, and he finds himself abusing the laws of hospitality by making love to his host's bride. According to the very laws by which he himself lives, his life is now forfeit to the man whom he has wronged; and from the moment of his discovery by Silva he hopes for nothing better than death. This same code prevents him even from accepting Silva's challenge to a duel.

ACT III

The Pardon

(Hugo: Le Tombeau)

The subterranean vault containing the tomb of Charlemagne at Aix-la-Chapelle.

The previous two acts have dealt entirely with the conflicts of individuals. Both run parallel in their situations, their conjunctions, their musical forms, even the cut of their melodies. But with the next act the opera opens out to wider horizons. Instead of the clash of personalities we have the sound of peoples on the move.

The act opens with a prelude for bass clarinet accompanied by two ordinary clarinets and bassoons—a masterly piece of tone-painting which foreshadows the start of the 'Miserere' scene from *Il Trovatore*. Even the melody, with its serpentine coils, carries an unusually heavy harmonic charge for early Verdi.

84

As it dies out on a low C Don Carlo enters with Riccardo. The vault, they understand, is to see the gathering of a conspiracy to murder Don Carlo on the very day when he is standing for election as Holy Roman Emperor. He dismisses Riccardo after telling him to have three cannon shots fired, if he himself should be elected; then the Electors must proceed to the vault, where the conspirators will have been unmasked. The clarinets and bassoons which have coloured the preceding recitative now give way to the brass choir as Carlo turns and apostrophizes the tomb of Charlemagne. Italian opera has no way of reproducing a speech of some two hundred Alexandrines such as Hugo here puts into the mouth of Carlo. It is of course the great speech of the play, in which he seems to weigh in his soul the world's glories and vanities. Verdi must make do with a brass-supported recitative, and an andante scored in chamber-music style (*Oh de' verd'anni miei*). Three cellos pizzicati and a double bass with its A string lowered a semitone set the rhythm, between whose beats another cello weaves a pattern of arabesques; full orchestra is not brought in until the nineteenth bar, where the opening phrase in its 'a^3' form is extended to make way for another, much nobler one which accompanies the 'punch line' of the text: 'e vincitor de' secoli il nome mio farò'. Here the doubling violins, the cello pizzicato semiquavers all emphasize the ungrammatical progression yet without detracting from the dignity of the theme itself (Ex. 85, overleaf).

There is no vocal cadenza for once, but—far more effectively—an extension of Ex. 85 into a delicate instrumental postlude. Carlo swiftly hides in Charlemagne's

85

tomb as the conspirators begin to pour into the vault. Ever since the second act of *Guillaume Tell* Italian composers have never lacked a model for conspiracy scenes. Verdi has made good use of it as regards the distribution of voices and orchestra while remaining quite individual in his melodic ideas and his scoring. The entire scene moves with sure-footed ease, from the first stealthily probing motif as the password (*Per angusta—Ad augusta*) is exchanged:

86

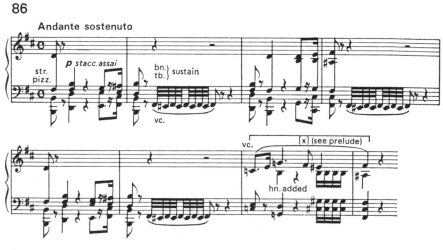

to the sinister suavity of the tune to which the conspirators unfold their plans. The lower instruments are used with particularly good effect throughout.

87

Foremost among them is of course Silva, and with him Ernani and Don Iago. They decide to draw lots for Carlo's murderer (here the music recalls Ex. 86 but with a chromatic scale for flute, oboe and bassoon in place of the warning dominant for bassoon, trombone and cellos). The lot falls on Ernani. Once again he has a chance to escape. Silva asks him to give up to himself the right of assassination; and once again Ernani is too proud to grant his wish. Thwarted, Silva is more resolved than ever to claim his share of the fatal bargain. 'A horrible death awaits you,' he tells Ernani, just as the chorus embark on a crescendo which will lead them to one of those unison hymns so loved by patriotic audiences of the time. *Si ridesti il leon di Castiglia* ('Let the Lion of Castile awake') belongs to the same genre as 'Va pensiero' and 'O Signore dal tetto natio' only it is more rousing than either. It is a battle hymn of the Venetian republic for those who mentally substitute the Lion of St Mark for the Lion of Castile. For the recurrence of the main theme Verdi has as usual increased the instrumentation and the rhythm of the accompaniment. Trumpets and trombones double the voices; the rest of the orchestra raps away peremptorily. For sheer crude force this passage has few parallels even in Verdi (Ex. 88).

But all their fine words are in vain; for at that moment the sound of a cannon is heard three times, and Carlo steps out of the tomb. For an instant the conspirators imagine that he is the ghost of Charlemagne; but he corrects them in a thundering voice: 'Charles V, you traitors!' At his words six trumpets are heard in a fanfare behind the scene as Don Riccardo, the Electors, their suites, and Donna Elvira enter the vault. Carlo orders the arrest of the conspirators. Only those who are dukes and counts are to be beheaded; the rest are to be sent to the dungeons (in Hugo they are to be set free). Ernani claims his right to the scaffold in a double-quatrain whose declamatory force and symmetrical setting reflect the stiff-necked pride of the Castilian. But there is no question of symmetry in Elvira's parallel verse (*Ah signor se t'è concesso*), a long lyrical outpouring which exploits the full range of the soprano voice. The melodic line goes on until it has exhausted its full charge of emotion. At her impassioned plea for mercy Carlo pauses. Again he turns to the tomb of Charlemagne, to apostrophize the dead Emperor in a piece well known to collectors of vintage gramophone records (*Oh sommo Carlo*) (Ex. 89).

Strings take over as he turns to the assembly once more and in tones as unsensational as those of Hugo's Carlos he pronounces a general amnesty. Ernani and Elvira are

88

89

to be united in marriage. 'All glory to Charlemagne!' And the chorus come to
life in a magnificent outburst—full orchestra and percussion with cymbals and
bass drum—as they cry, 'All honour and glory to Charles V!' The manner in
which the massive tuttis are worked in and contrasted with fragments of Carlo's

melody is something new; so too is the tactful transition to the admittedly less distinguished F major melody. Here at least there is a valid dramatic reason for the change. So Act III ends in a blaze of glory and happiness barely disturbed by the vengeful mutterings of Silva.

It is of course opera, not drama; and one can sympathize with Hugo's anger at the elimination of one of his most telling strokes. The original Hernani proudly recites the full list of his titles as he claims the right to be put to death. To Doña Sol's plea for mercy Carlo replies:

> Allons relevez-vous, duchesse de Segorbe
> Comtesse Albatera, marquise de Monroy

> (à Hernani)
> —Tes autres noms, Don Juan?*

Italian *melodramma* cannot jump ahead of its audiences in this way.

ACT IV

The Mask

(Hugo: La Noce)
A terrace in the palace of Don Juan of Aragon in Saragossa

The last act of *Ernani* consists of three elements only—a dance, a recitative and a final trio. Of the four leading characters of the drama one, Carlo, has left the arena. His moment of magnanimity, which has raised him far above either of his rivals, has formed the second turning-point of the action; but it has happened too late to affect the lives of the other characters. It only remains for Ernani to succumb to his private nemesis, for Elvira to follow him, and for Silva to plunge even deeper into a hell of his own seeking.

The act opens with a long stretch of banda music, of better quality however than that in Act II, even if unrelieved by orchestral intervention. The bolero-like melody trips along with unusual grace. It is part dance and part wedding song; hence the snatch of unaccompanied chorus (*O come felice*). But among the maskers is one in a black domino who seems to glide about like a malignant ghost. The others comment on his appearance, and the eyes beneath the mask that seem to mirror the fires of hell; and for once Verdi makes sure that these remarks are heard by holding up the flow of banda music, except for a few phrases here and there. The man in the domino disappears and the gay dance music is resumed in full. The stage gradually empties; and then Ernani—or Don Juan of Aragon as we should now call him— leads in his bride. As they gaze to the stars we hear the main theme of the prelude (Ex. 68) first given out on flute and oboe, then taken up by Ernani in what promises to be a full andante (*Vedi come gli astri stessi*). But Elvira magically interrupts the first cadence recalling the time when from Silva's castle she used to gaze at the same stars as she waited for Ernani. Now they will be together to all eternity; and the voices join in a unison climax (*Fin al sospiro estremo*) foreshadowing in its effect the equally illusory joy of hero and heroine in Act III of *Tosca*. As they come to rest

---

* *Hernani*, IV, iv.

on the final cadence the sound of a distant horn is heard. Ernani bursts out in a bitter curse—not loud enough, however, for Elvira to have heard; for her the next phrase breathes nothing but serene tenderness. Once again the final note is mocked by the horn, now coming closer. Ernani cries out, 'It is the tiger seeking his prey,' and to Elvira's horror he babbles about an old man's hellish leer among the shadows. Three more blasts on the horn—and Ernani seems to recover his self-possession, though the orchestra here and there betrays his hysteria. He tells Elvira that an old wound is troubling him; she must bring a healing lotion. There is a brief orchestral descrescendo, suggesting both Elvira's departure and Ernani's subsiding excitement. Left alone he is almost inclined to believe that it was all an illusion. He makes to go; whereupon the form of Silva looms up out of the darkness. To the sound of Ex. 67—more menacing than ever before in B minor sung by a bass voice—he reminds Ernani of his solemn oath. Will he after all break his word? Now that Elvira is at last truly his, Ernani for the first time is tempted to put love before honour. He replies to Silva with a double stanza (*Solingo, errante, misero*)— allegro assai moderato in C minor with a pathetic change to A flat major half-way through. Here is the rising-sixth motif in its most tragic guise:

90

Cannot the day of reckoning be put off a little? All his life he has been a fugitive, an outcast. Now that the cup of happiness is at his lips may he not be allowed to drain it? 'Here is your cup,' Silva snarls, holding out in one hand a dagger, in the other a phial of poison. The rhythm tautens without fundamentally altering as Ernani first refuses Silva's challenge. Then, taunted with cowardice and lack of honour, he is about to take the dagger when Elvira rushes in and hurls herself between the two men, her voice ringing high above the orchestral clatter with a sustained A (see Ex. 10).

She then begins what is the principal movement of the final trio (*Ferma, crudele, estinguere*). It is certainly a remarkable piece—the essence of early Verdi. This is not an unqualified compliment. For its length, which is considerable, it is constructed very primitively, scored in poster-like colours and crammed with cliché. Its strength lies in its consistency, its sureness of purpose and a simple but effective key-scheme which rings the changes on D minor, F major and D major. Elvira, cursing her uncle for a 'demon of Avernus' leads off her verse in D minor, moves into F and then returns. Just as she is about to stab Silva she has a change of heart, which is reflected in a switch to the tonic major (*Ma che diss'io? perdonami*), so producing the secondary pleading theme of the trio.

91

Interlocked with it is Silva's harsh reply (*È vano o donna il piangere è vano*), which is the trio's main subject. Elvira leads the music into A major with her protests of

92

(tutti on 1st beat)
w.w.

E va - no, o don-na, il pian-ge - re, è va - no,

love for Ernani; but Silva brings it back firmly to the tonic as he insists on Ernani's death. Elvira expresses her grief in a phrase which plunges downward from D minor, through F and back to D minor. Then Ernani in D major once more enters with a new tenorish theme which draws a 3/4 line across the prevailing 9/8 (*Quel pianto Elvira ascondimi*). Together he and Elvira again move towards the dominant from which point they approach Ex. 91. This is again answered inexorably by Ex. 92; but for its last two repetitions Verdi emphasizes the D major–F major polarity with what is in effect a hemiola—one bar of three slower beats in place of two bars in the basic pulse (Ex. 93, overleaf).

Throughout the trio instruments are used singly or together to bring out the individual colour of the voices; the oboe in particular giving an edge to Ernani's agony. 'The best piece in the opera?' Well, it would hardly bear taking out of its context. Yet the very relentlessness of the 9/8 rhythm helps to concentrate the drama and set in high relief the clash of the characters.

Again Silva reminds Ernani of his promise (Ex. 67); and unlike his counterpart in the play Ernani chooses not the poison, which has been tasted before him by Doña Sol, but Silva's dagger. Elvira tries to take it from him, but Silva holds her back. Ernani stabs himself; and there is a moment of silence broken only by the rolling of timpani and bass drum. High tremolo violins prepare us, as they will often do in the future, for the words of a dying man. The melody is evolved entirely from the Tosca-like phrase heard earlier on (*Fino al sospiro estremo*), into the scoring of which Verdi has by a happy inspiration brought the bass clarinet. There is a sonorous brass-filled climax, and Elvira falls fainting on the body of her lover, while Silva gloats in vengeful triumph. Melodramatic it may be, but it is less so than Hugo's original in which Hernani and Doña Sol die of a painful poison and Silva stabs himself.

VIENNA, *spring 1844(?)*—MILAN, *autumn 1844*. At one or other of these productions was first added Silva's cabaletta *Infin che un brando vindice*. A certain air of mystery surrounds it. Its earliest musical appearance is in a vocal score of *Ernani* issued as No. 9 in the series 'Standard Lyric Drama', published by Boosey in 1851, with an editorial note to the effect that it was not part of the original score. Ricordi first printed it in their 'Edizione Popolare,' *ca.* 1870. But its text can be found in a libretto published for a performance at La Scala, Milan, in the autumn of 1844. The reason for its inclusion is clear enough. *Ernani* as has been said was conceived as an opera for soprano, tenor and baritone principals with a large part for comprimario bass. When the great basso profondo Derivis, who had created Zaccaria, was engaged

93

for a performance at Genoa he aspired to the part of Carlo, much to Verdi's irritation when he heard about it. ('How will he manage to sing the delicate *Vieni meco sol di rose* with that great voice of his?' he said to Muzio.)★ Ignazio Marini, Verdi's first Oberto, chose more realistically to sing Silva, first in Vienna in April, later at La Scala in the autumn; but in token of his status as principal he had to be accommodated with a double aria.† The simplest way of doing this was to add a cabaletta of vengeance to the cantabile *Infelice*. Throughout the 1840s this cabaletta-text appears only in libretti published for performances in which Silva was sung by Marini. There is no autograph; and a slight doubt remains as

★ Letter from Muzio to Barezzi, 11.6.1844. Garibaldi, p. 165.
† As no one has yet found a libretto of the Vienna production with the cabaletta text included, we cannot be sure whether Marini sang it there also. But since the Viennese papers referred to a 'grand scene' for Marini it is probable that he did so.

to whether Verdi himself was the author. On the positive side is the fact that it appeared in scores of *Ernani* printed during the composer's lifetime without any objection from him. On tne other hand:

(1) Verdi was not personally associated with either of these revivals, so far as is known.

(2) A review of the Milan premiere in the *Gazzetta Musicale di Milano* of 8 September 1844 not only regrets the cabaletta but appears to hold Marini responsible for having introduced it.

(3) Ricordi's catalogue of 1855 advertised the piece separately as 'cabaletta eseguita da Marini', not, as one would expect, 'composta per Marini'.

(4) The coda of the cabaletta is musically identical with that of Nabucco's cabaletta in Act IV of the opera. Self-borrowing on that scale is without parallel in the rest of Verdi's output.

(5) It is clear from one of Muzio's letters that when *Ernani* was given at La Scala in the spring of 1845 for the first time under Verdi's supervision the opera had already been the subject of a rift between composer and both publisher and management.*

Happily, the mystery has at last been resolved by Roger Parker's recent discovery of an almost identical text in a libretto of *Oberto* printed for a revival in Barcelona in February 1842, in which Marini took part.† Clearly, then, it belonged to a new 'insert-aria', the rest of which is now lost, written by Verdi for that artist and therefore his exclusive property. In its new context it makes little sense; nor, significantly was it performed during a revival of *Ernani* in Verdi's presence at La Scala in 1881 with Edouard de Reszke in the role of Silva.

PARMA, *autumn 1844*. At Rossini's request, Verdi wrote a grand aria for the tenor Nicola Ivanoff who was making his first appearance in the title role.‡ Its point of insertion occurs in Act II after the oath in which Ernani puts his life and his services at the disposal of Silva; and it was doubtless intended to be sung in place of the duet with chorus which follows. Inevitably, dramatic values are completely overthrown. There is no attempt to maintain the momentum of the scene. In its context the aria must have sounded like a parody of stage-heroics even in the 1840s, though musically and technically it is not at all negligible. Don Iago enters to announce that Ernani's followers wish to speak with their leader. 'Father,' says Ernani, apostrophizing not Silva but his own murdered father, 'with these men at my side you shall be fearlessly avenged.' Fourteen bars of preparation lead to the andante (*Odi il voto, o grande Iddio*). This is a minor-major design, spacious and well proportioned, with a continuous pattern of violin semiquavers in the accompaniment, phrased and bowed in the minor, plucked in the major. The opening

---

* Letter from Muzio to Barezzi, 13.3.1845. Garibaldi, p. 188.

† R. Parker, '"Infin che un brando vindice" e le cavatine del primo atto di "Ernani"', *Bollettino dell'Istituto di studi verdiani*, no. 10 (1987), pp. 142–60.

‡ For this service the composer was paid 1,500 ducats. See letter to Rossini, 28.1.1845. *Carteggi verdiani*, II, p. 346. The autograph has recently been acquired by the Pierpoint Morgan Library, New York (Mary Flagler Cary Music Collection, MS. 205).

idea preserves the rising sixth that is so characteristic of the opera as a whole. Considered purely as a piece of writing for star tenor it is remarkably assured. The melting phrase that begins the C major quatrain, with pizzicato violins coloured by sustaining woodwind, is in the best tradition of tenor romanze.

During a brief transition featuring the unison chorus, Ernani commands his followers to renew their oath of allegiance. Then he launches a cabaletta of vengeance (*Sprezzo la vita ne più m'alletta*), so unusual in form and material as to be called experimental.

The central cadence is not V (E) but II (B); so that a longer passage than usual is needed to reach the reprise. The piece is unremittingly strenuous, with the chorus weighing in at every climax; and there is a certain roughness about it that sets it below the andante. But that is not unusual in the operas of this period.

Ernani has all the sureness and sense of purpose of *Nabucco*, fortified by an improved technique. From Hugo's play with its canvas of more than life-size figures Verdi distilled an 'Uroper' of emotional *scontro* like the *Trovatore* which it often foreshadows. Abbiati has called *Ernani* Verdi's inaugural lecture,★ rather aptly; for in this opera Verdi defines his basic terms of reference for the next few years. Even more than *Nabucco* it shows the crystallization of his musical personality. More important still, it was his first opera to qualify as a repertory piece for the international stage, as indeed it remained for more than half a century after it was written. Together with *Nabucco* it was the earliest to be heard in London in 1845

★ 'Prolusione accademica', Abbiati, I, p. 489.

at the Haymarket Theatre to which it returned with a regularity which attested its favour with the public. Inevitably it tended to arouse either enthusiasm or disgust. To Chorley of the *Athenaeum* it was an example of Verdi at his worst. In Vienna Nicolai did his best to prevent a performance of it, and would probably have succeeded if Donizetti had not stood valiantly by his countryman.* In Italy, at the time of the accession of the liberal Pius IX to the pontificate, patriotic choruses sang 'A Pio Nono sia gloria ed onor' to the final chorus of Act III.†
Later when Verdi had educated his audiences to a style less crudely immediate, *Ernani* still retained its place in the repertory if only because of its appeal to virtuoso singers. But by the early years of this century it had begun to fade out. Nowadays it stands high among the list of early Verdis that can be guaranteed to fill a theatre, even if its heroics strike a modern audience as mildly ridiculous.

Ernani was the first of Verdi's operas to be translated into English; and as an indication of how Verdi's musical personality impressed a perceptive but by no means uncritical music-lover, it is worth quoting from the translator's preface: 'That Verdi has made free use of other people's scores is past doubt. Here we have a scrap of accompaniment from Riccardo's first air in *I Puritani*;‡ there a recasting of the Terzetto from *Norma*§—anon a few bars of chorus from *Lucia*¶ to say nothing of the perpetual returns to the dozen other commonplaces which thrown into a Musical Kaleidoscope must come out in the shape of an imposing Italian opera as times go. But there is something beside, and better than mere quotation; a disposition to study new effects in the concerted music. . . . Signor Verdi's choruses are generally spirited. . . . A Grand Sextet at the end of the first part is admirable and new. The conspiracy scene too . . . is dramatic and effective. For new melody however the student may search in vain. . . . Signor Verdi's concerted music is far worthier and more individual than his arias and cavatinas.' So little in love does Mr Wrey Mould seem with his subject that one wonders why he undertook to translate the opera at all. Yet there is some truth in what he has to say. Like so many commentators he fails to distinguish between 'quotation' and the use of common stock. The essential individuality of Verdi's music shows itself not so much in details as in the whole.

Let us leave the last word to Bernard Shaw, for whom, despite his Wagnerian predilections, *Ernani* represented 'that ultra-classical product of Romanticism, the grandiose Italian opera in which the executive art consists in a splendid display of personal heroics, and the drama arises out of the simplest and most universal stimulants to them.' As for Carlos, 'In the play [he] is sublime in feeling, but somewhat tedious in expression. In the opera he is equally sublime in feeling, but concise, grand, and touching in expression, thereby proving that the chief glory of Victor Hugo as a stage poet was to have provided libretti for Verdi.'‖

* See Donizetti, letter to Giuseppina Appiani. Walker, pp. 111–12.
† See Muzio, letter to Barezzi, 13.8.1846. Garibaldi, pp. 258–9.
‡ A reference to the woodwind passages *Ernani*, *Ernani involami*.
§ The trio from Act II (Ex. 76).   ¶ See note on p. 158.
‖ *Shaw's Music*, II, pp. 724–5.

8 I DUE FOSCARI

I DUE FOSCARI

Opera in three acts
by
FRANCESCO MARIA PIAVE
(after Lord Byron's play, *The Two Foscari*)

*First performed at the
Teatro Argentina, Rome,
3 November 1844*

FRANCESCO FOSCARI,	PRIMO BARITONO	Achille De Bassini
JACOPO FOSCARI, his son	PRIMO TENORE	Giacomo Roppa
LUCREZIA CONTA-RINI, Jacopo's wife	PRIMA DONNA SOPRANO	Marianna Barbieri-Nini
JACOPO LOREDANO, member of the Council of Ten	BASSO COMPRIMARIO	Baldassare Miri
BARBARIGO, senator, member of the Giunta	SECONDO TENORE	Atanasio Pozzolini
PISANA, friend and confidante of Lucrezia	SECONDA DONNA	Giulia Ricci
OFFICER (Fante) of the Council of Ten	SECONDO TENORE	N.N.
SERVANT OF THE DOGE	SECONDO BASSO	N.N.

Members of the Council of Ten and the Giunta—
maidservants of Lucrezia—Venetian women,
people and masquers of both sexes

Walk-on parts: Chief of Police (Il Messer Grande)
Jacopo Foscari's two children—naval officers
(comandadori)—prison warders—gondoliers—
sailors—people—masquers—pages of the Doge

The action takes place in Venice

Epoch: 1457

By the time *Ernani* had begun its triumphal progress round the world Verdi found himself with so many commitments on hand as to require a more methodical habit of correspondence than he had employed hitherto. Hence the start in the spring of 1844 of the so-called *Copialettere*, consisting of file copies of important letters and memoranda, written out carefully in the composer's own hand. Here also we find a list of possible operatic subjects,* some of which he followed up, others not: *King Lear, Hamlet, The Tempest*; Byron's *Cain*; Hugo's *Le Roi s'amuse, Marion Delorme, Ruy Blas*; Grillparzer's *Die Ahnfrau*; Dumas père's *Kean*; Racine's *Phèdre*; *A secreto agravio secreta venganza* by Calderón, *Maria Giovanna* by Dennery, Chateaubriand's *Atala* and a few others by authors not named. All this was with an eye to the future. The immediate problem was to find an opera suitable to the Teatro Argentina in Rome, for whose winter season Verdi had been commissioned to provide the opera di obbligo with Piave. His first idea was to compose a *Lorenzino de' Medici*. He wrote to Piave asking him to resume work on the synopsis and to have it approved by the Roman authorities as soon as possible. 'But,' he added, 'just in case the police don't allow it we'll have to think of a quick alternative and I suggest *The Two Foscari*. I like the plot and the outline is already there in Venice; I sent it to the Presidenza, from whom I beg you to retrieve it. If you want to make some alterations to the synopsis do so but stick closely to Byron....'†
The Roman police did object to Lorenzino, as to all tyrannicides; so *I Due Foscari* it was.

'Everything about Venice is extraordinary—her aspect is like a dream, and her history is a romance.' So wrote Byron in the preface to the first and better of his two Venetian plays, *Marino Faliero*. But it was not the gay, sensual Venice, the carnival city of Hoffmann and Schumann, that caught his imagination, but the secret, mysterious Venice of Hugo's *Angélo*. It was the Venice of hidden cruelties, the seat of a vast maritime empire and the most repressive oligarchy in modern Europe, a city whose secrets are as deep as the ocean which symbolically she weds each year. He could identify this oligarchy with the English aristocratic society which, in a sense, had cast him out. Both his heroes—Faliero and Jacopo Foscari—are men who have set themselves against their peers. Of the two, Faliero conforms more strictly to the Aristotelian definition of a tragic hero; he is therefore a more interesting figure, and *Marino Faliero* a better play. (Doubtless Verdi might have considered it for an opera if Donizetti had not already forestalled him.) Jacopo Foscari is a noble victim and nothing more. Here Byron's self pity seems to have got the better of him. It is clearly not Venice to which the young Foscari refers when he talks about:

> That malady
> Which calls up green and native fields to view

---

* *Copialettere*, plate XI (facsimile). Modern scholarship, however, assigns this list to 1849. See Conati, pp. 256–7.
† Letter to Piave, 18.4.1844. Abbiati, I, p. 513.

> From the rough deep, with such identity
> To the poor exile's fever'd eye that he
> Can scarcely be restrain'd from treading them. . . .*

Venice has many beauties; but green fields are not amongst them.

As an opera *The Two Foscari* was obviously a dangerous subject for Venice. Marina, young Foscari's wife, gives an unflattering portrait of Europe's oldest republic:

> . . . keep those
> Maxims for your mass of scared mechanics
> Your merchants, your Dalmatians and Greek slaves,
> Your tributaries, your dumb citizens
> And mask'd nobility, your sbirri and
> Your spies, your galley and your other slaves
> To whom your midnight carryings off and drownings,
> Your dungeons next the palace roofs or under
> The water's level; your mysterious meetings,
> And unknown dooms, and sudden executions
> Your 'Bridge of Sighs', your strangling chamber, and
> Your torturing instruments have made ye seem
> The beings of another and worse world . . .†

She describes the Decemvirs and the Council of Forty:

> The old human fiends
> With one foot in the grave, with dim eyes, strange
> To tears save drops of dotage, with long white
> And scanty hairs, and shaking hands, and heads
> As palsied as their hearts are hard, they counsel
> And cabal and put men's lives out, as if life
> Were no more than the feelings long extinguished
> In their accursed bosoms . . .‡

No wonder Count Mocenigo of the Fenice had felt uneasy; and it was with the susceptibilities of his fellow-citizens in mind, so Abbiati tells us, that Piave had prepared a long antefatto to be printed along with the libretto. The main part of it runs as follows:

On 15 April 1423 Francesco Foscari was raised to the ducal throne of Venice, having successfully competed against Pietro Loredano. The latter, however, ceaselessly opposed his policies to such an extent that one day in a fit of impatience Foscari declared openly in the Senate that he could not consider himself truly Doge of Venice so long as Pietro Loredano was alive. By a fatal coincidence a few months later Pietro and his brother Marco died suddenly—from poison, it was said. So at least Jacopo Loredano believed and he had it inscribed on their tomb; and in his private business records he noted the names of the Foscari as his debtors for two lives for which he was patiently awaiting a settlement. Many years later on 5 November 1450 occurred the

*Byron, *The Two Foscari*, III, i. †*Ibid.*, II, i. ‡*Ibid.*

murder of Ermolao Donato, chief of the Decemvirs who had sentenced to exile the Doge's son Jacopo, husband of Lucrezia Contarini, for having accepted bribes from foreign rulers. The night before, Jacopo and his servant had been seen in Venice. For this they were both brought back to Venice, tortured and exiled to Crete. Five years later, having in vain sued for mercy, Jacopo Foscari felt unable to continue living unless he could see again his beloved fatherland; he wrote to the Duke of Milan, Duke Francesco Sforza, begging him to intercede on his behalf with the Venetian government. The letter fell into the hands of the Ten; Jacopo was again taken to Venice, and put to torture. He confessed to having written the letter but merely from a longing to see his country again even at the price of imprisonment.*

The five acts of Byron's play are concerned with the young Foscari's torture and confession, his final sentence of exile, his own death as he is led to the ship, and that of his father the Doge, whom the Council have forced to resign from his position. It is a monotonous, uneventful play pitched in a minor key throughout, and even Verdi on re-reading the synopsis realized that it would not be sufficient to 'keep close to Byron'. 'I notice,' he wrote to Piave, 'that the . . . play does not quite have the theatrical grandeur needed for an opera; so rack your brains and try to find something which will make a bit of a splash particularly in the first act.' In the same letter he writes: 'Take a good deal of trouble with it, because it's a fine subject, delicate and full of pathos.'†

Delicacy and pathos: these are the outstanding qualities of the opera. The characters are as sharply defined as those of *Ernani*, but so different as to reverse the normal Verdian hierarchy of vocal power: Jacopo Foscari, passively brave, romantically devoted to the city that has cast him out, a man who can face prison and torture more readily than exile; his father, an old man of eighty-four, a Venetian Captain Vere, determined to repress his own paternal feelings when they conflict with his duty to the state and her laws; Lucrezia, the wife (Marina in the play), to whom love of her husband means everything and her country's laws nothing; and, finally, Loredano, cold and implacable, not to be satisfied until the deaths of his father and uncle are wiped out by those of the two Foscari. Of these only the basso profondo (also a comprimario part, but a much smaller one) retains the character of his counterpart in *Ernani*. Tenor and baritone are both passive; and the vehicle of power is the soprano. But power in that raw, elemental form in which it appears in so many early operas of Verdi finds no place in *I Due Foscari*. After the prodigious discharge of energy in *Ernani*, it was natural that the next work should take on a milder, more intimate character. It becomes an opera of refinement, of consolidation; more streamlined in form and at the same time more fastidious, even recherché, in its invention. The pattern is to be repeated nine years later. After *Il Trovatore* with its pell-mell vitality comes the gentler, subtler *La Traviata*.

Indeed, when Piave's draft libretto arrived, Verdi felt that he had gone almost too far in that direction. Jacopo was in danger of seeming too weak—'I would give him to begin with a more forceful character,' the composer wrote to Piave.

* Abbiati, I, p. 523. For a translation of the complete antefatto see C. Osborne, *The Complete Operas of Verdi* (London, 1969), pp. 96–8.
† Letter to Piave (undated). Abbiati, I, p. 516.

'I wouldn't have him tortured, and after the tender address to Venice I would aim for something robust and that way we should make a fine aria.'* Accordingly the poet added the text of a cabaletta to the Act I romanza: but even this failed to satisfy Verdi.

> Two things are not quite right. The first is that Jacopo remains on stage at the end; and that always makes a bad effect. The second is that there is no contrast ['distacco di pensiero'] between the andante and the cabaletta. These are matters which are all right in poetry but all wrong in music. After the adagio have a little bit of dialogue between the Fante and Jacopo, then an officer to say, 'Escort the prisoner', after that a cabaletta but make it a powerful one because we're writing for Rome.†

So Piave changed the text; only to be told months later that he would have to change it again 'because the words "Io so ben" which are repeated twice keep reminding me of a comic aria by Donizetti, and I can't do anything with them'.‡ Few cabalettas gave Verdi so much trouble as this.

Having told Piave at the start to reduce Byron's five acts to three, Verdi originally intended Act II to end with Jacopo's departure and death. Piave's draft libretto however contained no such scene; and Verdi countered with the suggestion that it should begin the third act. 'I would start it with a scene representing the Piazzetta of San Marco with a chorus of men and women. Somewhere during this chorus you could have a gondolier far off in the lagoon singing a verse [*ottava*] of Tasso. Then let Jacopo enter accompanied by Marina, and make a really beautiful duet, etc.'§ From this and other letters on the same subject it is clear that all the ideas resulting in the opera's present arrangement originated with Verdi— Lucrezia's cavatina no less than Jacopo's, the Doge's solo, the duet-finale to Act I and the sequence of romanza, duetto, terzetto, quartetto, chorus and finale which make up Act II. Even the sunset at the beginning of Act III was his suggestion. The verse of Tasso however was not followed up; Rossini had, after all, cornered the market in distant gondolieri. For the rest Verdi repeated his usual injunctions ('Keep it short'—'Beware of long recitatives, particularly for Loredano and Barbarigo', etcetera).¶

Work on the opera proceeded smoothly throughout the summer of 1844, despite an occasional bout of ill health, a contralto who pestered Verdi to include a part for her in his new opera and a composer who tried to dissuade him from setting Byron's plot (he himself was writing an opera on the same subject and had

---

* Letter to Piave, 14.5.1844. Abbiati, I, p. 514.

† Letter to Piave, 22.5.1844. *Copialettere*, p. 426. Abbiati (I, p. 515) reads 'Roppa' for 'Roma'; later in the same letter where Verdi appears to recommend brevity in the duet finale to Act I he substitutes 'bello' for 'breve'. Whether or not these emendations are justified they certainly make better sense. Far from being short, the finale of the first act is one of the longest duets Verdi ever wrote. There is no evidence that the Roman public was more predisposed than any other towards forceful cabalettas. But Roppa was certainly a forceful tenor. Indeed it would not be the only time that this unfortunate artist has had his name misread. In a letter from Verdi to Mocenigo (26.7.1843), reproduced in M. Nordio *Verdi e la Fenice* (Venice, 1951), he appears as 'Raspa'. Abbiati (I, p. 471) gives the correct spelling.

‡ Letter to Piave, 9.9.1844. Abbiati, I, p. 521.

§ Letter to Piave, 14.5.1844. Abbiati, I, p. 514.   ¶ *Ibid.*

no wish to see it suffer the fate of Mazzucato's *Ernani*). So much we know from Emanuele Muzio, who had arrived in Milan in April to study with Verdi, and to play much the same role in his life as Ferdinand Ries in that of Beethoven—i.e., a non-paying pupil and general factotum.

The first night was not the success that Verdi had hoped for, though neither was it a failure. The audience were less favourably disposed than usual because the management had raised the price of the seats. Nor were the singers at their best. Yet at the end Verdi was called out seven times. Prince Don Alessandro Torlonia, the concessionaire of the theatre, gave a banquet in his honour, where Jacopo Ferretti, librettist of Rossini's *La Cenerentola* and a member of the Arcadians, paid him homage in a flowery ode. The critic of the *Rivista di Roma* was unreserved in his praise of *I Due Foscari*, maintaining that in it 'even more than in *Ernani* Verdi has endeavoured to shake off his former manner, to return to the springs of passion and affection. In this opera he wished to hark back to the pure and simple style of the Old Masters. . . .'*

Next year at Vienna Donizetti saw a season of Italian opera launched with *I Due Foscari* and *Ernani*. 'Was I not right to say that Verdi had talent,' he wrote to his friend Guglielmo Cottrau, 'even if *I Due Foscari* only shows him at his best in fits and starts?'† Verdi's own opinion was more equivocal. In his disappointment at the opening night he wrote to a Milanese friend, 'I had a great liking for this opera, perhaps I was wrong but before changing my mind I should like another opinion.'‡ And to Piave three years later: 'In subjects which are naturally gloomy if you're not careful you end up with a deadly bore—as for instance *I Due Foscari*, which has too unvarying a colour from beginning to end.'§

But Verdi's last thoughts on his operas were not always his fairest. He was one of those artists whose works give them little pleasure once they have been composed, and still less as time goes on. The composer of *Otello* and *Falstaff* could even say that his best 'opera' was the Home for Destitute Musicians in Milan. Revivals of his early works terrified him, as they terrified Rossini. Let them be given if they must as long as he had no part in it. Within a short time of its composition *I Due Foscari* had become an irrelevance, belonging to a musical past on which he had not the slightest wish to dwell. The fact is that it maintained a steady, unsensational popularity for many years. It was easy to mount, and therefore often in demand as an opera di ripiego.

Of the four operas composed since the ill-fated *Un Giorno di Regno*, it is by far the shortest, running to barely a hundred minutes. The same instrumental forces are used, including, momentarily, the banda, but more subtly and economically than usual. Wind instruments make a more individual contribution to the

---

* Quoted in Toye, p. 40.

† Letter to Cottrau, 26.2.1845. G. Zavadini, *Donizetti, Vita, Musica, Epistolario* (Bergamo, 1948), p. 797. For Donizetti's good opinion of Verdi see also the letter to Persico quoted by C. Gatti (1st edition, p. 240). 'Verdi has great genius. He lacks the imagination to find the right start of a number; but when he has it he goes ahead divinely.' The older master's enthusiasm and good-will over the Viennese premiere of *Ernani* is shown at length in a letter to Giuseppina Appiani of 24 May 1844 (Walker, pp. 111–12). But his much quoted encomium, 'Frankly this man is a genius,' supposedly called forth by *I Due Foscari*, cannot be traced beyond Monaldi's notoriously inaccurate biography (3rd ed., p. 78).

‡ Letter to Toccagni, 4.11.1844. Walker, p. 124.

§ Letter to Piave, 22.7.1848. Abbiati, I, pp. 751–2.

orchestral palette, particularly clarinets, which are less often combined in a garish line with flutes, oboes, trumpets and piccolo. At the same time there is more extensive and varied writing for strings alone. The harmonies are in general richer and less predictable than those of *Ernani*; the forms are remarkably streamlined, occasionally too much so for the balance of their proportions; and—more remarkable still—the opera associates themes with characters in a way that amounts almost to Leitmotiv.

Almost, but not quite. In 1844 Italian opera was no more geared to the systematic use of Leitmotiv than German or French. Even Wagner up to that time had merely hinted at its possibilities. The essence of Leitmotiv in the Wagnerian sense is that it should have the function of a 'subject' in a symphony, forming the thematic basis of the scene in which it first occurs. It must be restated, developed and woven into the fabric of the music. *Götterdämmerung* consists almost entirely of leading-motives and their development with hardly any 'free' material at all. Here Leitmotiv has completely ousted the closed form as the structural principle of music drama. Indeed where it co-exists with the closed form it is arguably not really Leitmotiv. Though it may contribute to the unity of the opera, it also tends to constrict, since it obliges the composer to return to a theme which may have no musical relevance to the scene in which it occurs. Dramatically it imposes on the character concerned a sameness of mood which inhibits the development of his or her personality. Wagner takes care never to imprison an important character within the same emotion. If he or she is characterized by a single theme, like Parsifal, it is not one with a heavy emotional charge. The theme which Verdi assigns to the heroine of *I Due Foscari* has a certain resemblance in mood to the motif of Freia in *Das Rheingold*.

96

But Freia is a minor character, who at her first appearance is not required to do more than register terror. When in the fourth scene she is restored to Valhalla her motif is suitably changed into the major key. Lucrezia is a protagonist, and her motif does not change at all. Nor fortunately does it accompany every one of her entries. If it did it would become intolerable. In the case of Jacopo Foscari, Verdi himself felt the risk of making him too passively sorrowful, but he incurred it all the more by stamping him with the motif (Ex. 97) on the opposite page.

The fact is that Verdi was far safer with the thematic reminiscence than with this crude labelling device, which merits far more than Wagnerian Leitmotiv Debussy's jibe about a 'carte de visite'. Never again did he apply it so consistently as here. He was always ready to learn from other composers, Wagner not least; but he must have realized that he lacked that faculty, possessed by Wagner to a unique degree, of concentrating a musico-dramatic image in a single, plastic motif. Leitmotiv could

97

never be for him the fundamental principle that it was for Wagner because he never completely abandoned the closed forms; he merely telescoped them. His greatest scenes can usually be analysed into a succession of basically symmetrical melodies (their regularity varied with phrase extensions and contractions) opening out one into the other like Chinese boxes. This applies to the love duet in *Otello* as much as to the duets in *Rigoletto* and *Traviata*. In such circumstances the use that can be made of single recurring themes is bound to be limited—and may even prove limiting. In *I Due Foscari* it results in a trim, consistent work, in which modesty of scope is compensated by finer workmanship than in any of his previous operas.

Like *Ernani*, *I Due Foscari* opens with a prelude, but one which does more than sum up the principal elements of the opera. Like the prelude to *Der Rosenkavalier* it begins the drama before the rise of the curtain. First there is a unison theme of nine bars for full orchestra in Beethovenian C minor, with a brutal tritone in the second phrase. It is repeated on brass and bassoons, stridently decorated by strings and high woodwind alternately. A sudden fortissimo breaks off leaving a clarinet to fill the silence with a long held note which presently anticipates the theme of Jacopo Foscari (Ex. 97), here dragging its harmonies painfully into G minor; for clearly he has just suffered those tortures which Verdi did not wish to represent on the stage. His motif is immediately followed by another in B flat quoted from Lucrezia's cavatina. It is harmonized more schematically however and scored for flute and tremolo violins—Verdi's instrumental shorthand for a prayer ascending to heaven.

98

After the third phrase the melody is interrupted by an orchestral crescendo like a wave, with horns and trumpets rapping out their triplets with all the force and excitement of the Act I finale of *Ernani*. The full orchestra bursts in with an unprepared modulation to D flat major; four bars of transition lead higher and higher to a climax in which C minor is finally re-established, and as the noise subsides the lower instruments can be heard grimly insisting on the tonic note, as on a sentence passed irrevocably. Two characteristically strong features are the double-dotted rhythms reinforced by bunched trombones six bars after the resumption of the original tempo, and the chromatic passing note turning the screw of anguish after the C minor climax.

ACT I

Scene 1: a hall in the Doge's Palace in Venice. At the back Gothic arches through which can be seen part of the city and the lagoon lit by the moon. On the left of the stage there are two doors, one leading to the Doge's apartments, the other to the main entrance; on the right two other doors giving respectively on to the Hall of the Council of Ten and the state prison. The scene is illuminated by two wax torches carried by brackets projecting from the wall.

The scene is one of sinister gloom, and therefore dominated by those two favourite instruments of darkness, clarinet and bassoon. The marking is *cupo* (hollow); and the music is heavily chromatic with murmuring phrases on the strings rising like coils of sea-mist. Slowly the hall fills with shadowy figures—the Council of Ten and the Giunta, so the stage instructions tell us, but the phrase needs a little explanation. The Council of Ten was a selection of magistrates who investigated and judged crimes against the state. They had the powers partly of a court martial, partly of a secret police, including the right to torture prisoners, however eminent, if they were believed to be concealing the truth. The vague word 'giunta' would appear to derive from a phrase of Byron's in Act V: 'The Ten / with a selected giunta from the Senate / of twenty-five of the best-born patricians.' The term has no historical significance. Verdi merely wanted an excuse to use the entire male chorus.

'Silence! Mystery!' The words are repeated again and again in overlapping phrases, ascending in semitones. From this pattern the main chorus motif begins to take shape, scored mainly for the lower instruments with clarinets and bassoons again prominent; and each bar punctuated by a demisemiquaver triplet on the kettledrums giving a touch of menace to what is a rather bland melody.

99 Andante con moto
CHORUS si - len-zio, mi - ste-ro Ve - ne-zia fan - ciul-la

Rossini has set the example in his *Le Siège de Corinthe*, where the Greek Council* are given a theme in the same key and the same triple rhythm (Ex. 100):

* In *Maometto II*, the original version of the opera, they are Venetians; hence perhaps the connection in Verdi's mind.

100

but Rossini's is more fragmentary in character and less consistently used. Verdi's is a complete melodic period and in the first scene it is developed at length. 'Silence and mystery watch over the infant Venice in her cradle of waters; silence and mystery made her mighty, mistress of the seas, wise and feared.'

The entire scene has been designed as a rondo, whose theme (Ex. 99) is stated four times, with intervening episodes. The second of these features a short exchange between Loredano, Barbarigo and the other senators. The Doge, they are told, has already preceded them calmly into the council chamber. Here the harmonies take on a studied richness evolved, however, quite logically from the chromatic figures that open the scene.

101

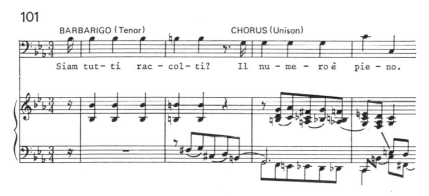

The composer's fondness for varying the accompaniment of a theme whenever it recurs hints at what one commentator has called of 'variation-form'.* Here it results in some rarely imaginative effects of scoring and figuration: the cello counterpoint that embellishes the second statement of Ex. 99; the groups of reiterated semiquavers rapped out successively by horns, trumpets and trombones

---

*P. Petrobelli, 'Osservazioni sul processo compositivo in Verdi', *Acta Musicologica*, XLIII (1971), pp. 125–42. It is not until the later operas when the themes become shorter and more plastic that Verdi subjects them too to variation.

in the third, driving it to a swift climax at the words 'Giustizia qui seggio posò';
the soft tympanum figure that seals the argument; the solo flute pattern decorating
the first episode; and the final 'exit' of the theme itself with a new 'off-the-beat'
countertheme. Verdi's operas have not so far shown such consistent refinements;
nor will they again for some time.

To the strains of Ex. 97 Jacopo is led in by the Fante, an officer of the Council,
who tells him to await the Council's summons. The Fante leaves and Jacopo
drags himself to a window and looks at the moonlit city.

> My beautiful, my own;
> My only Venice—this is breath! Thy breeze,
> Thine Adrian sea-breeze how it fans my face!
> The very winds fell native to my veins,
> And cool them into calmness. . . .*

Piave's lines are more pedestrian than Byron's; but Verdi has surpassed both
authors with an exquisitely scored arioso, based throughout on an instrumental
pattern whose main feature is a quasi-trill on the solo flute—an almost Ravel-like
effort.

102

He conjures up a similar atmosphere for the dying Doge in *Simon Boccanegra*,
Act IV. The music mounts to a climax for Jacopo's words: 'Queen of the Waters
I salute thee . . .' and so leads to the first movement of the cavatina describing the
exile's nostalgia (*Dal più remoto esiglio*). This is something new in Verdi, not so much
in design, which is the familiar a^1 a^2 b a^3 c a^3 and coda, as in the rhythm and scoring.
It is a delicate andantino in 6/8 whose first sixteen bars or so (up to a^3 and before
c) are scored for pizzicato strings only, with the usual clarinet and bassoon sus-
tainings confined to the two cadences. It is the kind of accompaniment which
allows the tenor voice to emerge in all its clarity and freshness, and it will be found
in many a tenor cavatina in the operas that follow. The melody has a resemblance
to a well-known Neapolitan canzone of the time 'Te voglio ben assai' but for its less
obvious harmonies. Everything about this aria is delicate; even the rhythmically
busy c with its woodwind figuration à la Bellini. At the return of a^3 Verdi has added
his favourite clarinet arpeggios to the accompaniment.

The Fante now returns to summon his prisoner to the Council. Jacopo is terrified
at the thought of meeting his father's eye, but the Fante assures him that he may
expect a merciful sentence. 'Liar, be silent!' Jacopo retorts, and he breaks into a
cabaletta of defiance (*Odio solo ed odio atroce*). His judges, he says, feel nothing but
hate; only the awareness of his own innocence and the fact that he is a Foscari

---

* *The Two Foscari*, I, i.

103

Andantino
JACOPO *con passione*

Dal più re-mo-toe-si-glio, sull'a-li del_ de-si - o,

str.
pizz.

gives him strength to endure their sentence. This cabaletta has none of the distinction of the andantino. Inserted to give a stiffening to Jacopo's character, it relies
too much on obvious expedients such as vocal syncopation, brash accompaniments and brilliant trumpet figures.

> *Scene 2: a hall in the Foscari Palace. A number of doors lead out of it,*
> *each surmounted by portraits of Procurators, Senators, etc., of the Foscari*
> *family; the back wall is broken up by Gothic arches through which can be*
> *seen the Canalazzo and the Rialto bridge in the distance. The hall is*
> *illuminated by a huge lamp hanging in the centre.*

Ex. 96 is heard on the strings, as Lucrezia hurries in followed by her attendants.
(In noting the generally energetic character of her music we should bear in mind
that Mme Barbieri-Nini was to be the creator of Lady Macbeth.) No, she will not
listen to them; she *will* go and see the Doge. He was a father before he became an
officer of state. Besides, she herself is a Doge's daughter and a Doge's daughter-
in-law. She has a right to demand justice for her innocent husband; and she affirms
that right with a downward leap of two octaves. In an agitated unison (*Resta: quel
pianto accrescere*) the waiting women try to hold her back. Why, they ask, does she
not put her trust in heaven? She yields to them so far as to address a prayer to God
(*Tu al cui sguardo onnipossente*). It is the melody already heard in the prelude (Ex. 98),
scored with a harp accompaniment, and woodwind touched in here and there.
Once again the young Verdi has achieved a miracle of translucent scoring. Particularly beautiful is the chorus's consolation in thirds (*c* of the design) against a
background of tremolando strings—an etherealized version of the choral comment
in Giulietta's cavatina in *Un Giorno di Regno* (q.v.). The autograph shows Verdi
to have taken great trouble with this aria, especially with the exact form of
Lucrezia's fioritura, which appears to have been more than once altered.

Pisana, Lucrezia's confidante, enters in tears. Lucrezia assumes that Jacopo must
have been condemned to death. 'No,' says Pisana, 'the Council have shown their
clemency in returning him to exile.' The word 'clemency' stings Lucrezia as it
had stung her husband. She, too, bursts out in a cabaletta of a curious, almost
experimental nature. Of the two quatrains only the second (*O Patrizii, tremate!
L'Eterno*) forms the material of the cabaletta proper. The first (*La clemenza!
s'aggiunge lo scherno*) is set as a minor key preparation for it in a strict, but slightly
slower tempo beginning with a 5-bar phrase. Lucrezia's wrath explodes all the

more effectively for this; but a formal consequence is that, whether because Verdi was short of words to repeat, or whether his feeling for rhythmic balance had momentarily deserted him, the middle limb of the cabaletta (bars 8–11 of the allegro moderato) has a curiously stunted quality.*

Scene 3: as for Scene 1

The purpose of this scene is partly to break up the sequence of entrance-arias and partly to remind the audience of the crime for which Jacopo was being tried.† Inevitably this means a return to Ex. 99 followed by a choral interchange between Barbarigo with one group of nobles and Loredano with another. 'The criminal was silent.' 'But the letter written to Sforza condemns him.' 'Let him return to Crete—alone.' 'His departure must be public and justice will be seen to have been done.' The only new material of any substance is a noisy chorus in fast 3/4 (*Al mondo sia noto*) in which the nobles sing the praises of Venetian justice that is no respecter of persons. The choppy rhythm of the opening theme contrasts well with the smooth unison sweep of the central episode (*Qui forte il Leon*). But its amiable naïveté hardly measures up to the needs of the situation. Rossini had written a far more imposing chorus for the judges in *La Gazza Ladra*. The scene ends with yet another re-statement of Ex. 99 by the orchestra, with a new, simpler counter-melody from the cellos.

> *Scene 4: the Doge's private rooms. There is a large table covered by damask,*
> *with a silver lamp placed on it; there is a writing desk and various papers;*
> *on one side is a large chair into which the Doge sinks as soon as he enters.*

The Doge, Francesco Foscari, is introduced by the last of the four Leitmotivs—and the most striking: a slow chordal melody sustained by cellos and decorated with a formal viola pattern like a frieze. The sound, though deep, is luminous:

104

'At last I am alone; perhaps really alone. Yet is there anywhere that the eyes of the Ten do not reach? All my words, my gestures, my thoughts are closely marked. . . .' The circumscription of the Doge's powers had become a basic

---

* Just how far Verdi had departed from the traditional plan can be seen by comparing this cabaletta with one which, consciously or not, must surely have provided its starting point, namely 'Ugo è spento' from Donizetti's *Parisina d'Este*. Here the key is the same, so too the basic tonal scheme with the change of mode accompanied by a brief dominant pedal, though without the excited Verdian quavers for pizzicato cello. The earlier piece, an orthodox rondò–finale cabaletta, is more gracefully designed, more sensitively scored even; but, predictably, it lacks Verdi's dynamism.

† Verdi himself had insisted on the necessity for doing this. See *Copialettere*, p. 426.

principle of Venetian statecraft since the conspiracy of Marino Faliero. Francesco Foscari cannot even intercede on behalf of his son; and in the romanza (*O vecchio cor che batte*) he laments the human weakness that makes him shed a father's tears. This provides yet another instance of that formal telescoping observed in Lucrezia's cabaletta. Normally the romanza in 'minor–major' form is a three-stanza structure (cf. Riccardo's 'Ciel che feci' in *Oberto*). Here Verdi has used two stanzas only, making the last line of the second debouch unexpectedly into the tonic major in a broad cadential phrase accompanied by full orchestra. The effect is wonderfully dignified and, in a sense, restrained, as though the Doge were expressing his feelings in the fewest possible notes. Characteristic too is the austerity of the opening stanza with its plain scoring for pizzicato strings in the manner of Jacopo's opening andante. Spiritually Francesco Foscari is the ancestor of that other Doge, but not of Venice, Simon Boccanegra. The bassoon following the voice in thirds in the coda is yet another indication of the sensitive use that Verdi makes of the woodwind throughout this opera.

Lucrezia is now announced, first by a servant then by Ex. 97 which never fails to make her seem in a hurry. Scarcely has her father-in-law greeted her than she breaks out in a tirade (tutti chords, tremolo strings, squealing piccolo), against the 'white-haired tigers' of the Council. Sternly the Doge bids her show respect for the laws of Venice. 'The laws of Venice,' she answers, 'are hate and vengeance,' and on the last word the orchestra launches an almost Berlioz-like torrent of sound rising and falling. What follows is basically the dialogue between the Doge and Marina which occupies most of Scene 1 of Byron's second act, and Verdi, very boldly, decided to work it up into a self-sufficient finale to the first act of the opera. Formally the duet anticipates that between Germont and Violetta in *La Traviata*, being a mosaic of contrasted basically symmetrical melodies which follow the natural shape of the verse, without any distortion of the metre beyond what the varying time-signatures require. This is a typically Verdian construction, not to be found in his predecessors, whose duets fall into fewer and much ampler sections usually diversified with recitative. It conveys wonderfully the cut and thrust of what may be called character-dialectic, which is among the secrets of Verdi's art. Piave makes no attempt to reproduce Byron's often complex arguments here; he is content with a succession of emotional attitudes.

Banal his lines may be, but they are such stuff as Verdi's genius feeds on. The following scheme will given an idea of how he divides out the text.

A. Andante 4/4 C minor ('Tu pur lo sai, che giudice')

LUCREZIA: You sat as judge amongst them; you saw the innocent victim at your feet; dry-eyed you condemned your son; give me back my beloved husband, cruel and unnatural father.
[*16 bars.*]

B. Andante 4/4 C major ('Oltre ogni umano credere')

DOGE: My mind is stricken beyond belief. Do not insult me; weep for me rather, I would give my worldly goods and my remaining days that my son might be guiltless and free.
[*16 bars with pertichini for Lucrezia.*]

C. *Andante 4/4 C major* ('*L'amato sposo rendimi*')
Extension of above based on last two lines of Lucrezia's and the Doge's
stanzas in combination, ending with cadenza.
[*15 bars.*]

D. *Allegro 4/4 C major–B flat minor* ('*Di sua innocenza dubiti?*')
LUCREZIA: Do you doubt his innocence? Do you no longer know him?
DOGE: Yes; but a letter intercepted accuses him all too clearly.
LUCREZIA: He wrote it only from a longing to see Venice once more.
DOGE: True, but it was a crime.
LUCREZIA: Then you should show some pity.
DOGE: I would; but I cannot.
LUCREZIA: Have pity. Hear me!
         [*Dialogue based on rhythmical orchestral motif modulating widely*
         and in strict tempo. 19 bars.]

E. *Meno mosso 4/4 B flat major–F minor* ('*Senti il paterno amore*')
LUCREZIA: If you could only feel a father's love.
DOGE: My heart is deeply moved.
LUCREZIA: Put aside your stern resolve.
DOGE: There is no sternness in me.
LUCREZIA: Forgive him; yield to my entreaty.
DOGE: No. The ruler of Venice has no power to do so.
         [*Another dialogue based on melody shared by the singers alternately;*
         only the final four bars modulate. 17 bars.]

F. *Allegro prestissimo 3/4 F minor* ('*Se tu dunque potere non hai*')
LUCREZIA: Then if you have no power come with me and sue for mercy for
         your son. My sorrow and your age will perhaps move them to pity.
         Let us make this last attempt. If the Doge is powerless let a father's
         love be your guide.
         [*42 bars.*]

G. *Allegro moderato 4/4 F major* ('*O vecchio padre misero*')
DOGE: Old and wretched father, what use is your throne to you if you
         cannot grant or even demand justice for a son sacrificed to his own
         unconscious guilt? Grief will bring me to my grave.
         [*19 bars. Pertichino from Lucrezia anticipating final section.*]

H. *Più mosso 4/4 F major* ('*Tu piangi? La tua lagrima*')
LUCREZIA: You are weeping? Your tears bring me hope.
DOGE: [*Repeats his last lines.*]
         [*34 bars, voices combining.*]

It would be possible to analyse this whole finale into a grand duet in three movements: A–C forming a 'dissimilar' andante; D–E a dialogue-transition; F a central
movement for Lucrezia alone (rare in the middle of a duet but not without precedent);* G–H a final dissimilar movement of a more compact type than the first.

* See Gennaro's solo 'D'un pescator ignobile' (*Lucrezia Borgia*, Prologue).

But in a piece such as this traditional divisions have lost their meaning. What we have here is a single structure in eight successive stages, of which only one (D) is of a purely transitional character. The unit in each case is 16 bars, as in any dance tune (32 in the case of F). The underlying symmetry is masked in two ways: by extensions of three or four bars in the final phrase with or without a cadenza in free time, and by making each section interlock with the preceding, so that the last note of A will be the first of B, and so on, thus achieving a sense of continuous momentum. As in the Germont–Violetta duet from *La Traviata* the baritone remains fairly constant; it is the soprano who traverses a wide range of emotion, from anger to entreaty, from despair to hope. In Lucrezia's *Senti il paterno amore* (E) the presage of Violetta's 'Conosca il sagrifizio' is plain for all to hear. It will be noticed too how very sparing Verdi is throughout in the use of full orchestra, reserving it only for moments of particular stress; how in sections like C where the voices combine the contours of each's melody reflect the singer's state of mind—stabbing accents and jerking rhythms for Lucrezia, smooth elegiac lines for the Doge; and how the start of B recalls, faintly, the Doge's motif by an arpeggiated cello pattern. Such are the admittedly primitive ways whereby the young Verdi with his still narrow harmonic range serves the interests both of structural harmony and of dramatic truth.

ACT II

Scene 1: the state prisons. A faint light penetrates through a vent high up
in the wall. On stage left there is a narrow staircase leading up to the Palace.

Never has Verdi written with such stark economy as in the prelude to this act—20 slow bars of E minor through which a solo viola and a solo cello trace a succession of wandering lines. The simple two-part string writing yields an astonishing variety of texture and harmonic suggestiveness.

105

The stage directions make it clear that Jacopo is confined in one of the lower prisons, the 'pozzi', so designed as to give the prisoner the impression that he was below the water-level. They were narrow and lightless; so it is not surprising that

Jacopo's first words recall those of Beethoven's Florestan. 'Night, perpetual night, that reigns here!' or in Byron's more elegant version:

> No light, save yon faint gleam which shows me walls,
> Which never echo'd save to sorrow's sounds. . . .*

But Piave and Verdi clearly decided that the opening scene needed something more sensational as well. Suddenly the full orchestra peals out as Jacopo springs up in terror. All around him ghosts are rising up. Among them he recognizes the giant figure of Carmagnola, the condottiere in the service of the republic, condemned and executed some years before for treachery in his conduct of the war with Milan. Carmagnola's ghost has a starkly brutal outline, pointing forward to Fasolt and Fafner in Wagner's *Rheingold*.

Terrified, Jacopo implores Carmagnola's mercy—it was the Council of Ten that had condemned him to death, as it now condemns the Doge's own son. But the spectre still advances, until Jacopo falls to the ground in a faint. All this is conveyed in a romanza (*Non maledirmi o prode*), almost an 'action aria' with a freedom of design characteristic of the entire scene. Basically the form is symmetrical: an agitato stanza in A minor expressing terror, and a pleading stanza, given out twice, in C major with an accompaniment of clarinet arpeggios. But twice he is cut short by a menacing gesture based on Ex. 106. The final return to A minor is free and totally unstrophic: a series of exclamations whose gradient, melodic and rhythmic, reflects Jacopo's rising hysteria. The style of cadence and orchestral decrescendo will be echoed in another, more famous hallucination: that of Azucena in *Il Trovatore*.

* *The Two Foscari*, III, i.

Lucrezia is announced by her customary Ex. 96. Seeing her husband lying still on the floor, she at first assumes that he must have been murdered. But she feels the beating of his heart (a process rather naïvely reflected in the orchestra) and is reassured. She awakens him in one of those transfiguring phrases that will assume a role of increasing importance in Verdi's art:

107

But his first words show that he is still in the throes of delirium. Not until she takes him in her arms does he recognize her as his wife, and the orchestra swells out a richer variant of Ex. 107. Restored to his senses, Jacopo wants to know whether his death has been ordered by the Council. 'Not death,' replies Lucrezia, 'a living death in exile.' Lucrezia breaks her news in the first movement of what is, despite Piave's lugubrious text, essentially a love duet (*No, non morrai, che i perfidi*) with a fresh bloom on it as in the scene between Gabriele and Amelia in *Simon Boccanegra*. Although the singers are in conjunction here, Verdi employs the familiar 'dissimilar' form doubtless for the sake of the melodic variety it affords; but the coda compensates with overlapping repetitions of the same phrase, like repeated assurances of love.

108

The sound of a barcarolle behind the scenes (*Tutta è calma*) strikes in with almost Mahlerian irony: a carefree Venetian melody, played by the banda off-stage with chorus joining in here and there. After the final cadence Jacopo bursts out in agony, cursing the men who sentenced him to prison and exile; but almost at once his mood changes to one of hope as he begins the stretta of the duet (*Ah speranza dolce ancora*); gentle in mood and completely orthodox in its 'similar' design. After the soprano statement there is another burst of singing behind the scenes and then the two voices join over an accompaniment of harp and tremolo strings in which we can almost hear the waters of the lagoon lapping against the walls of the pozzi.

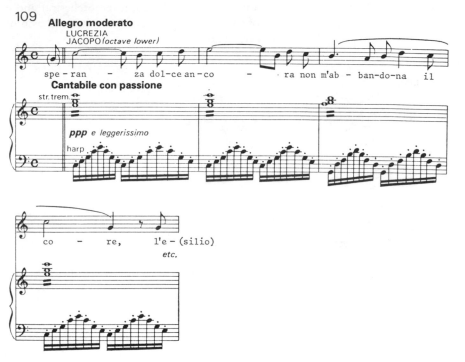

The door of the cell opens once more to admit the Doge. Perhaps because he is no longer in his robes of state, Francesco Foscari enters not to Ex. 104 but to one of those excited orchestral passages, with pounding string bass, which in Verdi betoken joyous reunion. According to traditional analysis the next five and a half pages of vocal score would be called the first movement of the trio. But the sense of forward drive is such as to make them seem a mere preparation for the andante that follows, especially when at the twenty-sixth bar a long dominant pedal is established whose influence reaches across to the grand cadential climax some thirty bars later. The more strophic andante (*Nel tuo paterno amplesso*) where Jacopo asks and receives his father's blessing begins with a tenor verse that harks forward to the *Rigoletto* quartet; and the parallel is reinforced at Lucrezia's entrance (*Di questo affanno orrendo*) with a succession of broken phrases in the manner of Gilda.

But the comparison merely shows how far Verdi had yet to travel to reach the dramatic truth of his middle-period works. The *Rigoletto* quartet defines in the narrowest space four personalities, four different worlds of feeling. Here the mood is uniform and to a greater extent even than the text implies; even Lucrezia's imprecations are expressed within the prevailing 'sweet sorrow'. Significantly, perhaps, the Doge's strophe contains an unconscious reminiscence of one of Verdi's favourite melodies, 'No, non ti son rivale' from Bellini's *La Straniera*,* also for baritone and also in D flat major. Again one is struck by the delicacy of the orchestration—the two clarinets alone in thirds above the pizzicato strings, the tiny bassoon solo at the start of Jacopo's second phrase, the liquid harp arpeggios which begin at the Doge's entrance and continue until the end of the movement; and above all the total absence of routine doubling. Only once does the full orchestra weigh in as the voices unite in the last cadential phrase. Over the final chord there is the instruction: 'They remain embracing and weeping.' The Doge must now take his leave; he will see them once again he says, as a high official of state. The father in him will suffer but be powerless. 'Oh God,' cries Jacopo, 'who will help me?' 'I!' replies the heavy bass voice of Loredano, who has just appeared at the door together with the Fante and four guards carrying torches. He tells Jacopo of the Council's sentence. 'The message is worthy of you,' says the Doge ironically. He embraces Jacopo and Lucrezia once more; but Loredano steps forward and parts them. Jacopo must hear his sentence read aloud at the Council and then set sail at once. Husband and wife turn and confront Loredano in unison. What would have been the stretta of the trio becomes a quartet (*Ah si, il tempo che mai non s'arresti*). Lucrezia and Jacopo invoke all manner of curses on Loredano. Loredano retorts that not even a Doge's authority can protect a man who is stained with the blood of his kinsmen; while the Doge stands between both parties, now calling on Jacopo and Lucrezia to restrain their fury, now joining in unison with Loredano as he proclaims the inexorability of Venetian law. Although it is scored quite heavily, most of the quartet is marked either piano or pianissimo as though to suggest deliberate restraint. The rhythm takes up that of Lucrezia's solo in the finale of Act I (*Se tu dunque potere non hai*). But the major tonality and slightly slower pace reveal more clearly its origins in the Viennese waltz.†

111

Only the passages for the Doge and Loredano in unison strike a genuine note of solemnity.

Scene 2: the hall of the Council of Ten. The Ten and the Giunta are assembling

The orchestral introduction is inevitably Ex. 99. Then the senators exchange a few words antiphonally and together about the need to get young Foscari shipped abroad as soon as possible; he has killed a Donato and has been treating with

---

* Letter to Somma, 19.11.1853. Pascolato, pp. 58–62.

† Clearly this is the passage referred to in a letter from Donizetti to Cottrau, 2.4.1845 (Zavadini, pp. 804–5): 'By a damned coincidence the Valz of the terzetto got a laugh. . . . They say it's a waltz by Strauss. . . . That's what four bars can do.' The Strauss would of course be Johann père.

foreign powers. All this in a unison chorus (*Non fia che di Venezia*) proclaiming yet again the incorruptibility of Venetian justice. The scoring is for wind and pizzicato strings with trumpets and drums playing an important part. Fragments of Ex. 99 are cunningly woven in, and the motif itself in its entirety rounds off the main melody with yet another variation of its countertheme. All stand as the Doge enters preceded by Loredano, the Fante of the Council and the Comandadori, and followed by pages. He proceeds solemnly to the ducal throne, and takes his seat, at which point the finale begins. He addresses a few dignified words to the assembly. 'Patricians, I am here at your bidding. Whether you wish to torment a father or a son I know not; but your will is law to me . . . I shall wear a Doge's face and conceal a father's heart.' The chorus murmur their approval; as the prisoner is now admitted between four guards to the accompaniment of Ex. 97, again with its opening harmonies slightly varied. Loredano hands the parchment roll containing Jacopo's sentence to the Fante; he in turn gives it to Jacopo, from whom it wrings a cry of anguish. As usual, the heightening of emotional temperature brings a change from free recitative into strict tempo. Jacopo's plea to his father to intercede for him, the Senators' objection, the desperate farewell of father and son—all these form a large period (F minor–A flat–F minor). But the last cadence is dramatically interrupted. Unheralded, for once, by Ex. 96 Lucrezia appears on the threshold of the hall. This is something unheard of for a woman, and the general astonishment is underlined by an elliptical sequence of progressions. With Lucrezia are her attendants, Pisana and her two children. Amid exclamations of outrage from the Senators, Jacopo calls his two sons to him. With an arm round each he breaks free from his guards and, to a cry of 'Miei figli' twice uttered to the familiar falling semitone of grief, throws himself at the Doge's feet, and begins the adagio of the finale (*Queste innocenti lagrime*)—a huge long-breathed cantilena moving from E flat minor to major and building up as it proceeds. Its model would seem to be the final scene in *Norma*, but as usual with Verdi the component ideas are shorter, and there are more of them. It is during this ensemble that for the first time in the opera Barbarigo detaches himself from Loredano with a plea for clemency (in the play his is the voice of moderation from the start). The others needless to say support his fellow councillor.

The final cadence is brutally interrupted by Loredano insisting that Jacopo leave forthwith. As a last favour the condemned man asks to be allowed to take his wife and children with him; but when this too is denied he breaks down with a muted pathos far more affecting than any cry of despair (see Ex. 112, facing page).

As if to set his loneliness in still greater relief the full chorus, ensemble and orchestra cover his last note with a restatement fortissimo and più mosso of the final melodic idea of the finale. So for the first time Verdi bypasses the stretta of a central finale and with it any possible sense of anticlimax.

ACT III

Scene 1: the Old Piazzetta of San Marco. The canal is full of gondolas passing to and fro. The scene, empty at first, gradually fills with people, many of them masked, who enter from various directions, meet and greet one another and stroll about together. In the distance is the Island of Cypresses, now called San Giorgio. The sun is setting. There is a general atmosphere of gaiety.

112

Andante

JACOPO
p con passione   dim.

Ve – di, al sepolcro in se – no,   il lacrimata polvere   fra poco scen – de – (rò)

str.

hn. sustain

dim.   smorz.   morendo

And not before time, the listener may well think. Verdi and Piave certainly did so. The so-called introduction and barcarolle add nothing whatever to the drama; but they provide a relief from the prevailing gloom. The opening chorus (*Alle gioie, alle corse, alle gare*) is just one of many in major common chords and military rhythm. Barbarigo and Loredano look on with a faint contempt. What does it matter to the populace who the Doge is—a Foscari or a Malipiero? They will always enjoy themselves. Loredano calls for a barcarolle to begin the regatta. All proceed to the water's edge waving white handkerchiefs to cheer on the gondoliers, singing the melody heard earlier on in the prison scene (*Tace il vento*). But here it is enriched by harmonies worthy of the mature Mercadante: a fine instance of what can be done with a melody once it has been taken out of the hands of the banda:

113

Allegro moderato

CHORUS-Unison

Ta–ce il ven– to,è que – ta l'on – da;mi – te u n'au –ra l'ac– ca–rezza

str.
w.w.

Two trumpeters now come out of the Doge's palace followed by the Chief of Police or Messer Grande (to give him his Venetian title). Three blasts from the two stage trumpets are enough to break up the happy throng, who scatter before the 'Justice of the Lion'. The gondolas, too, vanish as a galley is seen approaching. From it steps the magistrate known as the Sopracomito to whom Messer Grande hands a paper. Then, announced for the last time by Ex. 97 in its most complete form, Jacopo comes slowly forward from the palace surrounded by his guards and followed by Lucrezia, Pisana and her women. Husband and wife take a desolate farewell of each other. From now on, says Jacopo, Lucrezia will be the widow of a husband who is still alive. May the seas swallow up the vessel that takes him to

Crete. Better that than the living death of exile away from father, wife and children. And so from this moving and beautifully scored recitative to Jacopo's final aria (*All'infelice veglio*) in which Lucrezia, Loredano and the chorus have a part. He commends the children to her care, and when she cries out in sorrow he reminds her that she is a Contarini by birth and a Foscari by marriage. All this is too much for Loredano who steps between them and removes his mask with a melodramatic 'Behold me!' 'Loredano!' exclaims Jacopo, 'my devilish foe. . . . You have the heart of a tiger.' Then without any change of tempo the music moves into the major for Jacopo's last farewell (*O padre, figli, sposa*), which has the character if not the form of a slow cabaletta. The melodic line, scored for harp and wind, is twice echoed by soloists and chorus with full orchestral backing and doubled by trumpet. All are filled with compassion except for the odious Loredano. Jacopo is at last led aboard; Lucrezia faints in the arms of Pisana; Loredano and Barbarigo, friends no longer, go off in opposite directions and the populace disperses.

The whole scene is typical of the hybrid forms to be found in *I Due Foscari*. Although set in the minor key, Jacopo's melody does not follow the usual romanza design. It is that rare phenomenon in early Verdi—a large-scale andante which preserves its minor-key orientation to the end; while Lucrezia's entry after the first full close (*Cielo s'affretti al termine*) gives it the air of a 'dissimilar' duet. The sharing out of the final melody between soloist and ensemble is a stroke of the utmost simplicity and originality whereby the scene takes on the scale of a miniature finale.

Scene 2: the Doge's private apartments as in Act I

Again the Doge's motif (Ex. 104) is heard in full, note for note, as in the third scene of the first act. He is discovered musing sadly on Jacopo's departure in a mixture of recitative and arioso. Once he had three sons. Two died in their prime; and now the last one has been sentenced to a dishonourable exile—and he himself is alone. Brass unisons announce the entrance of Barbarigo with a letter, which he hands to the Doge. It was written by a certain Erizzo on his deathbed. In it he has confessed that he, not Jacopo, was responsible for the death of Donato. The Doge exclaims joyfully in a soaring expansive phrase (*Ciel pietoso il mio affanno hai veduto, a me un figlio volesti renduto*). But before he can reach his final cadence there is a desolate cry from Lucrezia, who enters with the news that scarcely had Jacopo stepped aboard the ship that was to take him to Crete than he collapsed and died. The Doge totters to a chair; and Lucrezia vents her grief in a cabaletta (*Più non vive . . . l'innocente*), which is one of Verdi's strongest. Most unusually it quickens after the central half-close,* breaking away into a brilliant Donizettian movement trailing clouds of fioritura and punctuated by those displaced accents of which Verdi was so fond in his early days. At the repeat not only are the words slightly varied, 'Più non vive' becoming 'egli è spento'; but there is also a substantial pause-decoration for the half-close before the change of tempo.

However life and Loredano have not yet finished with the Doge. No sooner

---

* Note the parallel with Lucrezia's cabaletta in the first act, where, as here, a change of tempo is accompanied by a dominant pedal. If, like Basevi (p. 68), you regard the earlier cabaletta as beginning with the G minor passage 'La clemenza . . .' the parallel will appear still closer.

has Lucrezia left than a servant announces a deputation from the Senate—in this case the Council of Ten as the familiar motif (Ex. 99) makes clear. Their spokesman is once more Loredano, 'a very Ovid in the art of hating'.* He tells the Doge that in consideration of his length of service to the republic, his great age and his recent private grief, the senate have decided to relieve him of his duties as Doge. Francesco Foscari rises indignantly to his feet.

> When I twice before reiterated
> My wish to abdicate, it was refused me;
> And not alone refused, but ye exacted
> An oath from me that I would never more
> Renew this instance. I have sworn to die
> In full exertions of the functions which
> My country called me here to exercise,
> According to my honour and my conscience—
> I cannot break my oath. . . .†

All this is paraphrased rather less elegantly by Piave. The Ten continue to insist that the Doge resign; whereat, as so often in Italian opera, his feelings are dissolved and transfigured in an outpouring of lyrical melody (*Questa dunque è l'iniqua mercede*). 'So this is the infamous reward that you would offer the aged white-haired warrior; is this the prize you would grant to one whose courage and honour have protected and increased the realm . . . ?' It is Verdian baritone music at its noblest, with rather more vigour than is ideally suitable for Byron's octogenarian Doge. The rough augmented fourths (D sharp–A–D sharp) enhance rather than spoil its beauty. It is a straightforward double quatrain setting with a

114

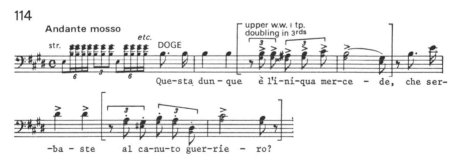

long coda in which the chorus joins telling him that he may now return to his dear ones. 'My dear ones? Give me back my son!' he cries, rising the second time to an F sharp of anguish; but 'yield, yield' the chorus insist, the lower brass adding a minatory tone to their words.‡ The Doge then sends for Lucrezia; next he hands the ring to a Senator, who in accordance with tradition consigns it to be broken.

---

* *The Two Foscari*, V, i.   † *Ibid.*

‡ For a similar design and rhythmic gait see the condemnation (also by the Council of Ten) of Israele Bertucci in Donizetti's *Marino Faliero*, with the male chorus chanting 'a morte, a morte' instead of 'cedi, cedi'. The part of Bertucci, being among Donizetti's most successful essays in the noble baritonic vein in which the singer Antonio Tamburini excelled, can hardly have failed to make a deep impression on the young Verdi. Francesco Foscari is Bertucci raised to a higher power of intensity.

Loredano makes as if to take the crown from Foscari's head; but this at least the Doge refuses to allow. 'Your hand is unworthy to touch it!' For the last time Lucrezia enters to the sound of Ex. 96. 'Father . . . Prince!' 'Prince no longer; those who have killed my son have taken away my throne.' At that moment the great bell of St Mark's begins to toll for Foscari's successor, Malipiero. Loredano's glee is too much for the other Senators, who demand that the old man's grief be respected. All this time the timpani are rolling steadily, horn and then bassoon sustaining a deep B flat pedal over which the strings give out a discordant C flat first inversion and Lucrezia exclaims in horror.

The Doge's final solo (*Quel bronzo feral*) points forward to parts of the Requiem with its cupo delivery and its austere accompaniment of pizzicato strings alternating with rolls on the timpani. The Doge already feels himself sinking into the grave. The chorus echo him massively, so intensifying the atmosphere of doom; but by the laws of Italian opera E flat minor must give way before the end to E flat major. So the Doge rallies in a più mosso sufficiently to protest against the hellish hate of which he has been a victim (*Dell'odio infernale*). Once again this is not a stretta but rather an extension, though a less convincing one, of the preceding movement. The tonic minor returns for an instant, together with the tolling of the bell. With a last agonized cry of 'My son, my son . . .' the Doge falls dead. Lucrezia and the others cry out that he has died of a broken heart; while Loredano takes out his book and opposite the names Pietro and Marco writes 'paid'.*

PARIS, *17 December 1846*. For the first performance of *I Due Foscari* at the Théâtre des Italiens Verdi was commissioned through the composer Prince Poniatowski to write a new cabaletta for the famous tenor Mario. The following year Mario sang it in London much to Verdi's annoyance, since no agreement had yet been reached as to the ownership of the music.† How the matter was settled we may never know. The parts used for the performance at Covent Garden doubtless perished in the fire of 1856. Nor has the autograph yet come to light. Fortunately a non-autograph manuscript score of *I Due Foscari* in the Bibliothèque Nationale‡ contains the new cabaletta bound, misleadingly, in the volume containing Act III.

Giovanni Matteo Mario Cavalier de Candia, the Valentino of the operatic stage,

---

* In the Museum of Busseto are preserved two pages from what is clearly a sketch for the entire final scene. These are of particular interest as being the earliest of Verdi's sketches to have survived. They are discussed at length and in relation to the complete sketch of *Rigoletto* by P. Petrobelli, 'Osservazioni sul processo compositivo in Verdi' (v.s.), who follows the thesis propounded by L. K. Gerhartz, *Die Auseinandersetzungen des jungen Giuseppe Verdi mit dem literärischen Drama—Ein Beitrag zur szenischen Strukturbestimmung der Oper* (Berlin, 1968), to the effect that up till 1850 or thereabouts Verdi designed his operas scene by scene in the manner of Bellini, and only thereafter as continuous, organic entities. Obviously until further sketches of the period come to light this must remain a matter for guess-work. On a more superficial level we may note in comparing the sketch with the finished result the care which the composer took to match vocal contours and emphasis to the exact sense of the text and the emotion of the speaker. Unfortunately the surviving fragments concern recitative and declamation only.

† See letter to Mario, 24.7.1847. *Copialettere*, pp. 40–1. See also letters to M. Escudier, 22.10 and 5.11.1846 (Abbiati, I, pp. 653–5); and to Mario, 17.10.1846, 23.11.1846 and ?1.1847 (Cesare Simone, 'Lettere al tenore Mario de Candia sulla cabaletta de *I Due Foscari*', in *Nuova Antologia*, 1934, pp. 327–34), in which Verdi first makes the astounding suggestion that if *Odio solo* were not to his taste Mario should use Oronte's cabaletta from *I Lombardi* instead!

‡ B.N., MS. D. 9699.

was not the kind of tenor that Verdi, or indeed any other composer, found very interesting. The only role of any importance that he created was the juvenile lead in Donizetti's *Don Pasquale*. A younger and better-looking Moriani, he specialized in the soulful rather than the dramatic. In England he was rated the perfect stage lover, with inexhaustible reserves of tenderness'. Therefore there was no question of writing for him the kind of forceful movement with which Verdi had taken care to provide Roppa. This time, instead of bursting out wrathfully, Jacopo must reply submissively to the Fante, putting his trust in God. The cabaletta (*Sento Iddio che mi chiama*) is of the measured, high-stepping kind such as the young Verdi more usually gives to his sopranos, though it also bears a kinship to Donizetti's 'Tu che a Dio spiegasti l'ali' from *Lucia*. The initial melodic idea is not particularly striking; the form is the routine Bellinian $a^1 a^2 b a^2$; the scoring strictly according to well-worn if self-imposed rules, but the codetta opens up a wider perspective, as a new, more varied rhythmic pattern is introduced, worked to a strong climax, then dissolved into the previous 'prancing' gait. Grace and intensity of feeling are happily combined:

Striking too is the unexpected coda—a three-bar phrase, twice stated before the conclusive resumption of the central ritornello theme. The syncopations, the displaced accents, the typically foreshortening effect created by the irregularity of the phrase length, all combine to give Mario's Jacopo a force and decision hitherto denied him. A high E flat in the second cadenza reminds us that for a while Mario had replaced Rubini in the famous 'Puritani' quartet, with Grisi, Tamburini and Lablache.

In certain respects the Mario cabaletta might seem more suited to the character of Jacopo than the one which it replaces. Formally, however, it bears too obviously the marks of an insert aria. The original movement, in conformity with the essentially streamlined structure of *I Due Foscari*, was dovetailed into the previous transitional passage with less than two bars of accompaniment to launch the soloist. Here Jacopo's 'Io la spero dal Signor' is worked up into a pompous half-close in total contradiction to the sense of the words; and the cabaletta proper begins conventionally with an instrumental statement of the first musical period. A world-famous tenor would expect no less by way of a platform; but it represents the kind of concession to the executant from which the rest of *I Due Foscari* is unusually free.*

* The score contains one enigma which only the discovery of the autograph could ultimately explain. The repeat statement of the cabaletta includes a cut of two bars without any indication of how the scoring should be altered to make this possible, since only the voice part is given. Admittedly it is not difficult to work out a satisfactory solution; and the abbreviation itself,

Until quite recently, writers on Verdi have been unduly harsh with *I Due Foscari*. As long ago as 1859, Basevi complained of the sense of monotony and relaxation resulting from over-use of 6/8 andantino, especially when accompanied by the pattern (𝅘𝅥𝅮 𝅘𝅥𝅮), which, he says, most people associate with a lullaby; and he contrasts this opera's 'tinta' unfavourably with the buoyancy of *Ernani* and *I Lombardi*.* It is quite true that *I Due Foscari* for all its streamlined construction has a more relaxed pace than most Verdi operas, and that if this allows one more time to notice the beauties of its craftsmanship it also allows an impatient audience more time in which to become bored. It must be said too that the occasional vulgarities (e.g., the quartet–stretta in Act II, Scene 1) obtrude more obviously when there is no exhilarating pace to sweep the listener off his feet.

The most serious obstacle to the popularity of *I Due Foscari* is its plot. Old-fashioned and preposterous as are the heroics of *Ernani*, we can none the less identify ourselves with the hero and share his loves and hates. But in the century of Auschwitz and Belsen it is impossible not to feel that there are worse fates than exile on the one hand and enforced retirement on the other. Then, too, the story of the opera is one of the slenderest, with barely enough action to cover one act, let alone Byron's original five. Indeed, Francis Toye's complaint that the libretto suffers from undue compression seems distinctly odd.† Piave has done his best to introduce as much variety as it will take. Yet such additions as Jacopo's hallucina-tion, Lucrezia's appearance in the council chamber with her two children, the two demon-king appearances of Loredano, remain no more than theatrical window-dressing and are quite insufficient to lift the drama out of its narrow groove. Elsewhere, far from being compressed, Piave's verses are infinitely repetitious (some-one should count up the number of times the word 'innocente' occurs). The one stroke of invention which might have borne fruit is the entrance of Barbarigo in Act III with the news of Erizzo's confession. It is Verdi who refused to allow the false hope to burgeon, cutting short the Doge's single phrase with Lucrezia's entry over a noisy diminished-seventh chord. Possibly in turning the screw of the Doge's suffering he was yielding to a little Byronic self-indulgence. He also knew what it was to suffer bereavement and disgrace in quick succession.

But for the musician there are many compensating virtues. Both in its merits and its defects *I Due Foscari* stands quite apart from its fellows. It strikes a note of intimacy not to be encountered again until *Luisa Miller*. No other of Verdi's early operas, apart from *Macbeth*, so effectively cuts the Gordian knots of tradition. Not one of the cabalettas begins with the usual instrumental anticipation. Neither of the concerted finales ends with a stretta. The numbers are welded together with greater coherence even than in *Ernani*. The scoring is more sensitive than in any of the operas written previously and a good many written after. The orchestra of

* Basevi, pp. 67, 71–2. † Toye, p. 251.

---

bringing the repeated climaxes in the codetta much closer together, is effective, if unusual. To this production also must be ascribed the altered fioritura in Lucrezia's first cabaletta to be found in the vocal score published by the Bureau Central de Musique, Paris; also the puntature in the Act II duet needed to accommodate the tenor part to Mario's range (see Simoni, p. 330). A score containing these exists in the Accademia S. Cecilia, Rome.

'salt-box, tongs and bones' (to use Browning's contemptuous phrase)★ is nowhere in evidence. Of course it is useless to look for great variety of style or vocabulary at this stage of Verdi's development. But the delicacy and pathos of which he wrote to Piave come through with remarkable freshness. *I Due Foscari* shows that he could write simple heartfelt melodies which do not rely on a headlong dramatic pace to sustain them. As with that other 'marine' opera, *Simon Boccanegra*, the sea-breezes play through it. Perhaps it is significant that in Germany, where audiences are less dependent on excitement, *Die beiden Foscari* or *Der Doge von Venedig*, as it is called in Günther Rennert's version, has already penetrated the repertory so far as to qualify for an entry in Lessing's *Handbuch des Opernrepertoires*. It may well survive the present Verdi boom more hardily than most.†

★'Bishop Blougram's Apology'.

† Since the above was written, a further discovery has come to light. In the second volume of his *Bibliography of the Works of Giuseppe Verdi* (London, 1978) the late Cecil Hopkinson drew attention to Ricordi's habit of publishing selected numbers from an opera before its première, at the risk of the composer's making substantial alterations to them during rehearsals, so that what first appeared in print might not tally with the definitive score. So it happened with the duet 'No, non morrai, che i perfidi'. By the time he completed the scoring, Verdi had arrived at a very different version of the first movement to the one that he had made available to his publisher in rudimentary short score as the basis for a piano-and-voice arrangement. Ricordi had meanwhile made the original plates available to his agents in Paris and London, with the result that separate copies of the duet can be found in the British Library and the Bibliothèque Nationale, Paris, in a form which pre-dates even that of the autograph score.

The original first movement is in 4/4 as distinct from the definitive 3/8; and the opening theme, though similar in shape to the revised melody, is more sedate.

As well as that, whereas in the first complete score Jacopo enters with a new idea ('O ben dicesti . . .'), in this early version he repeats Lucrezia's theme note for note. The revision is yet another instance of Verdi's moving towards a wider differentiation of his characters as well as a greater dramatic concision.

For a detailed consideration of this passage see G. Biddlecombe, 'The revision of "No, non morrai, che i perfidi": Verdi's compositional process in "I Due Foscari" *Studi verdiani*, II, pp. 59–77.

9 GIOVANNA D'ARCO

GIOVANNA D'ARCO

Opera in a prologue and three acts
by
TEMISTOCLE SOLERA
(after Schiller's drama *Die Jungfrau von Orleans*)★

First performed at the
Teatro alla Scala, Milan,
15 February 1845

CARLO VII, King of France   PRIMO TENORE   Antonio Poggi
GIACOMO, a shepherd in   PRIMO BARITONO   Filippo Colini
   Dom-Rémy
GIOVANNA, his daughter   PRIMA DONNA SOPRANO   Erminia Frezzolini-Poggi
DELIL, an officer of the King   SECONDO TENORE   Napoleone Marconi
TALBOT, supreme comman-   SECONDO BASSO   Francesco Lodetti
   der of the English army

Officers of the King—villagers—people of Rheims—French
soldiers—English soldiers—blessed spirits—evil spirits—
nobles of the realm—heralds—pages—children—marshals—
deputies—knights and their ladies—magistrates—halberdiers—
guards of honour

The action takes place in France: in Dom-Rémy, Rheims and near Rouen

Epoch: 1429

★ The librettist himself denied this (see below).

The genesis of *Giovanna d'Arco* is one of the least documented among all Verdi's operas. It seems probable that the contract arose out of an understanding with Merelli that Verdi should compose another opera for La Scala in 1845 to make up for the loss of his services in the previous year.* The librettist would be Solera as a matter of course; and his engagement would be Merelli's responsibility not the composer's.† Verdi himself had complete faith in the poet's judgment and sense of theatrical effect and may even have left to him the choice of subject. Too often it is assumed that *Giovanna d'Arco* marks the beginning of Verdi's love affair with the plays of Schiller, which was to prove so fruitful in later years. But a letter of Solera's to the publisher Ricordi suggests otherwise. Remembering the fine that he had had to pay when *Nabucco* was given in Paris, Ricordi had written anxiously to the poet asking him to make sure that his libretto involved no breach of copyright, since he had heard of a contemporary French play . . . Solera replied firmly:

I have absolutely no knowledge of the play you mention [*probably Soumet's*]; I assure you positively that my *Giovanna d'Arco* is an entirely original Italian drama. I merely wanted, like Schiller, to have Joan denounced by her own father; in all the rest I have not allowed myself to be imposed upon by the authority either of Schiller or Shakespeare, both of whom make Joan fall basely in love with the foreigner Lionel. *My play is original;* and in fact I would like to have it announced in the papers that I have been very careful to make it original knowing that people have been saying that I would naturally take my plot from Schiller.‡

No question then of 'staying close to Schiller' as Piave had been told to keep to Byron and Hugo. Indeed it might be asked just how far Verdi himself had the subject to heart, since there is no previous mention of it in his letters. He liked plots that were new; the story of Joan of Arc was already well worn. It had been set by Destouches, Conradin Kreutzer, Niccolò Vaccai, Giovanni Pacini, and Michael Balfe. Pacini's opera had had its premiere at La Scala in 1830. The libretto by Barbieri follows Schiller as closely as the *convenienze* will allow; indeed copies of it printed for the first performance contain an apology for having made the gentle Dauphin into a strong baritone role 'since Tamburini is not accustomed to play an insignificant character'. If in the new *Giovanna d'Arco* the lineaments of Schiller's drama are plainly discernible, it must be remembered that invention was not Solera's strong suit.

* Letter to I. Marini, 11.6.1843. *Copialettere*, p. 423.
† That this was standard practice at La Scala under Merelli is apparent from Verdi's letter to Brenna of 25.9.1843. Conati, pp. 87–8.
‡ Letter from Solera to Giovanni Ricordi (undated). Abbiati, I, p. 534.

Giovanna d'Arco was completed in four months, during which time Verdi had contracted also to mount a revival of *I Lombardi* for the opening of the carnival season. Trouble began with the first rehearsals. The orchestra was too small and badly arranged; the scenery and costumes were inadequate and the singers inclined to take too many liberties. Merelli, though a generous man, was a bad impresario, of whose judgment Donizetti was never tired of complaining, and the consequences of his slovenly direction were now becoming apparent. Muzio describes how 'La Frezzolini is always in tears because she says her voice isn't what it used to be; her husband Poggi fluffs continually; and Colini sings most sweetly, but the part is written for a basso profondo not a baritone so he can't be heard in the ensembles.'* No wonder that Verdi preferred not to attend the opening night. Yet these were the singers who were to figure in *Giovanna d'Arco*. The unpleasantness did not end there. Poggi wanted to break his contract, having been told that he would be hissed off the stage. (As the lover of the notorious Countess Samoyloff he was believed to share her pro-Austrian sympathies.) One of Verdi's Busseto friends advised him in all good faith to be careful before accepting a drink from anyone: 'Remember what happened to Bellini. . . .'†

One person who had no misgivings about the first night of *Giovanna d'Arco* was Muzio. No opera was more beautiful and philosophical, he wrote; even if Joan had not immortalized herself by her deeds, Verdi would have done it for her—and more to the same effect.‡ The public was to agree with Muzio, though a few lampoons were hurled at Poggi. Soon the streets were ringing to the sound of the demons' chorus (*Tu sei bella*) played on innumerable barrel-organs.

Yet in Verdi's mouth the taste of unpleasantness still lingered. He berated Ricordi for having printed a notice which damned the opera with faint praise.§ The fact is that the general tone of the press had stung him. *Giovanna* was his seventh work for the stage and all the critics implied that he was still, relatively speaking, a beginner; that he was improving certainly, but that with their guidance he could improve still further.¶ To crown everything, Merelli had, without Verdi's knowledge, begun to negotiate with Ricordi about the sale of the full score. It was the end of a friendship. The composer vowed never to set foot on the stage of La Scala again and never to speak to Merelli or any of his staff. Meanwhile he wrote to Piave: 'The opera was a success despite a huge party in opposition to it. Without doubt it is the best of my operas. . . .' ‖ So there! This assertion is too defiant to ring true. Although it would be quite wrong to speak of *Giovanna d'Arco* as a hack job, nevertheless both here and in the opera which follows Verdi played a more passive role than in *Ernani* or *I Due Foscari*. He was increasing his pace, from one to two operas a year; and to do this he was forced to capitalize his present assets rather than to develop new ones. Nor was there anything in the libretto to inspire him. For all his protestations of originality, Solera often has recourse to Schiller—or what he remembers of him—when at a loss for words.

---

* Letter from Muzio to Barezzi, 29.12.1844. Garibaldi, p. 179.
† For Verdi's sharp reply, see letter to 'Finola' Demaldè (undated), *Carteggi Verdiani*, IV, p. 80 '. . . . Bellini died of consumption and nothing else . . .' In fact he died of intestinal ulcers.
‡ Letter from Muzio to Barezzi, 9.12.1844. Garibaldi, p. 175.
§ Letter to Giovanni Ricordi (undated). Abbiati, I, p. 541.
¶ For a summary of the reviews see Abbrati, I, pp. 537–8.
‖ Letter to Piave, 16.2.1844. Abbiati, I, p. 538.

(The ending, for instance, with Joan dying not on a pyre but on the field of battle, is merely Schiller diluted.) *Die Jungfrau von Orleans* is a vast canvas of sharply drawn figures, and a treasury of classically chiselled poetry. Solera's libretto is neither. The characters are reduced to a minimum. There is no 'Rabenmutter' Isabeau, no Dunois, no Lionel or Duke of Burgundy. Talbot is a secondary part without even his famous dying line, 'Mit der Dummheit kämpfen Götter selbst vergebens'.* For poetry and humanity we are given theatrical sensationalism. Merelli's La Scala was not yet, or indeed ever, the Paris Opéra of Meyerbeer; but it was moving in that direction. The shadow of *Robert le Diable* looms over *Giovanna d'Arco*, with its invisible demons and angels, its storms and its instrumental trickery. But the cast only runs to three principals—Joan, her father (here called Giacomo),† and the Dauphin. Joan is a soprano, Charles the Dauphin (Carlo) a tenor. What more natural than that they should fall in love? This leaves Giacomo as the baritone villain—not too fierce a one however since Filippo Colini was a rather light singer, a Rossinian florid basso cantante rather than a true Verdian baritone like Ronconi. The duet for father and daughter should be one of reconciliation, allowing him to be convinced of her innocence after overhearing her soliloquize in a manner worthy of baroque opera at its most unreal. To Verdi all this meant a return to the grandiose manner of *I Lombardi alla Prima Crociata*, and a work which, as a whole, falls short of *I Due Foscari*, *Ernani* and *Nabucco* in unity of conception, though it contains some fine individual numbers and even scenes. It would seem too that the qualities of Erminia Frezzolini had inspired what is surely the composer's best soprano-role to date. He himself evidently thought well enough of it in later years to recommend it to Teresa Stolz.‡

The overture is Verdi's first since *Nabucco*, and the first one that does not pay even lip-service to the tonic–dominant principle of sonata form. It falls into three movements. The first is an example of storm music in which the stylized onomatopoeia of Rossini is combined with Bellini's more melodic approach. Verdi has something new to add in the pattern of flute quavers pianissimi that runs for twelve modulating bars between two thunderous outbursts. This is one of the rare instances of emotional undertones in Verdi's early descriptive music: for the flute retains here all its associations of innocence, reminding us that these are the clouds of war as well as weather. The point is made even clearer when a succession of brutal chords on the trumpets, trombones and cimbasso are answered by a flute cadenza and vanquished by it, rather as the orchestra is 'tamed' by the piano in the slow movement of Beethoven's fourth piano concerto. The next movement was described correctly as a pezzo concertato for flute, oboe and clarinet by the critic Lambertini—who then spoiled matters by adding 'in the style of the instrumental quartets of Handel and Mayseder'.§ In fact it is a delightful essay in the 'ranz des vaches' manner of Rossini. Formally it is a miniature rondo with the subject worked into a rudimentary canon at its second and third statements. The effect is

---

* Schiller, *Die Jungfrau von Orleans*, III, vi.

† At several points in the autograph the name Tebaldo is scored out and that of Giacomo is superimposed. It seems that Solera had originally intended to call Joan's father by the Italian equivalent of Thibaud, the name given to him by Schiller. In fact his name was Jacques d'Arc.

‡ Toye, p. 42. Teresa Stolz had a great success in the title-role at La Scala, Milan, 1865.

§ G. Morazzoni and G. M. Ciampelli, *Verdi: lettere inedite; Le opere verdiane al Teatro alla Scala (1839–1929)*, p. 80.

that of a celestial *Flötenuhr*, its mechanical element somehow emphasized by the 'circular', revolving shape of the melody.

116

As in the *Nabucco* overture there is a return to the *minore* allegro rising in a steady crescendo at the climax of which it opens out into the heroic major. This final movement hints at a transformation of themes, corresponding to Joan's transformation from shepherdess into warrior maid. The main theme for instance follows the main contours of Ex. 116:

117

The andante contains the following codetta theme:

118

In the allegro it appears thus:

119

If the result is noisy and trivial, we should remember that even in the works of Liszt, the father of thematic transformation, the subject rarely retains its dignity in all its guises. There is no second subject, merely an episodic restatement of Ex. 117, differently scored, in F major.

PROLOGUE*

Scene 1: a great hall in Dom-Rémy, adjoining the rooms hired by the court

* Originally *prologo* indicated a short, dramatic prelude to the main action setting forth the character of the drama. In pre-Metastasian opera prologues were generally sung by gods and goddesses or allegorical figures who never appeared again. In Verdi's day the distinction between a prologue and a first act is more usually the length of time separating it from the acts that follow. But the usage is in no way consistent. Act I of *I Lombardi* ought to qualify as a prologue. In the present opera the dividing line is presumably the relief of Orleans, which the audience hears about but never sees.

The opening scene is a tour-de-force of conventional operatic craftsmanship such as Solera could be guaranteed to devise. It is the Rossinian 'introduzione e cavatina' expanded into a huge 'quadro' with a variety of contrasting elements. The large chorus is divided into two—the officers of the French court, and the inhabitants of Dom-Rémy, male and female. In a choral dialogue the officers tell the people of the village that Charles has been driven from his throne, and Orleans is about to fall to the invaders. Then both groups unite in a chorus of execration against those who will not remain within the boundaries God has ordained for them. The opening of this scene is remarkably impressive. Here Verdi has drawn on his reserves of musical science to weave an instrumental backcloth as dignified and expressive as the opening of *Samson et Dalila*, though without Saint-Saëns's academic archaizing. Note the prominence of that universal symbol, the descending semitone of grief (*x*).

120

The main unison theme (*Maledetti cui spinge rea voglia*), doubled by trumpet and trombone, is a commonplace specimen of Verdi's Risorgimento manner, though there is some ingenious woodwind writing in the accompaniment, and the lamenting figure in Ex. 120 is neatly woven into the coda.

Delil (De Lisle) announces the Dauphin; and the semitonal figure Ex. 120(*x*) is hammered out with greater force. As Carlo enters the chorus comment on his melancholy appearance, 'so young and so unhappy'. He now issues his last command. An embassy is to go to Orleans to put an end to the fighting. Let the English king sit upon his throne; he himself absolves the French from their oath of allegiance. (All this is strictly according to Schiller.) Carlo's words have the force of a solemn pronouncement and are duly punctuated by full orchestra throughout. But as he moves into his narrative the scoring takes on a light intimate quality, as though he were talking half to himself. He describes how he prayed that God's wrath should be visited on him alone. Suddenly his senses thrilled; he fell into a blessed sleep and dreamed a marvellous dream. He was in the middle of a forest, reclining beneath an oak-tree on whose trunk a Madonna was painted. All at once the figure spoke to him. 'Arise . . .' she said, 'bring a sword and helmet and lay them at my feet.' Some of this is told in arioso, the narrative sensitively if naïvely illustrated by the orchestra. The dream itself forms the subject of a three-quatrain narrative aria (*Sotto una quercia parvemi*) only once interrupted gently by the chorus, who point out that there exists just such an oak-tree not far from the village. The character and texture of the movement are similar to Jacopo's 'Dal più remoto esiglio' (*I Due Foscari*): 6/8 andantino with pizzicato strings. But here the touches of woodwind colouring have a rhythmic as well as a harmonic function:

121

In the middle stanza (*Le tue parole, o vergine*) Carlo's exaltation is reflected by a move into the dominant and the favourite device of rapid pizzicato semiquavers in the bass. The final quatrain in which Carlo once more prays that France may be spared takes up more elaborately the cadential phrase of the first. Otherwise there is no more repetition than is needed to make the melody cohere. It is a graceful piece of writing, showing how the process of refinement continues ceaselessly even in Verdi's less distinguished works.

Carlo now determines to visit the sacred oak before nightfall, but the villagers try to dissuade him; for it is a place of horror and of death. In a chromatic passage heavy with the menace of chalumeau clarinets, bassoons and lower brass they describe how as twilight falls and the church bells 'peal out their last salute to the dying day', unearthly storms rage about the forest (and here they break out into a wild 6/8 allegro). 'Witches and warlocks celebrate their infernal rites and make their pacts with demons. Woe betide any man who intrudes upon them; for unless he gives his soul to the Devil he will never see the light of morning.' This chorus, Verdi's first essay in romantic *diablerie*, begins effectively in C minor; but the inevitable major section is only just saved from skittishness by rhythmic vigour and the headlong whirl of its progressions.

122

The climax is reached by a procedure which is soon to assume a vast importance in Verdi's musico-dramatic language: an unprepared leap on to a 6/4 chord outside the centre of the prevailing tonality.* All this recitation leaves Carlo unmoved.

* This procedure is to some extent anticipated in the chorus 'È dunque ver?' (*I Lombardi*); but there the effect is not so much one of emphasis as of routine exoticism.

Where there is an image of the Virgin, Hell can have no power. His only thought is to put aside the crown which has brought him so much unhappiness. Apart from a strong final cadence *Pondo è letal martirio* is a cabaletta of the gentle, languid variety as befits one of Carlo's melancholy character; and an unusually protracted choral coda is needed to wind up the scene with appropriate vigour. But the courtiers' attempt to rally the king's spirits is in vain, and he dismisses them with a gesture.

Scene 2: a forest. On the right there is a shrine which rises over a cliff, which may be climbed. On the left an oak-tree rises from ground level, and at the foot of it a stone seat. Upstage is the mouth of a cave. The sky is dark and stormy A near-by church bell sounds calling to prayers for the dead.

No bell, however, is marked in the score* which opens with storm music similar to the overture and in the same key. As the thunder dies away Giovanna's father Giacomo enters in a state of terror. He would never have ventured near this evil place if he were not haunted by a still greater fear that drives 'like a red-hot nail' into his soul—and a long tremolo on the open-string G of second violins and violas illustrates his word—a fear that under this oak-tree Giovanna may have sold herself to the Devil. Why else does she come here night after stormy night? After a brief arioso prayer (*Cielo, cielo m'attesti*) he withdraws into the cave to keep watch. This is his only solo music in the scene. But the intermittent storm noises throw it into a special relief. Another growl of distant thunder, and then Joan herself appears. The turbulent sky seems to her to reflect the war which is devastating France and in which she, a weak woman, can take no part. If only she could find a sword, a helmet and a suit of armour! During her recitative at the word 'battaglia' we hear a snatch of melody on the woodwind and lower brass which recurs in Act III as a 'battle theme'.

123

Giovanna's cavatina begins with a prayer to the Virgin Mary for weapons with which to fight (*Sempre all'alba ed alla sera*). The fresh, simple melody evolves, Donizetti-like, from a single rhythmic pattern:

124

Sem-pre al-l'al-ba ed al-la— ·se - ra qui-vi in-nal-zo a te— pre - ghie-ra;

The movement follows Verdi's usual 'extended' design (see previous chapters). From the first few notes is derived a martial figure rhythmically recalling Ex. 123,

* In the autograph the stage direction referring to the bell has been crossed out. Obviously Verdi and Solera decided that it would be an unnecessary complication.

part woodwind, part tutti, which forms the basis not only of *c* but of an additional coda as Joan falls asleep beneath the oak tree, her mind still full of the battle that she cannot join. This is, in its naïve way, Wagnerianism avant la lettre.* Her words merely beg forgiveness for having uttered so bold a prayer, but her inner-most thoughts are unashamedly militant.

The storm once more raises its head in the orchestra, as Carlo comes in and kneels before the shrine of the Virgin Mary, after first laying before it a sword and helmet. There he remains quite unaware of the curious sounds that are filling the air, seeming to arise from the last echoes of the dying storm. Soft chords on the harmonium and a trilling triangle (or sistro);† then a faintly heard chorus, bland and tuneful (*Tu sei bella*). They are demon voices audible only to Giovanna herself. 'You are young and fair,' they say; 'foolish maid, why not enjoy the sweet things of life? When you are past forty, that is the time to boast of virtue.' It might be the chorus of servants in Act II of *Un Giorno di Regno*.

125

This chorus sent Muzio into ecstasies: '... a pretty waltz, full of seductive themes; you can sing it straight away after two hearings ... original, popular, purely Italian'.‡ That of course is its fault. It has an innocent vulgarity which reeks of the Neapolitan café. However, if it does not precisely illustrate the proverb that the Devil has all the best tunes, it is more memorable than that of the Angel host which follows without a break in the same key. The clouds overhead disperse, bathing the forest in moonlight. Harmonium and triangle give way to harp and 'fisar-monica'§ and an angel choir of contraltos¶ tells Giovanna that she has been chosen by the Lord to save France, and woe betide her should she ever surrender to mortal love. Barely have the angels finished their melody than the demons are back again, and the two groups with their respective instruments do battle. Not a very serious battle however since the harmonies are blameless E flat major through-

---

* For this kind of counterpoint of thought and speech the locus classicus is Oreste's 'Le calme rentre dans mon cœur' from Gluck's *Iphigénie en Tauride*. That Verdi had this passage in mind is unlikely considering the opinion he held of Gluck (see letter to C. Bellaigue, 2.5.1898; *Copialettere*, p. 415).

† Nobody can be quite certain what a 'sistro' is, or was in Verdi's day; surely not the Egyptian instrument to be found in the Museo Archeologico in Florence. More probably it was a primitive triangle. The part nowadays played by the triangle in *The Barber of Seville* is marked *sistro* in the autograph.

‡ Letter from Muzio to Barezzi, 9.12.1844. Garibaldi, p. 175.

§ A kind of harmonium used in Italian theatres backstage—not a piano accordion, which is the present-day meaning of the term.

¶ Since an Italian opera chorus of those days was invariably divided into sopranos, tenors and basses, the 'contralti' probably refer to a separate unit altogether—boys or even children of both sexes.

out and fit perfectly. But in the end the angels' unison E flat conquers and Giovanna springs to her feet to see Carlo at the shrine. As in all the St Joan plays, she recognizes her sovereign straight away and tells him that the Almighty has answered his prayers. 'But who are you?' he asks. 'The warrior maid who invites you to glory,' she replies in what soon reveals itself as a trio-finale (*Son guerriera che a gloria t'invita*). It is a graceless melody, coarsely scored and over-syncopated, first cousin to the trio-stretta in the first act of *Ernani*. At the end of Carlo's stanza the orchestra cuts off sharply, leaving Giacomo to exclaim into a void, 'The King.' But neither Giovanna nor Carlo hears him. Giovanna is commending her flocks, her home and her father's white hairs to the care of the Blessed Virgin; Carlo is voicing his wonder at this maid who seems more than mortal; but to Giacomo it is all hideously clear. His daughter has compounded with Satan for the love of her King. All this Verdi sets forth in a curious little unaccompanied trio (*A te pietosa vergine*) poor as *a cappella* part-writing yet written with a good ear for the blending abilities of operatic voices. Formally this serves as a ritornello, after which all three singers resume in unison part of the cabaletta theme in all its banality, Giovanna and Carlo proclaiming their patriotism, Giacomo calling down a curse on his daughter's head.

ACT I

Scene 1: a lonely place with rocks scattered here and there. In the distance can be seen the city of Rheims. English soldiers are scattered about in groups. Women are weeping over the dying; others are tending the wounded.

The music which opens this act is that of a people in flight, with the same semi-fugal writing in the orchestra that marked the chorus 'Lo vedeste' (*Nabucco*). The English have only one thought—to return home as soon as possible now that Orleans is lost. Their commander Talbot tries to rally them. To his reproaches of cowardice they remind him how bravely they have all fought up till now. Mortal men hold no terrors for them, but against a fury from Hell they are powerless. In vain Talbot tells them that this is mere fanciful nonsense. They have come to fight soldiers, they reply, not armed demons; and once more they break into the fugal movement. More than one commentator has marked the similarity between the central homophonic part of the chorus (*O duce, noi sempre mirasti sui campi*) and the verse of 'Heart of Oak'.*

126

* See Toye, p. 256; Osborne, p. 116.

That this was a deliberate half-quotation seems quite likely. There is a good precedent for it in Donizetti who quoted 'God Save the Queen' in the overture of *Roberto Devereux* and 'Home Sweet Home' in the finale ultimo of *Anna Bolena*. Schumann tells us that in the 1840s England was renowned for two things—her navy and her choirs. A British gunboat was a frequent sight in any Mediterranean port where there was likely to be trouble, and the nautical songs of Dibdin and Boyce would doubtless have followed in its wake. The resemblance to the English song is just close enough to suggest a conscious reference; and it results in one of Verdi's more attractive choruses, particularly where the wind and side-drum accompaniment is garnished by a counterpoint of mobile pizzicato strings, following the model of 'Agli spaldi' (*I Puritani*). Before Talbot finds himself with a mutiny on his hands, Giacomo enters, 'his dishevelled hair and his gestures betraying the disorder of his wits'. This very night, he tells them, he will deliver into their hands the woman whom they fear. Sensation! Giacomo tells his story in an andante, *Franco son io*. Despite the love he bears his country he is resolved to fight against a king who has brought dishonour upon his white hairs. The soldiers take heart at once and talk of preparing the stake; but they cannot help pitying the old man's distress. The cabaletta (*So che per via di triboli*) shows Giacomo struggling to subdue his paternal feelings while Talbot and the soldiers vow to avenge his wrongs. As so often where the scena is conventionally designed the best is to be found in the transitions rather than in the principal sections. Sustaining horns where one would expect clarinets and bassoons, and a line that moves in slow painful steps, may give a sombre dignity to the andante, reminiscent of Silva's music in *Ernani*; but the movement is spoiled as a whole by a more than usually fussy and mechanical accompaniment. The cabaletta goes to great lengths to portray the feelings of a broken man—slow throbbing accompaniment, chromatic passing notes, a vacillation between major and minor. All the means are obvious and superficial, and in the absence of an exhilarating rhythm the formal bones obtrude. It is weary but in quite the wrong sense. Wonderfully effective on the other hand is the sudden blaze of E flat major at the end of Giacomo's opening sentence ('Questa rea che vi percuote sarà vostra prigionera')—a purely local key-change since the tonality reverts to C almost at once, showing how Verdi's use of strong modulation tends to be dramatic rather than architectural. The interventions of Talbot and the chorus are neatly calculated to express interest, suppressed excitement, resolution and, unexpectedly, compassion. This last is conveyed in a striking pianissimo passage scored for wind alone, to which Giacomo replies with the phrase that serves to introduce his cabaletta ('È memoria d'una figlia che tradiva il genitor'). In the context of Verdi's harmonic language at the time its plangent, Schumannesque appogiaturas stand out in sharp relief; and when it is recalled together with the preceding idea in the ritornello of the cabaletta the orchestra seems both to continue and to comment upon the thought that Giacomo cannot bring himself to complete (Ex. 127, opposite).

Scene 2: a garden at the Court of Rheims

It has been a day of rejoicing. For the first time in a hundred years the victors of Crécy, Poitiers and Agincourt have suffered a resounding defeat, and preparations are being made for the coronation of the Dauphin as King of France. But

127

Giovanna, the heroine of the hour, is tormented by a sense of her own unworthiness and a certain nameless guilt. The atmosphere of the court stifles her and she has fled into the garden still clad in helmet and breastplate. Yet even here the siren voices pursue her; and into the prelude for flute, clarinets and oboes is woven the song of the demons (Ex. 125), sounding even more beguiling in its innocence than before. Deep inside her she is aware of a new feeling that she dare not name. France is now saved; her mission is accomplished—why then does she remain at court? Ex. 125 breaks out *con tutta forza* and scored with deliberate brutality, trombones blasting away on an arpeggiated accompaniment. Giovanna quickly turns her thoughts to the pastoral life that she once knew: the little cottage, her old father, the mysterious forest. The *romanza* (O *fatidica foresta*) with its Rossini-like triplets, its snatches of flute obbligato, reverts to the 'ranz des vaches' style of the overture's second movement. It is a most beautiful expression of Giovanna's pure-hearted simplicity, and a reminder that beneath her armour she is a country girl.

128

Just as she has made up her mind to return to her native village, Carlo arrives looking for her; and so begins a grand duet which is to form the finale of the first act and in which the music for the first time reaches and even surpasses the heights of *I Due Foscari*. The best of Verdi's early duets are normally between soprano and baritone with both parties in a state of mutual tension. The great love duets between soprano and tenor come later, in *Otello*, *Aida* and *Don Carlos*; but perhaps the most striking of all these love scenes, the most wide ranging, and the most important in regard to the operatic structure is that of *Un Ballo in Maschera* where Amelia's sense of guilt acts as the grain of sand in the oyster shell, yielding pearl after pearl of musical inspiration. Of this the duet in Act I of *Giovanna d'Arco* gives a direct foretaste. The situation is much the same—the tenor ardent, the soprano tormented but unable to resist. The form is in no way unusual, being merely an elaboration of the standard tripartite scheme. The first movement is made up of two contrasted elements. An orchestral theme in quick-step rhythm, recalling the overture to *Un Giorno di Regno* and with the familiar trumpet and woodwind tinting provides the basis for the opening dialogue (*Chiede ognuno che mai fusse*); then as Carlo grows more pressing the music flowers into a stanza of vocal melody (*Dunque, o cruda, è gloria e trono*) repeated in anguished tones by Giovanna. She is no longer the chosen of Mary; she is betraying her divine mission. Why can he not respect her as before? To a return of the orchestral motif Carlo protests that his love for her is pure and spiritual. The quickstep gives place to an agitated pulsation for Giovanna is now unable to help herself, and after a long transition through key after key she throws herself into Carlo's arms, and the two voices sink into a rapturous cadence. But over the final note steal the angel voices as they repeat their warning. Terrified Giovanna breaks away from Carlo, who, of course, has heard nothing. To his repeated questions she remains silent, the strings answering for her with this obsessive figure:

129

Carlo rejoins with one of those soaring phrases which happen like a miracle in the course of many a Verdian scene.

130

For a time the rhythm of Ex. 129 persists as Giovanna seems to see in the shadows the apparition of her father, Carlo repeats his phrase and though both her words and her vocal line continue to betray agitation, the melting G major harmonies reveal that her heart is irrevocably his. A military tattoo without trumpets brings on a deputation of courtiers headed by Delil to summon Carlo to the cathedral for the coronation ceremony. Giovanna must go before him in the procession carrying the banner with which she had led the troops into battle. But as she receives it from Delil the men notice how her arm seems to tremble. Carlo dismisses them and then begins the final stretta, totally orthodox in its 'similar' design, as he takes Giovanna's hand and prepares to lead her away (*Vieni al tempio e ti consola*). It is a tender and dignified melody, but no sooner has Giovanna repeated it to more sorrowful words than the demons burst in with a chorus of glee, accompanied this time not by harmonium and triangle but by cymbals and the brass instruments of the banda. This is grafted quite easily on to the end of the melody without disturbing the harmonic scheme, and then worked into a ritornello punctuated by cries of despair from Giovanna and solicitous queries from Carlo. As a theatrical device it is clever but strictly two-dimensional. The demons make their effect, such as it is, through rapping semi-quaver rhythms and the garish scoring of their accompaniment. But of genuine horror there is not a trace. When one considers what Wagner had already achieved in that direction with his Act III of *The Flying Dutchman* it becomes clear that the extremes of *Schauerromantik* were not for Verdi. The entire episode is a tasteless and feeble excrescence on a remarkably fine duet.

ACT II

Scene: the main square in Rheims. In the foreground to the left is the Cathedral of St Denis. The stage is crowded with people.

A brief chorus of acclamation (*Dal cielo a noi chi viene*) is followed by a triumphal parade with banda and orchestra playing alternately and in combination. *The crowd is parted in the centre by a double file of soldiers*, run the stage directions. *The procession is headed by a military band; after them come a group of children robed in white, then the heralds, the halberdiers, pages, magistrates, marshals of the realm, nobles, cavaliers, ladies-in-waiting, ambassadors, etc. Finally the Maid carrying her banner followed by the King borne on a palanquin by six barons. Courtiers, servants and soldiers complete the procession.* As a spectacle it could doubtless be very fine; but the fact is that Solera's grand theatrical tableaux awake no response in Verdi until they are kindled by the spark of drama. His setting of this entire sequence is commonplace, not to say provincial.

The music plods relentlessly through 137 bars, giving the procession ample time to pass across the stage into the cathedral followed by the crowd, until only one person is left on the stage. It is Giacomo, now more than ever filled with a sense of his mission as an avenging angel. His recitative is twice punctuated by recollections of the storm in the overture, and the minor–major romanza that follows (*Speme al vecchio era una figlia*) opens with a meandering figure for unison violas and cellos which harks back to Ex. 120 from the first chorus of the Prologue. 'Once,' says Giacomo, 'I had a daughter, the hope of my declining years; one who would have closed my eyes in death; and now I must be her accuser. Yet all will have been for the best if I can save her soul from everlasting fire.' (This last thought, of course, is the burden of the major section.) It is a carefully scored piece, unencumbered by fussy accompanimental patterns, but the determined restlessness of the orchestral bass, doubtless intended to characterize Giacomo's state of mind, results in some ugly voice-leading unredeemed by any distinction in the melody. It is all too much like the Doge's 'O vecchio cor che batte' (*I Due Foscari*) without the latter's pith and concentration.

Fanfares are now heard inside the cathedral (six or nine trumpets are specified); then an *a cappella* hymn (*Te Deum lodiamo*) as flat and characterless as a religious postcard. The fanfare is repeated and the procession slowly files out headed by Carlo now duly crowned and anointed. With him is Giovanna, visibly perturbed as Giacomo notes with grim satisfaction. Carlo ascribes her behaviour to mere modesty. He takes her by the hand and amid cheers presents her to the people as France's saviour. A second cathedral, he says, should be erected in her honour; but his words are cut short by Giacomo. 'Spare God the blasphemy of her at whose feet you are kneeling!' Carlo reacts with fury. Giovanna cries out, 'My father!', the crowd echoing her with the appropriate change of pronoun. Twice during this scene Giovanna's agitation is expressed in an orchestral motif which at its second occurrence reminds us how thoroughly Verdi had studied his *Don Giovanni*.

131

Giacomo's denunciation (*Comparire il ciel m'ha stretto*) has a cabaletta-like gait and structure though it lacks repeat, ritornello and coda. God has forced him to bear witness that in the same forest where the King first met her Giovanna had sold her soul to the Devil. 'Now,' he cries, as the storm music peals out again and the crowd recoils in terror, 'dare to raise a church in her honour!' Orchestra and voices subside in a long decrescendo. There is a pause; and the adagio concertato of the finale begins. Giacomo is wrestling with his paternal feelings, Carlo is unable to believe in the guilt of one so like an angel; the crowd are helpless and bewildered. So far all has been convention, not to say routine. Apart from the sudden D flat major chords which interrupt the final F major cadence at *Coi demoni patteggiar* Giacomo's solo suffers from the not uncommon failing of the young Verdi: force without substance. But the movement which now follows is as powerful in its musical architecture as in its truth of dramatic expression. It begins with a duo for Carlo and Giacomo with chorus (*No! forme d'angelo*). The general numbness is reflected by the short-winded phrases, the lack of any defined melody and the largely unaccompanied texture. One figure stands out, however, underlined by orchestral strings:

132

The second part of the movement, as usual, takes on a more 'periodic' character, as the voice of Giovanna soars in a cantilena of limpid serenity, transfiguring the tragedy, dissolving the tears in an ideal world of lyrical sound. Once again clarinet arpeggios figure in the accompaniment.

133

GIOVANNA
cantabile con semplicità

L'a - ma - ro ca - li - ce   som - mes - sa io   be - vo,

One is reminded of the finale of Act III of *La Traviata*, where the ensemble is dominated by another falsely accused heroine. Giovanna, like Violetta, is resigned; she will drain the cup of bitterness in silence; God's will be done. Her final cadence is interrupted thunderously by Ex. 131, now sung to the words *O qual o qual orribile* and transformed into an even more menacing dotted rhythm. The smoother phrases of Carlo and Giacomo from the first part of the ensemble are recalled in a three-part counterpoint of soloists.

Ex. 133 is resumed, Carlo now singing in unison with Giovanna as if to show that he will stand by her, come what may. This time the accompaniment is derived from Ex. 132 now in the major key and developed into a single line of semi-quavers shared out among choral groups and doubled throughout by pizzicato strings, an effect to which Verdi was to return in the Act I finale of *Stiffelio*. In the coda the contrasts are epitomized even more steeply, with Giovanna's line culminating in a long high phrase in semiquaver triplets. From here on the musical level declines. Carlo calls upon Giovanna to defend herself; but the crowd note that she remains pale and silent. Her father takes her hand and three times, to the sound of trombone and bassoon chords, he asks her if she is guilty of sacrilege: in the name of God, of her family, and the soul of her mother. There is a burst of thunder. The crowd are now convinced that Giovanna is a witch. In vain Carlo cries out that he will save her. 'None but God can save her now,' replies Giacomo. 'Come, daughter.' The people hurl their imprecations in a noisy stretta (*Fuggi, o donna maledetta*). Once more Giovanna assumes the lead with a lyrical melody declaring that her sense of guilt has been purged by suffering, that she will now bear her cross gladly. Again Carlo shares her line at the reprise, though he is now powerless to help her. But while the adagio was tinged with Verdi greatness the stretta is a stretta like any other, except for unusual rhythm—a smooth rapid 2/4, without the usual sense of galop—and an initial dominant pedal.

ACT III

Scene: inside a fort in the English camp. A ladder leads up to the tower which commands a view of the whole camp. Giovanna is seated heavily chained on a bench; near by is a stake.

How she arrived here is unexplained. Presumably she allowed her father to lead her across the lines like a lamb to the slaughter. This is certainly not what happens in Schiller where the capture is a matter of chance, or divine providence. It is precisely during this intervening time that the psychological climax of Schiller's drama occurs; where Joan's mind is suddenly cleared of her sense of guilt and her faith in her mission restored. But Solera and Verdi are not concerned with psychology, merely with effective theatre. The first scene moves into action very swiftly. After four orchestral flourishes the sentinels can be heard calling out that the French have attacked. There are three cannon shots; then a long 'battle' based on Ex. 123. Compared with that of *I Lombardi* it at least has the virtue of coherence. There is no attempt to represent each side with a different motif and a different assortment of instruments. It is merely a trim Verdian march, less vulgar than some, yet redolent of the Sunday afternoon bandstand rather than a field of battle. Yet it makes Giovanna as restive as a tethered racehorse that has heard the starting signal. She sees in a vision the French charge, the English counter-attack, Carlo surrounded . . . taken prisoner—and she can do nothing! In her agony she does not notice that Giacomo has entered (evidently English security arrangements were casual even in those days). At first he thinks she must be wandering in her mind. But when she falls on her knees and implores God not to forsake her he begins to wonder whether he has not made a terrible mistake. During all this the battle music has been used ingeniously to provide the background to a duet-movement between two people, one of whom is unaware of the other's presence. In the andante that follows (*Amai ma un solo istante*) the situation is unchanged but the music transcends its absurdity. It is the familiar combination of soprano and baritone which rarely fails Verdi. Over an accompaniment of strings coloured here and there by sustaining horns and bassoons Giovanna opens her heart to God. She loved a man but only for a moment; she is still pure in body and soul, and all her thoughts are turned to Heaven. The opening phrase spans the first two lines of the stanza without the caesura which so often breaks up the line in Italian opera of the period; and surely no melody was ever more sensitively 'graced'.

134

It is a fine specimen of the dissimilar duet-movement with the voices kept mutually distinct until the last possible moment. Giacomo, now deeply remorseful, responds to her melody with another in the major key. She rejoins with a further idea couched in Verdi's noblest lyrical vein, and spun out so as to form a long codetta.

135

Only in the last six bars do the two voices converge in harmony.

Giovanna now rises to her feet, 'kindled by her faith', and prays for a miracle to set her free. This is strictly according to Schiller who knew his Old Testament far better than the author of *Nabucco*. 'Thou who didst break in pieces the chains of Samson.' But Solera's memory, normally excellent where other people's work was concerned, evidently failed him at this point and instead of Samson he wrote 'the chosen apostle'. Somebody must have pointed out the mistake, for in the autograph the word 'apostolo' is crossed out and 'Saulo' written over the top. And of course that is wrong too. However, it has found its way into the printed score.

But there is no need for a divine miracle since Giacomo is there, for whom the loosening of his daughter's bonds is literally the work of a moment. Giovanna is overwhelmed with joy. She asks for her father's blessing; then the two of them join in a 'similar' stretta (*Or dal padre benedetta*). However, being soprano and baritone, as distinct from soprano and tenor, they are confined to different keys. Normally one would expect the second voice to enter in the dominant or subdominant but here for once Verdi places Giacomo in a remote key—F major against the soprano's A. The procedure yields such a beautiful modulation at the point of return that one wonders why he never adopted it again. This same F major–A major polarity is driven home in the coda, so winding up the movement with an unusual strength of musical logic.

Giovanna now hurries away to join the French troops. Ex. 123 is resumed as Giacomo climbs to the tower to watch the progress of the battle. Giovanna seems to be everywhere at once. Now she has rescued Carlo; now the English are falling back in disorder (here the music takes on a momentary contrapuntal aspect). Then everything is hidden in a cloud of dust, and the next thing that Giacomo hears is the joyous shouts of the French as they storm the fort and burst into the prison cell with Carlo at their head. Giacomo implores the King's forgiveness, which Carlo readily grants. He had come, he says, at Giovanna's insistence to defend her father's life. At this moment Delil enters with the news that Giovanna has fallen. Giacomo buries his face in his hands, while Carlo laments her death in a romanza (*Quale più fido amico*), one of those panels of delicate colour that stand out with such clarity in Verdi's early scores. Over a sparse accompaniment of pizzicato strings the cello traces a pattern of semiquavers in the tradition of Rossini's 'Sois immobile', while the cor anglais moves in sixths and thirds with the voice. (This same combination of cor anglais and solo cello will recur in a similar context of grief in Act II of *Rigoletto*.) The melody, if not especially distinguished, has the dignified sincerity to be found in all Verdi's best tenor romances. Then to the strains of a funeral march Giovanna's body is borne in. Here the music takes on a certain primitive grandeur. The opening, scored for strings, lower woodwind, brass and timpani, is clipped, restrained, almost unthematic (Ex. 136).

Melody supervenes by way of variation with the sopranos' episode (*Non*

136

sembra un angelo), accompanied by pulsating chords on the upper woodwind, 'How serene she looks,' they say, 'how like an angel!' The full chorus enters in unison pianissimo with a line which modulates upward by semitones, the cellos busy with an accompaniment similar to that of Carlo's romanza. Finally, the opening theme, Ex. 136, reappears with a decoration of staccato semiquavers played by four desks of first and second violins. During the last section of the march Giacomo has heard a faint groan from Giovanna. She opens her eyes, slowly raises herself and the music rises to a triumphal climax as Carlo hails a new miracle. But Giovanna's recovery is only fleeting. In a brief recitative she takes a loving farewell of her father and her fellow warriors. The sight of her banner fills her with mystical joy, expressed in a lyrical cadence followed by a chord of E flat major which swells and dies. She sees the heavens open and the Virgin Mary coming to meet her—she with whom Giovanna had so often communed by the oak-tree in the forest. Recitative gives way to a slow 6/8, an extension of the marcia funebre rhythm, the voice accompanied only by snatches of solo clarinet. As the melodic thread is picked up by soloists, chorus and full orchestra, we can recognize the long, Verdian reach, the slow parade of interlocking themes from which the finest of the early finales are made. Only the solo clarinet, unfortunately reminiscent of the violin in Act III of *I Lombardi*, strikes a faintly jarring note. Carlo begs Giovanna not to forsake them: she must live for France, for her father, for him. But Giacomo is resigned and asks only for his daughter's blessing. Giovanna feels herself borne up on wings. The stage is filled with a strange light; angel voices are heard calling her home; and to the accompaniment of a brass band the demons metaphorically gnash their teeth, fortunately without much affecting the rhythmic or harmonic scheme. At last Giovanna sinks back; the light grows brighter; the soldiers lower their standards and fall on their knees. The curtain falls on a note not of tragedy but of triumph.

VENICE, *carnival-quaresima, 1845–6.* For the first revival of *Giovanna d'Arco* at the Teatro la Fenice Verdi composed a new cavatina for Sofia Loewe*—an *amende honorable* no doubt for the rondò-finale that he had failed to provide her with in *Ernani*. The music has not yet come to light; but the text indicates two movements each based on the standard Metastasian double quatrain: an andante ('Potrei lasciare il margine'), a short transition of two lines, and a cabaletta ('O se un giorno avessi un dono').† There is a final pendant in which Giovanna falls asleep to the same words as in the original aria.

The subsequent history of *Giovanna d'Arco* is less sensational than its tremendous success at Milan in 1845 might lead one to expect. It was more popular than *I Due Foscari*, less so than *Ernani* and the later *Attila*. From Milan it passed to all the other principal operatic theatres, undergoing some strange metamorphoses of title in places where religious susceptibilities were offended by the glorification of an as yet uncanonized heretic. For the French, of course, it had a patriotic appeal and so was assured of a temporary place in the repertoire of the Théâtre des Italiens,

---

* See letter to Sofia Loewe, 19.12.1845. *Copialettere*, p. 18.

† A copy of the printed libretto, issued by the Melenari press, can be found in the archives of the Teatro la Fenice.

and there were one or two surprisingly late revivals of it in Italy;* for with all its faults it remains an impressive vehicle for a prima donna. But in the recent neo-Verdian age it has not fared particularly well. Nor is this surprising. Whereas *Ernani* and *I Due Foscari* for all their faults show a homogeneity of style and structure *Giovanna d'Arco* remains a work of brilliant patches. At its worst it is provincial and childishly pretentious. But the best things in it surpass anything that Verdi had written up to that time. In the heroine he has created a soprano part of rare distinction, in which all the solo numbers and most of the ensembles are of a high calibre. At no point does Giovanna descend to the level of an ordinary prima donna. Almost everything she has to sing carries her own unique blend of simplicity and majesty. It is to be noticed too that even in the grandiose world of Solera Verdi never forgot his maxim of brevity. How typical, for instance, that in the funeral march in Act III two of the three sixteen-bar units should be fore-shortened by two bars—in contrast to the relentless symmetry of a similar march in Donizetti's opera *Belisario*. For all its variety *Giovanna d'Arco* is a remarkably short opera, lasting barely two hours, despite the fact that the proportions of, say, the finales to Acts II and III are much bigger than in the longest ensembles of *Nabucco*. In short, *Giovanna d'Arco* hints at the great works of the post-*Traviata* period.

---

* Monaldi, pp. 84–5, states that in 1885 Verdi removed the overture and 'placed it at the start of *I Vespri Siciliani*, where it still remains'. No satisfactory explanation of this extraordinary statement has yet been offered. The thematic connection observed by Osborne, pp. 112–14, on close examination is not quite as firm as the author would seem to imply.

10 ALZIRA

ALZIRA

Opera in a prologue and two acts
by
SALVATORE CAMMARANO
(after Voltaire's tragedy, *Alzire, ou les Américains*)

First performed at the
San Carlo Theatre, Naples,
12 August 1845

ALVARO, father of Gusmano } GUSMANO } Governors of Peru	BASSO COMPRIMARIO PRIMO BARITONO	Marco Arati Filippo Coletti
OVANDO, a Spanish captain	SECONDO TENORE	Ceci
ZAMORO } } heads of Peruvian ATALIBA } tribes	PRIMO TENORE SECONDO BASSO	Gaetano Fraschini Michele Benedetti
ALZIRA, daughter of Ataliba	PRIMA DONNA SOPRANO	Eugenia Tadolini
ZUMA, her sister	SECONDA DONNA MEZZO-SOPRANO	Maria Salvetti
OTUMBO, a South American warrior	SECONDO TENORE	Francesco Rossi

Spanish officers and soldiers—South Americans of both sexes

The action takes place in Lima and other regions of Peru

Epoch: towards the middle of the sixteenth century

After the prodigious success of *Ernani* in 1844 one of the first people to approach Verdi for a new opera was Vincenzo Flauto, impresario of the San Carlo theatre. Together with La Scala and the Fenice, the San Carlo made up the trio of leading theatres in Italy; and it had a far longer and more glorious tradition than either of the other two. During the eighteenth century Naples had been the cradle of classical opera, serious and comic. Its composers, mostly from the Kingdom of the Two Sicilies and all trained at its Conservatorics, had carried the latest operatic developments throughout Europe. But as so often happens the progressives of one century had become the diehards of the next; and by the early years of the nineteenth century Naples presented as conservative a face to the operatic world as could be imagined. True, in the next decade Rossini conquered there in the teeth of an entrenched opposition; and for some six years the San Carlo opera house was to offer him the same freedom for experiment as Haydn enjoyed at Esterház. Yet a glance at his Neapolitan operas shows that they were written for special conditions and even a special climate of taste.* In the time of Bellini and Donizetti these were fast disappearing. But Naples remained a city apart, immensely proud of its traditions and conscious of its standards. To the Neapolitan the northern Italian was scarcely less of a foreigner than the Frenchman or German. In 1845 the presiding musical genius was Saverio Mercadante, head of the Conservatorio and no friend to Verdi until many years later. 'To score a real success in Naples is always difficult, particularly for me,' Verdi was to remark on a future occasion.†
The real attraction of the Neapolitan contract was the opportunity it afforded of working with the house poet of the San Carlo Theatre, Salvatore Cammarano. Since the virtual retirement of Felice Romani, Cammarano was the foremost librettist in Italy. He may have lacked Romani's clarity and elegance; but he handled the traditional fustian of Italian *melodramma* with fluency and a certain distinction. He had a good sense of dramatic pace within the operatic conventions; he was more experienced than Piave, and had a surer touch than Solera who was only at home with the grand gesture. Several of Donizetti's greatest successes (*Lucia di Lammermoor, Roberto Devereux, Belisario*) had been written to Cammarano's libretti. Then, too, as a subject of one of the most repressive governments in Europe, he was adept at avoiding all those details of plot and language at which the censors were likely to baulk. There was no subject, however inflammatory, which he could not reduce to well-made romantic pulp. To Verdi, intent as he was on mastering all the standard procedures of his trade, the advantages of their collaboration were obvious.

But Cammarano's reputation, and perhaps the fact that his libretto was being paid for by the management, resulted in an even more passive attitude on Verdi's

* One curious feature of the Neapolitan scene, seemingly without parallel elsewhere in Italy, was a tradition of comic opera with spoken dialogue in place of recitative (e.g., Bellini's *Adelson e Salvini* (1st version); Luigi Ricci's *Piedigrotta* et al.). Naples was also the first Italian city to abolish recitative with keyboard in opera seria.
† Letter to V. Flauto, 1.11.1849. *Copialettere*, p. 86.

part than he had adopted over *Giovanna d'Arco*. The choice of Voltaire's *Alzire* was not his, as a letter to Cammarano makes clear. 'I have received the synopsis, and I'm delighted with it in every respect. I've read Voltaire's tragedy which should make an excellent opera in the hands of a Cammarano. I'm often accused of being too fond of noise and of treating the voice badly. Pay no attention to that; put plenty of passion into it and you'll find that I write quite passably. . . .'* Cammarano, after his fashion, complied. But just as *Lucia di Lammermoor* bears little trace of Scott's eerie Border novel, so in Cammarano's *Alzira* Voltaire might have found it difficult to recognize his own play.

This much needs stating if only because the Voltairian subject tends to let loose a flood of irrelevant and tendentious discussion about Verdi's agnosticism. For the devout Catholic the Sage of Ferney still represented the Antichrist among writers. Not that this prevented Rossini, that most uncomplicated of believers, from setting *Tancrède* and *Sémiramis* with a clear conscience. But *Alzire* is a rather different case. Here Voltaire has set himself up as a saviour of Christianity from itself. The play is based on an incident which took place in Peru in the sixteenth century when the Spanish governor Gusman was assassinated by a tribesman on the day of his wedding with an Inca princess. In his preface Voltaire writes:

> A barbarian's religion consists in sacrificing to his gods the blood of his enemies. An ill-educated Christian is scarcely any better. To him religion means observing useless practices with great assiduity while being false to his duties as a human being; offering up his prayers while clinging to his vices; fasting and yet hating; intriguing and persecuting. The true Christian looks upon all men as his brothers. He does good to them all and forgives the injuries he receives. Such a Christian is Gusman at the moment of his death.

Not, however, before. The true Christian virtues are embodied in the sympathetic but powerless figure of Gusman's father Alvarez. The hero is the assassin Zamore, the noble savage, inflexible in his loves and hates, yet capable of disinterested generosity. He is the converse of Gusman who stands for all that is worst in the forces of established religion and whose marriage to Alzire the Inca princess is merely a matter of politics. Alvarez, the retiring governor, is all for treating the Incas as friends but to Gusman:

> L'Américain farouche est un monstre sauvage
> Qui mord en frémissant le frein d'esclavage;
> Soumis au châtiment, fier dans l'impunité
> À la main qui le flatte il se croit redouté.
> Tout pouvoir en un mot périt par l'indulgence
> Et la sévérité produit l'obéissance.†

So much for the professions of Christendom to bring the light of civilization to the dark continents. *Alzire* is a play of ideas rather than of passions, and Alzire herself is as ready as any Shavian heroine with the witty thrust. She tells her father:

---

* Letter to Cammarano, 23.5.1844. *Copialettere*, p. 429. † Voltaire, *Alzire*, I, i.

> Jamais mon visage
> N'a de mon cœur démenti le langage.
> Qui peut se déguiser pourrait trahir sa foi;
> C'est un art de l'Europe; il n'est pas fait pour moi.*

Her father Montèze had already promised her in marriage to Zamore whom she loved and who loved her in return. But Zamore is said to have died under torture at the hands of the Spaniards. Montèze meanwhile has become converted to Christianity and is anxious to promote the match with Gusman as a means of honourably uniting conquerors and conquered. Alzire is willing to obey him in this as in everything else. She has no compunction in renouncing the gods of her youth. But if the new religion brings life beyond the grave, and if her heart has been given to Zamore once and for all, then whether or not he is dead in the earthly sense can surely make no difference. Her marriage to Gusman will be a lie in the sight of heaven: and is not the Christian god also a god of vengeance? Voltaire's Alzire is no wilting romantic heroine.

In the hands of Cammarano however the sting of scepticism is removed and the play's intellectual content reduced to a minimum. Religion and politics, the two raisons d'être of the drama, are scarcely mentioned; and the confrontation of different creeds, different civilizations and different worlds becomes merely another variant of the eternal triangle. Gusman is not so much the tyrant as the thwarted lover. Zamore is a South American Ernani; Alzira just another woman in love who sighs and suffers. Alvarez and Montèze (here renamed Ataliba) are comprimario and secondo basso respectively.

None of this worried Verdi. He professed himself highly delighted with the lines, especially those in the cavatina for Alzira in Act I. Yet even with Cammarano he was unable to refrain from one or two mild observations. Was it not just a little dangerous to have three cavatinas coming one after the other?† And would Cammarano please remember to err on the side of brevity rather than otherwise. Cammarano certainly did so, being no doubt unprepared for Verdi's rather plain manner of verse-setting which makes the lines pass much quicker than in Donizetti or Mercadante. The result was that *Alzira* proved too short; and the management decided to compound with Verdi for an overture outside the terms of the original contract.‡ Work on the opera progressed slowly due to a recrudescence of the throat and stomach troubles that so often affected Verdi during composition, so that the premiere had to be postponed. Cammarano was not displeased about this, hoping that the first night could be deferred until the soprano Tadolini had recovered from her confinement: therefore if the maestro could see his way clear to prolonging his ailment still further. . . . Verdi replied that the illness needed no exaggeration on his part as the enclosed medical certificate would make clear. When Flauto wrote suggesting that there was nothing wrong with him that tincture of wormwood and a little Neapolitan air would not cure, he received a very short answer. 'We artists,' Verdi wrote to Cammarano, 'are apparently not allowed to be ill.'§ By 24 June he was well enough to travel to Naples. Piano

---

* *Ibid.*, I, v. † Letter to Cammarano, 27.5.1845. *Copialettere*, p. 430.
‡ See letter from Muzio to Barezzi, 18.9.1845. Garibaldi, p. 217.
§ Letter to Cammarano, 2.6.1845. *Copialettere*, p. 13.

rehearsals began at the end of July, and the premiere was at last fixed for 12 August. On 30 July Verdi wrote to Andrea Maffei, 'I've finished the opera including the scoring. . . . I couldn't give you a proper opinion on it because I composed it almost without thinking and with no trouble whatever. . . . So even if it were to fail that wouldn't upset me unduly. But don't worry, it certainly won't be a fiasco. The singers enjoy singing it and some of it must be quite bearable.'* Composer's modesty, no doubt; for it seems that on the whole he had high hopes for *Alzira*. The cast of principals was a strong one. Gaetano Fraschini was a heavy heroic tenor, known as the 'tenore della maledizione' from his forceful delivery of the curse in *Lucia di Lammermoor*.† The baritone Coletti was generally regarded as a worthy successor to Tamburini and was much admired by, of all people, Thomas Carlyle. The Alzira was Eugenia Tadolini after all, no longer young but still one of the finest sopranos in Italy. So Verdi was spared the doubtful talents of Anna Bishop who would have taken her place. Even the mixed reception on the opening night failed to shake his optimism. 'It was just like the first night of *Ernani*,' he wrote to Piave. 'When I've said that I've said everything. I hope that later on it will be more appreciated and stay in the repertoire for who knows how long. Then if I'm not mistaken it will go the rounds fairly quickly because I think it makes a stronger effect than *I Due Foscari*.'‡ Certainly the correspondent of Ricordi's *Gazzetta Musicale*, Opprandino Arrivabene, was complimentary enough; writing of 'beauties so delicately contrived that the ear can hardly take them in at a first hearing'.§ Nevertheless Verdi's forecast was wrong. *Alzira* did not recover then or at any time; and a disastrous performance in Rome in November eventually convinced him that it had, in theatrical terms, laid an egg.

> Many thanks for your news about the failure of *Alzira* [*he wrote to the librettist Ferretti*], and also for the suggestions you were kind enough to make. In fact, though, I noticed all these faults before it went on stage in Naples and you can't imagine how hard I worked to put them right. The trouble is in the opera's vitals, and tinkering with it would only make it worse. . . . I did hope that the overture and the second act finale would have to some extent redeemed the rest and I see that at Rome they didn't. All the same, they should have done.¶

Next year a revival at La Scala earned Verdi the worst press notices he had received since *Un Giorno di Regno*. In years to come he was to refer to *Alzira* as 'downright bad'. ‖ This too is an exaggeration. *Alzira* has plenty of melody. The overture and finales are good, especially that of Act II which is arguably the one moment when the music rises to greatness. But there is no denying the fact that much of the score remains on a rather commonplace level of invention. Clearly Verdi's

---

* Letter to Andrea Maffei, 30.7.1845. *Copialettere*, p. 431.
† By the same token Napoleone Moriani was known as the 'tenore della bella morte' from his playing of the final scene in the same opera.
‡ Letter to Piave (undated). Abbiati, I, p. 566.
§ The entire notice is quoted in Muzio's letter to Barezzi, 18.9.1845. Garibaldi, pp. 217–19. For less flattering views see Walker, pp. 138–9.
¶ Letter to J. Ferretti, 5.11.1845. *Copialettere*, p. 432.
‖ *Copialettere*, p. 432.

imagination had been insufficiently fired. The fault was not Cammarano's for having traduced a strong play. By the standards of its time *Alzira* is quite a good libretto, but it was written for the wrong composer. Instead of a fast-moving dramatic scheme Cammarano had devised a succession of large-scale finite numbers. His arias for the tenor are particularly expansive, as though he had in mind that composer par excellence for the tenor voice, Donizetti. Verdi as yet lacked the craftsmanship to fill out these designs in the way that his audience expected. Even in the grand love duet of Act I he preferred to press swiftly ahead, sustaining a dramatic momentum which the text does not imply. This is one reason for the opera's disconcerting brevity. No wonder the canary-fanciers of Naples felt that they had been sold short. One suspects too that the very fluency of Cammarano's verse, the skill with which he deployed the elements of solo, ensemble and recitative, had given Verdi a false sense of ease in the composition. He had written it 'almost without thinking'—his own words.* And is there not perhaps a touch of cynicism in the large AMEN scribbled at the end of the overture, the last piece to be composed?

The overture was described by the critic Arrivabene as 'preserving the two-fold character of the opera—savage and warlike on the one hand, tender and romantic on the other. Its form is completely novel and it aroused the greatest enthusiasm.'† Like the overture to *Giovanna d'Arco* it is in three movements, none of them owing anything to sonata form. The first, an andantino scored for high woodwind and percussion, is an essay in exotic colour, with particularly effective use of piccolo and low clarinet.‡ Here and there the music strays into the territory of *Casse-Noisette*.

137

The second movement is introduced by three horn and trumpet blasts repeated in direct anticipation of *La Forza del Destino* and consists of noisy warlike tuttis from which at length a solo clarinet detaches itself to trace a long pathetic melody accompanied by pizzicato strings. The final allegro brillante is notable mainly for a variant of that theme which first saw the light in *Oberto*. It is the only quotation from the opera itself, where it forms the triumphal march of the Spaniards at the beginning of Act I (Ex. 138, overleaf).

In construction the movement runs parallel to the final part of the *Giovanna d'Arco* overture with one important difference: it begins in the wrong key, and with a subsidiary melody that never recurs later. In the hands of a Beethoven this

---

* Letter to A. Maffei, 30.7.1845. *Copialettere*, p. 431.   † See Garibaldi, p. 218.
‡ The San Carlo theatre seems to have been unique among Italian opera houses in employing two flutes *and* a piccolo (see Chapter 2).

138

procedure would have had a cogent sense of musical logic. In Verdi the climb up through a crescendo from G major to D major sounds strangely casual. On the other hand the central excursion into F major where Ex. 138 is accompanied by violin triplets and then developed in a piccolo solo is strongly approached and well quitted. Verdi, like Chopin, is far more certain in his feeling for the relationship of keys a third apart.

PROLOGUE

The Prisoner

*Scene: a vast plain watered by the Rima. The eastern horizon is covered by clouds tinged with purple by the rising sun**

There is no particular significance in the subtitle, beyond a typically Neapolitan love of pomp (Cammarano always gave his acts subtitles, not all of which found their way into the published scores). But 'Prologue' is strictly apt; for the episode on which the scene is based is alluded to in the drama as having taken place several years before the start of the action. Brought forward in time it makes for a highly effective 'Introduzione e cavatina' for the nobly savage hero.

During a long 'curtain up' crescendo with a brutal tritone prominent a group of Inca tribesmen headed by one Otumbo are seen dragging Alvaro in chains across the stage. They bind him to a tree trunk and then dance round him singing a blood-thirsty war chant (*Muoia, muoia coverto d'insulti*). The setting is as vigorous as one could wish, Verdi in his brashest 6/8 vein, somewhere between the crowd of mocking odalisques in *I Lombardi* and the chorus of villagers ('Nell'orribile foresta') in the prologue to *Giovanna d'Arco*. Like a true Christian Alvaro prays that God may forgive his murderers; but his prayer is cut short by the shouts of his captors who, 'uttering frenzied cries of joy advance on their prisoner, some with darts, some with whips, some with torches of burning pitch'. Suddenly their attention is caught by a tribesman steering a canoe up-river towards them. Strings with horns give out a characteristic figure in accordance with the rule (in force ever since Tancredi stepped ashore in 1813) whereby any form of navigation must be signalized in the orchestra.

The man is recognized as the Inca warrior Zamoro, who is believed to have died under torture. Otumbo and his fellow tribesmen throw themselves at his feet. Seeing Alvaro bound to the tree Zamoro commands his immediate release; he does not want the day of his return home to be stained with bloodshed. 'Return

---

* From a letter of Muzio to Barezzi (17.7.1845; Garibaldi, pp. 208–10) it seems that Verdi had originally intended to open the opera with a prelude depicting the sunrise and inspired by Félicien David's cantata *Le Désert*, which had recently been performed in Milan. See also Chapter 11.

to your people,' he says to Alvaro as he unties his bonds, 'and tell them that you owe your life to a barbarian.' Alvaro embraces him with tears of joy and is escorted away by a group of tribesmen. Zamoro now unburdens himself to the Incas in the andante (*Un Inca, eccesso orribile!*), not, for once, a sensitive, lightly scored movement with which Verdi usually launched his tenor roles, but a broad, intense melody with an elaborate accompanimental pattern and frequent outbursts from the full orchestra. Cammarano's hymn of hate against the tyrant Gusman could hardly have been set otherwise; and the unfamiliar design resulting from the text of three quatrains instead of the normal two marked a new and exciting formal solution. But for once the long Verdian reach is not long enough. The melodic trajectory is exhausted by the end of the second quatrain, to be artificially prolonged by mere battering force. This unremitting emphasis of expression, this total lack of chiaroscuro, is to make Zamoro the most two-dimensional of operatic heroes.

On being told that both Alzira and her father are in enemy hands, Zamoro determines to rescue them. The short solo (*Risorto fra le tenebre*) in which he describes the spirit of revolt which is abroad is technically a transitional passage, but the melody, strong and non-modulating, has the quality of a whispered cabaletta. The harmonic accompaniment by solo clarinet gives a foretaste of similar refinements in *La Forza del Destino*.

One cannot expect Zamoro to remain subdued for long; and, sure enough, the final line ('cento vendette e cento faremo in un sol dì') explodes in a fortissimo 'tutta forza'. The scene culminates in a unison battle hymn (*Dio della guerra*) shared out between Zamoro and the orchestra. If the melody is not in any way beautiful it has the strength of steel. Powerful use is made of the triplet on the word 'guerra', placed sometimes at the end, sometimes at the beginning of a phrase, always with propulsive effect.★

ACT I

A Life for a Life

Scene 1: the main square of Lima. To the cheerful sound of martial instruments the Spanish troops file into the square; the officers are gathered in a group.

The 'martial instruments' are of course the banda, here playing Ex. 138 and soon to be fortified by the orchestra. The soldiers chat amongst themselves about the latest rumour that the King of Spain has ordered fresh conquests in South America. Alvaro puts an end to their speculation by presenting to them their new governor, his son Gusman. The soldiers obediently hail him. Gusman leads Ataliba forward and, with a magnanimity quite foreign at this stage to Voltaire's tyrant, announces that his first step as governor will be to decree peace between the Incas and the Spaniards. He orders Ataliba to pledge his fellow-tribesmen's allegiance to the Spanish crown. Then, declaring the city of Lima open to Inca and Spaniard alike, he reminds Ataliba of a 'sweet token' promised to him 'to solemnize yet further the peace between our peoples'. Ataliba acknowledges the hint, but adds that Gusman would do well not to hasten matters, for Alzira's heart is not yet free. 'Too well do I know it,' says Gusman with a sigh. Cue for cavatina.

How is it, Gusman wonders, that he, the victor of a thousand battles, cannot conquer one human heart? He has never feared a mortal foe; but against a ghost, an eternal memory, he is powerless. The andante (*Eterna la memoria*) in 'unextended' form (a^1 a^2 b a^3 coda) has the usual cut of Verdi's grandiose aria-movements: but apart from a touch of chromatic subtlety in the harmonization of b at the words 'temer m'è forza estinto' it has little to mark it out from its fellows.

Alvaro advises perseverance; Ataliba suggests that Gusman wait a little longer. But the new governor is not accustomed to waiting. He tells Ataliba to order Alzira's compliance straight away. For all his fame and glory are as dust and ashes if he is deprived of the woman he loves. This last sentiment forms a cabaletta (*Quanto un mortal può chiedere*) of no great distinction and charged with the indiscriminate force that typifies so much of the score.

Scene 2: the apartments appointed for Ataliba in the Governor's palace

On a couch beneath a heavily draped canopy Alzira is lying asleep. Her sister Zuma and her attendants enter to a long whispering passage on tremolando muted strings combining a presage of Violetta's death scene with a reminiscence of the harmonic freedom in Giselda's prayer (Ex. 140). Zuma lifts a curtain and observes that her sister, worn out with weeping, has at last found peace; and the attendants murmur prayers for her comfort while the strings continue to discourse softly. Suddenly Alzira starts awake with the name of Zamoro on her lips. The violins and violas now set up a fluttering figure as she paces up and down the room.

★See note on p. 242.

Where is he? She has seen him just now. But no, it was a dream; and she proceeds to recount it in the form of a large-scale narrative aria (*Da Gusman sul fragil barca*), the first of a type that was to reach its apogee in *Il Trovatore*. Alzira dreamed that she was fleeing in a canoe from Gusman; a storm blew up and she was on the point of being drowned when from the heart of the storm-cloud Zamoro's arms reached out and gathered her to him; and at once love's power seemed to fill the universe. Graphic to the point of naïveté the aria begins with another 'rowing' or 'paddling' figure, with the harmonies deliberately left bare (Ex. 141). Quickly

the accompaniment is filled with storm noises; Alzira's terror is expressed in disjointed phrases and pulsating strings, until the moment when Zamoro takes her in his arms and the long cantilena which Verdi never failed to produce on such occasions is furnished with an almost Beethovenian climax in the form of a return from E flat to the original C major. But from there to the end of the movement the music relaxes into decorative triviality. The waiting women beg Alzira to dismiss such dreams from her mind in a short unison verse similar to that of Lucrezia's attendants in *I Due Foscari*. She however is convinced that he is alive in a land above the stars, where she will at last join him. The stars doubtless are the justification for her twinkling cabaletta (*Nell' astro che più fulgido*); but they are the Christmas stars of a department store rather than celestial bodies. Curiously enough this kind of soprano piece with its prancing gait, its tinselly scoring and its coloratura broken up into short snatches rather than laid out in long lines is one to which the young Verdi was evidently partial, since he returns to it several times in his next operas (Ex. 142, overleaf).

Ataliba now arrives to fulfil the mission imposed by Gusman. Alzira must make up her mind to marry the governor straight away. Alzira protests vigorously. Alvaro took away her father's kingdom but spared his life; Gusman has not only slaughtered and oppressed her people but has killed her lover to whom she was solemnly promised in marriage. How can Ataliba possibly think of uniting their

142

family with his? Ataliba tells her that it is the only way of avoiding further blood-shed—and besides Gusman loves her. He, Ataliba, orders her to marry him; and there is an end of the matter. No sooner has he left than Zuma announces that one of the Inca prisoners captured during the recent uprising begs to speak with her. Alzira consents and finds herself face to face with—her lover. The first movement of their duet (*Anima mia!*) is conducted entirely to the type of 'reunion' music first encountered on a large scale in Act II of *I Due Foscari*, brilliant, throbbing, excited and loosely anchored throughout to a dominant bass, all except one depressingly banal episode in the sub-dominant (*Qual mai prodigio renderti*) during which Zamoro learns with relief that Alzira is not yet married to Gusman after all. In a tiny eight-bar transition the lovers swear to be true to one another. Accompanied by oboes and bassoons only it is perhaps the most moving passage in the duet, by reason of its utterly unexpected restraint.

143

The last movement (*Risorge ne' tuoi lumi*) combines the functions of central andante and stretta: andante-like in so far as it is reached by a relaxing key-change from E major to G, but having the rapid gait of a final movement. The voices remain in sixths and thirds throughout, each protesting eternal faith in the other rather than in the false gods of their ancestors. Delicately scored at first with pizzicato strings and low clarinet arpeggios it degenerates all too soon into a welter of noisy doubling. Rarely can a love-duet have been dispatched so briskly.

The lovers are already locked in each other's arms when Gusman and Ataliba arrive on the scene together with Zuma, the attendants and an escort of Spaniards, and the music proceeds to gather itself for a grand first-act finale. Gusman's predictable reaction is to order Zamoro's arrest and torture; Alzira weeps and protests; Ataliba storms; Zamoro taunts his rival in a formal stanza (*Teco sperai combattere*) with a cabaletta-like accompaniment. He has so often demanded to fight him in fair combat; but all Gusman can talk of is prison, the rack and the scaffold. He is not a soldier but a butcher (the last word to a climactic high A). The rhythm, the thinly disguised symmetry all point forward to another tenor strophe placed with no less powerful effect in the centre of a finale before the slow concertato—Alfredo's 'Ogni suo aver' in Act II of *La Traviata*; but its parent—indeed the archetype of all such tenor interventions—is Edgardo's famous curse, 'Maledetto sia l'istante' (*Lucia*) on which Fraschini had built his reputation. Just as the soldiers are about to drag him away Alvaro enters, amazed to recognize Zamoro the noble savage who saved his life. He pleads with his son to let Zamoro go free; but Gusman, in the best melodramatic tradition, is inflexible in matters of the heart. If Zamoro had been anyone else but Alzira's lover, perhaps. . . . The situation is now set for the andante concertato (*Nella polve genuflesso*), which Verdi lays out in the form of a huge sextet with chorus, the characters taking up their several positions vis-à-vis the latest revelation. Alvaro begs his son to show mercy; Gusman remains obdurate but uneasy; Alzira, in a sad sweet melody, like Giovanna's in Act II of *Giovanna d'Arco*, laments the passing of her short-lived happiness; Zamoro expresses his faith in her constancy, Zuma and Ataliba their despair. Writing for Cammarano and the Neapolitan public it is not surprising that Verdi should once again have had before his eyes the great sextet from *Lucia di Lammermoor*, notably in the pairing of the voices (Ex. 144, overleaf). But the structure is altogether more varied and elaborate. The opening dialogue between Alvaro and Gusman is remarkably original with its persistent upward motion from key to key a fifth apart (Ex. 145, overleaf).

The impasse is broken by the sound of a military band heard in the distance—not a Spanish one however, to judge from the hollow minor harmonies and the bass throbbing like a tom-tom. The Spanish captain Ovando enters with the news that the Incas are on the march and are demanding the release of their leader Zamoro. At this Gusman makes up his mind. He will show himself his father's son, and grant a life for a life. Zamoro he says may go free; 'but', he tells him, 'be sure that we shall meet again—on the field of battle'. The hyper-conventional stretta begins with Gusman hurling threats at Zamoro (*Trema, trema a ritorti fra l'armi*), to which Zamoro replies that he intends to have Gusman's scalp. The others all join in the musical fray, whose only passage of interest is the un-Rossinian crescendo worked in the abrupt style of *Nabucco*.

ACT II

The Vengeance of a Savage

Scene 1: inside the fortifications of Lima

Once more the Incas have been repulsed, and the Spaniards are celebrating with a drinking chorus or 'brindisi' (*Mesci, mesci*) of marked undistinction. But in the middle there occurs a characteristic stroke. The general merriment is clouded

by a procession of prisoners in chains with Zamoro in their midst. Without a change of pulse the music takes on the rhythm of a funeral march, muted and with that desolate combination of oboe and bassoon in unison of which Verdi was to make especially effective use in *Macbeth*. The soldiers try to dismiss it from their minds with cries of 'Bevi!' ('Drink up!'), and the brindisi is resumed in all its vulgarity. Gusman arrives with Alzira, to be acclaimed as the hero of the hour. Ovando then presents him with Zamoro's death warrant, which requires only his signature. For Alzira's benefit Gusman reads aloud: '. . . condemned as a rebel to be burned alive at dawn.' She can save him, he tells her, by consenting to be his own wife. The situation is precisely the same as that of Leonora and the Count of Luna in *Il Trovatore*. But the way it is treated shows how far Verdi had yet to travel towards that masterpiece of his middle career. The duet (*Il pianto, l'angoscia di lena mi priva*) is a pale reflection of the trio in Act IV in *Ernani* with the same rolling triple rhythm, the same parade of kindred themes but without the perspectives afforded by the third voice and the ample key scheme. Alzira's anguish is graphically portrayed by the minor tonality, the wealth of 'lamenting' semitonal figures and gasping rests.

146

But as each idea develops one has the impression as so often in this opera that Cammarano's verses were just too ample for Verdi's purpose.

Alzira's pleas only make Gusman angry, and he is about to sign the death sentence, when she at last gives in. To a brilliant orchestral melody in buffo style Gusman then orders a wedding feast to be prepared, and both singers proceed to the final stretta (*Colma di gioia ho l'anima*). It is a duet of the 'dissimilar' variety and the nearest approach to the corresponding movement in *Il Trovatore* in mood and character. But in the later duet both singers are expressing joy of a kind. Alzira on the other hand is full of shame and remorse, rendered by Verdi with syncopations and displaced accents which merely result in bad prosody without increasing the emotional tension.

> *Scene 2: a desolate cave. The stage remains empty for some time; then Otumbo enters stealthily and beats a bronze shield which hangs from the side wall. At this an advance party of the defeated Incas issues from a remote part of the cave where they have been hiding.*

During this little manœuvre the orchestra plays an atmospheric introduction no less evocative for looking in short score somewhat like a learned organist's improvisation. It is a parade of musical science but harnessed to a dramatic purpose.

147

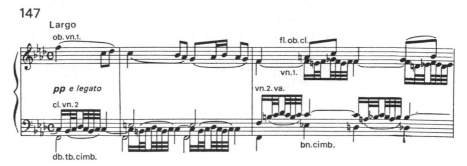

When the tribesmen have gathered Otumbo tells them a vital piece of news. By means of that accursed substance gold—so desired by the European, so useless to the Inca—he has managed to bribe Zamoro's guard, and to procure from him a Spanish uniform. Zamoro will shortly arrive, dressed as a Spanish soldier. And here, if he mistake not . . . But it is a Zamoro broken in spirit, his grief reflected in a varied resumption of Ex. 146 featuring a solo clarinet. The tribesmen try to comfort him, as he pours out his heart in an andante (*Irne lungi ancor dovrei*). He who had looked death in the face without flinching cannot bear the thought of life apart from Alzira. The opening is commonplace enough; but the music gathers interest as it proceeds. Like the first movement of his previous cavatina, it is a three-tiered structure, the middle section finishing rather unusually in the dominant *minor*, after which the music returns to the home key with a new phrase of heart-warming beauty, which the orchestra repeats later as though in sympathy and admiration. It is Zamoro's most human utterance to date.

148

Otumbo adds a final touch to his misery by telling him that Alzira has given herself to Gusman. That very night the city will blaze with the light of many torches. Does he not see in the distance the lights of the city burning with a new brightness? (As he says this Otumbo's baleful emotion is expressed in unusually rich harmonic and orchestral colours.) Zamoro 'gives a wild cry; clutches his hair frantically, and a violent shudder seizes his whole frame'. His despair is drowned in an access of fury. Ignoring his companions' attempt to hold him back he declares his resolve to set out to Lima that night and take his revenge. The time has passed for cowardly tears . . . a trite sentiment, and matched in a suitably trite cabaletta (*Non di codarde lagrime*).

> *Scene 3: a vast hall in the Governor's residence—with a balcony at the back from which can be seen the city, brightly lit; in the centre is a dais with three or four steps leading up to it. The scene is crowded with Spanish troops; the leaders stand on the dais, Alzira's attendants to one side; the hall echoes with singing.*

Like the last scene of *Ernani* this begins with a bolero chorus introduced by the banda (*Tergi del pianto America*), happily giving way to the orchestra at the point where the singing starts. Alzira's waiting women are acclaiming the marriage which will unite Inca and Spaniard, victors and vanquished in a lasting peace. Then Gusman steps forward and presents his bride to the assembled company. In a heroic stanza (*E dolce la tromba*), so ample and so fully scored as almost to have the character of a self-contained aria-movement, he declares that though the joys of victory are sweet, still sweeter is the joy of possessing the beloved. Alzira prays that the earth will open and swallow her up. She is about to place her hand in Gusman's when a soldier leaps forward from the throng and stabs him to the heart.★ 'It is I,' cries Zamoro, already surrounded by Spanish troops who threaten him with their swords. 'Rejoice, faithless woman, drink your fill of my blood; and you, Gusman, learn from me how to die.' 'I would teach you different virtues,' replies Gusman, now sinking to the ground supported by Ovando and his officers. 'Your gods urge you to take a violent and terrible revenge; but I listen to the voice of mine who bids me to forgive. Alzira's loving heart betrayed you only to save your life. Now you may live together in peace and happiness.' It is inevitable that an event such as this, a tyrant's change of heart, should suggest to Verdi a similar treatment to that of the third act finale in *Ernani*. The form is the same with a minor opening gradually blossoming into a major with increasingly elaborate participation of chorus and soloists. But he has not repeated himself. As with all composers, Verdi's inspiration had its low as well as its high tides; but like the true musical dramatist that he is, he could always rise nobly to the chief occasion. The finale of *Alzira* is worthy to be put beside those of *Il Trovatore* and *La Traviata*. The material is plain, often recalling the inspired simplicity of Bellini's *Norma*; the baritone line runs like a golden thread through the choral and orchestral tapestry. Towards the end the instrumental colour is enhanced by a harp and, as a final touch, the figure of Alvaro, grief-stricken at his son's death, is thrown unexpectedly into relief with a pattern of lamenting semitone figures traced alternately by cello and clarinet across the main pulse (Ex. 149, overleaf).

Downright bad? No, *Alzira* is certainly not that. A revival at the Rome Opera in 1967 under Bruno Bartoletti with Virginia Zeani (Alzira), Gianfranco Cecchele (Zamoro) and Cornell MacNeil (Gusman) proved that the score is genuinely alive. The rapid pace, even the composer's more than usually cavalier treatment

---

★In Voltaire, needless to say, the tragedy takes place offstage in accordance with Horatian precepts.

149

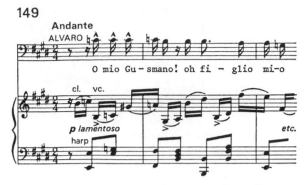

of the traditional operatic elements at least allow no time for boredom to set in. The two finales do indeed help to redeem the meagreness of the rest. No Verdi opera is totally negligible; and even the despised *Alzira* dropped a seed which was to bear fruit a generation later in *Il Guarany*, with which the Brazilian Carlos Gomes won his first Italian laurels.

Note: An autograph sketch for the battle hymn described on pp. 233–4 exists in the Bibliothek der Gesellschaft der Musikfreunde, Vienna. For a detailed description see P. Petrobelli, 'Pensieri per "Alzira"', *Nuove prospettive nella ricera verdiana: Atti del convegno internazionale in occasione della prima del 'Rigoletto' in edizione critica, Vienna, 12/13 marzo, 1983* (Parma, 1987), pp. 110–24.

11 ATTILA

ATTILA

Opera in a prologue and three acts
by
TEMISTOCLE SOLERA
(after Zacharias Werner's play, *Attila, König der Hunnen*)

First performed at the
Teatro la Fenice, Venice,
17 March 1846

ATTILA, King of the Huns	PRIMO BASSO	Ignazio Marini
EZIO, a Roman general	PRIMO BARITONO	Natale Costantini
ODABELLA, daughter of the Lord of Aquileia	PRIMA DONNA SOPRANO	Sofia Loewe
FORESTO, a knight of Aquileia	PRIMO TENORE	Carlo Guasco
ULDINO, a young Breton, Attila's slave	SECONDO TENORE	Ettore Profili
LEONE, an ancient Roman	SECONDO BASSO	Giuseppe Romanelli

Chieftains—kings and soldiers—Huns—Gepids—Ostrogoths—
Heruls—Thuringians—Quadi—Druids—priestesses—populace,
men and women of Aquileia—maidens of Aquileia in martial
dress—Roman officers and soldiers—Roman virgins and
children—hermits—slaves

The action takes place in Aquileia, the Adriatic lagoons and near Rome

Epoch: the middle of the fifth century

One of the inconveniences that Verdi had to endure after the success of *Ernani* was the importunity of Giovannina, wife of the publisher Francesco Lucca, Ricordi's chief rival in Milan. Her husband, it seems, could not sleep for thinking of all the money he was losing through not having an opera of Verdi's to publish. 'When we are in bed,' she told the composer, 'he does nothing but sigh and groan all night.'* At the time Verdi got rid of her by a coarse joke. But by January the following year Muzio was able to announce that 'the editor Lucca has at last got the ownership of an opera of the Signor Maestro's; it will be the one for Venice for carnival next year. He obtained it from Lanari for 13,000 lire.'† The transaction can only have come about because of the rift between Ricordi and the composer at the time of *Giovanna d'Arco*, since up to then Ricordi had been assured of the proprietorship of every score of Verdi's. A gap in the *Copialettere* from July 1844 to the following April prevents us from knowing more.‡ However as the archives of the Teatro la Fenice contain no record of business correspondence between Verdi and the management it would seem that all these matters were handled by Lucca on his behalf. About the same time Verdi contracted with Lucca for an opera that was to have its premiere at His Majesty's Theatre, London. It was the first instance of his writing for a publisher rather than a theatre (see Chapter 1). He was to compose *Stiffelio* and *La Battaglia di Legnano* for Ricordi in the same way; but by that time he was demanding royalties over a period of ten years, as well as a proportion of the hire fees. In the case of the three operas owned by Lucca the copyright was sold unconditionally to the publisher and the score was his to dispose of as he liked. Many years later he sold the autograph of *Attila* to a wealthy Englishman living in Florence; and it now lies in the MS. department of the British Library§—the one autograph of a Verdi opera not held either in the archives of Messrs Ricordi in Milan or in the Bibliothèque Nationale in Paris.

The idea of setting Zacharias Werner's play *Attila, König der Hunnen* seems to have been suggested during the spring of 1845 by Andrea Maffei, who, since Verdi himself knew no German, drew up a synopsis to be sent to Piave. Clearly the composer was mightily impressed by it,¶ though it is difficult to see why. Written in 1808, it springs from the wilder shores of German literary romanticism, of which no equivalent exists in England or Italy. Its roots lie partly in Christian mysticism, partly in a twilight of Nordic Saga (Attila, it should be remembered, figures as Ezil in the *Nibelungenlied*). All the Wagnerian apparatus is there—the Norns, Valhalla, the sword of Wodan, the gods of light and the gods of darkness. The

* Letter from Muzio to Barezzi, 18.6.1844. Garibaldi, p. 171.
† Letter from Muzio to Barezzi, 12.1.1845. Garibaldi, p. 181. Alessandro Lanari acted as impresario for the Teatro della Pergola, Florence, and the Fenice.
‡ The letter of Giuseppina Strepponi to Giovannina Lucca, 17.8.1844 (Abbiati, I, p. 519), in which the prima donna appears to be acting on Verdi's behalf, would seem to refer to the 'Sei Romanze' published by Lucca the following year.
§ British Library, Add. MS. 35156.
¶ Letter to Piave, 12.4.1844. *Copialettere*, pp. 437–8.

hero is another noble savage whose brutality burns with a flame of pure and holy innocence. The 'scourge of God', appointed by Wodan to chastise the degenerate, is as ruthless with his own people as with the enemy; merciful to those who fight bravely, merciless to those, friend or foe, who run away. His innocence, like Siegfried's, is betrayed; and in true Wagnerian style he considers the world well lost for love. His murderess is the Burgundian princess Hildegonde, whose family and betrothed he had killed in battle. An Ortrud-like figure, dedicated to the gods of darkness, she shows herself outwardly the most devoted of Attila's followers, spurring him on to greater deeds of violence and setting the example herself with her troop of warrior maidens, her aim being to marry him and murder him on their bridal night. So deeply is she dedicated to personal vengeance that she even thwarts a Roman attempt to poison Attila at a banquet. Then there is the Roman general Aetius, by a strange tradition Attila's former blood brother in arms, hated and distrusted by the Roman imperial house who are forced to rely on him none the less as their only hope of victory in the field. He is partly patriot, partly cunning powermonger, full of scorn for his fellow Romans but not above some double dealing on his own account. Finally, among the principals, the saintly Leo, here called a bishop, who embodies the Christian mystical aspect of the play. It is he who halts Attila before the gates of Rome and who reconciles him to death with the prospect of eternal life. Of the lesser characters the young emperor's sister stands out. It is she who is destined to be Attila's bride in the life to come; but she has no part in the opera. The play ends with a general bloodbath. Aetius has already been killed in battle; Attila and his young son are stabbed by Hildegonde, who then stabs herself before being finally dispatched by one of Attila's followers. She dies protesting everlasting love for her fiancé whom Attila had killed, and Leo observes that even the fires of hell may be sometimes cooled by the breeze of true love. It is an extraordinary Teutonic farrago to have appealed to Verdi; but he was not the only Italian to have been inspired by it.[*] One Malipiero composed an operatic version called *Ildegonda di Borgogna* which was given in Venice during the same season as Verdi's *Attila*, without much affecting the box office returns. The composer's letter to Piave makes it clear that he originally intended to keep close to the action of the play. There was to be a double chorus of Huns and Italians outside the burning Aquileia; a scene of fighting surveyed by Leo from the Aventine; an imperial banquet behind the scenes with Aetius 'on stage, pensive, considering the various events'. (Premonitions of *La Prise de Troie!*)

> Meantime there are three stupendous characters—Attila, who refuses to be thwarted by fate—Hildegonde, a proud and really fine character obsessed with the idea of avenging her father and brothers and her lover—and Aetius is very fine too, and I like that bit in his dialogue with Attila when he suggests that they share out the world between them. We ought to bring in a fourth strong character and I think it should be Walther who believes that Hildegonde is dead, and has somehow escaped, and you could make him appear among the Huns or the Romans and that would give you the opportunity of a good

---

* Beethoven also considered Werner's *Attila* as a possible operatic subject. Farinelli's opera *Attila* (1807), however, preceded the play and, to judge from the opening scene, may even have inspired it.

scene with Hildegonde. You could make him play a part in the poisoning scene but above all in Act IV where he should have an understanding with Hildegonde about the murder of Attila.

I don't want Aetius to die beforehand. I think he too should come into the last act with Hildegonde, etc.

He ended by recommending Piave to look at Werner's choruses 'which are tremendous' and above all to read Mme de Staël's *De l'Allemagne* 'which should shed a great deal of light on it all . . .'.*

But as the weeks passed Verdi evidently came to feel that the subject required a more powerful touch, a grander sweep than the poet of *I Due Foscari* was able to supply; accordingly he turned to his old partner, Solera. Piave was persuaded to relinquish the Venice project and stand by for other work. The Fenice was to have *Attila* with Solera's libretto. Eventually, however, Piave had a hand in it too.

Solera treated Werner's play even more ruthlessly than Cammarano had treated Voltaire's *Alzire*. He does not seem to have bothered about Mme de Staël's *De l'Allemagne*, the one link between the Latin world and that of German romanticism. He was concerned to appeal to Italian and, more specifically, Venetian patriotism. He retained therefore the two big dramatic scenes, though in reversed order: Attila halted by Leo before the gates of Rome; and the scene in which Hildegonde, or her equivalent, prevents the King from drinking the poisoned wine. To the latter he added an incident taken from a later point in the play where at the wedding ceremony of Attila and Hildegonde the candles are mysteriously blown out. To the opening scene at Aquileia he added another showing the foundation of Venice. For the rest Hildegonde becomes Odabella, an Aquileian warrior maid fighting on the Italian side when she is captured by Attila. Her betrothed is not Walther but the historical character Foresto. All the other characters disappear with the exception of Leo, who for reasons of ecclesiastical censorship is called 'an ancient Roman'. Attila is given a 'feed' in the person of the Breton slave Uldino. The result of all these changes is a gain in clarity if not in verisimilitude.

Verdi remained enthusiastic. He wrote to Léon Escudier, the French publisher, suggesting that he might expand it into a Grand Opera for Paris.† His letter to Ferretti after the Rome performance of *Alzira* ends: 'I'm at present at work on *Attila*. What a fine subject! The critics can say what they like.'‡

Once again Verdi found himself slowed up, partly by recurring bouts of ill-health, partly by the dilatoriness of Solera, who in the autumn of 1845 had followed his prima-donna wife to Madrid, not, however, before authorizing the composer if necessary to enlist Piave's help with the last act of which he had only drafted a sketch. Verdi did so, and whether because of ill-health or because familiarity with this most docile of collaborators was beginning to breed a slight contempt we notice for the first time a note of irritation creeping into their correspondence. Piave had suggested making use of the Kinsky band. Verdi

*Letter to Piave, 12.4.1845. *Copialettere*, pp. 437–8, where the letter is implausibly assigned to 1844. See Conati, pp. 142–4.

† Letter to L. Escudier, 12.9.1844. *Copialettere*, p. 439.

‡ Letter to J. Ferretti, 5.11.1845. *Copialettere*, p. 439.

replied with a tirade against stage bands in general: 'They're a continual absurdity and just make a row; and anyway I've written marches before; a warlike one in *Nabucco* and a solemn, ceremonial one in *Giovanna* and I shan't do any better than those. And why can't there be a grand opera without the din of a band? Aren't *Guillaume Tell* and *Robert le Diable* grand operas? Yet they don't contain a band. Nowadays the band is a provincialism and quite unsuitable any longer for a great city.'* If only he had kept to that opinion!

Solera had intended a choral finale. Verdi instructed Piave to avoid choruses at all costs and concentrate on the principals. 'And do take care, my dearest Piave, that we don't make a hash of it.' In the event, this was more or less what they did. After having vainly pestered Solera through the intermediary of the baritone Superchi to complete his libretto, Verdi finally sent him a copy of Piave's verses for the last act, so that he could make any changes he thought fit, '. . . but I warn you I've already composed the music for the most important passages.'†

Solera was horrified. 'Your letter was a shattering blow to me,' he wrote to Verdi. 'How on earth could the solemnity of a final hymn fail to inspire you? . . . The ending you've sent me seems nothing less than a parody . . . it seems to me to make nonsense of the characters as I've portrayed them. Fiat voluntas tua . . . you are the only person that has been able to convince me that the career of librettist is not for me . . .'‡

It was the end of a collaboration which had so far not produced a single failure. When Solera approached Verdi fifteen years later with another libretto the composer took evasive action. He had no wish to renew their partnership. In any case he had long since outgrown Solera's ideas of musical theatre.

Solera's *Attila* was far from being the masterpiece he himself considered it to be; yet his bitterness is justified up to a point. Verdi's last-minute attempt to give human identity to the stiff, cardboard figures does result in a theatrical anticlimax.

The first night, according to the press, fell short of expectations. Not all Verdi's fault however. The singers it seems were in poor voice, and, most unfortunate of all, the candles at Attila's feast in the second act were made of a substance which stank horribly when extinguished. 'The scourge of God,' remarked the *Gazzetta Privilegiata di Venezia* austerely, 'ought not to be the scourge of our nostrils.'§ *Il Gondoliere* found inspiration only here and there; for the rest 'only a noble effort at inspiration . . .'.¶ The applause, they implied, was more for Verdi himself than for his music.

But there the critics were mistaken. The Italian public had taken *Attila* to their hearts; and over the next few years it was to prove one of the most popular of all patriotic operas.

After two full-scale overtures Verdi returned to the prelude form which usually served him better. This one is based on a subject of Beethovenian simplicity, to which in the finale to Act II the Druids will utter their warning. The 'bow-shape' of the melody is almost as recurrent a feature of *Attila* as is the rising sixth of *Ernani*.

---

* Letter to Piave (undated). Abbiati, I, p. 591.
† Letter to Solera, 25.12.1845. *Copialettere*, p. 440.
‡ Letter to Verdi, 12.1.1846. *Carteggi Verdiani*, IV, p. 245.
§ Abbiati, I, p. 604.   ¶ Abbiati, I, p. 605.

150
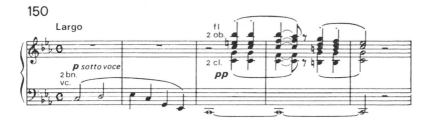

In the course of the movement it is treated in a rudimentary canon at the octave and finally thundered out by the bass instruments with a superstructure of busy figuration. Alternating with it is a more feminine idea which begins on a 6/4 chord of E flat major and returns each time fatalistically to the home key. The scoring is often thick and brutal (the staccato bassoon arpeggios are particularly primitive) but the whole piece forms a compact and cogent musical statement.

Prologue

Scene 1: the camp of Attila near Aquileia; the scene is crowded with Huns, Ostrogoths, Heruls, etc.

The action begins, as in Werner's play, after the sack of Aquileia in the middle of the fifth century A.D. The barbarians are celebrating their victory with naïve enthusiasm. Rape, pillage, bloodshed—this is their idea of Valhalla on earth; and Attila has discovered it for them. The chorus (F minor) is abrupt, uncouth, made up of irregular phrases which smooth themselves out in a contrasting C major unison episode. This in turn becomes an instrumental march over a dominant pedal of expectancy as Attila and his suite enter to a steady crescendo. The soldiers fall on their knees and hail him in a noisy F major coda. 'Arise,' he tells them. 'It is for the vanquished to lie in the dust and die. Stand about me, and raise the hymn of victory. . . .' It is a brief but highly effective recitative taking the great basso Marini down to an exposed A flat on the word 'muor'. The Huns respond with another chorus (*Viva il re delle mille foreste*) acclaiming their King as Wodan's chosen minister and prophet, the wielder of his irresistible sword. The music is unexpectedly quiet but its scoring for brass, bassoons and percussion gives it a sense of restrained power. A curious feature of this short choral scene is that for the only time in his Italian operas Verdi asks for four trumpets instead of the usual two. The result is a gain in brilliance and force even though there is only one point where each pair does not double the other.*

Attila is now surprised and annoyed to see Uldino his slave escorting in a number of women prisoners; he had given orders that no one was to be spared.

* An incomplete sketch for this scene can be found in the Bibliothèque Nationale, Paris (MS. 2208), very similar to that for the final scene of *I Due Foscari*. The principal items are set out on full-score MS. paper so as to form a continuity. The sketch breaks off at bar 72 of the score and resumes at bar 111, omitting Attila's intervening recitative; the fact that the second chorus is in the key eventually allocated to it suggests that the recitative had already been drafted, since the scheme of F–E flat major would not commend itself to a composer a priori. There are notable divergences between the sketch and the finished result, but it is clear that the notion of four trumpets was present from the start. The absence of Attila's recitative may be accounted for by the fact that Verdi had extracted it and sent it to Marini for his approval.

Uldino replies that he considered a troop of warrior maids fit tribute for a great king. Attila is astonished. Valour in women is something inconceivable to him. Who can have taught them the masculine virtues? One of the prisoners, Odabella, interrupts with the answer: 'Holy and boundless love of the fatherland'—delivered in three majestic phrases of recitative including a downward scale of more than two octaves. It is a striking entrance, all the more so because the previous interchange is set not as recitative but as a parlante in strict rhythm against an orchestral melody. This serves not only to bind the scene together more strongly, but also to increase the force of Odabella's declamation—and especially since the violins which carry the melody are playing tremolando, so giving the effect of a suppressed Rossinian crescendo. In fact composer and librettist, by a neat stroke of patriotic symbolism, have converted what began as a 'sortita' for Attila into an 'introduzione e cavatina' for Odabella, with the King reduced to an admiring comprimario. Not surprisingly, then, her andante (*Allor che i forti corrono*) has the most extended design Verdi has employed yet—a^1 a^2 b a^3 c b a^3. The all-important b is based on a suitably majestic phrase set to the words 'Ma noi donne italiche' which serves to launch a^3 on an unusually wide and powerful trajectory.

151

The aria is conceived very much in the manner of Abigaille's cavatina, calling for powerful low notes and trumpet-like brilliance above the stave; but it is more original, since the idiom is no longer Donizettian small change. 'Your women,' says Odabella, 'can only weep helplessly when they see their menfolk in flight. We Italian maids put on armour and fight.' During c Attila adds a little pertichino of admiration. So impressed is he with her warlike spirit that he offers to grant her anything she may ask. 'A sword,' she replied without hesitation. 'You shall have mine,' Attila declares; whereupon Odabella bursts out in a cabaletta of savage joy (*Da te questo or m'è concesso*). With this sword, symbol of divine justice, she will be revenged upon her country's foe. It is of course a typical footlight cabaletta. Apart from its brilliance, force and wide melodic range there is nothing to mark it out from many another composed by Verdi at this time.★

Attila now orders the slave Uldino to bring in the Roman ambassador. Not that he intends paying attention to anything that he might have to say. The issue

★For a deleted version set to a different, decasyllabic text and still visible in the autograph see M. Noiray and R. Parker, 'La composition d'*Attila*: étude de quelques variantes, *Revue de Musicologie* LXII, no. 1 (1976), pp. 104–24.

will be decided on the Campidoglio not at the conference table. To a martial theme scored for strings only, and strongly reminiscent of Rossini's overture to *Le Siège de Corinthe*, Ezio enters, to be greeted by Attila as an old friend and a worthy adversary. Attila hopes that he has not come to talk about peace. But peace, if not with honour, is exactly what Ezio has come to propose. In the andante of their duet (*Tardo per gli anni e tremulo*) he tells Attila that the Emperor of Constantinople is old and feeble; the ruler of the West is only a boy. Attila and himself between them could be masters of the entire Roman empire. But Ezio would be happy for Attila to rule the whole world—the universe—so long as Italy were left to him. As in so many of the composer's solemn baritone stanzas the closely patterned string accompaniment is coloured only by sustaining horns, oboes and bassoons being held in reserve for that climax that always drew frenzied applause from a contemporary audience:

152

Attila, disgusted, replies with a 'dissimilar' stanza in faster tempo and in the tonic minor. Are these the words of a hero? Where is the intrepid warrior he once knew? He is turned traitor to his country. A people so degenerate deserve God's scourge. Unperturbed Ezio repeats his offer; and so to a coda in which the interweaving voices are sharply distinguished by the scoring, Attila's line picked out by oboe, trumpet and bassoon, Ezio's in the softer colours of violins, flute, clarinet and cellos. Then Ezio changes tack. If Attila rejects his proposal, he says, he will revert to his role as Rome's ambassador; and here the string melody to which he entered takes on a more menacing aspect with a reinforcement of woodwind.* But Attila will not listen; it is no longer possible to halt the approaching hurricane in its course. The scene ends with a stretta of mutual defiance (*Vanitosi che abbietti e dormenti*). Attila intends to lay proud Rome in the dust and seize the power she no longer deserves to hold. Ezio reminds him that so long as he is in command Rome is still a force to be reckoned with—'witness the victory of Châlons'. It is a 'similar' type stretta, but the voices being unequal some adjustment is necessary. Verdi chooses the solution first adopted in *Oberto* in the duet between father and daughter in Act I, whereby the upper voice sings a third higher than the lower but in the same key. Here the melody itself is so rudimentary that the device is more successful than in the earlier, more lyrical instance, and it makes for a suitably bellicose final stanza, the sonorous thirds clashing over the accompanimental harmonies in the nineteenth-century Italian manner. If in this long duet there is not the great contrast between baritone and bass voices that we find in *Ernani* the reason would lie partly in Marini's style of singing which was

---

* This use of an orchestral melody before and after an andante movement with subtle variations in the recurrence to reflect the altered situation or mood can be found in many a Rossinian finale. For its occurrence in a duet and in a musical context very similar to this one see Donizetti's 'È men fier' (*Pia de' Tolomei*). Clearly it can be a most useful continuity device.

that of a low basso cantante rather than of a true basso profondo such as Selva or Derivis.

> *Scene 2: the Rio Alto* in the Adriatic Lagoons; a chain of small islands is visible with a few huts scattered here and there in which hermits are living. In the foreground is a stone altar dedicated to St James. It is just before dawn; a storm is raging.*

The scene opens with the noisiest of storms, calling at one point for a thunder machine. As it subsides we hear the steady tolling of a bell from one of the hermits' huts. At length the lightning ceases, the thunder dies away in the distance and all that is left is a swell of water portrayed by chromatic patterns in contrary motion on the lower strings.

The hermits, all basses, come out of their huts and give thanks to God for the passing of the storm, their simple unison phrases alternating over chords of trumpet, trombone and cimbasso. Gradually the dawn breaks, in a long instrumental passage which earned the composer much critical praise at the time. Muzio's correspondence enables us to trace the source of its inspiration to that forgotten favourite of Victorian choral societies and begetter of the Franco-Oriental style of the mid-century, Félicien David's *Le Désert*. Verdi had heard it in Milan just before setting out for Naples in 1845, and a comparison of this passage with David's particularly in the matter of scoring shows that the lesson of *Le Désert* had not been wasted. It is a long way from the soft-toned nature-painting of the German school but theatrically quite effective. Two figures are casually thrown out by flute and muted violins respectively.

153

As more and more instruments are added, as the space between the figures closes up, as the music forces its way through diminished sevenths to burst out into a brilliant C major and the chorus salute the morning, we can sense the stage slowly flooded with the beams of the rising sun. 'Praise be to the creator!' cry the hermits on their knees; and far away across the lagoon voices echo their words. The hermits turn and see a number of boats approaching with men, women and children aboard. As in *Alzira* the precedent of Tancredi's sortita is resorted to for the portrayal of a seascape alive with gently rocking craft.

154

---

* Literally 'high channel'—doubtless a piece of pseudo-antiquarianism on Solera's part suggesting the origin of the Rialto.

They are the fugitives from Aquileia, sacked by Attila and his army. Their leader is Foresto, a knight, who now steps ashore with the rest and in a brief double stanza like the start of a Rossinian stretta (*Qui, qui sostiamo*) he announces that in this very spot they will raise an altar. All present shout their approval and gratitude, then Foresto's thoughts turn to Odabella. Has she fallen into the hands of the savage Huns? Better death than such a fate. . . . This is the burden of an andante (*Ella in poter del barbaro*) with the long rhythmic thrust of a Verdi heroic aria, as well as the bow-shaped opening phrase peculiar to so much of this score. It is designed on a variant of the new extended plan of Odabella's previous andante—a^1 a^2 b a^3 c b a^4 coda, c being a consolatory choral intervention from sopranos and tenors rising and falling in thirds. The four variants of a reveal the master-hand that will one day give us the sustained melodic gradient of 'Tacea la notte'.

155

The Aquileians and hermits (a massive seven-part chorus) are more confident. The storm is past, the sun is shining all the brighter. So, they imply, it will be with the days ahead. In his cabaletta (*Cara patria già madre e reina*) Foresto reverts from lover to patriot. Rome, the once powerful, mother of heroes, is now sunk in misery and defeat; but on these barren marshes she shall rise again like a phoenix from the ashes. The chorus take up his last two lines in a *Nabucco*-like unison refrain, and in a more than usually substantial ritornello both parties urge each other on to fresh hope. A matching coda brings down the curtain in a fierce blaze of choral and orchestral sound—the 'Risorgimento' manner at its most crudely effective.

ACT I

Scene 1: a forest near Attila's camp; moonlight reflected in a stream
Several weeks have passed. Attila and his army have arrived within a few miles of Rome and have pitched camp ready to attack the next day. Odabella, meanwhile, has now become Attila's honoured guest. She has accepted her new position so as to have the means of murdering him; but she is unhappy in her dissimulation. Hence the sorrowful G minor melody for violins, not unlike the

cello cantilena at the start of Act II of *Norma*, which introduces the scene and is woven into the subsequent recitative. This is the hour when she likes to steal away from the camp and invoke the spirits of her murdered father, and of Foresto whom she believes to have been killed in battle. (The murdered father is of course a legacy from Werner's Hildegonde, and typical of the loose ends that librettists were apt to leave lying about when they departed from the original drama.) The idea of mystical communion in a lonely forest clearly drew from Verdi some of the most exquisite pieces of scoring to be found in his early operas. The romanza (*Oh nel fuggente nuvolo*) is a brightly coloured tapestry woven from threads of cor anglais, flute, cello and harp, and embellished, but never extravagantly, with vocal coloratura. As usual, flute and cello each have their own individual pattern from which they never depart; the harp enters at bar 42 with rippling arpeggios; the cor anglais mostly doubles the voice or moves in thirds with it, as in Carlo's romanza 'Quale più fido amico' (*Giovanna d'Arco*) except at the beginning, where it provides the sole accompaniment. The combination results in a beauty of sheer sound recalling Gluck's 'Che puro ciel' (Ex. 156, facing page).

Odabella, gazing upward, seems to see her father's image engraven in the fleeting cloud—but no, it is not his at all, it is Foresto's. Let the breezes be still, let the streams cease their murmuring so that she may hear the voices of the heavenly spirits. Suddenly there is the sound of footsteps, as the orchestra gives out a climbing motif very much akin to Ex. 13 (*Oberto*), here nailed to pulsating dominant harmonies in a way that signals an imminent reunion, if not at first a joyous one. All Foresto's worst fears seem to have been confirmed. He had searched for Odabella everywhere; he had even entered Attila's camp unobserved to find her feasting at the King's table, carousing with her country's enemies. Hurrying quavers give way to measured crotchets as Foresto pours out his reproaches. The resultant relaxation allows him to give weight to his words but bland major harmonies preclude emotional depth. In these, as in the primitive approach to the high G, one sees the limitations of the 'poster' idiom. There is dignity and even a hint of pathos behind the force, but not much humanity (Ex. 157, p. 256).

The transitional movement over, the lovers continue their altercation in a formal andante (*Si, quello io son ravvisami!*). Foresto denounces Odabella in a double stanza whose minor tonality is made even more poignant by the use of sustaining oboe. She replies in the major begging him to strike her dead. Their mutual opposition does not, of course, preclude a united cadence of particular beauty in the coda.

The situation is still unresolved, when Odabella reminds Foresto of the story of Judith and Holofernes. On the very day, she says, when she was told that he and her father had died in battle, she swore a solemn oath to do for Italy what Judith had done for Israel.

Foresto is at last convinced, and the two are reconciled in a rather paltry stretta (*Oh t'innebria nell'amplesso*) whose only distinguishing feature is the fact that for the first and only time in Verdi the voices remain in unison up till the coda.

Scene 2: Attila's tent. Attila asleep on an oriental couch covered with tigerskin.

A short orchestral preamble brings back the mood of the prelude, with an anticipation of Wagner's Norns, though differently harmonized (Ex. 158, p. 256).

156

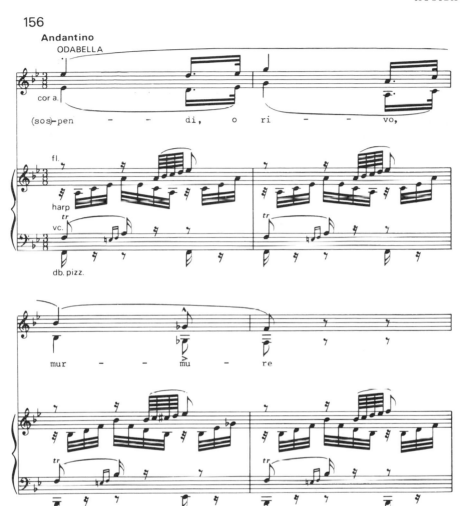

But it is not a Leitmotiv, even in the limited sense of the identifying themes of *I Due Foscari*. It is what Roncaglia would qualify as a 'tema cardine': a small memorable phrase nailing down a particular event or utterance on which the drama resolves as for the theme of Ernani's fatal oath;[*] and a little later it forms a most impressive central climax to the andante (*Mentre gonfiarsi l'anima*) in which Attila recounts to Uldino the nightmare from which he has just awakened. While he stood before the walls of Rome, preparing to attack, an old man appeared before him, grasped him by the hair and said to him, smiling but in a voice of thunder: 'Thou art God's appointed scourge for mortals alone. Approach no further, for this is the dwelling of God.' And for the first time Attila knew fear. The old man's words are declaimed over Ex. 158 sequentially extended over D flat minor, C minor, B flat minor—between an F minor opening section and a thoroughly conventional F major close. Having told his dream Attila is now no

[*] See Roncaglia, 'Il "tema-cardine" nell' opera di Giuseppe Verdi', in the *Rivista Musicale Italiana*, XLVII (1943), pp. 218–29.

157

Allegro

FORESTO

T'in - fin - gi in - va - no: ___ tut-to co - no - sco,

str.

tut - - to spi - ai ___

hn.

158

Andante

vn.va.trem.
ob.cl.

sotto voce

vc.

pp

longer frightened by it. To prove his resolution he orders Uldino to summon his druids, officers and men: the attack will take place at once, and so to a martial and quite undistinguished cabaletta of defiance (*Oltre quel limite, t'attendo, o spettro*).

Scene 3: the place of assembly in Attila's camp

To a swift crescendo of martial music the Huns, Heruls, Visigoths, and others assemble; among them are Odabella and Foresto, the latter presumably disguised. There is a brief hymn to Wodan (*Sia gloria a Wodan*) in blunt military vein, and a flourish of six stage trumpets. The chorus repeat their warlike shouts. Then the sound of high voices floats across the distance, singing an Italian version of the 'Veni Creator'. The doors of the tent are parted to reveal a procession of women and children in white. At their head is the old man of Attila's dream who greets the King with the same unforgettable words (Ex. 158). In his terror, Attila seems to see two gigantic figures in the sky menacing him with flaming swords (they are of course the St Peter and St Paul of Raphael's fresco).* His solo (*No, non è sogno*) passes from disjointed phrases in F minor to a canto spiegato of prayer (*Spirti, fermate*) in A flat, and from there the music gathers itself into a slow concerted finale based almost entirely on one shimmering melodic 'bow':

159

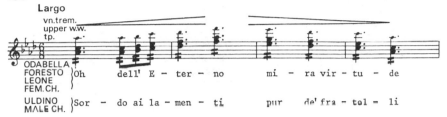

Odabella and Foresto join the Christian women and children in singing praises to God for the miracle. Uldino and the Huns look with horror at the spectacle of their King prostrate in the dust; while Attila continues to murmur fearfully. The entire scene is beautifully contrived, the unaccompanied 'Veni Creator' taking up the chords of chorus and stage trumpets in an ethereal echo. Here as later in *Don Carlos* Verdi has depicted the confrontation of two worlds by means of two full basses. But the Grand Inquisitor in *Don Carlos* is a principal; Pope Leo has the smallest of comprimario parts, his one solo line consisting of Ex. 158. For the rest he merely forms part of the ensemble. The scene has a hymn-like grandeur which even the rather naïve rosalia at bar 40 seqq. fails to diminish.

As in *I Due Foscari* no stretta follows. The miracle has quenched all the fires of emotion.

ACT II

Scene 1: the Roman camp

Ezio is reading a dispatch from the Emperor Valentinian recalling him to Rome, now that Huns and Romans have made a truce. The Emperor, he reflects bitterly, seems more afraid of his own troops than of the enemy. His mind goes back to the ancient heroes whose glory once filled the universe; if they could only rise once more, would they recognize their fatherland in the rotting corpse of present-day Rome? A deputation of Huns, escorted by Roman soldiers, come to invite Ezio to a banquet to be given by Attila to celebrate the truce. Ezio accepts, and the soldiers leave all except one, who asks for a private word with the general. He refuses to give his name (it is of course Foresto) and merely tells Ezio that when during the feast he sees a beacon lit on a near-by hill he must order his soldiers into the attack. Ezio is now jubilant. Here at last, he thinks, is a task worthy of a hero. If he is killed in the attempt his name will be recorded in history as the last of the Romans.

The whole scene is Ezio's, built round an andante and cabaletta. Of these the andante (*Dagli immortali vertici*) is a well-known 'cheval de bataille' for student

* Verdi had written to the sculptor Luccardi in Rome asking for details about the figures in this fresco, in particular the hairstyles. Letter to Luccardi, 11.2.1846. *Copialettere*, p. 441.

singers, being an archetypal Verdian baritone cantilena. What the piano reduction does not show is that here, for once, the wind instruments (clarinet, horn and bassoon) sustain throughout instead of intermittently, so giving an unusual intensity to the vocal line. Note the characteristic arch of the final phrase, so characteristic of the opera as a whole:

160

The cabaletta (*È gettata la mia sorte*) is an example of Verdi's patriotic style at its crudest, with the baritone confined to that area of his voice where he can make most noise. The best music in the scene is to be found in the stealthy exchange between Ezio and Foresto over a hushed theme on tremolo strings which combines an air of mystery with a high dramatic charge.

> Scene 2: *Attila's camp, as in Act I, arranged for a solemn banquet. The night is brilliantly lit by a hundred flames issuing from huge trunks of oak-trees treated for the purpose. Huns, Ostrogoths, Heruls, etcetera.*

While the warriors are singing Attila, followed by Druids, priestesses, captains and kings, goes to take his seat. Odabella is beside him, dressed as an Amazon. The Hunnish soldiers (tenors only) are as usual singing the praises of their King (*Del ciel l'immensa vòlta*) in Busseto homespun style.

Attila welcomes his chief guest Ezio, who replies with a suitable compliment to Attila's magnanimity in peace and prowess in war. But the Druids (chorus basses) murmur a warning in the King's ear to a sinister accompaniment of wind chords and rolls on the timpani (Ex. 150). The clouds are stained with blood. The spirit of the mountain has been heard howling into the night. Attila dismisses such childish fantasies, and bids the priestesses sing and dance. The ballabile (*Chi dona luce al cor*) is a choral variant of the type of aria represented by Alzira's 'Nell'astro più che fulgido' (*Alzira*). Its text is modelled on that of the Druid choruses in Werner's tragedy. 'Who can illumine the depths of the heart? Neither the stars in their courses nor the rays of the moon . . .' Gradually the language becomes more ominous; the trite tinkle is suffused with menace. Violins and cellos in alternation blow gusts of demisemiquavers across horn and woodwind chords at irregular three-bar intervals and in a violent tutti explosion ('Ah . . .' from the banqueters to a long E minor chord), all the candles are extinguished. In the silence that follows Verdi builds up the andante of his concerted finale. The Huns mutter in fear at the spirit of the mountain. Ezio reminds his host of the offer he made at their last meeting, to meet him in fair fight. Attila refuses to listen. Foresto whispers to Odabella that the moment of triumph is at hand, since Uldino has been won over to their side and intends to poison Attila's wine. Odabella observes, to herself (not Foresto), that she hoped for a more honourable revenge on the man who killed her father. The movement is constructed very impressively. The opening is unaccompanied but punctuated by string tremolos like a reminder of the fatal gust. It ascends through the steady addition of more and more instruments to a powerful climax, then subsides quietly into a pause; after which the music resumes in the major key as everyone hails the passing of the crisis. Once more the singing is unaccompanied, but with a new punctuating figure which recalls the clearing of the sky in the prologue (Ex. 153).

Attila commands that the torches be rekindled, and here the orchestra set out a 'party-music' theme which already contains an inappropriate hint of *Traviata*-like elegance.

Attila raises his glass and, over a succession of trombone and cimbasso chords, announces a libation to Wodan. But before he can raise the cup to his lips Odabella dashes it from him with the cry, 'It is poison!' Foresto steps forward and accuses himself, reminding the King that once before he had toppled the crown from his head (another reference to the fiancé of Werner's Hildegonde which must be obscure to anyone unfamiliar with the original play). Attila threatens a violent revenge. But Odabella insists that as a reward for saving Attila's life she alone should be allowed to punish the criminal. To this Attila agrees; and in token of his gratitude he announces that Odabella shall be his bride. He then launches the final movement of the stretta (*Oh miei prodi un solo giorno*), calling upon his warriors to resume the fight against Rome. Ezio may go and tell his servile Emperor that the King of the Huns is no longer frightened by dreams. Odabella urges Foresto to escape while he can; and he agrees to save his own life in order to exact a fuller revenge. But his heart is broken by what he considers to be Odabella's treachery. Ezio wonders at this strange behaviour on the part of a patriotic warrior-maid. Uldino fears for his own life. The Huns meanwhile respond joyously to the new summons to arms. The expository part is effective, particularly Odabella's entry in the minor key (*Frena l'ira che t'inganna*) immediately following Attila's stanza, the effect being momentarily that of a 'dissimilar' duet; but routine soon assumes its sway, and from then to the end is mere sound and fury.

Musically this finale is much the most elaborate in the opera; and there is no denying its powerful construction. A pity therefore that so much of it should remain on the level of mere theatricality. Even the andante concertato is essentially a triumph of pattern-making, being mostly made up of gestures which might have come from any Rossini comic opera. In the Druidesses' dance Verdi was merely trying to do what Wagner and Weber did so much better.

ACT III

Scene: the forest dividing the camp of the Romans and the Huns

Foresto is waiting for Uldino, from whom he hopes—and fears—to hear the news of Odabella's wedding to Attila. Uldino arrives to say that the wedding procession is just about to pass near by, conducting the bride to Attila's tent. Foresto tells him to join Ezio's company, who have need of every man they can get for the ambush. He then breaks out into a romanza of despair (*Che non avrebbe il misero*). How could such an angelic form as Odabella's conceal so false a heart? It is a conventional early-Verdian piece, whose minor-key opening bears the

Ernani hallmark of the rising sixth; but the *Attila* arch returns at the resolution into the major.

It is at this point that Piave took over, working strictly under Verdi's direction. Solera had clearly intended working up to a final hymn in the manner of *I Lombardi*. Verdi wanted to end with a confrontation of principals. The question was, how to bring them together at the same time without anyone else present. Piave had suggested that it might all take place in Attila's tent; Verdi objected that this was the last place in which Foresto would be found. But the solution eventually adopted was no less absurd. Evidently the Roman attack cannot go ahead without Foresto. Enter therefore Ezio to find out what is keeping him so long. The banda-like melody which accompanies his entrance apparently instils some martial spirit into Foresto, and he resolves with Ezio that not one of the Huns shall be left alive. But just then the sounds of a marriage hymn are heard offstage (*Entra fra i plausi o vergine*) set to a melody of pastoral freshness and simplicity whose kinship with the off-stage wedding chorus 'Pari all'amor degli angioli' (*La Straniera*) is doubtless occasioned by the similarity of the dramatic situation.

Ezio tries to recall his comrade's attention to the immediate task. But Foresto can only explode in futile curses—when Odabella herself arrives. How has she escaped from the procession? Why, as Solera so pertinently asked,* should she try to flee from a marriage in which she had placed all hopes of avenging her murdered father? And how else does she hope to avenge him, since, according to Piave, flight is certainly her intention. Foresto interrupts her soliloquy, crying that it is too late for repentance. Ezio points out that if Foresto continues to waste time it will certainly be too late for the ambush; Odabella protests that her heart belongs as it has always done to Foresto, and so the situation remains through a rather beautiful D flat major trio with harp accompaniment (*Te sol te sol quest'anima*), the lovers lyrical in their grief, Ezio's impatience breaking out in staccato semiquavers. Dramatically it prompts unworthy memories of the second-act trio of *Il Barbiere*.

Solera's complaints of parody were not so far wide of the mark. Hunnish kings like Roman generals do not like to delegate, it seems. So Attila himself comes in search of Odabella just as Ezio had come looking for Foresto. He is pulled up sharply at the sight of the two men. So! a conspiracy. He proceeds to hurl bitter accusations all round, in a voice 'cupo e terribile'. 'You, Odabella, once my slave, now my bride; you, Foresto, whose guilty life I saved; you, Ezio, whose city I have spared—you all dare to plot against me?' Like the trio in the first act of *Ernani* this quartet is intended to form the stretta of the preceding number; and, as

* Letter to Verdi, 12.1.1846. *Carteggi Verdiani*, IV, p. 245.

in the earlier opera, the formal allegro is launched from a taut declamatory stanza in strict time, voice and instruments alternating in brusque gestures. Attila's growing indignation is reflected in the rising vocal line.

162

They all have their answers however, which are unfolded in a long, many-limbed melody moving on an axis between the poles of B flat and D flat. Odabella reminds Attila of her murdered father, whose blood-stained ghost would haunt their marriage-bed; Foresto's defence is that life is a worthless gift from one who has robbed him of his country and his beloved; Ezio's that a world enslaved cries out for revenge. As the ensemble builds up to a lyrical climax, distant voices are heard crying, 'Death! Vengeance!' Evidently the attack has gone ahead quite smoothly without either Ezio or Foresto. Odabella stabs Attila to the heart ('Father, I sacrifice him to you!'). Attila dies, Caesar-like, murmuring, 'You too, Odabella!', as the Romans fall upon the unarmed Huns.

The only justification for such a finale is that it enabled Verdi to do something new. The quartet itself has a key-scheme akin to the final trio of *Ernani*, but also a dynamic character of its own, not unmixed with lyrical feeling. Nor like the *Ernani* trio does it rely on repetition. In a word, it is all real music, fresh and original. The build-up from Foresto's solo through a trio whose first movement is a duet for the two men to the final quartet is a notable instance of streamlining in the manner of *I Due Foscari*. Again Verdi follows his favourite method of short symmetrical interlocking statements and again the effect is a steady crescendo of lyrical and dramatic intensity. But whether one feels that this last act redeems the opera or merely lets it down, the fact remains that it does not really fit. If *Attila* had been an opera of individuals like *Ernani*, it would have been a logical consummation. But Solera had designed the first three acts as part of a grand pseudo-historical fresco, an opera of spacious gestures and theatrical effects. The result of the change is a disproportion in scale and an alteration to the fundamental character of the opera. Clearly Verdi had wanted to instil some humanity into his odious principals; but as Foresto reminds Odabella, 'the hour is late for repentance'. The fault was Solera's as well as Piave's. It would be easy to assume that as a German Werner would be biased in favour of Attila and the Huns; but in fact through all his obscurity he keeps the dramatic elements fairly well balanced. By making the changes that he did, Solera himself unwittingly tilted the scales against his own countrymen. The attempted poisoning of Attila makes better sense if it occurs, as in Werner, *before* his march on Rome; for it then becomes an attempt to save the Eternal City. If it takes place afterwards it is nothing more than a piece of treachery and spite. The final taunt from Ezio that Attila must fear the vengeance of a world that he has trampled underfoot comes ill from one who has already proposed that they divide the universe between them. Finally in her transformation from Hildegonde to Odabella the heroine has lost all plausible identity. Werner's Hildegonde is a villainess, though not a totally unsympathetic one. Odabella is not only the most unpleasant heroine in all Verdian opera; she is vocally and dramatically two people—an Abigaille-like dramatic soprano in the prologue, and a suffering *lirico* in the rest of the opera. Her role in Act III which so infuriated Solera was doubtless an attempt to make her character more palatable; but even that is contradicted by the final coup de théâtre. Musically and dramatically Odabella has none of the integrity of Giovanna.

TRIESTE, *autumn 1846*. In July, four months after the first performance, Verdi received a coy letter from Rossini. 'Just as the enamoured touch of the first kiss bestowed upon your fair hand calls for one more, so Ivanoff . . . mindful of that first precious embrace that you gave her (*sic*) when you composed a magnificent aria which brought him so much honour, now comes to ask for a second embrace, that is to say a second composition which will undoubtedly afford him much bliss. . . .'* Ivanoff was to sing Foresto in a performance of *Attila* in Trieste that autumn and wanted an aria of his own to sing in it, such as he had had in *Ernani*. Once again Rossini was to pay the composer on his behalf. For the text Verdi naturally turned to Piave: '. . . a romanza with recitative and two little verses. The subject is to be a lover complaining of the faithlessness of his sweetheart (old stuff!). . . . Five or six lines of recitative then a couple of quatrains in eight-syllable

* Letter from Rossini, 21.7.1846. *Carteggi Verdiani*, IV, p. 33.

metre. Have a break after each two lines, which always makes things easier. . . .
I would like them to be pathetic and lachrymose. Make this fool of a lover say that
he would have given her half his share of Paradise and ah! she has repaid him
with . . . horns! Long live the horns . . .' and more to the same untranslatable
effect.* From this it is clear that the romanza was to replace that in Act IV, *Chi
non avrebbe il misero*. We learn from Muzio that the piece was finished and sent off
some time in September.† The text, which can be found in libretti printed for
the Teatro Regio in Turin (1848–9), but not for some reason before,‡ begins:

> Sventurato! Alla mia vita
> Sol conforto era l'amor.

The music was never published, and the autograph, alas, is in private hands and
for the moment inaccessible.

MILAN, *carnival season 1846–7*. It was this revival that disgusted Verdi once and
for all with Merelli's management. On 29 December he wrote to Ricordi approv-
ing the contract for *Macbeth* on condition that it should never be given at La Scala.
'I have seen too many examples to be convinced otherwise than that they either
cannot or will not mount operas as they should be mounted—and especially
mine. I cannot forget the wretched way in which they put on *I Lombardi*, *I Due
Foscari*, *Ernani*, etc., etc. . . . I have another example before me at this moment in
Attila. I would ask you yourself whether this opera could possibly be worse
mounted despite a good company?'§ Muzio goes into greater detail, telling how
Verdi was asked to take charge of the production and refused; how Lucca had
demanded such an outrageously high price for the hire of the material that Merelli
applied to the Austrian police, who obliged the publisher to lower it. The performance, Muzio admitted, was quite good, but 'the mise-en-scène is villainous.
The sunrise occurred before it was indicated in the music. The sea, instead of
being rough and stormy, was calm and without a single breaker. The hermits had
no hovels; the priests had no altars; in the banquet scene Attila held a feast without
lights, without flaming torches, and when the hurricane and thunderstorm occurred
the sky remained clear and bright as on the finest of spring days. Everyone . . .
cursed Merelli for having treated *Attila* so abominably. . . .' He adds: 'The maestro
has written a romanza for Moriani to sing in the opera, and it was greeted with
frantic applause.'¶

This romanza, too, is a double strophe, beginning:

> O dolore! ed io vivea
> Sol pensando alla spergiura

* Letter to Piave 4.8.1846. Rome, Istituto del Risorgimento Italiano, Busta 551, n. 82 (4).

† Letter from Muzio to Barezzi, 10.9.1846. Garibaldi, p. 269.

‡ See D. Lawton and D. Rosen, 'Verdi's non-definitive revisions: the early operas', in *Atti del
IIIº Congresso Verdiano* (Parma, 1974), pp. 189–237.

§ Letter to Ricordi, 29.12.1846. *Copialettere*, pp. 34–5. From the same letter it would appear
that Verdi wanted the embargo on La Scala to apply to all of his operas written in the future.
Happily for his early benefactor he never insisted on this. The first Italian performance of
Jérusalem was given there in 1850.

¶ Letter to Barezzi, 27.12.1846. Garibaldi, pp. 303–4.

The autograph is in the Museo alla Scala with a brief accompanying note from the composer ('Here is the romanza, with which you can do what you like').* Unlike most recipients of substitute arias Moriani could hardly wait to sell his; which is why copies of it in piano reduction were available the following year.† It is an ample structure six bars longer than the *Chi non avrebbe il misero* which it replaces and introduced by an unexpected modulation from C minor to D flat major. Moriani was a lachrymose artist, always at his best in death scenes; and Verdi serves him rather as a tenor Silva (*Ernani*) with a slow-climbing melodic line. As in the romanza for la Granchi in *Nabucco* the return to tonic harmony precedes the melodic reprise, which is held in reserve for a final transcendent statement (Ex. 163). But here the design is enhanced by a far greater melodic and harmonic variety. Note the long reach, the widely separated pinnacles (*x*) each higher than the last, and the strong, if unorthodox, use of six-four harmony (*y*):

163

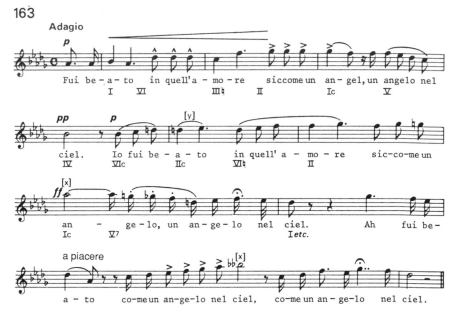

Striking too is the imaginative and unusual instrumentation. Clarinets, horns and bassoons for a^1 and a^2; strings alone for *b*, and the unexpected addition of harp for the words 'Ah fui beato in quell' amore' up to the end of the piece. It was more than Moriani deserved.‡

In his memoirs published in 1864 Benjamin Lumley wrote: 'None perhaps of Verdi's works had kindled more enthusiasm in Italy or crowned the fortunate composer with more abundant laurels than *Attila*.'§ The opera pursued a triumphant course throughout the Italian cities. Everywhere the words 'Avrai tu l'universo, resta l'Italia a me' brought forth spontaneous cheers. After 1860 the

---

* Letter to Moriani, 21.12.1846, Museo alla Scala, 11113 and 11114.

† Copies can be found in the British Museum (B.M. H.473—91) and in the Bibliothèque Nationale, Paris (B.N. Vm⁵ 1426). Both contain serious harmonic inaccuracies.

‡ For the part played in the life of Giuseppina Strepponi by this unscrupulous artist see Walker, pp. 38—95.

§ B. Lumley, *Reminiscences of the Italian Opera* (London, 1864), p. 214.

mood of bellicose patriotism to which *Attila* appealed began to pass, and with it the opera's popularity. But three successful revivals towards the end of the century showed that the embers could still be fanned into flame. On the whole biographers have treated it benevolently as a work which lies just below the horizon of repertoire but could repay revival better than most products of the 'anni di galera'. Did not Verdi himself describe it, with becoming modesty, as 'not inferior to my other operas'?* The experience of recent anniversary years (1951, 1963) have shown that the forecast has been over-optimistic. *Attila* in performance has more disappointments than surprises. In the heady atmosphere of the 1840s it was like a tract for the times. Nowadays it is easier to identify oneself with the romantic unrealities of *Ernani* and *Il Trovatore* than with the wiles and machinations of Foresto and Ezio. Ernani and Manrico can appeal to the unreasoning youth in all of us. The ideals of Solera's Romans have become shop-soiled after a hundred years. Paradoxically *Attila* repels because it is too sordidly modern. Ezio embodies all the more squalid aspects of resistance warfare.

As with the plot, so with the music. *Attila* is the heaviest and noisiest of the Risorgimento operas, blunt in style, daubed in thick garish colours; full of theatrical effects with no depth to them and containing more than its fair share of brash cabalettas. There are fitful gleams of a *Nabucco*-like solemnity, especially in the Prologue. There are moments of tenderness and beauty too (Odabella's romanza, her duet with Foresto, the final trio and quartet). But despite a genuine strength of construction much of it remains no less than *Alzira* on the level of commonplace vigour.

Yet the opera does show an advance in one respect: of all Verdi's essays in the grand manner composed to date none shows so great a consistency of language. Even *Nabucco* contains reminiscences of Donizetti and Rossini. In *Attila* every phrase is characteristic, each aria is an archetype of the composer's early manner. The melodic arch mentioned above may be a little too pervasive; but it gives to the score a quality of integration which is lacking in *I Lombardi* and *Giovanna d'Arco*.

In the main, however, the critics of the time were right. *Attila* is a work of consolidation; it is not the great step forward that they—and Verdi—foretold. For that we must wait until the next opera: *Macbeth*.

---

* Letter to Gina della Somaglia (undated). Abbiati, I, pp. 606–7. Also to Opprandino Arrivabene, 19.3.1846. Alberti, p. xxvii. It should perhaps be mentioned that *Attila* was completed during convalescence from a particularly severe bout of gastritis. The fact that Lucca insisted that he should fulfil his part of the contract despite his 'deplorable physical condition' was among the causes of Verdi's later hostility to the publisher. See letter to Piave, 14.1.1848. *Carteggi Verdiani*, II, p. 350.

MACBETH

Opera in four acts
by
FRANCESCO MARIA PIAVE
(after Shakespeare's play, *Macbeth*)

*First performed at the
Teatro della Pergola, Florence,
14 March 1847*

MACBETH } Generals in the army of King	PRIMO BARITONO	Felice Varesi
BANCO } Duncan	BASSO COMPRIMARIO	Nicola Benedetti
LADY MACBETH	PRIMA DONNA SOPRANO	Marianna Barbieri-Nini
WOMAN in attendance on Lady Macbeth	SECONDA DONNA MEZZO-SOPRANO	Faustina Piombanti
MACDUFF, a Scottish nobleman, Lord of Fife	TENORE COMPRIMARIO	Angelo Brunacci
MALCOLM, son of Duncan	SECONDO TENORE	Francesco Rossi
A DOCTOR	SECONDO BASSO	Giuseppe Romanelli
A SERVANT of MACBETH	SECONDO BASSO	N.N.
A MURDERER	SECONDO BASSO	Giuseppe Bertini
A HERALD	SECONDO BASSO	N.N.
FIRST APPARITION	SECONDO BARITONO	N.N.
SECOND APPARITION	SECONDO SOPRANO	N.N.
THIRD APPARITION	SECONDO SOPRANO	N.N.

Witches—King's Messengers—Scottish nobles and exiles—murderers—
English soldiers—bards—aerial spirits, apparitions, etc.

Walk-on parts: as above—Duncan, King of Scotland—Fleanzio—
Hecate, goddess of night (2nd version only)

The action takes place in Scotland, and on the Anglo-Scottish border
*Revised version. First performed at the
Théâtre Lyrique, Paris,
19 April 1865*

MACBETH	M. Ismael	MALCOLM	M. Huet
BANCO	M. Bilis Petit	DOCTOR	M. Guyot
LADY MACBETH	Mme Rey-Balla	SERVANT	N.N.
WOMAN IN ATTENDANCE	Mme Mairot	MURDERER	M. Caillot
MACDUFF	M. Montjauze	HERALD	N.N.

When in 1865 a French review greeted the premiere of the second and final version of Verdi's *Macbeth* with the remark that the composer clearly did not know his Shakespeare, Verdi was furious—far more so than if the critic had merely said that the opera was a failure. 'It may be that I have not done justice to *Macbeth*: but to say that I do not know, understand and feel Shachespeare (*sic*)—no, by God, no! He is one of my favourite poets. I have had him in my hands from my earliest youth, and I read and reread him continually.'* The ambition to set *King Lear* recurs as a rondo-theme throughout his life, though it was never to be realized. But a Shakespearian opera was inevitable sooner or later and it would be something very special—of that one could be sure. What subject to be given in what theatre at what time would all be determined like everything else in Verdi's early career by external circumstances.

After the premiere of *Attila* Verdi's plans included another opera for Naples, one for Paris (not necessarily new, but to be directed by himself) and two more operas for Francesco Lucca, including a world premiere for London (either *King Lear* or Byron's *The Corsair*).

Another more prolonged bout of ill-health prevented him from fulfilling any of his contracts abroad or in the south. Flauto agreed to release him, Lumley and Escudier to a postponement; and in the meantime Verdi accepted an offer from Lanari, manager of the Teatro della Pergola, Florence, for an opera to be given in the Carnival or Lenten season of 1847. 'The maestro is considering three possible subjects,' Muzio wrote, '*Macbeth*, *Die Räuber* (Schiller) and *Die Ahnfrau* (Grillparzer).'† The last of these was dropped. The choice was between Shakespeare and Schiller, the determining factor being whether or not Lanari could engage a tenor such as Fraschini for the part of Karl Moor. As it turned out he could not; so Verdi transferred his attention from a *Masnadieri*, which he had already begun, to *Macbeth*, though not before making sure that the baritone Varesi would be available for the title role. He also stipulated Sofia Loewe as the other principal. However, he was not unduly upset when it transpired that she was not available, and Madame Barbieri-Nini, heroine of *I Due Foscari*, was engaged in her place.

There can be little doubt that the possibility of setting all three subjects occurred to Verdi as a result of his growing intimacy with the Cavaliere Andrea Maffei and his circle. Maffei had some pretensions as a poet and man of letters; and the Casa de' Nobili had commissioned both him and Verdi to collaborate on a cantata in honour of a scientific conference in 1845. At the time Verdi took evasive action; but that year he set six Romances to words by Maffei, Romani, and Maggioni published by Lucca (the best known of them is 'Lo Spazzacamin'). During the composition of *Attila* Maffei had always been ready with advice; and

---

* Letter to Léon Escudier, 28.4.1865. J. G. Prod'homme, 'Lettres Inédites de G. Verdi à Léon Escudier', in the *Rivista Musicale Italiana*, XXXV (1928), pp. 187–8. Also *Music and Letters* (April 1923), p. 184, translated L. A. Sheppard.
† Letter from Muzio to Barezzi, 13.8.1846. Garibaldi, p. 258.

when Verdi went to take the waters at Recoaro in the autumn Maffei went with him. An ardent Shakespearian, Maffei was very taken up with *Macbeth*, of which he was later to make a translation; and as a would-be librettist himself, who was already collaborating with Verdi on *I Masnadieri*, it is likely that he had a hand in the more than usually extended synopsis that Verdi consigned to Piave with a letter:

> . . . This tragedy is one of the greatest creations of man. . . . If we can't make something great out of it let us at least try and do something out of the ordinary. . . . The sketch is clear . . . unconventional . . . and short. Please see that your verses are short too. Only the first act is rather on the long side but it will be up to us to keep the pieces themselves short . . . and you will need to write in a lofty, noble style throughout except in the witches' choruses; these must be trivial but in an extravagant original way. . . . When you've done the introduction please send it to me; it's made up of four little scenes and can do with a very few lines. Once this is done I'll leave you all the time you want, because I've got the general character and the colour of the opera into my head just as if the libretto were already written.*

Three weeks later (22 September): 'I've got the cavatina which is better than the introduction. But oh, how prolix you are! . . .' The whole of Lady Macbeth's recitative, including the letter, was too long and not sufficiently 'lofty' in style; the first line of her adagio was too commonplace and took away all the energy of her character. There were too many lines in the duet between Macbeth and Banquo; as for the chorus of witches—something was wrong though Verdi could not exactly say what. Perhaps if Piave were to make the lines short and irregular the result would be more effectively bizarre; and over and over again, written in insulting capitals, come the words 'POCHE PAROLE . . . POCHE PAROLE . . . STILE CONCISO' and so forth.† Having received Act II, he objected to the idea of Lady Macbeth's writing a letter to her husband urging him to murder Banquo; a soliloquy would be much better. (In Shakespeare the murder of Banquo is something that Macbeth deliberately keeps from his wife; in the opera it is she who persuades him to it. As usual it is the points where Verdi departs furthest from Shakespeare that give him the most trouble.)

Piave did everything that he was told; but meanwhile he had heard from Lanari that no dancing was allowed on stage during Lent so that the ballet of aerial spirits would have to be dropped. Verdi was unmoved. He wanted a ballet with chorus at that point (i.e., after the apparition of the eight kings) and he would have one. Would Piave therefore please write the words and not keep making ridiculous objections.‡ Meanwhile he continued to worry about the beginning of the second act. It should be neither a letter nor a soliloquy but a dialogue between Macbeth and his wife. He even sketched out their recitative as a guide for Piave:

---

* Letter to Piave, 4.9.1846. Abbiati, I, p. 643. The letters of Verdi to his librettist on the subject of *Macbeth* are among the most interesting parts of his unpublished correspondence that Abbiati has brought to light. The originals are, presumably, in the Gallini collection.

† Letter to Piave, 22.9.1846. Abbiati, I, pp. 644–5.

‡ See letter to Piave, 10.12.1846. Abbiati, I, pp. 667–8.

MACBETH*	But the unearthly women
	Foretold Banquo as the father of kings.
	Shall his sons then reign?
	Was Duncan killed for *them*?
LADY	He and his son live,
	But nature has not created them immortal.
MACBETH	That gives me comfort; indeed they are not immortal.
LADY	Therefore, if another crime? . . .
MACBETH	Another crime? . . .
LADY	Were necessary.
MACBETH	When?
LADY	As soon as night falls
MACBETH (*pretending*)	A new crime!!! . . .
LADY	Well?
MACBETH	It is decided. . . . Banquo, for thee eternity begins in a few moments.†

An aria for Lady was to follow, mainly so as to give time for Macbeth to arrange for Banquo's murder in the following scene. It was to take the form of a cabaletta on its own, so Verdi thought at the time.

In short Piave was given no peace. Everything he did was wrong or needed some kind of adjustment. The composer who had insisted at the time of *Ernani* that it never made the slightest difference to him what metre he was given now wanted hendecasyllabics changed into octosyllabics, regular stanzas chopped into irregular lines. Particular attention was to be paid to a chorus of exiles at the beginning of Act IV, 'the one moment of real pathos in the opera'.‡ It was to be the equivalent of 'Va pensiero' in *Nabucco*, the gist being taken from Shakespeare's dialogue between Ross and Macduff. More instructions followed about the final battle and the death of Macbeth including an idea for a scene change which had just come to Verdi when he was writing the letter, '. . . and try and do better than you did with the chorus of witches'.§ The libretto completed, Verdi turned on his collaborator with savage fury. 'Of course you're not the slightest bit in the wrong except for having neglected those last two acts in an incredible way. Ah, well! Sant Andrea [*a nickname for Maffei*] has come to my rescue and yours—and more especially to mine, since to be frank I couldn't have set your verses to music. Still we've managed to put it all right now—by changing almost everything,

* There is some confusion in the Italian nomenclature. Only Duncan, Banquo and Fleance are consistently italianized into Duncano, Banco and Fleanzio respectively. The rest retain their English names on the title-page, but euphonic -o endings are allowed into the text itself; so that, for instance, 'Macbeth! Macbeth! Macbeth! Beware Macduff!' becomes 'Macbetto! Macbetto! Macbetto! da Macduffo ti guarda prudente!' (at a recent performance in Verona the First Apparition cut off the final -o in each case, doubtless in order to forestall a laugh from any of Shakespeare's countrymen who might have been present). Both in the autograph and in the printed score as well as in Verdi's correspondence Lady Macbeth is always called 'Lady' for short, and her handwoman, rather quaintly, 'Dama di Lady'. For the sake of simplicity I have kept throughout to the original names, even when discussing the opera.

† Letter to Piave, 3.12.1846. Abbiati, I, p. 656. This last line is clearly inspired by 'Banquo, thy soul's flight, | If it find heaven, must find it out tonight'.

‡ Letter to Piave, 22.12.1846. Abbiati, I, p. 675.

§ Letter to Piave, 10.12.1846. Abbiati, I, p. 672.

however . . .'* The witches' chorus in Act III and the sleepwalking scene were rewritten entirely by Maffei. Exactly what other changes he made we shall never know; but they were sufficient to induce Verdi to omit Piave's name from the title page, which makes no mention of a librettist. Maffei was recompensed with a gold watch; Piave however was paid by Verdi in full, although the composer's last words on the subject were, 'I wouldn't have your drama for all the gold in the world.'†

Usually it was the librettist's business to instruct the management as to the mise-en-scène; but Lanari had found Piave's indications not nearly detailed enough. ('Lanari is complaining about you,' wrote Verdi, 'and so am I. The fact is that you've taken on too much work and I'm the one that has to suffer for it.')‡ But in fact Verdi had been in touch with Lanari from the start, urging him to spare no expense, especially as regards chorus and stage machinery. The witches were to be divided into three covens of no less than six each. For the apparition of the eight kings Lanari must make use of a magic lantern. The ghost of Banquo was to rise through a trap-door into Macbeth's seat. He must wear an ash-coloured veil and wounds should be visible on his neck. 'All these ideas I've got from London where they've been playing *Macbeth* continuously over the last two hundred years.'§ He insisted on overriding Benedetti's objection to appearing on the stage as Banquo's ghost. As for costumes and scenes he had equally strong views; indeed he had been into the matter very carefully and was prepared to read the designer Perrone (via Tito Ricordi) a lecture on English and Scottish history. The period was 1040–57, not, as the stage designer seemed to think, contemporary with Ossian or the Roman occupation. Therefore no silk or velvet in the costumes.¶

Most interesting of all, perhaps, are Verdi's instructions to Felice Varesi, the first Macbeth. Even before starting to compose the opera, Verdi had written to him, to make quite sure that he would be available in Florence during the whole of the Lenten season. Some time in January of 1847 he was in touch with him again.

> Herewith a duettino, a grand duet and a finale. You can make a lot of the opening duettino [with Banquo] even more than if it were a cavatina. Always bear in mind the dramatic situation: you have met the witches who predict a crown for you. You're bewildered by this and terrified; yet at the same time there is born in you an ambition to reach the throne. That's why you must start this duet sotto voce and make sure you give real importance to the lines, 'why do I yield to that suggestion whose horrid image doth unfix my hair?' Pay careful attention to the dynamic markings from *pp* and *ff*. . . . In the grand duet the first lines of the recitative where you give the orders to the servant can be thrown away. But when you're left alone you get more and more carried away and you seem to see a dagger in your hands which gives you the idea how to kill Duncan. This is a most beautiful passage, poetically and dramatically, and you must put a lot into it! Remember

---

*Letter to Piave, 21.1.1847. Abbiati, I, pp. 676–7.

†Letter to Piave, 14.2.1847. *Ibid.* p. 680. See, however, E. Baker, 'Le lettere di Giuseppe Verdi a Francesco Maria Piave, 1843–1865', *Studi verdiani* IV (Parma, 1986–7), pp. 136–66, where for 'dramma' the author reads 'danno', i.e. 'injury', which puts a very different complexion on the tone of the letter!

‡Letter to Piave, 3.12.1846. Abbiati, I, p. 656.

§Letter to Lanari, 22.12.1846. *Copialettere*, pp. 446–7.

¶Letter to T. Ricordi (undated). *Copialettere*, p. 448.

that it's night; everyone's asleep; so that this duet should be sung sotto voce but in a hollow voice such as will inspire terror. Macbeth himself—as though carried away for the moment—will sing one or two phrases in full voice, but all that you'll find explained in the score. So as to give you a clear notion of what I have in mind, I'll tell you that the whole of this recitative and duet is scored for muted strings, two bassoons, two horns and tympani. You can see that the orchestra will sound very quiet, and therefore you two on stage will have to sing with your mutes on!*

Particular emphasis was to be given to two extremely beautiful poetic ideas, one of them Shakespeare's ('Will all great Neptune's ocean wash this blood clean from my hand?'), the other concerning Duncan's 'avenging saintliness'. These were the only two phrases of the scene to be sung 'a voce spiegata'. Throughout Varesi is urged to serve the poet rather than the musician. 'I shall never stop telling you to study the words and the dramatic situation; then the music will come right of its own accord.'

In the next letter Verdi drew Varesi's attention to a cantabile 'which is sui generis' after the procession of the eight kings. This too is a departure from Shakespeare, Macbeth being made to try to attack the apparitions then pulling up short as he realises that they are only ghosts. 'Needless to say, *Morrai fatal progenie* requires one type of effect, and *Ah che tu non hai vita* another, that's to say that at this point you need two different styles of delivery; do it in the way that comes most naturally to you and then write and *tell me how you want it scored*.'† An interesting sidelight, this, on the collaboration between artist and composer in the 1840s.‡

The third act closed originally with a cabaletta (*Vada in fiamme*) based on Macbeth's lines:

> The castle of Macduff I will surprise;
> Seize upon Fife; give to the edge o' th' sword
> His wife, his babes, and all unfortunate souls
> That trace him in his line.§

Of this Verdi wrote to Varesi, 'It isn't in the usual form because after what has gone before this would sound banal. I had written another one which I liked when I tried it out on its own but when I joined it on to what had gone before I found it intolerable. . . .' It is indeed a very interesting and unusual cabaletta, but in the later definitive *Macbeth* it was replaced by another duet for Macbeth and 'Lady'.

Less relevant nowadays are Verdi's instructions about how the death scene is to be played, since that too was transformed in the final version, though modern performances often include it. It is set as a declamatory arioso like Don Carlo's 'Tu

---

* Three letters to Varesi, written between January and March 1847 and published by Giulia Cora Varesi, the baritone's daughter, in 'L'interpretazione del Macbeth', in the *Nuova Antologia* CCLXXXI (Nov.–Dec. 1932), pp. 433–40.
† Italics mine.
‡ Another letter to Varesi preserved in the Verdi Institute, Parma, includes alternative sketches for the death scene ('Mal per me che m'affidai'). Again Varesi is asked to decide between the two.
§ Shakespeare, *Macbeth*, IV, i.

sei Ernani' or Attila's 'Tu rea donna': 'pathetic, yes, but more than that, terrible. It must not be a death like Gennaro's or Edgardo's.' In effect it was the last piece in the opera, and therefore stood out in relief like the death of Violetta or Boris Godunov. In the later version the death takes place offstage; while the dialogue between Macbeth and Macduff is swallowed up in the orchestral fugue depicting the battle. The last word is given to the chorus.

During rehearsals the composer was more than usually exigent and unreasonable.* However on the opening night the public reception was as warm as could be desired, Verdi being called to take twenty-five bows and escorted to his lodgings by a vast cheering crowd. Those like Muzio who appreciated the opera talked about a 'sensation', a 'fanatical' enthusiasm on the part of the audience for this 'grand and magnificent' opera; those who did not maintained that the plaudits were for the composer not the opera. One envenomed correspondent wrote to the Florentine newspaper *Il Ricoglitore* describing *Macbeth* as a 'vera porcheria'.† Verdi himself was particularly irritated by a notice which criticized the verses of the witches' chorus as inept—they happened ironically to be Maffei's, not Piave's. (It says much for Verdi's sense of justice that he recalled this verdict ten years later in Piave's defence.‡) On the other hand he accepted almost too humbly a complaint made by the poet Giuseppe Giusti that in *Macbeth* he had not touched upon 'that string of melancholy which awakens the readiest echo in the hearts of our people'.§ It was the business of an Italian musician, Giusti maintained, not to go whoring after foreign and fantastic subjects, but to marry his genius indissolubly to the traditions of his country. Verdi agreed; but pointed out that it was not easy to find the poet who would express such ideals in an operatic libretto.¶ The fact is that, foreign or not, he himself was very pleased with *Macbeth*, as is shown by a touching letter to Antonio Barezzi, his father-in-law. 'For many years I have intended to dedicate an opera to you who have been my father, my benefactor and my friend. Here now is this *Macbeth* which is dearer to me than all my other operas, and which I therefore deem more worthy of being presented to you. I offer it from my heart; accept it in the same way, let it be witness of my eternal

---

* See Monaldi (3rd ed., pp. 90–3), who quotes the memoirs of La Barbieri-Nini to the effect that she was required to study the sleepwalking scene alone for three whole months and to rehearse the duet with the baritone more than 150 times.

† Abbiati, I, p. 687.

‡ Letter to T. Ricordi, 11.4.1857 (written after the quasi-fiasco of *Simon Boccanegra* at the Fenice, Venice, for which well-meaning friends blamed Piave's libretto). 'Ten years ago I took it into my head to write *Macbeth*; I drew up the plot myself—indeed, I did more than that, I laid out the whole drama in prose with the division into acts, scenes, numbers, etc. . . . Then I gave it to Piave to put into verse. And as I found certain things to object to in his versification I begged Maffei, with the consent of Piave himself, to go over the lines in question. and to rewrite entirely the witches' chorus in Act III and the sleepwalking scene. Well, would you believe it? Although the libretto didn't have the poet's name on it, everyone assumed it was Piave's; and the said chorus and sleepwalking scene were the most abused and held up to ridicule! Perhaps those two numbers could have been written better, but as they stand they're still Maffei's lines, and the chorus in particular has great character. There's public opinion for you!' *Copialettere*, p. 444.

§ Letter from Giusti, 19.3.1847. *Copialettere*, pp. 449–50.

¶ Letter to Giusti, 27.3.1847. 'Una lettera inedita di Verdi', in the *Corriere della Sera*, 12 May 1933, reprinted from a French periodical, *Dante*. Walker, p. 157 (in English); Abbiati, I, pp. 591–2.

remembrance and the gratitude and love of your most affectionate VERDI.'*

For years to come he continued to watch *Macbeth*'s progress with interest. He insisted that Ricordi should withhold it from La Scala until conditions there improved.† It was one of the few operas of which he was prepared to direct a revival. On the whole it proved scarcely less popular than *Attila* and the chorus of exiles in Act IV and especially the battle hymn *La patria tradita* were to rouse great enthusiasm in the revolutionary years. In 1848 it was to be staged for the first time at the San Carlo in Naples. Verdi, already in touch with the Neapolitan librettist Salvatore Cammarano over *La Battaglia di Legnano*, gave him plenty of advice about the production to pass on to the management. Having seen a performance of the play in London the year before, he considered himself an authority on how to present Shakespeare. The kings, for instance, must on no account be puppets. They must pass over a mound so that they appear to ascend as they come in and descend as they go out. What particularly disturbed him was the idea of Tadolini (the first Alzira) in the part of Lady Macbeth.

> Tadolini's qualities are too great for this role. A ridiculous thing to say, you may think. . . . Tadolini is a fine figure of a woman, and I would like Lady Macbeth to look ugly and malignant. Tadolini sings to perfection and I would rather that Lady didn't sing at all. Tadolini has a marvellous voice, clear, limpid and strong; and I would rather that Lady's voice were rough, hollow, stifled. Tadolini's voice has something angelic in it. Lady's should have something devilish. . . .
>
> Point out . . . that the chief pieces of the opera are two: the duet between Lady and her husband and the sleepwalking scene; and these pieces must not be sung at all:
>
> > They must be acted and declaimed
> > in a voice that is hollow
> > and veiled: without this
> > the whole effect is lost.
> > Orchestra with *mutes*.‡

It is an argumentum ad hominem (or feminam) rather than a statement of fact, rather like Richard Strauss's instruction to perform *Elektra* as fairy music. In other words to combat the narcissistic disposition of the Italian prima donna a touch of exaggeration was needed. The point was that *Macbeth* was first and foremost music-drama. As Verdi wrote to Flauto, 'The opera is a little more difficult than my others and its mise-en-scène is important. I confess, I care for it more than for the others and I should be sorry to see it fail.'§

When approached in 1852 about an opera for Paris Verdi wished to make it one of the conditions that *Macbeth* should be mounted in the same season,¶ with the addition of a ballet if necessary. But it was not until 1865 that this became a practical possibility. The suggestion came this time from Carvalho, impresario of

* Throughout Verdi uses the formal 'Lei'. Letter to Barezzi, 25.3.1847. *Copialettere*, p. 451.
† Letter to G. Ricordi, 29.12.1846. *Copialettere*, pp. 34–5.
‡ Letter to Cammarano, 23.11.1848. *Copialettere*, pp. 60–2.
§ Letter to Flauto, 23.11.1848. *Copialettere*, pp. 57–60.
¶ Letter to Roqueplan, 2.2.1852. *Copialettere*, p. 134.

the Théâtre Lyrique, whose resources were more modest than those of the Opéra, certainly; but he had already put on a truncated version of Berlioz's grandiose *Les Troyens*, and he too wanted a ballet, not to mention a final chorus. Verdi complied readily enough, though nothing would induce him to go to Paris for the production.* He sent to Ricordi for a full score of the opera, then found to his dismay that it needed far more overhauling than he had thought.

> To put it in a nutshell [*he wrote to his French publisher Escudier, through whom Carvalho's approach had been made*], there are various pieces in it which are either weak, or lacking in character, which is worse still. We shall need:
>
> (1) An aria for Lady Macbeth in Act II
> (2) To rewrite various passages in the hallucination scene in Act III
> (3) To rewrite completely Macbeth's aria in Act III
> (4) To revise the opening scenes of Act IV (the exiles' chorus)
> (5) To compose a new finale to Act IV removing the death of Macbeth.
>
> To do all this and the ballet as well is going to take time, so Carvalho must give up any idea of producing the opera this winter.†

Verdi's revision was even more extensive than that. The first act, he decided, could stand unaltered apart from a few adjustments to be made to the duet; but the choruses would remain as they were so the chorus members could start learning their parts straight away. The new chorus for the last act would have to be a victory hymn. The ballet was going to present a real difficulty. 'It can only come at the beginning of Act III after the chorus; the only people on stage are the witches and to have these delightful creatures for a quarter of an hour or twenty minutes will make a pretty frantic divertissement. It isn't as if we could bring on sylphs or aerial spirits since we've got them later on at the point where Macbeth faints.'‡

For the textual revisions Verdi turned to his old friend Piave, long since restored to favour. As usual it was a laborious business, Verdi quibbling over the length of this or that line, the placing of an accent and the choice of individual words. To judge from the letters to Piave (including one which Abbiati must surely be wrong in assigning to the year 1847)§ he virtually wrote the text of Lady Macbeth's aria in Act II himself, basing it on Macbeth's lines:

> Light thickens; and the crow
> Makes wing to th' rooky wood;
> Good things of day begin to droop and drowse;
> While night's black agents to their preys do rouse.¶

---

* The reason was probably the unpleasant scene that had taken place between Verdi and the orchestra during rehearsals for a revival of *Les Vêpres Siciliennes* in the summer of 1863. The composer had stormed out, vowing never to set foot in the theatre again. Cf. letter to L. Escudier, 19.6.1865, in the *R.M.I.* (1928), pp. 190–1, *M. & L.* (1923), p. 186.

† Letter to Escudier, 24.10.1864. *Copialettere*, pp. 451–2 (dated 22.10 in *R.M.I.* XXXV [1928], pp. 180–1, and *M. & L.* [1923], pp. 64–5).

‡ Letter to L. Escudier, 2.12.1864. *R.M.I.* (1928), p. 183, *M. & L.* (1923), p. 66.

§ Abbiati, I, p. 676. Part of the autograph, from the Gallini collection, is reproduced in facsimile facing p. 656. See also letter to Piave, December 1864. Abbiati, II, pp. 804–5. Here Verdi is less specific as to metre, merely asking for a double quatrain and two final lines 'di silenzio' and insisting that the word 'voluttà' be kept.

¶ Shakespeare, III, ii.

If the last lines have nothing to do with Shakespeare (*O voluttà del soglio*, etc.) it is because they are designed with a view to the musical form, which here requires the spirit of a cabaletta. Only the spirit however, since Verdi had by 1865 given up writing cabalettas entirely, while embodying their function and character in a handful of sweeping phrases in fast tempo.

The recomposition of *Macbeth* took most of the winter; and it is interesting to find the composer writing to Escudier in the same vein as Beethoven when he was engaged on the revision of *Fidelio*. Beethoven disliked 'patching up the old with something new'.* Verdi found it no less troublesome to 'take up a thread which had been broken so many years ago . . . I'll be able to manage it soon enough; but I detest mosaics in music.'† However by February all the problems had been solved to his satisfaction. The ballet became a mixture of ballet and mime with Hecate appearing but not dancing (Verdi was emphatic on this point). The last chorus of all was to be launched by Bards, 'who in those days regularly accompanied the armies into battle'‡ (was he thinking of Ossian after all?). Macbeth's final aria in Act III was to be replaced by a duet with Lady Macbeth. The instrumentation, he told Escudier, must on no account be tampered with. The appearance of Hecate should be accompanied by bass clarinet in unison with cellos and bassoon to give 'the austere hollow sound that the situation demands'. No less important was the little band under the stage which accompanied the procession of the eight kings. 'Two oboes, six clarinets, two bassoons and a contrabassoon will give a sonority which is strange and mysterious and at the same time calm and quiet, such as no other combination can give.'§ He continued to worry over the problem of Banquo's ghost and actually appended a sketch of the banquet scene as he envisaged it, explaining the advantages of the various placings. For the battle scene:

> You'll laugh [*he told Escudier*], when you hear that I've written a Fugue. A *Fugue*??? . . . Me, who detest everything that reeks of the schoolroom and it's almost thirty years since I wrote one!!! But I can tell you that in this case that particular musical form will be all right. The continual succession of subject and countersubject, the clash of dissonances, the general din, etc., etc., can describe a battle well enough. Ah if only you had our trumpets, with their rich tone, their brilliance!! These valve trumpets of yours are neither one thing or the other.¶

As to the translation Verdi insisted only on one point: that in the duet between Macbeth and Lady her words 'Follie, follie!' should be preserved where they stand since they give a vital clue to her character and attitude.

Carvalho behaved with the mixture of good-will and philistinism that had already driven Berlioz frantic two years before. Verdi had particularly asked for

---

* Letter to Treitschke, April 1814. E. Anderson (ed.), *The Collected Letters of Ludwig van Beethoven*, vol. I, pp. 454–5.
† Letter to L. Escudier, 31.12.1864, in the *R.M.I.* (1928), p. 184.
‡ Letter to Piave, 28.1.1865. Abbiati, II, pp. 812–14.
§ Letter to L. Escudier, Jan. 1865. *Copialettere*, pp. 452–4.
¶ Letter to L. Escudier, 3.2.1865. *Copialettere*, p. 456.

Duprez to make the French translation, since he was a musician as well as a poet. Carvalho entrusted the work to Nuttier and Beaumont. He also made what seemed to him an eminently reasonable suggestion: that the drinking song in the banquet scene should be sung by Macduff rather than Lady Macbeth, who had plenty to sing anyway whereas the tenor had only one aria. Verdi pointed out that much as he admired Carvalho's ingenuity it would have a disastrous effect on the drama. Nor would it help if Macduff were to use the drinking song as an opportunity to hint at his suspicions since this would conflict with the brilliant character of the music. The entire scene must be dominated by Lady Macbeth. He elaborated on this point in a final letter to Escudier:

> Abide by the rule that the main roles of this opera are, and can only be, *three*: Macbeth, Lady Macbeth and the chorus of witches. The witches dominate the drama; everything stems from them—rude and gossipy in Act I, exalted and prophetic in Act III. They make up a real character, and one of the greatest importance. Whatever you do to the part of Macduff you'll never make it very interesting. Indeed the more prominence you give it, the more it will reveal its emptiness. He has enough music to distinguish himself if he has a good voice, but he mustn't be given a note more.★

The performance was on the whole a failure. Even with its alterations and improvements it was too unsophisticated for a Second Empire audience. Critics complained, not unreasonably, of the march which announced the entrance of Duncan, finding it too trivial and homely. Verdi himself had been quite satisfied with the revised *Macbeth*, and its failure puzzled and disappointed him. ('I thought I had done quite well with it . . . it appears I was mistaken.')† The early *Macbeth* had enjoyed a favoured position among the Risorgimento operas. The later version has had to wait for the Verdi revival of the present century to take its rightful place in the Italian repertory.‡ The fact is that the new *Macbeth* as it was called is, despite the care with which it was revised, a patchwork of two styles, a mosaic, as Verdi put it. Not only do the least distinguished survivals from 1847 sound still worse in their new context; even the best lose their once dominating position. The skyline, so to speak, is altered. For instance the original Act II worked up steadily from a commonplace cabaletta (Lady Macbeth's *Trionfai*) through Banquo's murder, through the hallucination scene to a huge concerted finale in a steady crescendo of musical and dramatic interest which takes even the cheap banquet music in its stride. The highlight of the new Act II is Lady Macbeth's *La luce langue* which throws into shadow everything that comes after it. The famous sleepwalking scene of Act IV is rightly hailed as a master-stroke of early Verdi. But how naif and old-fashioned it seems after the new exiles' chorus, with its foretaste of the

★ Letter to L. Escudier, 8.2.1865. Autograph in the Teatro Colón, Buenos Aires; text published in 'Cinque lettere Verdiane', in the *Rassegna Musicale*, 1951, XXI, pp. 260–1. See also letter to the same, 28.5.1865. *R.M.I.*, pp. 188–9. His protests were too late however since Carvalho had already put his idea into effect.

† Letter to L. Escudier, 3.6.1865. *R.M.I.* (1928), pp. 189–90; *M. & L.* (1923), pp. 185–6.

‡ Important landmarks were the revivals at Glyndebourne in 1938 under Fritz Busch with Vera Schwarz, Valentino, Franklin and David Lloyd, and at the Maggio Musicale Fiorentino in 1952 under De Sabata with Callas and Mascherini. Nowadays there is even a fashion among Italian critics to claim *Macbeth* as the best of Verdi's Shakespearian operas.

Requiem. No blame, then, to the Paris audience of 1865 for finding the opera wanting. But granted the awkward bridging of an eighteen-year gap, *Macbeth* as we know it today is still an enthralling work. It shows Verdi more than ever before reaching out beyond the confines of contemporary Italian opera, striving however crudely for a *Gesamtkunstwerk* in the Wagnerian sense.

The *Macbeth* of 1847, without the battle fugue, the opening and final choruses of Act IV, the aria *La luce langue*, with both the hallucination and apparition scenes simpler and less effective, and with the sleepwalking scene as its musical climax, could be resurrected easily enough since copies of the full score exist in various libraries in Italy and abroad. We should find it more consistent in style than the later version, though it is doubtful whether that would compensate for the loss of the Parisian additions still less those retouches of genius where Verdi has contrived to re-enter and at the same time widen his original version. But we should see at once how even in 1847 the Shakespearian experience brought about what he had hoped for, mistakenly, from *Attila*; over and over again it lifted him out of the rut of operatic cliché which ever since *Giovanna d'Arco* had been threatening to canalize his invention. It had dispersed for a while those shades of the prison house that were closing about him. The 'anni di galera' were not yet over; and indeed they were to leave their mark on at least three operas to come. But in *Macbeth* there are glimpses of a new freedom.

'One of the greatest creations of man . . .' so Verdi described Shakespeare's play; but what drew him to *Macbeth* in the first place, rather than to *Hamlet* or *Othello*? On the practical level there was the fact that it called for a combination with which he was already familiar—that of baritone and dramatic soprano. More decisive, no doubt, was the character of Macbeth himself. Verdi was drawn to complex personalities; to men in whom an inner conflict between good and evil soars and plummets with each new situation. Such characters yielded the kind of variety which he knew so well how to draw from the baritone voice. *Hamlet*, it is true, is also complex and indeed was one of the possible subjects that Verdi would note down in 1849; but as one Shakespeare scholar puts it, 'Hamlet's tragedy is that he cannot begin; Macbeth's that he cannot stop.'[*] The inner conflicts which inhibit Hamlet drive Macbeth to ever more violent action. In 1847 crude, volcanic energy was very much Verdi's province. *Macbeth* was therefore a natural subject for him to choose, as *Hamlet* never was nor ever would be in the future. However he may have failed to give an adequate musical equivalent of the poetry, however ineptly he may handle some of the details of Shakespeare's plot, he had no difficulty in expressing its dramatic essence, especially in the first version, where the character of Macbeth is set more sharply in relief. One of the problems of reviving the 1847 *Macbeth* would be to find a baritone capable of sustaining the title role.

As an operatic character Macbeth has had many descendants, the greatest being Mussorgsky's *Boris Godunov*. The villain in whom there is a hero struggling to get out was becoming more and more common in nineteenth-century opera since Meyerbeer's *Robert le Diable*. Verdi's own Pagano, Don Carlo and Gusman are all examples of the type. Macbeth is another; but in his case the struggle is lost. There is no triumph, merely an ever-mounting violence. That even Macbeth should retain our compassion is the incredible achievement of Shakespeare the dramatist.

[*] G. Saintsbury, in the *Cambridge History of English Literature*, V, p. 203.

Not only that, but he devised for him the perfect partner in crime—perfect because her qualities are the converse of her husband's. Outwardly cold and ruthless, with nerves of steel, Lady Macbeth is rotting inwardly, like a diseased elm. While Macbeth retains to the end all the energy of a gored bull, she goes into a decline the nature of which she does not understand herself. Macbeth gains strength and courage from the ability to look into the abysses of his own soul, even when his nerves are shattered. Lady Macbeth's falterings are like unconscious reflexes. She herself would have murdered Duncan if only he had not looked like her father when he slept. She has no waking terrors like Macbeth; her unease lies unformulated in the subconscious mind. She lives the scene of the murder over and over again in her sleep. The result is not only psychologically convincing; it produces also a state of equilibrium between the two characters which remains until the end. If Verdi intended particularly in the later version to allow Lady Macbeth to encroach on her husband's territory this matters less in so far as in opera baritone and dramatic soprano contrast with and complement each other anyway and therefore do not need Shakespeare's razor-sharp definition of character in order to reach their full stature. For an Italian opera composer of the nineteenth century the narrow focus of the plot was a great advantage, slightly offset by the absence of a star role for a romantic tenor.

Another attraction, more superficial, was the fantastic element and the opportunity it afforded for clever scenic effects. This aspect of *Macbeth* was its bane from the start. It had led to Middleton's spurious additions, inserted during Shakespeare's lifetime; it also helped to popularize Davenant's travesty which passed for 'acted' Shakespeare right up to the end of the eighteenth century. Now Verdi as we have seen lacked the natural Germanic aptitude for *Schauerromantik*. Yet there are moments in *Macbeth*, particularly in Act III, where he comes nearer to making the skin crawl than in any of his other operas.

Together with most of Act I the prelude is the same in both 1847 and 1865* versions; a kaleidoscope of themes associated with the grimmer parts of the tragedy. Shakespeare opened with a brief scene for the three witches ('When shall we three meet again?'); Verdi, by implication does the same; for his first theme is associated with their chorus at the beginning of Act III, *Tre volte miagola la gatta in fregola* ('Thrice the brinded cat hath mewed'). The rhythmic ambiguity caused by beginning in the middle of the bar, the unison trill on the three wind instruments and above all the fidgeting figure on first violins culminating in a

---

* At the time of going to press no scholarly edition exists of either version. The score and parts hired out by Messrs Ricordi contain certain differences from both originals: i.e., the 1847 MS. in Ricordi's archives in Milan and the part-copyist, part-autograph score in the Bibliothèque Nationale, Paris (MS. 1075–8) which constitutes the Paris version. The most notable of these discrepancies is the inclusion of a harp both in the prelude and in the sleepwalking scene as backing to the cello pizzicato semiquavers (see Ex. 167). In Verdi's orchestration whether early or late the harp always forms a distinct element in the texture; it is never used as a discreet condiment in this way. No more authentic are the sophisticated dynamics ($p < $ subito $p < sf$.) sequentially repeated in the orchestral phrase that forms the introduction to Lady Macbeth's cavatina. Small wonder that Toye (p. 273) was reminded of Beethoven! The score contains a simple crescendo–decrescendo–sforzando following the contours of the melody. Just at what point these and similar refinements infiltrated into the Ricordi score and parts it is impossible to be sure. Clearly they represent the ideas of a particular conductor and as such are legitimate *for him*. There is no reason why they should be handed down as Holy Writ.

bare minor ninth all combine to suggest that shrill malevolence which is the special characteristic of Verdi's witches.

164

Next from Act III is the brass theme which heralds the apparitions; here it is combined with the devilish chuckling of the 'weird sisters' from Act I.

165

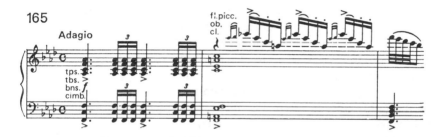

The rest of the prelude derives mainly from the sleepwalking scene with a few sequences of connecting tissue added. There is a hushed two-part sequential figure for violins, vividly suggesting the faint gnawing in the recesses of Lady Macbeth's unconscious mind:

166

and finally a mournful cantilena that owes something (not everything, as is sometimes implied) to Act II of Donizetti's *Anna Bolena* (see Ex. 167, overleaf).

Its resumption after a noisy episode is marked (so as to leave no room for doubt) *pppp* and accompanied by the stealthy padding of a low clarinet.

167

ACT I

Scene 1: a wood.* Three groups of witches appear, one after the other, amid thunder and lightning.

As usual there is a clear break between prelude and introduction, which begins in an unrelated key with a burst of storm music into which are woven the figures Ex. 164 and Ex. 165, both harmonically filled out. We are on the blasted heath, where the roar of the tempest seems to blend with the sound of eldritch laughter. The music falls into a triple pattern so as to allow each coven of witches to make a separate appearance, and the whole is filled with a driving rhythm that recalls the first movement of Beethoven's second symphony. The formal chorus is built round the tale of the sailor's wife (*M'è frullata nel pensier*).†

The sense of weirdness is conveyed by the unrelieved minor tonality, hollow harmonies, shrill orchestration, grace-notes, irregularity of bar structure and at one point, at the words 'Ma lo sposo', a displacement of the main accent from the first to the third beat of the bar. If all this does not add up to anything very terrifying it at least recaptures the essentially childish malice of the witches in the play ('and munch'd, and munch'd, and munch'd', 'I'll do, I'll do, and I'll do'). Verdi's witches, like Shakespeare's, are out of St Trinian's.

The sound of a side-drum (behind the scene) breaks in on their revels. 'A drum, a drum. [Who can it be?] Macbeth doth come [here he is].' If the additions indicated in brackets are no improvement on the original they at least allow for some impressive gestures on the brass. The witches then perform their round dance *Le sorelle vagabonde* ('The Weird Sisters, hand in hand, posters of the sea and land')

---

* The Italian word *bosco* can signify anything from a coppice to a wooded landscape. Doubtless Verdi found it very difficult to visualize Shakespeare's 'blasted heath'.

† The multiplication of witches at Verdi's own request (letter to Lanari 21.1.1846; *Copialettere*, pp. 447–8) makes nonsense of this story as well as contradicting the use of the first person singular. Also the librettist misses Shakespeare's point that the physical power of the witches does not extend beyond nuisance value.

to a faster melody, which forms the major complement of the one preceding. This is strictly according to the rules of Italian opera in 1847 but as so often the result is an anticlimax. *Le sorelle vagabonde* has all the deliberate vulgarity of its predecessor without any of the fantasy. It is just any chorus of gipsies or peasants, and no amount of piccolo and trumpet or decoration by violins playing sul ponticello can make it otherwise.

Macbeth and Banquo enter to the usual string recitative, the instrumental contribution having a suitably march-like flavour. The words are Shakespeare's abbreviated ('So foul and fair a day I have not seen'). With the witches' prophecies the music again takes up the triple pattern of the opening. The instrumentation, characteristic of all the high points of the 1847 score, assumes a particular spine-chilling air in relation to the plain string writing of the rest of the scene:*

168

The prophecies regarding Macbeth proceed in wider intervals than those of Banquo and mount a steeper gradient; but the first and last of them end on the dominant of a minor tonality. Banquo's hardly move, melodically, at all. Each one begins uncertainly over a diminished seventh then opens into an unclouded major chord through a crescendo to which violins tremolando add intensity. It is an effective way of indicating the difference in the destinies of the two men.

'So, all hail, Macbeth and Banquo.' 'Banquo and Macbeth, all hail.' Here the witches abandon their prophetic tone and sign off with a noisy, mock-military flourish, leaving Macbeth and Banquo to ponder separately and in unison. The announcement by Ross and Angus of Cawdor's condemnation and the settlement of his lands and title on Macbeth is entrusted predictably to a male chorus, set against a brash orchestral tune which as usual makes the words impossible to hear. It may be that the intention was to echo and so give point to the tone of the witches' final salutation. More probably it is just a typical case of the composer's 'public square' manner designed to form a jarring contrast with the private thoughts of the two generals. These now find expression in a masterly duettino *Due vaticini compiuti or sono* ('Two truths are told | as happy prologues to the swelling act | of the imperial theme'). Tradition would have required a cavatina at this point; and as always when Verdi strikes out on a new path he does so with tremendous certainty of effect. Basically it is a duet of the 'dissimilar' type but the contrast between the music of Banquo and that of Macbeth traces a far wider parabola than usual before the two voices come together in the obligatory sixths and thirds.

---

* The view of Dyneley Hussey, in *Verdi* (London, 1940), p. 52, that 'at their best [the witches] use the idiom of liturgical responses in church' takes no account of the all-important factor of scoring. If this passage is liturgical, it is the liturgy of the Black Mass!

Macbeth's probing imagination ('. . . why do I yield to that suggestion | whose horrid image doth unfix my hair?') sends the music modulating restlessly through related keys in such a way as to give the impression of an arioso rather than a formal stanza. Banquo, true to his more sceptical character ('And oftentimes, to win us to our harm, | the instruments of darkness tell us truths, | win us with honest trifles, to betray's | in deepest consequence'), tends to cling to the tonic; and when towards the end of the second stanza Macbeth takes the lead once more and propels the melody into a dominant cadence it is Banquo who pulls it back again in warning tone and Macbeth reacts by plunging into a remote key:

169

The coda logically spans the preceding key-contrasts and the air of brooding uncertainty is intensified by the addition of chorus basses, wondering why Macbeth is not more pleased at the good news. The duettino exploits one of the few dramatic advantages that opera possesses over a spoken play—its ability to present simultaneously the emotional content of two consecutive and contrasted speeches, each delivered as a soliloquy.

When Macbeth, Banquo and the messengers have left the witches reappear and wind up the scene with a chorus (*S'allontanarono*) which has no parallel in Shakespeare but it is logical enough in terms of operatic construction and quite appropriate dramatically. It is in essence a cry of triumph. The witches have planted their seeds of evil; they have only to wait for the tree to grow and the fruit to appear. Macbeth has gone; but he will return. The music is of the same genre as the opening chorus but here cast in a rapid 'plebeian' 6/8 and featuring a characteristic rhythm (♪ | ♫♫ ♫♫) which will recall the 'weird sisters' at a later point in the drama. Once again the minor section is superior to the major which sounds all too like a Neapolitan street song.

Scene 2: a hall in the castle of Macbeth

The scene is Shakespeare's I, v, which, as has been pointed out,* in itself anticipates the form of an Italian cavatina, with a messenger to provide the link between andante and cabaletta. Not only that; Lady Macbeth enters reading a letter. The convention whereby letters are spoken instead of sung enables Lady Macbeth to make the most arresting entrance of any prima donna before Adriana Lecouvreur. She is heralded with a worthy instrumental prelude—a trial of powerful gestures

---

* Winton Dean, 'Shakespeare and Opera', in *Shakespeare in Music* (ed. P. Hartnoll) (London, 1964), p. 93.

each like the sound of a hurricane blast. Everything in this scene is an expression of power; and at such times as always Beethoven is never far away—not only in the instrumental introduction which reminded Francis Toye of the 'Pathétique' sonata,[*] but also in the transition leading from recitative to the formal andantino. *Vieni t'affretta* is of course based on 'Hie thee hither, | that I may pour my spirits in thine ear'; and as might be expected presents Lady Macbeth as Abigaille enriched by the musical experience of five years. There are the same wide leaps and jagged rhythms. Both need a really powerful lower register; but nothing in Abigaille's music attains such a strenuousness as the climbing sequence whereby in this simple, unextended design the music returns to the home key without repeating his opening idea.

170

The attendant announces Duncan's arrival to another of those military interludes in which this score abounds. Lady Macbeth dismisses him, then launches into a cabaletta (*Or tutti sorgete*):

171

Note how the minims in the second, third and fourth bars act like dynamos storing up an energy which erupts in the fifth into a semiquaver flourish. (Verdi was to use this device to even greater effect in Hélène's first-act cabaletta in *Les Vêpres Siciliennes*.) Musically all this corresponds to the most terrifying speech that Lady Macbeth has to utter: 'Come, you spirits | that tend on mortal thoughts,

* Toye, p. 276.

unsex me here; | . . . that no compunctious visitings of nature | shake my fell purpose . . .' Lady Macbeth's only fear is of her own subconsciously motivated reflexes; and it is these that destroy her in the end.

Macbeth enters, and the dialogue between husband and wife, brief enough in Shakespeare, is telegraphic in Verdi. One notices how he seizes on the vital words 'O, never | shall sun that morrow see!' and underpins it with a sequence of hard, brass chords (trumpets, trombones and cimbasso) in a remote key (*Ma non ci rechi il sole un tal domani*). The distant sound of a band breaks in on their conversation. 'The king!' cries Lady Macbeth. 'Come with me and give him joyful greeting!' And her imperious nature asserts itself in an emphatic cadence preceded by a downward swoop of two octaves.

The piece which now unfolds has been harshly criticized, and no less extravagantly defended, even on Brechtian principles. Verdi's only 6/8 march has a jaunty impudence to modern ears, the cane-twirling, hat-at-an-angle air of a music-hall comedian. The fact is that like all banda music its function is purely scenic; it is not meant to be listened to and judged seriously as music. If played in its entirety, and not reduced to a skeleton in order to apologize for its existence, it lasts a full two and a half minutes, giving enough time for King Duncan to parade with full retinue across the stage and to exchange a few gracious words in dumb show with his host and hostess before retiring. This is the nearest Verdi comes to establishing him as a character; and the critics who regret that he went no further than this take no account of the economics of nineteenth-century Italian opera. To have done justice to Shakespeare's warm-hearted, over-trusting monarch would have required a cantabile at least. But this would have raised Duncan to the dubious rank of a heavy comprimario or semi-principal of which there are already two (Banquo and Macduff). To have created another, who is eliminated in the first act, would have been bad housekeeping. Likewise the omission of Macbeth's philosophic speech which begins 'If it were done—when 'tis done—then 'twere well | it were done quickly', and the subsequent vacillation is logical, in that Italians, unlike Germans, dislike philosophizing in music; nor have they the equipment to do so. Composers such as Verdi conceive of drama in its literal, etymological sense as 'action'. The speech just referred to is all speculation; and, like its counterpart in *Hamlet* ('To be or not to be'), it weakens the will to act. By leaving it out altogether Verdi concentrates the drama and reduces the first act to manageable proportions, but with one damaging consequence: Lady Macbeth is deprived of an important opportunity to resume the offensive. The full rounding of her character needs another aria, at a moment where circumstances demand that she put forward her whole strength. True, she is given a bravura aria at the beginning of Act II but by this time Macbeth has been launched on a torrent of morbid energy and has no need of further goading.

So the end of the march finds Macbeth preparing to carry out the assassination. The recitative that follows conforms throughout to the famous 'dagger' speech and has no parallel in any previous opera, at any rate by Verdi. Both it and the duet to which it leads must, in the composer's words, 'be sung sotto voce and in a hollow voice except for certain phrases marked *a voce spiegato*'; all this is made possible by a new and flexible use of selective orchestration. The entire scene is scored for flute, cor anglais, clarinet, horns, bassoons, timpani and muted strings.

But the colours are not maintained in unvarying intensity as in previous 'panels' of this kind. They shift and change with the images that pass through Macbeth's mind, luring him on as the sight of an abyss will lure a certain type of acrophobe. The cor anglais rarely plays alone. At all important points it is doubled with another instrument, clarinet, bassoon and in one place a solo cello. Macbeth's imagination leads the music into very strange regions indeed, witness the serpentine crawlings that match the lines, 'Now o'er the one half-world | nature seems dead, and wicked dreams abuse | the curtain'd sleep'. A reference to witchcraft that 'celebrates pale Hecate's offerings' harks back to the jigging rhythm of the 'stretta del'introduzione'; while the vocal line is suspended above a long held note low down in the clarinet. The recitative is the most powerful and the most melodic that Verdi wrote before 'Pari siamo' (*Rigoletto*) and as with the latter one is a little hard put to it to account for the sense of completeness and unity that this free monologue conveys. It certainly does not derive from the key-system or from any workings of themes or motifs. One may notice, however, two kindred phrases both occurring at points of repose in the speech. The recitative closes

with the ringing of a bell followed by the lines, literally translated: 'Hear it not, Duncan; for it is a knell | that summons thee to heaven or to hell'; and Macbeth enters Duncan's chamber to a muffled tutti pierced by the timbre of horns in unison. It dies away in a hushed sequence of string chords forming a rudimentary canon between the outer parts. The effect is of a silence made palpable.* At this point Lady Macbeth appears. Cor anglais in octave with bassoon evoke 'the owl . . .

---

* This startlingly evocative use of strings—so untypical of contemporary Italian opera—is echoed in Act II (1865 only) before the utterance of the third apparition (see p. 303).

the fatal bellman | which gives the stern'st good night'. 'Who's there?' Macbeth cries. Has he failed? she wonders. The next moment he appears at the doorway, dazed and swaying, a bloodstained dagger in his hand. His stifled cry, 'All is over!' is taken up by the strings and developed into the accompanimental pattern for the first movement of the formal duet (*Fatal mia donna! Un murmure*).

The Italian critic Massimo Mila rightly draws attention to this as being the most meaningful accompaniment that the composer had devised so far.* It is not just a reach-me-down figure, vaguely connoting agitation, such as had served him so often in similar situations. It grows organically out of its thematic context; and it has a natural energy which drives the music like a flywheel, creating precisely the right background for the tense exchanges between husband and wife. It ceases for the A flat major episode where Macbeth recounts how two courtiers in the next room awoke and one cried, 'God save us!' and the other 'Amen!' and 'Amen I would have uttered, but Amen stuck in my throat'. Here clarinets doubling the voice in thirds impart a pleading tone; but with Lady Macbeth's 'Follie!' Ex. 173 is restored, to make way eventually for her important dismissive figure which recurs in two movements of the original duet, and all three of the Paris version.

The central andantino (*Allor questa voce m'intesi nel petto*) is formed initially from the famous lines:

> Methought I heard a voice cry, 'Sleep no more!
> Macbeth does murder sleep . . .
> Glamis hath murder'd sleep, and therefore Cawdor
> Shall sleep no more. . . .'†

*Mila, p. 63. †Shakespeare, II, ii.

As in the opening theme Verdi has availed himself of the implied three-part structure, and so condensed the speech into three symmetrical phrases in which veiled scoring is made still more sinister by the edging of each climax with two trombones and bass drum (both instruments being foreign to the 'panel'). What follows is at first sight rather surprising, since it has no parallel in Shakespeare. It is simply a case of music asserting its formal rights. Lady Macbeth counters her husband's stanza line for line; but the melody is now in the major accompanied by pizzicato strings and a sinuous figure divided between cello and clarinet. The major tonality not only balances the preceding section; it prepares the way for one of those glorious lyrical outbursts with which Italian romantic opera transcends its most horrible situations. Macbeth's *Com' angeli d'ira* is of the same stamp as Carlo's 'È pure l'aere' (*Giovanna d'Arco*) with the same arch-like shape. It is interesting too that for the words Piave went back to the philosophic speech from Shakespeare's I, vii:

> . . . [Duncan's] virtues
> Will plead like angels, trumpet-tongued, against
> The deep damnation of his taking-off.

Verdi was repaying to Shakespeare some of the debt that the operatic medium had obliged him to contract.

175

The E natural in bar 6 is one of the emendations of the Paris version (originally it had been E flat). A characteristic of the mature Verdi was his ability to assimilate the richest chromaticisms of the mid nineteenth century without risk of cloying. Eighteen years' progress from 1847 to 1865 are epitomized in that one E natural.

It is at this point in the score that the revisions begin in earnest. Lady Macbeth's countermelody is simplified from a chain of semiquavers into a variant of Ex. 174. Then the original codetta with the voices subsiding in conventional semiquaver tenths and sixths over a tonic pedal is replaced by an epigram of modulation.

176

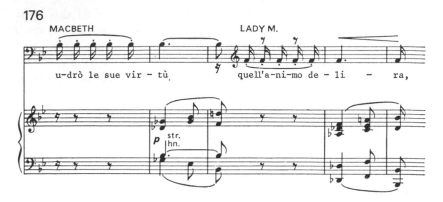

There follows a brief transitional moveme.t in the original fast tempo, during which the dialogue continues mostly in an orchestrally based parlante, culminating in Macbeth's melodic outburst ('Will all great Neptune's ocean wash this blood | clean from my hand?'). The only change here occurs in the accompaniment of the orchestral melody, which in the later version is embellished by academically 'interesting' inner parts and more lightly scored—a concession to the more sophisticated Parisian taste which in no way affects the musical substance. Meanwhile knocking has been heard. Having left the bloodstained dagger* in Duncan's room Lady Macbeth returns and begins the stretta conventionally enough as she tries to drag her husband off to bed (*Vien, vieni altrove ogni sospetto*). The movement is a presto in F minor. Throughout the entire duet and the preceding recitative there has been an unusual predominance of minor tonality. To have persisted with it to the end of the stretta would in 1847 have incurred the charge of 'abuso dei minori'. But in 1865 this rule had lost its validity. The switch into F major which occurs at the tenth bar of the original version brings a note of relaxation which is quite absurd in its dramatic context (see Ex. 177, facing page). It could have come from *Un Giorno di Regno*. In 1865 it was replaced by a continuation in the minor of the original idea, to which he added, very logically, Ex. 174 rhythmically adapted. The final 'vieni, vieni' with its Neapolitan modulation echoes Ex. 176 and thus in its final form the entire duet is a model of logic and consistency. Like Mendelssohn in his *Midsummer Night's Dream* music Verdi had managed to re-enter the world of his youth and enrich it with the fruits of experience. Only at one point does the seam show—and then more to the eye than the ear. The original nine bars of the stretta which Verdi retained have a conventional accompaniment of pulsating split chords. At the tenth bar this gives way to a real contrapuntal bass such as he would never have assimilated into his operatic style in 1847. But let us not minimize the importance of this duet as originally written in the development of Verdian music-drama. Here even more than in *I Due Foscari* the essentially static Rossinian 'gran duetto' is converted into a dynamic form with most of the conventional repetitions and all the ritornelli abolished. The staple unit of three movements and transition represents not three expanded moments but a single, unfolding action.

* Singular in Verdi though plural in Shakespeare.

177

For the finale he kept to the 1847 score as it stood, reasonably enough since, though old-fashioned by the standards of the 1860s, it is a magnificent specimen of its type—at once spacious and compact. Note the connection between the orchestral figure which surrounds Macduff's first recitative and a similar gesture in the duet, just at the point where Macbeth refuses to re-enter Duncan's room. Here it is worked up into a crescendo, as though Macduff's fear were growing tangible.

He has come to wake the king as ordered. With him is Banquo, Lennox having no existence in the opera (neither for that matter has the porter, for reasons which by now should be obvious); so when Macduff enters the king's chamber, it is Banquo who delivers the speech describing the 'unruly night'. He does so in a splendid arioso (*Oh qual orrenda notte*), its somewhat conventional fidgety accompaniment shaded by sustaining oboe and clarinet in unison. Then as Macduff comes out, incoherent with terror (*Orrore! orrore! orrore!*) the orchestra bursts out in tumultuous energy. He summons the household, Macbeth and his wife return with feigned bewilderment, and Banquo goes into the king's chamber. All this takes place to a long passage of four-bar sequences, made up of the most commonplace ingredients—rushing scales on the strings, violent contrasts of loud and soft, syncopations, rapping brass chords. Yet there is the same driving sense of purpose here as in the 'introduzione'; and was Verdi in his Scottish opera deliberately recalling the rhythm of the storm in Mendelssohn's Hebrides? As the noise subsides Banquo announces Duncan's murder in a phrase recalling almost note for note (though a tone lower) Macbeth's *Non potrebbe l'oceano questa mano a me lavar*. The finale evolves from the motif (*Tutto è finito*). Here the usual dynamic procedures are reversed: for the adagio concertato begins fortissimo, after Banquo has made his announcement in tones of hushed horror ('È morto assassinato il rè Duncano') (Ex. 178, below).

Inevitably at this point opera takes over from Shakespeare; the drama must freeze into a prolonged expression of dismay in adagio and stretta. Once again like situation produces like music. The model of the concerted adagio is therefore that of Act I of *I Lombardi* which also begins with the discovery of a murder. First there is a massive outburst (Ex. 178a), next an episode for chorus and principals in the minor key *a cappella* (b), then the major 'answer'. But of course the later work transcends the earlier in every respect. Such is the intensity of the unison vocal writing, and so taut the melodic span of Ex. 178c that the major key does

178

not give an effect of anticlimax. The final stretta, cut down to a mere pendant to the adagio, takes up the motion of *Orrore, orrore, orrore*. Particularly striking is the tiny oasis of quiet in which Lady Macbeth, her waiting woman, Macduff and Macbeth twice cry, 'Gran Dio!' to be answered each time by a ferocious unison outburst on the orchestra.

ACT II

Scene 1: a room in the castle

Again the falling semitone theme (recalling Ex. 173), this time scored as a flourish of fortissimo wind unison. It is followed by a lengthy quotation from the duet (*Fatal mia donna*). The scene is a skeletal precis of Shakespeare's III, ii, with a little extra information thrown in for the audience's benefit. Malcolm, we are told, has fled to England and is therefore suspected of Duncan's murder; so what has Macbeth to fear? Merely the fulfilment of the witches' prophecy that Banquo's sons shall be kings. 'If't be so . . . | for them the gracious Duncan have I murder'd; | put rancours in the vessel of my peace | only for them?' But in Shakespeare this speech is a soliloquy from the preceding scene. To his wife Macbeth only hints at what he has in mind to do, insisting that she be innocent of the knowledge 'till she applaud the deed'. In the opera the recitative closes with 'Banquo, thy soul's flight, | if it find heaven, must find it out tonight'; and he goes out to arrange for Banquo's murder, leaving Lady Macbeth to sing the aria which, dramatically, she should have been given earlier on when her husband was wavering. Here it is the expression of power in a vacuum; and the single cabaletta written in 1847 (*Trionfai, sicuri alfine*) sounds like a brash cousin of Elvira's 'Tutto sprezzo che d'Ernani', with more than a touch of Abigaille.

179

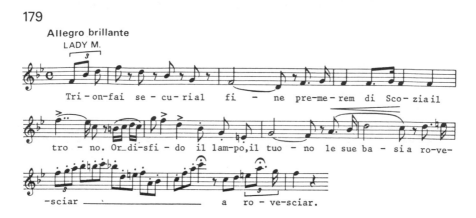

Not surprisingly Verdi was horrified when he came to re-examine the score after eighteen years. Hence the magnificent *La luce langue*, for which, as we have seen, he drafted out the words himself. In 1847 he could penetrate the essence of Shakespeare's drama; by 1865 he had come much nearer to matching his poetic language. As a result the aria in its context is an eagle among chickens. True, it is linked to the composer's earlier style, by providing the kind of patterned accompaniment that he had long ago given up writing in 1865. But this has a richness, a flexibility and a subtlety of orchestral colouring that makes even that of the sleepwalking scene appear crude by comparison. The sustaining woodwind overlap with each other; the horns no longer beat out the rhythm; the orchestral web is as coherent as the melodic line, with none of those irrelevant entries of trumpet or first violins merely to emphasize a particular corner of the melody. Half-way through the movement this pattern too is dropped, as the trajectory of Verdi's imagination carries him far away from the 1840s. Note first the introduction of this aria from bar 5:

180

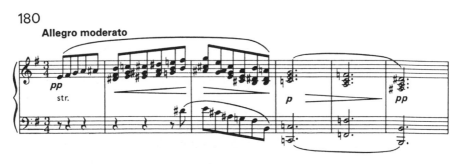

The Neapolitan sixth is strikingly followed up by a modulation to F major in the second half of the movement, which then proceeds incredibly to settle in A flat minor.

The wide span of the keys traversed is then epitomized in this tiny andante link:

The final section (*O voluttà del soglio*) has the function if not the form of a cabaletta, and consists of a series of sweeping phrases without any of the virtuosity that marks the cabaletta of Act I. Every note breathes the distinction of Verdi's later years. Already there is an anticipation of that strong, yet subtle style in which Verdi was to express Desdemona's anguished pleading:

183

Scene 2: a park with Macbeth's castle in the distance

This is Shakespeare's III, iii, the scene of Banquo's murder. As with the witches Verdi sees no reason to particularize the three murderers; they might just as well be the entire male chorus acting under royal orders. The music reverts to 1847, when Verdi, unable to provide the equivalent of one of Shakespeare's most striking night-pieces ('the west yet glimmers with some streaks of day') opts for a solution which is frankly operatic in the lowest sense: a stealthy chorus of the kind that might be more acceptable today if it had not been parodied so often. We have heard it many times before—in *I Lombardi*, in *Nabucco*—and we shall hear it again in *Rigoletto*. Apart from the rather absurd outbursts (*Trema Banco!*) and the unfortunate proximity to the great *La luce langue* the chorus *Sparve il sol, la notte or regni* is a worthy specimen of its type. The unaccompanied timpani figure which launches each phrase is a refinement of a similar idea in the first scene of *Ernani*. The off-beat accents in the second bar balanced by normal accents in the fourth add a certain piquancy to the melody; and, following the example of the soldiers' chorus in *Giovanna d'Arco*, Verdi decorates the reprise with a busy rhythmic pattern in the accompaniment—not this time a countermelody but an ostinato for violas joined by flute in the coda.

The murderers conceal themselves as Banquo enters with Fleance (the latter like Duncan a walking-on part). His romanza, to words from Shakespeare's II, i, and III, i,* is conventional in form with a minor start and a major ending. But for 1847 the scoring is remarkably powerful with bassoons, trombones and cimbasso bunched together on the accompaniment and the full strings doubling the melody in a Tchaikovsky-like unison, reinforced by oboe and clarinet (Ex. 184, facing page).

There is no pause after the final cadence, but a stealthy pulsation in the strings pointing forward to a similar passage at the end of 'Caro nome' (*Rigoletto*)—logically, since it is a similar situation. During this Banquo and Fleance leave the stage. Suddenly Banquo's voice rings out: 'O, treachery! Fly, good Fleance . . .' and to a huge wave of orchestral sound Fleance rushes across the stage pursued by one of the murderers. The curtain falls to a whisper on cellos and basses.

---

* 'Thou hast it now—King, Cawdor, Glamis, all, | as the weird women promis'd; and, I fear, | thou play'dst most foully for't'; and 'merciful powers, | restrain in me the cursed thoughts that nature | gives way to in repose!'

184

*Scene 3: a magnificent hall; a banquet prepared**

The banquet music which opens the scene is brash and trivial but theatrically effective, and Verdi saw no need to rewrite it for 1865. Macbeth and his wife are playing the gracious host and hostess to the nobles of Scotland. By an un-Shakespearian but in the circumstances legitimate operatic device, Macbeth asks his wife to lead the company in a drinking song. She responds with a melody (*Si colmi il calice*) entirely suited to the character of one who is to say later (though not in the opera), 'Stand not upon the order of your going, but go!'

185

The chorus repeat it obediently, with trumpets rapping out a semiquaver rhythm between the phrases. The same melody played softly by oboe and clarinet and with ominous bassoon countermelody provides the background for Macbeth's conversation with the murderers. The banquet music is then resumed to be interrupted violently by the first of Macbeth's hallucinations ('Which of you have done this? . . . Thou canst not say I did it, never shake | thy gory locks at me'). The Italian translation is quite literal at this point, and the setting, powerful enough in the original version, is infinitely more so in the later one. Only Macbeth's music is changed. The first setting recalls the dementia of Nabucco. It is a free, lyrical arioso over pulsating strings, which keeps strictly within the orbit of F minor. The second version is lower in tessitura, more declamatory in style and more instrumentally conscious with an accompaniment embellished by chromaticisms, foreign chords and sudden modulations. The comments of chorus and Lady Macbeth are identical in both versions. In other words Verdi adheres closely to the material of 1847 weaving back the new threads so as to make the joins invisible. Then too though both hallucinations as revised are more elaborate in design and more sophisticated harmonically than the original (Verdi could never have ventured the vertiginous chords at 'può render gli uccisi' nor yet the harmonics at

* Headed in the autograph: *Convito visione.*

'O poi che le chiome' in 1847) they are less indiscriminately noisy. The new harmonic subtlety goes hand in hand with a lighter orchestral touch, as can be seen very clearly at the end of the soothing D flat major episode (*Sedete, mio sposo*) with its string accompaniment. The melody is the same in both versions, but the final cadence into B flat is harmonized in the second with a chromatically moving bass; and it is precisely this harmonic interest which makes quite unnecessary the sustaining chords of clarinet and bassoon that point the original cadence. Changes in the scoring include a most unconventional use of trombones to reiterate chords that had originally been given to strings alone. Both settings are worth quoting at this point to show both how near to and yet how far from his original idea Verdi found himself in 1865, by which time the bold 6/4 progression had become a hall-mark of his style.

186

Macbeth's composure temporarily restored, Lady Macbeth once more repeats her brindisi but without its coda, for the last note of the choral refrain is cut short by Macbeth's second vision ('Avaunt! and quit my sight'). Here the revisions mostly take the form of elaborated inner parts—sighing appoggiaturas on the cellos and at the words 'Diventa pur tigre' a cursive violin figure evolved from part of the accompaniment to 'quel sangue fumante' which is common to both versions. The almost shouted climaxes 'Fuggi, fuggi!' are differently scored, so too the preceding chords (tutti in 1847, brass in 1865), but the marvellous E major cadence beneath tremolo violin at Banquo's final disappearance is the same in both versions. From there to the end everything is 1847. The concerted finale begins with Macbeth's 'they say blood will have blood' (*Sangue a me quell'ombra chiede*);

but this being an Italian opera he has to say it as an aside in the presence of his guests who murmur their dismay at great length. In other words it is a typical concertato of the kind that is dominated by one singer (cf. *Alzira*, II; *Ernani*, III). The Act I finale of *Nabucco* comes to mind since the soprano is also thrown into relief; and indeed Lady Macbeth's interventions are particularly Abigaille-like in this movement. No one would claim that the huge largo, to which there is mercifully no stretta, is one of Verdi's most sublime lyrical transformations. It is all strictly in his early manner, with the dramatic expression confined to the rhythm and melodic contours of the singers, yet the rock-like firmness of its structure, the momentum of its rhythm and the strength of its climactic cadences and modulations all redeem the rather commonplace material.

ACT III

Scene: a dark cavern; in the midst a boiling cauldron. Thunder and lightning

As in the opening scene of all the music combines suggestions of storm and demonic chuckling; only here everything is incomparably more powerful, with the characteristic figure from the stretta (*S'allontanarono*) rapped out by oboes, clarinets and bassoons.* As in so much of *Macbeth* the key is E minor. By a particularly daring stroke which Beethoven would have approved it opens with a chord of the German sixth. The home tonality is not unequivocally established until the tenth or eleventh bar and then only by implication. At bar 10 the new Verdian 6/4 chord puts in an unexpected appearance:

187

Ex. 164 is now heard again for the first time since the opening; the scoring is the same as before, and very sinister it sounds in the lull that follows the storm. It serves to introduce a theme associated with the stirring of the cauldron and played first of all by chattering strings reinforced by bassoons and—typically—low clarinets. Its second half features Ex. 165, also from the prelude; after which the entire scheme from Ex. 164 onwards is repeated in an amplified form with witches' voices added. 'Thrice the brinded cat hath mew'd . . .' It was about here that the composer's irritation with Piave's inadequacy seems to have reached boiling point. Certainly the verses here (*Tre volte miagola la gatta in fregola*) are Maffei's. What must strike everyone who can hear them is how carelessly they are draped over the music. The all-important 'tre' is tacked on to Ex. 164 in what amounts to a grace-note. The musical phrase is repeated in a threefold pattern mounting from E minor to G major–B minor, and with the 'tre' swallowed each time. With

* Trumpets, trombones and bassoons in Ricordi!

'Double, double toil and trouble' (*Su via, sollecite, giriam la pentola*) the prosody becomes more and more bizarre ('L'acqua già fuma, fuma, crepita e spuma, spuma'). Nor is there any improvement when the main choral melody of the scene takes shape, thrusting the orchestra into the background (*Tu, rospo venefico*), a piquant characteristic tune poised ambiguously between major and minor and repeated by each group of witches in the ascending progression of E–G–B.

Again one notices the inept scanning of 'aconito', also the extra quaver necessitated by the third syllable of 'venefico' which would weaken the melody if this were not at the same time being stated in its original form by oboe, clarinet, bassoon and first violins *without* the quaver. On the superficial level all this would indicate that Verdi had thought of the music independently of the text, as he frequently did. What is strange is that he should have been satisfied with the compromise that results. It is just possible that he considered that bad scansion added to the general *bizarrerie*. At a century's distance one is more critical, and tends to notice that while at the outset of the combination of thunderstorm and witches' glee presents a powerful musical image, the scene becomes less impressive as it unfolds and the witches themselves spring more clearly into focus. The stretta (*E voi spiriti negri e candidi*) ends in cheerful banality which the Parisian revision for once does little to improve. True, the three-part vocal writing is more varied, the harmonies are enriched by a light chromaticism. But we are still in the realm of opera buffa: the Neapolitan café has given way to the Savoy Theatre—that is all.

Verdi's letters to Léon Escudier make it quite clear that he intended the ballet which follows as a serious addition to the drama; and his insistence that the second movement, where Hecate appears, should be mimed and not danced is a proof of his anxiety to adhere to what he imagined to be Shakespeare's text, not realizing that the scene in question is an interpolation of Thomas Middleton's. In idiom and style the entire ballet is vastly more sophisticated than the music which has preceded it. Clearly Verdi's brief sojourns in the city of Gounod, Delibes and Berlioz had not been wasted. The opening rondo in which the cave fills with dancing demons opens with a theme for cornets and trombones which is as fantastic as anything in the ballet music from *Faust* (Ex. 189, opposite).

After the second recurrence of the theme the pace broadens and the music turns into E major as all the spirits gather round the cauldron and invoke Hecate in a majestic tune, played by the brass and bassoon against a background of semiquaver scales in contrary motion (an impressive, Beethovenian touch of which necessarily the published vocal score gives no hint). The appearance of Hecate is

189

framed by two snatches of storm music; and she advances to a melody of bland
string chords—major in mode but heavily charged. How far the Paris production
followed Verdi's instructions in keeping this as a mime for Hecate throughout we
have no means of knowing. But to have done so entirely would have strained to
breaking-point the semantics of nineteenth-century ballet. At the start Hecate
tells the witches that she knows what they are about and why she has been summoned. Twenty-three bars later she 'examines everything very carefully', after
eleven more bars she 'announces that King Macbeth will come to ask them about
his fate and they will have to grant his request'. Later 'if the visions which they
will show him overcome his senses they must conjure up the spirits of the air to
awaken and restore him'. But the music itself is well constructed and full of
striking ideas: the stately B flat melody, on which cellos and bassoon are joined
by bass clarinet; the bass-heavy thudding, reinforced by tympani and bass drum,
where Hecate examines the cauldron; the Beethovenian string writing that leads
up to the reprise and the flute countermelody that refers to the spirits of the air.
When Hecate has gone the dancers join in a rapid waltz, vividly scored, full of
boulevardier echoes, yet unmistakably a danse macabre (note the 'devilish' open
fifths at bar 43 seqq.). Verdi was clearly very pleased with the following passage,
over which he wrote in the autograph that it should be mimed rather than danced
to; or if that was impossible that the dancers should be reduced in number.

190

Great music it certainly is not but it is skilful and inventive and brings the dance
to an exciting conclusion. As a transition from the end of the ballet to the 'Gran

Scena delle Apparizioni' there is a quotation from the stretta of the previous chorus, embellished with an inner chromatic line.

The text of this scene is conscientiously Shakespeare with the poetry paraphrased or condensed. Macbeth demands to be allowed to know his fate though 'heaven and earth renew their ancient war'; the witches conjure up three apparitions one after the other: the armed head ('Macbeth! Macbeth! Macbeth! beware Macduff'), the bloody child who tells him that none of 'woman born' can do him harm; and finally the crowned child with a tree in his hand ('Macbeth shall never vanquish'd be, until | great Birnam Wood to high Dunsinane Hill | shall come against him'). But Macbeth still wants to know if Banquo's issue shall wear the crown. For answer the witches show him a procession of eight kings each with Banquo's features and followed by Banquo himself 'who points at them for his'.* For Paris Verdi overhauled the scene very extensively, widening the range of tonality, improving the instrumentation, altering the melodic contours here and there to aid the declamation and enriching the design with fragments of arioso and passages in strict time. The text remains the same however. The invocation of the witches (*Dalle basse e dall'alte regioni*) is preceded by Ex. 165, sounding far more powerful in the Paris version merely because Verdi had by this time learned that horns are much more effective when sustaining and that the trombones are the best instruments to give a bite to the semiquaver triplets. Less effective, because generally inaudible, is the gong added to the fortissimo which marks the appearance and disappearance of the apparitions. But the prophecies themselves sung offstage by baritone and two sopranos respectively are spine-chilling, with their accompaniment of bassoons, trumpets, trombones and cimbasso sounding like an organ in the distance. In all of these Verdi altered and strengthened the chord sequences for the Paris version; but the most spectacular—and necessary—improvement occurs at Macbeth's reaction to the second prophecy, where in the original score Verdi had contrived one of those rapid, off-hand changes of mood that so often start the audience tittering. Shakespeare's

> Then live, Macduff; what need I fear of thee?
> But yet I'll make assurance double sure,
> And take a bond of fate: thou shalt not live

is condensed into 'Macduff, I will spare thy life. No, thou shalt die, thy death shall be a double pledge on my regal breast'. The difficulty lies in the juxtaposition of the first two lines. In the Paris score Verdi amplified what was originally perfunctory recitative ('No, morrai') into a snatch of fast arioso in F sharp minor over a busy accompaniment. It is very short; but the tonal and rhythmic firmness give it a sense of finality, as of a resolution taken in the full awareness of what it will imply. The last note is interrupted by another explosive tutti; and Macbeth's wonder at the next apparition is expressed in a sequence of hushed string chords over a low clarinet.† The third apparition is followed by a much more extensive arioso of joy from Macbeth (*Oh liet'augurio*) which amounts almost to a cabaletta. (It replaces a single, drawn-out lyrical phrase in the Florence score.) But Macbeth

* Spike Hughes (p. 67) justly observes that the librettist has telescoped Shakespeare's instructions in making Banquo himself the eighth king with a glass in his hand.
† See note on p. 287.

still wants to know more, and he threatens the witches with death. To a vertiginous chain of tremolo diminished sevenths the cauldron vanishes. 'What sounds are these?' cries Macbeth. Shakespeare specifies 'hautboys', Verdi 'the sound of sub-terranean bagpipes'. But by cornamusa he meant not the Scottish bagpipe, how-ever appropriate to this context, but the gentler Italian variety which you can still hear on the streets of Rome round about Christmas or Easter. The keenness of aural imagination which had served him as early as Giselda's prayer came to his aid in 1847 too; and from the combination of two oboes, six clarinets, two bassoons and one contrabassoon placed under the stage he contrived one of the most unearthly sounds in nineteenth-century opera, all the more disconcerting for the simplicity of the music itself. But where does simplicity fall into banality? That was a question much more easily answered in 1865 than in 1847. A comparison of the first six bars of the procession in each version is instructive. In the later the trend towards a popular ditty is effectually arrested.

191

Macbeth's D minor strophe (*Fuggi regal fantasima*) is unaltered except for a much fiercer accompaniment; but the end of the procession is changed out of recogni-tion, the pedestrian groups of three bars each moving predictably from one related key to the next being replaced by a scheme in which the tonality changes first every two bars, then every bar and finally every half-bar, and the keys are some-times not related at all (the change from G sharp minor to E minor at the appearance of the sixth king is particularly gruesome). Although the revised version is actually shorter it opens up far wider musical perspectives, as of a line 'stretching out to the crack o' doom'. In Macbeth's strophe (*O mio terror, dell'ultimo*) Verdi has not only added an accompaniment which shows clearly enough that he had now conceived it as in a faster tempo; he also displaced the opening lines so as to make it dovetail into the previous interrupted cadence. The rather quaint result is that what was originally the first phrase of the tune now becomes the second, docked of one essential note and fitted to the words 'Splende uno specchio in mano'. But the basic shape remains the same in both cases; and by the seventh bar Verdi has returned into step with his previous self. The climactic phrase of each version gives a splendid illustration of how his melodic style developed over the years:

At the news that Banquo's progeny will live Macbeth faints. Once again the lines which announce an 'antic round' are Middleton's not Shakespeare's, and the dance of aerial spirits another interpolation. The 'coro e ballabile' with its prominent harp part (*Ondine e silfidi*) is palpably early Verdi,* and first cousin to the dance of Druidesses from *Attila*. For Paris the composer merely embellished the final cadence of the voices with new flute and violin obbligati and added a longish instrumental coda featuring a countermelody in the cellos and a good many trills in the flute.

* Toye (p. 277) and Hughes (p. 67) ascribe it wrongly to the later version.

Once more the two versions begin to diverge widely as Macbeth comes to himself. The Florence score wound up with a cabaletta of a most unusual cut (*Vada in fiamme*). The design might be described thus: *a* (A minor), *b* (A major), *c* (episode in A minor), *b* (A major) and coda. Not only does the line lie between A and F above the stave; the baritone sings continuously. Musically it may not be very distinguished, but as a supreme expression of crude baritonic power it is quite extraordinary and very fitting for one who has said 'From this moment the very firstlings of my heart shall be | the firstlings of my hand.' But it needed a Varesi or a Ronconi to sing it at the end of a long third act; and so, if only to take some of the weight from the baritone's shoulders, Verdi dropped the aria in favour of a duettino. ('I don't find it illogical that Lady, intent as she is on keeping an eye on her husband, should have discovered where he is.')* No sooner then has Macbeth returned to his senses and willed that '. . . this pernicious hour | stand aye accursed in the calendar' than the herald announces: 'The Queen!' Macbeth recounts the prophecies over a recitative played tremolo sul ponticello. Lady Macbeth punctuates each one with a mere 'Segui' ('Continue') and when he tells her that Banquo's descendants shall reign after him, she bursts out in terrible fury— 'Lies! Lies! Death to the evil brood!' Macbeth declares his murderous intentions; and Lady Macbeth welcomes the revival of his courage in a long swooping cadential phrase such as she has already uttered in *La luce langue* which leads straight into the formal duet (*Ora di morte e di vendetta*), a paean of vengeance not unlike the duet of Lysiart and Eglantine in *Euryanthe* or of Ortrud and Telramund in *Lohengrin*, though Verdi could not have heard either opera at the time. It is a case in which the departure from Shakespeare is justified in terms of opera. Psychologically it is all wrong. If Macbeth needed no goading at the start of Act II he needs it even less now. At this stage in the drama Lady Macbeth is a spent force—quite how spent will appear in the next act. It is utterly inappropriate to give her this new access of strength; and it would be fatal to the dramatic balance in a spoken play. But in this duet the two characters are in equilibrium. Its form suggests a compression of the similar duet for unequal voices in which one repeats the other's music at a different pitch. The imitation is confined to single phrases, which are increasingly telescoped as each singer presses harder on the other's heels. There is a hushed episode in B flat major and the imitation is resumed at still closer intervals culminating in a variant of Lady Macbeth's introductory cadential phrase. A rapid coda plunging from major to minor and back again brings the act to an exciting finish. The entire duet shows that one of the lessons that Verdi had learned in the last eighteen years was how to make his orchestral bass lines *move*.

ACT IV

Scene 1: a deserted place on the borders of England and Scotland. In the distance Birnam Forest.

Scottish geography has been rationalized here to allow for an amalgamation of two important scenes—Shakespeare's IV, iii, and V, iv. There is no time for the long colloquy of Malcolm and Macduff about Scotland's future ruler, nor for

* Letter to L. Escudier, Jan. 1865. *Copialettere*, pp. 452-4.

Lennox to break to Macduff the news that his wife and children have been murdered. But the woes of Scotland under tyranny, the 'new sorrows' that 'strike heaven on the face, that it resounds | as if it felt with Scotland, and yell'd out | like syllable of dolour' can be powerfully depicted in a choral lament. For his original setting of *Patria oppressa* Verdi had in mind a chorus on the lines of 'Va pensiero' or 'O Signore dal tetto natio'. But he hated to repeat himself; and the melody which finally gets under way is very different from either. Its design is like that of Donizetti's 'Una furtiva lagrima' with its progress of minor–relative major–minor–tonic major; and the final section could have come straight out of Bellini's *Norma*:

This is Verdi's Risorgimento style at its noblest—possible in 1847, irrelevant to 1865; so it was replaced by a setting that is not only a masterpiece of originality, but also far more harmonically daring that anything Verdi had yet written. The choral texture alone points forward to the Requiem and the Quattro Pezzi Sacri. Everything about it is arresting: the opening brass chorale with timpani rolls, the sustained hollow fifths of the second violins, the line of pizzicato cellos and basses with its modal inflections, the combination of 'lamenting' figures that results in ambiguities of chromatic harmony worthy of Liszt and Wagner. If the opening of the *Tristan* prelude poses difficulties of harmonic analysis, what is one to make of such a passage as this? (Ex. 194, opposite).

The G sharp gives the effect of an A flat until the C appoggiatura has resolved itself. The whole melody of which this is an excerpt is repeated with clearer harmony after a dominant cadence, but darker scoring heavily coloured by low trombones and cimbasso. The oboe figure takes up the motif last heard in *Alzira* and to be heard again associated with the lonely grief of King Philip in *Don Carlos*. A final stroke of unorthodoxy was to make all the voices move across the tritone from B flat to E for the final cadence—the diabolus in musica. From here the descent to Macduff's aria bewailing the death of his children (*Ah la paterna mano*) is inevitably rather steep. For this is a very orthodox 1847-style romanza in

194

Andante sostenuto
SOLI SOP. 1ᵢ *tristissimo*

D'or – fa – nel – li e di pian – gen – ti chi lo

spo – so e chi la pro – le al ve – nir del nuo – vo so – le

del nuo – vo so – le

minor–major form, though distinctively coloured by solo cello and clarinet. The maggiore section equiv..lent to 'front to front | bring thou this fiend of Scotland and myself' sounds especially benign with its placid clarinet arpeggios.* A military gallop brings in a very brisk Malcolm at the head of the English troops. After asking and being told the name of the near-by forest he orders his men each to seize a branch and carry it in front of him. He tells Macduff to take comfort from thought of vengeance; to which Macduff replies no less pithily, 'I cannot . . . he has no children.' The compression of Shakespeare's lines is both ludicrous and ineffective; and we may just surmise that it was Verdi's memory of his own bereavement that made him insist on including it. The scene ends with a rousing duet and chorus in which a melody begun by Malcolm and Macduff in unison is repeated phrase by phrase with full chorus—an effect not heard since the first act of *I Lombardi*.† The only Parisian addition is a section in faster tempo (*Fratelli gli oppressi corriamo a salvar*) before returning to the original instrumental coda.

* In a letter to L. Escudier (3 Feb. 1865, *R.M.I.* (1928), p. 186) Verdi speaks of having 're-touched and scored' the tenor aria. Yet the Paris MS. shows beyond all manner of doubt that the revisions concern the first three bars of recitative only. Otherwise the movement is identical in 1847 and 1865 versions.

† It has the additional, economic advantage of preserving Macduff's comprimario status. If he had sung a cabaletta on his own he would automatically qualify as a principal.

Scene 2: a room in Macbeth's castle, as in Act I

With the 'Gran Scena del Sonnambulismo' we reach the high point of the Florence *Macbeth*, a scene unique in all Italian opera of the time. As in the duet from Act I Verdi has had recourse to 'selective' scoring, muting the strings, cutting out all the brighter wind instruments and using clarinet and cor anglais as obbligati. None of this is altered in the Paris version. Like all the best things in the early *Macbeth* it is laid out on an unusually large scale. The scene is set by Ex. 166 and Ex. 167; while the effect of handwashing is suggested by a rapid gesture on muted strings. During all this we have heard only the whispered fearful comments of the Doctor and the Gentlewoman ('How came she by that light?' 'Why it stood by her; she . . .' 'Her eyes are open' 'Ay, but their sense are shut . . .'). When Lady Macbeth does begin to speak (*Una macchia!*) it is to the following well-known accompaniment:

195

That this dates from 1847 should surprise no one: it is the kind of elaborate self-perpetuating pattern which occurs in all the early operas and which Verdi first renounced in *Stiffelio*. Here for once it has real dramatic and musical force. As the scene unfolds it gives way to two other patterns no less expressive before petering out in plain string pulsations.

The whole of Lady Macbeth's speech is here, moulded from Shakespeare's prose with *ottonari*, and worked by Verdi into a design of modified symmetry—two stanzas of eighteen bars apiece, the first ending in D flat, the second in E major; a shorter verse of nine bars returning to the original key, and a sixteen-bar coda. The vocal line is marked as in the Act I duet *sempre sotto voce*, with a phrase here and there to be sung *a voce spiegata*; yet despite the pertichini from Doctor and Gentlewoman, the broken phrases ('Yet here's a spot. . . . Out, damned spot! out, I say! . . . One, two; why, then 'tis time to do it. . . . Yet who would have thought the old man to have had so much blood in him?') the effect is of one endless, uninterrupted, *unrepeating* melody. Two very personal harmonic effects call for mention: the melting C major 6/4 chord in the middle of an E major cadence at the passage 'all the perfumes of Arabia will not sweeten this little hand' and the sinister side-slip of two other 6/4s at 'Banquo's buried; he cannot come out on's grave'. Much of Lady Macbeth's line lies in the lower register of the voice; but her final phrase includes a high D flat marked *Un fil di voce* (an effect which most singers achieve by singing mezzo-forte as far offstage as possible). A reference to Ex. 166 over a thudding bass follows her exit, and ends a scene whose only fault is that it occurs so soon after the still more memorable chorus of exiles. A revival of the 1847 Macbeth would be of more interest to Verdi students than to the ordinary music-lover; but it would at least allow the sleepwalking scene to 'tower in its pride of place'.

Scene 3: a room in Dunsinane Castle

This opens to a clatter of orchestral sound, indicative of the battle raging outside. Macbeth is discovered musing on his destiny as in Shakespeare's V, iii: 'Fear not, Macbeth; no man that's born of woman | shall e'er have power upon thee.' So he is safe enough; but adagio string quavers depict his growing mood of listlessness ('my way of life | is fall'n into the sear, the yellow leaf') and make way for the hero's only lyrical adagio in the whole opera (*Pietà, rispetto, amore*).* The words correspond closely to Shakespeare's 'and that which should accompany old age, | as honour, love, obedience, troops of friends, | I must not look to have; but, in their stead, | curse not loud but deep'. The aria uses the simple design with a new breadth and freedom. The second limb of the melody (a^2) is extended with verbal repetition into a melting dominant cadence. There is no a^3; instead the music strikes out unexpectedly into E major, at the words 'Sol la bestemmia', returning to the home key of D flat within the final three bars. By way of compensation the main theme is restated as a full-throated melody for upper woodwind and divisi violins in octaves in a regular eight-bar period, remaining firmly in D flat throughout and joined by the voice as it moves towards the final cadence. This kind of orchestral intervention, as though the composer were associating himself directly with the singer's grief, is new and prophetic.

There is a commotion offstage, and a cry of women; then the Gentlewoman comes in to announce that the Queen is dead. Macbeth is permitted only a tiny fragment of his famous speech; but to Verdi what remained was of sufficient importance for him to want to improve his setting of it in 1865. 'Life's . . . a tale | told by an idiot, full of sound and fury, | signifying nothing.' For 'told by an idiot' the original score had a slow climbing figure underpinned by trilling clarinets and bassoons which give an appropriate foretaste of Iago's 'Credo'. 'Sound and fury' is sung fortissimo; 'signifying nothing' forms a straightforward cadence. More subtly in the later version the entire passage is sung over a brooding diminished seventh of accidie with hollow-sounding sforzandi low on the clarinet, and the last note is interrupted by military fanfares, as Macbeth's soldiers enter to tell him that Birnam Wood is on the move. Desperately he calls for his sword and shield and leads his men away to battle. As he does so the scene begins to change to a vast plain where fighting is in progress; and here the two scores diverge for the last time, never to come together again.

Battles do not show Verdi at his best—witness *I Lombardi* and *Giovanna d'Arco*. It was to the latter that he turned for his model in 1847. A series of rapid fanfares give way to a paltry theme which is repeated in various keys alternating between major and minor ad infinitum.

During all this a good deal happens. Malcolm, advancing at the head of his troops, orders them to throw away the branches; then there is a general charge. Macbeth and Macduff enter fighting. Macbeth taunts his opponent with the

---

* In a letter to Varesi of 4.2.1847 (*Nuova Antologia* (1932), pp. 438–9) Verdi had described this movement as 'an adagio in D flat major, tender and melodious, which you must colour [*miniare*—the word used for illuminating a manuscript] beautifully'.

witches' prophecy, then learns that Macduff 'was from his mother's womb untimely ripp'd'. They fight and Macbeth falls. The fanfares come to a halt and Macbeth has a short but impressive death scene in declamatory style. So impressive is it that certain productions beginning with Glyndebourne's in 1936 insert it into the revised *Macbeth*, which is going strictly against Verdi's wishes ('I too am of the opinion that we should change the death of Macbeth, but I can't think of anything better than a final hymn').* It has no direct parallel in Shakespeare—it is merely a bitter farewell to life, ending 'Vile crown, I despise you'.†

196

A single phrase from the crowd, hailing Malcolm as King, brings down the curtain.

The newer version however is more arresting. The battle is conveyed in a lengthy passage of 'theatrical' counterpoint. Despite a brilliant opening for trumpet and trombone it is rather ineptly scored, the orchestral weight being often wrongly distributed for this kind of writing; also it covers up the important exchange between Macbeth and Macduff. Its climax occurs at the point where women and children enter fleeing in terror; then it gradually subsides into silence broken by off-stage cries of 'Victory!' The crowd hail Malcolm with a hymn (*Macbeth, Macbeth ov'è*) laid out in three choral groups—bards, soldiers and women. It is an exciting chorus, very much of the new Verdi, open to cosmopolitan influences. Bizet's *Pearl Fishers* and the Scottish symphony of Mendelssohn could each have contributed to the invigorating melody with its tramp-tramp rhythm, its simple but brilliant scoring with piccolo prominent over widespread chords on woodwind and pizzicato strings.

---

* Letter to L. Escudier, 2.12.1864. *R.M.I.* (1928), p. 183; *M. & L.* (1923), p. 66.

† An equivalent exists in Garricks performing version, which was still current in nineteenth-century England. See V. Godefroy, *The Dramatic Genius of Verdi*, vol. I (London, 1975), p. 139.

197

The old *Macbeth* was to be heard in every opera theatre in Italy and abroad up till the 1860s. The new version had to wait until this century to be appreciated. Incredibly the first performance in England was that of Glyndebourne in 1938, where it was taken up again during the 1950's. Nowadays it ranks with *Nabucco*, *Ernani* and *Luisa Miller* as one of the four undisputed repertory pieces of the pre-*Rigoletto* epoch.

The 1847 *Macbeth* is an astonishing achievement, not only for its obvious novelties such as the sleepwalking and apparition scenes still less the lack of a conventional love interest.* Even the traditional elements are better handled than in *Attila* or *Alzira*. The arias grow organically from the implications of their own material, rather than from the deliberate elaboration of a formula. Throughout there is greater continuity and cohesion than ever before; while for the study of Verdi's stylistic evolution the early score offers a feature of unique interest—the unorthodox use of 6/4 chords in a remote key. It is remarkable how in his revisions Verdi has not only preserved but enriched the 'colorito' of the original, which is more marked even than in *Attila*. It shows itself in the prevalence of E minor tonality, the dark scoring, the number of themes based on the falling semitone and even in a characteristic contour to be found in certain opening phrases:

* Although often referred to by Italian critics as the 'opera senza amore' it is by no means unique in this respect, even for its period. Witness Donizetti's *Belisario*, *L'Assedio di Calais* and *Lucrezia Borgia*, to name only a few.

198

ACT II Scena ed Aria
(Lady Macbeth) 1865   Scena (Banco) 1847   ACT IV Chorus 1865

To this he added in 1865 the long falling lines of *La luce langue*, of the codetta to Macbeth's solo after the apparitions and of the final duettino to Act III. Yet certain problems remain. The revision of *Macbeth* eighteen years after its first performance is comparable to Beethoven's new *Fidelio* of 1814 and Brahms's refashioning of his trio, Op. 8, at the end of his life. But Brahms even in his youth had an intellectual maturity which Verdi was slow to attain. Beethoven when he revised *Fidelio* did so at far less distance of time and development. Despite the integrity of Verdi's genius, the passage of eighteen years was just too long to allow him to re-enter his original conception at every point.*

---

* One curious feature of *Macbeth*—unparalleled in any other of Verdi's operas apart from *Il Trovatore*—is the use of key, not architectonically, but for purposes of dramatic definition. Perhaps one should speak of 'areas of pitch' rather than keys, since both the modes are included, while the relation of one 'area' to another is not exploited. Three are of special importance: F major/minor which belongs to Macbeth himself; A major/minor which denotes the outside world, including the witches; D flat major which is associated with the idea of murder. There are two subsidiary areas: E connoting power and B flat escape. Against this more or less constant background the dramatic events spring all the more vividly into relief. Note how the idea of murder first insinuates itself into Macbeth's mind in the form of D flat major against the prevailing F major of the duettino in Act I; how Lady Macbeth's cavatina proceeds from an andante in D flat to a cabaletta in E major—i.e. from the idea of murder to that of power; how the unequivocal E major of the Act II finale is shaken by jagged rhythms as though Macbeth's newly acquired power were already tottering. Whether such a scheme was adopted by Verdi consciously we cannot be sure. But it is significant that the 1847 ending in which Macbeth dies on stage is in F minor, while the new finale of 1865 is in A major.

Since this chapter was written the version of 1847 has been several times resuscitated, notably in concert form in London in 1978 at the 84th season of Henry Wood Promenade Concerts under John Matheson with Rita Hunter, Peter Glossop, John Tomlinson, Kenneth Collins, and the BBC Chorus and Concert Orchestra, and at the Teatro Margherita, Genoa in 1986, under Gunter Neuhold with Olivia Stapp, Vicente Sardinero, Paolo Washington and Jesus Pinto. An earlier revival, at Danville, Kentucky, in 1977 under David Lawton, was the occasion of an international congress organized by the American Institute of Verdi Studies, out of which arose *Verdi's 'Macbeth': A Sourcebook*, ed. D. Rosen and A. Porter (London and New York, 1984). This published a number of newly discovered documents, including a copy in Verdi's handwriting of Piave's original libretto, edited by Francesco Degrada, with alterations by Maffei, not all of which Verdi accepted. Meanwhile it has been established that the starting point of the dramatic scheme was Carlo Rusconi's translation of 1838 together with August Wilhelm Schlegel's important Preface, a part-translation of which appears in the Milan libretto of 1850.

13 I MASNADIERI

I MASNADIERI

Opera in four acts
by
ANDREA MAFFEI
(after Schiller's play, *Die Räuber*)

*First performed at
Her Majesty's Theatre, London,
22 July 1847*

MASSIMILIANO, Count Moor PRIMO BASSO		Luigi Lablache
CARLO ⎫ his sons PRIMO TENORE		Italo Gardoni
FRANCESCO ⎭ PRIMO BARITONO		Filippo Coletti
AMALIA, an orphan, PRIMA DONNA SOPRANO		Jenny Lind
the count's niece		
ARMINIO, The count's TENORE COMPRIMARIO		Leone Corelli
steward		
MOSER, a pastor BASSO COMPRIMARIO		Lucien Bouché
ROLLA, one of Carlo's SECONDO TENORE		N.N.
companions		

Young men led astray, later bandits—women—children—servants

The action takes place in Germany

Epoch: the beginning of the eighteenth century

I Masnadieri, like *Macbeth*, originated in the convalescent holiday that Verdi spent with Andrea Maffei at Recoaro after the production of *Attila* in 1846. With Maffei at hand as librettist it seemed the most likely priority for Florence next year; so Verdi set to work on it in the autumn, and appears to have composed a good part of the libretto before he heard that the tenor Fraschini would not be available for the part of Carlo. He then postponed it for what promised to be a more momentous occasion: his first premiere outside Italy, to be given at that ancient stronghold of Italian opera abroad, Her Majesty's Theatre, the Haymarket, London.

The contract had been arranged through Lucca some time between July 1844 and April 1845. The subject was to have been Byron's *The Corsair*, for which Piave would write the libretto; and the opera would be performed in the summer of 1846. However, Verdi's long bout of ill-health following the premiere of *Attila* prevented him from going to London that year, nor was he amused when Lumley the impresario wrote prescribing the same treatment as Flauto.* But he had no wish to renounce altogether a project which promised to be the most lucrative he had ever undertaken. So in November he wrote to both Lumley and Lucca proposing to give the new opera in June the following year on condition that Fraschini and Jenny Lind were available.† Meanwhile he had decided against *The Corsair*. He had read Piave's libretto and found it 'dull and lacking in theatrical effectiveness'.‡ Accordingly, though it had doubled his expenses to do so, he had commissioned a new libretto from Maffei on Schiller's *Die Räuber*, of which he had already set a third.§ He hoped therefore that the management would see their way clear to accepting the change. The management did, but they were unable to guarantee Fraschini. Luckily Verdi was not disposed to insist.¶

In the meantime Lucca was clearly out to make up for his lost hours of sleep. Not content with demanding an outrageous fee for the mounting of *Attila* at La Scala in 1846, he was trying to drive impossible bargains with foreign publishers over the as yet unwritten *I Masnadieri*. || All this may well account for the irritable, not to say unreasonable, tone Verdi adopted towards him as the time for his London engagement drew near. At the end of March he acknowledged an advance payment on the rights of *I Masnadieri* to be given at Her Majesty's Theatre in early July

* Letter to Lumley, 4.12.1846. *Copialettere*, p. 33.
† Letter to Lucca, 3.12.1846. *Copialettere*, pp. 32–3.
‡ Letter from Lumley, 13.5.1846. *Copialettere*, pp. 21–2.
§ Letter to Lumley, 11.11.1846. *Copialettere*, p. 30.
¶ Emanuele Muzio, with his ear to the ground for news of the London opera season, shows that Verdi did well to be flexible in the matter. 'Generally speaking Fraschini wasn't liked. Of all the singers that Lumley has engaged the most popular were Gardoni, Coletti and Superchi; the others don't live up to the reputation they have in Italy.' (Letter to Barezzi, 22.4.1847. Garibaldi, pp. 315–17.) Later: 'It's possible that the Maestro will write for Gardoni instead of Fraschini, especially as Gardoni has been signed up by the Théâtre des Italiens in Paris and there'll probably be a revival there next winter.' (Undated letter to Barezzi. Garibaldi, pp. 319–20.)
|| Letter from Giuseppina Strepponi to Giovannina Lucca, 23.2.1847. *Carteggi Verdiani*, IV, pp. 252–3. 'The Escudiers are still gazing with open mouths and telescopes glued to their eyes ... at the figure you're demanding for *I Masnadieri*. ...'

1847, adding that he would restore it if, as he had heard might happen, Jenny Lind was not engaged as the prima donna.* Later:

> I'm glad to hear that La Lind is going to London after all. But it looks to me as if she's going rather late and I wouldn't want the season to be over-prolonged for the sake of my opera. Rest assured that I will not put up with the slightest shortcoming. I have been treated so shabbily in this whole affair that if my opera isn't put on at the proper time and with everything done as it ought to be done I tell you quite frankly I will not have it performed.†

However, he set out with Muzio during May, and made his way in leisurely fashion to Strasbourg and then down the Rhine to Cologne and across to Brussels. But Muzio was alone when he arrived in London on 3 June. It had come to Verdi's ears that Jenny Lind was set against learning any new roles; and unless he could be assured by Lumley via Muzio that this was not the case, he would not cross the Channel. Muzio, however, was able to write to him that La Lind was waiting eagerly to learn her part and Lumley was deeply mortified at not seeing him.‡ So a few days later Verdi duly arrived, still in a highly distrustful frame of mind. 'It's true,' he said to Clarina Maffei, 'that I'm late and the impresario has some cause for complaint, but if he says one word to me I shall say ten to him and go straight back.'§ This, after having made punctuality a condition of giving his opera at all!

The impresario had his problems too. Early in the year Benjamin Lumley had a serious quarrel with his leading singers and his conductor Michele Costa, who promptly walked out and proceeded to set up a rival organization at Covent Garden. Only the veteran bass Luigi Lablache remained loyal to Her Majesty's. The rebel company was formidable on paper. It included Ronconi, the creator of Nabucco, the contralto Alboni, and Mario, the Victorian operamane's favourite Latin lover; while in Michele Costa they could boast the most experienced and efficient opera conductor in England, far outclassing Michael Balfe, who succeeded him at Her Majesty's. Lumley staked everything on the three trump cards he hoped to play: Jenny Lind, an opera by Mendelssohn, and a new opera by Verdi—in that order. The Mendelssohn opera had become the shadowiest of possibilities, but Lumley had not given up hope. He had roused Romani out of retirement and obtained from him the promise of a libretto; he had from his own pocket commissioned a Tempest from Scribe (the only writer capable of doing justice to the subject, Mendelssohn had said); but when the opera season opened, composer and librettist were still arguing over the dramatic treatment, and when The Tempest was announced on the prospectus of Her Majesty's the opposing party wrote derisive letters to the Press, and with good cause. Mendelssohn's opera never came to fruition that year or any other, for by November he was dead; but the libretto, translated into Italian, eventually served Halévy for an opera which Lumley produced at Her Majesty's in 1850.

With Jenny Lind the situation was complicated by the fact that two years previously she had signed an agreement with Alfred Bunn, manager of Drury Lane

---

* Letter to Lumley, 23.3.1847. Copialettere, p. 35.
† Letter to Lumley, 10.4.1847. Copialettere, pp. 35–6.
‡ Letter from Muzio to Barezzi, 4.6.1847. Garibaldi, pp. 325–7.
§ Letter to Clarina Maffei, 9.6.1847. Copialettere, p. 457.

Theatre, to appear in the English premiere of Meyerbeer's *Ein Feldlager in Schlesien*. When it became clear that Bunn had no intention of mounting the new opera, she refused to come. Next year she signed a more lucrative contract with Lumley for the season of 1847 to sing the lead in an opera by her friend Mendelssohn and, possibly, one by Verdi, as well as some of the tried favourites. She then offered Bunn £2,000 to release her from the previous contract. Although the sum was more than twice what Bunn had intended paying her for the whole season, and although Drury Lane was not giving opera that summer, he not only refused her offer but put it about that she would be arrested the moment she landed at Dover. As a result she hesitated on the Continent so long as to threaten Lumley with ruin. Eventually she arrived in London not long after Verdi set out from Milan, and after still more vacillation ventured to appear in the part of Alice in *Robert le Diable*. Furore!—and Lumley was saved.* It merely remained for him to redeem the promise to the public of a new opera. Mendelssohn's was out of the question; there remained Verdi's. For most English music-lovers this was a poor alternative. Mendelssohn's name was already linked with those of Beethoven and Handel. Verdi was regarded by many as the noisiest of a degenerate brood. Although, ever since the first London performance of *Ernani* two years before, he had been building up a steady following, its enthusiasm was not shared by the press, the academics or even the pundits of Italian opera, for whom Rossini was still the touchstone of merit. H. F. Chorley of the *Athenaeum*, the champion of Mozart, Mendelssohn and Rossini, and J. W. Davison of *The Times* were as implacably hostile to him as they were later to become towards Wagner.

Certainly Verdi could not complain of his welcome. No sooner had he been seen at Her Majesty's than the papers were full of his arrival. He was showered with invitations, fêted whenever he was recognized, and in general everything was done to meet his wishes. Yet for most of his stay in London he lived like a recluse. He liked the country; he liked the people; he detested the climate (it must have been a particularly bad summer) which threw him into agonies of hypochondria. 'I am well enough,' is the burden of his letters, 'but am unlikely to remain so in this horrible weather.'† So he remained in his room, working—or 'with the intention of working'—and only going out at night to the theatre. Muzio meanwhile regaled his Busseto patron with fatuous tittle-tattle about the rival company and London life in general.‡ His remarks about Jenny Lind are interesting, since they probably represent Verdi's views as well: '. . . a marvellous artist in every sense of the word. . . . Her trill is without equal; she has an incomparable agility— indeed she's apt to show off her technique in fioriture and gruppetti and trills, the sort of thing which people liked in the last century but not in 1847.' On that sentence alone a musicological treatise could be written about nineteenth-century *Aufführungspraxis*. 'If she would come to Italy I am sure she would sing differently and abandon her mania for embellishments, because she has a voice even and flexible enough to sustain a phrase simply in La Frezzolini's manner. . . .'§

* For a full account of the affair, see B. Lumley, *Reminiscences of the Italian Opera* (London, 1864), pp. 156–93.

† Letter to Giuseppina Appiani, 27.6.1847. *Copialettere*, pp. 457–8. Also to Clarina Maffei (on the same day). Luzio, *Studi e bozzetti di Storia letteraria e politica* (Milan, 1910), p. 408.

‡ See Walker, pp. 158–63.

§ Letter from Muzio to Barezzi, 16.6.1847. Garibaldi, pp. 327–32.

All this helps explain the rather tinsel-like music that Verdi wrote for Amalia, and why in both her arias he left the cadenzas to the artist's invention. (Several of Jenny Lind's decorations and cadenzas for arias by Bellini and Rossini are transcribed by Rockstro in his biography, and remarkably tasteful they are, however old-fashioned.)* For the rest she needed more rehearsal than the other singers, being not very well versed in Italian, so Muzio explained. He added that she was solemn and rather ugly with large hands and feet and a huge nose and a 'Nordic quality about her which I find antipathetic'.† But she was clearly what the Americans call a 'very lovely person', and her dislike of the stage and all things theatrical endeared her to Verdi.

The other stars were worthy of the occasion and they shone all the brighter in that the rival company was in financial difficulties. As Massimiliano Moor there was the bass Luigi Lablache, who by an odd coincidence had created the same role eleven years earlier in Paris in Mercadante's *I Briganti*. Coletti (Francesco Moor) was already known to Verdi as the creator of Guzman in *Alzira*. Not so long since he had appeared at Her Majesty's before an audience who had been expecting the great Tamburini. The result was the famous 'Tamburini riot', described in the *Ingoldsby Legends*, in which several of the audience, including a prince of the blood royal, charged on to the stage. Since that time Coletti had won general acceptance, and even counted Thomas Carlyle among his admirers. For Carlo Moor Lumley had engaged Italo Gardoni, a twenty-five-year-old tenor previously unknown in this country, who, according to Chorley, 'by his charm of person and of voice, somewhat slight though the latter has proved, did more to reconcile the public to the loss of Signor Mario than could have been expected'.‡ All in all a successful premiere seemed assured. Muzio predicted confidently that 'Next to *Ernani* this will prove the Maestro's most popular opera.' Verdi himself was more cautious. 'I've already had two rehearsals with orchestra,' he wrote to Clarina Maffei, 'and if I were in Italy I could give you a cool appraisal of the opera, but here I can't understand anything . . . blame the climate . . . blame the climate . . .'§ The first night (22 July) was the greatest event of the season, with Queen Victoria, the Prince Consort, Louis Napoleon and the Duke of Wellington in the audience. Verdi himself conducted 'seated on a chair higher than all the others, baton in hand' (Muzio) and securing a most finished performance from the orchestra, so the *Morning Post* tells us. 'As soon as he appeared in the orchestra pit there was a continuous applause which went on for a quarter of an hour. . . .' At the end, 'The Maestro was cheered, called on the stage alone and with the singers. Flowers were thrown to him and nothing was heard but "Viva Verdi, *bietifol*" . . .'¶ Contemporary accounts show that Muzio was not exaggerating. It was after all the first time since Weber's *Oberon* (1826) that a world-famous composer had written an opera specially for London. Neither Rossini, Bellini nor Donizetti had, as Muzio put it, ever 'pitched their tents on the banks of the Thames'. ‖ Of the critics Chorley ran true to form: 'We

---

* Scott Holland and W. S. Rockstro, *Jenny Lind, the Artist* (London, 1891), II, p. 453 seqq. See also *Grove's Dictionary of Music and Musicians* (3rd edn, London, 1927), III, pp. 200–2.

† Letter from Muzio to Barezzi, 29.6.1847. Garibaldi, pp. 332–8.

‡ H. F. Chorley, *Thirty Years' Musical Recollections* (London, 1862), II, pp. 246–7.

§ Letter to Clarina Maffei, 17.7.1847. *Copialettere*, pp. 458–9.

¶ Letter from Muzio to Barezzi, 23.7.1847. *Copialettere*, pp. 459–60 (in full). Garibaldi, pp. 344–9.

‖ Letter from Muzio to Barezzi, 18.7.1847. Garibaldi, pp. 340–3.

take this to be the worst opera that has been given in our time at Her Majesty's Theatre. Verdi is finally rejected. The way is now open to an Italian composer.'* Davison of *The Times* was only a little less scornful. *Punch,* with the same good-humoured philistinism that it showed to Berlioz and Wagner, describes the opera as so noisy that each act 'was a Riot Act since it disperses everyone until the ballet'. 'A new opera by Signor Verdi . . . the music very noisy and trivial' (Queen Victoria's diary). The first night was glorious enough. On the second, the last to be conducted by Verdi himself, the plaudits were already diminishing, if we may read between the lines of Muzio's final letter from London: 'Verdi aroused a *furore* in London but the English are a matter-of-fact and thoughtful people and never give way to enthusiasm like the Italians, partly because they can't understand too well and partly because they think that well-bred people shouldn't make a lot of noise . . .'† Lumley had been all eagerness to secure Verdi's services as conductor for the next ten years with the obligation to compose an opera for each season. Verdi haggled rather perfunctorily; clearly he would need a fortune to compensate for the necessity of enduring ten English summers. He countered with a more limited project to produce three operas in consecutive years (1849–51), demanding for each exactly five times what he usually received in Italy, together with a house in the country and a private carriage.‡ But this too came to nothing. Later Verdi blamed Lucca, who had refused to release him from his contract to produce an opera for the spring of 1848 in Italy. But there is little doubt that Lumley's impresario's nose had smelled a hidden fiasco in *I Masnadieri.* Nor was he alone in this. An English writer in the Parisian *Gazzette Musicale* (admittedly hostile to Verdi) expressed the same view in considerable detail.§ After Verdi's departure *I Masnadieri* lasted out two more performances before the season ended on 21 August. There followed a few sporadic appearances in Italy. Elsewhere on the Continent it did little better, though it was in due course translated into French, Hungarian and German. It was even heard in Odessa under the title *Adele di Cosenza* before it joined *Alzira* in the limbo of Verdi's least performed operas.

At first sight this seems hard to understand. Not only does *I Masnadieri* belong to the same vintage as *Macbeth*; it was also a long opera to which Verdi had devoted considerable care, unlike *Alzira* thrown off with as little trouble as possible during a period of convalescence. Both operas, however, share one rather ominous circumstance—an exaggerated regard on Verdi's part for the librettist. By the time they collaborated on *Luisa Miller* and *Il Trovatore,* Verdi was clearly making his requirements to Cammarano in unmistakable if always respectful terms. At the time of *Alzira* he was all humility. With Maffei he never worked again after *I Masnadieri.* But Muzio was probably echoing his master's views when he declared that even Romani's verses were not to be compared with Maffei's.¶ Certainly Maffei's are elegant enough, and his vocabulary is far wider than that of the average librettist.

* Toye, p. 56.　　† Letter from Muzio to Barezzi, 23.8.1847. Garibaldi, pp. 351–3.
‡ Letter to Lumley, 2.8.1847; and Lumley's reply, 7.8.1847. *Copialettere,* pp. 42–4.
§ Holland and Rockstro, II, pp. 138–40.
¶ Letter to Barezzi, 9.11.1846. Garibaldi, pp. 291–3. Abbiati, I, p. 721. See also letter to M. Escudier, 12.1.1847. 'Cinque lettere verdiane' in *Rassegna Musicale,* July 1951, p. 258. 'I've already settled on *I Masnadieri* for London, the libretto of which is already completed and seems to me entirely successful as regards the dramatic situation, and has been beautifully versified in full by one of the most illustrious Italian poets.'

Theatrically he had already proved his worth (so Verdi thought) by coming to the rescue of Piave's botched *Macbeth*. So Verdi was prepared to leave almost everything to his discretion. There are no impatient letters exchanged between Milan and London; no demands for alteration of metre here or an extra strophe there; merely an isolated request that part of the second act be revised in the interest of theatrical effect.* Such complaisance on Verdi's part was a bad sign. Far better the endless harryings of Piave, of whose ability he thought so much less.

Maffei's preface to the printed libretto shows that he had not undertaken his work lightly:

> This melodrama is taken from the famous tragedy *Die Räuber* by Friedrich Schiller, the first drama to issue from that divine intellect before maturity and the study of human nature curbed the excesses of a fiery imagination. The harsh circumstances of his youthful upbringing combined with a spirit naturally inclined to melancholy to inspire this fearful drama which, as we know, so worked on the overheated imagination of the young men of his time that many ran away into the forests dreaming of setting the world to rights through crime and bloodshed.
>
> But if his frightening picture of society falls short of reality; if it fails to reveal that penetrating insight into the human heart that we admire in *Maria Stuart*, *Wallenstein* and *Wilhelm Tell*, it presents by way of contrast such vividness, such mounting tension, such a wide range of powerful emotions that *I cannot think of any other literary work which would lend itself so well to musical treatment*.† It is to situations of this kind, emotions of this intensity, that anyone attempting the difficult genre of melodrama must address himself, whether he takes his plot from history or fiction. Since the poet is confined within a narrow limit and cannot give to his thought the scale or the psychological depth the drama requires, he must work in broad simple strokes presenting the musician with a skeleton which will derive form and life and warmth not from words but from musical notes. He must turn a huge conception into a miniature without altering its physiognomy, like a concave lens which diminishes objects while preserving their shape.
>
> The libretto is in fact merely the seed of a poetic creation, which will ripen only when fertilized by musical ideas. . . .‡

This is not only logical but profound; and it is very different from the boorish attitude of Solera, who butchered a far better tragedy of Schiller's so as to produce what he impudently called 'an entirely original drama'. Yet where opera was concerned, Solera was a professional, Maffei a dilettante. Looked at superficially *Die Räuber* had everything to recommend it not only for opera but specifically for Verdi, the patent Shakespearian influence not least. Karl Moor is half Hamlet, half Coriolanus; Franz is descended from Edmund, Maximilian from Lear, and there is plenty of action, which is what Verdi liked. But there are also hidden traps which a more experienced, less intellectual librettist would have seen from the start.

Of all Schiller's dramas *Die Räuber* is the most firmly rooted in its time and place.

* Letter to A. Maffei, undated. *Copialettere*, pp. 32–3. Abbiati, I, p. 641.
† Italics mine.　　　　　　　　　　‡ Abbiati, I, pp. 718–19.

It belongs to that curious epoch in German literature which takes its name from Klinger's play *Sturm und Drang*, and which forms a rich loam that nourished the roots of the great German classics. It was a blind revolt against the age of reason in the name of emotion; a volcanic explosion against the walls of a static society. What distinguishes the *Sturm und Drang* from other movements of revolt is its essentially unconstructive quality. Its heroes are all rebels without causes. Their despair is not that of Hamlet, Lear or Othello; at its best it is the self-indulgent rantings of Richard II; more often it suggests a Young Angry of the 1950s. Karl von Moor is Jimmie Porter in Gothic script. In later life Schiller became thoroughly ashamed of him.

He is very much a young man's hero—wild, impetuous, extravagant, his father's favourite, though his escapades continually land him in trouble. While he is at Leipzig University his younger brother Franz poisons their father's mind against him and persuades him that only by threatening Karl with imprisonment will he teach him to mend his ways. Karl reacts to this threat by turning bandit, and in the course of his Robin-Hood-like career he sacks an entire city, murdering women and children, in order to save a comrade from the gallows. Meantime he receives word that Franz has spread a false rumour of his death, hoping that this will cause their father to die of grief, so that he can help himself to Karl's betrothed, Amalia. Both plans fail. Amalia is proof against all Franz's threats and pleas. The father survives, to be kept a prisoner in some remote tower. The hero then returns home with his band of robbers, determined to be avenged. He succeeds only too well. Tormented by a guilt which he supposed himself incapable of feeling, Franz hangs himself. But though vindicated in all essentials, the hero cannot bring himself to reveal his identity either to his father, whom he has rescued, or to Amalia. She however at last realizes who he is; his father on learning that his favourite son is a robber chief dies on the spot. Karl stabs Amalia and then gives himself up to justice.

Such is the original story, later modified by Schiller in his stage edition. For the youth of his time it has a message; indeed, it was not lost on Beethoven, whose letters at times speak the same language of tortured sensibility. Schiller's hero is the *ne plus ultra* of youthful egoism; one who even at his supreme moment of self-justification cannot relinquish his trump card of anonymity; of being, in a word, misunderstood. He embodies all his generation's hatred of a society which was more rigid in Germany than anywhere else in Europe. Transplanted into a less conformist age and set among a more pragmatic people, Karl von Moor speaks with less force, particularly in translation—since the charm of his rhetoric depends much on the lively prose of the original, earthy and fantastic by turns.

From Verdi's point of view *Die Räuber* had the further disadvantage that its earlier scenes are carried on in different places. Each of the participants begins in his or her separate world. Confrontation, which is the essence of Verdian music-drama, cannot happen until the end of the first act. Whereas in *Macbeth* the drama takes wing with the duettino of the introduction, the scheme of *I Masnadieri* imposes what was for Verdi the most uninspiring of all routines—a chain of cavatinas. Just how conscientiously Maffei went about his task of reducing a 'vast conception' to a small scale can be seen by comparing his libretto with the one by Crescini which had served Mercadante in 1836 and which hardly touches the fringe of Schiller's play. Like Cammarano's *Alzira* it cuts down the characters and situations to conventional romantic size. Ermanno (Karl) is a standard lyrical hero who gets up to nothing more serious than a drinking song with his robber mates. Corrado (Franz) is the most ordinary of baritone villains. Massimiliano does not appear until more than half-way through the opera, when Ermanno releases him from the tower. Incident is minimal so as to allow for a sequence of long decorated solos and duets for Grisi, Rubini, Tamburini and Lablache. The music, like so much of Mercadante's, has every admirable quality except spontaneity. Most striking are the choruses, which are worked out at more than usual operatic length; but even these are mostly spoiled by those rapid dotted rhythms which so often halt the flow of Mercadante's ideas. *I Briganti* deserved its failure.

A libretto such as this would have been little use to Verdi. It is much too slender. Maffei's suffers from the opposite fault of being too meaty. He preserved the main features of Schiller's huge straggling drama, retaining all the major characters except for Spiegelberg, cramming in as many of Schiller's scenes and actual thoughts as the length of an Italian opera would allow, so providing the composer with a succession of indigestible dramatic units.

None the less *I Masnadieri* is far from negligible. Verdi is never content to repeat himself—there is always some novelty of scoring or of structure where you least expect it. Compared to the early *Macbeth*, to *I Due Foscari*, *Ernani* or *Nabucco*, it is small beer. It does not even contain one memorable part, like the heroine in *Giovanna d'Arco*. But it marks a further stage in the perfection of a style that was to reach its apogee in *Rigoletto*, *Il Trovatore* and *La Traviata*.

The atmosphere of the drama is established by a prelude in the form of a cello concertino, written for Alfredo Piatti, who led the cellos at Her Majesty's Theatre. It is an instrumental romanza, in minor–major form, with material from the stormy orchestral introduction neatly woven into the coda. The grave beauty of the music is undisturbed by meretricious display; and indeed the piece itself would easily bear transplantation to the concert-hall, if it were not so short.

ACT I
Scene 1: a tavern on the frontier of Saxony

Carlo is discovered reading Plutarch's *Lives* ('O for a spark of that ancient heroism!'). The voices of his carousing student companions float in upon him as they sing of the glories of a bandit's life. Carlo's thoughts return to the green hills and forests of his home, to Amalia his chaste sweetheart. At that moment his comrades bring him a letter, which he is sure will contain the news of his father's forgiveness; but it is from Francesco, his brother, warning him not to return on pain of imprisonment. After an outburst of fury, Carlo yields to the suggestion of Rolla (the only one of his companions to be individualized) that they form a band of robbers with Carlo himself as their captain. General enthusiasm—and an oath of mutual allegiance.

All this is laid out in a 'scena e cavatina', unusually rich in the variety of its elements. Carlo's silent reading is accompanied by a march in Rossini-like triplets and scored with the same composer's ear for bright, contrasting colours. The recitative is punctuated by a snatch of offstage chorus. For the formal andantino

(*O mio castel paterno*) Verdi has reverted to the gentler style employed in the tenor cavatinas of *Giovanna d'Arco* and *I Due Foscari*—6/8 rhythm with pizzicato strings; but there is novelty in the luminous pattern of flute, clarinet and oboe chords which plays an increasingly important part in the accompaniment, forestalling a similar combination in Amalia's introductory scene (logically enough, since it is Amalia of whom Carlo is thinking). The melody has an unselfconscious charm—note the naïf tritone of popular song.

199

It follows the simplest of aria designs—with one difference: taking his cue from Maffei's quick rhyme Verdi has resumed the opening phrase straight away instead of at the beginning of the third line as had been his inevitable practice up till now. The coda comments on the same phrase, shifted from the beginning to the middle of the bar with an effect of subtle aplomb. The dialogue between Carlo and the chorus is handled with economy, each emotional change mirrored in the music without altering its steady flow. Rolla *speaks* the words of Francesco's letter after Carlo has rushed from the scene in a passion. It is a little unfortunate that the hero's next speech—a fearsome tirade against the 'crocodile brood of mankind . . . generation of hyenas'*—should fall on one of the least prominent parts of the conventional 'scena' structure. Verdi treats it as a discourse on a single phrase, first in free recitative then in strict tempo with powerful harmonic stresses. The result is an unremitting emphasis which comes near to upsetting the musical balance of the scene. The oath is summed up in a cabaletta (*Nell'argilla maledetta*) with a fine, generous swing to it.

200

The melody evolves in Donizettian fashion from one rhythmic motif and so avoids some of the literal repetition of phrases that one expects in this type of movement. The final limb is taken up excitingly by the chorus in unison.

Scene 2: a room in the castle of Massimiliano Moor
The G minor prelude forms an arsenal of the widely various orchestral figures that are to punctuate a recitative that Maffei has condensed from a speech three

* The quotations from Schiller's play are all given in the English translation of H. G. Bohn.

pages long. As the essence of Francesco's philosophy is inexhaustible malice, one of these figures forecasts the brutal flourish that opens Iago's 'Credo'. It was nature who created Francesco the younger brother, but it was also nature that gave him the means of being revenged upon her. The lamp of his father's life is burning low; nature will soon extinguish it; then why should nature not receive a little help? This thought is formulated in the andante (*La sua lampada vitale*) with its obbligato of pizzicato cellos. One method of conveying irony in music is to score a phrase inappositely, so as either to make the listener chuckle or to set his teeth on edge. The four bars of lyrical introduction are scored for horns and trumpets. As often with Mahler the effect is not so much bizarre as vulgar. Far from suggesting Francesco's cynicism, it exhales the piety of a Salvation Army band. But the andante as a whole is not to be dismissed. By repeating the second two lines of each strophe Verdi has enlarged the design so as to include a melodic idea that recurs with the insistency of a refrain. Beginning as a smooth elaboration of the plagal cadence which opens the aria it erupts in a wealth of accents in the composer's most savage baritonic manner, portraying the real face behind the hypocritical mask:

201

The coda sums up with yet another extended theme in which a striking key-change (A flat to E) and a series of violent tutti chords complete the picture of villainy. Francesco summons Arminio, a dependant of the Moors;* tells him to disguise himself and come to old Moor with the news that Carlo has been killed in battle. Without a doubt the old man will die of grief. This is conveyed in connecting material of no particular importance, though always thematic and with no slackening of pace. After a slight demur Arminio goes off to do as he is told, leaving Francesco to exult in the certainty of triumph. '. . . Now you shall see Francesco as he really is and tremble . . . haggard want and crouching fear are my insignia; and in this livery will I clothe you' (Schiller). The cabaletta (*Tremate, o miseri*) is not unlike the unison duet 'La patria tradita' from *Macbeth* but here the line has a downward trend like a sneer. Like Carlo's cabaletta it evolves from a single cell (*x*). The scoring throughout is particularly coarse (Ex. 202, facing page).

Scene 3: a bedroom in the castle

Massimiliano (Maximilian) Moor is lying asleep observed by Amalia. The scene is introduced by a prelude for flute, oboe and clarinet only—the same instrumental

---

* So in Schiller. In the score of *I Masnadieri* he is described as 'camerlengo', suggesting a bursar or steward of the estates. In the play he acquiesces in Franz's stratagem because he is Karl's rival for the love of Amalia. In the opera he is amalgamated with Daniel, an aged retainer.

202

formula as for Act I Scene ii of *Giovanna d'Arco*, but without any pastoral implications. Rather the aim seems to have been to create one of those brightly coloured backcloths of piquant, inchoate figures against which Meyerbeer likes to present his heroines (and Jenny Lind was a particular favourite of his). Amalia's entire recitative is sung softly: 'How venerable—venerable as the picture of a saint. . . . No, I cannot be angry with thee . . . sleep on . . .' and the woodwinds meanwhile appropriately flutter and caress. The text of the cavatina (*Lo sguardo avea degli angeli*) is a formal song which Amalia sings much later in the drama 'Bright as an angel from Valhalla's hall';* and its sensuous imagery contrasts oddly with the frigid, jerky arabesques of the vocal line. It is a song of regret for past happiness and memories of love; but its principal aim is to provide a vehicle for La Lind's particular style of virtuosity. In pace and character it recalls Alzira's cabaletta in Act I of that opera; nor is it any more striking apart from one curious feature of its design: it runs for fifty-four bars, through related and remote keys, without any element of reprise. Only a few tiny motivic links save it from formlessness. The final cadenza as has been noted was left by Verdi to the singer's invention.

Massimiliano stirs in his sleep, breathes the name of Carlo: 'Alas, how miserable you seem. . . . Ha, Francesco, will you tear him even from my dreams? . . .' At last Amalia succeeds in waking him, and with this the drama begins to stir into life. The duettino which follows (*Carlo io muoio*) is moving in its simplicity. 'Carlo, I am dying and you are far away from me. . . .' It is a lament in D minor, whose turn into the relative major falls naturally on the words 'Sweet the sound of mourning to a dying man, but who will mourn for me over my grave?' (Maffei). All this to a typically Verdian bass melody moving by small intervals in a wide sweep. In an answering idea Amalia expresses her longing for death, and an eternity spent with Carlo; and the dialogue resolves into a final D major section with the voices united in simple sixths and tenths. (There is an echo here—conscious or unconscious—of the romanza 'Cinta di fiori' which Lablache had sung in *I Puritani*).

203

Francesco enters with the disguised Arminio and relates how he fought with Carlo in the army of King Frederick at the battle of Prague. As Carlo lay dying of his wounds he asked him to carry a message to the father who had cast him off.

* *Die Räuber*, III, i.

'Tell him that his curse drove me into battle and to death; that I fell in despair.'
Massimiliano cries out in horror; but Arminio proceeds: 'His last word was
Amalia'—and here Francesco points to the words written in blood on the sword:
'Amalia, death has released you from our oath. Francesco, take her as your wife.'
This whole episode is carried on most effectively to a melody sustained on slow
notes, underpinned by driving allegro triplets. As it proceeds the melody becomes
more fragmented with the desperate anguished interruptions of Massimiliano and
Amalia and the promptings of Francesco; it culminates in a climax from which
Amalia's anguished cry: 'Carlo, you never loved me . . . never . . . never' emerges
to form as a link to the main movement of the quartet. This is unquestionably the
finest piece in the act. It is launched by a long strophe of Massimiliano (*Sul capo mio
colpevole*) in which remorse mingles with furious hatred of Francesco. Amalia
follows with a verse of consolation, scored for tremolo strings and arpeggios for
flute and clarinet, so as to indicate that her thoughts are heaven-bent. Francesco
gloats in triumph, his line whenever exposed pointed up by the busy accompaniment of hatred. Arminio sings of his shame in sixths with Amalia. The development of ideas, the contrasting and blending of emotions, are in every way masterly.
In the coda the wide key-range is summed up with one of Verdi's most striking
cadential epigrams, marked by the characteristic use of the 6/4 chord in a remote
key (see *Macbeth*).

204

There is the briefest of allegro strettas—in which Massimiliano cries yet again,
'Give me back my son,' and then collapses; Amalia cries out that he is dead, and
Francesco exults in a phrase more or less identical with that of Abigaille as she places
Nabucco's crown on her own head.

ACT II
Scene 1: the family vault of the Moors

Some months have passed. Francesco is now master of the household, and has
been making the most of his new freedom with feasting and revelry. Amalia, more
alone than ever, has stolen away from the banquet to shed a secret tear over
Massimiliano's grave. The mood is that of the opening prelude, bleak and sombre
with heavily charged D minor harmonies. Amalia's first words recall the cello
melody without actually quoting from it. The sound of a joyous chorus breaks in
on her thoughts—Francesco's guests, all out to enjoy themselves while they may
(*Godiam che fugaci*). It is remarkably long and elaborate for an unaccompanied off-
stage chorus* and it provides an effective contrast to Amalia's bitter denunciation

* This is the point at which Mercadante's opera begins. His opening chorus (on stage) is
more elaborate still.

of Francesco. At least, she thinks, her uncle has now gone to a place where his son's taunts cannot reach him, and her last falling semitone is echoed sepulchrally by low bassoon and trombone in unison (a bold orchestral stroke for Verdi at the time). Once again Amalia raises her eyes piously to heaven as she imagines Carlo and Massimiliano united in eternal bliss while she remains suffering below. Her adagio (*Tu del mio Carlo al seno*) is far more affecting than her cavatina in the previous act. It is a straightforward piece of canto spianato, beautifully and delicately scored with a persistent accompaniment of harp, one cello and one bass, touched in here and there with sustaining woodwind. Here again the voice of Bellini can be heard particularly in the expressive decoration. Victorian audiences would doubtless have responded to its echo of one of their own favourites, 'There is a flower that bloometh' from Wallace's *Maritana*.

205

Once again the cadenza, apart from a downward chromatic scale, is left to the artist's discretion. Arminio now bursts in hastily to break the startling news that both Carlo and Massimiliano are alive, and with that he hurries off, refusing to say more. Amalia vents her joy predictably in a cabaletta (*Carlo vive? Oh caro accento!*), conventional alike in character and design. The series of crotchet trills at the word 'sorriso' as well as the long shake over the final orchestral tutti are doubtless concessions to Jenny Lind's special accomplishment; and she would surely have filled in the pause before 'gli astri' with a flourish of grace notes. Disappointing too is the duet which follows. The odious Francesco now comes out and proceeds to fall at her feet, only to be spurned with fury and disgust. Why the andantino (*Io t'amo, Amalia, t'amo*) fails to live up to its beautiful opening strophe is a mystery; but a comparison with the kindred duettino in Act I of *Ernani* furnishes a clue. The situation is basically the same—baritone trying to seduce unwilling soprano, and it too is laid out in the 'dissimilar' pattern. There, however, the contrast between the two strophes is far greater, and consequently generates a more powerful tension, so that when the moment of *musical* resolution occurs in the joining of the two voices in sixths and thirds the emotional current persists. Dramatic truth is achieved in the teeth of the lyrical convention. One suspects that Verdi was not prepared to entrust to the Swedish nightingale the kind of idea that needs forceful delivery. In *I Masnadieri* the passage of conjunction bears a fatal resemblance to its counterpart in the duet between Amalia and Massimiliano; and its effect in the present context is distinctly flaccid. The movement is too long and too ordinary. In a brief transitional passage, with all the urgency of strict tempo, Francesco tries to drag Amalia away by force—not to be his wife, but his servant and whore ('druda'). She at first protests, then pretending to fall on his neck she snatches the dagger from his belt. She now has him covered, so to speak, and the scene is set for a stretta of mutual defiance (*Ti scosta, o malnato*), Amalia leading off in A flat major, Francesco replying with the same musical phrase, no less abusively, in F major. But there are no striking modulations from one to the other as in the F major–A major duet for baritone and soprano in *Giovanna d'Arco*. Nor can all the energy of its cello sextuplets disguise the fact that in style and character the movement is just too near Amalia's joyous *Carlo vive* to be convincing as an expression of fury and contempt.

Scene 2: a forest near Prague

A swift, panther-like motion is set up by the strings: C minor, subdued and ominous. Two groups of 'Masnadieri' appear from opposite sides of the stage and carve up the string melody in a series of staccato exchanges, as they tell each other the latest news. Rolla has been captured and put in prison. This very day he is to be

206

hanged. When the captain heard of this he vowed that he would make a holocaust of the whole town by way of revenge. The crotchets motion dissolves into flickering quavers, on unison violas and violins as flames are seen reflected in the backcloth. Ex. 206 is now thundered out by the full orchestra. High above the general din soprano voices rise in chromatic hysteria. Then a group of terrified women flee across the back of the stage, and their wailing can still be heard in the distance after the music has subsided. This is a brilliantly effective movement and one—we might add—that Verdi would never have risked unless he knew he had a strong chorus at his disposal. The fact that the melody is based on a two-bar figure gives it a sense of development as it progresses through the various related keys. The scoring is simple but sure—strings only, with occasional woodwind sustaining, and brief but telling outbursts on trombone and cimbasso. After such economy the tutti erupts with astonishing force, epitomizing a disaster quite adequately within the space of half a minute, before spending itself in a long diminuendo. Then the movement suddenly changes from triple to double time. Bustling triplets and an arpeggio figure reminiscent of Leporello's 'Catalogue Song' create an air of expectancy. The robbers, gazing offstage, are startled to see Rolla burst joyfully on to the scene with a group of his comrades—'snatched', he tells them all, 'from the gallows' noose' (a phrase, be it noted, for which he needs a low B). The others naturally want to hear more, but he feels unequal to the task of telling them, and in any case he is not a principal. So the story of his rescue is entrusted to his companions, all of whom are basses, in a brisk melody in Verdi's most winningly popular style (*I cittadini correano alla festa*):

207

It is the triumphant glee of Rustighello and his spies in *Lucrezia Borgia* ('Non far motto') with a higher voltage. Next Carlo enters with a sad, preoccupied air. He tells them they must be ready to leave at dawn. This they are happy enough to do and they resume their rollicking chorus of *Viva il masnadier* as they march away with Rolla, leaving Carlo alone gazing at the sunset, 'radiant and glorious, like a hero's death'. But the beauties of nature are not for him. Heaven and earth alike have rejected him. His companions are robbers; his occupation crime. And the memory of the sweet, innocent girl whom he left at home only adds to his sorrow. The romanza (*Di ladroni attorniato*) shows Carlo for the first time as a 'tenor of sensibility' in the Donizettian mould; and indeed despite the artificiality of the muted string accompaniment its affinity with that archetype of all nineteenth-century Italian tenor romances, 'Una furtiva lagrima', is proclaimed in the opening phrases:

208

It also belongs to that purely Italian genre of melodies which open in the minor and end in the relative major, with that sense of poignancy and longing after lost happiness that results from a cadence in which there is incomplete repose. There is an almost feminine suppleness about the vocal line, emphasized by the heavy, blunt choruses that precede and follow it. After the brief oasis of poetry Rolla and the rest of the band come in to announce that the wood has been surrounded. Carlo, once more the ruthless robber chief, rallies their spirits as brass fanfares launch a noisy final chorus (*Su fratelli corriamo alla pugna*) with the hint of a French march about it; otherwise of no great distinction.

ACT III
Scene 1: a deserted place by a forest near Old Moor's castle

So far Maffei's libretto has followed Schiller's play closely enough, merely condensing the action and altering the order of some of the scenes. Here he departs from it more radically. It was natural enough to omit the baiting of Father Dominic which occurs when the robbers are surrounded. But the decision of Carlo to revisit his home is vital to the drama. It is prompted by his meeting with a would-be recruit whose story is very similar to his own, and, in consequence, Carlo plans to spy out the land incognito, even to his beloved Amalia. Maffei needed a love duet at this point and altered the plot accordingly. The result is if anything rather more plausible than in Schiller, if not as strong. For how, one might reasonably ask, did Amalia manage to hold out against Francesco? That on one occasion she proved too quick for him means nothing. Yet in Schiller's Act IV she is calmly conducting the disguised Karl round the family portraits, sadly, but with all the conscious dignity of unsullied virtue. Maffei's heroine however, after her experience in the family graveyard, decides to flee from the castle. Act III then opens with a spate of agitato music—pounding cellos and basses, panting violins and violas, syncopations, displaced accents all mounting to a tutti cut short by Amalia's high F sharp as she rushes on to the scene. The vocal line then descends to a calm, peaceful cadence, supported by smooth string chords. Alone at last, and safe; but her relief does not last long. Almost at once the sound of rough voices breaks in on her thoughts; their melody is not unlike that of the banqueters in the previous act, but the words are more alarming: 'To rob, to wench, to burn, to kill is our delight', and she is

209

convinced rightly enough that she has fallen among thieves. Then she sees someone moving among the trees. The music becomes agitated again, as the stranger approaches her; there is a brief interchange, the music mounts to a climax and— Amalia and Carlo fly to one another's arms in a very short prestissimo movement of extrovert joy, full of wide leaps and high woodwind doublings (*T'abbraccio, o Carlo/Amalia*). Then Amalia remembers with a shudder the distant voices she has just heard. She and Carlo must fly quickly. Carlo tells her not to be afraid—she will be safe with him, but in an aside he prays that she may never find out to 'what infernal monsters' he has bound himself. The andantino of the duet (*Qual mare, qual terra*) is laid out, rather unusually, as a dialogue, a musical stichomythia, line by line, and designed therefore on a bigger scale than most of its kind and with more close repetition (Ex. 210, opposite).

Amalia relates how false word was brought of Carlo's death, and at length the voices come together as they seem to see the rainbow against the stormclouds of the past. In mood and character it is like a forerunner of the famous 'Ai nostri monti' (*Il Trovatore*), with its suggestion of delicate nostalgia. The conjunction in sixths as always has the effect of throwing the tenor more strongly into relief; but in deference to Jenny Lind's abilities there are some light embellishments for both voices. As in the soprano–tenor duet from *I Lombardi* effective use is made of displaced accents in the long cadential phrase leading down from the melody's climax.

The andantino concluded, the lovers continue their dialogue in a rapid transition. Amalia tells Carlo of his father's death and Francesco's attempt on her honour.

Now that she has found her Carlo she will follow him to death and beyond. 'Fair soul betrayed,' Carlo cries: but for the moment he accepts her view that they will be together in heaven. This thought is the basis of the utterly conventional stretta (*Lassù, lassù risplendere*) of which the most that can be said is that it must have provided the prima donna with a first-rate opportunity of showing off her famous trill.

Scene 2: in the forest—near by a ruined keep

Here presumably is the source of the singing that Amalia heard in the previous scene, and it is still going on. After a minatory introduction (bassoons, trombones and cimbasso alternating with strings), a steady orchestral crescendo brings back Ex. 209 (*Le rube, gli stupri*). It turns out to be the first of a chain of undistinguished choral movements, which form a setting of the song that appears in Schiller's IV, v. It is a blood-thirsty hymn to the glories of a bandit's life, the text as unremarkable as the music. A rapid waltz recalls the demons in *Giovanna d'Arco*:

After a reprise and coda, Carlo enters to be greeted in chorus. They may rest, he tells them; he himself will keep watch; and the robbers hum themselves to sleep with Ex. 211, here scored in the most tinkly manner imaginable, all violins and high woodwind. The scene is now set for Carlo's great suicide speech (Schiller, IV, v). In the original it is a powerful piece of Teutonic rhetoric—Hamlet's 'To be or not to be.' in terms of *Sturm und Drang*. Speculation brings Karl von Moor, like Hamlet, to the brink of the abyss. He gazes down and his eyes try to fathom the darkness. Then the will to live exerts itself. 'Shall I yield to misery the palm of victory over myself? No, I will endure it. Misery shall blunt its edge against my pride.' He might have said, with Beethoven: 'I will seize Fate by the throat.'

It is obviously one of the high points of the play, and ideally should be of the opera as well. Yet in all this theorizing and speculation there is very little for an Italian composer, except the final assertion of will. Verdi dispatches the entire soliloquy in the lightest of string-accompanied recitatives, merely adding a tutti at the point where Carlo throws aside his pistol.

A stealthy figure in the strings warns of someone approaching. Carlo steps back into the trees. It is the elusive Arminio, apparently carrying something and making for the ruined keep. He calls out softly and is answered by a hollow voice that seems to come from underground. He hands some food through the bars of the gate, and is just about to leave when Carlo leaps out and grasps him by the shoulder. Arminio is certain that this is one of Francesco's men and begins to babble excuses. Again the voice calls from inside the keep. Carlo dismisses Arminio who is only too glad to make his escape. Then he opens the gate of the keep and drags out a frail old man. The figure is scarcely recognizable, but the voice is that of Massimiliano. His ghost, thinks Carlo; and bassoons and trombones suggest a momentary frisson. But Massimiliano reassures him as a brief dialogue movement gets under way (*Ombra non son*): he is not yet a ghost, though only just alive. What villain has imprisoned him in this tower, Carlo wants to know? 'My son Francesco,' the old man replies; he proceeds to tell his story.

The 'Racconto di Massimiliano' (*Un ignoto tre lune or saranno*) is a step on the road to the great narrations in *Il Trovatore*, if a slightly faltering one. The narrative arias of the 1830s differ from those which express a state of mind only in that they are longer than two stanzas and usually include moments of pure declamation to draw attention to the important points of the story. Donizetti is particularly skilful at blending the lyrical and declamatory elements—cf. 'Regnava nel silenzio' (*Lucia di Lammermoor*) and 'Nella fatal di Rimini' (*Lucrezia Borgia*). In *Il Trovatore* Verdi was to recognize two kinds of narrative aria: the lyrical ('Tacea la notte') in which the story is recollected in tranquillity, and its details submerged in the melodic flow; and the dramatic ('Condotta ell'era in ceppi') where each event is intensely relived, the declamatory element is well to the fore, and the form itself much freer. Massimiliano's story ideally needs the second treatment but is given the first. Nowhere does it break the lyrical mould, being essentially a minor–major romanza inflated by an extra strophe to allow the full story to be given: how the news of Carlo's death caused the old man to faint, how he revived to find himself in a coffin; how Francesco, finding him still alive, had cried out, 'Old carcase, will you live for ever?' and finally thrown him into a dungeon. The accompanimental figure changes with each strophe but without any graphic effect; the aria as a whole seems artificially prolonged. His story finished, the old man swoons. Carlo leaps up, fires his pistol to awake the robbers. He points to the prostrate figure of Massimiliano and summons them to aid him in avenging his father's wrongs. His tense fury is conveyed by the strict march of his declamation (slow but within a fast pulse) and the chords for woodwind and brass which punctuate it. The final phrase reminds us that for Carlo the composer originally had in mind the 'tenore della maledizione', with his sustained power in the lower, 'baritonic' register and his ringing top.

212

Finally he makes them swear a mighty oath, far more terrible than the vow of brotherhood in Act I, to be the instrument of God's vengeance. Timpani, horns and bassoon create a suitably sombre backcloth for the trumpet blasts of Carlo's anathema (*Giuriam ognun*) taken up by the chorus line by line in harmony according to the standard 'giuramento' formula (as exemplified in Donizetti's *Marin Faliero* and Rossini's *Guillaume Tell*, amongst others). The downward minor arpeggio is to make a striking appearance later on as a symbol of retribution.

213

The final A major section (*Struggitrice ira di Dio*) has an emphatic swing to be recalled years later in a similar oath sworn by Otello and Iago (Ex. 214, overleaf).

ACT IV
Scene 1: a gallery in Moor's castle

There is a flurry of agitato music from the orchestra as Francesco comes rushing in terror from his room. He calls for Arminio and the servants and orders them to summon the minister. Can the dead rise again? Can dreams ever come true? (Brass and bassoon chords underline the horror that he feels.) Francesco's vision of the Day of Judgment (*Pareami che sorto da lauto convito*) is another narrative aria, far more ambitious than Massimiliano's. The poem teems with the kind of images that would be expected to appeal to the future composer of the 'Dies Irae'—the earth taking fire, the graves giving up their dead, the three shining figures on Mount Sinai—and finally the judgment on Francesco himself: 'As each hour passed some mortal sin was thrown into my scale; yet each was outweighed by the blood of

214

atonement. Then at last an old man wasted with hunger came up, plucked a white hair from his head and cast it into the scale; whereupon the cup of my sins plunged downward, the other was lost in the clouds, and a voice of thunder was heard: "Accursed one, the Son of God was not crucified for thee." . . .' This last quoted passage is beautifully and skilfully realized within a free lyrical design which reflects the sense of the words at every point, proceeding to a climax that is totally convincing in terms of musical logic. The early part is both too schematic and too diffuse. Every novel harmonic or instrumental effect is diminished by symmetrical repetition, yet the general shape is slack. The fact is that here, as elsewhere in the opera, Maffei has given the composer more verses than he knew what to do with. Even so there are some powerful moments—tuttis like hammerblows with rushing strings and squealing piccolo, that predict the infinitely more powerful day of wrath to be written in the 1870s.

Pastor Moser is announced by powerful unisons on trumpet, trombone and strings. Has Francesco sent for him in a spirit of mockery? Or is he beginning to be afraid of the God whose existence he denies? Like Pope Leo in *Attila* Moser provides an instance of Verdi using a strong bass voice for a special effect at a special moment of the drama. His words 'tu tremi' are accompanied fortissimo by an upward-thrusting arpeggio figure which plays an important part in the scene. So too does the slow *downward* arpeggio in which Moser parades the majestic extension of his voice.

215

Francesco affects to be sceptical as usual. If, he asks, the soul is immortal, what sins so provoke Moser's God as to annihilate it. 'There are two,' the minister replies. 'Patricide and fratricide.' Arminio returns with the news that a crowd of horsemen are attacking the castle. 'Away to the chapel,' cries Francesco, 'and pray for me.' Distant voices are heard crying out that the bastion has fallen. Francesco begs Moser to grant him absolution. To a still more impressive version of Ex. 215(b) set in a minor key and outlined by trumpets, trombones, bassoons and cimbasso Moser declares that only God can forgive. The duettino with chorus that follows (*Trema iniquo*) has just the three-dimensional quality that Francesco's solo lacks. Both arpeggio figures are combined in the opening theme with its unmistakable reference to Carlo's 'giuramento'):

216

Francesco's despair finds expression in agonized descending phrases which fall like waves on the breakwater of Moser's inexorable line. For the first time in his life Francesco finds himself praying. Then all at once he rises. Hell shall never make sport of him, he says, and as chorus and orchestra mount to a climax he rushes out.

Scene 2: a forest—as in Act III, Scene 2

In the delicious string tremolos which open the scene, Verdi gives another foretaste of his later style, with its side-slipping sixths (Ex. 217, overleaf).

The atmosphere is peaceful, almost idyllic, in the greatest possible contrast to what has gone before. Massimiliano is seated on a stone; Carlo is beside him. The old man feels deeply remorseful about both his sons. He has no wish to be revenged on Francesco, and, as always, he hopes that the spirit of his lost elder son will forgive

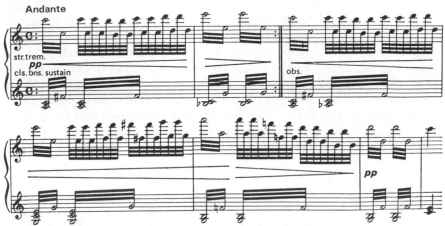

the wrong he did him. Carlo, moved, still cannot bring himself to reveal his
identity. True to his calling he demands a ransom for the old man, but he also
begs Massimiliano for a father's blessing, and the old man readily grants it. The
scene is suffused with a Bellinian tenderness, with phrases of recitative so lyrical as to
sound like fragmentary arias. Bellini-like too is the duet *Come il bacio d'un padre
amoroso* with its see-saw accompaniment of second violins. But the form is purely
Verdian—a dissimilar duet condensed so that its sections are merged into an
apparently monolithic structure. Tenor and bass entries are for once only slightly
contrasted (one idea is almost a variation on the other). Where the voices join, the
cellos add richness and warmth to the bass line. The tranquillity is soon shattered.
A stealthy footfall of strings brings back a group of robbers, with the news that
someone has escaped; someone so indefinite as not to need a pronoun in Italian.
But Carlo knows that they refer to Francesco and—improbably for Schiller's
hero—gives thanks to heaven. 'Mercy be henceforward our watchword!' he cries.
But now another band of robbers is heard approaching in triumph. They have
captured a rare prize—Amalia. The rhythm reverts to the tense 6/8 that preceded
the swearing of the oath in Act III. Amalia cries out to Carlo, 'her bridegroom', to
protect her. Massimiliano exclaims in surprise; Carlo becomes hysterical. 'Tear her
from my neck! Kill her! Kill him! Kill me—yourselves . . . let the whole world
perish. . . . Die, father! These your deliverers are robbers and murderers; your
Carlo is their Captain!' At these words Schiller's Moor dies, but Verdi's Massimiliano is needed for the final trio with chorus and must therefore remain in this
world a little longer. After a thunderous explosion of anger and despair, Carlo
begins the final number (*Caduto è il reprobo*). It was compared at the time with
the closing trio of *Ernani*; but there is an important difference. After tenor and
soprano the third element in the tug-of-war is not Massimiliano, the bass, but the
chorus who enter with shattering brutality at the twenty-third bar. Carlo is prepared to pay his debt to the society he has outraged and spend the rest of his life in
prison. His resolution is expressed in a strophe of desolating sadness to which the
orchestra chords give declamatory bite (like Macbeth he is no Edgardo or Gennaro).
In melting, lyrical contrast Amalia replies that she will never leave him whether he

be angel or demon. Massimiliano's entry still harping on the string of remorse is hardly noticed. In this final crisis he has no role to play other than to fill out the vocal design and in one or two crucial places to keep the rhythm going. Yet altogether it is a worthy finale, with all the spaciousness and grandeur that one expects of Verdi's best ensembles. We may notice again the arpeggio figure of retribution as the robbers remind Carlo of his solemn oath to share their lives. In a last snatch of declamation Carlo cries: 'Hear me, you fiends! Each of you staked for me a life full of infamy and shame. I sacrifice an angel to you.' And with that he stabs Amalia to the heart. Collapse of elderly gentleman may be expected to follow.

It is difficult to find a single overriding cause for the failure of I Masnadieri as a work of art. Maffei's indigestible libretto was partly to blame together with Verdi's reluctance to ask so distinguished a poet to change his verses. For instance, Carlo's long solo (Vedete quel vecchio) leading to the 'Giuramento' of the third act is too protracted to make its full effect; also it puts an intolerable strain on the soloist who has to keep up the tension that finally explodes in the andante (Giuri ognun) and leads to that besetting sin of Verdi's early style—emphasis without depth. Then, too, Schiller's plot is less suitable material than might appear. His characters have all the high emotional voltage that could be desired; but they are too turned in on themselves. Amalia is a nullity; and her part was being taken by a singer whose voice Verdi found to be less interesting than he had hoped. The part of Carlo needs ideally more force and variety than a tenor voice can afford. To Francesco Verdi made an interesting reference eight years later when he was in correspondence with Somma about King Lear. He found that Somma had made the bastard Edmund too savage in his villainy—'I would make him a frank scoundrel, but not a revolting one like Francesco in Schiller's Die Räuber, but one who mocks and despises everything and commits the most atrocious crimes with the greatest indifference. . . . I would be for giving Edmund a mocking character because this will result in more musical variety; if you represent him differently I should have to give him one of those huge, shouting phrases. Contempt and irony are expressed in mezzo voce. . . .'[*] Clearly, then, Verdi liked his villains offhand where possible; otherwise he felt obliged to make them shout. Francesco has all the villainy of Iago but without Iago's lightness of touch.

There remain some fine things in I Masnadieri: the prelude, the tenor cavatina and the quartet finale to Act I; the choruses and tenor romanza of Act II; the love duet in Act III; the duet between Moser and Francesco and the trio finale to Act IV. But they are isolated, not part of a general scheme like the best of Macbeth.[†] To account for this seemingly backward step we should remember that I Masnadieri, although completed after Macbeth, was conceived in all essentials before, during the composer's long convalescence at Recoaro. It has more in common with the world of Attila than with that of the middle-period masterpieces which here and there it prefigures.

A brief epilogue: In December 1869 Léon Escudier wrote to Verdi announcing a revival of I Masnadieri at the Théâtre des Italiens and asking for any special

---

[*] Letter to Somma, 8.1.1855. A. Pascolato, Re Lear e Un Ballo in Maschera (Città di Castello, 1902), pp. 70–4.

[†] See also Basevi, pp. 121–2, on the lack of a consistent 'colorito' throughout the score.

instructions regarding its performance. Verdi replied. 'I can't tell you anything about it because I don't have it to hand and can't remember it. I know that the last two acts are better than the first two, in which perhaps you'll need to make some cuts—*possibly nothing more than the repetitions of the so-called cabalettas.*'★

Ponder well this last statement, all ye purists for whom the omission of cabaletta repeats in nineteenth-century Italian opera constitutes an act of sacrilege!

★Italics mine. Letter to L. Escudier 14.12.1869, transcribed S. Casale, *Newsletter of the American Institute of Verdi Studies*, xi (March 1983), p. 9.

14 JÉRUSALEM

JÉRUSALEM

Opera in four acts
by
ALPHONSE ROYER AND GUSTAVE VAËZ

First performed at the
Académie Royale de Musique, Paris,
26 November 1847

GASTON, Vicomte de Béarn	PRIMO TENORE	Gilbert Louis Duprez
THE COUNT OF TOULOUSE	BARITONO COMPRIMARIO	Charles Portheaut
ROGER, brother of the Count	PRIMO BASSO	Adolphe Louis Joseph Alizard
ADHEMAR DE MONTHEIL, Papal Legate	SECONDO BASSO	Hippolyte Bremont
RAYMOND, Gaston's squire	SECONDO TENORE	M. Barbot
A SOLDIER	SECONDO BASSO	M. Prévost
A HERALD	SECONDO BASSO	M. Molinier
THE EMIR OF RAMLA	SECONDO BASSO	M. Guignot
AN OFFICER OF THE EMIR	SECONDO TENORE	M. Koenig
HÉLÈNE, daughter of the Count	PRIMA DONNA SOPRANO	Mme Julian Van Gelder
ISAURE, her companion	SECONDA DONNA	Mme Muller

Knights—ladies—pages—soldiers—pilgrims—penitents—Arab Sheiks—
Women of the Harem—people of Ramla

The action takes place in Toulouse and Palestine

Epoch: 1095–1099

Sooner or later an aspiring Italian composer of the nineteenth century was bound to want to make his debut at the Paris Opéra; and not for financial reasons only. On the whole, Italians, little as they liked to admit the fact, produced their best work for Paris. The grandiose scale of French serious opera with its choruses and ballet offered them more scope, while the more intelligent, more dramatic quality of the average French libretto forced them to take greater thought for the drama instead of relying for their effects mainly on the quality of the human voice. The whole apparatus of French serious opera had been designed to outweigh the lack of really good native singers. Moreover, it had been born during the Grand Siècle. It served the same audiences that frequented the plays of Racine and Corneille, who expected similar qualities from their opera. They loved artifice; but it had to be artifice for adults, with something to engage the intelligence as well as to delight the senses. Not surprisingly, those who in the late eighteenth century wished to drag Italian opera seria out of its rut of mindless sententiousness looked to France for their models. Traetta set translations of Rameau's librettos; Mozart wrote *Idomeneo* to a libretto based on one which had already served Campra; Gluck's *Orfeo* even in its original form is essentially a French-type opera in miniature, complete with choruses and ballet. The same pattern was maintained well into the following century, surviving the Revolution, the Napoleonic Wars and all those changes of taste and fashion which the romantic age brought about. More and more Italians crossed the Alps having found Italy too narrow for their talents—Cherubini, Spontini, Paër, then Rossini. Bellini, before he died, was making plans for a French grand opera. Donizetti's last years were divided mainly between Paris and Vienna; but it was for the Paris Opéra that he produced what is arguably the greatest of his tragedies—*La Favorite*, in strict obedience to Parisian taste. For the canary-fanciers and Italophiles there was always the Théâtre des Italiens. Lovers of serious music drama preferred the Académie de Musique, as it is still officially called to this day.

The 1830s and '40s were the golden age of the Paris Opéra. It had begun when, following the Revolution of 1830, the Opéra, previously a state institution, run by government officials and financed by taxes levied on all other operatic performances in France, was leased out to a private entrepreneur. The new manager Véron used all the resources of publicity and advertisement to make the theatre in the Rue le Pelletier the foremost lyric stage in the world. The presiding dramatic genius was Eugène Scribe, an accomplished playwright as well as a librettist. The musical pillars of the new establishment were Auber, Meyerbeer and Halévy, at whose hands grand opera achieved a complexity and scale undreamed of before. Schumann and Mendelssohn might sneer; yet, so long as one does not mistake Meyerbeer and his colleagues for great composers (and many Frenchmen at the time *did* so mistake them), there is no harm in admitting that Parisian grand opera was a stimulating influence all over Europe; and that it played an important part in the genesis of Wagnerian music-drama—though, paradoxically, it was the Frenchmen Auber and Halévy that chiefly influenced Wagner's style, whereas Verdi, as we shall see, had more to learn from the German Meyerbeer.

Verdi's first invitation to Paris came in 1845, shortly after the production of *Giovanna d'Arco*, through Léon Escudier.* At the time Verdi was already behind schedule with his Italian commitments; and for two years he held out against a definite engagement. Finally in 1847, with *I Masnadieri* safely behind him, he accepted a contract to provide an opera for the autumn season of that year.† There was no time, he maintained, to write an entirely new work; he proposed instead to follow the precedent of Rossini and fit up an old opera, grafting it on to a new plot and composing fresh numbers where necessary.‡ Of his eleven operas to date the one most suited to such treatment seemed *I Lombardi*, which became *Jérusalem*, much as Rossini's *Maometto II* became *Le Siège de Corinthe*. On Scribe's advice the new libretto was entrusted to the poets Alphonse Royer and Gustave Vaëz (authors of Donizetti's *La Favorite*), who kept the crusading ambience of Solera's original but little else. Preparations went ahead smoothly enough. Pillet had been succeeded by two directors, Nestor Roqueplan and Charles Duponchel, who spared no trouble and expense. The premiere was indeed a success, or as much of one as the restless state of the French capital would allow. Louis-Philippe had two acts of it performed at the Tuileries and created Verdi a Chevalier de la Légion d'Honneur. Financially, it was no less profitable, since Verdi had been paid for it as for an entirely new opera. Later he sold the Italian rights to Ricordi who brought out the score of *Gerusalemme* with a dedication to the ex-singer who was beginning to play an ever more prominent part in Verdi's life—Giuseppina Strepponi.

Biographers, English and Italian alike, have all followed Basevi§ in denigrating *Jérusalem* as a cheap money-spinner, vastly inferior to *I Lombardi*. Even the fairminded Frank Walker finds this refashioning of an earlier work together with the hasty writing of *Il Corsaro* among 'the least conscientious actions of Verdi's career'.¶ But the way in which Verdi describes the progress of *Jérusalem*, and his negotiations with Ricordi over the Italian version, do not suggest indifference or lack of conscientiousness. To Léon Escudier he wrote:

> I've examined the second act over and over again and find two faults which are absolutely basic. The first is that the pilgrims' chorus will fall quite flat if it follows straight after Roger's aria because it has the same character and it will seem too long; the other fault is that Hélène's aria has no dramatic interest, nothing to set it off and is utterly useless where it stands. For myself, I'm quite convinced that at that moment Hélène must have had a surprise. Something unexpected and pleasurable must have happened to her to make her break out in a cabaletta full of enthusiasm. It seems to me, the only way to set this right is to put Hélène's aria immediately after Roger's and it doesn't matter if that means two arias one after the other because one of them is solemn and the other very brilliant so that the musical effect is of one aria in two contrasted movements. Please pass all this on to Royer and Vaëz. As you know, in this

* See letter from Muzio to Barezzi, 26.5.1845. Garibaldi, pp. 202–3. For subsequent overtures from Pillet, see Walker, pp. 180–2.

† See letters from Muzio to Barezzi, 8.8.1847 and 23.8.1847. Garibaldi, pp. 349–53. Surprisingly there is no letter of acceptance in the *Copialettere*.

‡ *Le Siège de Corinthe* (1826) and *Moïse* (1827) were both constructed in this way.

§ Pp. 123–32. For a far more objective re-appraisal see G. Pugliese, 'Jérusalem e Gerusalemme' in *Quaderni dell' Istituto di Studi Verdiani 2: Gerusalemme* (Parma, 1963), pp. 45–86.

¶ Walker, p. 184.

opera [*I Lombardi*]—no matter whether it's performed well or badly—the pieces which never fail to come off are this aria, the chorus and the trio. If we leave the scheme as it is we run the risk of letting two of them go for nothing.*

The pilgrims' chorus is not the 'Processione' from Act III of *I Lombardi* but 'O Signore dal tetto natio' from Act IV; Hélène's aria is, of course, the Cabaletta della Visione, and Roger's aria is Pagano's romanza from Act II—the only one of the three to keep its original position in the drama.

Royer and Vaëz saw their way to meeting Verdi's demands; and once rehearsals were under way, the composer waxed enthusiastic. 'Transformed out of recognition' is how he described the new *Lombardi*.† Biographers insist that in remaking the original opera Verdi had taken away its character; for which, like Sheridan's Sir Fretful Plagiary, we should be—at least to some extent—obliged to him.

Verdi was no less concerned about the proposed Italian version. 'If I can find an Italian poet here,' he wrote to Ricordi more than a month before the premiere, 'I'll get the Italian version made myself; if not, I'll send you the French score, but on condition that you get Muzio to see to the underlay.'‡ He also insisted that Ricordi should exact a fine of 1,000 francs from any theatre which dared to give the work in a mutilated or truncated form. Only the ballet could be omitted. This is not the behaviour of one who does not care. When at a performance at La Scala in 1850 he heard that the duettino in Act II and various other pieces had been cut, he expressed his annoyance to Ricordi.§

The accepted view then is due, one suspects, partly to Italian chauvinism, partly also to the conviction that music designed for one context can never be effective in another. Some writers may have been misled by the cynical tone of Verdi's letters to his friends in Milan, with their tales of showing impresarios the door, wanting nothing to do with music and so forth; as if this were anything more than the tone with which Brahms and Elgar liked to tease their more earnest female admirers. In an age when every artist is supposed to be in touch with the infinite, it is merely Verdi's claim to the right of being a hard-worked professional like any other, and one who would be only too willing to lay down his tools the next day.

But of course the real evidence against the traditional judgment lies in the score itself, which hardly anyone seems to have taken the trouble to examine. The revisions are very extensive and, with the exception of the uninteresting ballet, nearly all are improvements. The diffuse drama which Solera had distilled from an epic poem is replaced by a far tauter, more concentrated plot which not only makes fewer demands on our credulity than *I Lombardi* but also avoids the problem of a second tenor who needs to be weightier and more heroic than the first. The various numbers, some newly composed, others repositioned and sometimes elaborated, are soldered together by linking passages of far greater significance than the string-accompanied recitative which they replace. The entire opera, as befits one designed for the French stage, is more 'through-composed' than its parent work; and only a sentimentalist could regret the omission of all that was most embarrassingly naïf in the original score. If the final result is something less than a masterpiece, this should

---

* Undated letter to L. Escudier, 1847. J. G. Prod'homme, *R.M.I.* (1928), p. 7.
† Letter to Countess Appiani, 22.9.1847. *Copialettere*, p. 464.
‡ Letter to Giovanni Ricordi, 15.10.1847. *Copialettere*, pp. 44–5.
§ Letter to Giovanni Ricordi, 5.1.1851. *Copialettere*, p. 112.

not surprise us either, if we know *Macbeth*. One of the drawbacks of Verdi's essentially conservative turn of mind was that in revision he rarely discarded enough. Having observed that the Cabaletta della Visione never failed to make an effect he insisted on giving it prominence in *Jérusalem*; whereas, in fact, it is the type of piece which he was beginning to outgrow. A high point in *I Lombardi*, it is a low point in *Jérusalem*. This and other weaknesses taken into account, *Jérusalem* remains to anyone but an Italian chauvinist the better of the two operas.

Verdi's first improvement (a pressing one) was to give the opera an adequate prelude. The opening of *Jérusalem* is no longer a series of commonplace disjointed phrases but a coherent dissertation on a theme which he introduced into the last act; a short, plastic motif foreshadowing that of the prelude to *Aïda*. Its first appearance (*x*), unharmonized on unison cellos, is almost casual: a feminine reply to the sombre menace of the opening two phrases (both from Act III), with their colouring of bassoons, cornets and lower brass.*

218

Both key and character recall the slow movement of Beethoven's G major piano concerto. A few bars later, after a powerful rejoinder, Ex. 218 returns to be developed in a canon. Later still it emerges as a full-blown cello melody decorated with violin semiquavers in the manner of the *Ernani* prelude; and a coda based on the same theme leads us through one of those Neapolitan modulations (E minor–F major) of which Verdi was becoming so fond to a supreme climax, triple forte, then dies away with reminiscences of the opening. The piece is full of effective detail in both harmony and scoring; the harmonic clashes of the canon softened by its uniform string tone; the scale of pizzicato quavers, not indicated in the vocal score, that decorates Ex. 218 as it turns into F major—all these should be proof enough that Verdi was not scamping his work. Interesting, if slightly crude, is the rapid trumpet figure at bar 10, like an urgent call to battle. It was Verdi's first attempt to avail himself of the distinction between trumpets and cornets, both of which existed in the orchestra of the Paris Opéra. Cornets normally took over the melodic aspects of high brass writing, but a rapping figure such as this could only be effective on a trumpet.

* For the brass bass the Paris Opéra provided not the cimbasso but the nimbler, thinner-sounding ophicleide. At no point does Verdi seem to have turned this difference to particular use.

ACT I

Scene: a gallery connecting the Count of Toulouse's palace with his private chapel; at the back are steps leading to the garden.

The year is 1095, as in the first scene of *I Lombardi*. The Council of Claremont has taken place and a crusade is in the air; but we are no longer concerned with the Lombard contingent, still less with an apocryphal Arvino, destined to lead them to the Holy City. The man in command is that authentic, historical figure Count Raymond of Toulouse, who, with Boemund, can claim to be a real leader of the First Crusade. (If he is not referred to as such but only as 'the Count', this is because, by some surely remediable coincidence, the hero's squire is also called Raymond.) Hélène, the new Giselda, is the Count's daughter. When the curtain rises she is discovered keeping a clandestine appointment with her lover, Gaston, Vicomte de Béarn. Their scene is framed by a crescendo and decrescendo of tremolo strings, like the rustling of a night breeze. Gaston's first words, as he hastens to Hélène's side, are 'Non, ce bruit n'était rien'—a cunning use of operatic convention for naturalistic ends and completely lost in Bassi's translation, 'Van' è il timor'. But dawn is not far off and Gaston must leave. 'Without having promised to renounce your hatred of my father?' Hélène asks. Gaston has good reason to hate the man who killed his own father in a civil war; but he is ready to give up the feud if the Count permits him to marry Hélène. The lovers then take their leave in a tiny duet of fifteen bars (*Adieu mon bien aimé*), unaccompanied except for a solo horn, which adds a third real part. An interesting example, this, of the greater flexibility of French as distinct from Italian operatic forms, since no Italian opera of the time would have accommodated a love duet as small as this, while the solo horn accompaniment is an instrumental refinement characteristic of Meyerbeerian French opera, to be compared with the viola d'amore accompaniment to Raoul's aria in *Les Huguenots*.

219

As Gaston leaves a bell is heard tolling the Ave Maria for Angelus. Isaure, Hélène's maid and confidante, comes out of the palace; and Hélène suggests that they both kneel and offer up a prayer for Gaston's safety. The prayer is of course Giselda's 'Salve Maria'. The scoring is for reduced strings, flute and clarinet, as in *I Lombardi*, and very well the music sounds in its new context. Hélène and Isaure now retire into the Count's palace while the orchestra plays a short interlude depicting the sunrise. It is of the same order as the clearing of the sky in *Attila*, both pieces standing beneath the shadow of Félicien David's *Le Désert*. There is the same clever if essentially shallow scoring with effective use of bright instruments, particularly trumpet, flute and piccolo. Also the reduced string strength of the previous number has enabled Verdi like David to achieve a particularly subtle crescendo by adding more stringed instruments every few bars. Towards the end, the gallery has begun to fill with people, the lords and ladies of Count Raymond's entourage. It then comes as a slight shock to hear the naïf banda music from the first scene of *I Lombardi*, fortunately scored for orchestra and unencumbered by any narrative, since the dialogue between Hélène and Gaston has told us all we need to know for the moment. Shorter than the original, *Enfin voici le jour propice* is merely a chorus of unambiguous joy. This day shall see an end to civil war, and all Christendom united in a holy enterprise. The A flat major episode (*Non plus de guerre*) is here set not for men only as in *I Lombardi*, but for full chorus in unison. Finally the Count comes out of the palace with his brother Roger, Hélène and Isaure. At the same time Gaston arrives from the outside with his squire and a company of knights. The Count is the first to extend the hand of brotherhood. Before they set forth on the Crusade, he says, their two families are to be reconciled by the Holy Church. In token of their new friendship he will bestow his daughter's hand on the Vicomte de Béarn, son of his old enemy. Amid the general happiness there is one dissident voice: that of Roger, the new Pagano, consumed by an incestuous passion for his niece. Strong meat for the 1840s! But it solves the generation problem, which besets *I Lombardi*. Roger's jealous fury is suggested by tremolo violins, diminished seventh harmony and a fidgeting figure on cellos and basses, similar to the one which will recur throughout *Simon Boccanegra* when a spirit of vengeance is in the air. It contrasts most effectively with Gaston's suave expression of gratitude:

220

then the voices gather together in the sextet with chorus (*Je tremble, je tremble encor*) which corresponds to the quintet ('T'assale, t'assale un tremito'), similarly scored but with, inevitably, certain differences in the vocal layout, partly to accommodate the extra tenor (Gaston's squire), and partly because the Count himself is a baritone, and there are no baritones in *I Lombardi*. In the thickest parts of the ensemble Roger is given the line which belonged to Pirro in the earlier work, Pagano's being taken by the Count. Otherwise Hélène equals Giselda; Isaure, Viclinda; Gaston, Arvino. Dramatically, one great advantage of the new version is that it presents the piece, like the quartet in *Fidelio*, as an ensemble of soliloquies, whereas Solera had certain of his characters whispering to each other. Hélène is apprehensive on her own account, not her father's; Roger has no equivalent of Pirro to conspire with. The chorus, as before, keep their suspicions to themselves. The only disadvantage of the new version is that the Count, having relinquished his musical role to Gaston, makes a rather ineffective first entry, in unison with Gaston's squire. Otherwise, like the prayer, this piece stands up very well in its new surroundings.

The next passage is composed strictly in the manner of French opera, remaining in a steady march-like tempo throughout. Gaston protests eternal allegiance to the Count. Roger again gives vent to his fury; but his sinister intentions are conveyed not by the three trombones and cimbasso but by depth of voice alone as he sinks down to a low G,★ accompanied by strings, and quickly goes out. The Count then states the first of the two melodies on which the passage is based. As it stands it is almost Bizet. A gruppetto in the fourth bar might turn it into Halévy or early Wagner:

221

The second theme on brass and wind ushers in the Papal Legate, Adhémar de Monteil:

222

★ It is noticeable that principal *basso profondo* roles associated with the French and German stages from Sarastro to Cardinal Brogni (*La Juive*) and Marcel (*Les Huguenots*) plumb the depths far more often than those written for Italy. To singers such as Derivis and Marini, for whom the terms 'principal bass' connoted 'basso cantante', too many low notes almost amounted to a breach of the *convenienze*. Such things were best left to the *comprimarii*. In the opening scenes of *Nabucco* and *Attila* Verdi takes his leading basses down to G and A flat respectively; thereafter he keeps them to the middle and upper part of their compass. It is the subsidiary characters such as Moser and Pirro who are allowed every opportunity of parading their full extension.

He has been sent by Pope Urban to nominate Raymond, Count of Toulouse, as the leader of the French crusaders. The Count, to an extension of Ex. 221, presents Gaston with his own white cloak in token of their mutual loyalty; while two pages place it round Gaston's shoulders and a development of Ex. 222, invested with the pomp of a Lully overture, leads into the grand ensemble which forms the conclusion of the first scene (*Cité du Seigneur, Saint Sépulcre*). It is merely a far more effective arrangement of 'All'empio che infrange', being designed for a chorus that does not need discreet orchestral support during awkward key changes. There are no meaningless brass flourishes and the contrast between a cappella and accompanied phrases is more sharply pointed. As in *I Lombardi* it ends in a march with side-drum (Ex. 53), applied not mechanically as in the Italian original, but with a little ornament at the start of each phrase, which gives it an extra kick of energy. Gaston, being unlike Arvino a lyric tenor, is doubled by his squire, and the male chorus is joined by another trio consisting of Hélène, Isaure and the Papal Legate, so that the crescendo is far better graded than in *I Lombardi*. The more sophisticated final stretta is extended into a longer instrumental postlude, based not on Ex. 53 itself as in *I Lombardi*, but on a theme rhythmically derived from it.

The organ (a real one this time) sounds from inside the chapel playing a different prelude to its equivalent in the earlier opera, but leading to the same chorus, here entitled *Viens, ô pécheur rebelle*, and doubled by organ throughout. The coda is expanded by a back reference to the preamble; and the curious 3/2 bars are retained. During the singing Roger has entered. In much the same words as Pagano he grimly apostrophizes the nuns, before beginning his cavatina *Oh dans l'ombre, dans le mystère*, the same as Pagano's 'Sciagurato' but written a tone down and with a simpler accompaniment. Verbally too the emphasis is less on vengeance, more on the criminal nature of his love. Hence the bleak chromatic scales in the bass of the orchestral part replacing the over-elaborate figuration of the original. What follows is entirely new. A soldier comes in and tells Roger that all is ready for the coup. He himself is unknown in Toulouse and therefore no suspicion will fall on him. Roger assures him he will not go unrewarded. All this is carried on to a swift, conspiratorial motif, developed in strict tempo; but it is in recitative that Roger gives his final instructions loud and clear. In the chapel the soldier will see two knights in golden armour. One will wear a white cloak; he is Roger's own brother, whom he loves. It is the *other* who must be murdered. The soldier slips into the chapel while a number of his comrades enter in festive mood to sing what was once the notorious 'Coro dei Sgherri'. Set to Solera's bloodthirsty words its humour is purely unconscious. But as a chorus of jollity sung by soldiers who know nothing about an impending murder (*Fier soldat de la croisade*) it is acceptable enough—a welcome moment of light relief. No Arab maid, they sing, can resist their gifts of baptism and good wine. Like Solera's Sgherri the soldiers too are implicitly rebuked by the distant voices of the nuns. Then comes Roger's cabaletta (*Ah viens démon, esprit du mal*) which is substituted for Pagano's 'Speranza di vendetta'. Longer than the original, with a ritornello and a coda of carousing soldiers, it is the only new addition which is less distinguished than the piece that it replaces. But the scène à faire which follows is so infinitely superior to the original that one wonders why it has not attracted more attention. Here Verdi makes use of that tense, rapid 6/8 rhythm, measured but with lightning bursts of semi-quavers, which he had employed to such good effect in *I Masnadieri*, and which is to figure again in the tumult scene of *Don Carlos*. The basic theme is as taut as a bow-string:

223

There are sounds of commotion inside the chapel and cries of 'Murder!' Roger is delighted at the success of his plan, then horror-struck, for the first person to come from the chapel is Gaston. 'Who has been murdered?' 'Your brother,' cries Gaston, and runs to support the fainting Hélène. By now the knights have captured the assassin. 'Save me,' Roger whispers as they drag him by, 'and I will save you.' The wounded Count is borne from the chapel accompanied by the Papal Legate, who demands to know the instigator of the crime. 'It was he,' says the soldier, indicating Gaston. 'It is false,' cries Gaston's squire, but to no purpose. All are now pointing the accusing finger at the Vicomte; and the scene is set for the adagio of the concerted finale (*Monstre parjure homicide*), half a tone below the original 'Mostro d'averno orribile'. This too has been extended and improved, partly so as to give greater variety of texture and dynamic and also to set Gaston in greater relief since he and not Roger is the object of general horror. But Roger, devoured by remorse, retains some of Pagano's most powerful asides (see Ex. 55). At length the Papal Legate pronounces an anathema on Gaston. He must surrender his sword and go into exile; every Christian must refuse him salt and bread. All recitative, this, but far grander than the corresponding passage in *I Lombardi*, if only because of the use to which Verdi has now learnt to put a solitary bass voice. The stretta (*Sur ton front est lancé l'anathème*) is again the original improved. The anticlimactic turn into the major cannot be avoided any more than in the adagio preceding, but in the latter we are spared the rather flippant tune that went with it in *I Lombardi*. Moreover, Verdi in the new version prepares us for the change of mode with a tiny episode in the submediant where previously he had kept a C minor orientation. No one could possibly say that in this work his professional conscience deserted him.

By now someone may be asking how Count Raymond could have led the First Crusade if he was murdered before it set out? Do not worry, dear reader. History is not mocked. The Count, you may rest assured, will have recovered by the time the curtain rises on Act II.

ACT II

Scene 1: the mountains of Ramla in Palestine, a few leagues from Jerusalem;
a cave beside which stands a cross crudely made; in the distance the Arab town
of Ramla.

With a slight change of locality this is the second scene of Act II in *I Lombardi*. The cavern music of the prelude is unchanged except for two timpani rolls at the beginning; but the recitative is quite different, preserving only the 'redemption motif' (if such it can be called) with flute arpeggios lightened by the omission of sustaining wind. Roger once more announces himself as a basso profondo with one of those slow downward arpeggios which never fail of their effect. Indeed, throughout the whole scene there is no attempt to add colour, as in *I Lombardi*, with trombone chords. Vocal timbre alone is sufficient. Roger is kneeling before the cross. After years of wandering in the Holy Land his hair has turned white, and he hardly recognizes the worn face that he sees reflected in the streams. Yet he still hopes that God may at last grant him pardon. Everywhere he seems to see the ghost of his murdered brother; and it is this, not the Holy Crusade, which forms the subject of his aria (*Ô jour fatal, ô crime*). Hence a striking difference between its opening phrase and that of the original:

a) I LOMBARDI

b) JÉRUSALEM

Solera's verse had included the words 'Iddio lo volle', one of the key phrases of Grossi's original poem, which needed a considerable degree of musical emphasis at an awkward point in the melody. Ideally, the second phrase should come to an equally strong cadence; and this, of course, does not happen. 'Iddio lo volle' stands out then like a climax in the wrong place; and the melodic architect in Verdi wisely simplified the French version, reserving his climaxes for later in the movement. The coda is prolonged by means of a cadenza-like phrase in which the singer parades the full extension of his voice from gamut F two octaves downward.

A speciality of French grand opera is the vividness of its mime music; not surprisingly, since Paris was the cradle of the romantic ballet. In what other city would it have been possible to write a grand opera with a non-singing mime as heroine, as Auber did in *La Muette de Portici*? Verdi, it must be said, unlike Wagner, rarely achieved anything very striking in that field; but there is a new, almost plastic quality about the music with which he introduces a pilgrim nearly dropping from fatigue. It might almost have come from Adam's *Giselle*:

Collapsing at the mouth of the cave the pilgrim gasps for water. Roger takes a gourd from his belt and puts it to the pilgrim's lips. He is not the only victim; there are others on the mountain, all dying of thirst. Roger decides to go to their aid; and he leaves to the last line of his previous aria—a phrase which here assumes a greater musical importance than in *I Lombardi*:

226

Adagio
ROGER
vn.cnt.bn. double

fais_ ô mon Dieu que je _ sau - ve_leurs jours

It is repeated twice by the orchestra after he has gone, each time with new harmonic refinements and subtleties—partly to allow Roger to make his exit before encountering the next two arrivals, who enter to a march *thème à la française* on the strings. They are Hélène and the faithful Isaure. Believing firmly in Gaston's innocence Hélène had resolved to seek him out. He was said to have gone to Palestine and there to have met his death. Hélène has come to seek the advice of the old hermit, revered by Saracens and Christians alike. At that moment, they notice the pilgrim. Is there not something familiar about him? Yes, it is Gaston's squire (four years have not changed *him*). Hélène asks for news of her lover in an urgent 'through-composed' dialogue, almost a duet with a lamenting figure on oboe and bassoon (Ex. 227, overleaf).

On hearing that Gaston is alive and a prisoner in Ramla she vents her feelings in one of those glorious long phrases which are becoming increasingly frequent in Verdi by this time (Ex. 228, see overleaf).

Then comes the 'Cabaletta della Visione', here set to the words *Quell'ivresse, bonheur suprême* and called by the French publisher, rather quaintly, 'Polonaise'. If its brilliance seems less out of place than in *I Lombardi*, this is because Ex. 228 has taken some of the emphasis away from it, so that it becomes merely a joyous kick of the heels. The structure is amplified by a new ritornello in which Hélène states her plans. She has plenty of money; she will somehow contrive to enter Ramla and see Gaston again; and so to the cabaletta repeat.* Both lamenting figures (Ex. 227) are heard again thundered out by the full orchestra in unison and followed by the sound of distant voices imploring God's mercy. A crowd of pilgrims, ragged and weary, drag themselves on to the stage. Like Gaston's squire they are dying of thirst; and they offer up one last prayer (*Ô mon Dieu ta parole est donc vaine*). It is, of course, 'O Signore dal tetto natio', identically scored except for cornets instead of trumpets on the melody line. At the end distant trumpets sound from the wings. The pilgrims take heart at once. Heaven has heard their prayer; the crusaders are at hand. As in *I Lombardi* they make their entrance preceded by a band, for which Verdi, happily, provided a new march. As usual he wrote it on two staves like a

---

* This extension bears out the sense of a letter of Donizetti to his old teacher Simone Mayr about the changes needed in his opera *Poliuto* to adapt it to the Parisian stage. 'Music and poetry for the French theatre have a cachet all their own to which every composer must conform . . . for example, no crescendos etc. etc., no routine cadences ('felicità, felicità, felicità,'), and between both statements of the cabaletta you should always have some lines which heighten the emotion . . .' Letter to Mayr. G. Zavadini, pp. 494-5.

227

228

piano part; but for once a few pages at the end of the autograph, written in a copyist's hand, enable us to know how the band was constituted and the notes apportioned. Very strange and modern it must have seemed to Verdi (in the autograph he refers to it not as 'banda' but as 'fanfares théâtrales'), being composed entirely of the instruments of Adolphe Saxe, then at the height of his fame. One little saxhorn in E flat, two cylindrical cornets in B flat, two B flat saxhorns and two in E flat; two B flat cylindrical trumpets or sax-trombas, one baritone and one bass saxhorn, both in B flat; a contrabass saxhorn and two side drums. It is a long march, complete with trio in the form of a sustained melody for cylindrical cornet and saxhorn, and it is made still longer by being repeated in full with the orchestra joining in. During this time the soldiers not only debouch in full procession on to the stage but are seen attending to the sick pilgrims and their own wounded. At length Count Raymond enters with the Papal Legate. His first words are to give thanks to God for having preserved his life from the hand of an assassin. To Ex. 226 Roger returns while the soldiers murmur their respect for the saintly hermit. The Count implores him for his blessing; but Roger, understandably perturbed, can only prostrate himself before his brother. He begs to be allowed to join the crusade, hinting at a crime to be expiated. The Count, surprised, grants his request. Then, led by the three basses in unison (the Count, Roger and the Legate), all join in a final chorus (*Le Seigneur nous promet la victoire*), in which the rhythm of *Ô mon Dieu ta parole est donc vaine* serves as the basis for a more virile melody. At the end all leave the stage to a reprise of the march, played by band and orchestra together.

229

Scene 2: a room in the Emir's palace at Ramla

Gaston, now a prisoner, has been summoned by the Emir. As he waits in the antechamber his thoughts turn to Hélène. There is a new plasticity in his Massenet-like arioso, traceable both to the French language and to the influence of French music in general (Ex. 230, overleaf). *Je veux encore entendre* is the new version of Oronte's cavatina from *I Lombardi*, shorn of its cabaletta and more lightly scored (no trombones and rolling timpani at *Ah bel ange mon idole*). Sited half a tone lower than in *I Lombardi* it includes a new 8-bar coda leading up to a high C, delivered forte, obviously for the benefit of Duprez, the creator of Gaston, who used to startle Rossini with his 'ut de poitrine' in *Guillaume Tell*. And for good measure Verdi has added another high C (pianissimo) to the final cadence.* The Emir tells Gaston that

* In the autograph the new 8 bars are marked with an optional cut, presumably for the benefit of those tenors who lacked the *ut de poitrine*. The final C, being pianissimo, would be taken falsetto.

he has spared his life only because he does not want to bring the wrath of the crusaders about his ears. Meanwhile Gaston is to consider himself a hostage and not try to escape under pain of death. An officer brings in Hélène who has been arrested

230

in Arab disguise. The Emir is relieved to hear from her that the Christians will not attack Ramla so long as she is within its walls. But he is disturbed by the signs of mutual recognition that have passed between her and Gaston. He leaves them alone together after arranging for them to be observed. There follows what was once the love-duet from Act III of I Lombardi with the melodic ideas all unchanged, even those embedded in the recitative. Only the formal andante, Une pensée amène (a tone lower than the original and without harp), is simplified by the omission of the soprano asides. Unlike Giselda, Hélène does not have to worry about having betrayed her faith; she has merely lied to a heathen—a no more than venial sin. There are sounds of confusion outside; Hélène leads Gaston to the window and points to the standards of the crusade fluttering down in the valley. Now is the time to make their escape. To distant cries of 'Aux armes' the lovers begin the final stretta Viens viens je t'aime, but their attempted flight is less successful than that of Giselda and Oronte, and, as the curtain falls, they find themselves surrounded by guards.

ACT III
Scene 1: the gardens of the harem at Ramla

A few hours have passed. Hélène has been placed in the Emir's harem as punishment for her duplicity. Her fellow-houris dance around her and mock her as they had mocked Giselda and to the same music (Ô belle captive). This is followed by a full-length ballet, the first that Verdi ever wrote. Musically there is not much to be said for it. Verdi inevitably took the coarse, flashy style of composers like Pugni as his starting-point. Admittedly the classical steps in vogue, both then and later, required a vigorous type of music, to lift the ballerinas off their feet. It was not until Delibes and Tchaikovsky devised an orchestral manner which was both strong and fine-grained that ballet music really came of age. Nothing illustrates quite so dramatically Verdi's progress in sophistication as the difference between the dance music in Jérusalem and that in Macbeth. The ballet in Jérusalem (which for once does not have a programme to it) consists of fifteen movements, comprising four separate numbers—pas de quatre, pas de deux, pas seul and pas d'ensemble. Here and there one finds special effects of scoring—the flute solo in the pas de deux (No. 2B); the melody for oboe and piccolo at the octave (No. 1E); an episode for the cornet (omitted in the printed score) during the E flat waltz (No. 3D). Most interesting of all from the technical point of view is the adagio of the pas seul (No. 2A) in which flute, oboe, clarinet and harp weave arabesques of the most ingenious complexity. It is the kind of effect to which Verdi will return in his next two overtures and also in the ballet music to *Il Trovatore*. Here it amounts to no more than a patch-work quilt, cloaking the most commonplace ideas. The most that can be claimed for the ballet in *Jérusalem* is that it is no worse than those in Wagner's *Rienzi* or Halévy's *La Juive*. Meyerbeer, on the other hand, was better in this field.

The women scatter among the gardens 'like a flock of birds' as the Emir enters with his officer and suite. The Christian army, they know, is marching on the city. If their chief should enter Ramla, says the Emir grimly, he will receive the head of his own daughter. They leave to man the defences, while Hélène prays to God to set her free (*Mes plaintes mes plaintes sont vaines*). This is a carbon copy of Giselda's 'Se vano se vano è il pregare', with the usual semitonal transposition and an enhanced cadenza; but so similar is the sense of the words that Verdi even repro-duces note for note the cello tremolos and trombone punctuations. Then all is confusion. The women rush shrieking across the stage, crying that the Christians have entered the city. In the meantime, Gaston has managed to break free from his guards and now hurries to Hélène's side. All this takes place to the same complex string figurations and woodwind countermelodies as in *I Lombardi*, though more dexterously worked. Then the Count enters, furious at seeing his daughter with his own would-be assassin. While the knights lay hold of Gaston, Count Raymond denounces her, as Arvino had denounced Giselda; and she, like Giselda, retorts with a rondò-finale (*Non, non votre rage*), here somewhat compressed because there is a much grander finale to follow. It is worth noticing too that, whereas in *I Lombardi* the opening phrase was delivered over a continuously pulsating accom-paniment, here the vocal phrases gain in declamatory strength by being left free, the pulsations being confined to the melodic interstices. Also an entry of the Count deflects the music from G minor to F for the final burst into the major, the effect being to emphasize still further the new transitional nature of this aria. At the end Hélène's father seizes her by the arms and drags her away.

Scene 2: the public square of Ramla

There is no break between this scene and the preceding. While the curtain is lowered the orchestra play a funeral march, melodically rather dull, but effectively scored, with striking use of low clarinets and percussion. Again there is a cornet solo of no distinction whatever. During the last few bars Gaston, heavily under guard, is led on. Behind him in the procession are a group of penitents who carry his sword, helmet and shield. A vast crowd have gathered to witness his public disgrace and execution, among them his fellow knights led by the Count and the Papal Legate, whose duty it is to pronounce sentence. Here for the first time in Verdi we find that canvas of contrasting musical and scenic elements which will yield impressive results in the operas to come. The Papal Legate proclaims, with all the authority of a basso profondo, that Gaston's name and escutcheon are henceforth to be dishonoured. Gaston pleads with his accusers in a moving andante (*Ô mes amis, mes frères d'armes*), which hints at Leonora's 'Madre pietosa vergine' from *La Forza del Destino*:

231

An interesting feature of this movement is its changes of mood and tempo—restless and sustained by turns, as he alternately pleads and despairs. The major section (it is basically a romanza in form) culminates in a high B suitable to a tenor of Duprez's calibre.

Gaston's pleas are all to no purpose. The knights demand his execution. Amidst silence, broken by soft string chords and thuds on the kettledrum, a group of penitents hand Gaston's helmet to the executioner. The herald proclaims it the helmet of a traitor. 'You lie!' cries Gaston; but the knights interrupt with a brutal, 'No mercy for the traitor.' Gaston's helmet is shattered to a simultaneous stroke on the gong and the bass drum. The penitents raise a supplicating plainchant backed by solo bassoon; and as it rises to its peak, the women of the crowd, moved to pity,

232

reply with a downward, compassionate phrase. It is the opening of the prelude (see Ex. 218) but with the second phrase effectively twisted into the major key. The entire sequence is repeated twice more for the sword and shield respectively, each time a tone higher. Then the Legate announces that Gaston shall be put to death the next day; but to Gaston, at the height of his despair, next day will be too late; and in the final stretta (*Frappez bourreaux frappez*), he begs them to kill him at once. Cast in the most commonplace of stretta rhythms (♩. ♫ | ♩. ♫ etc.) it avoids a sense of anticlimax by maintaining a minor orientation throughout, with only the winding-up cadences in the major. It is also suitably brief.

ACT IV

Scene 1: near the Crusaders' camp in the Valley of Jehoshaphat; there is a distant view of Jerusalem

The scene is set for the famous 'Coro della Processione' (Jérusalem); here preceded by a slow recitative from Roger to give added perspective. As he gazes at the ramparts of Jerusalem, he feels that the end of his earthly journey is near. Then distant voices break in on his thoughts; cries of 'Jerusalem!'; and so the chorus begins much as in *I Lombardi*, but with one difference in the opening phrase:

233

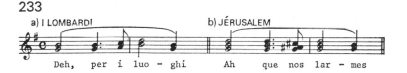

The larger Parisian chorus with sopranos in three parts instead of two clearly favoured a full triad at the outset rather than a simple third even if the consequent flattening of the melodic contour means a slight loss of charm. For the same reason the harmonies are redistributed towards the first cadence ('. . . dernière fête un jour si beau'), the chromatic line being transferred to the bass. Likewise the instrumental doubling is dropped as unnecessary. An unexpected reward, however, is the 8-bar oboe solo in E minor which intervenes before the first episode at Hélène's words 'Il est là!' Doubtless it depicts her private grief amid so much pious exaltation. The second half of the solo for chorus basses ('Des oliviers saluons la montagne') is also new and an improvement. It has greater solemnity than the original and avoids its jerky rhythm. As the procession passes into the distance a diminishing fanfare of cornets and trumpets replaces the more prosaic string 'busyness' in the earlier work. This in turn gives way to the exquisite coda based on the main theme in its new guise (Ex. 233b) but scored as in *I Lombardi*.

Before he leaves to join the procession the Papal Legate commands Roger to grant absolution to the condemned man. So Hélène and Roger remain behind, as Gaston is escorted from his tent. It is at this point that Verdi introduces that figure (*x*) from Ex. 218 which formed the main subject of the prelude. In her despair Hélène, like Giselda, comes near to cursing God; but Roger, to the same music to which Pagano had baptised Oronte, assures her that God's justice will soon be proved and Gaston's innocence vindicated. As there is, fortunately, no solo violin, the 'angelico' arpeggios are played by the much more appropriate flute; and so prepare the way for the famous trio (*Dieu nous sépare, Hélène*). Like so much of *Jérusalem* this is a semitone lower than the original, and there are a few minor improvements in the voice leading. The absence of solo violin from an otherwise identical score is a further advantage since it relieves the piece of its 'concertante' element and so permits a more dramatic ending than the long-drawn-out coda in *I Lombardi*. Sounds of battle cut across the final cadence.

At the sound of fighting Roger pricks up his ears like a warhorse. He restores Gaston's armour to him, and the two rush off into the fray. The curtain is then lowered for a perfunctory battle interlude, the same as that in *I Lombardi*, but with the two melodies removed and with no banda.

Scene 2: inside the Count's tent

Hélène and Isaure are awaiting the outcome of the battle. To their joy the Count enters in triumph followed by the Legate and an unknown knight, his face covered by a visor. The Count, who has seen him performing deeds of incredible valour, demands to know his name. For answer, the knight drops his visor and reveals himself as Gaston, now calling for justice on his executioners. But at that moment Roger staggers in mortally wounded. The death scene in which he reveals who he is and confesses his crimes begins in the same way as Pagano's but is necessarily shorter. There is no place here for the melting phrases with which Giselda attempted to console Pagano (they might have been misunderstood) and a single melodic sweep in the major key given out first by the soloists then with chorus added and the Count's cry of 'Mon frère!' thrown into relief must make do instead. As his dying request Roger begs to be allowed a last sight of Jerusalem. The tent flaps are parted, and as the sun's rays fall on the ramparts of the Holy City, all join in a shortened version of the original final hymn (*À toi gloire ô Dieu de victoire*). This time there are no half-dozen bars for the 'caro maestro' to score before mid-day.

Jérusalem's subsequent career was not very glorious either in the original or in the wretched translation of Calisto Bassi. One reason was that Verdi himself had made conditions which priced it out of the market, as Giovanni Ricordi explained to him in great detail.* Besides, *Jérusalem*, even without the ballet, calls for larger resources than most theatres of the time could muster. (The meeting of pilgrims and crusaders alone needs a stage the size of the Paris Opéra.) Then, too, history went against *Jérusalem*, particularly in Italy. In the days of frustration and of smouldering rebellion which followed the events of 1848 *I Lombardi* took on a new lease of popularity.

In such an atmosphere 'O Signore dal tetto natio' still created vibrations, while *Ouvre nous à la France un chemin* most certainly did not, least of all after the French suppression of the Roman republic in 1849. Even in revivals at the Paris Opéra *Jérusalem* was not to go unscathed.†

Yet as late as 1857 a French critic proclaimed that with *Jérusalem* Verdi had won

---

* Letter from Giovanni Ricordi, 26.1.1850. *Copialettere*, pp. 87–93.
† See letter to Roqueplan, 10.11.1852. *Copialettere*, pp. 150–1; also a review of the revival that year in the *France Musicale*: 'The fine march at the beginning of the second act was cut: the dances which are quite delightful were removed in order to end the evening with a mediocre ballet: *La Vivandière*. The entire final scene was left out, no account being taken of the fact that if the curtain falls on the terzetto the opera becomes a nonsense. . . .' *Copialettere*, p. 151.

his papers of French nationality and the Paris Opéra another masterpiece.* This is clearly an exaggeration. There is no substitute for integrity of conception, and a new plot grafted on to an old score with fresh musical additions will always result in a slight disparity of style. The most valuable addition—the final scene in Act III —is not free from that flat two-dimensional quality that marks so many of Verdi's early essays in the grand manner. The real importance of *Jérusalem* lies in the fascinating study it provides of the way in which he first came to terms with French opera, which was to play such a vital role in the formation of his mature style. It fired his dramatic imagination, refined his scoring, sharpened his harmonic palate; and in general made possible the amazing advances of the next few years.

*Rolandi, p. 9.

15 IL CORSARO

IL CORSARO

Opera in three acts
by
FRANCESCO MARIA PIAVE
(after Byron's poem, *The Corsair*)

*First performed at the
Teatro Grande, Trieste,
25 October 1848*

CORRADO, Captain of the pirates	PRIMO TENORE	Gaetano Fraschini
GIOVANNI, a pirate	SECONDO BASSO	Giovanni Volpini
MEDORA, Corrado's beloved	SOPRANO COMPRIMARIO	Carolina Rapazzini
SEID, Pasha of Coron	PRIMO BARITONO	Achille De Bassini
GULNARA, favourite slave of Seid	PRIMA DONNA SOPRANO	Marianna Barbieri-Nini
SELIMO, an Aga	SECONDO TENORE	Giovanni Petrovich
A EUNUCH	SECONDO TENORE	Francesco Cucchiari
A SLAVE	SECONDO TENORE	Stefano Albanassich

Corsairs—guards—Turks—slaves—odalisques—
Medora's handmaidens—Anselmo, a corsair

The action takes place on an island in the Aegean and at the city of Coron

Epoch: The beginning of the nineteenth century

The Corsair figured very early amongst Verdi's operatic schemes, as did a number of Byron's works. It had been considered along with *The Bride of Abydos* and *The Two Foscari* as a candidate for the Venice Carnival season of 1844, only to be dismissed since no baritone of the order of Ronconi was available, whether for the hero or the villain is not clear. That same year *The Two Foscari* came to fruition in Rome. All this suggests that like many of his generation Verdi was going through a Byronic phase at the time. It was a young man's enthusiasm; and he grew out of it much faster than Liszt or Berlioz (if the latter can be said ever to have grown out of it at all). When *Il Corsaro* first became a practical possibility Verdi was hot on the scent; when he actually came to compose it the trail had to some extent gone cold.

Some time in 1845, as we have seen, Verdi signed a contract with Lucca to produce an opera at Her Majesty's Theatre, London, the following summer. His first thoughts, as so often, were of the *Re Lear* that was never to be.* Later he recognized *Il Corsaro* as the obvious choice, and Piave, who had already proved his skill in adapting Byron, as the most suitable librettist. Lucca agreed to the subject, but took the liberty of approaching one Manfredo Maggioni, an Italian resident in London, for the book. Verdi stood firm; he was committed to Piave, and Lucca must sort out the muddle over Maggioni as best he could.† Meanwhile he drew up a synopsis with Piave and sent it to Lucca, asking him to forward it to Lumley.‡ Giovannina Lucca now took a hand, offering a different subject altogether— *Ginevra di Scozia*, hardly a novelty since Ariosto's heroine had been treated operatically by several distinguished composers in the past, including Handel and Mayr. Anyway Verdi would have none of her. 'I may be making a big mistake,' he replied, 'but it is either *The Corsair* or nothing. All your arguments against it only make me like the subject more.' Byron's poem was much in vogue in Italy at the time. Verdi himself could think of no plot that was 'finer, more full of passion or easier to set to music'.§

But the severe bout of ill-health which followed the premiere of *Attila* postponed the London visit for another year. Meanwhile, during his convalescence at Recoaro in the company of Maffei, Verdi began to cogitate on the more ambitious projects of *I Masnadieri* and *Macbeth* (in that order) with a view to his next engagement at Florence. But that he had not lost sight of *Il Corsaro* is demonstrated by an unpublished letter to Piave written as late as August. The poet asked for his libretto back, so as to relieve himself of a pressing commitment. 'Give you back *Il Corsaro*,' Verdi exclaimed:

> . . . that *Corsaro* which has always fascinated me and which I've thought about so much, and which you've put into verse with more than your usual care?

* Letter to Piave, undated (December 1845). Abbiati, I, pp. 590–2.
† Letter to Lucca, 25.1.1846. Abbiati, I, pp. 598–9.
‡ Letter to Lucca, undated (Jan./Feb. 1846). Abbiati, I, pp. 599–600.
§ Letter to Giovannina Lucca, 24.1.1846. Abbiati, I, p. 601.

It's true it was arranged for London, but even if the London business has fallen through I still have to write the opera for Lucca. And I've been composing this *Corsaro* almost without noticing: I've already sketched out a few of the things I found most congenial, the prison duet and the trio in the last act. And you want me to give it up? . . . Go on, go to the hospital and get your head examined. . . .

Towards the end of the letter he begins, perhaps significantly, to relent:

. . . Well, do as you think best, and if you really want me to give up the *Corsaro* I will, but only on condition that you write me another libretto with the same loving care with which you wrote this one.*

But evidently Piave did not press the matter; for next month, with *Macbeth* already about to be put in hand, composer and librettist were still discussing details of *Il Corsaro* and whether or not Turkish costumes would be permitted on stage.†

By the end of the year, the situation had changed completely. Piave was rapidly sliding out of favour for failing, in Verdi's opinion, to bring to Shakespeare's drama the care and attention it deserved. So when Lucca and Lumley announced the renewal of the London contract, Verdi replied to the latter that he had changed his mind about the subject, having found *Il Corsaro* 'dull (*freddo*) and theatrically ineffective' when reduced to a libretto.‡ But he still kept it in hand for a future occasion.

I Masnadieri finished and performed, one of the three contracts with Lucca remained outstanding, and Lucca much to Verdi's annoyance was insisting on its fulfilment. It is the only one included in the *Copialettere*, having been signed in October 1845. In it Verdi bound himself to 'write for you an opera to be performed in one of the leading theatres of Italy with a first-class company of singers in the carnival season of 1848 provided that in the said carnival season I am not engaged to write an opera for some theatre outside Italy; if that were the case I would write the opera for you in some other season to be arranged by mutual consent within the year 1849'.§ The agreement was to be valid unconditionally for five months; its continuance depended on whether in the meantime Lucca had duly fixed the performance of *Attila*. Lucca did all that was required of him; but by the autumn of 1847 it was Verdi who wanted to back out. He had acquired a thorough dislike of the publisher, who 'forced me to finish *Attila* in a deplorable physical condition'.¶ Letters to his friends in Milan are full of complaints about that 'most irritating, ungrateful' Lucca, and how he had 'prevented me from getting an engagement worth 60,000 francs'.‖ 'I would have returned to London next year,' he told

---

*Letter to Piave, 27.8.1846. Autograph in the Accademia dei Concordi, Rovigo (MS. 595).

† Letter to Piave, 14.9.1846. Morazzoni, pp. 27–8.

‡ Letter to Lumley, 4.12.1846. *Copialettere*, pp. 33–4. (See also letter to Lucca, 3.12.1846; *Copialettere*, pp. 32–3: 'As you know, I have changed my mind about *Il Corsaro*.') That Verdi was being less than frank to the London impresario appears from his statement later in the same letter that he would have time to complete *I Masnadieri* of which he 'had already written nearly half', but not to compose *Il Corsaro* from the beginning.

§ Letter to Lucca, 16.10.1845. *Copialettere*, p. 16.

¶ Letter to Piave, 14.1.1848. *Carteggi Verdiani*, II, p. 350.

‖ Letter to Clarina Maffei, 3.12.1847. *Copialettere*, pp. 461–2.

Emilia Morosini, 'if the publisher Lucca had accepted 10,000 francs to release me from my contract with him. So now it will be two years before I can return.'* As so often to his admiring countesses Verdi was telling less than the truth. A glance at the terms of the contract with Lucca will show that it could not possibly have prevented him from writing for London in 1848 had he wished to do so. But Verdi could be very unreasonable with people he disliked.

As Piave's libretto for *Il Corsaro* had been written and paid for, Verdi offered it again to Lucca with the alternatives of *Die Ahnfrau* (Grillparzer) or Romani's *Medea*; or if Lucca had any better ideas he would be prepared to consider them.† By way of reply Lucca sent him a new libretto using Giuseppina Appiani as intermediary. Verdi burst out in fury, 'I shall never compose an opera of the slightest importance for that tiresome and indelicate Signor Lucca and I wonder how he has the nerve to encourage Signor Giacchetti to send me a plot like this *Giuditta* . . .'‡ He returned to Piave's libretto of *Il Corsaro* and set it as it stood, omitting only a line or a couplet here and there. On 12 February 1848 he dispatched the completed score to Lucca by way of Muzio, authorizing the publisher to make whatever use he chose of poetry and music both in Italy and abroad.§ In no other opera of his does Verdi appear to have taken so little interest *before* it was staged.

Lucca decided to place *Il Corsaro* at the Teatro Grande, Trieste. As Verdi had no intention of going there himself, Muzio wrote to Barezzi that he would be prepared to direct the performance if the publisher would make it worth his while.¶ The management were quite content to have as second best the man who had assisted Verdi with the preparation of most of his operas since *I Due Foscari* and who would be presumed to know his intentions better than anyone. The première, however, was not until October, by which time much had happened: the glorious Cinque Giornate, the not-so-glorious retreat of the Piedmontese army, the Battle of Custoza and the overwhelming reassertion of Austrian strength in Lombardy-Venetia, nowhere more in evidence than in the essentially Austrian city of Trieste.

* Letter to Emilia Morosini, 30.7.1847. *Copialettere*, pp. 460–1.

† Letter to Lucca, 2.8.1847. *Copialettere*, p. 42.

‡ Letter to Giuseppina Appiani, 22.9.1847. *Copialettere*, p. 461. Evidently Piave remained for a long time blissfully unaware of Verdi's hostility towards Lucca, as can be seen from four letters he wrote to the publisher between August and September 1847. The autographs are in the Museo alla Scala, and the texts have been published in part by G. Barblan in his article 'La lunga quarantena del Corsaro' printed in the programme book for *Il Corsaro* (pp. 299–303) prepared for the opera's revival during the 1970–1 season at the Teatro la Fenice, Venice. *Il Corsaro* was still the most likely choice for the fulfilment of Verdi's contract, with Grillparzer's *Ahnfrau* as a fairly close second; but it is interesting to note that Piave was seriously considering the possibility of a *Don Rodrigo* based on Manzoni's *I Promessi Sposi*. In the last of these letters (13.12.1847) we find Piave having to rebut the suggestion that Verdi might have lifted the sunrise in *Jérusalem* from *Attila*. The composer's distaste for Lucca may not have been as unreasonable as it seems.

§ Letter to Lucca, 12.2.1848. *Copialettere*, p. 48. See, however, a letter written two days later to the sculptor Vincenzo Luccardi: 'I have written an opera for the publisher Lucca of Milan and I was counting on taking it to Italy myself, but I decided to send it because I didn't feel fit to undertake the long and tiring journey at this time of year. . . .' E. Faustini-Fasini, 'Una lettera inedita di Giuseppe Verdi' (in *Le Cronache Musicali*, 1.2.1901), quoted in translation by Walker, p. 185. That Verdi was expected in Italy about that time is clear from Muzio's letter to Barezzi of 17.2.1848: 'Here's a disappointment to all my hopes and yours too of seeing the Maestro. This morning I found instead of Verdi a letter saying that the night before he was due to leave he caught a slight feverish cold and didn't want to make the journey. . . .' Garibaldi, p. 361.

¶ Garibaldi, p. 361.

Muzio was no hero. During the summer he had stayed in Switzerland discharging commissions for Ricordi by post. So the opera was rehearsed by Luigi Ricci (known nowadays if at all as joint composer with his brother Federico of the opera *Crispino e la Comare*). Its reception from both public and press was disastrous. Only the designer won a second curtain call. The leading newspaper critic remarked that since Maestro Verdi had now filled his pockets with English guineas and French francs he could afford to study the classics a little.[*] 'Trieste deserves a better opera than this' was the general verdict. *Il Corsaro* vanished from the repertoire after three performances.

Three revivals followed in 1852 at Cagliari, Modena and the Teatro Carcano at Milan, the last of which drew an unusually kind notice from the *Gazzetta dei Teatri*;[†] though it is clear that in each case the score was subjected to those 'modifications' from which Verdi was so anxious to protect his other stage works. Mounted at Venice the following year as an opera di ripiego it enabled Felice Varesi to restore his reputation as Seid after his disastrous Germont in *La Traviata*.[‡] The last important performance was at the San Carlo, Naples, in 1854. Verdi hearing about it remarked, 'Not a happy inspiration—least of all for the San Carlo.'[§]

With all these facts before them it has been too easy for writers on Verdi to dismiss *Il Corsaro* out of hand. If he was over-optimistic about a work while it was in gestation, *a fortiori* how much worse must be an opera to which he was apparently indifferent almost from the moment he received the libretto. Alone of his operas this one seems to have been 'thrown away'. A glance at the score might show that in 1848 he was able to write a confessedly minor work without a lowering of artistic standards; what is more, that such a work might come across the years more unscathed than some of its more ambitious fellows.

Among Byron's works *The Two Foscari* had been a rather unusual choice. *The Corsair* lay much more in the main-stream of the poet's work. It had all those qualities which endeared him to romantic Europe, especially those countries to which German romanticism at its most profound had never penetrated. It is set in the Aegean landscape, already glamorized by the Greek War of Independence in which Byron himself died. Its hero was typically Byronic: a Lucifer, proud, solitary, ironic and melancholy. It was an image as attractive to the youth of the time as James Bond's in our own day.[¶] Antisocial he may be, but the fault is society's not his:

> Yet was not Conrad thus by nature sent
> To lead the guilty—guilt's worst instrument—
> His soul was changed, before his deeds had driven
> Him forth to war with man and forfeit heaven. . . .
> Too firm to yield, and far too proud to stoop,
> Doomed by his very virtues for a dupe . . .

[*] Article in *Il Costituzionale*, 29.10.1848. Abbiati, I, p. 764.
[†] See Barblan, p. 304.
[‡] See letter from Varesi to Lucca, 10.3.1853. Abbiati, II, p. 229.
[§] Letter to Cesare De Sanctis, 6.7.1854. *Carteggi Verdiani*, I, pp. 25–6.
[¶] See, for instance, Berlioz: 'Je suivais sur les ondes les courses audacieuses du Corsair;

> Lone, wild, and strange, he stood alike exempt
> From all affection and from all contempt . . .

But he is allowed the characteristically Byronic heroine, the frail flowerlike woman who lives for him alone and dies when he is killed. This too suited the sentimental spirit of the age. So far the parallel with *I Masnadieri* appears almost exact. Corrado is Carlo in seafaring terms, Medora is Amalia; which brings home yet again how much closer the so-called English romanticism was to *Sturm und Drang* than to the romanticism of Germany. To Goethe 'the romantic was the diseased'. But he approved of Byron.

In view of Byron's immense and lasting reputation on the Continent a mere Englishman might well hesitate before criticizing a famous work of his, especially one of which he himself thought so highly. Even so, I suggest that nowadays *The Corsair* will be found far more unreadable than *The Two Foscari*, if only because of its artificial mould—three cantos of heroic couplets, as though Wordsworth and Coleridge had never existed. The simple story is encumbered with a succession of epigrams, inversions and antitheses. One can still admire some of the description, the sheer skill of its versification, the sense of action, direct and vivid, which Byron infuses into the most unlikely passages. But mostly it is an empty tour de force with characters of cardboard, except for the hero who is the usual romantic projection of Byron himself. Pasha Seyd, into whose hands Conrad delivers himself by an act of chivalry, is a villain from a boy's adventure story; Gulnare who kills him is just another woman in love with Conrad, and less distinctive even than Medora. Yet in Piave's and Verdi's scheme, Gulnara is the prima donna, Medora the comprimaria.

But the basic reason why *The Corsair* hardly makes for music-drama is that it is a *narrative*. Not being conceived in dramatic terms it offers no opportunity for the generation of musical power through conflict and the clash of personalities. Therefore the qualities that raise the best of Verdi's earlier operas above the level of their musical language are hard to find in *Il Corsaro*. It has neither that steady crescendo of dramatic interest that lifts us off our feet in *Ernani* nor the cut and thrust of character dialectic that informs *I Due Foscari*, nor yet the sense of grand theatre that transfigures the great moments in *Giovanna d'Arco* and *Attila*. Nor is there any question of capitalizing on the formal advances of *Macbeth* since, as we have seen, its genesis like that of *I Masnadieri* belongs to an earlier period. The shape of an *ottocento* opera is to a great extent conditioned by its libretto. Even if Verdi had not begun work in desultory fashion on Piave's text as early as 1846 its distribution into the traditional self-sufficient scenes would have imposed the treatment which he gave it two years later. Outwardly, then, Verdi's *Il Corsaro* conforms to the pattern of Pacini's work of 1830 on the same subject. But there the similarity between them ends. Pacini's opera with its contralto hero and tenor villain has all the expansive artificiality of the Rossinian age. One of the most striking features of Verdi's score is its economy, thematic no less than formal. This is achieved partly by the (for him) unusual frequency with which he evolves movements from a single melodic cell, and partly

---

j'adorais profondémont ce caractère à la fois inexorable et tendre, impitoyable et généreux, composé bizarre de deux sentiments opposés en apparence, la haine de l'espèce et l'amour d'une femme.' *Mémoires* (Paris, 1870), I, Chapter 36.

by a kindred principle which can loosely be described as 'strophic variation', and whose nature will, I hope, be made clear during the analysis that follows. All this, if it cannot raise *Il Corsaro* from the category of minor Verdi, gives it a unique character. In no other opera does Verdi extract so much from so little material. The relative modesty of its scope, combined with the subtlety of its craftsmanship, often results in that quality of 'delicacy and pathos' which Verdi sought in his other Byron opera.

The opening of the prelude comes as near to pure cacophony as anything that Verdi ever wrote. The music is based on Corrado's short but powerful solo in the third act where he lies in prison. It is an orgy of Byronic despair against a backcloth of tempest. Violent orchestral tuttis with the high wind instruments trilling in semiquavers alternate sequentially with a distracted falling motif on violins and

234

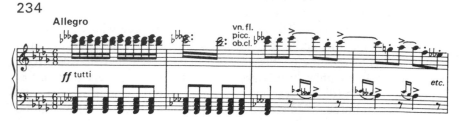

high woodwind. The harsh symmetry of the opening idea gradually loosens up in a slow transitional andante unusually long for its immediate function which is merely to prepare for the main melodic idea of a very short prelude. The entire passage is evolved from the figure of two side-slipping sixths (x) extended and developed in rhythmic diminution. The luscious chromatic harmonies accented off the beat will appear again in Gulnara's cavatina in Act II. The new harmonic subtlety—including the skilful way in which unequivocal D flat major tonality is withheld until the final three bars—is set in relief by the plainness of the scoring.

235

The melody which follows is associated with the dying Medora. It is only eight bars altogether; but even here there is room for a strong harmonic ellipsis (see

236

Ex. 8). At the sixth bar the final cadence is interrupted by a more or less conventional winding up tutti of no great thematic interest but balancing by its length (Ex. 235.) It subsides over a long timpani roll with reminiscences of Ex. 236. There is no other Verdian prelude quite like this one. It is both long and short where you least expect, but the sense of proportion is unerring.

ACT I

Scene 1: the Corsairs' Island in the Aegean

The stage is empty, but a roistering chorus can be heard in the distance (*Come liberi volano i venti*). It is, more or less, the opening of Byron's poem:

> 'O'er the glad waters of the dark blue sea,
> Our thoughts as boundless, and our souls as free,
> Far as the breeze can bear, the billows foam,
> Survey our empire, and behold our home.'

237

In mood it is a pirates' chorus like any other with here and there a strong progression to give it grit (the unexpected F flat chord at bar 6 and the jump from F major to D flat major at bar 24). But the rhythmic cut is subtly different from any we have encountered so far. Here for the first time the favourite decasyllabic metre of 'Va pensiero' and 'O Signore dal tetto natio' is bent to fit the movement of a French cavalry march.* The music is no longer subjected to the tonic accent of the verse. A small gain, but a significant one in a native tradition where like metre

* This point has been made by G. Vecchi, 'Il libretto', in *Quaderni dell'Istituto di Studi Verdiani*, 1: *Il Corsaro* (Venice, 1963), pp. 12–13.

tends to impose like rhythm. A still more flexible setting of decasyllabic verse will be found in Act III of *Il Trovatore* in the chorus 'Squilli, echeggi la tromba guerriera'. The example of French opera doubtless inspired both. Between the two verses Corrado who has entered slowly apostrophizes his followers in two phrases of recitative each launched over an orchestral tutti: 'Fiero è il canto de' prodi miei consorti.' Not a very significant remark; but the music conveys his heroic stature with a certain crude effectiveness—not of course to be compared to the way in which Otello will one day 'plant' himself in all his glory. After a violent tirade against the human race Corrado presents himself directly to us: 'Warp'd by the world in Disappointment's school'. Like Byron, Piave hints at some misfortune that drove him to become a moral and spiritual outlaw. The andante of the cavatina (*Tutto parea sorridere*) is a noble movement with the smooth melodic gradient rising to a hammered-out climax in a manner eminently suited to heroic, slightly baritonal tenors of Fraschini's type. The principal section is straightforward enough with both quatrains ending in a similar cadence. But then what begins as a coda in the manner of Macbeth's 'Pietà, rispetto, amore', with the main melody restated in the orchestra, is extended to form a varied reprise of almost the entire movement. The opening of this section is wonderfully delicate, with a pattern of pizzicato strings replacing the more commonplace accompanimental figure of the opening:

238

If in Macbeth's aria the effect is ternary, in Corrado's it is that of 'strophic variation', even if the variants can be unexpectedly drastic. For this time the words 'ma un fato inesorabile' provoke a dramatic interruption—a tense rising phrase leading towards F minor like a sudden stiffening of the musical sinews—after which the tenor proceeds to his second quatrain cadence as before. Yet there is nothing illogical here since the new departure is itself derived from the opening phrase of the movement, with harmonies altered and the melodic contour steepened.

239

Giovanni brings Corrado a letter from a 'Greek spy'. Its contents prompt Corrado to summon his men and tell them to make ready to set sail that evening. Like much else in *Il Corsaro* the cabaletta (*Sì, di Corsari il fulmine*) expresses more neatly and economically what we have often heard before. Indeed the commonplace sequence to the words 'All'armi all'armi intrepidi' is lifted note for note from Carlo's cabaletta in *I Masnadieri*. But note how at the outset the essence of masculine heroics is encapsulated in the upthrusting figure which takes in a full arpeggio from A♭ to A'♭ with powerful off-beat leverage. The same phrase is taken up by chorus in canon with soloist by way of a codetta.

240

Scene 2: the apartments of Medora
Strings alone prepare us for this most vulnerable of Byronic heroines.

241

The elegiac quality is enhanced by cellos doubling the line of the first violins at the lower octave. Medora is waiting for Corrado as she has done so often in the past; and once more to while away the interminable hours of his absence she takes up her harp and sings. The Romanza (*Non so le tetre immagini*) is based on the strophic song in which Byron for once departed from his perpetual heroic couplets:

'Deep in my soul that tender secret dwells,
Lonely and lost to light for evermore,
Save when to thine my heart responsive swells,
Then trembles into silence as before.'

It is mostly pianissimo with a certain bias towards the lower, veiled register of the soprano voice. Flute and clarinet figure in the introduction. Otherwise the accompaniment is confined to harp, single cello and single bass. As the first instance in Verdi of purely strophic form in a solo this romanza merits a little attention. For the next five years this design will be used mostly for 'set pieces' such as would be sung in a straight play.* Not until the narrative of *Il Trovatore* is the strophic song drawn into the mainstream of operatic language. Like Germont's 'Di Provenza', Medora's romanza is evolved, though not quite so closely, from its opening phrase; but, unusually, the second verse is encrusted with decorations which extend through a compass of two octaves. The basis of these embellishments is the figure (*x*) which also serves as a unifying element in a melody which contains no reprise. In this way the romantic melancholy is shot through with a sense of obsession.

242

During the last two bars Corrado has entered softly, and his first few words of recitative take up the same note of tender sadness; and the duet which follows is similarly on a note of wistful lyricism rather than of passion. Corrado tells Medora that her love is all that remains to him on this earth: that without it life holds nothing for him.

'But—oh Medora! nerve thy gentler heart,
This hour again—but not for long—we part.'

* The two most obvious exceptions to this rule are so in appearance rather than reality. 'Quando le sere al placido' (*Luisa Miller*) is strophic with a difference, having more affinity with the couplet form—that is, two parallel verses in which the words of the last line or lines are identical in each case, so giving the effect of a refrain ('Ah mi tradia, mi tradia!'). The Duke's 'Quest' o quella' (*Rigoletto*) is entitled 'Ballata', which would seem to indicate that the composer thought of it as a set-piece; though this is not necessarily implied by the dramatic content any more than is the case with Cherubino's 'Non so più cosa son cosa faccio'—which is emphatically *not* a set-piece.

In the first movement of the duet-finale (*No tu non sai comprendere*) Medora's distress (Ex. 243 a) is conveyed partly in the nervous double-dots of the melodic rhythm, partly in the broken triplet figure on flutes and violins with its characteristically falling semitone, partly too in the meanderings of the vocal line suggesting a mind distraught. Against this Corrado's reply (b) strikes a note of reassurance, with its simpler accompaniment, firmer thrust, slower pace and its turn into the relative major. Yet the rising motion and the fact that both melodies move within the same compass (G–G) make his music seem like a variation of hers. Finally, at a still slower tempo, the two voices combine in the tonic major in a chain of melting sixths (c) in what is unequivocally a variation of (b). The effect is of three different facets of the same idea each evolving from the other.

243

But . . .

> Hark—peals the thunder of the signal gun!
> It told 'twas sunset and he cursed that sun.

In the stretta of the duet (*Tornerai ma forse spenta*) Medora predicts that by the time her lover returns she will have died of grief, while Corrado gives what comfort he can. It is Edgardo and Lucia at the end of Donizetti's Act I—the same rhythmic movement, the same guitar-like accompaniment of pizzicato strings, the same simple pathos that tries to smile through grief. Indeed the resemblance in character and situation to 'Verranno a te sull'aure' is so close as to set the difference between the composers in the sharpest possible relief. Donizetti's melody is a straightforward sixteen-bar double quatrain with nothing more unusual than a codetta which presses hard on its heels. Verdi's is set to a sestina yet with the musical character of a double quatrain telescoped into fourteen instead of sixteen bars. But if the last six bars seem rhythmically like a foreshortening, melodically they give the effect of an expansion, lifting the vocal line up to its highest point at an unexpected moment:

244

Note too the elliptical false relation at bar 3; the dominant G held across bars 3 and 4 in the bass so as to give added force to the tonic C which coincides with the climax of the melody. The academic composer would have brought the bass up to C at the start of bar 4. But it is as pointless to talk of crudity or incorrectness in Verdi's case as in that of Berlioz. It is touches such as these that give his melodic style the strength that Donizetti's so often lacks. At the third statement of the melody the voices sing not in unison, as in Donizetti, but in dialogue over an enriched accompaniment with arpeggios on flute and clarinet. In case we should have forgotten about it, the signal gun is fired again during the coda.

ACT II

Scene 1: the apartments of Gulnara in Pasha Seid's palace

Needless to say this scene does not occur in Byron. Its function is merely to introduce the prima donna by means of the most conventional of all formulae, the cavatina with chorus (Pacini had introduced his own Gulnara in the same way). The opening chorus of odalisques (*Oh qual perenne gaudio t'aspetta*) has suggested to Verdi the instrumental palette that he employed for the houris in *I Lombardi*—an abundance of piccolo, high woodwind, cymbals and a triangle which here tinkles like an electric bell. It is a far neater piece than its predecessor: more delicate, apart from the brutal interruptions (bars 6–7, 13–14, 24–7) intended no doubt to suggest the lurking menace of the Pasha. Also it is less insistently repetitive, for this time the odalisques have no malicious intent. They are merely telling Gulnara how lucky

she is. But Gulnara, like Elvira in *Ernani*, feels nothing but hatred for her benefactor, and she longs to escape from her gilded cage into a 'heaven of love'. In the
andante (*Vola talor dal carcere*) the key (F major), the time (6/8), the pizzicato
accompaniment all bring to mind the coquettish charm of Mozart's Susanna
('Deh vieni non tardar') but there is depth, and a touch of oriental voluptuousness
in the vocal line, marked successively *espressivo, sensibile, dolcissimo*, all within
six bars. The design is the familiar a^1 a^2 b a^3 c a^3 coda but a glance at a^3 and the beginning of c will show how far Verdi's technical craftsmanship had progressed since
the days when he had first adopted the scheme.

245

It is a striking instance of his growing skill in reinforcing a melodic climax by
harmonic and rhythmic means no less than by the contours of the melody itself.
The fact that each semiquaver in (x) carries its own harmony coupled with the
cross-grained slurring gives the effect of a broadening out, an expansion of the
rhythmic frame. The balance is restored in the second half of the bar with its
unsupported pianissimo flourish. And how vastly preferable to the routine woodwind chatterings is the pattern of flute and clarinet (y) at the start of c.

To an orchestral march tune in whose tutti outbursts there is a hint of the
Pasha's authority a eunuch enters to bid Gulnara to a feast held by Pasha Seid to
celebrate his forthcoming victory over the corsairs. Gulnara replies in proud
recitative that she will come, but not alone. Her handmaids shall accompany her.

Before going she confides to us her hope that one day heaven may grant her heart's desire. The cabaletta (*Ah conforto è sol la speme*) is one of the 'prancing' type and has no distinction whatever, though apparently the expertise of its vocal writing gained it a place in a number of published 'methods'.*

Scene 2: the banqueting hall of Seid's Palace

High in his hall reclines the turban'd Seyd;
Around—the bearded chiefs he came to lead.

At present these same chiefs are singing a festive chorus, based on a rhythm which Verdi will put to more effective use in Act III of *La Forza del Destino* ('Sol grido di feste'). Seid promises them fresh laurels in the next day's battle. Then he leads them in a hymn to Allah (*Salve Allah! tutta quanta la terra*). Cast in the familiar decasyllabic rhythm, set this time in the traditional manner, it recalls the early patriotic choruses from *Nabucco* or *I Lombardi* with Pasha Seid less like a soloist than a larger than life-size choregus. But there is a concentrated boldness in the opening ritornello with its fierce gestures of alternating brass and strings. The brass choir, pounding in a rhythm of (♩♫ ♪, ♩♫ ♪) forms the sole accompaniment to the Pasha's melody, the rest of the orchestra entering where the chorus takes up the Pasha's last two lines as a refrain. Once again the strophic form indicates a 'set piece'. Most unusually, however, the second verse presents the theme in the minor, reverting to the original key only for the refrain (*Santo in pace, terribile in guerra*). This, incidentally, is based on an idea that occurs as early as the quartet from *Oberto* (see Chapter 3). But Verdi is not the only composer to use up in a minor work the unexhausted potential of earlier material.

The slave Selim introduces a Holy Dervish who has come to beg the Pasha's protection from the Corsairs. Dervish and Pasha engage in a telegraphic dialogue over a restless throbbing accompaniment of strings and bassoons.

'Whence com'st thou, Dervise?' 'From the outlaws' den,
'A fugitive—' 'Thy capture where and when?'

Three months ago the Dervish was taken prisoner. He had escaped; and a humble fisherman had brought him ashore to the Pasha's domains.

'How speed the outlaws? stand they well prepared,
Their plunder'd wealth, and robbers' rock, to guard?'

With the Pasha's question begins the formal duettino (*Di que' ribaldi tremano*) where for the first time in this opera there is an element of vocal 'scontro'. Seid's first words are a prodigious assertion of baritonic vehemence, set to a variant of the

---

* A. Soffredini, *Le Opere di Verdi* (Milan, 1901), p. 111.

phrase which opened the cabaletta of Corrado's cavatina.* The Dervish, replying that as a prisoner he saw nothing but the sky, heard nothing but the roar of the waves, speaks in soft tones and smooth rhythm, with a displaced accent in the second bar suggesting the whine of some priestly character-tenor:

246

The contrast is maintained even at the point where the voices join: Pasha's Seid's line descending in savage staccato semiquavers, the Dervish's rising in smooth semi-staccato quavers. Only in the last eight bars does this excellent little duet tail away facilely in the manner of a comic opera.

The Pasha would like to question the Dervish further; but:

> 'What star—what sun is bursting on the bay? . . .
> Ho! treachery! my guards! my scimitar!
> My galleys feed the flames—and I afar!'

All is now confusion. The eunuchs and chiefs cry out in terror. Seid orders the Dervish's arrest. But the Dervish flings back his hood and cloak to reveal Corrado, armed for battle. He takes a horn from his belt and summons his followers. By this time flames have reached the harem, from which desperate cries can be heard. With fatal gallantry, Corrado orders the rescue of the women, so giving his enemies

* The curious statement made by Roncaglia, p. 133, and taken up by M. Mila, 'Lettura del Corsaro', in *Nuova Rivista Musicale Italiana* (Turin, Jan.–Feb. 1971), pp. 54–5, that both themes are directly derived from Bellini's 'Ah bella a me ritorna' demonstrates the dangers of 'theme-spotting'. The similarity is irrelevant; what matters is the difference. Verdi's phrase takes in all four notes of the common chord in an emphatic upward movement; Bellini's takes in only three, and its centre of gravity remains relatively fixed around the dominant—two of the reasons which make Verdi's the essence of masculine assertion, whereas Bellini's is no less appropriate to the Druid priestess who sings it.

time to rally and counter-attack. The corsairs are easily overcome, and Corrado himself falls wounded. During all this the musical interest may be said to retire. The basis of the scene-à-faire is a four-bar idea of bustling semiquavers stated no fewer than five times, each a semitone higher than the last, in the manner of 'hurry music' for the silent screen. It is as near to mechanical writing as Verdi ever came, and vastly inferior to a similar scene in *I Masnadieri*. With Corrado's capture, the Pasha's Abigaille-like taunting of the fallen hero (*Prode invero, rapitore di donne*), and Corrado's defiant retort (*Chiudi il labbro, superbo*) the stage is set for the adagio of the finale. Both here and in the stretta we find for once not a parade of successive ideas but a steady development of one rhythmic motif with a bare minimum of contrast. The opening phrase of the adagio (*Audace cotanto mostrarti pur sai*) with its double and even triple dots is instinct with the Pasha's restrained fury: to which suave clarinets give a smile of sarcasm. (The obsessive repetition of a motif set in the major key and scored for clarinets in thirds and sixths is a favourite device of Verdi's for creating that twilight of emotion—irony, bitterness and anger.)

247

Corrado's reply merely continues the melodic monolith. Gulnara's line as she sings in thirds with the odalisques of the dawning of her love for Corrado is the only thematic departure in the movement, providing the contrast of a second subject, but still with the double-dotted pattern embedded in it.

248

The male chorus of Turks keep up the momentum here and there with a discreet triplet between phrases. Meanwhile the music rises in a Bellinian groundswell to a powerful climax at bar 68, then winds slowly down to its close. The scale seems all the larger for the extreme concentration of the material.

Selim and a group of soldiers now enter escorting in those of the corsairs who have not been killed or made their escape. Seid has no wish to pursue the fugitives, now that he has their leader; and he leaves his victim in no doubt that he is to be horribly tortured. The stretta (*Sì, morrai di morte atroce*) at first sight looks like any of a dozen by Donizetti or Rossini:

249

But this too is subjected to close thematic workmanship. Gulnara and the odalisques turn it into the minor key when they beg for mercy for Corrado (Ex. 250 a) on the same principle of strophic variation observed in *Salve Allah*. All the bustle ceases where Gulnara confronts the Pasha (b) in the language of Cenerentola pleading with Don Magnifico (*Ah sempre fra le ceneri*). But rhythmically the derivation is still from Ex. 249. While to a further extension of the same idea (c) Corrado heroically asserts his spiritual freedom. A resumption of Ex. 249 by all voices in an exhilarating unison recalls the movement to its familiar path.

Paradoxically, and contrary to traditional practice, his own included, Verdi individualizes his characters more powerfully in the stretta than in the largo—a welcome novelty in itself. In both movements there is a degree of concentration here that has not appeared in any of the previous operas. It will appear again—and to a theme very similar to that of the stretta—in the overture to *Luisa Miller*.

ACT III

Scene 1: the private apartments of Seid

Like Gulnara's in the previous act this scene is the most conventional of concessions to a principal singer. Its object is to extend the baritone throughout his emotional and technical range. But Seid in isolation is the least interesting of villains, and the composer wastes no more time on him than is strictly necessary. The opening recitative has some strong moments: the fortissimo unison trills by full orchestra (the most powerful of all vehicles of negative emotion, as in the revised *Simon Boccanegra*), the crawling chain of diminished sevenths that depicts the serpent of jealousy that 'from its eyes drops cold poison into the heart'. But the andantino (*Cento leggiadre vergini*) in which Seid reflects on the irony of his position—courted in vain by a hundred lovely maidens, spurned by the only woman of his choice—Verdi dispatches in a tight little 6/8 melody of the kind in which this score abounds. The design is approximately that of Macbeth's *Pietà, rispetto, amore* with the unexpected modulation occurring in the same place, though in a more obviously explosive form. Once again the opening idea is repeated by the melodic instruments of the orchestra over a vocal parlante but with a new inflexion given to the

250

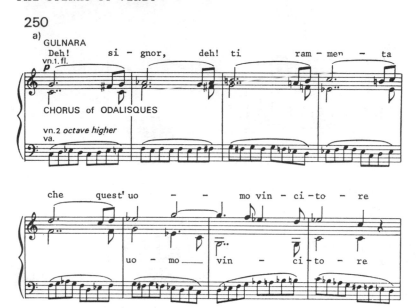

third phrase (A sharp instead of A). Once again the composer's instinct for developing melody remains to redeem a movement whose only merit is that it exploits the baritone's faculty for passing between extremes of emotion, from tenderness to fury, within a few notes.

Selim is called and told to summon Gulnara; meanwhile the Pasha breaks out in a cabaletta of vengeful savagery (*S'avvicina il tuo momento*), very much according to a well-tried but now rather tasteless recipe.

Very different is the passage where Gulnara enters and the two begin to fence verbally with each other. In the first movement of their duet (*Vieni Gulnara*) the dialogue is carried on over an orchestral melody in the manner of Donizetti's duet of the two spies ('Qui che fai') in *Lucrezia Borgia*. The sinuous line conveys the slyness, the bland scoring for violins and clarinets the Pasha's false suavity; while the sinister thud of horns, bassoons and cimbasso tells of the mailed fist behind the

251

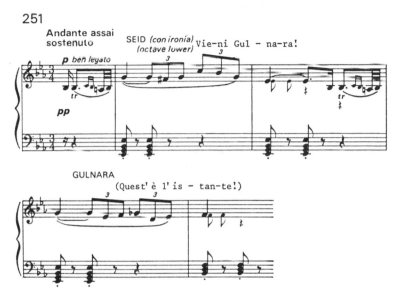

velvet glove. Gulnara suggests that though Corrado fully deserves to die he would be more useful alive since there will be a vast price on his head. But this the Pasha is not prepared to do for all the treasures of his Sultan's harem. Nevertheless, Gulnara insists, if Corrado were alive he could be made use of. But the Pasha has heard enough. Gulnara loves Corrado—so much is clear; and the music breaks away into a rhythmic declamation which anticipates the dialogue of Sparafucile and Maddalena.* Seid reviles his favourite, sometimes over tremolo strings with sweeping scales in the bass, sometimes with a still more terrifying quietness (Ex. 252, overleaf).

> 'Thou need'st not answer—thy confession speaks,
> Already reddening on thy guilty cheeks;
> Then, lovely dame, bethink thee and beware:
> 'Tis not *his* life alone may claim such care.'

For this final thrust Verdi has devised a musical period which spans two centuries of style and feeling. Beginning in a world of eighteenth-century elegance and suavity with what is almost a direct quotation from Mozart's 12th piano sonata it turns suddenly into an expression of upsurging revolutionary violence. Significantly the three-note figure which introduces each phrase is sited on middle C, in the centre of the high baritone's area of maximum strike. The same note will play an especially important role in Rigoletto's famous monologue, 'Pari siamo'.

* The parallel is effectively demonstrated by Mila, 'Lettura del Corsaro', pp. 64–5.

252

SEID

ma ba-da,o per-fi-da, al mio con-si-glio; non è il cor-

str. col canto

tutti

-sa - ro so-lo in pe-ri - glio

Finally in the stretta (*Sia l'istante maledetta*) the Pasha's fury erupts in full force.

> 'accursed was the moment when he bore
> Thee from the flames . . .'

> Ah, little reck'd that chief of womanhood—
> Which frowns ne'er quell'd, nor menaces subdued;
> And little deem'd he what thy heart, Gulnare!
> When soft could feel, and when incensed could dare.

A particularly interesting feature of this stretta is that at no point do the two voices merge their identity in the usual chain of sixths and thirds. Gulnara's line, mostly minor in contrast to the major of Seid, is marked *sotto voce* up to the final cadence, just after Seid has stormed out.★ Only then does she venture a high fortissimo B flat. He on the other hand remains fortissimo throughout making his exit to a phrase which contains a high G flat unaccompanied except by a roll on timpani. Not great music, perhaps; but it represents one of those steps towards dramatic truth which are apt to pass unnoticed in a minor work.

Scene 2: a prison cell

This scene has been compared to the start of *Fidelio*, Act II.† As in *I Due Foscari* Verdi has used solo cello and viola to create an atmosphere of gloom and bleakness supported this time by a murmuring accompaniment of the other strings in which

---

★ You know better than I that anger is not always expressed by shouting, but sometimes by a choked voice, as is the case here.' Letter to Marianna Barbieri-Nini, 6.10.1848, M. Conati, *Interviste e incontri con Verdi* (Milan, 1980), pp. 308–9—another proof that Verdi was not as indifferent to the opera's fate as is so often assumed.

† Toye, p. 284. Medici, p. 64.

the 'lamenting' semitone is prominent as in Ex. 243 a,* But whereas in the earlier work the texture was for the most part deliberately bare, here the writing abounds in poignant harmonic effects.

253

Corrado, like Florestan, is in chains. Like Florestan again his thoughts are with the woman he loves. The news of his death will surely kill her. If only he had a sword—but what is the use? Worn out with the day's events he lies down to sleep. Then Gulnara, with the stealth of Otello entering his wife's bedroom, comes into the cell. She gazes at the sleeping Corrado, who gradually stirs into wakefulness. Assured that she is real and not a spirit, he listens to what she has to say. So begins the formal part of the duet (*Seid la vuole*). Seid, Gulnara says, is impervious to her pleadings: none the less Corrado shall go free. She herself will help him. Corrado will have none of this.

> 'Unfit to vanquish, shall I meanly fly,
> The one of all my band that would not die?
> Yet there is one to whom my memory clings,
> Till to these eyes her own wild softness springs.'

Gulnara is saddened to learn that Corrado's affections are pledged elsewhere. She envies Medora with all her heart; and she hastens to disabuse Corrado of the idea that she herself is in love with Seid.

> 'I felt—I feel—love dwells with—with the free.
> I am a slave, a favour'd slave at best,
> To share his splendour, and seem very blest!'

She will bribe Corrado's gaolers; a ship will be awaiting them in the harbour. As for Seid—she has a dagger with which she will dispatch him as he lies asleep. But this only increases Corrado's unwillingness to escape. He will be no party to an act of treachery. Their argument concludes with repeated pleas from Gulnara, and repeated refusals from Corrado.

Sketched in 1846, this can be seen as the prefiguring of a new kind of duet which

---

* That this is intended as a deliberate reminiscence seems unlikely. The falling semitone has been a commonplace of Verdian language ever since *Nabucco*.

will emerge in greater perfection in Act I of *Macbeth*; it is not the duet of symmetrical, contrasted movements to be found in *I Due Foscari* or *La Traviata*, but one in
which the musical discourse adapts itself to the course of the dialogue sentence by
sentence, as will happen for instance in the great duets of *Don Carlos*. As yet the
technique is somewhat rudimentary. The problem of unifying 101 bars of freely
moving andante mosso is solved partly by a series of self-perpetuating patterns of
accompaniment in the composer's early manner, and partly by an element of
reprise at the 55th bar. But note how any a priori impression of symmetry is forestalled at the outset by two 5-bar phrases; how Gulnara's words 'Schiava son io,
Corsaro' are isolated from the musical flow in a kind of recitative. Of course there
is no trace here of the urgency which gives the grand duet in *Macbeth* so much of
its power. But each moment in the dialogue finds its appropriate expression within
the essentially conversational character of the setting: the brusque heavily scored
progression where Corrado first refuses Gulnara's help, the lamenting semitonal
figure where he refers to Medora, the access of rhythmic energy where Gulnara
denies any love for Seid. The duet enters a new phase (already prepared by an
accelerando) as she points out the danger which hangs over her own head and begs
Corrado to save them both, for her sake as well as his. There is a change of time
signature here, but the tempo reverts to andante mosso, so blurring the division
between what could be analysed as two separate movements. Gulnara's phrase
(*Non sai tu che sulla testa*) is superbly concentrated in its expression, with its Puccini-
like doubling of melody and bass. There is an echo here of *Aida* at her most tormented.

254

For the rest of the movement the two parties restate their position in flights of
pleasant if more conventional lyricism. At last she tears herself away; but the sinister
brass chords that punctuate the recitative tell us that her resolution is as unshaken as
his own. Then follows a stormy interlude for Corrado and orchestra recalling the
opening music of the prelude. Its presence at this point of the opera needs some
explanation. In the course of telescoping the narrative Piave understandably
resorted to some re-arrangement. In Byron, Gulnare twice comes to Conrad in
prison and it is between the two visits that she tries to prevail on Seid to spare his
life. Piave, however, has rolled both occasions into one, without allowing several
days to elapse between them. It was on one of those days that . . .

Came storm and darkness in their mingling might.
Oh! how he listen'd to the rushing deep,
That ne'er till now so broke upon his sleep . . .
He rais'd his iron hand to Heaven, and pray'd
One pitying flash to mar the form it made:
His steel and impious prayer attract alike—
The storm roll'd onward, and disdain'd to strike.

Based on Ex. 234 the entire episode is conveyed in two and a half pages of vocal score as a transition between two movements of the duet. It is an effective piece of writing for the 'tenore della maledizione', but little else.

The storm having died away Gulnara returns softly and with unsteady step. 'The deed,' she whispers, 'is done.' She has murdered the Pasha in his sleep. Once more the spirit of chivalry is aroused in Corrado. If he cannot love Gulnara he can at least save her. In the final stretta (*La terra, il ciel m'abborrino*) he replied to her anguished minor opening strophe with a verse in the major key, after which they join voices in their resolution to flee. Convention has again resumed its sway. This is formally a stretta like any other. But it is expressive, grateful to sing, and free from undue noise. The final resumption by full orchestra of the codetta theme *Fuggiam che salvo almen t'avrò* is apt and effective.

Scene 3: the island of the Corsairs

This final scene is inevitably all Piave. In Byron Gulnare dies on the ship that carries her and Conrad to the corsairs' island; while Medora by that time is already dead. So for the beginning the librettist has taken his cue from a scene earlier in the poem where those of the corsairs who have escaped return to tell Medora of Conrad's capture.

Ponderous orchestral gestures set the scene of desolation. The recollection on the oboe of Medora's opening song (Ex. 242) as she enters supported by her maidens is a beautiful touch (it may have been observed that oboe, as distinct from clarinet, melodies are rather rare in early Verdi and usually associated with extreme grief). Medora asks the corsairs for news of Corrado, but their dispirited appearance seems to tell her the truth that she has feared long since. She can only repeat, 'Corrado is no more,' to a desolate little three-bar phrase in D minor. She is already dying and will soon be with him in another world. Suddenly a ship is sighted—Corrado's. As he comes ashore the music mounts to a glorious lyrical climax on voices and orchestra, as though the whole world were joining in the lovers' embrace. But as in the last act of *Tristan* it is too late. Nevertheless before she can legitimately die Corrado has a certain amount of explaining to do, such as will require more than just a few lines of recitative. Hence a new complete movement (*Per me infelice*) based on a single rhythmic pattern and making use of the same principle of 'strophic variation' noted earlier.

The second strophe, shortened and at the same time harmonically varied, begins with Gulnara's *Grazie non curo* as she gently refuses Medora's thanks for having saved Corrado's life. The same cell generates a transitional passage during which the accompaniment takes on a pulsating motion with Medora's faltering breath; the

255

chorus murmur their sorrow, and the adagio finale begins with Ex. 236 of the Prelude sung by Medora, as she begs Corrado to draw near so that she may die in his arms. The use here of timpani to suggest a labouring pulse at the words *Del giorno i rai s' oscurano* is like an anticipation of Strauss's *Tod und Verklärung*. Medora's phrases are soft and broken with semiquaver pauses, Corrado's taut with despair; Gulnara's have a profound lyrical sadness. From these three threads is spun a beautiful if rather loosely knit finale. Only the final bars of the opera may cause a slight smile. Medora dead, Corrado in an agony of despair leaps from a rock into the sea. Gulnara and the chorus exclaim in horror and the curtain falls.

Il Corsaro is certainly minor Verdi. It is mostly conventional in form, with routine cabalettas, some undistinguished choruses and echoes of what he has done more adventurously in the past; also, like *Alzira*, it is awkwardly brief for an age when opera evenings are not filled out with ballets. But with all its shortcomings there remains much that is fine and characteristic: moments of lyrical poetry which are almost totally absent from *Alzira*, and a greater sense of its own limitations than is to be found in *Attila* and *I Masnadieri*. Medora's solo, her duet with Corrado, the andante of Gulnara's cavatina, the scene in the prison cell all have that depth which comes from Verdi's increasing harmonic range. The finale of Act I from the adagio concertato is a tour de force of thematic workmanship, all the more striking for being an exception to the usual Verdian rule. Then too there is an increasing sureness of touch in the realization of personalities. If Pasha Seid is the most two-dimensional of villains (and the subject hardly allows any other way of depicting him), Medora is a real, individual character, and all the more so for being conceived strictly within the framework of a comprimaria. A note more and she would have lost her identity, as surely as in Pacini's opera, where the plot itself is altered so as to give her parity with Gulnara. (As if Byron's heroine would have the 'unwomanly' courage to try to rescue her lover!)* But above all *Il Corsaro* shows the gradual precipitation of Verdi's mature style through contact with the French opera of the time. It is an influence which, paradoxically, will be even more marked in the next opera, which ought to be the most Italian of them all.

---

* Pacini's opera is a travesty in every sense of the word. Byron's manly hero is played by a contralto. The womanly Medora puts on man's clothes and goes in search of her lover. It is she, not Gulnara, who kills Seid; while Gulnara and Corrado sail away to live happily together ever after. The opera, commissioned for the opening of the Teatro Apollo, Rome, was as badly received as it deserved to be. Mendelssohn, who was present at the opening night, described the music as being beneath criticism. See A. Cametti, *La Musica Teatrale a Roma 100 anni fa* (Rome, 1931), pp. 19–20.

16 LA BATTAGLIA DI LEGNANO

LA BATTAGLIA DI LEGNANO

Opera in four acts
by
SALVATORE CAMMARANO
(after Joseph Méry's play, *La Battaille de Toulouse*)

*First performed at the
Teatro Argentina, Rome,
27 January 1849*

FEDERICO BARBAROSSA, German Emperor	BASSO COMPRIMARIO	Pietro Sottovia
FIRST CONSUL of Milan	SECONDO BASSO	Alessandro Lanzoni
SECOND CONSUL of Milan	SECONDO BASSO	Achille Testi
MAYOR OF COMO	SECONDO BASSO	Filippo Giannini
ROLANDO, a leading soldier of Milan	PRIMO BARITONO	Filippo Colini
LIDA, his wife	PRIMA DONNA SOPRANO	Teresa De Giuli-Borsi
ARRIGO, a soldier from Verona	PRIMO TENORE	Gaetano Fraschini
MARCOVALDO, a German prisoner	SECONDO BARITONO	Lodovico Butia
IMELDA, maidservant to Lida	SECONDA DONNA MEZZO-SOPRANO	Vincenza Marchesi
ARRIGO'S squire	SECONDO TENORE	Mariano Conti
A HERALD	SECONDO TENORE	Gaetano Ferri

Knights of death—magistrates and leaders of the people of Como—
Lida's serving maids—people of Milan—senators of Milan—soldiers
from Verona, Novara, Piacenza and Milan—German army

The action takes place in Milan and Como

Epoch: 1176

Verdi's next two operas have a mutually entangled history. At the time of the production of *Alzira* Verdi had signed a contract to write another opera for Naples in the summer of 1847.* He then spent the next three years trying to withdraw from it on one pretext or another, partly because of the attention he received from the Neapolitan columnists, partly because, as he told Count Arrivabene, 'the censorship is too strict to permit interesting subjects'.† The events of 1848 gave him the excuse he wanted. After five days of street fighting the Austrians were driven from Milan by the citizens in revolt; Venice threw out its Austrian governor and proclaimed a republic; the Duke of Parma fled into voluntary exile; the King of the Two Sicilies was obliged to grant his people a constitution. In the general turmoil the management of the San Carlo Theatre changed hands, and Verdi, receiving no word from the new impresario, regarded his contract as null and void. He returned to an idea which he had adumbrated shortly before his visit to London; that was, to compose with Cammarano an opera for Ricordi to place at whatever theatre he chose, provided it was not La Scala, Milan.‡ By this time a patriotic subject was clearly indicated. He wrote to Piave, now a citizen-soldier of the Venetian guard:

> Imagine whether I wanted to stay in Paris when I heard that there was a revolution in Milan! I left immediately when I heard the news, but I've been unable to see anything except those marvellous barricades. All honour to our brave champions. Honour to all Italy who at this moment is really great.
>
> You may be sure that the hour of her freedom has struck. The people will have it so . . . and there is no power on earth that can resist them! . . . So you're in the national guard? I'm so glad that you're only a private soldier. If I could have joined up I should want to be just an ordinary soldier but now I can only be a tribune and a wretched one at that because I'm only eloquent by fits and starts.§

Verdi had another reason besides patriotism for his sudden visit to Italy. He wanted to buy the Villa S. Agata, near Busseto. The purchase arranged, he then returned to Paris. There was nothing he could do to help the patriots on the spot; and in any case the war was starting to go badly for the Italians. The insurgents could not agree among themselves on the type of government to be set up. There

---

* Letter to Antonio Barezzi, undated (June 1845). *Copialettere*, pp. 14–15.

† Letter to Arrivabene, 19.3.146. Alberti, p. xxviii.

‡ Letters to Giovanni Ricordi, 20.5 and 24.6.1847. *Copialettere*, pp. 37–40. It is in these two letters that Verdi for the first time suggests that in his contract with the theatres Ricordi should make it illegal to modify the score whether by transposition or omission of individual numbers —apart from the dances, which could always be left out. It was an unrealistic proposal at the time, but it sheds a revealing light on Verdi's growing insistence on the integrity of dramatic composition since the all-important experience of *Macbeth*.

§ Letter to Piave, 21.4.1848. A. Bonaventura (ed.), *Una lettera di Giuseppe Verdi finora non pubblicata* (Florence, 1948).

were three possibilities—a federation of Italian republics under the presidency of the Pope; a single republic; and annexation by the House of Savoy, which had at least granted its subjects a constitution. To all hopes of the first the Allocution of Pius IX put an end. More and more people in Lombardy inclined to the third solution, particularly if it brought a standing army to their aid. So, led by their King Carlo Alberto, Piedmontese troops crossed their frontier and marched to attack Radetzky's army which had concentrated itself in the so-called quadrilateral, enclosed by the fortified towns of Verona, Mantua, Peschiera and Legnago.* On 27 July Ricordi wrote sadly to Verdi in Paris: 'After three days of fighting during which the battle went in our favour . . . Radetzky attacked our men in the rear and we were forced to withdraw to the Mincio.'† The Battle of Custoza followed; the Piedmontese retreated through Milan, jeered at by a populace convinced it had been betrayed. Then came the armistice of Salasco; and Milan was once more Austrian territory.

In Paris Verdi did what he could to help his country. He signed a petition which was presented to General Cavaignac begging him as the chief of the French army to go to the aid of a sister republic.‡ But Cavaignac was already fully occupied in putting down the July insurrection, and the government was in no position to help the people of a foreign country. At the suggestion of Mazzini whom he had met in London Verdi set to music a patriotic poem by the young poet Mameli. The completed work was dispatched to Mazzini in October with a letter expressing the hope that 'Suona la tromba' might soon be sung on the plains of Lombardy amid the roar of the cannon.§ Indeed, ever since the spring revolution Verdi had brooded on more than one subject with which to come forward as 'tribune' for the new Italy. *Cola di Rienzi*, based on Bulwer Lytton's *The Last of the Tribunes* and considered as early as 1843, was soon dropped, mainly because Cammarano could not see an effective way of treating it. The love interest, he said, was tepid, and the end of the story did little credit to the Italian people. Why not, Cammarano pursued, return to the great days of medieval Italy—to the Lombard League that had defeated Frederick Barbarossa in 1175? The date and the occasion could be grafted on to an already existing plot by the French poet Joseph Méry. 'A story like that,' he added, 'should stir every man with an Italian soul in his breast.'¶ Verdi was convinced, and so was Ricordi.

On Cammarano's side work on *La Battaglia di Legnano* progressed so slowly that during the summer of 1848 Verdi had leisure to consider another operatic subject, about which he wrote to Piave: Guerrazzi's novel *L'Assedio di Firenze*, of which more later. This too had a patriotic inspiration, clouded, however, by a pessimism that the events of the summer made understandable. *La Battaglia di Legnano*, on the other hand, was conceived in the springtime of Italian hopes, when it seemed that the Austrians might have left Italy for good. If it was not finished until the first month of 1849 the fault was largely Cammarano's, who took his work as a librettist more seriously than most and would not be hurried. He was much less biddable than Piave.

* Not as Toye evidently believed (p. 60) the modern name for Legnano.
† Letter from Giovanni Ricordi, 27.7.1848. Abbiati, I, pp. 763–4.
‡ Joint letter to Cavaignac and Bastide, 8.8.1848. *Copialettere*, pp. 466–7.
§ Letter to Mazzini, 18.10.1848. *Copialettere*, p. 469.
¶ Letter from Cammarano, 20.4.1848. *Carteggi Verdiani*, II, p. 59.

Written in 1828, Joseph Méry's play *La Bataille de Toulouse* was well known in Italy and admired out of all proportion to its value, possibly since Méry was a nostalgic Bonapartist and Napoleon's name was still associated with the cause of Italian freedom. The story, set in the last days of the Peninsular War, concerns the personal tragedy of three people. Isaura, a young Spanish girl, has been separated from her French lover Gaston de Verville. Believing him to be dead, she marries at her dying father's request a Major Duhoussais to whom she bears a son. But Gaston is not dead. He has followed his Emperor all over Europe, and now, sole survivor from the Battle of Leipzig, he has returned to take part in the last desperate defence of France. He is an old friend of Duhoussais, whom he regards as a second father; and he is determined not to break up the older man's home whatever his own personal feelings. It is Isaura herself who insists on a word with him in private if only to excuse her apparent betrayal of their love. Worse still, she visits him in his lodgings to bid him a last farewell before the battle. They are betrayed by Gaston's landlord Dandrey, a dastardly Anglophile. Duhoussais comes to Gaston's room and in due course discovers Isaura hiding on the balcony. He repulses her with bitter scorn, while on the friend to whom he had entrusted the care of his wife and son should he himself be killed he inflicts the most humiliating punishment that can happen to a patriot—not to be allowed to fight for his country. He locks the supposedly guilty pair in the room. Gaston in despair leaps from the balcony to his death as the curtain falls.

In Méry's play, the patriotic motif is implicit, and all the stronger for being understated; for his heroes are as tight-lipped as the English they are fighting. The element of emotion is provided by Isaura, who being a foreigner cannot be expected to have the self-control of the two men (strange how Wellington's values seem to have crossed the lines of battle!). Cammarano's task was to bring patriotism into the foreground without upsetting the balance of the drama. Hence the various choral and scenic effects which have no counterpart in Méry: an introductory scene which shows the gathering of the Italian contingents and the reunion of the two heroes ending with a 'conjuration' in the style of *Guillaume Tell* Act II: a second conjuration where Arrigo (Gaston) joins the 'Knights of Death' (a kind of suicide squad); a grand finale in which Arrigo is borne in mortally wounded, having saved the day for Italy. Like Cherubino he has survived his leap from the window to kill Barbarossa in battle, and see his friend and his friend's wife reconciled in the knowledge that 'he who dies for his fatherland cannot be so guilty in his heart'. All this is routine musical theatre. But it was Verdi's own idea that the two patriots should at one point confront Barbarossa, and it gave Cammarano 'much food for thought'.* Indeed the problem of uniting the grand tableaux with the drama of individuals, of passing from public to private emotions was never very happily solved. The strength of Méry's Gaston lies not in what he says but in what he refuses to say. Clearly this is no use for Italian opera, especially in a part written for Italy's foremost dramatic tenor, Gaetano Fraschini. Therefore Arrigo must be equally emotional as lover and patriot. To give him a motive for joining the 'Knights of Death', Cammarano added an unpleasant scene between him and Lida, in which the jilted lover hurls hysterical abuse at her for having married someone else in the belief that he himself had been killed. When forced to rely on their own

---

* Letter from Cammarano, 11.7.1848, *Carteggi Verdiani*, II, p. 59.

invention Italian librettists were ill at ease, and Cammarano was no exception. It is possible that he considered Arrigo's arguments reasonable; to most people they will appear childish and egotistical, their only justification being that they maintain the high emotional voltage that every Verdian grand duet requires. Then, by the most bewildering of non sequiturs, there follows the scene with Barbarossa in which the male parties in the eternal triangle are seen collaborating in perfect harmony, no trace of awkwardness between them.

When it came to details of theatrical effect, Cammarano was on surer ground altogether. He had a fund of stage experience of which Verdi was only too willing to avail himself, so long as the poet's advice did not run counter to his own ideas. The text of the last two acts arrived in Paris together with copious suggestions for the musical treatment.* The word 'infamia' in the trio-finale of Act III was to be sung by all three voices together over a cadence; the entire effect of the line 'un vile, un infame egli è' would lie in the 'No!' which follows, and which should therefore be repeated several times. The 'Coro dei Morti' (i.e. 'Chorus of the Knights of Death') should be preceded by a 'grave ritornello as befits the solemnity of time and place'. The instructions for the final tableau are even more detailed, and include ideas for the entry and placing of the stage band as well as for the manner of Arrigo's death.

Some of these Verdi observed, others not.† Both in the Chorus of Death and in the trio of Act III he did almost everything Cammarano asked, except in the final movement. In the scene between Rolando (Duhoussais) and Marcovaldo (the equivalent of Dandrey with an added motive of thwarted love), he compromised by having the letter sung not spoken, in accordance with Cammarano's invariable prescription, but keeping the string-tremolo which he had been asked to avoid. In the death of Arrigo he went his own way entirely, even to the extent of dispensing with a banda of the conventional type.

His own contribution to the scheme included as well as the scene with Barbarossa a part for Arrigo's 'squire' in Act I, the extended recitative for the guilt-ridden Lida at the start of Act III, Scene 2, the duettino in which Rolando blesses his infant son, and the simultaneous cantilene of Lida, monks and populace in Act IV— a clear inspiration from the Parisian stage, though Cammarano insisted that it had occurred to him as well. Generally speaking the poet's instinct was for tradition, and he apologizes when forced to break with it, as in the unusually long passage between the cantabile and cabaletta for Rolando in Act III, or when reducing Lida's part to a minimum in Act IV. Verdi on the other hand was all for speed and novelty: if he wanted four more lines for Arrigo and Rolando in the Barbarossa scene it was merely to avoid repetition of words. With three weeks to go before the opening night he wished Cammarano to replace the two quatrains in the duettino between Rolando and Lida with two couplets, so as to maintain the dramatic temperature.‡ But as always the arguments between Italy's leading composer and senior practising librettist were fruitful, and contributed no little to Verdi's growing sense of dramatic craftsmanship.

The first night of *La Battaglia di Legnano* was fixed for the carnival season at the

---

* See letters from Cammarano, 9 and 29.10.1848. Abbiati, I, pp. 771–3.
† See letters to Cammarano, Sept. and 23.11.1848. *Copialettere*, pp. 55–6, 60–1.
‡ Letter to Cammarano, 6.1.1849. Abbiati, I, p. 781.

Teatro Argentina in Rome. Both time and place were well chosen. Rome was one of the cities that had not yet succumbed to Austrian pressure. Pope Pius IX had found it less easy to reverse the current political trend than he had hoped. His minister Rossi had been murdered by fanatical Republicans; he himself was forced to disband his Swiss guard and so remained virtually a prisoner in his own city. In November he contrived to escape to Gaeta in the Kingdom of the Two Sicilies, from where he tried unsuccessfully to negotiate his return to Rome with the diplomatic aid of King Ferdinand. Within a fortnight of the premiere of Verdi's opera Rome had declared itself a republic.

Not surprisingly the work itself enjoyed a *succès de scandale*, the last act being repeated in its entirety. A similar reception awaited it eleven years later in Parma when it was revived under the title *La Sconfitta degli Austriachi*. But both were exceptional cases linked respectively to the dawn of the Roman republic and the unification of Italy. Elsewhere the opera did not escape the taint of a *pièce d'occasion*, somewhat to the composer's mortification.

During the 1850s *La Battaglia di Legnano* inevitably fell foul of the censors. With Verdi's own consent it was changed into *L'Assedio di Arlem*, Barbarossa becoming the Duke of Alva; but this did nothing to increase its circulation. One reason was that in his contract with Ricordi, Verdi had over-reached himself. As in the case of *Gerusalemme* he had demanded such a high proportion of the fee for hire and purchase of the score that in order to show a profit Ricordi had to demand prices which the average theatre could not afford to pay. After a grand remonstrance from Ricordi* the contracts for *La Battaglia di Legnano* and *Gerusalemme* were modified accordingly. But the first opera had lost its novelty appeal; the other had never had any, since most Italians regarded it as a mere debasement of *I Lombardi*. Both operas continued to do badly.

But Verdi himself thought very highly of *La Battaglia di Legnano* and in the years that followed the spectacular flowering of his mid-career with *Rigoletto*, *Il Trovatore* and *La Traviata* he hoped to rescue it from oblivion with the help of Leone Bardare, the poet who had completed *Il Trovatore* after Cammarano's death. 'I don't want a mere change of names and title with a few lines and words here and there; I want an entirely new subject, of the same character and no less exciting. As regards plot and action this shouldn't be too difficult, but as regards *colorito* [that mysterious but significant word] it will be very difficult indeed. To retain all the enthusiasm for fatherland and freedom without actually mentioning either will be a hard task, but we can try . . .'† Whatever Verdi had in mind Bardare evidently failed to provide. His synopsis included an aria for Arrigo in the middle of the 'Coro dei morti', which the composer objected to on the grounds that it would spoil the shape of the scene. Otherwise he gave the new scheme cautious approval, merely stipulating that Bardare should keep as much of the original text as possible.‡ But early in 1856, with a similar work of rehabilitation on *Stiffelio* almost completed, he took up the matter once more with his Neapolitan friend De Sanctis. '. . . You will need to go to Bardare and try and persuade him to change the subject again. To tell you the truth I don't like this *Lida* of his. Always the same

---

* See previous chapter.
† Letter to C. De Sanctis, 6.7.1854. *Carteggi Verdiani*, I, pp. 25–6.
‡ Letter to C. De Sanctis, 17.2.1855. *Carteggi Verdiani*, I, pp. 29–30.

things—meanness of setting and costumes, and all so hackneyed. For instance couldn't the scene be transferred to Spain at the time of the Moors? To Granada which is such a beautiful country? . . . the period of the Moorish invasion is too well known: better the time of their defeat or rather a period between the two. I'm just talking roughly . . .'* Meanwhile there was a new opera to compose for Venice the following spring,† and time was running out. Two months later Verdi admitted privately to De Sanctis that if Bardare was too busy to rewrite the libretto he would be happy to pay him off for the work already done;‡ and there the project ended. Many years later a French version entitled *Pour la Patrie* was prepared for the opening of the Théâtre Château d'Eau in Paris in the 1880s, but the performance never materialized. Nevertheless the opera was published with the new translation, and according to Muzio in a letter of 1886 it was extremely popular in the provincial theatres.§ This is significant. For one of the paradoxes of this most consciously Italian work is that it could only have been written in Paris, against a background of French opera and above all the French military march, whose tradition had flourished in full vigour ever since the days of Napoleon. The operas of Auber are often a series of marches thinly disguised. In a word the march is to early nineteenth-century French opera what the waltz is to Viennese operetta. Verdi was reaping the fruits of his first encounter with French opera in *Jérusalem*, just as he was to do on a much larger scale and to still better purpose in the works which followed *Les Vêpres Siciliennes*. Nobody is likely to miss the echo of the 'Marseillaise' in the overture to *La Battaglia di Legnano*.

Not that there is any lack of Italian melody in the opera. But it is subjected as never before to a process of refinement and elaboration. The fidgeting, mechanical accompaniments which are a hallmark of Verdi's early style are far less in evidence here than in the opera which follows, even though *Luisa Miller* is generally held to mark the beginning of the composer's so-called 'second manner'. Such self-perpetuating patterns as do occur in *La Battaglia di Legnano* (mainly in the choral scenes) are unusually studied, obviously with Rossini's French operas in mind. Everything is deliberately made 'interesting'; nothing is repeated without harmonic variation wherever possible. Even the scoring is calculated with greater care than one expects from Verdi at the time. In no opera before *Les Vêpres Siciliennes* does the composer seem so eager to parade his French lessons.

One result of all this is to emphasize the dichotomy inherent in Cammarano's scheme, a shortcoming of which Verdi was less aware in that he had not read the original play.¶ The grand scenes are more imposing than ever; the domestic ones have an intimacy and feeling which is new. But they remain on different levels. More even than *Il Corsaro* (if for a different reason) *La Battaglia di Legnano* is an opera of individual scenes, rather than a unified whole. But what lends it particular interest is the fact that it was the first opera to be *conceived* in the post-*Macbeth* era.

---

* Letter to C. De Sanctis, 28.3.1856. *Carteggi Verdiani*, I, p. 33.

† *Simon Boccanegra.*

‡ Letter to C. De Sanctis, 5.5.1856. *Carteggi Verdiani*, I, p. 35.

§ Letter from Muzio, 24.4.1886. *Carteggi Verdiani*, IV, p. 219.

¶ 'I think poor Cammarano took this libretto from something by a French playwright—Méry, I think—and I think the title was *The Battle of Toulouse* or *The Siege of Toulouse* but I'm not at all sure.' Letter to De Sanctis, 6.7.1854. *Carteggi Verdiani*, I, pp. 25–6. Nor, it appears, are most of Verdi's biographers. Only Abbiati and Luzio appear to be aware of the source of this opera.

It contains evidence of a dramatic sensibility not to be found in the three operas preceding it, all of which had their form determined before the composer's first encounter with Shakespeare.

The overture is so arresting that one can only wonder why it should not be heard in the concert halls at least as often as that of *Nabucco*. In basic form it could be called the overture to *Giovanna d'Arco* writ large, just as Rossini's *Semiramide* overture is an amplification of the design first used in *La Scala di Seta*. But that is only half the story, since in Verdi's case the later piece contains so much more than the earlier even implies. The first movement alone offers a fine example of what he could do with a single idea. It opens with what is in effect the signature tune of the Lombard League: a march-like melody with the archetypal quality of a leitmotif.*

256

Trumpets, trombones and cimbasso—the most cutting combination that Verdi knew, with no horns or bassoons to blunt the edge. Woodwind take up the theme against a soft background of strings, then propel it through various keys to a melting A major cadence, beautifully delayed, which breaks off just before its final note. There is a pause and Ex. 256 explodes on full orchestra in C major. Then after ten bars of violence and self-assertion the horns and bassoons lead gently into D major for the andante.

257

The theme, later to be associated with Arrigo as he sits writing to his mother the night before the battle, is worked into what sounds superficially like an accompanied four-part canon at the third above between clarinet, oboe, flute and bassoon. On closer hearing it turns out to be as much a piece of charming 'trompe

---

* A variant of this archetype, no less memorable, is the Liverpudlian folk-song 'Johnny Todd', familiar to thousands as the signature-tune of the television series *Z-Cars*.

l'oreille' as the pseudo-canon in the *Giovanna d'Arco* overture. But the parts have genuine contrapuntal independence and the texture, though more elaborate than in the earlier work, is no less transparent. Moreover, the rondo-structure which was embryonic in the overture of 1845 is here fully formed. Ex. 257 recurs twice, each time with the solo instruments succeeding each other, stretto-fashion, at intervals of one bar instead of two. The last appearance is decorated with cascades of demisemiquavers from the flute, recalling a similar movement in the ballet music from *Jérusalem*. Between the three statements are two episodes based on this idea:

258

The second episode includes a huge outburst in D minor vaguely hinting at the music of the second conjuration scene, after which Ex. 258 is resumed in D flat major. That this should give an effect of almost Beethovenian surprise shows how well Verdi has managed to preserve the tonal orientation—usually a very minor consideration for him as for his compatriots.

The final allegro brings back Ex. 256 unchanged except for a figure for timpani between the main beats. Then comes a variant on that melodic idea which first occurred to Verdi in *Oberto*:

259

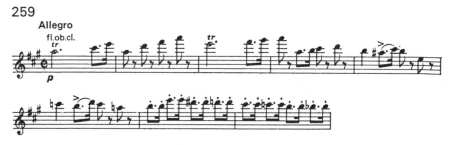

Starting on woodwind supported by lower brass it passes in a two-stage crescendo to the full orchestra. For the moment it seems to have ousted Ex. 256 in importance. Not only does it carry the main burden of the development, but its appearance in F major over a shifting bass gives it the quality almost of a second subject; and as in a similar context in the first movement of Mozart's 'Haffner' Symphony the sharp ear will detect the original theme (Ex. 256) persisting in the heart of the texture. In the reprise, reached by a long dominant preparation most unusual in Verdi, the two subjects are combined again; but this time Ex. 259 appears as a fife-like countermelody to Ex. 256, and as such it will appear in the final scene of the opera. The true relationship between the themes has now been made clear and it remains merely to introduce a powerful coda with an echo, perhaps unconsciously, of Europe's most famous revolutionary song (Ex. 260, facing page). After a series of bold, unorthodox cadences—F major, A, B flat major, A, C major, A—all featuring Verdi's idiosyncratic use of the 6/4 chord and all recalled in the con-

260

juration scene of Act III, the piece winds up with a final, triumphal statement of Ex. 256. It is all in the last resort too consciously theatrical to rank with the world's greatest overtures; yet it is difficult to find another which deploys its themes in a more original way.

ACT I

He lives*

Scene 1: a part of rebuilt Milan near the walls

(From one part of the city the soldiers of Piacenza are advancing together with detachments from Verona, Brescia, Novara and Vercelli. The street is crowded with people, so too the balconies of the near-by houses which are hung with festive garlands and gaily coloured bunting.)

The opening scene is laid out with an almost classical symmetry: march—chorus—cavatina (Arrigo)—chorus—romanza (Rolando)—chorus ('Giuramento')—march. The opening instrumental movement is extended in a crescendo as the various detachments march on to the scene, and a decrescendo where they march off at the end. The chorus which follows it is the hymn of the Lombard League (*Viva Italia! sacro un patto*) sung to an unaccompanied version of Ex. 256.

'A sacred pact binds all the sons of Italy; it has made our country a land of heroes. Unfurl the banners of the Lombard League and freeze the marrow of proud Barbarossa!

> Viva Italia forte ed una
> Colla spada e col pensier!

At the final lines the women from their balconies chime in with a 'Viva Italia!' and the piece ends as a full chorus. Among the soldiers from Verona is young Arrigo, who comes forward and apostrophizes his beloved in a simple cavatina (*La pia materna mano*). It is a simple double-quatrain design very much in the tradition of the gentle andantes and andantinos with which Verdi liked to launch even his most forceful tenor parts; but it is longer-breathed than most, with an unusual rhythmic cut which will be recalled in Ulrica's invocation (*Un Ballo in Maschera*)—see Ex. 261, overleaf.

The melody is of the continuous kind. Not a single phrase is repeated either at long or at short range; every idea leads to something new and often surprising—as

* It was Cammarano who insisted, according to his custom, on calling the four acts 'Parts', each with a separate title. Letter to Verdi, 29.10.1848. Abbiati, I, pp. 772-3.

261

Andante sostenuto

ARRIGO *dolciss. ed espress.*

La pi - a ma-ter-na ma -'no   chiu - se la mia fe - ri - ta; ep-

- pur   da te lon-tan, da te lon-ta - no io non sen-tia la vi - ta:

for instance the sequence of quick-changing harmonies just before the half-close in the second quatrain ('parea sepolto sepolto il mio cor') or the almost uncannily Chopinesque coda. As always the most harmonically complex moments are entrusted to strings alone.

Another detachment of soldiers is heard approaching, again to the strains of Ex. 256. They are the troops of Milan led by Rolando. He and Arrigo exchange an incredulous greeting—for Arrigo was believed to have been killed at the Siege of Susa. In fact he had been carried home wounded to his native Verona and nursed back to health. Their dialogue is set as a free arioso over a rapid orchestral accompaniment of studied elaboration (Ex. 262, facing page).

Rolando's line is characteristic of the music that Verdi liked to provide for the smooth, high baritone Filippo Colini, for whom explosions of force had to be kept to a minimum. His grief at the supposed death of his comrade is conveyed in desolate minor ninths and broken triplets which seem to echo the 'Lachrymosa' from Mozart's Requiem. The Romanza (*Ah m'abbraccia d'esultanza*) is also very much *sui generis*, fast in tempo, but profoundly tender, the vocal line doubled at the third above by an unfamiliar combination of flute and bassoon (Ex. 263, p. 400).

If at first blush this seems like a cabaletta to complement Arrigo's andante* in form it is not a cabaletta at all but an air *à la française* with an A–B–A design such as can be found in Gounod and Bizet passim, the central section ('O buon Dio la tua possanza') forming a contrast in texture, tonality (D minor leading to F major) and even pace (*meno mosso*). Off-stage trumpets herald the arrival of the two consuls who have come to command the army to swear allegiance to the new cause. Both full basses, they make an impressive entrance. But they are secondary parts, not principals. Therefore it is Arrigo and Rolando who in rough alternation launch each phrase of the oath (*Tutti giuriam difenderla*) which is taken up and repeated by the rest as in *Guillaume Tell*, *Marin Faliero* and countless others. However, reluctant to forego the effect, so often exploited before, of downward arpeggios sung by the basso profondo voice, Verdi allowed his consuls a striking unison phrase ('Milan defendere tutti giuriam') before the end of the movement. In a final allegro vivo (*Domandan vendetta gli altari spogliati*) the music rises twice from bare unison sonority (pp) through a series of short sequences to a cadence of great splendour in E flat major, after which the soldiers leave to a decrescendo of the same march theme that played them in.

★ See Osborne, p. 193.

262

Scene 2: a shady spot surrounded by a group of trees. Near by are the moats, new-filled with water, which surround the city walls. Lida comes forward wrapped in thought, followed by her women, and sits down in the shade. There she remains absorbed, gazing up at the sky

The women cannot understand why on this day of triumph she alone seems unable to share in the general rejoicing. Their chorus *Plaude all'arrivo Milan dei forti* starts in the vein of 'Si festevole mattino' from *Un Giorno di Regno* with identical rhythm and scoring. But here the rustic simplicity is overlaid with various sophisticated devices—piquant instrumental figures in the style of Meyerbeer, with chromatic inner parts recalling the Mercadante of *Il Giuramento* (Ex. 264, overleaf). Violins playing semiquavers on the point of the bow decorate the return of the main theme, and a characteristic epigram of modulation embellishes the coda.

Rousing herself from her reverie, Lida tells her ladies that she too loves her

263

264

country; but how can she be happy with her brothers and both her parents killed in the war? Tears are her only consolation. The andante of her cavatina (*Quante volte come un dono*) takes us straight into the world of Chopin's nocturnes—a Chopin experienced directly, not through the medium of Bellini. True the affinity between the Polish composer and his Italian predecessor is not easy to rationalize in terms of mutual influence, since it is clear that the basic style of each was formed independently of the other. As early as *La Straniera*, in the trio 'No, non ti son rivale', Bellini had arrived at harmonic effects implying a pianistic rather than vocal configuration long before he could have heard a note of Chopin's music. Likewise the early piano music of Chopin was composed some years before *Il Pirata* had carried Bellini's fame across the Alps. The chief difference between them lies in Chopin's infinitely greater subtlety and sophistication—a quality no less evident in Lida's andante: in the twisting accompaniment with its flattened sixth, wonderfully expressive of grief; in the clarinet sigh (*x*) which leads from A flat major to E flat minor at the start of the second quatrain; and by an avoidance of the obvious throughout (Ex. 265, facing page).

How often has Lida prayed for death; but she is a mother and has her duty. Though the movement is cast in the time-honoured simple design (a^1 a^2 b a^3 and coda) the keys shift more freely than usual. The coda, interrupting the final cadence

265

of the melody, seems like an extension of it rather than a new idea. Twice it soars up to a peak above the stave, each time with a different harmonization, before subsiding into a cadential phrase with a progression of Lisztian daring. An allegro agitato heralds the German prisoner Marcovaldo, who has come to force his un-welcome attentions on Lida. Before she can repulse him, Imelda enters to say that Rolando has returned, and with him is—Arrigo. Lida pronounces the fatal words: 'He lives!' on the summit of an orchestral crescendo and in a tone of ecstasy which does not escape Marcovaldo. She then breaks into a cabaletta of joy (*A frenarti o cor nel petto*) brilliant and mostly piano since she cannot afford to make her feelings too plain. To suggest a joy that ill conceals itself Verdi does deliberately what in Oronte's cavatina from *I Lombardi* he had done as a matter of course: he throws in the full orchestra together with trombones just before the reprise of the opening phrase. In the earlier opera the result was needlessly heavy. Here it has genuine dramatic point. Otherwise the cabaletta is a commonplace affair complete with an introductory orchestral statement of the kind with which Verdi was beginning to dispense in similar contexts, and also a central ritornello in which Imelda and the women contribute a characteristic comment on their mistress's change of mood. Only an ominous D flat (flattened submediant) in the accompaniment links this movement with the mood of the andante.

Rolando enters, greets his wife affectionately, presents her to Arrigo. But why is Arrigo trembling? His friend mutters something about an old wound. 'Liar,' says Marcovaldo to himself. Rolando continues unnoticing. Arrigo, he says, often stayed in her father's house in the course of his duties; now he is to be their guest. He signs to Marcovaldo and the women to leave them, when once more trumpets are heard off stage. A herald enters and announces that their spies have reported German troops gathering on the Alpine approaches. Rolando, as leader of the Milanese army, is summoned to a council of war. He leaves the former lovers, Arrigo and Lida, to confront one another in a remarkably original duet (*È ver, sei d'altri?*), a unique synthesis of old and new. Already in *Il Corsaro* Verdi had experimented with continuous dialogue in a single movement. Here the principle is carried still further, the entire duet being comprehended within the initial allegro. If it retains certain aspects of the two-movement plan which Donizetti and Bellini often used, it evolves in a manner that can only be called classical: a variant of sonata form to be found in operas written about the turn of the century, with exposition, development and a new idea where one expects the recapitulation (compare 'Gut, Söhnchen, gut!' from *Fidelio*). Arrigo's opening gambit (Ex. 266 a) with its declamatory pauses after each phrase develops on Rossinian lines into a more periodic structure, including Rossini's favourite rhythm of cadential preparation (♫♫ ♫ ♫♫ ♫ etc.) but unexpectedly it modulates, loses sight of the B flat tonic and finishes in the dominant; so that Lida's 'dissimilar' reply (Ex. 266 b) takes on the character of a second subject.

266

This too is extended into a self-sufficient period, ending unequivocally with an F major cadence. It is an exposition in a literal as well as a musical sense. Both parties have stated their position, Arrigo his horror and outrage that Lida should be another's after she had sworn eternal faith to him, Lida the reasons why she acted as she did—the belief that Arrigo had been killed and her father's dying wish that she should marry Rolando. What follows is an orthodox development adapted to the special requirements of Verdian dialectic, each vocal intervention being accompanied by a change of key. Most of the argument falls to Arrigo either in long, smooth phrases of sardonic fury or in declamatory outbursts leaping from one end of the compass to the other. Like the future Stiffelio (a part also created for Fraschini) Arrigo is an Otello in embryo. The modulations are typically steep and sudden:

ARRIGO	When the fatal news of my death reached you, What grief and mourning it cost your Sensitive soul! The sudden wedding proves it only too well.	*F minor–C minor*
LIDA	Arrigo!	*F minor*
ARRIGO	This was the faith you had pledged to me! Remember that at the feet of the Eternal God You shall be brought face to face with the defender of Italy If he should die for her.	*D flat major– C sharp minor*
LIDA	Woe is me!	*D major (implied)*
ARRIGO	Answer! speak! Can you excuse yourself?	*D minor*
LIDA	Father!	*F major (implied)*
ARRIGO	The guilty are always ready to blame others for their misdeeds.	*F minor*
LIDA	You are more cruel than the fate I suffer.*	*B flat minor*

And here for a while the music remains with an emphasis on the dominant in preparation for a return to the original key. The reprise is replaced by a cabaletta in which the voices sing not in alternate periods but in overlapping phrases, and continue throughout ritornello and coda; but the 5-bar structure of the opening phrase helps to maintain the sense of forward drive and avoid any lapse into form.

267

T'a- ma - i, t'amai   qual an - ge-lo, or qual de-mon· t'ab-bor-ro!

Note how the bar containing the high A is harmonized differently for each voice, giving an effect of contradiction similar to that of 'Süsse Thränen, bitt're Thränen' in the aforementioned trio from *Fidelio*. Arrigo once loved Lida as an angel; now he hates her as a she-devil; Lida wonders that she can suffer so much and still be alive. If the melodic material is entirely new a link with the previous section exists in the form of a pulsating figure (*x*) which, beginning as a musical

* This is merely an approximation to the sense of the original. A word-for-word translation of Cammarano's fustian would be intolerable.

embodiment of Arrigo's brutal gesture, is then transformed into a symbol of his persistent, all-pervasive fury. It is ironical that this most illogical of operatic arguments is set with a musical logic worthy of the Viennese classical masters.

ACT II

Barbarossa!

Scene: a magnificent room in the town hall of Como. The shutters at the back are closed. The Dukes and Magistrates are assembling.

The magistrates and city fathers of Como are in Council, the mayor presiding. A sub-fusc orchestration of strings, clarinets, bassoons, horns, and cimbasso gives the proceedings an air of conspiracy; yet the councillors are not actively conspiring, they are merely furtive and frightened, as they exchange comments on the latest rumours. Is it true that the proud city of Milan is stooping to make a pact with Frederick Barbarossa? Too late! The scoring darkens still further (clarinets, bassoons, violas) for their chorus (*Sì tardi ed invano*) in which they gloat over the discomfiture of a rival city. The major sequel (*Dai padri, dagl' avi in noi fu trafuso*) in which their hatred finds a noisy outlet is, as usual, less distinguished.

268

The mayor now announces the arrival of delegates from the 'impudent' Lombard League. Arrigo and Rolando enter while the brass plays Ex. 256 yet again. Rolando briefly explains the situation. Another army of Germans has made its way down the Adige and is at present being held by the Veronese. Frederick Barbarossa is at Pavia, and must be prevented at all costs from linking up with them. Only the Comaschi can bar his way, making use of the natural defences of their lake. A solo violin playing part of Ex. 268 indicates the resistance to Rolando's words. The city fathers murmur something about their pact with Frederick—whereat Arrigo bursts in passionately. How can they speak of such a pact without blushing for shame? In the duet (*Ah ben vi scorgo*) Rolando and he plead with all the lyrical eloquence at their command. The men of Como have the faces of Italians but the hearts of barbarians. The time will come when their grandchildren will be ashamed to bear their name. May history never have to call them the murderers of their brothers, nor their race be cursed by posterity. It is another instance of the device noted in *Il Corsaro* whereby an essentially bland theme in the major key, doubled by clarinets in thirds, is repeated obsessively so as to convey intense bitterness and irony* emphasized by such details as the accenting of the words 'assassini, assassini'. Throughout the movement a powerful crescendo of feeling is built up. Restless

---

* For a similar denunciation couched in the same key and conveyed in the same musical language see the concertato 'Maffio Orsini, Signora, son io' from *Lucrezia Borgia*.

figuration on the violas conveys the reaction of the council to these patriotic sentiments. At length Arrigo asks what reply he should give to those who sent him. '*I
will give it*,' cries a bass voice like a thunderclap. It is Barbarossa. The action then
freezes into the adagio of the finale (*A che smarriti e pallidi*) which is as schematic in
its design as any that Verdi wrote. Federico and the two patriots confront each
other in a succession of 8-bar ideas. The first (A flat minor) is jerky, almost neutral,
as Federico remarks sarcastically on his enemies' pallor and confusion. They reply
quietly but firmly, again in thirds doubled by clarinets (*Detti . . . non val rispondere*);
while twice a demisemiquaver figure on the strings indicates the faint stirrings of
repressed emotion. With the change into the major key the two attitudes become
more defined. Federico's next phrase is a magnificent assertion of power. His own
pitiless heart, he says, has sealed their doom. It is a bass line in every sense, carrying
the harmonies above it as happens so often in the arias of Handel's time.

269

Arrigo and Rolando reply that they will all three meet again on the field of battle.
As before their voices are doubled by clarinets but the major key gives a new boldness to their words and the feeling expressed by the violin demisemiquavers here
focuses itself in a rapping trumpet figure (♪ ♪ etc.). The three voices are
combined as Federico develops Ex. 269 which is then extended into a codetta, after
which the Comaschi reaffirm it in harmony (basses of course taking the theme itself)
and backed by full orchestra fortissimo, so forming the climax of the movement.
They have weighed in rather prudently on Federico's side, and are now rejoicing
at the prospect of Milan's destruction. There is a long winding-down passage over
an implied tonic pedal with Arrigo's voice soaring high over the ensemble as he
repeats once more that they will meet again in battle.

A brisk march tune is heard behind the scenes played by the six stage trumpets,
together with four trombones and two side drums, so forming what was known
on the French stage as 'fanfares théâtrales'—a most agreeable substitute for the
miscellaneous wind band in vogue in Italy. At Federico's orders the balcony
shutters are thrown back to reveal the near-by hills thronged with German
troops. 'Here is my answer,' Federico announces. Rolando retorts that mercenary
swords will never conquer a people that aspires to freedom. 'They shall not alter
Italy's destiny,' Arrigo adds. '*I am Italy's destiny*,' cries Federico, a Teutonic Roi
Soleil, so beginning the stretta of the finale (*Il destino d'Italia son io*). It is laid out even

more formally than usual as a cabaletta complete with ritornello and coda. Verdi's use of self-perpetuating patterns à la Rossini is nowhere more complex than here.

270

The melody itself is based on the rhythmic cell (*a*) repeated no less than twenty-four times; while both (*b*) and (*c*) are rarely absent in one form or another (in the coda they appear modified and with positions reversed). The shift from tonic minor to tonic major within a single period is put to good dramatic use in the final phrase of the melody where Arrigo and Rolando proclaim the greatness of free Italy. The Comaschi, always on Federico's side, join in the ritornello and coda—both in the major key—whipping up the last to an overwhelming climax by means partly traditional to Verdi and partly novel, the fruit of his sojourn in Paris. Purely Verdian are the unison three bars (*Guerra dunque terribile*) followed by the explosion into harmony and a remote key (the six-four chord again!) at 'a morte'. Quite new is the sequence of modulations that comes after (F–B flat minor–G flat/F sharp–diminished seventh–E major) with the final cadence reinforced by the stage trumpets and trombones. It is an astonishing tour de force especially when one bears in mind that, for the first and only time in a finale of this magnitude, Verdi had dispensed entirely with the female voice. The element of contrast is supplied by the high cutting tenor of Arrigo, whose line is exposed at certain crucial points, e.g. before each statement of the main melody. The individual human interest is minimal; and indeed the extreme formality of the music emphasizes the essentially fresco-like character of the scene. The steady crescendo of power from the moment of Federico's entrance to the final pages is something unique in Italian romantic opera, not to be equalled until the first act of Puccini's *Turandot*.

ACT III

The Disgrace

Scene 1: a subterranean vault in the basilica of St Ambrose. Here and there are recent tombs, giving access to the vault. The scene is lit dimly by a lantern; at the back there is a stairway. Down which come the Knights of Death, a few at a time; each of them wears a black sash and gorget imprinted with a human skull.

The knights have come to renew their solemn oath either to avenge their slaughtered kinsmen or to die in the attempt. It is very much a Grand Operatic Tableau which Verdi has learned to treat far more sensationally than he treated a similar scene in *Ernani*. Both introduction and opening chorus (*Fra queste dense tenebre*) are scored for bassoons, trumpets, trombones, cimbasso, together with lower strings and timpani whose part, curiously, is written in minims since it is important for the player not to damp the sound. In this atmosphere of gloom the Knights call upon the spirits of their fathers to bless their enterprise. Throughout the wind are used as a chorale, strings intervening with abrupt gestures and an occasional tremolando. Melodically it may not be particularly memorable; its rich chromatic harmonies may not raise the scalp; but the whole movement has a sombre impressiveness that compels attention. The chain of dominant sevenths (Ex. 271 a) is strictly in the Parisian Grand Opera tradition (see overleaf).

Arrigo now appears at the head of the steps and announces that he has come not only to join them, but to request the foremost place in their ranks. Deeply moved, the eldest amongst them takes off his sash and places it on the shoulders of the kneeling recruit. Then follows the oath sung in rough two-part harmony (*Giuriam d'Italia por fin ai danni*)—a wonderfully 'big' sound (see Ex. 272, p. 409).

The A major concluding stanza (*Siccome gli uomini Dio l'abbandoni*) is a little facile—a reversion to the more naif world of *Ernani* Act III with less conviction—but the instrumental texture remains inventive throughout. As in the end of the overture a succession of unusually approached cadences (C major–A major–F major–A major–B flat major–D minor–A major) closes the scene which again has something of the carefully-wrought grandeur of Act II of *Guillaume Tell*.

Scene 2: Lida's apartments in Rolando's Castle

The curtain rises to disclose Lida pacing up and down in the utmost agitation, watched apprehensively by her maid Imelda. She is consumed by an unreasoning sense of guilt, having heard of Arrigo's death-vow in the vault. After a series of distracted outbursts she gives Imelda a letter for him.

This is certainly one of the most remarkable of Verdi's earlier recitatives—a magnificent tribute to one of the most gifted sopranos of the time, both lyrically and dramatically.* It is essentially a 'mad scene' without an aria at its core. Cantilena

---

* Teresa De Giuli had already proved her worth seven years before when she took over the role of Abigaille from Giuseppina Strepponi at La Scala in the autumn of 1842 and for the first time made the audience aware of its possibilities. Verdi was anxious if possible to secure her services for *Rigoletto* (q.v.).

271

and declamatory recitative are combined in a way that transcends both. Between the passages of broken phrasing where the orchestra portrays Lida's sobs and palpitations there are snatches of Bellini-like arioso which are the perfect expression of thoughts one hardly dare formulate. One is not surprised to find an anticipation of Violetta's 'Amami Alfredo' in the phrase 'Ma Dio mi volle ad ogni costo rea'. Yet when she had admitted everything to Imelda the same idea re-appears transfigured into a tranquil melody (*Questo foglio stornar potria*) introduced by the clarinet—as though the confession itself had brought a certain release. Just as Imelda is about to leave with the letter Rolando enters and calls her back. From here on the scene belongs to him. He wants to see his child once more before leaving for the battle. A wistful flute and clarinet phrase in D minor paints the grief he is vainly trying to repress. Imelda returns with the little boy; and Rolando embraces son and wife. He is certain that victory will be theirs, but at the price of much blood. The duet with Lida (*Digli ch'è sangue italico*) is one of the most moving pieces in the opera. Clasping his son to him, Rolando begs Lida to teach him that he is of Italian stock; that next to God he must honour his fatherland. Rolando's minor-key opening has something of the melancholy grandeur of the later Mercadante (see Ex. 273, facing page). Lamenting figures and phrases on the oboe give poignancy to Lida's consolatory reply. Harp is introduced in time for a long coda suddenly moving from G major to E flat as Rolando places his hand on the boy's head and gives him his blessing.

272

273

'After God the fatherland,' Lida echoes, her private grief temporarily assuaged, and the duet closes against a background of harp and shimmering strings, as she goes out with the child. A mere thirty-eight bars in all, and a remarkable instance of 'multum in parvo'.

Arrigo arrives in answer to Rolando's summons. They talk of the dangers they shared in battle, of how Rolando once saved his friend's life. But now, as a husband and a father, for the first time Rolando feels afraid. He himself must lead a surprise attack against the Germans; Arrigo shall remain with the Veronese troops to guard the city. 'If I should fall in battle,' Rolando goes on, 'I entrust my wife and child to your care.' The andante (*Se al nuovo dì pugnando*), which maintains the smooth 'soft' baritonic style both of the previous duet and of Rolando's romanza in Act I, is like an anticipation of Germont's 'Di Provenza il mar, il suol' (*La Traviata*), with the same simple scoring and the same inclination to repetitiousness countered by the most delicate vocal nuances. Against the powerful downward tendency of Rolando's phrases (Ex. 274 a) Arrigo's intervention (b) with its upward climb and resolution in a stylized sob sounds especially affecting.

274

The movement ends in D flat as expected; but the final farewell between the two men is delayed through 7 bars of allegro declamation. Between the two 'Addios', the rhythm (*x*) of Ex. 266 and 267 makes an unobtrusive appearance; and a chromatic progression decorates the aftermath of the final cadence. Both features have a bearing on what follows, the first forming the rhythmic basis for the long transition to Rolando's cabaletta, the second preparing for the wrench from A flat major to A minor like a breath of cold wind, as Marcovaldo enters to tell Rolando he has been betrayed. He mentions the name Arrigo; whereupon Rolando's hand flies to his dagger and the instrumental texture begins to dance with serpentine clarinet arpeggios. At length Marcovaldo produces the note. 'I know everything. You have pledged yourself to die with the sacred company of knights. My husband will lead the field against Frederick. I must see you again before the battle, Arrigo, in the name of our . . . ancient . . . love.' (The words die on Rolando's lips, say the stage directions, but his flashing eyes and the convulsion of his limbs bear witness to his extreme fury.) Indeed the scene is remarkable for its restraint. Only when Marcovaldo pronounces the words 'Arrigo e Lida' does it rise to forte, to be constantly repressed. Right up to the German's final gloating comment 'Di mia vendetta è già maturo l'ambito istante', feeling is expressed only in the writhings of the orchestra. Then at last Rolando explodes into the cabaletta (*Ahi scellerate alme d'inferno*)—an unusual one, however, with no instrumental prelude, no central ritornello leading to a restatement, and a coda in which the singer continues without respite until the end. As in 'Vada in fiamme' from the first *Macbeth* Verdi doubtless felt that an orthodox movement would cause the dramatic interest to flag; possibly, too, he was following the principle of concentrating the gentle Colini's outbursts in as small a space as possible. At all events, if the form is novel the content is only too conventional and generally speaking unworthy of what has gone before.

Scene 3: a room high up in the tower. On one side an iron door, at the back a balcony giving on to the moat. Arrigo's black sash hangs on the back of a chair.

The orchestral introduction for strings only is a beautiful piece of musical pattern-making even if its pictorial function is obscure. The curtain rises to discover

275

Arrigo standing on the balcony looking out into the night. After a while he sits down to write a last letter to his mother. As he does so, the oboe plays the main theme from the andante of the overture (Ex. 257), joining it very happily to Ex. 275. During this time Lida has entered unnoticed. She confesses that she loves Arrigo but they must avoid each other, she for her son's sake, he for his mother's. She mentions the note—'but I never received a note', exclaims Arrigo. Suddenly there is a knock at the door. Rolando's voice is heard outside. Lida swiftly hides on the balcony behind the closed shutters. Rolando entering tells Arrigo that he knows of his vow, and that if he wishes to join the Company of Death, he must set out at once. 'It is still dark,' Arrigo objects. 'You are wrong,' replies Rolando, and he opens the shutters to reveal—Lida. She and Arrigo attempt an explanation, which Rolando cuts short with a cold 'I have not accused you; why do you make excuses?' (the lines are Méry's translated, and represent Cammarano's one concession to the manner of the original Duhoussais). Then his fury erupts in full operatic force. Inevitably it is not the fury of a Ronconi or a Varesi. In the first movement of the trio finale (*Ah d'un consorte o perfidi*) it finds expression less in terms of sheer lung power than in the extension and sharp contours of his line with its wealth of dotted and double-dotted figures. As always in this opera the harmonic interest is greater than usual, but there is a faint air of contrivance in the long irregular solo at the beginning, while the four-bar orchestral figure introduced at his words 'Taci, arretrati' does not really gain from being stated four times, each a semitone higher than the last, so recalling the most mechanical passages in *Il Corsaro*.

The concertato movement (*Vendetta d'un momento*) is a different matter. Rolando had decided to kill Arrigo and cast Lida from him; then he caught sight of the door and a better idea occurred. He does not say what it is, but his line is instinct with sinister irony, to which the timpani and bass drum beats give an additional twist (Ex. 276 a). Effective too is the ambiguity of mode. The replies of Lida and Arrigo, (b) and (c), begging for instant death, anticipate uncannily the lines of Leonora and Manrico in the famous 'Miserere' scene. All the usual pictorial devices are laid under contribution; sharp rhythms for Rolando's determination

276

a)
Andante mosso
ROLANDO
(con voce soffocata dalla rabbia)

p Ven-det – ta d'un mo-men – to sa-reb – be il tru-ci-dar – ti

b)
ARRIGO

Ah no:___ ah! no: tra-fit – to, e-san – gue

c)
LIDA

Ah! ces – sa tu l'in-gan – ni...

(♩♩ ♩♪♩ ♪, etc.), tremolos for Arrigo's shuddering despair. As the tension grows, so the instrumental texture becomes more elaborate.

Trumpets sound again off stage. 'Your punishment,' cries Rolando, 'shall be infamy.' Despite their protests he bounds out of the room and locks the door behind him; so that the stretta of the trio becomes a duet. Its basis is an anapaestic theme in march rhythm of the type which will become very familiar in *Don Carlos*. To this Arrigo cries that he has not betrayed his friend's honour; and the fourth bar with its displaced accents in the orchestra vividly suggests someone rattling vainly at a locked door. To complete his misery the side drums are heard beating a tattoo, then the 'fanfares théâtrales' with Ex. 256. Arrigo can bear it no longer. Below is the Company of Death. If he is not there to lead them posterity will brand him as a coward. The music becomes taut to the point of incoherence, marching trumpets alternating with tremolo strings, and with a cry of 'Viva l'Italia!', Arrigo leaps from the balcony into the moat. A most original ending, quite different from the cabaletta-finale that Cammarano appears to have envisaged.

ACT IV

To die for the fatherland

Scene: the porch of a church in Milan

Imelda and Lida are among the crowd kneeling in prayer. There are three loud unison chords, then the organ sounds from inside the church followed by a chorus of monks (basses) singing Psalm 83 in plainchant: 'Oh my God make them like a wheel; as the stubble before the wind. . . .' Meanwhile in a whispered recitative Imelda tells her mistress that Arrigo escaped safely to join the Company of Death.

While the monks continue their psalm with a single line from the organ to support them, the main chorus pray to the God of lightning for victory (*O tu che desti il fulmine*) in a succession of chords to which Lida adds her own prayer (*Ah se d' Arrigo e di Rolando*) that moves in freer rhythm and with occasional fioritura high above the other voices. To call this, as Verdi did, a combination of three separate melodies is to stretch a point. Once again it is a case of theatrical make-believe—three different elements of sonority which give the impression of going their own separate ways. As an essay in the grand opera style it is at least striking and Lida's line is effective in its lyrical eloquence.

A distant cry of 'Victory'; a faint trumpet fanfare; and now begins the triumphal parade of the Lombardians to Ex. 256 in all its glory, growing from a far-off march on trumpets and trombones and gradually swelling to a climax. Soon Ex. 258 enters as a counter-tune, all the more effectively for having been heard separately in the overture. Meanwhile the second consul announces that the Germans have been defeated and Frederick Barbarossa killed by Arrigo of Verona. 'Let the Hymn of Victory be raised!' The whole chorus and orchestra with chiming bells give out a simple but stirring melody (*Dall'Alpi a Cariddi echeggi vittoria*) as the victorious troops march in with Rolando at their head. From the Alps to Charybdis (i.e., Messina) Italy is free. But as the last cadence dies away a funeral cortège is heard approaching to the sound of a trumpet with typically 'mourning' figures on the strings and timpani.

Arrigo is carried in mortally wounded by the Knights of the Company of Death, and laid on the steps of the church. With his dying breath he calls Lida and Rolando to him. Swearing by the holy fatherland that Lida is guiltless and pure as an angel, he begins the final trio (*Per la salvata Italia*). A typical death-scene with harp, it begins with a combination of oboe and the low clarinet, giving the dark lugubrious colour to be found in Banco's short solo preceding the discovery of Duncan's murder (*Macbeth*) (Ex. 277). The movement wanders freely through B flat–D flat–E

277

major as the voices interweave, and somehow we are convinced that Rolando and his wife are reconciled by Arrigo's heroism. The concluding G major phrase, 'Chi muore chi muore per la patria alma sì rea non ha' (He who dies for the fatherland cannot be wholly wicked) contains the essence of the opera's philosophy, stated with that simple, heart-warming sincerity of which Verdi knew the secret better than anyone (Ex. 278).

The chorus repeat it; then the organ and choir from the chapel are heard briefly as the first consul enters in the triumphal chariot. Rolando embraces Lida, gives his hand to Arrigo who as his last request asks for the standard to be brought to him.

278

Largo
LIDA

Chi muo - re, chi muo-re per la pa - tria, chi muo-re per la

pa-tria al-ma sì re - a non ha!

While the chorus and orchestra thunder out Ex. 278 complete with organ and bells, he kisses the banner and falls dead.

La Battaglia di Legnano is the last of Verdi's youthful works written deliberately in the grand manner. It stands at the end of a line which begins with the altogether exceptional *Nabucco*, passes through the chaotic jumble of *I Lombardi*, acquires a basic consistency of style with *Attila*, and in the latest opera reveals a refinement of technique which Italy alone could not have supplied. The blunt instrument of Verdi's bombast has here developed a cutting edge. Side by side with the improved expertise in handling the massed scenes, there is evident a deepening of poetic feeling in the solo numbers. The emotions of the individual characters no longer have that unvarying two-dimensional intensity that characterizes *Ernani* or Jacopo Foscari. Yet curiously enough these same virtues which make *La Battaglia di Legnano* so fascinating in detail detract from its integrity as a whole. A comparison with *Ernani* is instructive. There Verdi moves in the third act from the personal to the public level all the more easily for having portrayed his individuals in a broad, grandiose style. In *La Battaglia di Legnano* the levels do not match so well. The conjuration scenes, the finales to Acts II and IV, are isolated set pieces which interrupt the personal drama (or vice versa) and prevent that 'long reach' which we find in *Ernani* and *Macbeth*, neither of which is designed as grand theatre like *Attila* or the present work, but which have all the inborn grandiosity of Verdi's early music. The cavatinas of Lida and Arrigo, Lida's recitative in Act III and her duet with Rolando are something new to Verdi: an anticipation of that intimacy of sentiment that finds its perfect expression in *La Traviata*. Arrigo illustrates this dilemma in the confusion of his motives—for as so often the fault in the musical design is paralleled by a fault in the drama. Is his heroism prompted by patriotic ideals, or is it that of the jilted lover who goes to Africa to hunt big game? In either case his reviling of Lida in Act I does him little credit. According to his argument no widow would be justified in remarrying. Méry's Gaston was a fatalist. Arrigo is a hysteric.

If then the opera to some extent suffers from its divided aims, it remains a rewarding work none the less, and is well worth the occasional revival. In purely musical terms it is the most consistently accomplished that Verdi has yet written. The second conjuration and the introduction to the scene in the tower are designed and scored with an attention to detail for which one looks in vain in *Attila* or *I Masnadieri*. Only *Guillaume Tell* can provide a proper standard of comparison; and if on the whole Rossini is more successful in yoking to the chariot of his opera the twin horses of love and patriotism, it should be remembered that Verdi's horses are more spirited.*

---

* For some reason *La Battaglia di Legnano* has always had a better press in England than in Italy. Gatti (I, pp. 315–16), while acknowledging isolated merits in it here and there, describes the opera as mainly 'laboured, mannered stuff'. Abbiati (I, p. 786) talks of a 'slackening of lyrical impulse'; Roncaglia (p. 194) shrewdly discovers a discrepancy between the often conventional forms and the novel implication of the material. Dyneley Hussey, on the other hand (*Verdi* [London, 1940], p. 61), calls the opera 'an advance upon anything that Verdi had done in the past both in its breadth of outline and in its elaboration of orchestral and choral writing'. To Toye (p. 290) it is 'of its kind an excellent opera which but for the prejudice aroused by the circumstances in which it was born, aggravated not improbably by its uninviting title, might deservedly have escaped the oblivion into which it has fallen'. Osborne (p. 198) describes it as 'on its own terms as viable a piece of *Musiktheater* as *Don Giovanni*, *Otello* or *Tristan und Isolde*, though by no means the exalted masterpiece that each of these is'.

17 LUISA MILLER

LUISA MILLER

Opera in three acts
by
SALVATORE CAMMARANO
(after Schiller's drama, *Kabale und Liebe*)

*First performed at the
Teatro San Carlo, Naples,
8 December 1849*

LUISA MILLER	PRIMA DONNA SOPRANO	Marietta Gazzaniga
MILLER, her father, a retired soldier	PRIMO BARITONO	Achille De Bassini
COUNT WALTER	BASSO COMPRIMARIO	Antonio Selva
RODOLFO his son	PRIMO TENORE	Settimio Malvezzi
FEDERICA, Duchess of Ostheim, the count's niece	CONTRALTO COMPRIMARIO	Teresa Salandri
WURM, the count's steward	BASSO COMPRIMARIO	Marco Arati
LAURA, a village girl	SECONDA DONNA MEZZO SOPRANO	Maria Salvetti
A PEASANT	SECONDO TENORE	Francesco Rossi

Federica's maids—pages—retainers—bodyguards—villagers

The action takes place in the Tyrol

Epoch: the early seventeenth century

In August 1848 Verdi wrote from Paris formally cancelling the contract that he had entered into three years earlier to write an opera for the San Carlo theatre, Naples.* But it was not to be got rid of quite so easily. The management turned on Cammarano and threatened him with imprisonment for having failed to supply the libretto. He was not a wealthy man, and he had a wife and six children to support. He wrote a desperate letter to Verdi begging him to renew his Neapolitan contract for the following year; and Verdi with a rather bad grace consented, 'just so that you won't have to suffer anything . . . I'm making this sacrifice for your sake only.'† A letter from Flauto followed thanking him for getting Cammarano out of his difficulty in a way which 'does great honour to Italy's supreme Maestro'.‡ But it was some time before Cammarano felt completely secure. 'Just in case I should be forced to write to you what I don't want to write as has happened to me before now, please regard letters beginning "Amico sempre a me caro" as coming from me personally.'§ Life could be dangerous in the Naples of King Bomba.

Verdi insisted that the new opera should be a 'brief drama with plenty of interest, action and above all feeling—which would all make it easier to set to music'.¶ He also wanted something spectacular to suit the size of the San Carlo theatre. He himself had the perfect subject in mind—*The Siege of Florence*. This was the opera about which he had written to Piave a month earlier. He already had ideas of his own how it should be treated. Ferruccio the hero he considered 'of gigantic stature, one of the greatest martyrs to the cause of Italian freedom'.‖ Would Piave please send him as full a synopsis as possible? But possibly Piave was too busy soldiering for the short-lived Venetian Republic. At all events he made no move; and Verdi took up the subject with Cammarano, in a way which shows that he had been thinking about it very deeply. Indeed, next to *King Lear* this was to be the most fascinating of Verdi's unrealized projects. Its basis was a recently published historical novel about the fall of the Florentine Republic in 1529, by Guerrazzi, who was a member of the republican faction that expelled the Grand Duke from Tuscany in 1848. Verdi himself sketched in an impressionistic form the scenario of the last scene.** Further ideas are set forth in two letters to Cammarano.††

All three documents shed a most interesting light on how Verdi's mind worked when he was in the grip of a strong dramatic idea. As with *Macbeth* his vision took in not only the form of the opera but also its scenic details. Noticeable too is the deepening of his concern for the purely human element, already evident in *La*

* Letter to Guillaume, 24.8.1848. *Copialettere*, pp. 49–50.
† Letter to Cammarano, 24.9.1848. *Copialettere*, pp. 55–6.
‡ Letter from Flauto, 14.10.1848. *Copialettere*, pp. 56–7.
§ Letter from Cammarano, 9.10.1848. Abbiati, I, pp. 771–2.
¶ Letter to Cammarano, 24.9.1848. *Copialettere*, pp. 55–6.
‖ Letter to Piave, 22.7.1848. Morazzoni, pp. 28–9.
** *Carteggi Verdiani*, IV, p. 219.
†† 14.2.1849 (summarized in *Copialettere*, p. 69); and 24.3.1849 (Abbiati, II, pp. 4–7).

Battaglia di Legnano, as well as his insistence that it should not become confused with the patriotic—a danger of which the earlier opera may already have made him aware. It is clear equally that at the time he was still partly under the spell of grandiose Parisian spectacle; nor had he forgotten the banquet scene in *Lucrezia Borgia* with its plethora of male secondary roles. Two passages stand out with particular significance: his suggestion of blending 'the comic and the terrible in Shakespeare's manner'; and his reference to a scene at a military camp in Schiller's *Wallenstein* in which 'there is a friar who preaches in the most comic and delightful way imaginable'. The first was to be realized in *Rigoletto*, the second not until *La Forza del Destino*.*

But *The Siege of Florence* was doomed from the start. As if a government of Naples ranged firmly on the side of exiled Pius IX could possibly accept a drama which represents Pope and Emperor as the enemies of Italian freedom! Cammarano might change the name of the opera and its characters (he was prepared to call it *Maria De' Ricci*) but everybody would recognize Guerrazzi's story. So in April 1849 the poet wrote regretfully to Verdi that *The Siege of Florence* had been forbidden by the censors, and he offered as an alternative a subject that Verdi had himself proposed some time back—Schiller's *Kabale und Liebe*. He also suggested a *Cleopatra*; but he made it clear that whatever Verdi decided he would do well to avoid any story which had a revolutionary tinge.†

At first sight *Kabale und Liebe* seems an odd choice. The last and best of Schiller's early prose plays, it is a bitter and comprehensive indictment of society under an absolutist government. Some of the *Sturm und Drang* manner persists but disciplined by a concentration of purpose. There is no rebellion here for its own sake, no self-indulgent torrents of rhetoric as in *Die Räuber*. The high-powered language is subordinated to a ruthlessly objective portrait of innocence destroyed by corruption. The archvillain of the piece—in the sense that he bears the greatest responsibility for the evil of others—never appears at all. He is the prince of one of those tiny states which made up so much of eighteenth-century Germany. He oppresses his subjects, sells the young men as mercenaries to his more warlike neighbours, ravishes any young woman who takes his fancy. Those who hold high offices about him have reached their positions through intrigue or worse and are obliged to use the same means to retain them. The drama centres round the tragic love affair of Major Ferdinand Walter, son of the President of the Council, and Luisa Miller, the daughter of a music master. The President is determined to improve his standing at court by marrying his son to the Prince's mistress, Lady Milford, a noble and passionate character who has used her position to alleviate the sufferings of the prince's subjects. With the aid of his secretary Wurm, himself a suitor for the hand of Luisa, the President contrives to smash the lovers' idyll. Miller is arrested and Luisa forced to write a letter of assignation to a certain Hofmarschall as the only means of releasing her father. The letter is conveyed to Ferdinand who in jealous desperation poisons Luisa and himself, then too late learns the truth from her dying lips. There are strong scenes: between Luisa and Lady Milford when the elder

---

* Monaldi (pp. 99–100) states that it was at this time that Verdi, prompted by the news of Nicolai's success with *The Merry Wives of Windsor* (1849), just conceived the idea of an opera built round the character of Falstaff. See Gatti, I, p. 337.

† Letter from Cammarano, 14.4.1849. *Copialettere*, pp. 71–2.

woman tries to make Luisa give up Ferdinand only to be shamed herself by the girl's innocent goodness into a decision to leave the court; between the President, Ferdinand, Luisa and her father when the President's obscene insults are countered by Miller's respectful defiance, and when the music-master's arrest is prevented by Ferdinand's threat to reveal his knowledge of how his father came to power. There is comedy, too, and some rather hectic emotionalism between Luisa and Ferdinand. But the play as a whole is tough and hard with a strong element of social criticism at its centre.

This aspect, however, was one which Cammarano could no more have reproduced than he could have recaptured the border-ballad grimness of *The Bride of Lammermoor*. So he softened the drama into an operatic *Giselle*, Act I. In the play Miller is aware from the start of his daughter's love for the major and disapproves of it heartily. In the opera Ferdinand (his name changed to Rodolfo) appears incognito as just another peasant and therefore an eminently suitable match for Luisa. Peasants are always more romantic than the petit bourgeois; so Miller becomes a peasant ex-soldier instead of the music master that Schiller made him. It is Wurm who, like Hilarion, reveals the fact that Luisa's suitor is the son not of anyone so prosaic as the President of the Council, but of the *new Count*. A prince's mistress has no place in Cammarano's world: therefore Lady Milford is replaced by one Federica von Ostheim, whom Schiller's play mentions only in passing. (She is used by the President as a ruse to trap Ferdinand into admitting that it is not Lady Milford's reputation that daunts him so much as the idea of marrying anyone but Luisa.) Cammarano has provided her with a history; she is a cousin of Rodolfo, and a childhood friend, married and now widowed. The Hofmarschall is also eliminated, and Luisa's letter addressed to Wurm himself.

Verdi received Cammarano's synopsis in May.* He was not entirely satisfied with it. As usual he was concerned to retain all that was best in the original. He wanted Lady Milford 'in the full extension of her character'. He felt that the 'infernal intrigue between Walter and Wurm which dominates the drama like fate lacked the strength and colour that it has in Schiller'.† He saw no reason why Luisa's letter should not be addressed, as in Schiller, to someone other than Wurm. Also he had various modifications to make to the scheme of Act II: instead of an aria for Luisa a duet for Luisa and Wurm, followed by another between Wurm and Walter, and an ensemble of some kind to finish rather than the aria for Rodolfo Cammarano had planned. And could not Wurm's character be strengthened by a clownish twist? The only one of these points on which Verdi had his way was the duet for Walter and Wurm. To the others Cammarano brought irresistible arguments, based on his own many years of experience, his knowledge of conditions at the San Carlo and above all on considerations of the 'convenienze'. No leading singer would ever undertake the part of a prince's mistress in Naples; to make Wurm sing two pieces in succession would be to enlarge the role unduly and make it very difficult to cast in an opera which calls for a baritone lead and another heavy comprimario bass (Walter). ('It is true that at Naples we have De Bassini, Selva and

---

* The synopsis is printed in full by Abbiati (II, pp. 10–16). For a simpler, schematic lay-out of the opera see letter from Cammarano and Flauto, 17.3.1849. *Copialettere*, pp. 78–80. The scheme was to be expanded by a cantabile for Walter and a duettino for Walter and Wurm.

† Letter to Cammarano, 17.5.1849. *Copialettere*, pp. 470–2.

Arati, but what about elsewhere?')* An aria for Rodolfo would end the second act perfectly if chorus were to be added and provided Verdi himself set the dialogue with Walter between andante and cabaletta in a fast tempo.† Elsewhere compromise prevailed.

Indeed, the correspondence between composer and librettist is of considerable interest, because of its spirit of give and take. For the finale of Act I, where the Count orders the arrest of Luisa, Verdi was most anxious that there should be no stretta, and that the tension should be screwed down precisely as in Schiller:

FERDINAND   Father, if I cannot prevent it she must stand in the pillory—but by her side will also stand the son of the President. Do you still insist?

PRESIDENT   The more entertaining will be the exhibition. Away with her.

FERDINAND   I will pledge the honour of an officer's sword for her. Do you still insist?

PRESIDENT   Your sword is already familiar with disgrace. Away, away, you know my will.

FERDINAND   Father—sooner than tamely see my bride branded with infamy I will plunge this sword into her bosom—do you still insist?

PRESIDENT   Do it if the point be sharp enough.

FERDINAND   God be my witness that I have left no human means untried to save her. Forgive me now if I resort to hellish means. While you are leading her to the pillory (*whispering loud in the President's ear*) I will publish throughout the town a pleasant history of how a President's chair may be gained. (*Exit.*)

PRESIDENT   (*thunderstruck*) What was that?—Ferdinand!—(*to the guards*) Set her free at once. (*Curtain.*)‡

Cammarano was quite agreeable to this on the condition that the act did not end in slow tempo but should quicken towards an animated finish. Verdi concurred and ended with an allegro in three mounting stages; but it is nothing like a conventional stretta. Nor is there any operatic model for this type of ending. Verdi had gone far beyond the example of his Italian predecessors in allowing the original drama to dictate his formal ideas.

About Act III composer and librettist were in full agreement, Verdi merely insisting that Cammarano should spread himself over the two duets (Luisa and Miller, Luisa and Rodolfo finishing in a terzetto with Miller), Cammarano that certain of his verses should be sung only in succession and never simultaneously. The poet wrote: 'If I were not afraid of being thought Utopian I would be tempted

---

* Letters from Cammarano, 4 and 11.6.1849. *Copialettere*, pp. 472–4. In accordance with the loose terminology of the time Verdi and Cammarano referred to 'three basses' of which the principal was to sing the part of Luisa's father. By an odd coincidence Bellini, who also appears at one time to have considered an *Amore e raggiro*, suggested a similar distribution: '. . . Tamburini must play Eloise's father, not the tyrant'. Letter to Florimo, 6.8.1828. *Epistolario*, pp. 148–51.

† Letter from Cammarano, 28.7.1849. One reason for Cammarano's refusal to end Act II with the quartet was a reluctance to repeat himself. He had already written a similar final scene for Mercadante's *Elena da Feltre*.

‡ Schiller, *Kabale und Liebe*, II, vii. Translation by R. D. Boylan and Joseph Mellish.

to say that to achieve the peak of perfection in an opera the same mind should be responsible for both words and music. From this idea of mine it follows that as the authors are in fact two they must work together like brothers and that if the poetry should never be the slave of the music neither should it be its master. . . .'* Such is the spirit of Verdi's and Cammarano's collaboration; and in *Luisa Miller* it worked remarkably well.

Verdi remained in Paris until midsummer 1849, during which time he again tried to have the Neapolitan opera deferred or given in his absence:† but Flauto remained obdurate on both points. Meanwhile in Italy the political situation had worsened still further. In March Carlo Alberto, King of Piedmont, had decided to renew the war against Austria, only to be heavily defeated at the Battle of Novara. The 'anciens régimes' were restored with Austrian backing in Parma and Tuscany. Brescia held out stubbornly and was treated on its capitulation to the most atrocious reprisals from the army of General Hanau. Venice put herself in a state of siege and resisted until August. In Rome the republic was overthrown and the Pope restored—by French troops! It is generally assumed that this, as much as the fear of a cholera epidemic, determined Verdi to leave Paris and return to Busseto; and it was here in the Palazzo Orlandi, bought by him some time before the Villa Sant' Agata, that work on *Luisa Miller* was begun.

At the beginning of October Verdi set out for Naples taking with him his father-in-law Antonio Barezzi. Having arrived in Rome they found themselves detained in quarantine because of a cholera epidemic. At the same time he received a disquieting letter from Cammarano regarding Bettini, the tenor whom they had cast for the part of Rodolfo, and who was now being sued by the management for bad singing, and also about the state of the San Carlo's finances. 'I tell you that so that you can take appropriate measures.'‡ Verdi did; no sooner had he arrived in Naples in late October than he wrote officially to the management via Flauto demanding the guarantee of his 3,000 ducats: otherwise he would dissolve the contract.§ This so incensed the Duke of Ventignano who was on the board of directors that he threatened to invoke a law whereby if Verdi failed to supply the opera he could be detained in Naples at the government's pleasure. In the end tempers cooled on both sides; Verdi had his payment guaranteed and rehearsals proceeded smoothly enough.

On the whole *Luisa Miller* was a great success, though press reviews are lacking. Abramo Basevi, in a famous passage, has described it as inaugurating Verdi's second manner.¶ Yet anyone who hopes to find in it a style obtrusively different from that of his preceding operas will be disappointed. The advance in orchestration, the broadening of language noticeable in *La Battaglia di Legnano* is not consistently maintained in the newer work. There is even a regression here and there to habits of doubling and fussy aria-accompaniments as though with his return to Italy Verdi had left some of his Parisian manners behind him. But the backsliding is more apparent than real. If the refinements are less marked than in the preceding work it is because they have sunk below the surface to effect a subtle

---

* Letter from Cammarano, 11.6.1849. *Copialettere*, pp. 473–4.
† Letters to Flauto, 1.6 and 26.7.1849. *Copialettere*, pp. 80 and 83–4.
‡ Letter from Cammarano, 17.10.1849. Abbiati, II, pp. 37–8.
§ Letter to Flauto, 1.11.1849. *Copialettere*, pp. 85–6.
¶ See Chapter 20.

transformation of the whole.* If the cut of certain scenes is conventional the reason must be sought in the essentially conservative influence of Cammarano, who was operating on his home ground and therefore better able to enforce his point of view than in *La Battaglia di Legnano*. Nor was this necessarily for the worse. It did Verdi no harm to forget his preoccupation with speed and excitement and to set a clear and comfortably paced libretto.

The overture is astonishing, a tour de force of musical science; as though Verdi, having in *La Battaglia di Legnano* at last legitimized his own personal type of overture, was determined to show that he could beat, or at least equal, the German composers at their own game. Unlike its predecessors it is in one movement only, and based throughout on one theme, later to be associated with the sadness of Luisa in Act III. According to the autograph it is to be played on the G string.

279

Not only the theme itself but the concentration of its working out had already been hinted at in the Act II finale of *Il Corsaro*. But here it is developed with a wealth of contrapuntal ingenuity. The lithe gait and much of the string writing recalls the Weber of *Der Freischütz* particularly in the tutti.† The transitional passage following the first of these is remarkable for the way in which tension is worked up by strictly symphonic means, that is by accelerating the pace of the modulations as well as their boldness, and at the same time diminishing the phrase lengths in the manner of the romantic symphonists. Having by both rapid and devious means reached the dominant of G minor the music hovers there for a while then slips with delightful unexpectedness into E flat major, where the same subject is transformed into a graceful clarinet melody. The development is stranger yet. Beginning with a touch of canon it then presents the theme embellished with a

---

* A manuscript score, originally hired from Ricordi's and now in the library of the Royal Opera House, Covent Garden, contains the revealing instruction: *Conductors are requested not to add the bass drum at any point in the opera, and are recommended to omit it even in the overture*— G. VERDI

† The influence is not surprising when one considers that this is Verdi's first essay in what might be called tutti scoring: i.e. scoring in which the full orchestra is treated as an organism based on the supremacy of the strings rather than as an opaque wall of sound to be split up into multicoloured sections whose tint at any moment is determined by the predominance of one or more wind instruments. In other words Verdi became for the purpose of this overture what he would describe as a 'quartettista'. See letter to Filippi, April 1878. *Copialettere* p. 626.

counter-subject on the upper strings (violins and violas), and dissolves both in a chromatic sequence worthy of Mozart's G minor symphony (K. 550). Mozartian

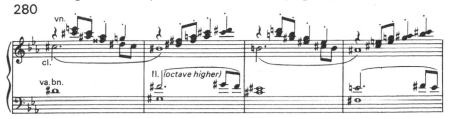

280

influence (the finale of the 'Haffner' Symphony) can be sensed in the unusually expert string writing in such a passage as this:

281

There is a touch of Schubertian romanticism in the sequence of tender vale-dictory phrases preceding the reprise, overlapping and mounting between pauses from F sharp major through A major to C. In one respect the piece remains purely Italian. In the German overture no less than the German symphony the great moment of drama is the recapitulation where for the first time since the beginning the main theme returns in the home key, generally with a dominant preparation. There is no such moment in the overture to *Luisa Miller*, though the autograph score shows that an orthodox reprise was in fact written, and followed immediately by the second subject as in many a Rossini overture. Doubtless Verdi decided that in a monothematic piece the effect was altogether too repetitious. At all events he scored out the thirteen bars of first subject, leaving the movement as it is today. From this point on native Italianism asserts itself more and more. As usual Verdi elaborates when he restates both in rhythm and instrumentation; and there is no denying that as it gets nearer its coda the texture coarsens. But taken as a whole the overture remains perhaps Verdi's most striking *musical* achievement in this field. That of *Les Vêpres Siciliennes* may have more grandeur; that of *La Forza del Destino* more verve; but in no other of his overtures is so much musical thought concentrated in so few notes.

ACT I
Love

Scene 1: a pleasant village. On one side Miller's humble cottage; on the other a country church; up stage the towers of Count Walter's palace are glimpsed through the trees. A clear spring day is dawning on the horizon; the inhabitants of the village are gathered to celebrate Luisa's birthday.

It is an idyllic country scene like those from *La Sonnambula* or Donizetti's *Linda* and Verdi has invested it with a similar dewy freshness. He begins it with a kind of

ranz des vaches on the first clarinet (which incidentally plays a most important part
in the entire opera, doubtless because the performer Sebastiani was a virtuoso).*
We have the impression of people entering on tip-toe, one by one, as strings and
woodwind alternate in tripping staccato phrases. For once oboe, though not
piccolo, is omitted from the entire woodwind group. Soon the reason becomes
clear. It will be used to outline the melody of the chorus itself (*Ti desta Luisa regina
dei cori*) in a beautiful combination with clarinet, bassoon and horn, piccolo adding
an occasional chirrup. The village youths and maidens bid her rise up and greet the

282

bright spring morning whose charms cannot compare with her own. The chorus
abounds in clarinet and flute decoration in the Rossini manner. It is one of the most
sensitively scored in all early Verdi.

At the conclusion the tempo quickens and the music plunges into the still
brighter key of E major as Miller and his daughter come out from their cottage and
exchange greetings with the villagers. Laura, Luisa's friend, suggests that they all
go to the church and invoke God's blessing. Miller thanks them all in a recitative
of great nobility and tenderness. But Luisa is clearly looking for somebody who
should be there and is not. Miller notices and is uneasy. Nobody knows anything
about the young man Carlo, he reminds her; he arrived in the village about the
same time as the new count; there could be danger. But Luisa is convinced that
Carlo has a noble heart and loves her as she loves him. 'Love at first sight' is the
theme of her cavatina (*Lo vidi e'l primo palpito*). Like Amalia's in *I Masnadieri* it
has the hint of a cabeletta in its gait with the Metastasian double quatrain extended
into the kind of ternary design with coda, more usually associated with a fast
concluding movement. Also it has the primitive scoring typical of the operas that
precede *La Battaglia di Legnano*. But here there is purpose in it. Luisa is an artless

* In Verdi's early letters to Cesare De Sanctis at Naples, Sebastiani regularly figures among
those to whom he wished to be remembered. The opening passage in question bears strong
resemblance to the clarinet solo in the beginning of Meyerbeer's *Le Prophète*, the premiere of
which took place in April 1849. Verdi was in Paris, and it is unthinkable that he was not
present.

village maiden whose joyous, trusting nature is perfectly expressed in this way. Later, a no less blatant melody—also in C major but confined to the orchestra—will depict Rigoletto's Gilda, as she comes rushing out of the house to greet her father. Here, as there, the natural brightness of the key is enhanced by an approach from the subdominant side.

The opening phrase of the melody is resumed by orchestra with choral intervention as the villagers present Luisa with flowers, and the movement seems about to settle down to a quiet close when there is a sudden pause as she recognizes a young huntsman who comes to offer his posy. Amid movements of growing excitement from the crowd he greets first Luisa then her father; and a long dominant pedal with the lovers' voices united in sixths leads into the terzetto 'che chiude l'introduzione'* (*T'amo d'amor ch' esprimere*), whose main theme has a lithe grace that recalls the Donizetti of *Linda di Chamounix*.

283

As befits both the dramatic context and the conventions of a final movement the melody is repeated by soprano and tenor successively. It is the doubting Miller whose entry is entirely different ('Non so qual voce infausta') with a minor key orientation. Throughout this whole movement he remains musically apart. His voice soars up in a prayer ('Ah non voler buon Dio ch' a tal destin soccomba') before the first reprise. He then joins the chorus basses in their staccato accompaniment, but only for a few notes here and there and as if unwillingly. When the melody is resumed yet again after a magical episode during which the villagers hear the bells calling them to church, Miller is entrusted with a bass line of restless, muttered semiquavers. His obstinate prescience of evil seems to be embodied in the horn note which dominates the final string cadence.

With the end of the terzetto the musical design comes to a halt even if there is no change of scene. A finite 'introduzione' was strictly according to Cammarano's essentially traditional thinking. But it is worth while to observe the entirely individual way in which this time-honoured Rossinian ground-plan is developed. There is not a bar of inert recitative. All the transitions are in strict, fast tempo; yet they accommodate single expansive phrases of great beauty and significance such as Luisa's 'Di letizia colma son'io' with its effusion of soaring crotchet triplets, and her whispered 'Abbraccialo, t'ama qual figlio'. The long dominant pedal before the terzetto is a typically Verdian device for suggesting the joy of reunion. Most remarkable of all is the terzetto itself, not only for the truth of its characterization but for the breadth of its structure. As in the previous two operas nothing is repeated without being varied. But in the new atmosphere of expansiveness the variations seem to evolve naturally from the implications of the material, rather than to serve merely as a device for avoiding monotony.

Breadth is the characteristic also of the next scena, a thoroughly conventional

---

* See letter from Cammarano, 15.5.1849. *Copialettere*, pp. 78–80.

affair built round a double aria for Miller. About to re-enter his house he is detained by Wurm, the Count's secretary, who has come to renew his suit for the hand of Luisa. Miller replies that he cannot force his daughter to marry anyone but the man of her choice. Now Wurm reveals the truth about Carlo's identity; then he slips away leaving Miller to reflect bitterly on the justice of his suspicions. Nothing is more disconcerting than the reversion to the fussy accompanimental writing at the beginning of Miller's andante (*Sacra la scelta è d'un consorte*). But it was some time before Verdi could be induced to give up doing what he knew he could do supremely well. Miller, written for De Bassini, the creator of the elder Foscari, reveals himself as the epitome of the '*baritono nobile*' quarrying still more deeply the vein of 'Questa dunque è l'iniqua mercede'. His cavatina is in the early grandiose style (indeed the opening phrase is marked *grandioso*) with an underlying toughness which one looks for in vain in anything written for Colini. It is one of those move-ments which evolve from a short rhythmic pattern and thus contrive to avoid repetition except at short range. But despite the quaver rests which give it a frag-mented look on paper the cantilena is extraordinarily long-breathed, each pair of lines in the double quatrain furnishing the basis of a complete musical sentence. There is a nod towards eighteenth-century tonality not only in the central domin-ant cadence but in the preparation for the tonal reprise ('Non son tiranno ... padre son io' ... etcetera). As usual glory is reserved for the final two lines which sum up the mood of the piece.* Here the throbbing string chords of the accompaniment give way to rippling clarinet arpeggios, while the melody instruments double the voice part. In the transition Wurm expresses himself in the suave conspiratorial

284

manner reminiscent of the exchange between Foresto and Ezio in *Attila* Act III. But here the characterization is more pointed, with a slithering bass line of semi-quavers to suggest a serpent-like evil. The final cabaletta (*Ah fu giusto il mio sospetto*) is notable for its use of staccato semiquavers at the end of a phrase as an expression of fury—a device to be repeated in the more famous *Di quella pira*. Otherwise it maintains the ample scale of the andante even taking the baritone somewhat unusually to high G in the final phrase.† It is not unknown for Miller to steal the show on the basis of this one scene.

* 'On earth a father is like God in his kindness but not in his severity.' As usual the sense of Cammarano's lines does not bear close scrutiny, especially when he has to invent something which is not in the original play.

† Normally G flat represents Verdi's idea of the baritone's upper limit. The high G in the final cadence of Rigoletto's famous monologue is not in the autograph or any of the printed scores.

285

Allegro moderato

WURM

(Co) - star - - ti, o vec-chio de - - bo-le,

ca - ro il tuo cie - co af - fet - to do-vrà, ben ca - ro!

Scene 2: a hall in Count Walter's castle

The early part of the scene is built round a solo for Count Walter which paints the Count in much softer colours than his counterpart in the play. The dominant characteristic of Schiller's President is his ruthlessness. When he claims to have pursued power entirely for the sake of his son, we know he is sincere only in so far as like most men of his type he regards his son as an extension of himself, his own passport to a kind of immortality. Like the rulers that he served he has the dynastic mind. Cammarano's Count Walter is a more ambivalent character. The scene opens in the middle of a conversation between him and Wurm. The Count's exclamation tells us at once that Wurm has revealed Rodolfo's secret romance. 'And the Duchess about to arrive at any moment! Tell him that I wish to see him at once.' When Wurm has gone to find Rodolfo the Count buries his head in his hands. Fortune has favoured him in everything; but—cruel irony—the son for whose sake he has built his career opposes his wishes. May he never know just how far his father would go or has gone in order to see him happy and powerful! The cantabile (*Il mio sangue la vita darei*)* is a minor–major romanza, which effectively

---

* The idea of this cantabile for Walter seems to have been a late addition to Cammarano's original scheme. Unfortunately the incompleteness of the surviving correspondence between Verdi and his librettist makes it difficult to follow the course of events. Clearly the casting of Walter was a problem. In his letter of 23.7.1849 (*Copialettere*, p. 475) Verdi wrote: 'For various reasons which would be too long to tell you in a letter I think it would be as well to keep to Selva for the part of Walter, so it's pointless to have the duet in Act I [*what duet, and why was it pointless?*] but bear in mind that the part of Walter must be a principal (*primario*).' He can only have meant 'principal' in relation to Wurm since at no point does Walter have anything more substantial than this one cantabile. In his letter of 8 August (Abbiati, II, pp. 26–7) Cammarano speaks of having transferred the cantabile from Act II to Act I so as to avoid giving Walter three pieces in a row. One reason why Verdi may have wished to fill out the part of Walter may have been that Antonio Selva was his own discovery (see *Ernani*).

sounds the full depths of Count Walter's character. It has grandeur, pathos, and a suggestion of force held in reserve. Like many Verdi basses Count Walter is a quiescent but not an extinct volcano. There is an infinity of sadness in the opening phrase with its crunching discord in the third bar; but also the anger of an outraged authoritarian when he speaks of Rodolfo having dared to flout his wishes:

286

Much of the effect is due to the incursions of tutti in an otherwise lightly scored aria. A no less impressive outburst occurs in the course of the major section where Count Walter speaks of the crime whose memory torments his conscience (*Pena atroce, supplizio d'inferno*). The flow of the melody is not interrupted but the chord of C flat (♭ VI B) rears its head with a Tchaikovskian menace. The final section is extended by a short episode in the minor and a slightly elaborated repeat, both of which are often cut on performance—which is a pity, if only because we lose the variety of accompanimental patterns in which this aria abounds. The shifting restlessness of the violin sextuplets in the episode foreshadow the agony of King Philip in *Don Carlos*.

Rodolfo enters to be told straight away by the Count that he is to marry his cousin and childhood friend Federica. She had long been in love with him before her father compelled her to marry the Duke of Ostheim. Recently her elderly husband was killed in battle, leaving her a title connected with royalty. Rodolfo protests that he has no ambitions in this direction. His father sounds a velvety warning; Rodolfo, he suggests, had better keep his counsel. On the contrary, the young man, as always candid to a fault, wants to explain everything; only at that moment festive music off stage indicates that the countess has already arrived and

Rodolfo is to be presented to his cousin immediately. All this has been carried on in straight recitative except for a brief arioso notable for a passage in Verdi's new chromatic manner describing the Duchess's youthful love ('ebra di gioia mi rivelò').

Federica's entrance is about as conventional as can be imagined; and the choral number (*Quale un sorriso d'amica sorte*) can be justified only by the consideration (which as we know from his correspondence weighed much with Cammarano and the management) that the chorus must be used somehow, and in the world of Italian opera it is quite natural that anyone as rich as Federica should be preceded by a host of attendants who sing her praise. Anyway Verdi has taken little trouble here. The melody is undistinguished, the introduction and postlude both flashily scored (though as in the introduction to Act I the texture is frequently softened by the omission of the oboe). There is a brief recitative in which Walter presents his son to Federica. Then he leaves to make preparations for the hunt, and with the departure of the servants the two cousins find themselves alone. Federica opens the conversation. Verdi has tried to endow her with as much of Schiller's Lady Milford's qualities as he can. Federica too is passionate and accustomed to having her own way. Like Lady Milford she is in love with Rodolfo and has no doubt that her feelings will be requited. After all, she has not changed, she says, underlining her words with a magnificent cadenza-like flourish, and she assumes that neither has he. The first movement of their duet (*Dall' aule raggianti di vano splendor*) is a beautiful piece which makes plentiful use of tonic pedal and has something of the quality of a Schubert Ländler. The old device of pizzicato violins and cellos contrasted with sustaining violas has never sounded more magical.

The scoring becomes more elaborate as both probe their memories of a happy

287

childhood when they told all their secrets to one another. Rodolfo wishes once more to confide in her, but she gradually realizes that his is not the kind of secret she wishes to hear. It is a masterpiece of dramatic writing. With Federica's dawning suspicions the melody wanders into darker keys, over a more and more turbulent accompaniment; it emerges again clearly, more Schubertian than ever, with Rodolfo's plea for compassion; then dissolves into peremptory declamation as Federica learns the truth. The music is now poised on the dominant of a new key preparatory to the stretta (*Deh, la parola amara*). This, alas, is an anticlimax. Federica like Lady Milford is not prepared to give up her intended bridegroom so easily. The emotional deadlock is conveyed in one of those 'similar' duets with the two voices singing the same subject in different keys (Rodolfo in G major, Federica in D major). But here the music carries so low a charge of emotion that the mere contrast of key is not sufficient to convey the situation. When the two voices come together at the end, Federica, unable to sing in unison with Rodolfo because of their respective tessiture, is given a mere filling-in part thinly disguised as a counter-melody. Having entered the scene with a bang Federica leaves it with a whimper.

> *Scene 3: a room in Miller's cottage. Two doors on either side of the stage,*
> *one leading to Miller's room, the other to Luisa's. By the first there hangs*
> *a sword and an old military uniform. At the back are the front door and*
> *window through which part of the church can be seen.*

Distant horn calls introduce an offstage hunting chorus (*Scioglete i levrieri*), divided into two antiphonal groups in opposite wings—a device which will be used again to begin the first version of *Don Carlos*. It is a nice pictorial touch, which stresses the rustic setting. The Count's hunt is in full cry and Luisa is waiting in her cottage for her lover, who has promised to break away from his fellow huntsmen and come to see her. The man who now enters is not Rodolfo but her father. Still against the background of distant hunting cries he tells her that 'Carlo' is the Count's son; what is more he is betrothed to someone else, and the bride has already arrived. He was a seducer after all; and Miller vows, by the uniform that he once bore,* to have vengeance. At that moment Rodolfo arrives, having overheard Miller's words. Miller advances on him threateningly; Luisa throws herself between them; and before either can speak Rodolfo swears that his intentions were honourable. With that youthful impetuousness which is his chief trait in the opera (Verdi's hero is every inch a Latin) he takes Luisa's hand and kneels before Miller with the words 'I am your husband!'—Again the clarinet plays an all-important part, formulating the thought which Rodolfo is struggling to express (see Ex. 288, opposite).

Miller is no longer angry but deeply apprehensive. How can the young man possibly overrule his father's wishes? Rodolfo replies that he can bring his father to heel by threatening to disclose a certain secret; and a sinuous figure on clarinet and bassoon beneath tremolo strings leaves no doubt that it is a very murky secret indeed. The music quickens into the first movement of the finale as someone is heard approaching. It is based on two orchestral themes, each in slightly differing tempo (Ex. 289 a and b, opposite).

* That Miller should be a retired soldier, not a music-master, was Cammarano's idea. See letter of 4.6.1849. *Copialettere*, p. 472.

The first is used sequentially modulating from key to key. The second is more in the nature of a stable melody. Both could have been written by Donizetti; but the boldness and rapidity of the modulations and the feeling of urgency are entirely Verdian. The newcomer is of course Count Walter, followed by the villagers. As in Schiller he reviles Miller and his daughter. He has come, he says, to rescue Rodolfo from a scheming woman. Miller protests that his honour as a soldier has been insulted and demands satisfaction. Father and son defy one another till at length the Count calls in his guards and orders them to arrest Luisa and Miller. Luisa falls at his feet and begs for mercy, but her father is ashamed that she should prostrate herself before anyone so worthless. She is innocent and should kneel only to God. With these words he begins the adagio concertato of the finale, a movement quite different from most of its kind. The andantino 3/8 persists unvaryingly but without the familiar sense of automatic propulsion. The elements are separated as never before, not even in the quintet from Act I of *I Lombardi*. In each case the effect is achieved partly by irregularity of phrase-length, partly by difference of accompanimental pattern, only here the procedures are carried much further. Miller, the principal figure in the canvas, offers two ideas contrasted in everything but pace:

290

The first (a) has a 3-bar structure together with a very sparse accompaniment; (b) has the regularity suitable to an assertion of faith and is backed by a rich instrumental sonority. The interventions of Rodolfo (*Foco d'ira e questo pianto*) and Walter (*Tu piegarti, tu, non io*) are both based on 5-bar units, the first set over an excited throbbing of strings, the second over peremptory chords. It is Luisa who restores the four-bar pattern, first with her F major melody (*Ad immagin tua creata*) over tremolando strings, then with a resumption of Ex. 290 b riding high above the vocal ensemble in what seems like a separate world of lyrical beauty. The tonal scheme is more than usually fluid with excursions to F sharp minor as well as F major; and for the final statement of Ex. 290 b Rodolfo adds his voice to Luisa's* propelling the movement to an astonishingly bold climax—an extended cadence (D major) prepared by a 6/4 chord in a remote key (B flat). It is like the ending to the Act I quartet of *I Masnadieri* but infinitely more powerful.

The last part of the finale has already been described—an exciting crescendo of drama with Rodolfo's voice cutting across it like a knife. Here at least Rodolfo must be a real 'tenore spinto' (Ex. 291, opposite). It is a pity that the threat whispered into the Count's ear has in the event to be trumpeted out in front of everyone; but that is opera.

ACT II

Intrigue

Scene 1: as before

Headed by Laura, Luisa's friends come pouring into the cottage in great agitation.

* Compare the concertato in the finale to Act II in *Giovanna d'Arco*. As so often with Verdi like situations breed like procedures.

291

They have seen Miller being marched off to prison in chains by the Count's guards. All this is described at some length in the unison chorus (*Al villaggio dai campi tornando*). The melody is not in any way striking; but the minor tonality emphasizes the general distress in a way that the young Verdi might have thought unnecessary. Nor is there any complementary section in tonic major, only an episode (harmonized) in the relative major punctuated by Luisa's anguished cries and then interrupted by the appearance of Wurm. As in Act I the musical form is merged into the dramatic scheme as the chorus slowly shrink away with a hushed prayer and the clarinets and strings take up the theme of their episode very quietly but in a different key. In its suggestion of impending danger this passage surprisingly anticipates the motif which heralds the final entry of Don José in *Carmen*. The villainy of Wurm is well established by showing the effect of his presence on others. Left alone with Luisa he tells her that her father is in prison for having insulted the Count. The only way in which Luisa can save him from the gallows is to write a letter to Wurm himself that he will now dictate, saying that she never loved Rodolfo and ending 'come to me tonight and let us fly together'. Wurm does not speak the letter; he sings it over a tiny string ostinato with shifting harmonies.* Sudden starts in the orchestra give us Luisa's reactions, while her resignation is expressed in a figure which calls to mind a similar scene in *La Traviata*.

292

Before signing the letter she breaks into an andante (*Tu puniscimi, O Signore*) may God punish her if she has done wrong, but not leave her to the mercies of these cruel men. It is very much in the grand manner, the village maiden becoming nearly engulfed by the prima donna. The striding rhythm, the major tonality, the patterned accompaniment all suggest a Verdi of the more distant past; yet even here there are unexpected touches of dramatic truth—such as the tendency to harp on the dominant of the relative minor (III ♯) thereby extending what would otherwise be a normal two quatrain structure. Wurm remains unmoved; and to a still more melancholy version of Ex. 292 played by all the woodwind Luisa signs her

* Cammarano seems to have had a rooted objection to the convention whereby letters were spoken, not sung. See previous chapter.

name. But Wurm has not yet finished. She must swear by her father's head that she wrote the letter of her own free will; also she must come that day to the castle and declare before the Duchess that she loves Wurm himself. Luisa agrees, and 'a diabolical smile springs to Wurm's lips', say the stage directions. Just the moment for an orchestral anticipation of Iago's credo:

293

Luisa's cabaletta (*A brani, a brani o perfido*) is of the rondò-finale type* in a minor–major design. A touch of chromaticism in the first part produces a momentary tonal ambiguity, beautifully emphasized by the clarinet in the chalumeau register. It will be recalled in A*ida* (IV, i) to convey the anguish of Amneris.

294

In the first part of the movement she inveighs against Wurm's cruelty; in the second, to a much smoother accompaniment, she takes comfort from the thought that she will have her father with her again. The contrast of modes thus reflects the sense of the text, as has not always happened in the past. Wurm adds pertichini to ritornello and coda.

Scene 2: a room in the Count's palace

Following a device first noted in the last act of *Il Corsaro* the scene begins with an orchestral reminiscence of the Count's aria from Act I, stated first rather pathetically then with a tortured emphasis, but always on strings alone. The Count is discovered alone and brooding on his son's disobedience. Wurm enters and tells him that their plan has worked. Luisa will shortly come to the castle, and meanwhile he himself has had the letter conveyed to Rodolfo. But why, he wants to know, was Miller not arrested earlier? For answer the Count reminds Wurm of his

---

* Cf. 'Era desso il mio figlio' (*Lucrezia Borgia*).

own predecessor's murder. In the impressive duet (*L'alto retaggio non ho bramato*) the two men tell the story in alternation, maintaining an unbroken melodic line. The fact that both are basses adds to the sense of two people in bondage to a terrible memory. They are talking not to each other, but to themselves. There is no opposition or clash of personalities as in so many Verdi duets. Almost in a dream they relate how Wurm brought the news that the previous Count, Walter's cousin, was about to marry and so jeopardize the succession of Rodolfo. At Wurm's own suggestion the Count had his cousin murdered at night in the forest, 'and everyone,' Wurm says, 'thought it was the work of robbers'. 'Not everyone,' the Count corrects him. Rodolfo, it seems, came upon the wounded man and heard from his dying lips the name of his assassin. Wurm is seized with terror. But in the final movement, Count Walter reassures him (*O meco incolume sarai, lo giuro*). Either he will be safe or they will both go to the scaffold together. It is a 'dissimilar' duet since Wurm's fears are by no means lulled. The Count's melody is doubled in the old style by trumpet, flute, oboe and clarinet—appropriately enough. Outwardly at any rate Count Walter is a tower of strength even to his partner in crime.

The rest of the scene is less interesting. Federica arrives, to hear Luisa's false confession. As she seats herself Wurm opens a secret door and introduces Luisa. He and the Count address the girl in long phrases as smooth as silk to which subdued but abrupt orchestral gestures give the lie. Federica's graciousness is accompanied by a wheedling melody for oboe and violins which shows Verdi's growing expertise in devising what may be called 'conversational' music.

295

As Luisa gives all the answers expected of her it becomes transformed into a jaunty theme vaguely recalling Abigaille's triumph in Act III of *Nabucco*. This in turn is broken down into sequences and interspersed with recitative and so leads into the unaccompanied quartet (*Come celar le smanie*). Here Verdi has abandoned his usual dramatic methods of construction with contrasting melodic patterns held together by an orchestral continuity. Instead he gives us an essay in pure music—in imaginative craftsmanship. The form is binary (minor–major) with the second section repeated and extended. The problem with all such ensembles is that they are almost invariably ineffective in practice because of the overtones in the average operatic voice, even when singing softly. Moreover the wide tonal range of the movement makes heavy demands on the musicianship of the participants. (What quartet of singers could ever manage accurately the jump from G major to a B major 6/4 and back again that precedes the coda?) And surely Federica deserves a more effective exit.

Scene 3: the castle gardens

To one of those orchestral motifs which seem to have grown out of the overture Rodolfo rushes in holding Luisa's letter. He is followed by a peasant to whom he throws a purse and sends for Wurm, then abandons himself to grief rather in the manner of Schiller's hero. But at such moments music has the advantage of prose. Nothing in Schiller can equal the beauty of his andante recalling the happier times spent in her company (*Quando le sere al placido*). Few of Verdi's early andantes have quite such a delicate orchestral frame. Paris and Chopin had not been forgotten.

296

The string chords, the rising cello phrase, the clarinet arpeggios, the touch of oboe in the final bars—all contribute to the unique quality of this movement. Were it not for the cabaletta that follows it would certainly be called a 'romanza', especially since it is cast in a mould not unlike that of Medora's 'Non so le tetre immagini', but—significantly—with no ornamentation on the second verse;* and indeed the non-repeating design of each stanza combined with the verbal refrain 'Ah mi tradia' gives it the quality of a French couplet, but with the heart of an Italian folk-song. As usual Verdi's giant hand makes itself felt at the climax, where the tenor's highest notes coincide with a swift modulation.

dalla sua man sen - ti - a. Ah!

con espressione

ah! ah! mi tra- di - a, ah! mi tra-di -

Wurm now appears. Rodolfo shows him the letter, then produces two pistols and asks him to choose one. But Wurm in a panic fires his pistol in the air and runs away. The sound brings servants and courtiers hurrying in and with them the Count. Once again the music resumes the overture-like motion of the opening. The Count with cruel irony now announces that he withdraws opposition to his son's wedding with Luisa. But when Rodolfo pours out his story, which his father affects to hear for the first time, he suggests that Rodolfo be revenged by marrying Federica. Rodolfo is now in a desperate state. He has given up all hopes of happiness either in this world or in the next; and there is a swaying, almost demented quality in his cabaletta (*L'ara o l'avello apprestami*) despite the clear major tonality and conventional accompaniment. Yet it would be pointless to pretend that it measures up to the andante as music.

ACT III
Poison
Scene: a room in Miller's cottage

The third act is undoubtedly the best of the three and Verdi's greatest achievement so far in combining large-scale structure with depth and intimacy of feeling. Basically the act resolves itself into three pieces—an ensemble for Luisa and

---

* The alteration of contour at the fourth line of the second verse is due to the words 'Amo te sol', which Verdi wanted to set in the strongest possible relief.

chorus, a duet between Luisa and Miller and one between Luisa and Rodolfo ending in a terzetto with Miller. All three are carried on a single developing musical thought no less than the numbers which make up the second scene of *Ernani*; only here there is no reliance on sheer excitement, but rather a calm intensity of lyrical expression which goes to the heart of the tragedy.

When the curtain rises Luisa is seated at the table, sad and abstracted. Her friends stand round her, wanting to bring her comfort yet hardly daring to speak, except to each other. The prelude is based on a variant in 3/4 time of the overture theme (a). It is announced by strings; two flutes* supply a gentle reminiscence of the duet *T'amo d'amor ch' esprimere* (b).

298

The chorus itself (*Come in un giorno solo*) is made up of three separate elements—Ex. 298 on the strings, a quiet succession of chords for the women and a melodic line for Laura. It is the same device as that in the last act of *La Battaglia di Legnano*, but used on a more modest scale and with more touching, less pretentious effect. At length Laura timidly suggests that Luisa should take a little food; but Luisa like the statue in *Don Giovanni* is not interested in earthly sustenance. A low clarinet figure underlines the import of Cammarano's melodramatic words; and celestial arpeggios on the flute make it clearer still. Luisa looks out of the window and sees lights burning in the church. Her companions look away uneasily. They dare not tell her that Rodolfo is about to be married to Federica. Here the opening melody (Ex. 298) returns, soon to be transformed into a more joyful motif in the major as Miller enters and his daughter throws herself into his arms. There is the usual subsidence over a dominant chord, but it is Laura who comments on the reunion, father and daughter being too moved to speak. The other women retire, leaving Luisa alone with Miller. In the short but exciting recitative that follows Miller notices and is shown the letter Luisa is about to send to Rodolfo suggesting a suicide pact. Again the orchestra plays a more than usually vital role in the elucidation of the drama. There is the familiar unison of oboe and clarinet poised over a drum roll as he takes up the letter; while at the mention of the place 'where oaths have no power' another variant of Ex. 298 apears in the bass. The formal duet begins with Luisa's reply (*La tomba è un letto*)—a simple melody in the Italian popular style, with the usual bitter-sweet discords of clashing thirds (Ex. 299, opposite).

Very much the village maiden once more, Luisa explains that the grave has terrors only for the guilty; for the innocent it is a couch strewn with flowers, a bridal chamber for two loving hearts. The duet develops in a sequence of short

---

* As this is the first instance in which Verdi uses two flutes to carry an orchestral melody it is perhaps worth mentioning that his first thoughts, according to the autograph, were for two clarinets. Then presumably he remembered the unique amenity offered by the San Carlo opera house.

299

Andantino

LUISA *delicatissimo*

La tom-ba è un let-to spar-so di fio-ri

movements. First (F minor, più mosso) Miller tries to convince her of the sinfulness of taking one's own life; then (D flat minor–major, meno mosso) he pleads with her to think of her sorrowing father. Miller, like Rigoletto, has no one in the world except his daughter; he therefore begs her to live for his sake with the same fervour, almost the same notes, as those with which Rigoletto implores the courtiers to give back Gilda to him. Note the upward portamento of a sixth in the most telling register of the high baritone voice.

300

Più mosso

MILLER

mes - se di pian-to e di do-lor? Ah! nel-la tom - ba

che schiuder vuo - i

Luisa yields and tears up the letter; and in a long crescendo over dominant harmony with offbeat wind chords, father and daughter find each other again. Musically the method is the same as in Act II of *I Due Foscari*, with the grading of rhythms and of phrase lengths so much better contrived. Miller and Luisa decide that they must leave the village. They may have to go begging from door to door, but they will at least be together. The final movement (*Andrem raminghi e poveri*) is marked *con molta passione* but the music is remarkably restrained. Already the fires of Verdian melody are beginning to sink to a rich glow. The design is an enriched variant of the 'stretta del duetto', the first quatrain being sung successively by the two singers, but ending in a different cadence. The second quatrain (*Forse talor le ciglia*) begins as an extension of the opening idea sung by the baritone, but Luisa instead of repeating *x* enters with a new idea of her own in faster tempo. This is developed in overlapping phrases, winding up in a cadential phrase in tenths ('Iddio benedirà'). In place of a ritornello a short dialogue leads back to the opening theme. It is decorated with the simplest of descants—a chain of quavers which Verdi marked on the orchestra *come un lamento* and in the voice part *hardly audible* (Ex. 301, overleaf).

Basevi's remark that in *Luisa Miller* Verdi draws away from Rossini and nearer to Donizetti is here particularly à propos, since the starting-point of this movement would appear to be the duet 'Dunque andiam: de' giorni miei' (*Belisario*). The situation is more or less identical, with father and daughter about to set forth into

301

the unknown as vagrants. If the verses, also by Cammarano, are in different metre, the character and rhythm of the music remain the same (measured crotchets in a 4/4 allegro). But Donizetti's design is totally conventional (a 'similar' movement at different pitches) and its effect more static. The access of warmth given by Luisa's 'me sempre al padre accanto' is the kind of inspiration which would not have occurred to Donizetti. It will be echoed, however, by the tenor in 'Parigi o cara' (*La Traviata*).

Miller goes into his room; the organ is heard playing from the church; and Luisa falls to her knees in a last prayer in the village where once she was happy (*Ah l'ultima preghiera*). Tomorrow she will say her prayers elsewhere. There is a touch of Parisian opera in the simplicity of the line, free and asymmetrical, strengthened here and there by a few grace-notes, in the manner of early Wagner, with an accompaniment of tremolo strings and the sound of the organ between each phrase. While she is still kneeling Rodolfo enters followed by a servant. He orders the servant to go and tell Count Walter that in this cottage 'the fatal rite will be accomplished'. He watches Luisa in silence; and from this point to the next formal number—i.e. 117 bars—the orchestra plays an increasingly prominent part expressing the feelings that the singers are trying to conceal. For instance a loud unison and a series of abrupt flourishes on strings and low clarinet indicate the point where Luisa looks up startled; but she says no word. Rodolfo produces the letter and asks her quietly whether she did in fact write it. After a painful hesitation (again portrayed orchestrally) she forces out a 'yes'. At once a furious tutti breaks loose; yet when Rodolfo speaks he is outwardly calm. He complains of thirst, and points to a cup that is on the table. Luisa offers it to him and he drinks. 'This draught is bitter,' he says, and he commands her to drink it after him. Luisa obeys him to a crawling passage in the orchestra which might have come straight from *Macbeth*—flute and low clarinet in unison, alternating with rapid gestures on viola and cello, then a long horn note and a major cadence in the sinister light of the flattened super-tonic. 'All is over,' says Rodolfo. 'No!' from Luisa followed by a long drum roll, while the voice lines are marked *silenzio terribile*. Rodolfo has of course poisoned the drink while Luisa was praying; and if this all-important event usually passes unnoticed it should be remarked that the taking of poison in full view of an audience was something to which Italian censors were inclined to object.[*] (In Schiller Ferdinand poisons the drinks *after* Luisa admits to having signed the letter.) If Cammarano is intentionally vague here, Verdi's orchestral writing is almost too explicit, making it hard to believe that Luisa does not yet understand that she has been poisoned.

At length the tenor rantings give way to a formal andante (*Piangi, piangi il tuo dolore*). It is worth quoting the purple passage in Schiller which, no less than Cammarano's verse, must have inspired Verdi to such heights of musical poetry:

LOUISA   Weep, Walter, weep. Your compassion will be more just towards me than your anger.

FERDINAND   You are wrong! These are not nature's tears! Not that warm delicious dew which falls like balsam on the wounded soul and drives the chilled current of feeling swiftly along its course. They are solitary ice-cold drops! The awful, eternal farewell of my love.[†]

Luisa's line moves between E minor and G major, Rodolfo's between G minor and B flat major, until both finally establish themselves in G major—a typically Italian and above all Verdian scheme. The principal phrase (a) returns in two variants (b), (c), the emotion mounting further towards the surface in each (Ex. 302, overleaf). Once again grief is transcended in lyrical beauty.

The bell chimes. Rodolfo for the last time asks Luisa whether she loves Wurm; and he tells her that the drink was poisoned. Freed from her vow she confesses her innocence and reveals the true explanation of the letter. The lovers' agitation breaks out in the G minor stretta (*Maledetto, maledetto il dì che nacqui*) and here at least there is no major-key complement. Miller's entrance leads to the trio-finale (*Padre ricevi l'estremo addio*) which is on a rather more conventional level, beginning haltingly then filling out into a rolling rhythm of three intertwining vocal lines. But the orchestration has some fine touches—the muted strings creeping up and down in diminished seventh arpeggios, the harp that adds lustre to the final section in the

---

[*] See letter from Jacovacci to Cammarano, 18.11.1851, about *Il Trovatore*. *Carteggi Verdiani*, I, p. 8.

[†] *Kabale und Liebe*, V, vi.

302

major. The ending is essentially Cammarano, not Schiller, with all the sensationalism of Italian melodrama. As Luisa dies Walter comes in followed by Wurm, his guards and the villagers. Rodolfo gathering his remaining strength runs Wurm through with his sword, then dies himself. Miller remains on his knees; Walter exclaims, 'My son!', the chorus, 'Ah!', and the curtain falls.

There is a well known story recounted by Gatti about a Neapolitan maestro, Capocelatro, who was believed to have the Evil Eye. All during the first night of *Luisa Miller* Verdi's friends formed a protective shield around him; but at one point the vigilance was relaxed, and Capocelatro embraced the composer, who only just escaped being crushed immediately by the fall of a heavy curtain.* It sounds like nonsense, and we may be sure that Verdi himself never believed it, since Capocelatro remained a lifelong friend of his. One is reminded of the incident only because despite the unanimous praise bestowed upon it by Verdi's biographers *Luisa Miller* has proved, if not precisely accident-prone, at least uncertain in the response it evokes. Both at its premiere and at a later performance in Rome the third and finest act was received coolly. Translated into French it was mounted at the Paris Opéra in 1853 where not only was it taken off after eight performances, but it became the source of a protracted quarrel between Verdi and his publisher. In London it did no better. It was given at Her Majesty's in 1858 and Covent Garden in 1874; in neither case did it survive into the following season. In Italy it circulated satisfactorily enough; but Verdi himself tended to discourage its revival except under the most favourable circumstances.

Certainly the vocal distribution poses problems. No previous opera of Verdi's contains so wide a cast of individuals. Probably it was the first Schiller subject in which he set himself to do justice to the original, wherever possible. But not all the parts reward the singer in proportion to the demands they make of him, or her. Wurm, written for Arati, a very modest bass but a great 'character',† must express his villainy only through pertichini, recitatives, one duet shared with the Count and a quartet. Federica's role is all the more thankless for beginning so promisingly, with a chorus of servants to prepare her entry and a striking recitative to mark it. One is almost disposed to forgive the contralto who in the English performance of 1858 omitted the duet with Rodolfo and substituted Leonora's cavatina from *Oberto* in its entirety transposing it down a semitone.‡ But Naples like every other city was subject to the convenienze as well as the talent that was available. Walter is a different matter—a typical Verdian bass whose character is fully rounded within comparatively few notes, and whose cantabile in Act I is worth many a two-movement cavatina. Miller too is a fully extended baritone role in the manner of Carlo in *Ernani*, though with a greater bias towards tenderness. Luisa herself presents difficulties of another kind. Verdi described her part as 'ingenuous and extremely dramatic'.§ In fact she is almost three people—in Act I a conventional ingénue, in Act II a somewhat less conventional tragic heroine; only in the last act does she reach her full stature with a simple pathos that has something of greatness in it—a conception already hinted at in *Giovanna d'Arco*. If the transition from the Luisa of Act I to that of Act III is wholly logical in terms of the drama, the aria in Act II strikes a faintly jarring note. The most consistently successful creation of all is Rodolfo. In the character with which Cammarano endowed him he provides the perfect channel for all those emotions which Verdi associates with the tenor voice. He is the epitome of youthful impetuousness and also youthful poetry. Given the iron framework of his father's authority his most passionate utterances have a force

---

* Gatti, I, p. 338.

† See *Carteggi Verdiani*, I, p. 4 *n.*

‡ Likewise the tenor substituted Carlo's 'All'argilla maledetta' (*I Masnadieri*) for *L'ara o l'avello* and omitted the final part of the act I finale which ended with the concertato. Did the London audience realize, one wonders, that this Rodolfo had seduced and abandoned Federica and that on believing Luisa false he had decided to form and lead a band of robbers made up of his father's retainers?

§ Letter from Flauto, 6.8.1849. *Copialettere*, p. 477.

and vividness denied to such as Corrado (*Il Corsaro*) and Carlo (*I Masnadieri*), who by comparison seem to be bombinating in a vacuum. He is not supposed like Ernani to be pitting his strength against others on equal terms. Like all romantic tenors he is a loser but for once his failure is built into his character and circumstances. It is wholly convincing that at the height of his anguish in Act III at the duet it is Luisa, the wronged innocent maid, who takes command of the situation. In the summer of 1850 Verdi heard of a project to put on *Luisa Miller* at the Carcano Theatre in Milan: he opposed it on the grounds that the company as a whole was weak and the opera above all needs a tenor of the front rank. *Luisa Miller* is a tenor's opera.

The best of it sets a new standard in Verdian opera. By comparison even the finest of the earlier works takes on a poster-like quality—bold, exhilarating, maybe, yet lacking in depth. In *Luisa Miller* buds of poetry hinted at in *I Due Foscari* and parts of *Il Corsaro* and *La Battaglia di Legnano* burst into full flower. There is a new refinement of musical thought, a new concentration of lyrical elements within the dramatic scheme, in sum a more thorough resolution of the drama into terms of pure music. All this despite a superficial reversion at times to certain stock procedures which are absent from *Jérusalem* and *La Battaglia di Legnano*. The reform is within. Nor can the question of environment be ignored. *Luisa Miller* was the first opera of Verdi's to be written against a background of comparative leisure. It is also the first for which he seems to have made extensive sketches in the manner of Beethoven,* though these are not publicly accessible. Less preoccupied than formerly with the demands of the moment he was able not only to allow the newly acquired Parisian elements to become assimilated into his Italian style, but also to let the influence of the German and Italian classics absorbed in his youth rise to the surface. The advance is most apparent in Act III – in the sensitive scoring, the flexibility of the musical forms, the growing importance of the role which Verdi assigned to the orchestra and which permits him to write two lengthy dialogue recitatives (Luisa—Miller; Luisa—Rodolfo) such as he would have avoided in his youth for fear of boring the audience. It is in this act too that the fussy accompaniments are abandoned, leaving a distilled essence of melody.

Like *Macbeth* and *Nabucco*, *Luisa Miller* has had to wait until the present century to be accorded its proper place in the Verdi canon. To most people it is the gateway to the great three—*Rigoletto*, *Il Trovatore* and *La Traviata*—with nothing of importance intervening. But as to the last part they are wrong. For the next opera, recently unearthed in its original form, is a work of no less significance.

---

* Gatti, I, p. 340. Abbiati (II, pp. 32–5) describes at some length a sketch of Rodolfo's aria in Act II, in which the andante *Quando le sere al placido* appears to have been jotted down straight away in its final form though a tone higher, while the cabaletta was drafted in more than one version.

18 STIFFELIO

STIFFELIO

Opera in three acts
by
FRANCESCO MARIA PIAVE
(after the play by Émile Souvestre and Eugène Bourgeois, *Le Pasteur, ou L'Évangile et le Foyer*)

First performed at the
Teatro Grande, Trieste,
16 November 1850

STIFFELIO, a minister of the Gospel	PRIMO TENORE	Gaetano Fraschini
LINA, his wife	PRIMA DONNA SOPRANO	Marietta Gazzaniga-Malaspina
STANKAR, an elderly colonel and count of Empire, Lina's father	PRIMO BARITONO	Filippo Colini
RAFFAELE, a nobleman	TENORE COMPRIMARIO	Rainieri Dei
JORG, an elderly minister	BASSO COMPRIMARIO	Francesco Reduzzi
FEDERICO DI FRENGEL	SECONDO TENORE	Giovanni Petrovich
DOROTEA, Lina's cousin	SECONDA DONNA MEZZO SOPRANO	Viezzoli De Silvestrini

Members of Stankar's household—friends and followers of Stiffelio

The action takes place in Austria at Stankar's castle by the river Salzbach [sic]

Epoch: the beginning of the nineteenth century

Before Verdi left Busseto for Naples in September 1849 he had already written to Flauto promising him another opera for the following year to be given round about Easter. The most likely subject appeared to be Hugo's *Le Roi s'amuse*—'a fine drama with marvellous situations in which there would be two magnificent roles for La Frezzolini and Bassini'.* But by the time he returned after the premiere of *Luisa Miller* his disgust at the management's behaviour both towards himself and the opera's prima donna† decided him to write the new work with Cammarano for Ricordi alone, to be placed in the autumn of 1850 at some theatre of the publisher's own choosing—always excepting La Scala, Milan. (It was the system employed for *La Battaglia di Legnano*.) In January he wrote to Ricordi that the subject had already been settled with Cammarano and the opera would be ready in about five or six months' time.‡ It was not, however, to be *Le Roi s'amuse*. Encouraged by the success of *Luisa Miller*, Verdi had ventured to revive the long-cherished project of a *King Lear*.

> At first sight [*he wrote to Cammarano in February*], *King Lear* seems so vast and so involved that it would be impossible to make it into an opera. But after having examined it thoroughly I think that the difficulties, great as they undoubtedly are, would not be insurmountable. You'll have realized that we can't make it a drama with the forms that have been more or less continuously in use up to now. It must be treated in an entirely new way on a large scale without any regard to the convenienze. The main parts could be reduced to five principals . . . two comprimarie women . . . two comprimari basses . . . the rest secondary parts . . . The scenes could be reduced to eight or nine . . .§

The detailed synopsis as well as the later correspondence with Somma must be left for another occasion. Cammarano was willing enough to discuss Verdi's ideas sympathetically; but it is fairly clear that they were much too advanced for him. By June 1850 Verdi had to reconcile himself to the fact that as far as Cammarano was concerned *King Lear* was adjourned sine die.

Curiously enough, during that year Verdi had two other offers of Shakespearian subjects. Benjamin Lumley wanted to interest him in an Italian version of *The Tempest*—the opera that Mendelssohn had never lived to write and that Halévy was now writing, also for Lumley. In a general way Verdi was quite attracted to the idea. But he did not like the prospect of competing with Halévy. It sounded too much like an impresario's stunt ('Lumley can be a gentleman when he chooses, but he is fundamentally an impresario').¶ A few months later Maffei's friend Giulio

---

* Letter to Flauto, 7.9.1849, *Copialettere*, pp. 84–5.
† Letter to C. De Sanctis, 28.12.1849. *Carteggi Verdiani*, I, p. 34.
‡ Letter to Giovanni Ricordi, 31.1.1850. *Copialettere*, pp. 93–5.
§ Letter to Cammarano, 28.2.1850. *Copialettere*, pp. 478–82.
¶ Letter to Marie Escudier, 7.3.1850. Abbiati, II, pp. 56–7.

Carcano offered him a libretto of *Hamlet*; but this too he declined regretfully for the time being.

> Alas, these great subjects take too much time and for the present I've even had to give up *King Lear* after having commissioned Cammarano to prepare a libretto for a more suitable occasion. If *King Lear* is difficult *Hamlet* is still more so. With two pressing commitments on my hands I've had to choose subjects which are shorter and easier so as to fulfil my obligations. However, I won't give up hope of our being able one day to get together with you and treat this masterpiece of the English stage.*

The commitments were in fact two—the opera for Ricordi to be given in the autumn and another for the Teatro la Fenice in Venice. Both contracts had been signed in April 1850 and for both Verdi had recourse to Piave, whose reputation as a librettist was already growing.† As subjects Verdi offered *Le Roi s'amuse*, *Manon Lescaut* (Prévost), *Kean* (Dumas), *Gusmano el Bueno*—this last having been already suggested by Väez and Royer in Paris. Piave countered with *Le Comte Herman* (Dumas), *Don Cesare* (of uncertain provenance), *Stradella* and *Stiffelius*. All were scouted by Verdi with the exception of *Gusmano el Bueno*, which he quite liked, and *Stiffelius*, which he had never seen.‡ In the meantime he had been brooding over *Le Roi s'amuse* and was becoming more and more fascinated by it. It had been banned at its first performance; it was, politically speaking, dynamite. But after all Venice had permitted *Ernani*; might it not also permit *Le Roi s'amuse*?

This then became the subject chosen for the Fenice, where Piave was thought to have some influence with the management; and here we leave it until the next chapter.

Eventually the sketch of *Stiffelio* arrived, and Verdi pronounced it 'good and exciting'.§ The literary source was a French play by Émile Souvestre and Bourgeois which had enjoyed some success in Italy in a translation by Gaetano Vestri. It is concerned with adultery in the household of a Protestant minister. Not, one might have thought, a very promising theme for Catholic Italy; but in the context of his feelings at the time it is not difficult to see why Verdi chose it. He was tired of stock subjects; he wanted something with genuine human, as distinct from melodramatic, interest. In December of 1849 he had written to De Sanctis in Naples that in the new opera which he was to write with Cammarano he hoped there would be some 'good sense, a very rare commodity in the theatrical world, but worthy of being attempted by conscientious artists such as Cammarano and myself'.¶ *Stiffelio* had the attraction of being a problem play with a core of moral sensibility; the same attraction, in fact, that was to lead Verdi to *La Traviata* a little later. Émile Souvestre, who appears to have been the moving spirit of the partner-

---

* Letter to Carcano, 17.6.1850. *Copialettere*, pp. 482–3.
  † That year he was to write a 'fantastic comedy' for the brothers Ricci, *Crispino e la Comare*, a former favourite of the Italian stage, occasionally revived to-day.
  ‡ The correspondence between Verdi and Piave that led to the choice of *Stiffelio* runs between March and May of 1850. The autographs are in the Gallini collection. Extracts are published in Abbiati, II, pp. 57–63.
  § Letter to Piave, 8.5.1850. Abbiati, II, pp. 62–3.
  ¶ Letter to C. De Sanctis, 28.1.1850. *Carteggi Verdiani*, I, p. 3.

ship, was well known for the high moral tone of his writings. After his death he was awarded the Prix Lambert as the contemporary writer most useful to society. A fulsome tribute was paid to his 'burning passion to be of service to the community, expressing those generous sentiments of which his heart was full' and to 'his defence of those moral truths that are denied, proscribed and forgotten by this materialistic century'.* Curiously enough, *Le Pasteur, ou l'Évangile et le foyer* passed almost unnoticed at its first performance in February 1849, though it was sympathetically reviewed in the *Journal des Débats* as a piece which deserved better attendance than it received from a public surfeited with cheap vaudevilles. Stranger still, Vestri's translation had already appeared the year before; and by the time that Piave made its acquaintance, *Stiffelius* was probably better known in Italy than in the land of its origin.

Le Pasteur, then, was for its time a modern piece, symbolizing that trend towards realism and a wider, more understanding view of humanity that marks the literature of the late nineteenth century. It deals not with a type, but with a special case. A Protestant minister, head of a sect, renowned for his goodness, eloquence and steadfastness in the face of persecution, finds that during his absence his wife has been unfaithful to him. His instinct suggests to him a course of action which his cloth forbids. This is the central problem from which the dramatic conflict is born; but it is not the only one. There is also the problem of Lina, his wife, who for all her frailty still loves her husband and whose repentance confers on her a genuine dignity. Finally there is her father-in-law, Stankar, the embodiment of conventional social values, anxious on the one hand to keep his daughter's adultery from her husband's ears, and on the other to avenge the honour of his family on the person of the adulterer. So by an ironical twist the man who seems at first to be soothing the conflict in the name of Christian charity is the one who will later push it to a violent and bloody outcome.

'Is this Stiffelio a historical person?' Verdi asked in a letter to Piave. 'In all the history I've read I don't remember coming across the name.'† There were indeed two historical figures of Stiffelius, both Protestants. The first, and more famous, was a converted monk who became a personal follower of Luther at the age of thirty-seven, and was sent by him as chaplain to another Lutheran convert, Christoph Jorger of Upper Austria. Several years later he was obliged to flee into Saxony, where he ended his career as Professor of Mathematics at the University of Jena. The other Stiffelius was a follower of one Professor Müller, a painter who taught at the Academy of Dresden in the early nineteenth century, and claimed to be a miracle-worker. It is fairly clear that Souvestre and Bourgeois availed themselves of both these sources not for facts but for names. Their Stiffelio has an alias Rudolphe Müller, forced on him by the need to hide from his persecutors. An elder member of his sect, and one who is particularly anxious to keep him in the oath of religious zeal, is called Jorg. The venue of Salzburg was probably chosen less because the historical Stiffelius was active there than because that part of Austria was noted for its religious intolerance, and had as recently as 1837 expelled its 'Inclinanti'. The sect of the Assasveriani, of which Stiffelio is supposed to be the

---

* Quoted by Hellmut Ludwig, 'La fonte letteraria del libretto', in *Quaderni dell'Instituto di Studi Verdiani 3: Stiffelio*, p. 12.
† Letter to Piave, 8.5.1850. Abbiati, II, pp. 62–3.

leader, was a pure invention on the part of the playwrights. The name is derived from Ahasuerus, the Wandering Jew, 'considered as the personification not of heartlessness eternally punished, but rather of an aspiration towards a happiness ever in flight and ever pursued'.*

As an operatic subject *Stiffelio* had one notable drawback: it was too complex to be treated in its entirety. As usual the smaller vignettes are expended: the vain, blasée Dorothea, the feather-brained Frédéric von Wrangel (an Austrian Bertie Wooster) become secondary parts with only a phrase here and there. Even Dr Raphael de Leuthold, 'half Faust, half Don Juan', who lays siege to Lina with the cold-blooded cynicism of Aldous Huxley's Dr Obispo, is reduced to a comprimario tenor of indeterminate character. In particular the circumstances which led up to Lina's adultery have to be omitted: the long absence of Stiffelio, the intercepting of his letters by Raphael, the worldly influence of Dorothea, and even the stratagem by which Raphael enters her room. In the play all this explains, if it does not excuse, Lina's faithlessness. In the opera it is only hinted at. The advantages of beginning at the start of the action had already been demonstrated in *Luisa Miller*. The characters can then develop in music as they do in the play. *Stiffelio* is hampered from the outset by a history of events which it is quite impossible to make clear in the course of the opera itself. Add to this the always dangerous omission of a conventional 'romantic' love interest, the undercurrent of realism, the nineteenth-century setting (Italians liked their operas 'period'), and the inevitable difficulties with a Catholic censorship, and it is surprising that *Stiffelio* succeeded as well as it did. The fact that while writing *Stiffelio* Verdi was busy with plans for *Rigoletto*, which fired his imagination far more, has misled certain writers into assuming that the earlier work was undertaken without enthusiasm or any real sense of commitment—a chore to be dispatched as competently, and with as little trouble, as possible. The score itself tells us otherwise; so too does Muzio who wrote to Ricordi in July that '*Stiffelio* is making gigantic strides and Verdi is working with the greatest enthusiasm on such a fine and congenial subject'.†

Ricordi decided to place it at Trieste, in the same theatre that had given such a poor reception to *Il Corsaro*. Here for the first time since *I Lombardi* composer and librettist encountered real trouble with the censor. At one point it seemed as though the opera would be forbidden altogether. But at last Verdi and Piave submitted with a bad grace to certain changes. Stiffelio was to be called not a minister but a sectarian; even the words 'evangelico pastore', which occur in Act I, were disallowed and the phrase 'la purezza dell'onore' pleonastically inserted in their place. The key phrase in Act III, in which Lina, having failed to move Stiffelio by appealing to him as her husband, demands that he should, as a minister, hear her confession, was to be rendered totally futile. 'Ministro, confessatemi' became 'Rodolfo, ascoltatemi'. The last scene of all was reduced to the most pointless banality. In the original libretto, as in the play, Stiffelio goes into the pulpit to preach, his heart still full of bitterness towards his wife; he opens the Bible and reads the story of the woman taken in adultery. At Christ's words, 'He who is without sin among you, let him first cast a stone at her,' he looks at Lina kneeling among the congregation and adds significantly: 'and the woman rose up and went

---

* E. Souvestre and E. Bourgeois, *Le Pasteur*, I, iv.
† Letter from Muzio to Giovanni Ricordi, 26.7.1850. Abbiati, II, p. 67.

her way forgiven'.* Dramatically it is an understatement, but it makes its point effectively and economically. In the altered version Stiffelio merely preaches in general terms about the desirability of forgiving one's enemies. Part of the Press—notably Francesco Hermet of *La Favilla*—reacted vigorously and in a manner obviously gratifying to Verdi, holding the censor up to the most deadly ridicule. But the reviews as a whole were mixed.† Hermet found Verdi's music 'sublime and philosophical'. *L'Italia Musicale*, on the other hand, considered it too studied, too much in the French style (a shrewd comment, if not a sympathetic one). *Il Diavoletto* found fault with the music, the subject and, above all, the nineteenth-century setting, which it regarded as the root of the opera's failure as a work of art. Modern costumes, it said, lacked beauty and harmony of form. Besides, poet and composer had made a great mistake in treating a religious question on an operatic stage. 'It is true that we tolerate monks, nuns, the organ, church bells, the outside of a church, a chorus of people at prayer, but one should never exceed these limits.' Religion in opera, it seems, should never be allowed to invade the sanctity of private life. In Florence the following year the opera was revived under the title *Guglielmo Wellingrode* with the hero turned into a German prime minister, but this did nothing to change its fortunes. In Italy in the 1850s censorship was more vigilant than ever before; and as early as 1851 Verdi was writing regretfully to Ricordi that if the opera was going to be butchered and truncated by the censors, it might be more sensible to wait until he had remade the last scene altogether before hawking it round the opera houses of Italy.‡ By 1854 he was convinced that the opera had no future as it stood;§ and with Piave's collaboration he rewrote it to a different, less convincing story (*Aroldo*). The theme of adultery and Christian forgiveness remains, but the hero, no longer a minister, becomes an English crusader. So certain was Verdi that *Stiffelio* was doomed that he constructed *Aroldo* from the autograph of the earlier work, throwing away certain numbers and adding others. The result is that no autograph of *Stiffelio* exists. It was only the discovery of two copyists' scores—one of *Stiffelio*, the other of *Guglielmo Wellingrode*—in the archives of the Naples Conservatory that made possible the recent revival at the Teatro Regio in Parma and also the discovery that, far from being an inferior version of *Aroldo*, *Stiffelio* is actually superior to it in the integrity of its dramatic conception. This is not to say that the musical changes were for the worse: many of them are improvements; but in most cases they were forced on Verdi by the altered setting and should not be taken as evidence that he regarded the pieces which they replaced as musically weak. It is significant that a few years later Verdi himself coupled it with *La Battaglia di Legnano* as one of two operas which he would not like to see forgotten. Both are, in a sense, pioneering ventures in which the stimulus of an unusual dramatic problem led Verdi to enlarge his vocabulary and to widen his stylistic range.

---

* Thus the libretto, using inverted commas to indicate a Biblical quotation. But the Gospel story ends with the words: 'Neither do I condemn thee: go thy way; from henceforth sin no more.' (John, viii, 11).

† A summary of the Press reaction is to be found in *Stiffelio* (Quaderni, 3), pp. 101 ff.

† Letter to Giovanni Ricordi, 5.1.1851. *Copialettere*, pp. 112–13.

§ Letter to C. De Sanctis, 6.7.1854. *Carteggi Verdiani*, I, p. 25.

The overture is not one of Verdi's most inspired, even if he saw fit to retain it with one or two modifications for *Aroldo*.* In fact its conventional blend of the lyrical and the heroic makes it better suited to the later work, with which in any case its thematic links are far closer. Of its five principal motifs only three occur later in the course of *Stiffelio*, whereas all five are used in *Aroldo*. The opening bars of the andante are based on the psalm-tune 'Non puniscimi Signore nel Tuo furor', neutralized out of all recognition into a succession of dry sequences of string chords with a characteristic comment for flute and clarinet at the end of each phrase†— (Ex. 303 a). The first subject of the allegro is taken from the first act chorus (*A te Stiffelio un canto*) each note accompanied by a side-drum (Ex. 303 b); the second is a variation in 4/4 time of the chorus which begins the Act I finale (*Concordi qui regnin la gioia, la pace*, Ex. 303 c).‡

Of the two 'free' melodies the most important is the Donizettian trumpet canti-lena which occupies most of the andante introduction and is treated with some ingenious woodwind decoration at its reprise. The other is a brash, martial theme, vaguely recalling the world of *Rienzi*, which first appears directly after Ex. 303 b, but not again until the coda. As in the overture to *Luisa Miller* there is a develop-ment but no first-subject reprise. The only passage which stamps itself on the mem-ory is the Verdian (not Rossinian) crescendo which follows the second subject. It is based on a figure too slender to be called a theme, but scored and harmonized with the piquancy of a Saint-Saëns.

* According to Abbiati (II, p. 72) it was composed the night before the first performance.
† Omitted in *Aroldo*.
‡ Compare the overture to *Nabucco* for a similar rhythmic transformation.

304

ACT I

Scene 1: a hall on the ground floor of Stankar's castle in Salzburg: upstage centre is a door; to the audience's far left a window; on the right a hearth with a fire alight. In front of the window towards the centre of the stage is a large table with several books on it, among them a rather large one, expensively bound and fastened with a clasp. Writing materials to hand.

The opening scene shows a more radical break with convention than any attempted by Verdi so far. Instead of an opening chorus, normally de rigueur, a brief but highly charged arioso, for the comprimario bass Jorg, an elderly minister of the Assasveriani (*Oh santo libro, oh dell'eterno Vero*). Very striking are the means used to create an atmosphere of other-worldly piety. Four bars of unison strings wipe away all sense of tonal orientation. Jorg's first phrase with its overlapping plagal fourths and its avoidance of anything that could be construed as a leading note takes on the character of modal plainchant. Only at the end of the second phrase does A major establish itself in retrospect, through its dominant.

305

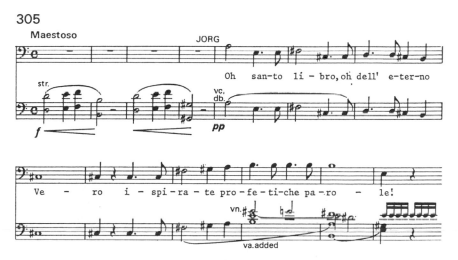

'Oh sacred book, words divinely inspired, that prophesy eternal truth! Go forth, Stiffelio, and let your word be a destroying tempest, a devouring wave, a blasting thunderbolt to all God's enemies on this earth.' Here too the tonality is reluctant to declare itself. The line moves in a characteristic tonal orbit which embraces the related keys of A major and A minor. With each admonition it rises higher, reaching its climax as well as its furthest point of distance from the home key in a high

E flat on the word 'God', from which it descends through an unprepared triad of
A flat to a solemn cadence in C major. Then woodwind and horns interrupt the
pious meditations of Jorg with a jaunty tune reminiscent of the 'Galop general'
from Act I of Adam's *Giselle*.*

Stiffelio has returned from one of his missions, and his wife is with him. In
another passage of recitative leaning heavily on the dominant of A minor, Jorg
expresses the hope that Stiffelio's marriage will not cause his religious zeal to slacken.
Then the cheerful theme is resumed to a fuller orchestration as Stiffelio enters
with Lina on his arm; and with them Stankar, Raffaele and Lina's cousins Federico
and Dorotea. So within a very brief space the two elements from which the tragedy
will be distilled—piety and worldly frivolity—are set in the strongest relief. What
Rossini called 'the moral ambience of the drama'† has been defined in the most
vivid chiaroscuro.

None of the next few numbers follows the usual pattern. Stiffelio's cavatina takes
the form of a short 'racconto' with pertichini of great dramatic importance from
the bystanders. He describes how a certain Walter 'the good boatman' one morning saw a man jump out of a high window into the river watched by a woman who
seemed out of her mind with terror. A letter fell out of his pocket, however, which
the boatman brought to Stiffelio. Clearly it related to some guilty intrigue; and
like the forgiving Christian that he is Stiffelio now produces the letter and throws
it into the fire.

The song (*Di qua varcando sul primo albore*) is basically strophic in form with the

---

* It could be heard as a rhythmic derivative of Ex. 304 with the quaver figure displaced on to
the first beat of the bar.

† A. Zanolini, 'Una passeggiata in compagnia di Rossini', quoted in L. Rognoni, *Rossini*
(Parma, 1956), pp. 313–19.

second verse extended to accommodate two extra lines and a flamboyant 'madrigal-ism' in the form of a long downward scale to suggest the young man's leap. In between verses the listeners react in various ways that will become more clearly defined in the septet which follows. As in *Alzira* and *Attila* the image of rowing is embodied in the accompaniment; while the melody itself is coloured by three horns and touches of chromatic harmony. The effect is not merely picturesque; it helps to suggest the type of cool reflective character not normally associated with a Verdian tenor. Doubtless it was passages like these that caused *Stiffelio* to be regarded at the time as too studied. When people complained that Verdi was forsaking the pure spring of Italian melody, they were doubtless comparing this barcarolle with something like the narrative chorus ('Come vinti di stanchezza') from the first scene of *Lucia di Lammermoor*.

307

In a continuation, to the same 6/8 rhythm, tension mounts as Stiffelio supplies details of time and place and is resolved in a manner more typical of Brahms than of Verdi—a broad cadential phrase sung by Stiffelio in which crotchets drive a rhythm of 3/4 across the prevailing 6/8 (*Ardan col nome del seduttor*).

The dramatic situation is now crystallized in a septet (*Colla cenere disperso*) launched by Stiffelio with an authoritative phrase about the virtues of forgiveness. In the coda this is taken up in diminution by all the voices 'all' unisono' and then transformed into a succession of melting chords. It is tempting to regard this com-bination of overlapping fourths as a Schoenbergian 'Grundgestalt' standing for the religious element in the opera—passive in Jorg's arioso and therefore descending; active and ascending in Exs. 308 and 309.[*] But if such was Verdi's conscious or unconscious purpose at the outset he failed to carry it through with any consistency. In any case his operas are not constructed motivically in this way. What matters is that in all three examples the sense of religious idealism is present and finds its precise musical expression according to the requirement of its context, while remaining within the stylistic framework of the whole. The second main theme of the septet is that to which Jorg, Dorotea and Federico express their approval of Stiffelio's action.

[*] The use of rising overlapping fourths to denote a kind of religious aspiration can be found in the works by at least three romantic composers—Liszt's *Les Préludes*, César Franck's Symphony in D minor and the fourth movement of Schumann's Rhenish Symphony. But in all three cases one of the fourths is always diminished.

308

309

310

JORG (Ah per-fi-no la me - mo - ria ei) di-sper-de dell' er -(ror)
FEDERICO Ei)

Clearly it is the forerunner of the conspirators' motif in the first chorus of *Un Ballo in Maschera* with its soft, padding motion and suggestion of counterpoint in its treatment, but it has not the same sharpness of character and association. It is little more than an instrumental figure such as Verdi, like Rossini, often entrusted to the lower voices in his ensembles for reasons of rhythmic architecture. The same theme, displaced by a semiquaver, serves Stankar at the point where he begins to voice his suspicions. The difficulty of *playing* such a figure off the beat with iron precision will be clear to anyone familiar with the last movement of Borodin's Polovtsian Dances; to expect it from a singer, however gifted, is surely unreasonable, nor is it particularly effective. Otherwise the piece is a musical gem, with plenty of fine sustained lyrical writing for tenor and soprano and skilful interweaving of vocal strands. Theatrically it is awkward, since the number of voices taking part makes it impossible for Verdi to sum up the attitude of each in a characteristic phrase, as in the quintet that occurs in a similar position in *I Lombardi*. At the same time, important information—Lina's remorse, Raffaele's cool suggestion for another assignation—is submerged in what is essentially a design of sonorities. We find ourselves plunged into the centre of an intrigue by complex characters with whom we have not yet become sufficiently acquainted. *Aroldo* follows a safer, more orthodox course at this point.

Stiffelio's friends and followers now start crowding in. They hail their leader in a chorus (*A te Stiffelio un canto*) based on Ex. 303 b, which here undergoes some striking transformations since it has to accommodate not only the joy of reunion between the minister and his flock but also Lina's remorseful anguish. The pizzicato decoration is a Bellinian legacy already encountered in *Giovanna d'Arco*.

Stiffelio's next aria is something new in Verdi. Strictly speaking it falls into the category of 'aria con pertichini', like Luisa's scene with Wurm in Act II of *Luisa Miller*. But there Luisa has only two positions (before and after writing the letter), which can be embodied in andante and cabaletta respectively. Here each of Lina's reactions, however fragmentary, evoke a different response from her husband and with it a new movement. The result is that the aria carries all the dialectical quality of the duetto-finale in Act I of *I Due Foscari* and is constructed accordingly. To begin with Lina is permitted a short arioso, as she begs to address Stiffelio as Rodolfo Müller, the name by which she first knew him. Then, she implies, he spared a thought for her; but since that time he has been enjoying the pleasures of the great world outside her. Stiffelio replies in a powerful G minor movement (*Vidi dovunque gemere*) in which he describes the squalor and degradation that he encountered on his travels. Here it becomes apparent that the part of Stiffelio is unlike any tenor role that Verdi had written so far. His early tenors are all young, with a vulnerable quality even in their most forceful utterances. Stiffelio is a mature man, happily married (or so he thinks), who has more on his mind than the roses and raptures of youthful passion. His line is sustained, weighty, baritonic almost, with an unusual emphasis on middle and lower registers and a tendency to move by step in wide spanning phrases buttressed by strong harmonies:

311

Noticing Lina's distress Stiffelio breaks off to assure her that she has restored his faith in marital fidelity (andante, D flat major). Now his wife's agitation begins to find concrete expre. ion in the orchestra with a characteristic semitonal motif.

312

She rallies sufficiently to suggest that his own greatness of soul would easily forgive a wrong done to his honour. There is exquisite irony in his reply (*Ah, no, il perdono è facile*—allegretto 6/8 in B flat major) with its sparse accompaniment, its gentle cello and clarinet arpeggios, and its tender concern for those sinned against rather than the sinners. Lina is tongue-tied and the orchestra takes over completely the task of conveying her feelings with further developments of Ex. 312.

Now Stiffelio realizes that there is something seriously wrong. He begs her to confide in him; or at least to smile at him as she did when they were first married (*Allor dunque sorridimi*—andante 4/4 in A flat major). The suave melody is abruptly halted in mid-phrase as Stiffelio notices for the first time that she is no longer wearing his mother's ring; and so through a turbulent allegro dialogue to the cabaletta (*Ah! v' appare in fronte scritto*) in which Stiffelio accuses his wife. It is the only orthodox movement in the aria, but totally different from most of its kind. The voice-part, marked 'hollow with rage', remains curiously level and restrained; only the orchestra smoulders and seethes with fury.

The cadence of the second statement is interrupted noisily as Stankar arrives to tell Stiffelio that his friends are waiting for him. Before the short, explosive reprise of the theme by all three voices in unison, which serves as coda, Stiffelio cries in recitative, 'I will come back soon' ('Tosto verrò'); which Lina at once picks up at the start of her 'scena e preghiera': 'Tosto ei disse' ('Soon, he said'). In this way a dramatic continuity is maintained despite the apparent finality of the preceding piece. Twenty-one years later Verdi will employ this procedure even more impressively with the words 'Ritorna vincitor'.

Lina's prayer for forgiveness (*A te ascenda, O Dio clemente*) has the simplest design imaginable: two parallel phrases each repeated (*a a b b* and coda); like her solo in Act II it is exquisitely scored, with a pattern of pizzicato cello beneath sustaining horns and bassoons and with soft string chords on first and third beats. Note the poignant Bellinian discord on the word 'Dio' (see Ex. 314, overleaf).

As in Gulnara's cavatina (*Il Corsaro*) the cadence of *b* is approached by a chain of chromatic harmonies accented off the beat.

Lina at last decides to write her husband a letter confessing that she is no longer worthy to be his wife. She has got no further than the first line when Stankar arrives, and reads what she has written. As in Stiffelio's own, the form of their duet is modified by the fact that Lina is too guilt-ridden to argue. The first movement therefore (*Dite che il fallo a tergere*) is essentially a solo for Stankar. Not content with betraying Stiffelio, he says, Lina is prepared to kill him with shame and grief. The melody, high-lying and with chromatic inflexions is in that vein of bland bitterness which the 'honeyed' baritone Colini would have realized to perfection.

314

315

In the andante (*Ed io pure in faccia agli uomini*) with its sparse pizzicato accompaniment the mood is further intensified, culminating in a violent outburst (*Voi l'indegna che disprezzo*) of almost unsupported declamation. Must he himself, Stankar asks, undergo the dishonour of having to acknowledge as his daughter a self-confessed adulteress? Lina's 'dissimilar' reply anticipates Gilda's part in the quartet in *Rigoletto* with a chain of broken semiquavers that suggest twisting and turning in an effort to escape.

In vain she protests that she was an unwilling partner in the intrigue. What is important, Stankar tells her, is to keep the whole affair quiet. They conclude their duet with a stretta (*Or meco venite, il pianto non vale*), in which Lina submits to her father's wishes. The design is 'similar' but the second quatrain differs in each case to suit the respective compass of soprano and baritone. The melody is carefully neutral varying in character according to the nature of the accompaniment. In Stankar's verse the crisp, almost military orchestral pattern gives it a suitable air of inexorability. With Lina it assumes a throbbing agitation. The final reprise has a purely decorative accompaniment with arpeggios on piccolo and pizzicato violins; and the movement winds up with a lyrical coda, somewhat protracted, so as to allow the voices at long last to unite in tenths. At the end there is a modulatory epigram (A flat–E major–A flat) highly characteristic of Verdi's maturing style.

When they have gone out Raffaele enters furtively with a letter which he inserts in a large bound volume of Klopstock's *Messias*. No sooner has he done so than Jorg returns unobserved. He sees Raffaele locking the book; he also hears Federico asking for Klopstock's poem. Federico comes in and takes it and then goes out with Raffaele. Jorg puts two and two together and makes five. It is a clumsy piece of stagecraft, very difficult to follow, especially since it takes place to a swift and furtive theme played by the strings. Verdi was to be faced with a similar problem at the end of the first scene of *Simon Boccanegra*, Act I, where he has to show Boccanegra's best friend turning into his worst enemy, and he solved it in a similar, no less unsatisfactory way. Curiously enough the solution was retained in the revised *Boccanegra*; whereas in *Aroldo* it was avoided altogether, so that the scene ends with the duet.*

Scene 2: the reception hall in Stankar's castle, illuminated in preparation for a soirée

Friends of Stiffelio and the Count have been invited to a reception in honour of the minister's return. The atmosphere is one of gaiety, and the festive chorus (*Plaudiam! Di Stiffelio s'allegri il soggiorno*) is based on a commonplace waltz-like theme which is in fact Ex. 303 c in 3/4 instead of 4/4 time. The same theme, now unaccompanied, now reinforced by a rather blatant orchestration, forms the background to a rapid dialogue between Jorg and Stiffelio, during which the old man recounts what he has just seen. Klopstock's *Messias* is being used as a cover for an intrigue involving Lina; and he indicates Federico as the guilty man. When the waltz has wound to a noisy conclusion Dorotea asks Stiffelio what will be the subject of his sermon. Fixing Federico with a steady eye he says that he will speak

* At the first revival of *Stiffelio* in modern times, which took place in Parma in December 1968, this little movement was placed earlier, between the cabaletta of Stiffelio's aria and Lina's prayer. The result was of course to make nonsense of Lina's words 'Tosto ei disse' which immediately followed.

about betrayal—not merely of him who sold Jesus Christ to his enemies but of all who would betray the laws of hospitality and the vows of marriage. Stiffelio's solo is remarkably baritonic, beginning with declamation in short phrases in dialogue with the orchestra:

316

The climactic high A in the penultimate bar is reached after ten bars of smooth gradually climbing melody, in the manner of Macbeth's 'Sangue a me'.

He takes up the *Messias*, as though to read a passage in illustration of his thesis, but of course it is locked—'but Lina has the key,' puts in Dorotea with supreme lack of tact. 'In that case,' Stiffelio says to his wife, 'do *you* open it,' and with Lina's hesitation the scene freezes into the adagio of the concerted finale (*Oh qual m'invade ed agita*). From Stiffelio's hesitant G minor melody is woven a texture of rare complexity, a tour de force of vocal instrumentalization in the manner of Rossini, with Jorg, Stankar and the chorus between them keeping up a continuous movement of demisemiquavers reinforced by pizzicato strings. The concluding G major section brings some beautiful modulations and a general smoothing of the rhythm into a lyrical conclusion, as in the earlier septet, with a similar use of overlapping fourths.

At length Stiffelio decides to force the lock himself; as he does so a letter falls out. He reaches to pick it up, but Stankar forestalls him and immediately tears the letter into shreds. Now for the first time Stiffelio gives full rein to his anger in the stretta (*Chi ti salva o sciagurato*—Ex. 317 a).

Amid the usual mêlée associated with a stretta Verdi has found room for an entirely contrasting idea in which Stankar covertly challenges Raffaele to a duel in the cemetery (Ex. 317 b). The minor key is maintained right up until the short, unthematic 'più mosso', which forms the coda; and all sense of anticlimax is averted.

ACT II

> Scene: An old graveyard. In the centre a cross with steps up to it. On the left a church doorway, lit up, above a large flight of steps. On the right Stankar's castle can be seen in the distance. Moonlight dapples the tombs which are shadowed by thick cypresses. One of the tombs is of recent construction.

The scene opens with a remarkable piece of scene-painting. Studied, in a sense, it certainly is; and the elaborately chromatic passage beginning at bar 11 falls so

317

easily under the hand as to make one suspect that it may have been worked out at the keyboard. Yet unlike the sunrises in *Attila* and *Jérusalem*, it is not just an exercise in instrumental sonorities (the orchestration is unusually simple and austere). It conforms much more nearly to Beethoven's criterion of good tone-painting: 'Mehr Ausdruck der Empfindung als Malerei'. The chromatic scales in cellos and basses suggest not only gusts of wind but waves of dread. The climbing motif of broken triplets that herald Lina's entrance would not be inappropriate for the fleeing Sieglinde. In a word the prelude has *depth*. Nor must one overlook the rhythmic ambiguity of the germinal motif to which Tito Gotti has drawn attention.*

318

For a long time (fifteen slow bars to be exact) we cannot be certain where the first beat of the bar falls. In the gloom of a graveyard at night even the rhythmic landmarks are obscured.

Aware of the duel that is about to take place between her father and Raffaele, Lina has come to the graveyard, impelled by an instinct she cannot even understand. Every breeze seems to accuse her; every tomb seems inscribed with her guilt. Then she recognizes the grave of her mother; at which point Ex. 318 takes on a calm, luminous quality as it passes from flute to oboe and then to bassoon over open fifths in the strings (see Ex. 319, overleaf).

The music warms to F sharp major; and Lina invokes her mother in the largo *Ah dagli scanni eterei*. The diaphonous accompaniment is one of the most subtly calculated in all Verdi—two solo violins and a solo viola, all playing in unison, and three 'ripieno' groups: the first consisting of four violins and two violas, the second of one violin, one viola and a cello, the third of all the remaining strings con sordino and all giving an effect of soft radiance. The melody itself evolves in an extended,

* 'L'opera: appunti per un' analisi', in *Quaderni 3: Stiffelio*, p. 66.

319

non-repeating design: plain to begin with, it gathers strength and interest as it proceeds, twice modulating to the dominant and always returning to the original F sharp major as though pleading for reassurance. Towards the end it draws effectively on the keys related to the tonic minor. One curious feature: a comparison with the corresponding piece in *Aroldo* shows the latter to be shorter by two bars, having bypassed the impressive upward climb to the climactic A sharp in bar 36 (VI–II–VII–IV–V–I). The previous two bars are scored out even on the copyist's scores of *Stiffelio* and *Guglielmo Wellingrode* in the Naples Conservatoire, which would seem to indicate that Verdi had decided to cut them after the vocal score of the original opera had gone to press—not, one suspects, because they are redundant but because they put a huge strain on the singer.

Suddenly Raffaele enters, and a whispered dialogue takes place between him and Lina over a pattering allegro of strings in 6/8 rhythm like a Mendelssohn scherzo, which lets up only to expose the passage in which she protests that she never loved him (*Fui sorpresa, non v'ama il mio core*) and he replies that he will always love her. He would rather fight for her, he says, than return her ring and her letters. (The cold-blooded unpleasantness of his character in the play is considerably softened in Piave's libretto.) Lina remonstrates in a flashily scored and utterly conventional cabaletta (*Perder dunque voi volete*) which adds nothing to the situation. This together with the preceding allegro was replaced in *Aroldo*. Having failed to move Raffaele, Lina now declares that she will tell Rodolfo everything. But once again her father arrives in time to forbid her. When she has gone, he proceeds to provoke Raffaele to a duel. At first, Raffaele refuses to fight an old man; till Stankar states roundly that his noble lineage is a fraud and that Count Raffaele is, to put it politely, a mere foundling. The young man allows his pride to get the better of his chivalry. The dialogue is carried on to a four-bar Donizettian orchestral motif, with an explosion in the fourth bar giving an urgency that is purely Verdian (see Ex. 320, opposite). Characteristic too is the pattern of quavers added at bar 22. For his final insult, Stankar abandons this melody altogether for a stanza of smoothly savage baritonic irony, clarinets doubling the vocal line in thirds (*Nobil conte Raffaello, tu non sei che un trovatello*).

At this Raffaele demands a sword; and before joining battle the two men unite in a brief duettino of sixths and thirds (*Nessun demone, niun Dio*), twice punctuated by sweeping scales on the orchestra. As the swords start to clash, Stiffelio appears at the door of the church. Speaking in broad authoritative phrases and without any

320

modification of the allegro vivo pulse he calls upon the two men to put up their swords and not profane the holy place. No matter how grave the offence, the true Christian must forgive his brother. At this point the accompaniment takes on a simple austerity which anticipates the final scene. A model can be found in certain pages from *La Straniera*, but here the underlying tension is infinitely greater.

321

Raffaele as the younger man must initiate the reconciliation, he says; and he takes Raffaele's hand. This is too much for Stankar. That his son-in-law should grasp the hand of his wife's seducer! All resolutions of silence forgotten, he blurts out the truth about Raffaele. Stiffelio, thunderstruck, turns to Lina who has come back, drawn by the sounds of fighting. Can she not say one word in her own defence? But Lina is too overwhelmed to do more than vent her distress; Stankar continues to threaten Raffaele; Raffaele to maintain an air of scornful defiance. The situation is summed up in a slow quartet in Verdi's most forceful manner (*Ah, era vero? . . . Ah no! è impossibile!*), the three principals standing out from one another with all the vividness observed in the finale to Act I of *Luisa Miller*. In no previous ensemble was Verdi able to incorporate in one ensemble music phrases quite so heterogeneous as those of Stiffelio and Lina. This Stiffelio pours out his agony in a tense, half-declamatory melody which sways between D minor and F major; Lina replies with a long phrase of semiquaver sextuplets in F minor which extends itself into a bar of 4/4 (Ex. 322 b). The scheme of tonality, D minor–F major–F minor–A flat major–F major, with its emphasis on the relationship of keys a minor third apart, is of course entirely typical.

322

a)

Largo

STIFFELIO

e-ra ve – ro? Ah no! è im-pos-si-bí-le! Che ho men-ti – to al-men mi

con disperazione

di – te un ac – cen – to, un ac-cen-tó pro-fe – ri – te

b)

spaventata si allontana da Stiffelio

(da sè)

LINA

Ah! ____ scop-pia-taè o-mai la fol-go-re, scop-pia-ta e o –

– ma-i _ la _ fol-go-re _ che rug-gi – a, _ che rug-gi – a sul-la mia testa

Stankar is now more than willing for Stiffelio to avenge his honour. Stiffelio seizes his father-in-law's sword and challenges Raffaele. Again Raffaele is reluctant to fight; whereupon Stiffelio threatens him in the language of high melodrama (*Non odi un suon terribile*). Does he not hear a voice from the tombs calling for vengeance? Here Stiffelio's line has an almost hysterical force recalling Arrigo's denunciation of Lida in Act I of *La Battaglia di Legnano*. Wide leaps, double-dotted rhythms, and in the orchestra continuous tremor of strings punctuated by explosions on timpani, bass drum, trombones and cimbasso (see Ex. 323, opposite).

Then suddenly from the church a 'still small voice', the sound of the faithful at prayer: 'Lord do not punish me in Thine anger'. It is the melody which begins the overture, here accompanied by organ. At the same time Jorg appears on the church steps and calls Stiffelio to return to his flock. But for the moment Stiffelio's personal tragedy has too strong a hold on him. His stanza (*Me disperato abbruciano l'ira, infernal furore*) takes up the vocal and harmonic character of his line in the stretta of Act I, here carried to a still higher pitch of excitement. Again the psalm is heard from the church. Stiffelio tries to collect his thoughts; prays God to inspire him with the divine word. The other principals murmur about 'peace and forgiveness'. But at the word forgiveness, Stiffelio starts up in fury. Never can he forgive the woman who has betrayed him. Jorg joining his voice to the melody line of the congregation points to the cross from which Christ forgave all mankind and Stiffelio falls down in a faint. The contrast between Stiffelio's agony and the quiet, peaceful prayers of the congregation is effective if a little theatrical. The psalm, like its fellow in *La Battaglia di Legnano*, is musically neutral and flat. It is used for the superficial associations of its style and as a counter of dramatic irony. Its piety is of a lower order than that expressed in Jorg's opening recitative.

323

Allegro

ACT III

*Scene 1: an antechamber in Stankar's castle with doors leading into various
other rooms. On the table are two pistols and writing materials.*

After a stormy prelude Stankar enters reading a letter, from which it appears
that Raffaele has decided to flee and Lina intends to follow him. His name dishonoured, his hopes of vengeance thwarted, Stankar has no further use for life. The
recitative has some fine moments; the unexpected C major chord at bar 37 for
trumpets, trombones and bassoons accompanied by a drum roll where the idea of
suicide occurs; the sobbing motif for flute and violin (bars 55–8) prompted by
thoughts of Lina and the tears that he cannot shed for her. But in the andante (*Lina
pensai che un angelo*), a lighter, high-lying melody in 'simple' double-quatrain
design amplified by a central couplet, it would seem that Verdi had his eye very

much on the virtues and limitations of Colini.* The reprise is even decorated in a slightly old-fashioned way, while the cadenza calls for real agility. Inevitably there is a loss of drama here: but in the cabaletta which follows (*O gioia inesprimibile!*) the balance is ingeniously redressed. Stankar is sitting down to write a letter of farewell to Stiffelio when Jorg enters and tells him that Raffaele will be returning to the castle. At this Stankar is overjoyed, but his happiness is not expressed quite as one might expect. The entire movement is marked *pianissimo* up to the final eight bars, Stankar himself being directed to sing 'con voce soffocata e convulsa'. Not that there is much sign of mental disturbance in the melody—a suave, attractive cantilena with more harmonic incident than usual. Then suddenly into the protracted coda, apparently dying away in repeated pianissimo cadences, the opening phrase explodes con tutta forza to the words *Vendetta! ah vieni, affrettati*, the voice-part climbing to a high G against full orchestra. Compared to Desdemona's equally unexpected outburst at the end of the 'Willow Song' it is artificial; but the dramatic point is made.

No sooner has Stankar left than Stiffelio enters with Jorg. He has recovered his self-possession at last and decided on a course worthy of his calling. He tells Jorg to inform the congregation that he will shortly join them in the church. Meanwhile, he has two painful interviews to conduct. The first is with Raffaele, who enters immediately Jorg has left. Raffaele is half ashamed, half defiant. But the minister disconcerts him with the question: 'If Lina were given her freedom what would you do?' As Raffaele hesitates, Stiffelio summons the servant Fritz (a silent part) and orders him to send for Lina. Meanwhile he conducts Raffaele into a near-by room from which he will hear what the minister has to say to her. 'We shall see what matters to you most—a sinful freedom or the future of the woman you have destroyed' (this to a phrase of unobtrusive nobility and grandeur) (see Ex. 324, opposite).

Lina enters, submissive and afraid. Without wasting time, Stiffelio talks of an immediate separation. The duet which follows is the high point of the opera, dramatically and musically. Here even more explicitly than in Stiffelio's aria in Act I we find a 'dialectic' of movements. In the opening allegro sostenuto (*Opposto è il calle*) the restrained bitterness of Stiffelio is canalized into a melody whose poignancy is all the greater for being confined within extremely formal bounds. Its accompaniment is of the simplest: a see-saw of strings in Bellini's manner. More than any other of Stiffelio's solos it requires a tenor with baritonic values (Ex. 325, opposite).

Stiffelio explains that a divorce will be possible since at the time when she married him she did not know his real name. Lina reacts in a contrasting movement (*Ah fatal colpo attendermi*), a wild outburst of grief (E minor–C major), but Stiffelio is not impressed by any of this. In a moderato assai (C major–*Speraste che per lagrime*) with the measured tread of Bellini at his most solemn he hands her the paper to sign; but no sooner has she done so than she takes on a new and unexpected dignity. Having appealed in vain to him as his wife, she will now appeal to him as her minister. Her melody is notable for its idiomatic use of hollow harmonies. The austerity is there as before yet warmth is slowly breaking in. For once the original version is scored more lightly than the revival (see Ex. 326, overleaf).

The movement culminates in the sweeping phrase 'Ministro confessatemi'; then

* 'We shall be able to make something of the company . . . as it is; though Colini isn't completely suited to the part of Stankar.' Thus Verdi to Ricordi, 25.6.1850. Abbiati, II, p. 65.

324

Allegro moderato

STIFFELIO *(alzandosi)*

Sa-per____ s'è a voi più ca — ra col-pe — vol li-ber-ta — de,

str. trem. *pp*

o l'av-ve-ni — re di don — na che per-de-ste

ff

325

Allegro sostenuto

STIFFELIO *con espressione*

Op — po-sto è il cal — le che in av — ve-ni — re

pp str.

to an andante (E minor) embellished by a cor anglais obbligato she declares that she never loved Raffaele; she was betrayed by him; that her heart is true to the husband who wishes to cast her off (*Egli un patto proponeva*). All the restrained pathos in the scene is concentrated in the cor anglais melody (Ex. 327, overleaf).

Stiffelio is astounded, as well he might be. If what Lina says is true then he himself has the right to dispatch Raffaele. He opens the door of the room in which he had hidden him. However, it is not Raffaele but Stankar who comes out, his sword stained with blood. The adulterer has paid the penalty that his crime demanded. (For his exit line Stankar descends, somewhat improbably, to an F below the stave!) Before Stiffelio can recover, Jorg has entered to summon him to the church. The minister is too dazed to think of anything but escaping from a house which has seen so much dishonour and bloodshed. At least in church he may find peace. The stretta (*Ah, sì, voliam al tempio*) is a 'dissimilar' movement, Stiffelio leading off in the minor key, Lina replying in the major to an accompaniment full of chromatic

326

327

scales and continuous drum rolls, as though the earth were opening beneath her feet. At the end Stiffelio allows himself to be led away by Jorg.

> *Scene 2: the interior of a Gothic church with a large arcade. No altar is to be seen, only a pulpit placed up against one of the piers and mounted by a double stairway.*

Dorotea, Federico and the congregation are in church. Lina enters, heavily veiled, and takes her place to the right of the pulpit. Stankar is on the left. All are kneeling and praying to the accompaniment of an organ.

Here again Verdi had reverted to his idea of combining three distinct musical elements in a kind of theatrical counterpoint. After an organ prelude the congregation sing the psalm that was heard at the end of Act II, over which Stankar superimposes a theme of his own (*Se punii chi m' ha tradito*) and Lina the most rudimentary descant (*Confido in Te*). Of the three strands only Stankar's can be said to be melodic. At the conclusion Stiffelio enters with Jorg and together they ascend the pulpit. At first the minister fails to recognize his wife; a moment later from the pulpit he does so and becomes visibly agitated. Jorg whispers to him to stand firm. Let him read from the Holy Bible and take inspiration from the word of God. Stiffelio opens the Bible at random, finds himself reading aloud the story of the woman taken in adultery and ends by publicly forgiving his wife. What is most striking about this scena finale is its deliberate avoidance of thematic interest. The continuity is maintained chiefly by repetition of pregnant hieratic motifs in the orchestra, of the kind which have appeared at various points of the score as symbols of religious faith.* The trumpet figure which heralds Stiffelio's entrance keeps to one note with shifting harmonies beneath. Stiffelio's reading of the Bible is backed by an orchestral pattern that we shall meet again in the duet 'Solenne in quest'ora' (*La Forza del Destino*). His own line is in measured recitative. The entire procedure is more typical of the Berlioz of *L'Enfance du Christ* than of a mid-nineteenth-century Italian composer. Its purpose becomes clear, when first Stiffelio and then the congregation take up the word 'Perdonata' in a heart-easing cadence. Short as this finale is, it represents a unique solution in all Verdi.

328

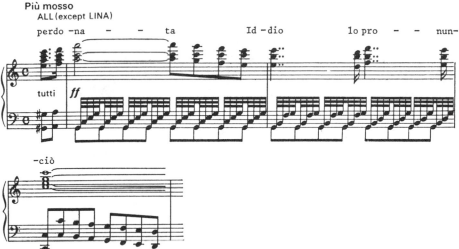

The later history of *Stiffelio*, strictly speaking, belongs to that of *Aroldo*. It had a few performances in the form of *Guglielmo Wellingrode*, which Verdi himself detested.

Outside Italy *Stiffelio* was produced only at Barcelona. Although both Ricordi and Escudier brought out vocal scores it made no appeal even in Protestant countries. With the refashioning into *Aroldo*, it faded out of sight altogether. Now that it has been rediscovered, one might ask what are its chances as a repertory piece. Probably less good than it deserves. Although Souvestre's plot may no longer shock religious sensibilities it is in the last analysis too complex and sophisticated for an opera. It has too many twists and turns; and of its four acts only the last two were reducible to operatic terms at all. Some of its scenic faults are remedied in *Aroldo* with its new last act, its greater thematic richness and—in certain passages— its clearer definition of the musical thought. Yet the original opera has an integrity which the later one never quite recaptures if only because in the course of revision the religious element is cut by half. Religion, of the inner personal kind, is, after all, what the opera is about. The title role is a unique conception. His music is all of a

---

* At this point Verdi requires the double-basses to lower their A strings by a semitone, as only in this way could the three-stringed instrument then in use reach the lower octave, so essential to this as to the 'Miserere' scene in *Il Trovatore* where the same procedure is prescribed.

piece.* It is designed for a man of authority, of religious zeal and blameless moral life 'somewhat declin'd into the vale of years', who is assailed by desperate jealousy. He is a controlled, less vulnerable forerunner of Otello. From him the opera takes its basic character. The religious solemnity expressed in the choruses of Acts II and III, the sense of guilt and terror in the graveyard scene; all these grow out of the original setting and belong with the stark restraint of Jorg's opening arioso and the finale ultimo. There is no substitute for the unity of style evident in a work which has been composed in a single flight of creation. With all its imperfections *Stiffelio* is worthy to stand beside the three masterpieces which it immediately precedes.

---

* He is the only character in Verdi's early and middle period operas who is not given a single cadenza.

19 RIGOLETTO

RIGOLETTO

Opera in three acts
by
FRANCESCO MARIA PIAVE
after Victor Hugo's drama *Le Roi s'amuse*)

*First performed at the
Teatro la Fenice, Venice,
11 March 1851*

THE DUKE OF MANTUA	PRIMO TENORE	Raffaele Mirate
RIGOLETTO, his court jester,	PRIMO BARITONO	Felice Varesi
SPARAFUCILE, a professional assassin	BASSO COMPRIMARIO	Paolo Damini
COUNT MONTERONE	SECONDO BARITONO	Feliciano Ponz
Courtiers:		
MARULLO	SECONDO BARITONO	Francesco De Kunnerth
BORSA	SECONDO TENORE	Angelo Zuliani
COUNT CEPRANO	SECONDO BASSO	Andrea Bellini
A COURT USHER	SECONDO BASSO	Giovanni Rizzi
GILDA, Rigoletto's daughter	PRIMA DONNA SOPRANO	Teresa Brambilla
GIOVANNA, her duenna	SECONDA DONNA SOPRANO	Laura Saini
MADDALENA, Sparafucile's sister	CONTRALTO CONPRIMARIO	Annetta Casaloni
COUNTESS CEPRANO	SECONDA DONNA MEZZO-SOPRANO	Luigia Morselli
A PAGE	SECONDA DONNA MEZZO-SOPRANO	N.N.

Knights—courtiers—halberdiers

Walk-on parts: Ladies—pages

The action takes place in Mantua

Epoch: the sixteenth century

Verdi's contract to produce a new opera for the Teatro la Fenice in Venice was signed in April 1850;* librettist Piave, production date carnival–quaresima 1851, subject as yet unchosen but Dumas's *Kean* high on the list of possibilities.† In fact Verdi and Piave had not yet even agreed on the opera for Ricordi due to be ready by the autumn. Then towards the end of the month, while he was still waiting to know more about the plot of *Stiffelio*, Verdi wrote to Piave with a new idea, broaching it with an almost furtive caution which shows that he was well aware of the risks involved.

> Probably we shan't find anything better than *Gusmano il Buono*, although I have in mind a subject that would be one of the greatest creations of the modern theatre if the police would only allow it. Who knows? They allowed *Ernani*, they might even allow us to do this and at least there are no conspiracies in it.
>
> Have a try! The subject is grand, immense and there's a character in it who is one of the greatest creations that the theatre of all countries and all times can boast. The subject is *Le Roi s'amuse* and the character I'm speaking about is Triboulet; and if Varesi has been engaged there could be nothing better for him or for us.
>
> P.S. As soon as you get this letter put on your skates [lit. 'four legs']; run about the city and find someone of influence to get us permission to do *Le Roi s'amuse*. Don't go to sleep; give yourself a good shake; do it at once. I shall expect you at Busseto, but not now, after they've agreed to the subject.‡

A few days later, in the same letter in which he agreed to *Stiffelio* for Ricordi, Verdi wrote:

> Oh, *Le Roi s'amuse* is the greatest subject and perhaps the greatest drama of modern times. Triboulet is a creation worthy of Shakespeare!! Just like *Ernani* it's a subject that can't fail. You remember that six years ago when Mocenigo suggested to me *Ernani* I exclaimed: 'Yes, by God . . . that can't go wrong.' Now going over the various subjects in my mind *Le Roi* came on me like a flash of lightning, an inspiration, and I said to myself the same thing . . . 'Yes, by God, that one can't go wrong.'§

It was hardly love at first sight; Verdi already suggested Hugo's play to Flauto as a possible subject for Naples the previous year. Not until both Cammarano and Shakespeare had dropped temporarily out of sight do the full possibilities of *Le Roi*

---

* *Scrittura Teatrale*, 23.4.1850. *Copialettere*, p. 103.
† Letter to Brenna, 18.4.1850. *Copialettere*, pp. 102–3.
‡ Letter to Piave, 28.4.1850. Abbiati, II, pp. 59–60.
§ Letter to Piave, 8.5.1850. Abbiati, II, pp. 62–3.

s'amuse seem to have been envisaged. Piave, as usual, did as he was told. He obtained vague assurances that the subject would be permitted and as early as June, with *Stiffelio* still under construction, was discussing with Verdi the way Hugo's tragedy should be treated. As always Verdi had his own ideas. Piave was to keep as closely as possible to the original, even down to the divided scene in the last act and the body in the sack (he had demurred over both). If they could not retain Victor Hugo's title (which would be a pity) the opera should be called a *La Maledizione di Saint-Vallier* since the whole plot devolves on the working-out of that curse. As in the play Saint-Vallier should only appear twice.[*]

In August came the first intimation of danger. At the time Piave was at Busseto. Verdi at once sent him back to Venice with a letter for Marzari, the President of the Teatro la Fenice:

> The doubt you express about whether *Le Roi s'amuse* will be permitted puts me in a very embarrassing position. I was assured by Piave that there would be no difficulty about this subject and I, trusting his word, set myself to study it and ponder deeply on it and the whole idea and the musical colour ('tinta') of it were already settled in my mind. I may say that the main part of the work has been already done. If I were now obliged to apply myself to another subject I wouldn't have enough time at my disposal to do the necessary study and I couldn't write an opera which would satisfy my artistic conscience. . . .[†]

By October he had the complete draft of Piave's libretto and he authorized Ricordi to pay him the first instalment accordingly.[‡] Then while Verdi and Piave were still in Trieste for the rehearsals of *Stiffelio* a still more ominous letter arrived from Marzari asking them to send him the libretto so that it would be submitted to the *Direzione d'Ordine Pubblico* for approval.[§] Rumour had it that the drama *Le Roi s'amuse* had been unfavourably received at its first production in France and also in Germany because of its 'abundant immorality'. The Direzione Centrale trusted none the less that in view of the honesty of poet and maestro the plot would be treated in a fitting manner. . . . It seemed as though history was about to repeat itself.

Le Roi s'amuse was first given in Paris at the Théâtre Français in November 1832. Its reception was stormy. The following day Hugo found a notice attached to the theatre billboard stating that by order of the Government all further performances of the play were suspended. He pleaded his case before the Tribunal de Commerce, but in vain. *Le Roi s'amuse* was not performed again in Paris until 1882. It was published however, and Hugo did not let slip the occasion to print a massive defence of his work in the preface.

> Triboulet is deformed; Triboulet is sick, Triboulet is a court jester—a triple misfortune which makes him evil. Triboulet hates the king because he is a

---

[*] Letter to Piave, 3.6.1850. Abbiati, II, pp. 63–4.
[†] Letter to Marzari, 24.8.1850. *Copialettere*, pp. 106–7.
[‡] Letter to Piave, 22.10.1850. Abbiati, II, pp. 71–2.
[§] Letter from Marzari, 11.11.1850. *Copialettere*, pp. 485–6.

king, the nobles because they are nobles, his fellow men in general because they have no humps on their backs. His sole pastime is to set the nobles against the king, letting the weakest go to the wall. The king he depraves, corrupts and brutalizes; he urges him on to tyranny, to vice and ignorance; he unleashes him against all the highborn families continually pointing out to him the wife to seduce, the sister to carry off, the daughter to dishonour. In the hands of Triboulet the king is nothing but an all-powerful puppet who destroys the lives of all those among whom his jester sets him. One day in the middle of a fête just at the moment when Triboulet is urging the king to carry off the wife of Monsieur de Cossé, Monsieur de Saint-Vallier makes his way into the royal presence and reproaches him in a loud voice for having dishonoured |his daughter] Diane de Poitiers. This father whose daughter has been taken from him by the king is mocked and insulted by Triboulet. The father raises his arms and curses Triboulet. The whole play evolves from this. The true subject of the drama is the curse of Monsieur de St-Vallier. Now observe; we are in the second act. On whom has this curse fallen? On Triboulet the king's buffoon? No, on Triboulet the man, who is a father, who has a heart, and a daughter. Triboulet has a daughter, that is the point. He has nothing else but his daughter in the whole world. He hides her away in a deserted quarter of the city, in a lonely house. The more he spreads the contagion of vice and debauchery throughout the city, the more he keeps his daughter isolated and immured. He brings up his child in innocence, in faith and chastity. His greatest fear is that she may fall into evil, since being evil himself he knows what suffering it causes. Well, the old man's curse will strike Triboulet through the one being whom he loves in the world, his daughter. The same king whom Triboulet is urging to rape, will ravish his, Triboulet's, daughter. The jester will be struck down by Providence in exactly the same manner as Monsieur de St-Vallier.

Then once his daughter has been seduced and ravished he will lay a trap for the king in order to be revenged; it is his daughter that will fall into it. So Triboulet has two pupils, the king whom he instructs in vice, his daughter whom he rears in virtue. One will destroy the other. He wants to carry off Madame de Cossé for the king but it is his own daughter whom he helps to carry off. He wants to murder the king to avenge his daughter, and it is his daughter whom he murders. The punishment does not stop half-way. The curse of Diane's father will be fulfilled on the father of Blanche.*

Verdi's letter to Piave shows that he had read this preface and believed quite firmly in the moral intention of the play. Where precisely lay the danger? Partly in Hugo's reputation as a republican; partly in the picture he presented of royal profligacy in action—a king making plans to abduct a courtier's wife, keeping low company in a tavern, and worst of all entrapping a virtuous young girl. The play contains a scene in the palace, omitted in the opera, in which the abducted Blanche is confronted by King François whom she had believed to be a poor student. Realizing at last his intentions she takes fright, runs into a near-by room and locks the door. But the king triumphantly produces a key from his pocket, opens the

* Hugo, *Le Roi s'amuse*, Preface.

door (it happens to be that of the royal bedchamber) and goes in laughing. . . . Curtain. Verdi, foreseeing that some concessions might have to be made, wrote to Piave authorizing him to change words if necessary here and there but to keep all the situations intact with the one exception of the scene with the key. They could probably work out something better in any case. But François must still be shown in the tavern of Saltabadil, the hired assassin, since without this scene the drama made no sense.*

Then early in December came the news that the Military Governor of Venetia had absolutely forbidden *Le Roi s'amuse* to be given, with or without amendments. He deplored strongly the fact that the poet Piave and the celebrated Maestro Verdi had not chosen a more suitable field for their talents than in the 'repulsive immorality and obscene triviality'† of the plot of *La Maledizione*. Verdi reacted by throwing the entire blame on Piave. It had been his business, he said, to get the subject passed; and it was on his assurances that Verdi had set to work on the opera. Meanwhile as there was no possibility of composing another piece in time for the scheduled date he suggested giving *Stiffelio* instead, which would be at least new for Venice. If the final scene was unacceptable to the censors he would write a new one.‡ Marzari considered this a very poor substitute, and decided rather to continue with Piave the struggle to find a way round the Austrian ban on *Le Roi s'amuse*. He had a sympathizer in the Director of the Ordine Pubblico, Martelli, at whose suggestion Piave refashioned the libretto into a *Duc de Vendôme*. But this Verdi found quite unacceptable. From his reply to Marzari we may gather that the Duke was to be a man of irreproachable character who did not go about seducing and abducting the wives, daughters and sisters of his subjects; nor is he encouraged by his jester to do so. Therefore . . .

> the courtiers' anger with Triboulet has no sense. The old man's curse, so sublime and terrible in the original, here becomes ridiculous because the reason for it is not nearly so vital; and besides it is no longer the case of a subject speaking out boldly to his king. The Duke is a nullity. The Duke must be an utter libertine; otherwise there is no reason why Triboulet should be afraid to let his daughter out of concealment and therefore the drama is impossible. . . . And how on earth would the Duke find himself alone in a remote tavern in the last act without some kind of invitation or rendezvous? I don't understand why the sack has been taken out. What does the sack matter to the police? Are they afraid it will not be effective? But allow me to say: why do they think they know better than I do in this matter? . . . There was the same sort of difficulty over the horn in *Ernani*, yet who laughed when they heard that horn? Take away the sack and it is most unlikely that Triboulet should speak for half an hour to a corpse before a flash of lightning shows it to be the body of his daughter. Finally I notice that you have avoided making Triboulet ugly and hunchbacked!! A hunchback who sings? Why not? . . . Will it be effective? I don't know; but if I don't know neither, I repeat, does

---

* Letter to Piave, undated (but clearly from Nov. 1850). Abbiati, II, p. 84.

† Memorandum from I. R. Direzione Centrale d'Ordine Pubblico to Marzari, 21.11.1850. *Copialettere*, p. 487.

‡ Letter to Marzari 5.12.1850. *Copialettere*, pp. 108–9.

the person who suggested the change. To me there is something really fine in representing on stage this character outwardly so ugly and ridiculous, inwardly so impassioned and full of love. I chose the subject precisely because of these qualities, and if these original features are removed I cannot write the music. If you tell me that my music will do as it stands, set to this drama, I reply that I cannot understand your reasons for saying so and I tell you frankly that, good or bad, my music is not just written casually for any situation; I try to give it a character appropriate to the drama. In sum a powerful and original drama has been turned into something trivial and dead.*

At Marzari's suggestion† and with Martelli's approval Piave and Brenna went to Busseto to settle with Verdi once and for all the question of the new opera for a carnival season that had already begun. A six-point memorandum was drawn up and signed by all three.‡ In it they proposed: (1) to remove the venue from the court of France to that of an independent duchy in either France or Italy;§ (2) to keep the characters of Hugo's play but to change their names; (3) to omit the scene with the key of the bedchamber; (4) to have the Duke enticed to Maguelonne's inn by a ruse; (5) that whether or not any modifications were necessary to the scene in which Triboulet discovers his daughter's body in the sack should be left to Verdi to decide on the spot; (6) that because of all these changes the first night of the opera should be postponed until the end of February or early March. All these suggestions were approved by the censor and in the event implemented. François I became Duke of Mantua, possibly even the famous, or infamous, Vincenzo Gonzaga, patron of Monteverdi and Titian. True his name was not to be mentioned, but 'by now everyone knows who was ruling at that time'.¶ Triboulet became Rigoletto; Blanche, Gilda; Saltabadil (the assassin), Sparafucile; his sister Maguelonne, Maddelena; and so on. MM. de St-Vallier and Cossé underwent a double transformation, since the names first decided upon for them belonged to existing noble families (Castiglione and Cepriano), who might be expected to take offence. They became Monterone and Ceprano respectively. The opera itself, originally to be called *La Maledizione*, now took its title from the protagonist. By 26 January Piave was able to announce with a 'Te Deum laudamus' that *Rigoletto* had arrived back at the Presidency, 'safe and sound without fractures or amputations'.‖ It was an astonishing triumph of patience and diplomacy.

The casting too had presented problems. Felice Varesi, the creator of Macbeth, was eminently suited to the title role. The Duke, Raffaele Mirate, was a comparative newcomer—'a young Moriani', so Piave described him,** and therefore just the man for one of the most gracefully lyrical of all Verdi's tenor roles. The

---

* Letter to Marzari, 14.12.1850. *Copialettere*, pp. 109–11.
† Letter from Marzari, 23.12.1850. *Copialettere*, pp. 488–9.
‡ Memorandum: Busseto, 30.12.1850. *Copialettere*, pp. 489–90.
§ Both in this document and in Marzari's letter the name of Pier Luigi Farnese, a former duke of Parma, is mentioned—possibly with a deliberate allusion to the despot who was at that time oppressing Verdi's native state. For a discussion of this point see G. Marchesi 'Gli anni del Rigoletto' in *Rigoletto: Bollettino dell'Istituto di Studi Verdiani* Vol. III, No. 7 (Parma, 1969), pp. 1–26.
¶ Letter from Piave, 24.1.1851. *Copialettere*, pp. 492–3.
‖ Letter from Piave, 26.1.1851. *Copialettere*, p. 494.
** *Ibid.*

question of the heroine took some time to settle. Verdi had wanted Teresa De Giuli, his heroine from *La Battaglia di Legnano*. When this was refused he began to sulk. He refused to consider the statuesque Sanchioli although the theatre had already engaged her for *Luisa Miller* during the same season, and he demurred at the idea of Sofia Cruvelli since she had the reputation of an eccentric (how true that reputation was Verdi would soon find out in *Les Vêpres Siciliennes*). 'I tell you frankly,' he wrote to Brenna, 'I don't like these caricatures of Malibran who have only her oddities without any of her genius.'* Of the other two singers suggested by the management Teresina Brambilla, sister of a famous contralto, Marietta, in Verdi's opinion 'sings better and has more attack'.† Piave meanwhile had approached Brenna with a suggestion that came originally from Verdi himself for a certain Boccabadati. Verdi scouted it irritably (he had heard that she was now singing badly).‡ So Gilda fell to Teresina Brambilla. Of the subsidiary parts the basso profondo cast for Sparafucile, Feliciano Ponz, had 'a strong voice and was artistically convincing'.§ The contralto Annetta Casaloni was happy to take the part of Maddalena even if there was no solo for her.¶ But Piave warned the composer to be on his guard against the baritone De Kunnerth who had a totally colourless voice, and made a poor impression on the audience, but happened to be a close friend of Varesi. || In the event he was given the part of Marullo where he acquitted himself without dishonour. Curiously enough there is no mention of what to many may seem the most surprising feature of the score: the lack of women in the chorus. In fact this was by no means unusual in ottocento opera, though there is no other instance of it in Verdi's own works. *Il Barbiere di Siviglia*, *Tancredi*, *L'Italiana in Algeri*, all dispense with female choristers. So, in effect, does *Lucrezia Borgia*, the nearest opera to *Rigoletto* in form and dramatic content.**

As usual Verdi's requests for last-minute revisions of the text are interesting. In the duet finale to Act II he insisted most of Gilda's lines should be addressed to her father and not spoken aside, 'since in *fast tempi* it is always ineffective to have two singers speaking about their own affairs without reference to each other'.†† Clearly the Duke's aria in the same act gave him some trouble, for Piave was required to rewrite the text of the cabaletta re-arranging the verbal stresses. In the adagio Verdi particularly wanted the second verse 'more beautiful'‡‡ than the first—acknowledging perhaps his own penchant for increasing the interest of a movement as it proceeds.

Rehearsals had already begun when Verdi arrived in Venice on 19 February with only a few bars of the duetto-finale to complete.§§ The premiere followed three

---

* Letter to Brenna, 5.10.1850. Conati, *La bottega della musica*, p. 219.

† *Ibid.*

‡ Letter to Brenna, 19.10.1850. *Ibid.*, p. 221.

§ Letter from Marzari, 14.1.1851. *Copialettere*, pp. 490–1.

¶ *Ibid.* She was also to play Federica in *Luisa Miller*. Verdi, asked to provide a part for her in his new opera, 'had no objection to writing for a contralto. It will depend on circumstances and the subject that we have to choose.' Letter to Brenna, 18.4.1850. *Copialettere*, p. 101.

|| Letter from Piave 24.1.1851. *Copialettere*, pp. 492–3.

** A feature of Verdi's French operas, and also of *Giovanna d'Arco* and *La Battaglia di Legnano*, is the use of a male *and* a mixed chorus side by side.

†† Letter to Piave, 20.1.1851. Abbiati, II, p. 98.

‡‡ Letter to Piave, 14.1.1851. Abbiati, II, p. 97.

§§ Letter to Marzari, 29.1.1851. Conati, pp. 249–50.

weeks later. As far as the public was concerned *Rigoletto* was an immediate success. The Press on the other hand seems to have been somewhat bemused. The critic of the *Gazzetta di Venezia* declared that an opera such as this cannot be judged on a single hearing. He went on to talk of bewildering novelty—in the music, the style, the form of each piece and the splendid and no less novel instrumentation; even the vocal writing he found quite different from anything he had heard before, and not altogether for the better. To another later reviewer, Verdi appeared to be archaizing, returning to the style of Mozart and his contemporaries. Another found the opera totally lacking in invention or novelty, 'and not at all in the best of taste'. One could go on quoting indefinitely the bizarre criticisms of *Rigoletto* made by those who were hearing it for the first time—including that of our own Chorley who pronounced the music 'puerile and ridiculous, full of vulgarity and eccentricity and barren of ideas . . . Verdi's weakest opera'.* They all seem to have heard a different piece. Yet each (apart from Chorley) was describing an existing facet of one of the most remarkable artistic syntheses in Italian opera. *Rigoletto* could be compared in Verdi's output to the 'Eroica' Symphony in Beethoven's. Verdi himself was not afraid to describe it as revolutionary, which it certainly is not in the sense of making a clean break with the past. The elements are in themselves mostly traditional, but they are fused together in a new and exciting way. At certain points we find new forms, or at least forms which Verdi had not used until that time. Elsewhere the old forms are dissolved within a wider perspective. The barriers between formal melody and recitative are down as never before. In the whole opera there is only one conventional double-aria. *Rigoletto* is also unique among Verdi's works in containing no concerted act finales. The nearest equivalent is the conclusion to the first scene where (incredible stroke!) the concertato is floated on the banda melody.

To the egregious Borsi, who wrote to him the following year to ask if he could compose an extra aria for his wife Teresa De Giuli to sing in *Rigoletto*, Verdi replied humorously but firmly:

> If you could have convinced yourself that my talent limits me to being unable to do any better with *Rigoletto* than I've done already, you wouldn't have asked me for another aria. . . .
>
> In fact where would you find a place for it? . . . Well, there is one place—but God forbid we should try it—we should be flayed alive! We would have to show the Duke and Gilda in the bedroom!! You see what I mean?! . . . In any case it would be a duet . . . Let me say that I conceived *Rigoletto* almost without arias, without finales but only an unending string of duets . . .†

He certainly considered it a landmark in his career. To Antonio Somma, the future librettist of *Un Ballo in Maschera*, he described it as: 'the best subject as regards theatrical effect that I've ever set to music. It has powerful situations, variety, excitement, pathos; all the vicissitudes arise from the frivolous, rakish personality of the Duke' (note the slight shift of emphasis away from Hugo for whom Triboulet himself was the prime mover). 'Hence Rigoletto's fears, Gilda's

---

* For a summary of the Press reaction see Abbiati, II, pp. 110–11.

† Letter to C. Borsi, 8.9.1852. *Copialettere*, pp. 497–8.

passion, etc., etc., which make for many excellent dramatic moments, among others the scene of the quartet which as regards effect will remain one of the best our theatre can boast.'* In a letter to De Sanctis *Rigoletto* was 'my best opera'—*tout court*.† To Piave he used the word 'revolutionary'‡ (he was comparing it with *Ernani*). All these letters were written with *Il Trovatore* and *La Traviata* already behind him. Admittedly one looks in vain in Verdi's writings for any consistent statement of his dramatic ideals. They varied according to the needs of his developing creative personality, which is one reason why as he grew older he repeated himself less and less. At one time he needed subjects that 'harp on one string' in order to focus his own invention. Later he began to demand a wider canvas. *Rigoletto* remains a miracle, and as such not to be explained by any amount of analysis; but two observations are in place. Both in his plans for *L'Assedio di Firenze* and in his thoughts about *Luisa Miller* Verdi had shown a desire to bring comedy into his music, to avail himself of those resources of that world from which the failure of *Un Giorno di Regno* had banished him. The plot of *Rigoletto* for the first time gave him the opportunity of doing so. The entire first scene from the prelude up to the entrance of Monterone is conceived in the language of comic opera—set, however, in the wider context of tragedy, which it serves to deepen by contrast. Hence the 'variety of effects' about which Verdi waxed so enthusiastic in retrospect; hence, too, his rather unkind jibes to Piave about his 'monotonous, tearful subjects, and elaborate verses . . . written to delight the ears of fickle seamstresses'§ (a reference to the librettist's unsuccessful amours). Then, too, in discussing the subject of *King Lear* with Cammarano, he had talked of treating it in an entirely new way without regard to singers' etiquette.¶ The 'convenienze' receive scant attention in *Rigoletto* with its cast of three principals, two comprimarii and five secondary roles. As we have pointed out *Le Roi s'amuse* was not new to Verdi; he had considered it many times before as an operatic subject, but it was not until *King Lear* had been put aside for the time being that he seems to have fallen in love with it. Is it too fanciful to suppose that his new-found enthusiasm for Hugo's play proceeded from the same creative mood that has inspired him to try his hand at Shakespeare's? That the searchlight which had penetrated the intricacies of *King Lear* was merely shifted on to *Le Roi s'amuse*? Both are dramas of paternity. Both feature a court buffoon. Certain it is that after Verdi had finished *Rigoletto* he returned for a while to more conventional operatic methods. *Il Trovatore* and *La Traviata* (particularly the former) are formally speaking nearer to the operas of the past. *Rigoletto* I suspect is one of the *King Lears* that might have been. But this is not to diminish Victor Hugo's part in the opera's greatness. It was not the first time that Verdi felt the concentrating force of the hard logic which underlies the Frenchman's romantic rhodomontade.

Before turning to the opera itself we should mention one of the most remarkable

---

* Letter to Somma, 22.4.1853. Pascolato, pp. 45–8.
† Letter to De Sanctis 20.1.1855. *Carteggi Verdiani*, I, pp. 28–9.
‡ Letter to Piave, Oct. 1854. Abbiati, II, pp. 279–80.
§ Letter to Piave, undated. Abbiati, II, p. 109. Relevant too is the observation made in the letter quoted above to Somma that 'our theatre suffers from excessive monotony'—presumably in contrast to the Paris Opéra. Both *Robert le Diable* and *Le Prophète* include scenes of comedy.
¶ Letter to Cammarano, 28.2.1850. *Copialettere*, pp. 478–82.

documents in Verdian scholarship, the so-called *Rigoletto* sketch published in facsimile by Carlo Gatti in 1941.* It consists of 56 pages of which the first two and the
last are filled with jottings of isolated phrases and ideas, some of which are used in
the final result, others not. Here for instance we find the first draft of the orchestral
theme that underlies the Rigoletto–Sparafucile duet from Act I, Scene 2, together
with attempts to work out the passage in which Rigoletto mocks the aged Monterone. On the last page *La donna è mobile* is found in the following variant:

329

Which goes to show that in Verdi as in Beethoven the most simple spontaneous-
sounding melodies often have to be chiselled into their final shape.

But the bulk of the 'abbozzo' consists of an uninterrupted draft of the entire
opera, mostly on one or two staves, and with only 24 bars crossed out. In his
preface Gatti quotes an observation of Verdi's to the effect that 'to compose
well one must do so in a single breath, merely reserving the right to fill out
and polish up the general sketch; to do otherwise is to run the risk of producing
a work in the manner of a mosaic, without style or character'.† None the less the
sketch appears to have been written over a fairly long period, since in the first act
the names of the characters are those of the original drama italianized (Triboletto,
Il Re, etc.) whereas in Acts II and III they have been changed into those of the opera
as we know it, except for Monterone, who has become for the present Castiglione.
No other sketch of Verdi's on this scale has ever been unearthed. Those for *I Due
Foscari* and *Attila* are concerned with one scene only. Whether the fragments printed
in facsimile by Gatti in his *Verdi nelle immagini* belong to continuous sketches in the
Rigoletto manner cannot be known for the present; but the page relating to *La
Traviata* suggests a less systematic, more impressionistic method. After a few bars
the notes give way to stage directions. ('Margherita si sente male, etc.') Possibly
then a work so complex, so unorthodox in form yet so organically conceived as
Rigoletto needed a firmer guide line from the start, akin to the 'cue staff' employed
by Beethoven in some of his later compositions. At several points the sketch
differs significantly from the finished result. Gilda's confession *Tutte le feste* occurs
in F minor instead of E minor, proving yet again the absence of large-scale
key-systems in Verdi, and at the same time making clear the source of her melody as

---

* *L'Abbozzo del Rigoletto di Giuseppe Verdi* (Edizione Fuori Commercio a cura del Maestro
della Cultura Popolare, 1941). The original is preserved at the Villa S. Agata. For a discussion
of this sketch and its relation to the finished product, see G. Roncaglia, 'L'Abbozzo del *Rigoletto*
di Giuseppe Verdi' in *Galleria Verdiana—studi e figuri* (Milan, 1959), pp. 87–100; and, more
important, Petrobelli, *Acta Musicologica* XLIII (1971), pp. 132–42.
† The original source of this quotation seems to have been Monaldi. See 2nd ed., p. 208.
Verdi supposedly continues, 'The exception of Meyerbeer doesn't hold; and anyway for all
the power of his genius he had to spend a great deal of time setting his libretti and not even he
managed to avoid a dislocation of style which is sometimes so palpable in his masterpieces that
you might think they were the work of two different composers.'

the duet between Raoul and Valentine in Act IV of *Les Huguenots*. Most remarkable of all is the ultimate definition of the opera's key motif: the phrase which embodies Rigoletto's memory of Monterone's curse. This is how it first appears in the sketch at the start.

330

RIGOLETTO

Quel vec - chio ma-le - di - va-mi

etc.

The explosive charge is detonated in the most obvious way with an ascent from soh to a climactic high tonic F. In the definitive version the climax is marked internally by means of a harmonic progression in the orchestra. What is more, the charge is *not* detonated; the urge towards a resolution in F minor is repressed. Musically the phrase is infinitely stronger, while the persistence of dominant sense vividly conveys the feeling of being 'hag-ridden' by a memory as it will do to no less effect in *Il Trovatore*.

331

Andante mosso

RIGOLETTO

cls.bns.

pp

(Quel

va.vc.
db.

vec - chio ma - le - di - va -mi!)

vc.solo(*muted*)
pp

morendo

Following the example of his own *Ernani* Verdi has based his prelude on the key-motif of the drama (Ex. 331), scoring it for a similar combination of brass. Here its orientation is tonic rather than dominant. Why then does it not lose part of its identity? Partly because in Verdi pitch is more important than tonal ambience. Partly because the phrase itself is pregnant with different implications, as Verdi himself unconsciously recognized when at a later stage in the autograph he wrongly notated the D sharp and F sharp as E flat and G flat respectively. Equally it could be said that the establishment of C minor at bar 5 is paralleled by the decisive turn into C major at the end of the monologue *Pari siamo*, where the motif (Ex. 331) receives its fullest exposition. There is no contrasting theme as in the prelude to *Ernani*. Melodically the motif is vague, amorphous, with an irregular three-bar structure, and only the sketchiest of melodic contours. Its germinating power is concentrated in the double dotted rhythm of trumpet and trombone, which within a nine-bar crescendo carries the music to a fortissimo climax, dissolving in a chain of sobbing figures on violins and upper woodwind. There is a brief recall of the subject twice moulded into a cadential phrase, then a six-bar coda of hammer-blows—including an important timpani solo—increasing in force up to the final cadence.

ACT I

Scene 1: a magnificent hall in the palace of the Duke of Mantua, with doors at the back giving on to the other rooms all splendidly lit

It is a little surprising to meet the banda once more, which had seemed to be banished some time ago from Verdi's operas. Indeed the opening of the *introduzione* can awake awkward memories of *I Lombardi*. But there is a powerful difference. In the earlier opera the banda was used merely to create an atmosphere of neutral festivity; here it depicts the corruption and triviality of the Duke of Mantua's Court. In *I Lombardi* the sense of anticlimax following the prelude is unintentional; here Verdi has achieved a deliberately jarring effect—the sombre menace of the prelude dissipated in a guffaw. The banda melodies are gay and profuse (there are five of them) and the voices are deployed against them with great skill. As usual the music is written out on two staves only, but at certain points Verdi specifies *pochi istrumenti*, for the sake of variety. There is also a pleasing touch of rhythmic ambiguity about them, to tease the listener into attention. Nos. 1 and 2 give the impression of beginning on the first beat of the bar, whereas in fact they begin on the third. No. 3 raises doubts. But it is only in the middle of No. 4 that the doubts are resolved and the rhythmic design emerges clearly.

332

Allegro con brio

Melody No. 5 begins unequivocally on the first beat.

Against this background the Duke of Mantua briefly confides to his courtier, Borsa, the story of the beautiful young girl he has been following every Sunday from church to her home in a dark back street. It is the same point at which Victor Hugo's play starts; and once again Verdi reaps the advantage of taking in the entire drama from the beginning. Inevitably Piave's exposition is much shorter than

Hugo's, which occupies a whole act. He cannot drive home, as Hugo does, the ceaseless malice of Rigoletto-Triboulet, his barbed insults, the thousand little acts that decide the courtiers to take their revenge. But he provides what was for the time a very unusual type of exposition, and one which Puccini and the Veristi always found congenial: a series of apparently disconnected events which take on significance only in retrospect.

Meantime the Duke's attention wanders to the Countess Ceprano. Borsa suggests that he had better not praise her too freely in front of her husband; he might repeat his remarks in the wrong quarter. The implication is that this might cause the Duke to lose his present mistress—a rather fatuous interpolation of Piave's; but it gives the Duke an opportunity to proclaim his philosophy. What does it matter if he loses one woman for another? He enjoys flitting from flower to flower. During the last part of the dialogue the orchestra has taken over discreetly from the banda with a leaping crotchet figure on flute, oboe and violins, which presently changes the 4/4 rhythm into the 6/8 of the Duke's Ballata (*Questa o quella*).

333

In the sketch the words run *Dian'Agnese per me pari sono*. However, since the mistress is no longer Diane de Poitiers, the proper names become inappropriate, as well as very difficult to make out at that tempo.

It is of course pure comic opera. The simple strophic form with its jigging 6/8 accompaniment in broken quavers is as remote from the usual cavatina as could be imagined. A new dimension was being added to Verdi's art, allowing him to kick off the tragic buskin and so produce this epitome of light-hearted elegance without damaging the integrity of the dramatic conception. The same qualities are apparent in the Duke's flirtatious duettino with the Countess Ceprano (*Partite . . . crudele*) which was doubtless the piece that caused Verdi to be accused of archaizing.

334

He uses here a second stage band composed of violins, violas and basses, for which he writes in the purest classical style of Mozart and Boccherini. The nearest equivalent in a previous opera is the first-act trio of the comedy *Un Giorno di Regno*. Both pieces derive from the stage minuet in the much studied *Don Giovanni*;* and both have the same air of wistful tenderness. Inappropriate perhaps for people as worthless as the Duke and Countess? No matter; Mozart lavished similar music on characters no less shallow. An empty bar and a half at the end of the final cadence allows Rigoletto the court buffoon to make his entrance with a typical jibe. 'What thoughts are running through your head, Signor di Ceprano?' The Count turns away angrily and follows the Duke into another room. Rigoletto remarks to the courtiers that the Duke seems to be enjoying himself ('le Roi s'amuse', in fact). It is a curiously unemphatic entrance for the chief character of the opera, but there is point in it. In this scene Rigoletto must appear as far as possible the stage-manager of the festivities. He does not take the floor himself; he merely intervenes to help the action along. It is possible that Count Ceprano has not understood the Duke's intentions with regard to his wife. Rigoletto sees to it not only that he understands, but that everybody else does so. Here melodies 2 and 3 of the first banda give way to a Perigordino played by the stage strings. This, too, is a graceful piece of music, despite its primitive texture with violas doubling the melody at the lower octave. Evidently it was in some sense an afterthought since the 'abbozzo' contains a different and less elegant melody at this point. The banda music then returns (melody No. 4) as another courtier, Marullo, comes in and with comical gravity breaks the news that Rigoletto has a mistress. Sensation! Just then Duke and jester return and the Count of Ceprano not far behind. How, the Duke wants to know, can he get rid of the tiresome Count—and he lays his hand on Ceprano's shoulder, half in jest and wholly in earnest. Rigoletto suggests various ways: prison, exile on some trumped-up charge, or even execution—what use is his head to him anyway? This jibe is underlined by an isolated orchestral intervention in a sequence of banda music and its effect is diminished when the stage band part is cued into the orchestral wind parts. The Count reacts violently, and even the Duke thinks that this time Rigoletto has gone too far. But the jester has unlimited trust in the Duke's protection. The courtiers meanwhile start murmuring about vengeance; the Count Ceprano proposes that they gather at his house the next day to work out a suitable plan. Beneath the pulsating dominant there are no less than four separate melodic strands all competing in a rough counterpoint yet all comprehended within the banda's dominant seventh harmony. Not real counterpoint, then, but it creates an extraordinary sense of forward propulsion. Verdi seems to have been at pains to derive Rigoletto's line from the first banda melody—a wasted effort since this is a passage which most Rigolettos reserve the right to omit. Why should they waste their lung power in a passage where their contribution is scarcely distinguishable from anyone else's? (Otellos apply the same argument to the ensemble in Act III of that opera.) At the start of this concertato, where orchestra and banda come together for the first time, Verdi exploits the rhythmic ambiguity in the banda's melody No. 4 to create a genuine counterpoint of stress with the orchestral part that supports the Duke. It is not the first time that he has combined melodic strands vertically; but for the manner in which it is done here the only model, however remote, is *Don Giovanni*. The material is now worked up into a richly

---

*For a study of the influence of Mozart's opera on *Rigoletto*, see Petrobelli, 'Verdi e il "Don Giovanni": osservazioni sulla scena iniziale del *Rigoletto*, *Atti del I° congresso internazionale di studi verdiani* (Parma, 1969), pp. 232–46.

335

Allegro con brio

DUKE and ORCHESTRA
vn.1.picc.ob.

Ah sem - pre tu spin - gi lo scher-zo all'- es - tre-mo

Banda

tuneful codetta. As the final chord ceases the voice of Monterone is heard outside demanding to be admitted.* He has come to reproach the King for having dishonoured his daughter. At this point Piave and Hugo diverge. M. de St-Vallier of the play is the father of Diane de Poitiers, the King's reigning mistress (even if he has not said a word to her for eight days, as we are told by the gossiping courtiers). She has sold her honour to him in order to secure a reprieve for her father who was under sentence of death for conspiracy. St-Vallier had given Diane in marriage to an elderly, gouty captain. He has no constructive purpose in coming to confront François; he no more wants his daughter back than Alfred Doolittle wants his Eliza. He merely wishes to protest about the blot on his escutcheon and to say that he would have preferred to die than to be saved at such a price. Triboulet takes it upon himself to reply. M. de Saint-Vallier, he says, was himself in the wrong for having married his daughter to such an ancient ruin as the captain. He ought to be grateful to the King for having usurped his son-in-law's marital rights. Had Diane remained a virtuous wife, St-Vallier himself would be plagued with deformed children, hunchbacked like Triboulet himself, or pot-bellied like Monsieur (and he indicates M. de Cossé, the original of Count Ceprano). Now there is every likelihood that St-Vallier will have happy, healthy grandchildren to delight his old age. . . . All this is shortened and bowdlerized in the opera, and with no great dramatic loss. Monterone is given a single, declamatory line of accusation above tremolo strings, reinforced twice by chords on horns, bassoons and cimbasso and a roll on the drum. Rigoletto replies with a parody of regal pomp, 'Sir, you have conspired against us and we have graciously pardoned you; you must have lost your reason to come here complaining about your daughter's honour.' This is one of the most carefully worked-out passages in the score, as the sketch reveals. The problem was to devise an idea that would express not only buffoonery but evil. Hence according to one view† the use of orchestral unison (Ex. 336, opposite).

After each phrase there are rapid gruppetti on violins and woodwind representing explosions of suppressed laughter. Then, too, there is deliberate bathos where the

* For this part Verdi specified 'the best baritone in the company'. Letter to Piave, 5.2.1851, Abbiati, II, p. 105. The point is worth mentioning since nowadays by tradition Monterone is given to a bass.

† P. Pal Varnai, 'Contributi per uno studio della tipuizzazione negativa nelle opere verdiane', in *Atti del primo Congresso Internazionale Verdiano*, pp. 268–75.

336

measured opening 'voi congiuraste' dissolves into free semiquavers—dignity treading on a banana skin. Monterone replies with a terrible outburst. Against his high held F the entire orchestra raps out a bar of ascending semiquavers fortissimo —an effect that only Verdi would have risked. Quietly but with recurrences in the orchestral texture of this same figure, Monterone declares to the Duke that dead or alive he will haunt him for the rest of his days. His one thought is to be avenged. The climax of the whole passage provides another striking instance of Verdi's use of the major 6/4 chord in a tragic context. Once again the effect derives principally from the Neapolitan relationship of the chord itself (D flat) to the basic key (C minor).

337

The Duke calls for Monterone's arrest. Monterone pronounces an anathema on both Duke and jester: 'It was an act of baseness, Duke, to set your dog on the dying lion. And you, serpent, who mock a father's grief, be you accursed!' It is this second curse directed solely at Rigoletto that makes the jester freeze with horror. In the play the act ends at that point with Monterone being led off to prison. Verdi is obliged by the laws of musical structure to wind up the scene with a stretta expressing the courtiers' dismay at the intrusion. Beginning quietly with voices in unison it works up to a climax in which the conventional effect of the switch into the major key is offset by strong and unconventional harmonic progressions. The entire scene lasts less than twenty minutes. It is constructed as a single organism from first note to last and there is no formal precedent for it in the whole of Italian opera.

Scene 2: the deserted end of a blind alley

The scene is divided into two. One part represents the courtyard of Rigoletto's house ('of moderate appearance') with a large and ancient tree and a marble seat. On the first-floor level of the house itself is a balcony sufficiently high to overlook the street, and supported by an arcade. Access to it is given by a small flight of stairs leading up to it from the outside. The second half of the scene represents the street itself flanked by a high garden wall with the Count of Ceprano's palace visible on the far side.

It is night. Rigoletto enters; his mind still full of Monterone's curse. The atmosphere is set by a typically dark-hued orchestration of clarinets, bassoons and lower strings. Out of this vague limbo of sound Rigoletto's voice emerges sharp and distinct with Ex. 331.* Then straight away a new idea takes shape in the orchestra: a sinuous melody played by muted cello and double bass with a pulsating accompaniment of clarinets, bassoons, four violas, bass drum, another solo cello and the rest of the cellos and basses all pizzicato.

338

This serves to introduce the hired assassin Sparafucile, and forms the background to his duet with Rigoletto (*Signor . . . va non ho niente*). He has come to offer his services to get rid of any rival for the young woman whom Rigoletto keeps under lock and key. As a decoy for his victims, he has a sister who runs a lonely tavern on the outskirts of the town. This extraordinary duet in which the voices never join and the entire melodic interest rests with the orchestra has an ancestor in the duettino 'Qui che fai?' from Donizetti's *Lucrezia Borgia*. Both pieces derive from the comic opera procedure of two buffo basses parlanti against an orchestral melody. Appropriately enough, each depicts a situation in which there is an element of grotesque humour—in one two spies are trying to checkmate one another; in the second a hired assassin is setting forth his terms with the self-conscious rectitude of an honest tradesman. If in *Ernani* the sardonic wit of Don Carlo had eluded Verdi, here in the false suavity of the melody, the thudding of the accompaniment, the sinister phosphorescence of the orchestration, he recaptures all the gallows-humour of the original.† Typically Verdian too is the elaboration of the accompaniment where the melody returns after an episode. The coda phrase where Sparafucile first gives his name is a masterpiece of Verdian ellipsis made possible by that identification of the major and minor mode that is part of his melodic thinking. Note the unprepared 6/4 in what is by classical standards a remote key.

Rigoletto's famous soliloquy *Pari siamo* is a classic instance of a recitative which has all the formal strength of an aria. 'We are alike, I kill with my tongue, he with his sword.' Then Rigoletto laments his fate as a jester—to make his master laugh at all times no matter what his own feelings. He inveighs against the heartless

* Curiously enough, from the jottings that accompany the sketch it is evident that Verdi originally wished the scene to begin with the three-note quaver figure which we first hear in the middle section of the duet that follows. This he discarded in favour of what is thematically a direct quotation from Rolando's first scena in *La Battaglia di Legnano*.

† The form in which this melody was first drafted on page 1 of the *Rigoletto* sketch suggests a more purely conversational theme such as had introduced the quartet in Act II of *Luisa Miller*. It was by altering the third bar so as to touch on the minor mode that he not only defined the dramatic ambience more sharply but also conferred on the melody itself a unique character.

339

courtiers; then a tender phrase on the flute brings back thoughts of his daughter, and the change which comes over him when he enters his own house. Like the clown's prologue in *I Pagliacci* which it so clearly inspired* this solo explores the entire range of baritonic expression. The tempo is partly strict, partly free, but there are two unifying factors. One is the recurrence once just after the beginning, once just before the end, of the curse theme, 'Quel vecchio maledivami,' always in the same key and with the same instrumentation. The other is the unusual symmetry of the tonal scheme (F–D flat; B flat; D flat; E–C). The three central progressions are by keys a minor third apart, while the jump from F to D flat at 'O uomini e natura' is mirrored by the descent from E major to C after 'Ma in altr'uomo qui mi cangio' —or nearly. An ominous B flat in the accompaniment brings back the 'hag-ridden' dominant sense of Ex. 331.

340

* Tonio's final 'Incominciate' appears to be an almost literal quotation from Rigoletto's 'È follia'. But the penultimate high G which all Rigolettos sing is not Verdi's. The highest printed note is E.

Only by a deliberate effort does Rigoletto succeed in banishing the memory of Monterone's curse and at the same time heaving the music out of an implied F minor into C major sunlight. As Rigoletto opens the door of his garden and Gilda rushes joyfully to meet him the orchestra takes charge with a typically festive tune shrilly scored in Verdi's early style.* This is Gilda's tune, just as Ex. 338 was

341

Allegro vivo

Sparafucile's; and Gilda, only sixteen, and an immature sixteen because of her sheltered existence, has all the unrestrained demonstrativeness of a child. When she notices her father's unhappiness the melody takes a turn into the minor key with discordant ninths and an increasing jumble of displaced accents. When it returns in its original form the scoring is lighter, and the total effect more subdued. Gilda loves her father, but she wants to know more about him and about her family. She questions him in one of those minute phrases that stand out like pearls, despite their transitional nature.

342

As Rigoletto's only reply is to ask if she has ever been out of the house, she has to repeat her question this time in E flat with still more ravishing effect. Who, she wants to know, was her mother? The andante (*Deh non parlare al misero*) approximates more closely to an orthodox central movement of a grand duet. But here the two double-quatrains are not merely 'dissimilar'; they have acquired complete independence within a larger organism. Rigoletto's solo in which he speaks of the 'angel' who took pity on his deformity is like an aria movement in miniature—a compressed equivalent of Macbeth's 'Pietà, rispetto, amore' which it resembles to the extent of having a similar modulation to E major ('Ah . . . moria') just where a reprise would be expected. Gilda's minor-mode answer with its broken triplet semiquavers then takes charge of the movement, yielding the string of heavenly phrases with which it concludes. The allegro, which starts as a transition, brings a succession of new ideas, each defining more sharply the attitudes of the two singers. It is the dialectic of *I Due Foscari* (duetto-finale of Act I) carried to

* The sketch contained a different melody at this point in the same rhythm as the festive tune that breaks in upon Jorg's pious meditations at the start of Act I of *Stiffelio*—which is doubtless one reason why Verdi ultimately changed it.

a higher pitch of perfection. Rigoletto's expansive phrase, telling her that she is his entire world (*Culto, famiglia, la patria, il mio universo è in te*) brings out that vein of childlike demonstrativeness in Gilda noticed earlier. But soon the strings begin to wheedle as Gilda begs to be allowed to see more of the city.

Rigoletto's panic is expressed in a long chromatic climb culminating in a no less protracted dominant pedal as he calls for Giovanna, the duenna, and questions her anxiously. Reassured he begins the final movement (*Ah veglia o donna questo fior*), a remarkable instance of a dramatic variation on an orthodox stretta design. Rigoletto instructs Giovanna to keep a strict watch on her charge. Gilda exclaims at her father's kindness, taking up the same theme in the subdominant key. Both stanzas (cast in the Bellinian $a^1\ a^2\ b\ a^2$ mould) are strictly symmetrical, so as to set in the strongest possible relief the point where Rigoletto, having resumed his verse, breaks off in the middle of a word at the fourth bar. He has heard a noise outside and rushes out to investigate. As he does so the Duke disguised slips into the garden, throws the duenna a purse and hides behind a tree. Rigoletto returning repeats his questioning of Giovanna to much the same music as before. The last bars are extended so as neatly to accommodate important information as well as dramatic irony. Giovanna asks if she must refuse entrance even to the Duke. 'Him most of all!' cries Rigoletto; and turning to Gilda, 'Farewell my daughter.' ('His daughter!' the Duke exclaims softly.) Rigoletto takes up once more the main theme of the movement, embellished by a simple descant from Gilda, so calculated as to cover all the pauses in the melody. The classical symmetry of the movement is rounded off by a coda (più mosso) of successive ideas of diminishing length, each repeated. The pianissimo cadences as father and daughter bid each other farewell are followed by a noisy instrumental wind-up, designed both to suggest the release of pent-up emotion and to stimulate applause. A wretched tradition prescribes a cut in this movement which makes Rigoletto break off the melody at its first statement, so making nonsense of the entire structure, as well as bringing the two questionings of Giovanna too close together.

Alone with Giovanna (or so she thinks) Gilda feels a certain sense of guilt. She has said nothing about the young man who follows her home every day from church; and she shyly confesses her attraction in a repeated half-phrase (*No, chè troppo è bello*), which is yet another premonition of Violetta's famous outpouring. With her eye on the tree Giovanna begins discreetly to praise this unknown wooer. (In Hugo each epithet is worth a gold piece to her.) Surely he must be a great lord, she says. But Gilda would rather have him poor like herself, and the clarinet melody accompanied by oboes and pizzicato strings gives a touch of innocent coquetry to her words.

344

Suddenly the Duke emerges from hiding and completes her half-uttered 'T'amo'. She calls out for Giovanna but the duenna has tactfully withdrawn. To the Duke's ardour she puts up a feeble resistance, which he proceeds to overcome with the poetical melody that forms the first movement of their duet (*È il sol dell' anima*). It is a song in praise of love the all-powerful, and its words seem to have been suggested by the much later scene in the play outside the royal bedchamber. The Duke may be insincere; yet it is refreshing, after the relentless ardour of most early Verdian tenors, to meet one who takes love lightly. Particularly enchanting is the shy, almost mesmerized quality of Gilda's answer with its pulsating octaves on flute and first violins. It is not strictly speaking a dissimilar answer because it echoes part of the tenor line, as though she were able to grasp only part of what he was saying:

345

In the coda the same phrase is taken over by the tenor while Gilda sings what was originally the second violin countermelody now doubled by flute and low clarinet; meanwhile violins and violas gently continue the throbbing Fs high up in a light semistaccato—a delicious effect, slightly offset by the over-elaborate cadenza which follows. Gilda, always curious, now asks to know her lover's name. 'Gualtier Maldé, a poor student,' he replies knowing that that is what she wants to hear. Just then the voices of Borsa and Ceprano bring Giovanna rushing out of the house to warn the lovers. In a short stretta (*Addio, addio, speranza ed anima*) the Duke and

Gilda take leave of each other. Though it lasts barely two minutes this movement too is often subjected to a cut, presumably on the grounds that in a work as dramatically convincing as *Rigoletto* there is something rather ridiculous about people in danger wasting precious time with repeated farewells. As if anyone understood the virtue of brevity better than Verdi himself! The fact remains that the andante requires an equally formal movement to balance it. To cut it down is pointless and impertinent.

Gilda is now left alone to dream happily about her lover, 'Gualtier Maldé'—a name that will for ever be engraved on her loving heart—in what is to be her only aria in the opera (*Caro nome*). The instrumental opening is one of the finest examples of woodwind writing that Verdi has yet given us. On paper *Caro nome* appears to lie in the tradition of those 'prancing'* movements that Verdi liked to give to his early heroines. But appearances are misleading. The composer wrote to De Giuli's husband: 'As for the cavatina in the first act, I don't see where agility comes into it. Perhaps you haven't understood the tempo which ought to be *Allegretto molto lento*. At a moderate pace and sung *sotto voce* it shouldn't give the slightest *difficulty*.'† In fact there is nothing brilliant about it. On the contrary it offers one of the most striking instances of vocal figuration used, so to speak, introspectively. Gilda weaves fantasies of semiquavers round her lover's name. In form no less than in character the aria is unique—a simple a^1 a^2 b a^2 design evolving in continuous variations in the manner of the Liszt–Paganini study 'La Campanella'. In between each phrase the solo first violin interpolates a cicada-like figure. The coda is a locus classicus of harmonic subtlety. Note the unexpected G major at (*x*) where a strict sequence would have required an F.

346

il mio de - sir a te o - gno - ra

As usual with Verdi refinements of harmony and scoring go hand in hand. After Gilda's final cadenza, strings and woodwind take over the melody off the beat, while the solo violin continues its figure in octaves. During this time Gilda twice repeats the name of Gualtier Maldé as she climbs the stair on to the terrace where she is in full view from the street. Over her last hushed reprise of the melody, tremolo violins and cellos, thudding timpani and a chromatic figure on flute and

---

* 'Melodia staccata' is the term used by Basevi, referring not merely to the rests between the notes but to the lack of those *appoggiature* which create a *binding* (legato) effect by making one note seem literally to 'lean' (*appoggiarsi*) towards the next.
† Letter to Borsi, 8.9.1852. *Copialettere*, pp. 497–8.

bassoon sound an unmistakable warning. (The unexpected use of *low* flute to colour another solo instrument is indicative of the composer's ever-widening orchestral imagination.) Meanwhile the street has been filling with masked courtiers all watching her and commenting on the beauty of 'Rigoletto's mistress'.*

Rigoletto now returns to the street drawn by a vague apprehension. The memory of Monterone's curse (Ex. 331) is recalled yet again. There follows a brisk scène-à-faire as Rigoletto encounters the courtiers. At the suggestion of Marullo he is persuaded to take part in his own daughter's abduction in the belief that it is the Countess of Ceprano who is being carried off. He is to hold the ladder while the others climb into the courtyard. Under cover of masking him like the rest Marullo binds Rigoletto's eyes and ears with a handkerchief. The theme which accompanies this exchange is full of abrupt, almost grotesque dynamic contrasts such as Verdi often uses to express 'negative' emotions (Ex. 347 a). A similar explosive tendency marks the gleeful chorus (*Zitti zitti moviamo a vendetta*), much in the manner of the 'Coro dei sicarii' (*Macbeth*) if more sophisticated (Ex. 347 b).

347

To an orchestral variant of the same melody they swarm on to the balcony and enter the house from which they drag Gilda gagged and bound. A moment later we hear Gilda's cries followed by shouts of 'Victory!' from the courtiers. Rigoletto however has heard nothing and cannot understand why. At last he tears away the mask and with it the handkerchief, sees the door of his house wide open, picks up a shawl which he recognizes as Gilda's, rushes in and comes out dragging the terrified Giovanna. He tears his hair and tries to speak but cannot. During all this the orchestral accompaniment has been rising chromatically as though coming to the boil. It is the mechanical formula seen in the Act II finale of *Il Corsaro* used with a new concentration and sense of purpose. At last Rigoletto bursts out, 'Ah . . . Ah . . . The curse!' and faints.

ACT II

Scene: a hall in the Duke's palace

Two doors on either side, and a larger one closed at the back of the stage. On either side of it are two life-sized portraits, one of the Duke, the other of his wife. There is a large chair and by it a table covered with a velvet cloth and various other articles of furniture.

The omission of the scene with the key meant a substantial departure at this point from Hugo's play. 'Doubtless we shall find something better,' Verdi had said; but

* It may occur to some literal-minded listeners to wonder how the courtiers can perceive Gilda's beauty when it is too dark for Rigoletto to see *them*. The play provides the answer. While Blanche is standing on the parapet thinking of her wooer she is holding a lighted torch in front of her face. No singer could be expected to do this!

the best that he and Piave could devise was an eminently conventional scena and double aria. In the play the King is a party to Blanche's abduction. In the opera it happens without his knowledge; hence his despair. She has been taken from him! She, the one person in the world who could have inspired him with a lasting love. The adagio (*Parmi veder le lagrime*), based on sestinas instead of the usual quatrains, is a beautiful piece of music in which the Bellinian formula (a^1 a^1 b a^2 and coda) is treated with a new breadth and flexibility. Inevitably one asks why should the Duke be given such a magnificent piece of musical poetry as this? Does it not conflict with everything we know about his character? Not at all. It is psychologically most apt, provided that we regard the Duke as a human being and not a monster. For the rich, spoiled child there is always a prettier doll in the shop-window. The biggest fish is always the one which got away. To the compulsive amorist the woman he desires but is prevented from seducing is precisely the one with whom he could happily have shared the rest of his days. It is not so much an insincere as a self-deceiving emotion. Again it is Mozart who in *Così fan tutte* demonstrated once and for all that people who deceive themselves require a musical expression as intense and serious as those whose sentiments are pure, noble and self-aware. The Duke's seriousness is genuine enough, but transitory. The moment he knows that Gilda is in the trap he changes from the poet to the strutting peacock.

After his final cadenza the courtiers troop in very pleased with themselves, and proceed to recount in unison the adventures of the previous night (*Scorrendo uniti remoto via*). One reason why the words are more than usually inaudible is that it is one of those melodies with a completely autonomous rhythmic life. But it is fully characteristic of the heartless jocularity of the courtiers, of whom it could be said that, like the witches in *Macbeth*, they constitute a leading member of the cast (Ex. 348 a, overleaf).

The music works up to a dominant half-close which serves to introduce the Duke's cabaletta (*Possente amor mi chiama*) often omitted in performance. True, it is an ugly piece of music scored very much in the style of Verdi's youth; also it is an old-fashioned cabaletta-in-parenthesis delivered just at the moment when the singer might be expected to have left the stage. On the other hand its omission results in a jarring harmonic non sequitur, with the half-close on the dominant of D major leading nowhere. Finally, the cabaletta is necessary to redress the formal and psychological balance of the scene and to make it clear in musical terms what kind of man the Duke really is.

Next Rigoletto enters humming a tune 'with affected nonchalance' (Piave's stage directions). Hugo too describes him as 'self-controlled but very pale'. Yet how many Rigolettos today make their entrance with that simian crouch which serves them throughout the opera, parading their anguish with inappropriate slurs and displaced accents? (Ex. 348 b, overleaf.)

In fact the more controlled he appears at this point the more impressive will be his later outburst. The courtiers greet him with ironical good humour but they notice how his eyes search every face and every corner. He snubs Ceprano with a return of his old manner: 'What's the news, buffoon? . . . Only that you're more tedious than usual.' But in the central limb of the melody (*Son felice che nulla a voi nuocesse*) is an undercurrent of bitter irony brought out in typically Verdian fashion by clarinets in sixths, as Rigoletto asks Marullo whether he did not find the night

348

a)

Allegro assai moderato

MARULLO, CEPRANO, BORSA and CHORUS

Scorren-do u-ni - ti re-mo - ta vi - a

b)

vn.

air rather chilly. 'I was sound asleep,' Marullo replies innocently. 'Ah then I must have been dreaming.'

349

RIGOLETTO

Son fe-li - ce che nul-la a voi nuo - ces - se

cls.

vc. pizz.
db.

Still singing his desolate little melody Rigoletto picks up a handkerchief; no, it is not Gilda's. Just then a page comes from the Duchess's apartments to say that she has asked to see her husband. 'He is asleep,' says Ceprano. 'But he was here with you just now.' . . . 'He's out hunting.' . . . 'What, without his pages, without weapons?' (Pages, being cadet members of the nobility, never hesitated to answer back their superiors.) 'He cannot be disturbed,' the courtiers cry out impatiently. In this and the following passage there are three separate dramatic points to be put across: the page's intervention, Rigoletto's realization of exactly what it implies, and his revelation that Gilda is not his mistress but his daughter. The conventional procedure would have admitted only two. The page and courtiers would conduct their dialogue in a transitional passage and Rigoletto's despair would have been expressed in a cabaletta. Here Verdi operates far more subtly. The dialogue is floated on a varied extension of the previous movement, with the dotted rhythm twice as fast and a pattern of cello pizzicato quavers derived from Ex. 349. The change to a bustling allegro transition is reserved for Rigoletto's words 'Ah ella è qui dunque'; while the words 'Io vo' mia figlia' are accompanied by a violent tonal wrench from F major to E flat as an implied dominant of A flat minor. In this way the ascending gradient of the drama is exactly reflected in the music by changes of rhythmic texture, movement and tonality. Finally Rigoletto's fury is discharged not in a cabaletta but in a slow movement (*Cortigiani, vil razza*) with one of those busy accompaniments usually associated with the operas written before *Luisa Miller* (Ex. 350 a). But it is no longer a mere pedestal for a larger-than-life character. It absorbs the impetus of the preceding movement and at the same time embodies all Rigoletto's impotent despair as he hurls insults at the courtiers. The entire aria is strictly symmetrical even at its fortissimo climax where Rigoletto throws himself at the door of the Duke's chamber, only to be repulsed by the courtiers. Its three sections are not unlike the quatrains of a usual romanza; but the tonal sequence is quite different, following as it does the graph of Rigoletto's emotion. Each stage in his abjection is marked by a further move to the flat side of the key. The meno mosso (*Ebben io piango, Marullo . . . signore*)* is in F minor against the original C minor. Here the pattern is one of pleading, to which the violas give an added poignancy by doubling part of the violin line at the lower octave (Ex. 350 b). At last, his pride and defiance gone, Rigoletto humbly begs the courtiers to forgive him and restore to him his daughter. Here the melody emerges into D flat major, and the instrumentation takes on the character of chamber music, with the voice line doubled by cor anglais at the sixth above and the accompaniment pattern given to a solo cello (Ex. 350 c).

350

It is the world of *Guillaume Tell* and 'Sois immobile'. There is the same pathos, the same underlying nobility all expressed in terms of the purest Italian lyricism. But Rigoletto's line has a more personal note to it. The expression is more concentrated in the voice, less in the cello obligato which here is used mainly to colour the texture. Rossini would never have aimed at the glorious, purely vocal climax at the words 'Ridate a me la figlia'—a Verdian speciality deriving from his unique feeling for the expressive powers of the baritone voice. Within the highly formal mould the declamation is always psychologically exact: a savage downward line, reminiscent of Francesco Moor for the first stanza; an increasing fragmentation of phrases in the second, suggestive of a man breaking into sobs; an idealized 'groan' in the third. How could the courtiers resist such a heart-rending appeal? The matter is never put to the test for at that moment Gilda comes rushing out of the ducal apartment. Rigoletto's first reaction is one of relief. She is at least safe. It was all a joke, perhaps? But Gilda's tears tell him otherwise, and she begs to be left alone with her father. The agitato music subsides. With unexpected dignity Rigoletto orders the courtiers to leave them. His stark dismissal (*Ite da qui voi tutti*), largely confined to the note C, stands out all the more impressively in that it is flanked by two quite

---

* Clément Marais, the original Marullo in the play, is a poet and man of the people, not a heartless noble, and might therefore be expected to show some compassion for a fellow professional.

separate musical ideas. Abashed, the men shuffle away murmuring that children and madmen must sometimes be humoured.

Gilda then recounts the story that we all know in the first of a sequence of tiny movements which make up the duet. (*Tutte le feste al tempio*.) As in Rigoletto's aria the modulations are used only to mark the stages of emotional dialectic, not as part of a tonal scheme. In the main each verse movement keeps to one tonality; but Gilda's recitation with its beautiful oboe introduction twice steers from the initial E minor into C major, where it ends. It is as though the sweetness of her love for 'Gualtier Maldé' continually overcomes her sense of guilt. Rigoletto responds with

351

a verse più mosso in A flat (*Solo per me l'infamia*) whose introspective quality is emphasized by rich harmonies beneath a somewhat static line. He had sought infamy only for himself: the lower he fell the higher he wished his daughter to rise; he had built an altar beside a gallows and now the altar was overturned. Here the music turns into E flat major for the most deeply felt movement of all (*Piangi, piangi, fanciulla*) 'Weep, child, weep'—again very short. It consists of a single phrase for Rigoletto stated four times, twice plain, twice embellished; an intervening phrase for Gilda; and a long coda in which the singers combine. The instrumental palette is calculated to bring out all the velvet depths of the baritone voice—clarinets, horns, bassoons and pizzicato cellos. Flute, oboe and violins give an added sense of plangency to Gilda. The mood is cathartic, one of grief purged by weeping and transfigured into serene melody. Throughout, Verdi makes abundant use of 'lamenting' figures in voice and orchestra without disturbing the sense of lyrical calm (Ex. 352, opposite).

Monterone is heard again as he passes through the hall, on his way to prison escorted by guards. As before he commands the full orchestra in each of his utterances. He stops for a moment in front of the Duke's portrait and reflects that his curse was uttered in vain. 'No,' cries Rigoletto, 'you are wrong, you shall have an avenger.' At this point in Hugo the curtain falls. Verdi concludes with what he called a brilliant sfarzoso cabaletta—the most famous and memorable of all those in which two characters sing the same music successively in different keys (*Sì, vendetta, tremenda vendetta*). When Verdi specified the metre and character to Piave it is difficult not to believe that he already had the melody in his mind. Its ancestor is generally held to be the vengeance duet between Othello and Iago in Rossini's *Otello*, but other examples of the same pattern and character can be found, as for instance the stretta of the Act I finale from Donizetti's *Fausta*. Verdi's melody is infinitely more vigorous than either.

Rigoletto is all fire and fury, Gilda timidly restraining, because, as she tells us in

her last two lines, she still loves the Duke. The tonic–subdominant seesaw wonderfully conveys this antithesis. Of course in the end the tide of Rigoletto's anger carries all before it, as the curtain comes down. Few will mind the fact that in the excitement of the moment Verdi has reverted to some very coarse orchestration.

ACT III

Scene: the right bank of the Mincio

As in the second scene of Act I the stage is divided, on one side the interior of a tavern so dilapidated that passers-by can look in through the cracks in the walls; on the other a road running alongside the river Mincio. Inside the tavern Sparafucile is seated at the table polishing his belt. Outside are Gilda and Rigoletto. The act opens with a tiny sombre prelude of nine bars—just enough to serve as backing to a low-keyed conversational recitative such as is usually avoided in the earlier operas. Rigoletto had already promised to take his daughter away from Mantua but he has been slow to do so. 'I have left you enough time to cure yourself of your love,' he says; and Hugo makes it clear that this amounts to a month, during which Blanche/Gilda has been the King's mistress. Piave only hints at this, while making it clear that she still loves the Duke and is convinced that he loves her. Rigoletto now shows her otherwise. Together they peer through the tavern wall in time to see the Duke arrive dressed as a simple cavalier, sit down at the table and order some wine and a bed for the night. While Sparafucile goes to arrange this, the Duke breaks into song. That he should of all people sing about the fickleness of women is a nice touch of irony that derives from the original play. It is not the first time that Verdi has included a canzone (i.e., what would have been sung even in a play) in the course of an opera. Medora's romanza from *Il Corsaro* is of the same order. The difference here is that the song is used naturalistically, as a dramatic 'prop' rather than an expression of character. Up to a point *La donna è mobile* does convey the Duke's shallow gaiety and virile swagger—there is a touch of his ruth-lessness too in the way in which the first orchestral statement is bitten off after seven bars in a parody of one of Italian opera's most primitive mannerisms. But the Duke is an aristocrat; this is a frankly popular not to say plebeian melody, and as such stands out in high relief from the rest of the score—even the comparatively neutral banda music. Its very catchiness, so essential to the drama, has in the past given the opera a bad name. To the uninformed *La donna è mobile is Rigoletto*.

While Sparafucile brings the wine, the first half of the melody is extended in repeated variations, fading out on a bassoon solo with a characteristic 'fidget' pattern in the cellos. With Maddalena's entrance the famous quartet begins—the Duke flirting with the attractive girl in gipsy costume, she half-heartedly repelling his advances, Gilda and Rigoletto commenting from outside. The first movement (*Un dì se ben rammentomi*) consists entirely of dialogue against a brilliant orchestral melody. Note the pizzicato cello quavers of excitement as well as the reminiscence of the violin figure in *Caro nome*.

354

Here we learn that Maddalena herself has enticed the Duke to the inn; and that, like his ancestor the Don, he is prepared to offer marriage to get what he wants. The pith of the quartet lies in the concertato andante (*Bella figlia dell'amore*), some-times said to mark a new stage in the evolution of ensemble-writing. Yet in *Luisa Miller, Stiffelio*, even *I·Lombardi*, Verdi had written more daringly constructed ensembles in which the individuals were even more sharply characterized. His real achievement here was to apply the differentiating technique *vertically* and within a regular, almost classical design. Structurally *Bella figlia dell'amore* belongs to the 'bi-partite' tradition of Bellini's 'A te o cara' (*I Puritani*)—which also begins with a tenor solo—and Donizetti's 'Chi mi frena' (*Lucia di Lammermoor*), though it is more extended than either. Only Mozart has achieved a comparable result, as in the sextet from *Le Nozze di Figaro* and the quartet from *Don Giovanni*.* The Duke is characterized by soaring phrases, Maddalena by staccato semiquavers, Gilda by legato semiquavers with rests like sobs or by a drooping line like a wail as in her duet *Piangi, piangi, fanciulla*; Rigoletto's part is more neutral, but at times his grimness is reflected in a static slow-moving line such as Verdi writes more usually for his basses rather than his baritones. All this is expressed simultaneously within the most pellucid lyrical writing imaginable:

355

Gilda's pattern of broken semiquavers in the coda has already been anticipated in *Stiffelio*. Here it has a new poignancy, which reaches its climax in a glorious harmonic 'dissolve' in what might be called the second coda.

From now on the act departs from all previous operatic norms. What follows could be described as a scène-à-faire against the background of a storm and with a tiny formal trio at its centre, but its design defies any detailed analysis, so rich is it in reminiscences, motifs and a variety of vocal and orchestral texture. First in a passage of quite unsupported recitative Rigoletto orders Gilda to return home, dress herself as a man and set out at once for Verona. Then he goes to the back of the tavern and returns with Sparafucile, to whom he gives ten scudi, the remaining ten to be paid on delivery of the body. When Sparafucile asks to know the victim's name Rigoletto replies: 'His name is crime, and mine is punishment.' The dialogue is

---

* This is not to imply, with Ildebrando Pizzetti 'Contrappunto e armonia nell'opera di Verdi', *Rassegna Musicale*, vol. XXI, pp. 189–200, that *Bella figlia dell'amore* is superior to such examples as the quintet from Wagner's *Die Meistersinger* where, as in the quartet from *Fidelio* and the trio from *Der Rosenkavalier*, the characters are all caught up in a reflective dream.

preceded by an orchestral motif which is to play quite a prominent part in the scene but whose dramatic as distinct from musical function no commentator has ever been able to explain:

356

It is a most arresting effect—the solitary oboe note gleaming above the hollow harmonies of the lower strings. What is more the sketches indicate that Verdi had imagined the notes *and* the scoring together. But one looks in vain for any definite dramatic image however crude. The same oboe note and hollow fifth underpin the recitative itself which is marked to be sung 'without the usual appoggiaturas'—an instruction which must have caused many a singer of this century to turn back the pages feverishly wondering what appoggiatura he ought to have sung and has not. In fact it is no more than a safety precaution. The position with regard to the appoggiatura had been fluid since the beginning of the century. Niccolò Vaccai in his *Metodo Pratico di Canto Italiano* insisted that it was obligatory; but by the time Lablache wrote his *Méthode complète de Chant* it was already regarded as optional; which meant that a composer who wanted appoggiaturas was advised to write them out rather than leave them to a singer's discretion. By 1851 this had become Verdi's regular practice, as a glance at the preceding recitative will show. Gilda's 'or venite' is written A flat–G flat–G flat–F. Donizetti would have made the third note an F, while expecting the soprano to sing G flat. Yet more than thirty years later when every singer might be expected to be familiar with his own practice Verdi still thinks it necessary to repeat his instruction on a similarly expressionless recitative in *Otello*.*

As Rigoletto leaves the first grumblings of the storm sound in the distance. Unlike most musical storms this one is not continuous even at the height of its fury, but is designed so as to seem ever-present. Musically it is embodied for the most part in three motifs in fast time and of regular construction (Ex. 357): far-off thunder and lightning (a), (b) and (c) moaning wind, portrayed with startling novelty by a wordless chorus† (d), heavy rain or hail (e).

Throughout the opening part of the scena (a) and (b) alternate with other motifs —notably Ex. 356—to give a formal punctuation to the otherwise amorphous recitative. The opening phrase of *Bella figlia dell'amore* on the clarinet reminds us that the Duke and Maddalena are still flirting. Sparafucile, re-entering, is treated by the Duke with off-hand insolence. Maddalena, already half in love with the young man, tries to persuade him to leave the inn at once; but the Duke accepts Sparafucile's offer of his own bedroom for the night. Again the clarinet recalls *Bella figlia dell'amore* as he whispers something to Maddalena—presumably an invitation

* Compare also the instructions written on the MS. full scores of *Luisa Miller* and *Macbeth*. In the score of the latter held in the Conservatorio Luigi Cherubini in Florence the grand duet from Act I is inscribed with the words: *Gli artisti sono pregati di non fare le solite cadenze.*

† In fact, a precedent exists in Auber's *opéra comique Haydée* (1848) which Verdi could certainly have seen during his stay that year in Paris.

357

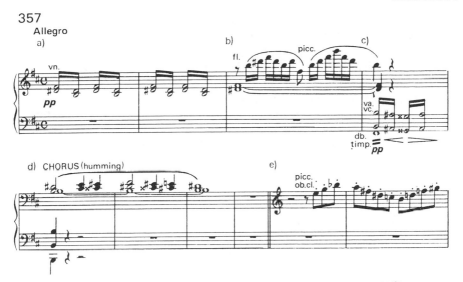

to visit him later. He mounts the stairs to Sparafucile's room, stretches himself on the bed and sings himself to sleep with *La donna è mobile*, clarinet taking over the phrases which he is too tired to utter. Finally he loses the melody altogether and murmurs repetitiously until cut off in the middle of a word.

From here on the motifs are more closely juxtaposed as the drama gathers momentum. With the closer approach of the storm Ex. 357 a is reinforced by cellos, basses and a soft roll on the bass drum. A new rhythmic element in crotchet-triplets is introduced both to compensate for the evaporating free recitative and to build a transition to the strictly formal trio that lies at the heart of the scene. Here Maddalena begins to coax her brother to spare the Duke's life. He merely tells her to go and make sure the victim is asleep and to fetch his sword. She obeys with a bad grace. Such a nice-looking young man and surely worth more than twenty scudi! Another burst of thunder, lightning and moaning wind directs our attention to someone approaching along the road. It is Gilda, dressed as a young man, drawn back to the scene by a determination to save the Duke. She looks in through the tavern walls to see and hear Sparafucile telling his sister that her young Apollo is to be killed and his body put in a sack. Maddalena thinks there must be a way out. Could they not kill the little hunchback when he comes back with the other ten scudi? But the suggestion is an affront to Sparafucile's sense of professional etiquette. He has never yet betrayed a client and does not intend to begin now. However, if by any chance some unknown traveller should arrive before midnight demanding shelter . . . With the body in a sack Rigoletto would not know the difference. The conversation between brother and sister is conducted for the most part to the crotchet-triplets, which gradually coalesce into a regular period of 32 bars. Apart from the flexibility of this procedure—neither recitative, arioso nor formal number —what must strike any student of the early operas is the direct quotation from *Il Corsaro*. Maddalena's 'Eppure il denaro . . . salvarti scommetto', etcetera is identical with a passage in the duet between Seid and Gulnara. True, the voices are different, but the situation is similar. A woman is pleading obliquely for the life of the man she loves, using *argumenta ad hominem*—or rather *ad virum*. Whether the reference is coincidental we can only speculate. By the time Sparafucile makes his final concession the storm has taken over completely. The triplets have become engulfed in a rising murmur of Ex. 357 a, and the rhythmic design switches abruptly to crotchets and quavers for the formal terzetto (*Se pria ch'abbia il mezzo di notte toccato*). The storm cuts off for the opening part of the melody (Ex. 358 a) only to burst out in all its fury in the final, major-key limb.

It is almost primitively schematic (24 bars of 8 + 4 + 8 + 4) but there is no formal cadence; merely a diminished-seventh outburst and a lessening of the storm to allow the chime of a near-by church bell to be heard striking half an hour to mid-

358

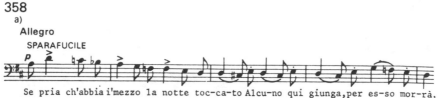

night. Gilda's knock at the door introduces Ex. 357 e for the first time. The others do not open immediately, since the formal balance of the scene requires a repeat of the trio. After that Gilda knocks once more, is admitted and stabbed by Spara-fucile to the most violent orchestral outburst yet heard, for which the score indi-cates the thunder machine should be used on the stage. But the music itself is here so powerful, so utterly free from formal trammels that this device is nowadays unnecessary. The storm then dies away in a long diminuendo in which Ex. 357 e plays an important part.

When all is quiet Rigoletto appears outside the tavern, musing on his approach-ing triumph. With his monologue (*Della vendetta al fin giunge l'istante*) we return to pure recitative with string chords and distant reminiscences of Ex. 357 c. After the clock has struck midnight* he knocks at the door of the inn. Sparafucile comes out with the sack and offers to throw it in the river. But Rigoletto wants to savour his vengeance a little longer. Sparafucile bids him a sepulchral good night and returns to the inn. Rigoletto's monologue reaches its climax with a splendid phrase of sombre gloating.

359

Just as he is about to cast the sack in the river, he hears a familiar voice singing

* Six strokes only—church clocks in nineteenth-century Italy never chimed more than that.

La donna è mobile. (To leave the audience in no doubt the Duke is directed to cross the back of the stage.) For a long time Rigoletto remains as if paralysed. At last, when the voice has died away in the distance, he cuts open the sack. A flash of lightning reveals for a moment the body of Gilda. He still cannot believe his senses. Gilda is on the road to Verona—it is all a dream. But a second flash of lightning leaves him in no doubt. He knocks at the tavern door wildly, but no one answers. Then a faint voice from the sack tells him that his daughter is still alive, but dying. The music has by now taken on the familiar throbbing motion with off-beat violins, and the way is being prepared to a final duet between father and daughter (*V'ho ingannato*). This is of course strictly in the operatic tradition. Even if Victor Hugo had not provided an equivalent, convention would have required Verdi to finish the act with something of the kind. But the tradition—now fortunately obsolescent—whereby it is cut is utterly foreign to the spirit of the drama. Melo-dramatic *Rigoletto* may be, but it is not Grand Guignol. As with any Greek tragedy its ending should contain a note of resolution, with a sense that 'nothing is here for tears'. Such a note is provided by the second half of the duet (*Lassù in cielo*) where Gilda talks of being united with her mother in heaven. The high violins and flute arpeggios are stock Verdian props for a death scene, familiar since *I Lombardi*; but even these undergo a miraculous transformation where at the repeat of the D flat major melody the first and second violins take over the arpeggios, alternating in octaves divisi while the flute trills on a high A flat. Gilda's final four bars contain

360

a harmonic side-slip worthy of the Requiem. She dies, and Rigoletto breaks out with a cry of 'La Maledizione!' as over repeated chords of D flat minor the curtain falls.

Right from the start *Rigoletto* was always popular with audiences, though for some time the critics continued to flay it and censors especially in the Papal States and the Kingdom of the Two Sicilies did their best to emasculate it. In Rome and Bologna it became *Viscardello* in 1851 and 1852 respectively. In Naples the follow-ing year it was performed as *Clara di Perth*, the text altered by the young poet Leone Bardare who had completed that of *Il Trovatore* after Cammarano's death; and in 1858 at the same theatre as *Lionello*.

Of the famous trio of operas which it introduces (*Il Trovatore* and *La Traviata* are the others) *Rigoletto* will always be the musician's favourite.* No other opera, it is

* Vaughan Williams considered it Verdi's greatest achievement.

sometimes said, maintains such a perfect balance between lyrical and dramatic elements; no other is so well proportioned, so tightly crammed full of ideas precisely arranged and organically related to the whole. Certainly it was a long time before Verdi surpassed it in the operas to come in that density of invention so organized as to cheat the clock. Again Beethoven's 'Eroica' comes to mind. But in one respect the parallel breaks down. The 'Eroica' established a bigger scale of musical thought than the symphony had ever known before, and one that Beethoven never exceeded until the Ninth and the last quartets. The scale of ideas in *Rigoletto* remains small. It is very much tied to the 16-bar melodic unit. Passages in freer time sooner or later require a symmetrical period to give 'composition' in the pictorial sense. There is an interesting contrast here with the mature Wagner. The first act of *Die Walküre*, possibly the most perfect single act that he ever wrote, is built up from small motifs worked into a huge scheme. But when in the 'Song to the Spring' he introduces a formal, self-contained melody, the smaller organism obtrudes on the greater, and the general design suffers, if only slightly. Verdi in the Storm Scene of *Rigoletto* needs such a closed form, a quasi-cabaletta stated not once but twice, in order to carry the freer passages which follow it. In a word Verdi's organization is as yet more primitive than Wagner's. None the less transalpine sophistication was making notable advances in his art, witness the increasingly important role assigned to the orchestra.

The name part of *Rigoletto* remains the greatest part ever written for a high baritone, requiring every emotional stop of which the voice is capable. It is of course murderously high, not so much in the solos as in the duets with Gilda, which call for a real beauty of tone. The new comic opera dimension has enabled Verdi to achieve a unique characterization both of Gilda and the Duke. The first is a light, lyric soprano, childlike, simple, utterly unselfish ('O buona figliuola,' she exclaims when Maddalena announces that she will tell the Duke to escape), the second an epitome of heartless, elegant charm, noble only when frustrated. Of the comprimarii Maddalena is a half-fledged character, individualized in the quartet but nowhere else. Sparafucile on the other hand is a brilliantly effective creation, with his sombre, sardonic humour combined with the vigour which makes his role so different from that of the 'ancient' or 'hermit' bass beloved of Italian opera. That function is taken by Monterone who, though baritone, is the apotheosis of the comprimario basso. At each of his entrances his is the Voice of God. Finally there is the chorus with its triple head (Borsa, Marullo, Ceprano); infinitely malicious and therefore dangerous, it forms a vital thread in the musical and dramatic texture of the first two acts. The nearest precedent is once more Donizetti's *Lucrezia Borgia* where the male chorus expresses itself in the same jocular style. Likewise Verdi had a precedent for his storm accompanied by murder in Rossini's *Otello*. In each case the original is infinitely transcended.

It has been said that all the turning points of musical history occur in the right places at the beginning or in the middle of the century. Opera was born about 1600; Beethoven's first symphony and Op. 18 string quartets were published in 1800. Just after 1850 at the age of thirty-eight Verdi closed the door on a period of Italian opera with *Rigoletto*. The so-called ottocento in music was finished. Verdi will continue to draw on certain of its forms for the next few operas, but in a totally new spirit.

INDEX

Figures and titles in **bold** type indicate whole chapters devoted to operas discussed in detail
Opera houses, theatres, etc., are under the names of their towns or cities.